THE EUROPEAN 1955 CUP 1980

JOHN MOTSON
JOHN ROWLINSON

Queen Anne Press

Macdonald Futura Publishers

London

First published in 1980 by
Queen Anne Press
Macdonald Futura Publishers
Paulton House
8 Shepherdess Walk
London N1 7LW

ISBN 0 362 00512 5

Text set in 10/11 pt Linotron 202 Times, printed and bound in Great Britain at The Pitman Press, Bath

CONTENTS

ACKNOWLEDGEMENTS

The thanks of the authors are due in no small measure to journalists Martin Tyler, Brian Glanville and Keir Radnedge for their patience in reading the proofs and suggesting improvements; and to Charles Balchin for his extensive photographic research.

We would also like to express our appreciation of the efforts of Anne Motson and Nicola Rowlinson, who researched and typed most of the statistics which appear in the appendices.

To all those who willingly gave up time to recount anecdotes, confirm or deny popular theories, or to add information not otherwise available, we would like to place on record our sincere gratitude.

PROLOGUE

The European Cup is the province of the privileged. For 25 years it has enjoyed an unchallenged reputation across football's oldest continent, simply because only champions are allowed to take part. It is a fine and necessary qualification. One which was laid down when the competition was launched in 1955 on the back of a campaign by a French newspaper, although the rule was not enforced in the very first season, when entry was by invitation.

The European Champion Clubs' Cup, to use its full, original title, might never have been established at all but for the perseverance of those early pioneers, and but for the powerful presence of the great Spanish club, Real Madrid, who gave it instant credibility. In winning the first five tournaments with a glittering team assembled from all over the world, Real had a cataclysmic effect on international club football. They broke down frontiers in the interests of obtaining better players and the quality of their play sometimes hovered on the edge of perfection. Real's pursuit of excellence manifested itself through the formative years of the European Cup, giving the new competition a shape and a style from which other ambitious clubs took their example.

First to do so were Benfica from Lisbon, their team blessed with lithe, adroit footballers from the black Portuguese colonies, and cunningly coached by the little Hungarian, Bela Guttmann. Benfica's bold belief in attacking football followed in the tradition set by Real Madrid, but in the mid-1960s it was superseded by the sinister approach and sharp practice of two Italian outfits from the same city – AC Milan and Internazionale.

It was a Scottish club entering the European Cup for the first time who broke the stranglehold of cynicism. Glasgow Celtic injected the competition with a renewed sense of adventure when they became the first non-Latin winners in 1967. A year later, Britain won again. This time with Manchester United, whose long love affair with the European Cup was a tumbling mixture of tragedy, romance and emotion.

From the Netherlands, there then came a rarified concept called 'total football' – a sort of players co-operative movement in which the free expression of intelligent, versatile footballers made hackneyed nonsense of restrictive team formations. It brought the European Cup to the Netherlands four years in a row – first to Feyenoord in Rotterdam, then to Ajax of Amsterdam, whose three consecutive titles thrilled the continent at the start of the 1970s. Their achievement was promptly equalled by Bayern Munich, whose Teutonic resilience brought West German football to a summit of technical awareness. The European Cup continued to be a mirror reflecting advanced football thinking.

Next it was the turn of Liverpool. Winners two years running, they showed how the best English club had discovered the right chemistry for European success. They harnessed the patience and poise of the continentals to thoroughbred British assets like speed and endurance.

So it was that English teams, who shunned the first European Cup in 1955–56, broke new ground in 1979 when Nottingham Forest became the third club from the birthplace of football to win the trophy. No other country provided three different winners in the first 25 years. But if the European Cup has been a kaleidoscope of dazzling images, a succession of swiftly fusing patterns over a quarter of a century, these winning teams had at least one thing in common – great players.

Real Madrid had so many that they sometimes kept famous internationals brooding in the reserves, unable to break the monopoly of giants like Alfredo Di Stefano, Ferenc Puskas and Francisco Gento. The Spanish club started in the 1950s what became an accepted trait in the 1980s – unashamedly buying a star player from abroad purely in the short term interest of winning the European Cup.

Benfica, too, relied on colossal individual flair, in the presence of Eusebio, Germano and Mario Coluna; from Milan, for all the hardened grip of *catenaccio* defence, there came the grace of Gianni Rivera, Luis Suarez and Sandro Mazzola. Three Manchester United players – Bobby Charlton, Denis Law and George Best – won the coveted individual prize: European Footballer of the Year. Yet Johan Cruyff, talisman of Ajax, carried off the award three times. Perhaps the only individual to bestride Europe quite as imperiously as Di Stefano and Cruyff, was the captain of Bayern Munich and West Germany, Franz Beckenbauer. His cool arrogance and natural leadership earned him the nickname *Der Kaiser*.

But none of these prolific players were elevated to the peerage of their profession until, or unless, they proved themselves in the most testing theatre of continental football – the European Cup. The same applied to Kevin Keegan. Liverpool's chief protagonist when they first won the trophy in 1977, Keegan went to West Germany to polish his skill, widen his experience, and enhance his international reputation. He surpassed even his own expectations by twice being voted European Footballer of the Year and leading Hamburg in their European Cup campaign in 1980 – another in the long line of gifted footballers to leave an indelible mark on the game's most glamorous club competition.

Keegan is among many of his kind who willingly found time to talk to us about their feelings for the European Cup and about the part they played in its development. Without the ready co-operation and enthusiastic response of players, coaches and observers across the continent, this book, which we see as a mark of respect for 25 years compulsive football action, would not have been written.

As we shall see, the European Cup has not been without its troughs, its conspiracies, its darker side. Neither have we made any attempt to hide the bitterness it has engendered or the shortcomings it has displayed. But without competitiveness and conflict, there would be no football. And all that is hopelessly addictive about the world's greatest game has been strikingly portrayed in what we believe to be the best club tournament yet devised.

John Motson
John Rowlinson
August 1980

CHAPTER ONE

FOOTBALL'S FRENCH REVOLUTION
(The Path Towards a European Cup)

It was Nelson who started it.

Not that the Lord Admiral's sinking of the French fleet off Cape Trafalgar had anything to do with football, for the game was then half a century away from being recognised in Britain. And it was not that the French had compensated for their nautical failures with some fine sporting inventions, of which the European Cup was just one.

No, Nelson's unwitting contribution was to give his name to an English town. So began a chain of events which led, exactly 150 years after the Battle of Trafalgar, to the inauguration of a competition which aroused as much fervent patriotism on the football field as England's greatest sailor had experienced on the high seas.

For that, we have to thank one Matthew Pollard, who farmed in the north country at the start of the 19th century. He shrewdly sold part of his land for the building of two turnpike roads, and built at their junction an alehouse which became a meeting place for settlers and travellers alike. Pollard perpetuated the late Admiral's memory by calling his hostelry the Lord Nelson Inn.

As the textile industry in Lancashire developed, the surrounding parishes of Great Marsden and Little Marsden merged into one. Factories sprang up around the junction where the Lord Nelson stood, and by 1850 the new township assumed the name Nelson.

In 1882 a football club was formed in the town. It did not grow quickly enough to be among the crop of Lancashire teams who inspired the formation of the Football League six years later, but when the league expanded Nelson FC joined, subsequently achieving rapid success. They were among the original members of the third division north when that section started in 1921. In the first season Nelson finished a modest 16th, but in the next (1922–23) they were champions.

The players' reward, as well as promotion to the second division, was an unexpected one – an overseas tour. For an English club to travel abroad was still something of an event in 1923, but for a third division team to spend part of the summer in Spain was highly original. Not that the game had been slow in spreading. From the turn of the century, British enthusiasts had taken football to Europe and South America. Just as engineering and industry had been successfully pioneered by the English and the Scots, so their exporting of soccer was taken up with a native respect for the inventors of the game.

While football abroad was in its infancy, the visit of professional teams from England and Scotland was little more than a gentle educational process. To put it simply, the visitors won as easily as they pleased. But the formation in 1904 of FIFA (Fédération Internationale de Football Associations), a world football body, showed that the continent meant business. Although the four British associations at first remained coldly aloof, one of the enthusiasts present at the inaugural meeting in Paris was a Spaniard, Carlos

Padros. He later became a leading light in the formation of Madrid FC. Students in Madrid had started the team at the turn of the century, playing their early matches on a strip of grass within charging distance of the city's main bull ring. In 1920 they were recognised by King Alfonso XIII, who bestowed on the club the title *real* (royal), thus effectively starting the proud reign of Real Madrid. But the club took time to throw off its humble origins, and when they moved to a new ground at the Velodromo, in Ciudad Lineal, in April 1923, their first visitors included the aforesaid Nelson.

Real agreed to play the English club twice, as part of Nelson's five-match tour. The first game ended in a 4–2 win for the third division team, but a few days later Nelson discovered how quickly their hosts were learning. Real Madrid won the second match 4–1. Nelson's players were surprised at the standard of the Spaniards' play, especially captain Mick McCullough, who was moved to write home to his local newspaper, the *Nelson Leader*.

'Real Madrid would give the best clubs in Europe a run for their money', wrote McCullough. 'They play beautiful, cultured football. The ball is trapped correctly and played along the ground. People at home would hardly believe the strides football has made in Spain.

'There is no kick and rush, but method in every movement. Their heading is also in the best British tradition. Perhaps the day is not too far distant when we shall have regular international club games with our friends from across the sea.'

McCullough's last, prophetic thought was shared by a Real Madrid player of that time. Santiago Bernabeu had joined the club as a junior at the age of 14, and by the time of Nelson's visit he had been a first team player for over 10 years. Soon, Bernabeu became club trainer. Then, from 1929 to 1935, Real's secretary. As a director, he received the ultimate accolade when, in 1943, they made him president. Only then was Bernabeu able to give weighty support to an idea which had lingered in his mind, too, after that visit of Nelson in 1923. Namely, regular competitive matches between leading clubs from all parts of Europe.

A year after the matches against Nelson, the Spaniards confirmed their progress with a 3–2 victory over the English FA Cup winners, Newcastle United, in a friendly match to mark the opening of yet another new stadium – this time in the Madrid suburb of Chamartin. It was in this district that Bernabeu would fulfil another dream: the construction, years later, of a vast, open air stadium with space for more than 100,000 people. His vision was to play an integral part in the implementation of the European Cup.

Poor Nelson's moment of glory was soon over. They were relegated after just one season in the English second division, and in 1931 found themselves voted out of the Football League when they finished 11 points adrift at the bottom of the third division north. By chance, the town made another valuable contribution to the development of European football. Nelson was the birthplace of Jimmy Hogan, one of the first professional players to make an impact as a coach. He did so not in England, but on the continent. Having played first for Nelson on wages of five shillings a week, he moved to Rochdale and then to Bolton Wanderers, where he helped win the Second Division Championship in 1909.

Bolton went on a victorious tour of the Netherlands where Hogan made contacts and later returned to coach a club side. In 1912 he went to Vienna and met Hugo Meisl, a Jewish banker's son, dedicated to advancing football in Austria. The Austrians had joined FIFA in 1905, when the British relented and also came into the fold, and in that year a crowd of 10,000 thrilled to an exhibition match in Vienna between Everton and Tottenham Hotspur, who were both on tour.

Meisl was a confirmed anglophile, and saw in Hogan the logical extension of the British influence. Together they drew up the first coaching scheme of its kind, and Austrian football moved forward to an exciting future. Hogan encouraged the Austrians, and later the Hungarians, to base their game on the so-called Scottish style of play, with the emphasis on close, accurate passing. A similar approach was working well in Czechoslovakia, where leading club sides like Sparta and Slavia, in Prague, were coached at that time by Scotsmen.

It was Sparta's success in three small international club tournaments that prompted Hugo Meisl to suggest in 1924, the year he established professionalism in Austria, the idea of a European club competition. It took him three years to get his way. In 1927, when Meisl became full time secretary and team manager of the Austrian FA, his Mitropa Cup began.

The man who launched the Mitropa Cup, forerunner of the European Cup, was the Austrian Hugo Meisl (right). (*Presse Sports*)

Because it was designed for leading teams in Central Europe, it was given the name *Mitteleuropa* and later shortened. Austria, Czechoslovakia, Hungary and Yugoslavia each entered two sides in the inaugural competition. The word had yet to spread to Bernabeu and western Europe. But from the start, there were striking comparisons between the Mitropa Cup and the European Cup, which was to come into being some 30 years later. The matches were played on a knock-out basis over two legs, home and away, and if the aggregate score was level the winner was determined at first by the toss of a coin.

By such a method Sparta Prague qualified for the first final, but once there they emphatically defeated Rapid Vienna. The second leg was marked by angry crowd scenes, with stones and bottles being thrown at Czech players by Austrian supporters. As the Mitropa Cup grew in popularity, fans began to cross the border to watch their team play away matches. There was clearly a public demand for international club football on the continent.

By 1930 countries further west were interested. A tournament held in Geneva that year attracted the champions and cup winners of France, Spain, Italy, Germany, Belgium and Switzerland. But the more experienced Mitropa competitors from Hungary, Czechoslavakia and Austria filled the first three places. The final, between Ujpest of Budapest and Slavia of Prague, was refereed by an Englishman, Stanley Rous. It was a first taste of competitive club football in Europe for a man who, as president of FIFA for 13 years, was to become the most famous football statesman in the world. Of the match, he said:

'Slavia had been involved in a rough semi-final, and on the day of the final they found themselves a couple of players short owing to injuries. I remember they went round the hotel trying to enlist some Czech waiters.

'Some of the matches had been very physical, so I went into both dressing-rooms before the final and warned the teams about their conduct. They took it so much to heart that when I blew the whistle for the first foul, neither side wanted to take the free kick.'

Rous still retained, 50 years later, a small pocket book in which he had made a careful note of his expenses for that trip to Geneva. They amounted to just £25. But although the continentals were delighted to welcome a referee from the home of football, they were still a long way from persuading English clubs to take part in such a tournament. Parochialism and politics were to blame.

England, Scotland, Ireland and Wales had resigned from FIFA in 1920. The British associations were opposed to playing international matches against enemy powers in the wake of the first World War. They went further, and proposed a boycott of any neutral countries who *did* play against the likes of Germany, Austria and Hungary. But allies like Belgium and France disagreed with the British stand. The rift lasted for four years, with the British associations rejoining the world body in 1924. Four years on, they were out again. This time, over an argument about amateurism and the policy of 'broken time' payments in connection with the Olympic Games.

This breach was not as fierce, because internationals continued to take place. But the fact that the British were officially part of FIFA for only four years between the wars, missing out on three World Cups as well as the early club tournaments, scarcely encouraged a marriage with pioneers like Meisl.

One man who did take an interest in what was happening overseas was Herbert Chapman, the first true visionary among English managers. Having played a part in a hat trick of first division championships with Huddersfield Town, he moved south to make Arsenal Football Club one of the most admired in the world. Chapman's foresight ranged far beyond teams and tactics, even though Arsenal dominated the English game in the 1930s. He supervised the rebuilding of Highbury so that, half a century later, it is still regarded as one of the league's best grounds. He talked enthusiastically about floodlights, air travel, white balls and weather-proof pitches. His friendship with Meisl led to Chapman agreeing to pay a fee of £2,600 to Rapid Vienna for their Austrian international goalkeeper, Rudi Hiden. He was to be paid £8 a week, the wage received by the other Arsenal players at that time, and to supplement his income by working as a chef.

But Hiden never got as far as London. Three times he made the crossing from Ostend to Dover, and three times he was turned back by immigration officials. The Ministry of Labour refused him a permit on the grounds that he would put an English player out of work.

Arsenal made regular visits to Europe, starting, in 1930, a series of prestige friendly matches against Racing Club of Paris, and it was the French who ultimately fostered the dreams of Meisl and Bernabeu, and processed plans for a proper European Cup.

The French journalist Gabriel Hanot, whose enthusiasm for international football reached fruition in 1955, 21 years after he first advanced the idea of a European competition for clubs.

Racing Club's president was another ambitious football figure named Jean-Bernard Levy, whose attention was caught, in 1934, by an article in the French magazine *Le Miroir des Sports*. It was written by the editor, Gabriel Hanot. He suggested improving international football relations by incorporating two club sides from other countries in one's own league championship. In other words, Rapid Vienna and Juventus, say, would play for a season in the French league, with a similar exchange scheme operating across Europe.

Levy thought this impractical, but did believe the time had come if not for a European League, then for a cup competition with each country across the continent nominating one representative. 'The greatest difficulty', he surmised with prophetic understatement, 'will be to get the English involved'.

Before very much more could be done, the English and the rest of Europe were involved in something more fearful than the future of football. Levy was killed fighting for freedom, and the continent was left to scoop up the ashes left by six years of war. But Gabriel Hanot was a patient and persistent man. He had been player and manager with the French national team, blessed with the same energetic zeal as Meisl, Bernabeu and Chapman, although the Arsenal manager had died in 1934.

CHELSEA FOOTBALL & ATHLETIC CO. LTD.

Official Programme

Directors :—Capt. J. H. MEARS, R.M. (Chairman), J. F. C. BUDD,
C. J. PRATT, H. J. M. BOYER, L. J. MEARS.
Manager-Sec. :—Wm. BIRRELL.
Ground :—STAMFORD BRIDGE, S.W.6.   Phone :—FUL. 3625.

COMMEMORATING THE FIRST VISIT OF A
RUSSIAN CLUB TO ENGLAND.

CHELSEA F.C.
v.
DYNAMO F.C.
(MOSCOW)
(U.S.S.R. CHAMPIONS)

Tuesday, November 13th, 1945
KICK OFF 2.30 P.M.

ДОБРО ПОЖАЛОВАТЬ!   WELCOME !

PRICE TWOPENCE

The first Soviet side to play in
Britain drew 3–3 with Chelsea.

Many of Chapman's futuristic ideas died with him, some to be revived many years later. British football remained in a cocoon, which is why the appearance at the end of the war of a party of Soviet footballers calling themselves Moscow Dynamo had such a startling effect on those who saw them. The first Soviet side to visit Britain attracted an estimated crowd of over 100,000 to Stamford Bridge in November 1945, to see them play Chelsea. The official attendance was 85,000, but many more squeezed into vantage points which included the roof of the stands and the edge of the pitch.

Out of curiosity came a lasting impression: these strange, sad looking men who walked on to the field wearing long shorts and carrying bouquets of flowers for their opponents, could actually play the game. They drew 3–3 with Chelsea, but their delightful football might easily have won them the match. Tommy Lawton, the England centre-forward signed by Chelsea from Everton only a week before the match, said the only department in which the Dynamos fell short was their shooting. But in their three other tour matches, the Soviets beat Cardiff City 10–1, an Arsenal side strengthened by guests 4–3, and drew 2–2 with Glasgow Rangers. Nine years later, Lawton faced them again, this time playing for Arsenal in Moscow in 1954. Dynamos won 5–0. Somewhere along the way, they had obviously learned to shoot.

Such a misconception was typical of the patronising attitude adopted by British football people to overseas teams and players before and after the war. In Lawton's case, it was perhaps forgivable since he scored twice in Great Britain's 6–1 victory over the Rest of Europe at Hampden Park, Glasgow, in May 1947. This match was staged to celebrate the return, yet again, of the British associations to FIFA. Now, for the first time, the island which introduced the game to the world was prepared to enter the World Cup; providing their Home International Championship was cast as a qualifying group.

The British emerged from their first competitive international exercise with no credit at all. England, as home champions, went to Rio in 1950, only to be humiliated beyond all expectations by a bunch of casual part-timers representing the United States. Scotland, who as runners-up in the home tournament were also entitled to play in the World Cup finals, adopted a dog-in-the-manager attitude. They refused to go to Brazil because they had not qualified as British champions.

Such an introspective attitude to what had now truly become a world game was based on the obdurate illusion that the British were still best at playing the game they had invented. The clubs themselves were largely to blame. Although a few, like Chelsea and Hibernian, had followed Arsenal's example with friendlies against European opposition, the vast majority in England and Scotland were concerned only with the domestic business of league and cup.

On the continent, efforts to revive the Mitropa Cup after the war had been somewhat thwarted by the ominous presence of the Iron Curtain; while the Latin Cup, suggested by Spain and Portgual, got off to a bad start in 1949 when one of the most attractive competitors, the Italian team Torino, was wiped out in the dreadful Superga air crash on the way back from a friendly in Lisbon.

Even so, British clubs had shown no interest in taking part in the tournament; neither in 1949 nor in the four years which followed. Typical of their homebound instincts was the decision to celebrate Coronation Year in 1953 with a cup competition in the summer for leading clubs from England and Scotland. No European sides were invited, but the continent was poised to make the British suffer for their blatant lack of respect.

It was the Hungarians, who learned their football originally from Jimmy Hogan, who inflicted on England the punishment which had been imminent for some time. The team which shattered England's unbeaten Wembley record against overseas opposition by winning 6–3 in November 1953, emphasising their utter superiority by winning 7–1 in Budapest the following May, included players like Ferenc Puskas, Sandor Kocsis and Zoltan Czibor, all of whom would make their mark in the European Cup.

These international defeats marked not only the eclipse of English football in its accepted form, but enabled the enlightened thinkers in the British game to convince the diehard traditionalists that things had to change; even in the stubborn surroundings of the Football League. Three friendly matches on successive days in December 1954 gave the pendulum a further nudge. The first, and the one which inadvertently got the European Cup off the ground, involved the first division champions at that time, Wolverhampton Wanderers.

In many ways, Wolves under their stern manager Stan Cullis, were an excellent example of the strengths of the English game: a fast, powerful team, ardent users of the long pass, high on the endurance needed to survive the demanding conditions of an English winter. It would be fatuous to say they had no skill, but when a friendly was arranged between Wolves and the Hungarian champions-elect, Honved, those who saw how the game was developing knew the match would be the ultimate clash of styles. For six of the Honved team, including Puskas, had played against England; and Billy Wright, who as captain of Wolves now had the opportunity to exact a kind of revenge for what he had suffered as leader of the fallen England brigade, was not the only player who saw the friendly that way.

Roy Swinbourne, not a full international but a fearless centre-forward in the best British tradition, said later: 'Wolves never played a match in which there was so much pride involved as the Honved game. The Hungarians had given us such a hammering in the internationals that people built up the club match as our opportunity to show we were still as good as the continentals.'

Among the apprentice professionals on the Wolves ground staff at that time was a 16-year-old Liverpool lad called Ron Atkinson, destined 25 years later to manage a West Bromwich Albion team in European competition.

'On the morning of the match, Stan Cullis sent for me and two of the other apprentices, and told us to go out and water the pitch. We thought he was out of his mind. It was December, and it had been raining incessantly for four days.

'When I watched the match in the evening, I understood what he was up to. The Hungarians were two up in about 15 minutes, and playing superbly. It was the best football I have ever seen, brilliant first-time movement.

'But the pitch was getting heavier and heavier. In the second half, Honved were still leading 2–0 but they gradually got bogged down. Billy Wright and

The *Daily Mail* salutes Wolves' victory over Honved in December 1954. Gabriel Hanot cast doubts on the claims and in the same week launched plans for the European Cup. (*Associated Newspapers*)

England's Masters win in the mud

Hail, Wolves 'Champions of the world' now

By DAVID WYNNE-MORGAN

SALUTE the wonderful Wolves this morning for giving Britain her greatest football victory since the war. Last night

The Paris offices of *L'Equipe*, the newspaper whose enterprise led to the formation of the European Cup. (*Presse Sports*)

Ron Flowers kept slinging these huge long passes up to the Wolves forwards. The mud just wore the Hungarians out.'

When Johnny Hancocks scored for Wolves from a penalty, the roar of the 54,998 capacity crowd inside Molineux must have helped to dishearten Honved for, in the last 15 minutes, Swinbourne scored twice, and Wolves won 3–2. The euphoria which greeted the English champions' recovery was heightened by the special atmosphere engendered by the Molineux floodlights, under which Wolves had earlier crushed the Soviet side, Moscow Spartak, by four goals. It was given added impetus, too, by the ecstatic reaction of the English newspapers the following morning. 'Hail Wolves – Champions of the World', was the headline in the *Daily Mail*. Across the English Channel, Gabriel Hanot took a more sober view. He wrote in the French sports daily *L'Equipe*: 'We must wait for Wolves to visit Budapest and Moscow before we proclaim their invincibility. And there are other clubs of international prowess, like Milan and Real Madrid. There is a strong case for starting a European championship for clubs. Bigger, more significant, less irregular than the Mitropa Cup.'

Hanot, now 65, had waited a long time to improve on the idea he first put up 20 years earlier. His mention of AC Milan was apposite, because the night after the Wolves-Honved match the Italian side visited Upton Park and beat West Ham United 6–0. John Bond, another who took such salutary lessons into club management in England years later, played right back for the London club that Tuesday evening: 'It was the first time we had come across a team assembled from all over the world. Milan paralysed us with all that was good about continental football. Malcolm Allison was in our side, and he was one of the first to enthuse about overseas players, and to insist that we had to get back to improving the basic skills in our own game.'

The following afternoon, 15 December 1954, the Hungarian champions of the previous year, Voros Lobogo (Red Banner) came to Stamford Bridge and drew 2–2 with Chelsea. The London club, who later that season won the first division title, included at centre-half Ron Greenwood, later to manage West Ham and England in European competition. Of that match he said:

'The Hungarians only emphasised what I had believed for some time – that there was more to football than running round the pitch during training, which is what most English clubs used to do.

'Not only were they brilliant players, but they knew how to look after themselves. I was marking Nandor Hidegkuti, who had scored a hat trick against England at Wembley the year before, and on one occasion he fouled me quite badly. I told him he had no need to stoop to that with his sort of skill.'

Still in that same week, Hanot and *L'Equipe* produced their blueprint for a European tournament. They proposed that each country should nominate one club side, and that matches should be played in midweek both at home and away with points awarded as in the league system. The French had a reputation as pioneers in sport: two journalists from *L'Auto*, talking in a Parisian café in 1903, dreamed up the idea of a Tour de France cycle race; Baron de Coubertin inspired the modern Olympic Games; and two French football officials, Jules Rimet and Henri Delaunay, piloted the World Cup and the European International Championship.

European reaction to Hanot's plan was mixed, but predictable. There was a favourable response from Austria and Hungary, agreement in principle from Belgium and Switzerland; but most countries favoured a knockout competition, because it would involve fewer matches. The number of games worried Germany, whose players in 1954 were still part-time and their league still regional. English interest was restrained, although sports columnist Desmond Hackett, of the *Daily Express*, liked the idea of a cup for eight or 16 clubs.

Significantly, the most enthusiastic reply came from Madrid. The president of the Spanish Football Association, Juan Touzon, wrote to *L'Equipe* in January 1955: 'This project appeals to me enormously and to my friend, Santiago Bernabeu, the president of Real Madrid. We are ready to receive, in his stadium which has room for over 100,000 spectators, all the top teams in Europe and also those from behind the Iron Curtain.'

Thus encouraged, *L'Equipe* sent out a month later invitations to take part in the first European Cup, together with a draft of proposed rules. The 18 clubs approached were selected by Jacques Ferran, editor-in-chief of the paper, Jacques Goddet, its managing director, and Hanot himself.

It was not intended that the clubs taking part in the first tournament should necessarily be champions of their country, since *L'Equipe* needed to know who would take part before the end of that 1954–55 season. But they did stipulate that the cup should be reserved for champions alone from the second season onwards. The 18 clubs they approached were: Rot-Weiss Essen (Germany), Chelsea (England), Rapid Vienna (Austria), Anderlecht (Belgium), BK Copenhagen (Denmark), Hibernian (Scotland), Real Madrid (Spain), Stade de Reims (France), Holland Sport (Netherlands), Voros Lobogo (Hungary), AC Milan (Italy), Sporting Lisbon (Portugal), FC Saarbrucken (The Saar), Malmo (Sweden), Servette Geneva (Switzerland), Partizan Belgrade (Yugoslavia), Moscow Dynamo (USSR), and Sparta Prague (Czechoslovakia).

Despite Wolves' delusions of grandeur, Chelsea were a logical choice as English representatives. Not merely because they were in line to win the first division championship, but because, like Arsenal, they had established overseas connections. Moscow Dynamo had been followed to Stamford Bridge by other continental sides, and in the 1946–47 season Chelsea had fielded full back Willi Steffen, a popular Swiss student who came over to learn English. The following summer, they tried unsuccessfully to sign Carlo Parola, the Italian centre-half then playing for Juventus.

But it was from England that Hanot received his first warning, albeit a friendly one from Sir Stanley Rous, then secretary of the Football Association. Rous recalled later:

'I knew Hanot well because I helped to place his daughter in the home of an English family in Brighton, so that she could learn the language. But when he came to see me in London about starting a European Cup, I told him he would need to get the approval of the national associations before the clubs could compete. And they would not approve of a competition organised by a newspaper.

L'Equipe took the point. To market their new product, they had to get it accepted by one of football's ruling parliaments. They went first to FIFA, and Jacques Ferran recalled the lukewarm reception the pioneers received.

'We got a polite reply from William Seeldrayers, of Belgium, the FIFA president. He said there was no provision in the statutes of FIFA for them to organise this type of competition. They were more concerned with national teams than with clubs.'

There was a veiled threat, too, in what Seeldrayers went on to say: 'I have no doubt that, if it is possible to fit in the dates of your European Cup matches in an already full calendar alongside the national programme, and alongside the international dates, this idea will prove extremely interesting and will be a great success.'

FIFA had played Pontius Pilate. So Hanot and Ferran went next to UEFA, to put their proposition to the executive committee of the European Football Union, who themselves had only been in existence for a year. 'We admitted that we at *L'Equipe* did not have the experience or the resources to organise a competition of this importance. We did not wish to carry out the christening of our baby ourselves, rather to hand it over to the correct organising body.'

The committee listened with some uneasiness, then referred the matter to the UEFA congress, meeting in Vienna in March 1955. But there was no carte blanche there, either. Sir Stanley Rous, speaking now on behalf of UEFA, said the European Union was not there to organise competitions, but to represent certain common interests.

Ebbe Schwartz of Denmark, UEFA's first president, said it was up to individual federations and football associations to authorise their clubs to take part in such a tournament. Among the reasons why UEFA were reluctant to support the European Cup at that time was their fear of a proliferation of club competitions. The Mitropa Cup was being revived, and the imminent Inter Cities Fairs Cup would also add to the fixture list. At least Ferran and his team now knew exactly where they stood. As Ferran has said:

'Neither FIFA nor UEFA were prepared to take the initiative in organising a competition which so many people wanted. It was up to us to act ourselves.
'Gabriel Hanot and I returned from Vienna convinced that, although neither body would give official approval, they could not prevent the ultimate progress of a scheme so far advanced.'

Ferran said as much in his *L'Equipe* editorials in March 1955, stating the limbo in which the European Cup found itself.

'The clubs concerned have said yes. The Federations are behind the idea. It only remains for the cup to be organised by an interested body. We shall probably be asking ourselves, in a few years time, why such a cup was not started sooner.
'Perhaps then the young and timid UEFA, who for the moment are sitting on the fence, will be able to take charge of a competition which, in effect, should be one of the reasons for their existence.'

On the back of such a sharp rebuke, *L'Equipe* pressed on regardless. They invited their 18 clubs to a meeting in the Ambassador Hotel, in Paris, on 2 April; all expenses paid by the newspaper. Only three clubs failed to send a representative. Hibernian expressed support by letter, but two of the East Europeans, Moscow Dynamo and Sparta Prague, remained behind the Iron Curtain.

The Soviets wrote to say they could not compete because they were

The famous meeting of delegates at the Ambassador Hotel in Paris in April 1955. Santiago Bernabeu, whose enthusiasm for the European Cup so impressed his colleagues, is third from the left.

unable to play home matches during their bad winter, and their spring fixture list was too crowded. But those who did come were united in their enthusiasm. Nobody more so than Santiago Bernabeu, who was accompanied by Real Madrid's business manager, Raimondo Saporta. Together they would shape the early years of the European Cup, and at that historic meeting in Paris it was Bernabeu who impressed Ferran: 'His sometimes shaky French was good enough for all of us to understand. His friendliness and courtesy hid a strong and forceful personality. This, and the importance of his great club, were vital factors in the way the meeting went.'

John Battersby, Chelsea's representative, remembered the gathering in Paris for rather different reasons. He had worked with Stanley Rous at the Football Association for 15 years, acted as liaison officer for football at the 1948 Olympic Games in London, and joined Chelsea as secretary a year later. When *L'Equipe's* invitation arrived at Stamford Bridge, Chelsea chairman Joe Mears encouraged Battersby to attend the meeting, and to take his wife Joan with him to Paris for a short holiday.

'Joan went shopping while I attended the first morning session, and when this was over I found myself sitting next to Jacques Goddet, the paper's managing director, at the lunch table.

'I was a non-drinker and had suffered in the past from food poisoning, but I remember eating oysters followed by duck with orange, and Goddet persuading me to take a glass of wine.

'Early in the afternoon session, I started to feel ill. I could not concentrate on what was being said, so I shuffled out of my seat and went upstairs to our bedroom. I was violently sick, and then collapsed. Joan fetched a doctor, who gave me an injection, put me to bed, and prescribed a diet of charcoal biscuits.'

Thus, for England, the European Cup began with a thumping great stomach upset. And there was to be much upheaval of another kind before the birthplace of soccer was to take part in its newest competition. His colleagues in Paris voted Battersby on to an executive steering committee, which consisted of Ernest Bedrignans of France as president, Bernabeu and Gusztav Sebes of Hungary as vice-presidents, then Battersby, Keller (FC Saarbrucken), Piazzalunga (Servette Geneva), and Jansen (Rot-Weiss Essen) as members.

The committee ensured their place in European Cup history when they performed their first task: 'fixing' the draw for the first round of the 1955–56 competition. The eight ties they arranged were the only ones never properly to be drawn: Chelsea v Djurgarden; Real Madrid v Servette Geneva; AC Milan v Saarbrucken; Rot-Weiss Essen v Hibernian; Honved or Voros Lobogo v Anderlecht; Reims v BK Copenhagen; Rapid Vienna v Holland Sport; Partizan Belgrade v Sporting Lisbon.

Ferran said later: 'The Paris meeting was the turning point in getting the European Cup off the ground. It was, in effect, a bluff by a committee who had neither the means nor the experience to apply themselves to such a difficult task as running this type of competition. It would have been inconceivable for directors and secretaries of clubs to organise a cup of this kind, because there would be new teams involved each year.'

But the bluff worked. In the corridors of FIFA there grew an unsettling feeling that if the world body did not ratify the European Cup, it would go ahead without their approval. Mutiny was in the air.

A month later, on 7 May 1955, FIFA met in London and decided to authorise the new competition on three conditions.

1 Participating clubs must receive permission to compete from their national football association.

2 The tournament must be organised by UEFA, who should accept responsibility for it.

3 The title 'European Cup' must be reserved for a proposed championship between national sides. (When this came into being, it was known first as the European Nations Cup, then simply as the European Championship.)

Two weeks after FIFA's announcement, UEFA's executive committee met in Paris and knew they could hedge no longer. They assumed control of the new competition and christened it: 'The European Champion Clubs' Cup'. They paid L'Equipe's steering committee the compliment of adopting in their entirety the rules, entries and first round draw suggested by the committee. Everybody, it seemed, was satisfied at last. But across the channel there was still strong dissatisfaction with the idea.

The English Football League held their annual meeting in London exactly a fortnight after UEFA had given the European Cup the green light. And the diehards of the league could only see red. President Arthur Drewry referred in his address to the great interest stimulated by the friendly matches Wolves and other clubs had played against continental teams in the 1954–55 season.

'Spartan struggles these, watched by millions on television, and welcome victories upon which we are glad to renew our congratulations . . .

'Although the interest of the public was quickened by these matches, the season generally was a bad one from an attendance point of view, with a drop of over two million in the aggregate figure for league matches.

'These figures are inclined to make one think that the league's Saturday fixtures are suffering as a result of all the extra matches which are being played, outside the league programme. The time has come to give serious consideration to a curtailment of the number of friendly and other matches which clubs are arranging.'

Among those who sat listening to Drewry's warning was
J. H. W. 'Joe' Mears, a member of the league's management
committee and chairman of Chelsea. His club were drawn to play
Djurgarden in the inaugural round of the European Cup, but the
League whose championship they had just won, far from wishing
them bon voyage, were frowning on the increase in ancilliary fixtures.

Remember, Chelsea still had to receive domestic approval to enter
the European Cup. That meant, in effect, the agreement of the
League management committee. Predictably, they followed Drewry's
line of thinking and 'suggested' to Chelsea that it would be
'inadvisable' to add the new tournament to their already crowded list
of fixtures. Battersby's stomach could have been forgiven for turning
over again. 'Joe Mears was torn. He was keen for Chelsea to be
involved from the club's point of view, but he was a member of the
League management committee as well. In the end, he bowed to
their pressure.'

Chelsea's dilemma did not attract detailed examination in the
national press. The European Cup had been drawn but not started.
When the English champions' timid withdrawal was announced on 27
July 1955, it merited just three paragraphs on the morning sports'
pages. Neither did Chelsea's manager, Ted Drake, feel particularly
bitter at the time: 'The decision was not as disappointing or as far
reaching as it would have been years later. The European Cup was
still at an experimental stage, and we had no idea what we might be
missing.'

Chelsea's place in the draw was taken by Gwardia Warsaw of
Poland. There were two other changes: PSV Eindhoven took over

Chelsea's withdrawal from the
European Cup in July 1955
raised few eyebrows in England.
(*Associated Newspapers*)

GE 16   DAILY MIRROR Wednesday July 27, 1955

ATTENTION MOSCOW!   **Wolves ar**
'Play hard

THEY LOOK

IN

Mirror

PORT

4 PAGES

Chelsea drop
out of the
European Cup

CHELSEA, Football
League cham-
pions, have with-
drawn from the
European Cup.
Their notifica-
tion to the Foot-
ball League that they were entering the competition came before the League's Management
Committee recently and after careful consideration the committee decided to ask Chelsea to consider the matter. The Management
Committee felt that the additional fixtures
might prove difficult to fulfil.

From BOB

I HAVE be
watching.
Wolves prepar

TODAY'S DIARY
way.—England v Australasia (5th
Birmingham, 7 0
.—Tournaments at Southend. Felix
Brighton, Ryde and Ilfracombe
Tennis.—Slazenger's £1,000 tourna
carborough Tournaments at Bed-
ide Worthing and Tunbridge Wells

from Holland Sport as the Dutch representatives, and Aarhus replaced BK Copenhagen for Denmark. Voros Lobogo (who later changed their name to MTK Budapest) were confirmed as the Hungarian choice. But there were those with foresight who rued the Football League's insensitive attitude. One of them was Roy Swinbourne, the Wolves forward whose goals against Honved precipitated the fulfilment of Gabriel Hanot's dream. 'Our attitude to the European Cup was comparable to our later approach to the European Common Market. We would have been better off if we had gone in sooner. The fact that we waited, meant that we had a lot of catching up to do.'

Curiously, the scepticism of the League was English, rather than British. Because north of the border, Hibernian were armed with the support of the Scottish Football Association and approached the new challenge with unbridled enthusiasm. Happily for Hibs, their chairman Harry Swan was not just a confirmed believer in European football, but also happened to be president of the SFA. His dual interest took him in the opposite direction to that of Joe Mears.

Hibernian had made a number of overseas tours since the war and were one of the first clubs in Britain to install floodlights. Evening friendlies against overseas opposition were a regular feature at their Easter Road ground in Edinburgh before the European Cup started. Swan was a great friend of George Graham, then secretary of the Scottish Football Association, who became a member of the executive committee formed by UEFA to run the European Cup. Graham's assistant in Scotland at that time was Willie Allan, who said later: 'When the idea of the European Cup came up, Harry Swan jumped at it straight away. He was a very forward looking man. He wanted smaller leagues in Scotland long before they arrived, and showed equal foresight when it came to mixing with the continentals.'

Hibernian had won the Scottish championship in 1951 and 1952, finished second on goal average in 1953, then fifth in 1954 and 1955. They boasted a celebrated forward line of Smith, Johnstone, Reilly, Turnbull and Ormond, although by the time they entered the European Cup, Bobby Johnstone had moved on to Manchester City and been replaced by Bobby Combe. Combe and outside right Gordon Smith had made their débuts for Hibernian during the war, both aged 16, and Smith was to play a unique part in the early years of the European Cup.

'We knew a little bit about overseas football because soon after the war Hibernian went on tour to places like Brazil and Czechoslovakia. The continentals had great players all right, it was just that in Britain, we did not know about them, or want to know about them. The European Cup changed all that.

'Mind you, it was only thanks to Harry Swan that we got involved. The Celtic chairman, Bob Kelly, had no time at all for European football in 1955.

'There was an insular, even ignorant attitude in Scotland, as well as in England. They still believed it was our game, and that the continentals should not be taken too seriously. When a Scottish team lost abroad there was always some excuse. It was either the ball, the referee, or unfair tactics used by the opposition.

'When Hibernian toured Germany early in the 1950s, I remember the thing that struck us most about our opponents was their footwear. We had never seen rubber studs before. This was just one of the ways in which the continent had caught up, and overtaken us.'

Hibernian's international winger Gordon Smith, who made history when he became the first man to appear in the European Cup for three different clubs. (*Popperfoto*)

Hibernian had the latest footwear by the time they went back to Germany for their first European Cup tie against Rot-Weiss Essen on 14 September 1955.

British soldiers serving along the Rhine swelled a crowd which saw Hibs win comfortably 4–0. Smith had a fine match, although Essen were without the injured Helmut Rahn, scorer of Germany's winning goal against Hungary in the World Cup final a year earlier. Smith, centre-forward Lawrie Reilly and goalkeeper Tommy Younger all missed the second leg at Easter Road, as they were late getting back from international duty.

But the pattern for the European Cup was already set. Having done the hardest part by playing away, Hibs found the home leg a formality. It was drawn 1–1, and refereed by Englishman Arthur Ellis from Halifax.

'The day before the match, I received a surprising telephone call asking me to find two linesmen to take with me to Scotland. They had forgotten to appoint any! I got hold of Jimmy Cattlin, from Rochdale, and my younger brother Frank, who was then officiating in the Yorkshire League. Frankly, some of the organisation in the early stages of the European Cup smacked of a chip shop approach.'

The Ellis trio handled the match in Edinburgh so competently that UEFA asked them to take charge of both legs of Hibernian's next tie against Djurgarden. The Swedish side, who had beaten Chelsea's replacements Gwardia Warsaw, asked if they could play both matches in Scotland because of the bad winter in Scandinavia. Hibernian were only too happy to oblige.

Djurgarden's 'home' tie was played on Partick Thistle's ground in Glasgow, where Hibs won 3–1. They also won the second leg, thanks to a penalty awarded for a foul on Willie Ormond, later Scotland's manager, and converted by Eddie Turnbull, himself to manage Hibernian.

For the moment, the ambitious Edinburgh club were in the semi-final of the first European Cup. And were playing an essential part in the growing appeal of a tournament which was beginning to fulfil the demand Hanot had sensed existed among public and professionals alike.

The acceleration in convenient air travel, and the acquisition by many clubs of floodlights, had quickened the pulse rate of football on the continent. From the Netherlands to Norway, from Scotland to Switzerland, there was a bristling anticipation for the battles to come. From uneasy beginnings, the European Cup now promised a glittering future. *L'Equipe*'s baby was not only christened. It was starting to grow.

CHAPTER TWO

THE REAL THING
(Real Madrid 1956–60)

The badge of Real Madrid Football Club.

A lion guards the entrance to the Lisbon stadium where the European Cup got under way. The animal, made of white porcelain, is the symbol of Sporting Club of Portugal, who staged the first match in the competition against Partizan Belgrade. The ground has changed since the afternoon of 4 September 1955. It now boasts a large concrete stand and a running track. What has not altered is Sporting's record in the competition. They went out in the first round to the Yugoslavs, and in subsequent attempts have failed to keep pace with the exploits of their neighbours and bitter rivals Benfica. Which is perhaps why there is no plaque at the José Alvalade stadium to commemorate the historic match with Partizan.

In some ways the two teams, like Hibernian, were fortunate to be in this first tournament at all. Neither were national champions: indeed Sporting had finished third behind Benfica and Belenenses in 1955. But at the time when entry for the European Cup was discussed by the Portuguese Association, the league programme had not yet finished. So Sporting, champions the previous season, were nominated.

Unlike Hibernian, they failed to take advantage of the favour. At home, they could only draw 3–3 with Partizan, whose team included Branco Zebec, a member of the FIFA side which had drawn with England at Wembley two years earlier. Later he became a coach, and in 1979 took Kevin Keegan's SV Hamburg into the European Cup. In this match, however, he spent much of the time hobbling on the wing after injury. In the return, it was his colleague Milos Milutinovic who proved the greater inspiration, scoring four times in Belgrade, as Partizan won the second leg 5–2. Their reward was to be drawn against the club which was to give the European Cup its glamour and its quality.

Yet in 1955, it must be emphasised, Real Madrid were neither the most popular, nor even the most successful Spanish club. Their recent championships, together with victory over Stade de Reims of France in the Latin Cup final in the summer, had placed them among the favourites for the first European Cup. But in terms of domestic honours, they trailed behind Barcelona and Atletico Bilbao.

The man who revolutionised Real's standing in Spain and Europe was Don Santiago Bernabeu. When he became president in 1943, the club's ground at Chamartin was a cramped affair, with a capacity of about 16,000. The team had finished 10th out of 16 clubs the previous season. But Bernabeu was not dismayed. He launched a membership scheme to finance a new stadium, to include not only facilities for football, but swimming pools and tennis courts, a gymnasium, and even a hospital.

It was an immense gamble, but Bernabeu had read the times correctly. Antonio Calderon, then Real's secretary, recalled:

'We got no money from the banks or the government. Nothing at all. All we had was a model of the new stadium and the belief of the president in our supporters.

'We issued shares for members amounting to about 45 million pesetas (then around £200,000), and sold out in two hours. Later there was a second issue of 15 million, which sold out in even less time. With the money, which I suppose would be worth about 20 times as much today, we built the first two tiers of the stadium and later added a third.'

The president's dream became a reality, and later the stadium was named after him. Bernabeu never forgot the faith shown by the members in his plan. For him, he once recalled, the ground 'held a smile in every stone'.

Less poetically, the president realised he needed a team to match, if the outlay on the stadium was to pay dividends. To that end, in 1952, he enlisted a business manager, Raimondo Saporta, who had impressed him with his handling of a basketball tournament at Real's headquarters. Saporta professed ignorance in matters of football, but proved a genius when it came to contracts. In the years ahead that genius would be frequently tested, as it was by Real's first major signing, the Argentine Alfredo Di Stefano.

He was the most complete footballer of his generation. Born in July 1926, Di Stefano joined his father's old club, River Plate of Buenos Aires, in the same year Bernabeu became president of Real. Di Stefano was then 16, and for a while he was loaned to Huracan, before River Plate brought him back.

In 1947, he won a championship medal, and the first of seven caps for Argentina, but two years later, lured like several English professionals by promises of higher wages in Columbia, he joined the Bogota club Los Millionarios. They were part of a rebel league which had broken away from their national association, and hence from FIFA. No longer required to pay transfer fees, Millionarios were able to offer huge inducements to star players. But by 1953, the party was over. The exiles made their way home, in most cases to a lukewarm reception.

Not so Di Stefano. His reputation had reached Europe. Indeed he had played on Real's ground as a Millionarios player. Now, like a Hollywood novelist with a bestseller on his hands, he sat and waited for the offers to come in. The field was quickly whittled down to two: Real, whose emissary Saporta had signed an agreement with the Columbians; and their rivals Barcelona, who had negotiated a fee with River Plate. Di Stefano's arrival in Spain taxed the wisdom of the Spanish association, who decreed bizarrely that he would play his first season with Real, then alternate in succeeding years with Barcelona.

Their tug-of-love scheme was never tested. Barcelona, growing weary of the affair, offered to renounce their option, if Real would reimburse them the money paid to River Plate. That decision helped shape the destiny of the European Cup, a competition that even by 1980 Barcelona had yet to win. Di Stefano became the sole property of Real and soon celebrated with four goals – against Barcelona. His total was 27 goals in 30 games, as Real took the Spanish title in 1953–54, for the first time since the war. The following season he managed to score 26 when Real were champions again. A great side was taking shape under the command of a former soldier, their coach José Villalonga. In goal, Juan Alonso remained first choice until lung trouble forced him out of the side, after playing in three European finals. At half-back Miguel Muñoz, later the club's manager, was a reassuring figure, while on the other flank the tenacious José Zarraga had gained his first cap for Spain against England in the summer of 1955.

So too had Francisco Gento, a young winger from Santander in northern Spain, who arrived in 1953, just before Di Stefano. Gento, would later establish a record number of appearances in the European Cup – 88 in all – but as a shy 20-year-old took time to settle among the celebrities in Madrid.

'In those days I was just a novice with many famous men around me. I was helped by Luis Molowny and, when he retired, my partner was Hector Rial, who also came from Argentina.

'He understood me very well, and made sure I had plenty of the ball. I always had great speed, but he taught me when to use it. He was a patient man and helped me to learn the game.'

Gento's education was taken a stage further in Geneva in September 1955, in Real's first European Cup match. Their opponents were Servette, coached by the Austrian, Karl Rappan. He had perfected the defensive system known as 'the bolt' which the Swiss national team had employed with good effect in the previous year's World Cup finals. For a time it baffled Real as well, until Muñoz broke the deadlock, and Hector Rial added a second in the last quarter of an hour. In Madrid, the Swiss were beaten by five clear goals. Real were on their way.

Their next match, against Partizan, was played on Christmas Day, but Real showed little charity, winning 4–0. Football was a victor here, for the tie went ahead smoothly, despite the lack of diplomatic relations between the régimes of Tito and Franco. In the years ahead, the tournament was to be less fortunate in eluding politics.

The return in Belgrade in January was played in freezing conditions. Not surprisingly, the Slavs adapted to them more easily, and were a goal up in 13 minutes. To make matters worse for the Spaniards, Rial missed a penalty. When Milutinovic scored for Partizan with a penalty, Real found their margin halved, and abandoned any thoughts of artistry. They were pelted with snowballs by a disapproving crowd, and conceded another goal to Milutinovic near the end, but still managed to hold on for a semi-final place on a 4–3 aggregate.

In these early days, there was little attempt by UEFA to have ties played simultaneously. Indeed the quarter-finals took almost three months to complete. It was not until mid-February that Real learned that they would meet AC Milan in the last four. The other semi-finalists were already decided: Hibernian had beaten Djurgarden at the end of November; and their opponents were to be Stade de Reims, champions of France.

The rise of Reims was the life's work of Albert Batteux, a remarkable manager, who dominated the post-war era in France, much as Matt Busby did in England. Son of a railway worker, Batteux was born in Reims in the summer of 1919, and served his local club first as a player, skippering them to their first professional championship in 1949, and then as a coach. By the time he left the club in 1962, Reims had won five more titles, including the double in 1958, and reached two European Cup finals.

Later, after four seasons in the wilderness with Grenoble, Batteux would be summoned by St Etienne in 1967, and lead their entry into the European Cup. That Batteux would one day leave Reims in a state of some disillusion would have been unthinkable in the 1950s. His 1955 championship side was a fine one, containing possibly the best defender, and certainly the best forward France has ever produced.

The first, Robert Jonquet, was an accomplished, elegant centre-half, who had played with Batteux after the war. In 1951, playing for France at Highbury, he had been the master of England's Milburn. In August 1955 he was a member of the Rest of Europe side which thrashed Great Britain in Belfast. In the same side was his Reims colleague Raymond Kopazewski, the famous Kopa. Born in 1931, he was the son of a Polish miner, who had settled in France between the wars. Kopa himself started work as a pit boy and had suffered a crushed forefinger before his talent for football was recognised.

Kopa spent two years at Angers before Batteux secured him for Reims, where the older man infused his pupil with a strength of purpose and a tactical awareness which never left him. Even when Reims, never a rich club, had to bow to Kopa's transfer to Real Madrid, the influence of Batteux remained strong. Their partnership helped France take third place in the 1958 World Cup finals.

At Real, Kopa operated mainly on the right wing, but his true value – as in Sweden – was at centre-forward, where his awareness made him the nucleus of the French team, the inspiration for the goals of Just Fontaine. Kopa returned to Reims in 1959 to win two more championships, and at 31, despite a troublesome knee, was still capable of exposing England's defence in the European Nations Cup match in Sheffield in 1962.

His début in the European Cup came in Copenhagen, where Reims beat Aarhus 2–0 in September 1955. Leon Glovacki, also of Polish origin, and Kopa's professed favourite partner in attack, scored both goals. The return, drawn 2–2, passed almost unnoticed in France, for on the same day Racing Club of Paris drew more than 36,000 spectators to the Parc des Princes for a friendly against Honved. For Reims, constantly struggling for funds, such enthusiasm was worth enlisting. From now on they would play their home legs in the European Cup in Paris.

Their next match was against Voros Lobogo, rivals to Honved in Hungary, who included another legendary forward, Nandor Hidegkuti. But in Paris, in front of another large crowd, he was outshone by Kopa, who was quite irresistible. Reims led 4–1 in this first leg, but a late penalty by Lantos, another of England's conquerors at Wembley, gave the Hungarians hope.

If the French were meant to expect defeat in Budapest, Batteux had other ideas. Glovacki put Reims ahead, and at one stage they again led 4–1. The match eventually finished 4–4, leaving Kopa and his colleagues the winners by an aggregate of 8–6. To a continent which had grown accustomed to the near infallibility of Hungarian football, it was as if the forces of nature themselves had been disturbed.

But as Reims celebrated came first rumour, then confirmation, of unhappy news. In March 1956 it was announced that Kopa had been promised to Real Madrid at the end of the season. A year earlier he had aroused the interest of the Spanish club with a flawless performance for France against Spain in Madrid. Real's offer of 52 million francs, plus 80 million to Kopa for a three-year contract, proved decisive. In May, while technically still a Reims player, Kopa made his début for Real in a friendly against Vasco da Gama. He scored twice in a 4–2 win, the crowd rising to acclaim one of Europe's favourite sons; a player fit to rival, but not, as we shall see, to outrank Real's own Di Stefano.

A month earlier, he had helped Reims beat Hibernian to reach the final of the European Cup. For the first leg in Paris, the French were forced to reshuffle after a cartilage injury put out Penverne, their combative wing half from Brittany. Siatka stepped in, and there was a place found on the wing for Michel Hidalgo, later manager of the French national side in the 1978 World Cup. Reims went ahead against the Scots with a goal by Leblond in the second half. Little René Bliard, the other winger, got a second goal near the end.

At Easter Road, a fortnight later, the crowd was more than 47,000, swelling Hibernian's return from the tournament to a healthy £25,000. The Scots attacked incessantly, but Reilly found life hard against Jonquet, particularly when the ball was in the air. In the second half Kopa set up Glovacki to beat Younger from the edge of the area, and Reims were in the final without losing a match.

Gordon Smith put Hibernian's defeat down to inexperience: 'Reims were easily the best side we faced, and we matched them for most of the game. But we didn't know how to be patient. And when it comes down to it, there was another main difference between the sides, and that was Kopa.'

The brilliant Frenchman's transfer to Real was achieved in the face of competition from another of the 1956 European Cup semi-finalists, AC Milan. Now a proud and prosperous organisation, it had been founded by English businessmen in 1899 as a joint football and cricket club. Indeed its English origins persisted in the name Milan, rather than the Italian Milano, though Mussolini forced a change briefly in the Fascist era.

Milan's rivals in the city were Internazionale, with whom they shared a stadium, San Siro (the stadium was renamed in 1979 as explained in Chapter 11), and a taste for imported talent. Overshadowed by Inter before the war, Milan moved boldly in 1949 to buy three Swedish players – Gunnar Gren, Gunnar Nordahl and Nils Liedholm – architects of their country's Olympic victory a year earlier. The trio Grenoli, an acronym of the first few letters of each surname, helped AC Milan to the Italian championship in 1951, their first for 44 years.

The dark and powerful Nordahl was a consistent goalscorer, who had been selected for the Rest of Europe against Great Britain in 1947, and again for the FIFA team which drew at Wembley six years later. In 1951 he scored 34 of Milan's 107 goals, the last championship side in Italy to score more than 100 goals in a season. In 1955, with Nordahl again their leading scorer, Milan won the championship again.

By then they had acquired another star forward in the Uruguayan Juan Schiaffino, scorer of the famous equaliser against Brazil in the deciding match of the 1950 World Cup. Four years later in Switzerland he had tormented the Scots in Uruguay's 7–0 win. Tommy Docherty once recalled: 'The game was played in blistering heat and this man murdered us. Poor Willy Cunningham was out of breath trying to catch him. I think he finished the game with a sunburnt tongue!'

Milan teamed him in midfield with Liedholm, a superb all round player who in 1958, aged 35, would grace both the European and World Cup finals, 10 years after his Olympic win. Handsome and greying, he later became a coach in Italy, taking Milan to the championship in 1979.

The Italians' first appearance in the European Cup was far from distinguished. They were drawn against the Germans Saarbrucken, allowed to enter along with Rot-Weiss Essen, since the Saar was technically still not part of Germany.

In Milan, the home side led 3–1, despite the absence of Nordahl. But in torrential rain the Saarlanders continued to battle, and were rewarded when their wing half Phillipi reduced the deficit despite an injury received earlier in the match. In the second half Saarbrucken added two more in a minute to win 4–3 – the first real sensation of the European Cup.

Milan's Buffon dives in vain. Rial's shot, watched by Di Stefano, beats him to score Real Madrid's first goal of the 1956 semi-final in Madrid. Real won the first leg 4–2 and reached the first final of the competition on a 5–4 aggregate.

It proved short-lived. With Nordahl restored, the Italians won the return 4–1, and then accounted for Rapid, drawing 1–1 in Vienna and crushing the Austrians 7–2 in Milan.

But in the semi-final against Real, the Italians themselves were swept aside in Madrid. Hector Rial scored in the seventh minute, and though Milan rallied briefly at two goals each, the Spaniards finally won 4–2. When Joseito scored in the return, Real went three up on aggregate. Though two penalties gave the match to Milan 2–1, the tie was beyond their reach.

So *L'Equipe*'s courage in setting up the competition was rewarded. Real Madrid versus Reims in Paris was for them a natural final, featuring a French team playing virtually a home match, against a side whose reputation in France was already assured. Real's Latin Cup success had been digested, and there was also the small matter of Kopa's transfer.

Even in a bigger stadium – the Parc des Princes began to bulge badly beyond 38,000 – the final would have been a certain sell out. Those who did find room were rewarded with a game of high drama, in which Di Stefano confirmed that he was without an equal in Europe.

The Spaniards, though, began badly and were two goals down in 12 minutes. First a free kick by Kopa was sliced away by full back

The first final – Reims and Real Madrid line up in front of the European Cup before the match in Paris. Real won 4–3, the first of five successive victories in the competition. (*Presse Sports*)

Lesmes, only for Leblond to reach it with his head and watch the ball loop over Alonso. The goalkeeper claimed later that the ball never crossed the line, but soon he was beaten again, when Templin scored at the second attempt.

It was then that Di Stefano came into his own, featuring in a move which began in his own half and ending it with a shot from inside the area, which left Reims' goalkeeper Jacquet helpless. On the half hour Madrid were level, when the faithful Rial headed in from a corner. If anything, Di Stefano raised his game still more in the second half, coming deep to direct operations, then drilling a pass forward for Joseito to beat Jacquet, only for the goal to be disallowed for offside by the referee, Arthur Ellis. Instead it was Reims who went ahead 3–2, when Hidalgo headed in another Kopa free kick. With more than an hour gone, Real's reputation, and in hindsight their destiny as a club, hung in the balance.

Gento recalled:

'It was a very hard match for us, the most difficult of all the finals we played. And we had to win to stay in the European Cup, because we had lost the Spanish championship to Atletico Bilbao.

'We were always behind in the match, and the crowd of course was with the French team. But we had a little luck, like we did in the snows of Belgrade.

'It came with our third goal which was scored by Marquitos, our big defender who was not known as a skilful player. He came from his own half on a long run, but when he finally shot, the ball was going wide of the goal. But it hit one of the Reims players and rebounded off the shin of Marquitos into the goal. As I said, all teams need a little luck.'

Gento himself help set up the winning goal 10 minutes from time; his pace giving Rial time to score his second and Madrid's fourth. Templin hit the bar near the end of the match, but soon Ellis called a halt to an epic encounter. Real had won the first European Cup by four goals to three.

The post mortems centred on the two famous forwards. Hanot

Real Madrid players pose with the trophy after their 4–3 victory against Reims (left to right): Alonso, Di Stefano, Muñoz, Atienza and Gento. (*Presse Sports*)

wrote in *L'Equipe*: 'Di Stefano is the most complete player we have seen. Equally outstanding in defence and attack, he eclipsed Kopa.' Some went further, implying that the Frenchman played as though he were already part of the Madrid team. But the comments were cruel and incorrect. Kopa himself, who had been very closely marked, was philosophical: 'After what I have seen in this game I don't know why Real need me. Their team is complete.'

UEFA president Ebbe Schwartz presented the trophy to Real's captain Miguel Muñoz. A celebratory banquet took place at the Eiffel Tower the following day. It was a time for congratulation; the tournament had succeeded beyond the dreams of Hanot and his fellow pioneers. In all, the 29 games had been watched by 912,000 spectators and produced 127 goals, an average of more than four per match. The gospel of the European Cup had been spread by newspapers and radio, and by the emerging attraction in the home, television. Despite the Football League's reluctant interest in the competition, the BBC did transmit live the second half of the final from Paris.

The worries of adolescence were still to come. For the moment, Europe rejoiced in a cup which provided entertainment for the fans, made money for the clubs, and which had produced an exhilarating climax. The attitude of the English had been the only sour note, but that, as we shall see, was about to change.

In May 1956, a month before the Paris final, the directors of Manchester United met under the rebuilt stand at Old Trafford. Their mood was cheerful: the club had just won the league championship for the second time in five seasons, and won it by the overwhelming margin of 11 points. Moreover the team, unlike the 1951–52 champions, was a young one, christened by the press, with their customary eye for a headline, the Busby Babes, after United's manager Matt Busby.

Busby himself had recently completed 10 years at Old Trafford, during which the club had progressed from an ailing outfit without a pitch to play on, to one of the giants of the first division. His position and reputation were already secure; and it was to him the board now turned for advice on an item new to their weekly agenda, the question of entry to the European Cup. Busby recalled:

Manchester United's manager Matt Busby who realised at an early stage the vast potential of the European Cup. (*Sun*)

The Busby Babes on their way to Madrid (left to right): Curry (trainer), Taylor, Clayton, McGuinness, Colman, Jones, Viollet, Byrne, Wood, Whelan, Edwards, Bent. Berry is framed in the doorway of the Elisabethan aircraft, similar to the one which crashed at Munich. (*Press Association*)

'At the time I was very friendly with Harry Swan the chairman of Hibernian and he was full of it. I had the feeling at this time that football was no longer an English game or a British game but a world game. I said this to the board, and of course they were very happy about it.

'The invitation to compete had arrived from UEFA via the Football Association who had no objections. But the next thing was that the League management committee wrote a letter to the club saying they didn't like the idea of us going in. We had a meeting again and I felt very strongly about it, that this was the new avenue to go into, and we just went on with it.'

United's chairman at that time was Harold Hardman, who had won an FA Cup winner's medal with Everton exactly 50 years earlier, and had become a respected solicitor in the city. Despite his slightness of build, he had the energy of a man half his age, and would constantly amaze office staff by walking the four or five miles to his home at the end of the day. His determination matched Busby's vision. United stressed that tickets and itineraries for the first round had already been fixed, and the League found itself outflanked.

The management committee minutes of September 1956 record that because 'the club had entered the competition in good faith at the invitation of the Football Association, and because all the arrangements for the home and away games with Anderlecht FC have been completed . . . we accept that at this stage Manchester United could not cancel their arrangements.'

If Busby now dreamed of Europe, he had once had thoughts of America. Born into a Scottish mining village in 1909, he lost his father and three uncles during the first war, and, as for so many other boys at the time, the price of family survival was the harsh world of the pit. His mother, however, had other ideas. She prepared to join her sisters across the Atlantic, but while waiting for the emigration papers to come through, Busby, a useful junior player, received an offer from a Manchester City scout.

The family stayed in Scotland, while Busby moved to Maine Road where he became at first an indifferent inside forward, then a classic wing half, winning a FA Cup winners medal and a Scottish cap in

1934. What he lacked in pace he made up in his thoughtful passing and control. Stan Cullis, later Busby's rival as a manager in the 1950s, recalled: 'I grew up in Ellesmere Port and as often as I could I would go to watch Matt Busby, and try to model myself on him.'

In 1936 Busby moved to Liverpool, and then during the war took charge of a star-studded Army team which included men like Joe Mercer, Tommy Lawton and Frank Swift. He also captained Scotland in a number of wartime internationals. Before the hostilities ended, Liverpool offered him a coaching post, but Louis Rocca, Manchester United's famous veteran scout, tempted Busby with an invitation to become the boss at Old Trafford.

In October 1945, Busby arrived to find a stadium blitzed by German bombs, a club chronically short of funds, and a team which had promise, but which had finished a moderate 14th in the first division in the season before the war. Busby, like Bernabeu in Madrid at about the same time, set about building a club as well as a team. He solved the most pressing problem by borrowing the Maine Road pitch from his former club for United's home matches. Later he would do the same for the early rounds of the European Cup.

More significantly, he signed as his assistant an old wartime friend, Jimmy Murphy, to begin a bold and fruitful partnership. With his foresight and fine words, Busby was a superb ambassador for the club. Murphy, on the other hand, was a Welshman with a penchant for plain speaking, a motivator, and most important of all, an excellent judge of young players.

In 1948, United won the FA Cup in a marvellous final beating Blackpool 4–2. In the League, they were runners-up for four out of the first five seasons of post-war football. In the sixth they were champions. But even as they celebrated, Busby and Murphy were preparing to break up the side. From the start their policy had been to find, and then secure for United, the very best of the nation's schoolboy footballers. That in itself was hardly revolutionary – clubs had courted young players since the league began – but Busby and his staff were the first to organise the search for talent.

What is more, having acquired it, they provided a setting in which it would flower. The boy stars who joined United were made to feel as much a part of the club as the members of the first team. Busby, who had known homesickness himself as a youngster in Manchester, even supervised the choice of digs.

'There were one or two of us who sensed what Matt was doing', recalled his old friend Joe Mercer. 'For one thing Stan Cullis had similar ideas at Wolves. But the important thing in life is to be first with something, and in this case Matt was first.

'At the time the first division was full of players like myself at the Arsenal, men who had played before the war. We were the old guard, and people used to moan that there were no players to match the Carters and the Lawtons. But Matt never believed that. He believed in the kids.'

It was Mercer who helped Busby sign the finest kid of all at Old Trafford, a young giant from the midlands called Duncan Edwards. Said Mercer: 'I used to help out with the coaching of the England schools' side, and I saw Duncan when he was 13, a year younger than the others in the team. Mind you he was a man among boys even then. One day Matt came into my grocer's shop asking about a lad

called Alec Farrell, but I told him the one he wanted was Edwards.'
Busby needed little persuading, and nor as it turned out did Edwards.
As for so many other youngsters the name of United, and the
reputation Busby had built, was irresistible. At 16 he was in the first
team, at little more than 18 he became the youngest winner of an
England cap.

'But there were so many other good youngsters', said Mercer. 'I mean you
had Eddie Colman at right half, sharp as a needle, a brilliant little player. To
be honest, I fancied him more than Edwards. I thought big Duncan might
have had a few weight problems later on, but Matt never thought so.

'Mark Jones was a terrific centre half, and then you had the Irish boy Billy
Whelan, who was some player, and David Pegg on the left wing. And
Tommy Taylor. He had a bit of knee trouble when he came to United from
Barnsley, but he was getting over it. He had a lovely touch for a big man,
and I tell you, he was like Lawton in the air.'

Taylor, in fact, was one of the few players United bought, in March
1953. The fee, in a typical piece of Busby diplomacy, was fixed for
£29,999, so the youngster was not burdened with a £30,000 tag.
Jimmy Murphy had trailed the modest Yorkshireman for months, and
at one stage almost called off the chase, when Taylor asked him for a
favour. Murphy sensed a request for an illegal signing on fee; it
turned out to be a plea for two tickets for his parents at Old
Trafford. The United official offered him a standful of seats if he
wished, and soon Taylor took his place among the young celebrities
in Manchester.

Within weeks he was in the England side, and in April 1956 it was
his goal against Blackpool which virtually clinched the championship
for United, and with it the passport to the European Cup. Taylor's
partner in attack was a Manchester boy, Dennis Viollet, who had
played in the England schools side, and joined United in 1949.

'Actually I was a mad keen City supporter – I used to live less than a
quarter of a mile from Maine Road – but when the chance came to go to Old
Trafford that was it.

'I arrived with Jeff Whitefoot and Mark Jones, who had been in the
schools side with me. It seemed all the best young players ended up at
United. I remember a bit later on Bobby Charlton came. Everyone knew he
was going to come through, it was just a question of when.

'But the thing I remember most about those early days was the real family
atmosphere at the club. Jimmy Murphy would swear and curse at us, but he
and Bert Whalley, the coach, were a great influence on young players.

'The older players were helpful too. I can recall Roger Byrne fighting my
battles for me in the "A" team. And off the field we would all stick together
and meet for meals in digs. There were some real friendships made. I know
it's easy to be sentimental about the Busby Babes because of what happened
later, but I can honestly say that it was a rare experience in my life.'

To Viollet fell the distinction of scoring Manchester United's first
goal in the European Cup in the 2–0 defeat of Anderlecht in
Belgium. United's team selection caused Busby few problems. In goal
there was Ray Wood, who had won three England caps since arriving
from Darlington. At full back were two more England internationals:
Bill Foulkes, who was to play more European Cup matches for United
than anyone else, and the captain Roger Byrne. He was a survivor
from the 1952 championship side, in which he had also played outside
left. England capped him at left back against Scotland in 1954, and
Byrne played 33 consecutive internationals, before his death in the
Munich disaster.

At half-back there was a late change caused by an injury to Edwards. Colman and Jones were joined by Jackie Blanchflower, an Irish international of great versatility, who challenged Jones for centre half, and later in the season performed heroically as a makeshift goalkeeper in the FA Cup final. Johnny Berry, known as Digger to his colleagues, was a winger with a proven record as a goalscorer, who had been capped again by England during the summer of 1956. He had joined United from Birmingham in 1951, and like Byrne, now had two championship medals. Berry's partner at inside right was Whelan; Taylor and Viollet played perfectly together in the centre, and the line was completed by Pegg on the left wing.

Anderlecht had lost to Voros Lobogo in the 1955–56 European Cup, but had qualified for the competition again by winning the Belgian league for the seventh time since the war. They were managed by Bill Gormlie, once of Blackburn Rovers, and led shrewdly in attack by the captain Jef Mermans. Said Viollet:

'We didn't really know how strong they were, or what to expect. In those days even flying to a game was quite an experience. We found they were quite a good side, but the game turned when Mermans missed a penalty. The ball was cleared downfield and I scored almost at once. Tommy Taylor got a second goal, but 2–0 flattered us a bit.'

The return, played at Maine Road because the Old Trafford floodlights were not yet ready, proved a memorable night. The Babes produced a show to startle Europe, winning 10–0, with Viollet, playing on the ground where he had been a spectator as a boy, scoring four.

'It rained for much of the match and for the first quarter of an hour it was really hard going. But once we scored, everything we hit seemed to go in. There was nothing they could do. The only forward who did not score was David Pegg, who was far and away the best player on the field. In fact we might have scored more if we hadn't been trying to give him a goal near the end. Against Borussia Dortmund in the next round we nearly blew it. We were 3–0 up at half-time with two from me and a shot from Pegg which was deflected in. We thought we would get another bagful, but in the second half the Germans scored twice, and we had to hang on a bit to preserve our 3–2 lead.'

The crowd at Maine Road was a massive 75,598, proof of the new competition's drawing power. Dortmund's president longed for a stadium as big, but had to be content with a capacity 45,000 for the second leg.

United, with Viollet injured, threw in another young reserve Wilf McGuiness, and moved the indomitable Edwards up front. While Viollet listened to an experimental hospital radio broadcast in Manchester, his team-mates fought hard on a freezing surface to save the tie. Wood, with his tracksuit trousers tucked into his socks to combat the cold, played well, and United drew a sporting match 0–0 to reach the last eight.

The influence of the competition extended beyond the match. At the banquet the players held a singsong, and the speeches, translated by Bert Trautmann (the former German prisoner-of-war, who played in goal for Manchester City, and had been invited to join the United party for the match) stressed the need for friendship between the two countries which had been at war little more than a decade ago. The sentiments were uncontroversial and sincere. The European Cup was not yet a divider of nations, but politics could not be kept out for long.

On 29 October, the players of Honved, one of the favourites for the tournament, left Budapest for a short tour prior to their away leg against the Spanish champions, Atletico Bilbao. Five days later came the news that Soviet tanks had moved into the Hungarian capital, that the provisional government had been ruthlessly set aside, and that thousands of refugees were heading for the border. For Puskas and his colleagues, anxious for news of their families, the following few days were grim. Not surprisingly they lost 3–2 in Bilbao, and no one seemed sure where the second leg would take place, if at all.

In this confused atmosphere, the players reached Madrid, where Puskas learned that his wife and daughter had reached the Austrian frontier safely, after a long journey on foot. Negotiations with Bilbao continued, while letters from the Hungarian FA demanded Honved's return. Some of the younger players fretted for home, but the club's three most famous names – Puskas, Kocsis and Czibor – held firm.

Honved continued to play a number of friendlies in Europe, including a 5–5 draw with Real Madrid, before the second leg with Bilbao was arranged to take place in the Heysel stadium in Brussels. There, on 12 December, Honved ran into more trouble. They were a goal down within five minutes, and then trailed 3–1 after Czibor was forced to take over in goal from the injured Farago. But in a glorious finish, the head of Kocsis and the left foot of Puskas – how else? – put them level, but they could not save the tie.

The revolution marked the end of a brief but remarkable era in European football, which had begun with Hungary's victory at the Olympic Games in Helsinki four years earlier. That country, with its comparatively small population, had dominated the continental game, and its influence, not least in England, would not be forgotten. Now, after a South American tour, the rebels of Honved broke ranks, with some, like Puskas' lifelong friend Boszik, returning to Budapest. But the three illustrious forwards remained in exile, and were to play a further part in the European Cup.

Bilbao's next opponents were the English champions, who arrived from Manchester in January to find weather as miserable as their own. Of United's players, only Byrne and Edwards had ever played in Spain: for England in Madrid some 20 months earlier. But there was a fragile link with the Bilbao ground for trainer Tom Curry, who had played there while touring with Newcastle United in the 1920s. Even he could not have foreseen that a blizzard would add to the heavy conditions soon after the start of the match; nor that the home side, with their five internationals, would take an early grip on the game.

Dennis Viollet was an early victim of the playing surface: 'I had a chance when the score was 0–0, and I shot past the goalkeeper, only for the ball to stick in the mud on the line. They went straight down the other end and scored, and at half-time Matt blamed me! We were 5–2 down near the end, when Billy Whelan got an absolutely brilliant goal. He carried the ball past about four defenders in a sort of slow run. Finally he reached the edge of the area and just crashed the ball in.'

Whelan's goal gave United hope, and the banquet at the Carlton Hotel in Bilbao was again a friendly and hospitable occasion. The only sour note concerned United's journey home. Their plane had had problems landing on the small airfield, and on their return the players found the aircraft covered in ice and snow. Digger Berry recalled: 'It was far from sunny Spain, believe me. We thought we'd just be stuck there, but Matt was worried what would happen if we were not back for Saturday's league match. He had us all sweeping the snow off with long brooms, and eventually we could leave.' The return flight was not without incident either, for the plane bounced badly as it landed in Jersey to refuel.

When the Bilbao team touched down in Manchester, their manager Ferdinand Daucik told reporters that he refused to believe his team could lose by three goals. But at Maine Road, in a match played at fever pitch, United squeezed through, to the delight of another huge crowd, and thousands more who followed the closing stages on the radio. United started anxiously, but found a way through just before half-time when Viollet scored. Two more goals were needed, and two were disallowed by the German referee, who remained calm amid the bedlam around him.

Taylor, whose duel with the Spanish international Jesus Garay was a barometer of the match, put United two up in the second half, and a play-off in Paris looked likely; but with six minutes left Taylor, for the umpteenth time in the match, made a run down the line. This time he rolled the ball into Berry's path. The winger beat Carmelo to put United through on a 6–5 aggregate. It was exactly a year to the day before the Munich disaster.

Meanwhile Glasgow Rangers had begun with hopes of a semi-final place themselves. They were, after all, champions of Scotland, unlike Hibernian the year before. But in the first of a number of dismal attempts in Europe's new venture, Rangers went out in the first round to the French champions OGC Nice, after a play-off. The French, who had sold Just Fontaine to Reims in the summer of 1956, lost 2–1 in the first leg at Ibrox Park. The match which had simmered throughout, with the Scots reacting angrily to the bodychecking of the continentals, had an extraordinary ending involving referee Arthur Ellis.

'It was not a pleasant game, and at one stage I had to stop play and just get everyone to calm down. Towards the end I was hit by the ball on my wrist and it broke my watch. The outcome was I only played 40 minutes in the second half. I blew for time, but in the dressing-room of course I realised my mistake. We had to go back outside, have a bounce up, and play another five minutes. Luckily there was no more addition to the score.'

When the Scots arrived in Nice, they found the Riviera ground under water, and the second leg out of the question. They returned on 14 November, when conditions were scarcely better, but this time the match went ahead. Rangers led with a penalty by Johnny Hubbard, but in another bad tempered affair, Nice scored twice in a minute in the second half to force a play-off. Near the end Rangers' Willie Logie was sent off for fighting, and not for the last time in the competition a referee, this time the Italian Pieri, was escorted from the pitch by police.

Rangers, somewhat naïvely, agreed to hold the third match in Paris, where, without the substantial presence of centre half George Young, they lost 3–1. Nice now moved on to a quarter-final tie against Real Madrid, who had also profited from their opponents' acquiescence over a play-off. Rapid had lost 4–2 in Madrid, but beat Real 3–1 in Vienna, thanks to a hat trick by Ernst Happel, who was later to manage Feyenoord and Bruges in European Cup finals.

Under the present system, Real would have gone out of the competition on the away goals rule. As it was, they offered the Austrians a guaranteed £25,000 if the play-off was held at Chamartin. Madrid won 2–0, and in the quarter-final found the French easier to cope with and won both ties. The second leg in France was watched by Matt Busby, whose United side would meet the winners in the semi-final. Di Stefano made a lasting impression.

'He was the one of the greatest, if not the greatest footballer, I had ever seen. At that time we had forwards and defenders doing separate jobs, but he did everything. When I saw him down there in France I said to the press afterwards "I don't think I've seen a better player", and at the time there was a wee bit of criticism over this statement.

'Later when we played Real ourselves there was a reception, and Di Stefano came over and said "I want to take you on as my publicity agent" – but I think time has proved that what I said after that one glimpse of him was right.'

The two teams line up for the 1957 semi-final first leg in Spain. Right, Manchester United (left to right, standing): Berry, Viollet, Wood, Byrne, Foulkes, Edwards; (kneeling): Pegg, Whelan, Taylor, Blanchflower, Colman. United lost 3–1. (*Popperfoto*) Below, Real Madrid (left to right, standing): Alonso, Becerril, Marquitos, Lesmes, Muñoz, Zarraga; (kneeling): Kopa, Mateos, Di Stefano, Rial, Gento. (*Keystone*)

The prospect of United's semi-final with Real filled the newspapers of both nations for weeks. Busby's team were on course for a unique treble, virtually having won the League again, and already having earned a place in the 1957 FA Cup final. The adventures of United's youngsters had won them admirers everywhere; their power and potential being an antidote to the drab pessimism of post-war football. Some saw in the Babes the sporting expression of the 1950s rock and roll era, but that may be too fanciful. Though they had youth in common, the insistence on the learning of skills and the value of teamwork at Old Trafford were old fashioned ideals.

On the morning of the first leg in Madrid, Busby ran into problems: 'There was so much excitement going on there, and young David Pegg and Eddie Colman became sick. I didn't think I would be able to play them. But eventually we went on to the field with them, but it was quite an occasion for anyone in Madrid that day, let alone young players.'

Even for a United side accustomed to high standards, the facilities at Chamartin seemed special. So too did the atmosphere produced by a 125,000 crowd in the tall birthday cake stadium. Bobby Charlton, then a young United reserve, recalled: 'I was right up in the gods, way above the pitch, and to be honest I was terribly pleased I wasn't playing. I saw Di Stefano and these others, and I thought to myself these people just aren't human. It's not the sort of game I've been taught.'

Nevertheless, Real did not find the game easy. For an hour United, in an all red strip, held on until Gento, who troubled Foulkes with his pace throughout the match, crossed for Hector Rial to score. Then Di Stefano, who had earlier reacted angrily to the attentions of Colman and Blanchflower, added a second. United's reply was a header by Taylor from a Whelan cross, but Mateos made it 3–1 just before the end. Real's fans rose to acclaim their favourites. But United's Berry had reservations about the Spaniards. 'There was no doubt they were a good side, but they could be a bit naughty at times, and that includes Di Stefano. There were a lot of what you'd call professional fouls, and Leo Horn, who was a famous referee, let them get away with a lot. On the day it was Gento who gave us the most trouble, while David Pegg was magnificent for us.'

Pegg's performance persuaded Real to bend the rules a fraction. For the second leg they replaced full back Becerril with Torres, officially only on loan from Zaragoza. For United, Charlton replaced the injured Viollet – his first European match. Under the new floodlights at Old Trafford, Real cruised into a two-goal lead with Kopa, the outstanding player on the night, and Rial scoring. In the second half the visitors were content to kill the pace of the game. United's display, for all their effort, was untidy and at times ill-tempered. They drew the match with second-half goals by Taylor and Charlton, but Real were by then beyond reach. There were lessons to be learned by United's young team.

Said Viollet: 'Even though we lost, we felt the European Cup had been a great experience. There was a glamour and colour about it. I felt playing in one game was worth about 20 league games. We knew that a good side had beaten us, but we were looking forward to entering the next season, because we felt we could only get better.'

The potential of United was obvious to Gento also. 'For us the semi-final against Manchester was the final. They were a powerful

Tommy Taylor (right, dark strip) scores for Manchester United in the second leg of their semi-final against Real Madrid at Old Trafford. The match was drawn 2–2 and Real reached their second final on a 5–3 aggregate.

and difficult team, and we were very impressed with Tommy Taylor. And like all British teams they played right until the end of the match. All they needed was more experience.'

The 1957 final against Fiorentina was a rather tedious affair, which Real, on their own ground in Madrid, won 2–0. The Italian champions had found goals hard to come by. In six matches up to the final, they had managed only eight, despite the talent of the Argentine Montuori and the Brazilian Julinho in attack. They had put out Norrköping, Grasshoppers of Zurich, and Red Star Belgrade, but in Madrid showed little inclination to attack. Real needed a disputed penalty – awarded by Leo Horn when Mateos was fouled even though a linesman had already flagged him offside – to break down the Fiorentina defence. Di Stefano scored from the spot, beating Guiliano Sarti, later to play in three more finals for Internazionale. The second goal was set up for Gento by Kopa, eager for his first winner's medal. Miguel Muñoz again received the trophy, this time from General Franco.

For Muñoz it was the last European match as a player, though he was to hold the cup again as a manager three years later. Real

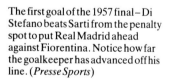

The first goal of the 1957 final – Di Stefano beats Sarti from the penalty spot to put Real Madrid ahead against Fiorentina. Notice how far the goalkeeper has advanced off his line. (*Presse Sports*)

replaced him at wing half with Juan Santisteban, and there was a change also at the top. The 1957–58 campaign would be led by Luis Carniglia, manager of the Nice team which had recently lost to Real.

More significant was the arrival from Uruguay of José Santamaria, perhaps the most impressive defender of the 1954 World Cup finals. Once again Saporta, like some modern mountie, had been despatched to South America to bring back a player and for £45,000 Real had acquired a centre half who could provide a ruthless touch on occasions, but who, by any standards, was a gifted footballer.

'He transformed the way we played', claimed Gento later. 'In Spain we used to have some defenders who were heavily built to make you afraid. They were easy to run past. Santamaria was a player with great technique, who could start attacks himself.

'This was a big difference between ourselves and other teams. Sometimes we would play with only two men in attack, with Kopa and myself coming deeper and Di Stefano almost in defence. But we were so quick to break into attack, that we scored a lot of goals that way. Many of them started with Santamaria.

'Of course Di Stefano was very important to us also. Most of all because he would make us want to win. Whenever we practised, even when we played cards or basketball in the gym, he would want to win. When I became a manager, I realised how important it was to have a player like that on the field. When I was a young player, I would have some bad games. But Di Stefano would keep me going, would always demand the maximum from me, and in the end he helped me.'

Santamaria's first game in the European Cup was in Antwerp, where Real began their 1957–58 campaign with a 2–1 win. Di Stefano scored twice and the second leg was a formality, the Spaniards winning 6–0. In the next round they were to play their fellow countrymen from Seville, allowed to enter after finishing second to Real in the Spanish Championship in 1957. Since then they had lost their coach Helenio Herrera to Malaga, but he was to make his own indelible mark on the European Cup in the next decade.

Seville, who had beaten an undistinguished Benfica earlier, were unimpressive in Madrid, and had defender Campanal sent off. Real's

Di Stefano scores the first of Real Madrid's four goals in the first leg of the 1958 semi-final against Vasas Budapest. Real won 4–0 in Madrid and reached the final on a 4–2 aggregate.

Marsal went with him, but this was scarcely an inconvenience. Real won this first leg 8–0, with four goals from Di Stefano. A 2–2 draw in the return match took Real into the semi-final. Their opponents now were the Hungarians, Vasas, conquerors of Ajax who, like Benfica, were making their first appearance in the competition. Real beat Vasas 4–0 in Madrid – 18 goals scored in three home matches – and lost only 2–0 in the return to reach their third successive final.

There they might have been expected to meet Manchester United again, but that hope disappeared on the runway at Munich. More than 20 years later the memory of the disaster, in which eight players and three officials lost their lives, is still clear. As in the case of the first Kennedy assassination, the news fixed the time and the place in the memories of those who first heard it, late in the afternoon of 6 February 1958. Furthermore, for those connected with the club, particularly the players who survived, the crash left an important legacy. For United the European Cup became an immense, and at times an oppressive symbol, until it was won finally at Wembley 10 years later.

United's early form in that tragic season was mixed. They started as though a third successive championship was within their grasp, taking 11 points from the first six games, at an average of almost four goals a match. But Bolton beat them in September, as did the new first division leaders Wolves. Blackpool and Portsmouth had unexpected wins at Old Trafford. Only in Europe did United find their real form again, beating Shamrock Rovers 6–0 with Whelan quite magnificent on his native soil. United won the return match 3–2, and then Dukla Prague were beaten 3–0 at Old Trafford in a match watched from the stands by the injured Viollet.

'I thought the Czechs were a very good side, and they played some great stuff up to the edge of the area. They had Pluskal and Masopust at wing half, and to be honest, I think Masopust was one of the best midfield players I ever saw.

'Colin Webster played in my place and scored, and I can tell you we were really pleased to have won 3–0. Afterwards one of the Czechs played *Harbour Lights* on the violin when we went back to the Midland Hotel. There was usually a good feeling after these matches.'

United lost 1–0 in Prague in December, and were now drawn in the quarter-final against Red Star Belgrade.

By the time the first leg took place the following month, Busby had lost patience with United's League form, and dropped five internationals. Blanchflower, Whelan, Berry and Pegg were replaced by Jones, Charlton, Ken Morgans and Albert Scanlon. Goalkeeper Wood, carried off in the FA Cup final on a stretcher a few months earlier, made way for Harry Gregg, signed from Doncaster for just over £23,000, then a record fee for a goalkeeper.

Red Star had been the first foreign team to play at Old Trafford, in the Festival of Britain friendlies in 1951. Their wing half Rajko Mitic was the only survivor of the game to challenge United again seven years later. In the Old Trafford mist, the Yugoslavs led 1–0 at half-time, but were finally beaten 2–1 with goals by Colman and Charlton.

The second leg on 5 February was preceded by a match at Highbury which was to serve as an epitaph for the Babes. United beat Arsenal 5–4 in a whirlwind display. They raced ahead to a 3–0 lead, Arsenal drew level, and then United pulled away again like true champions.

In Belgrade, United again went three goals ahead – Charlton scoring twice and Viollet once – but were finally forced to concede a 3–3 draw.

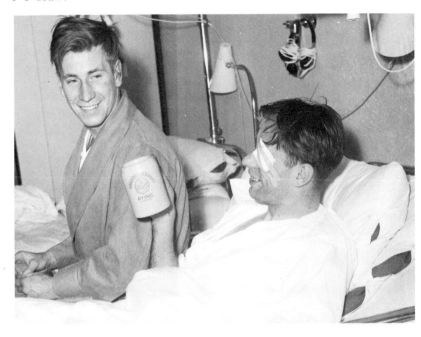

A youthful Bobby Charlton (left) and the Manchester United reserve goalkeeper Ray Wood recovering in the Rechts der Isar hospital after the Munich disaster in February 1958. (*Keystone*)

'Obviously we thought we had won it when we got those early goals', said Viollet, 'but we finished up struggling to hold them. It all got a little unsavoury in the second half, and big Duncan had his hands full with little gypsy Sekularec, who was a tough nut.

'The big outside left Kostic scored, and then they got another back through a penalty. We had players limping, especially Ken Morgans who had a really bad gash. Near the end, they got a free kick outside the box, and the shot hit me in the wall and dropped past Harry Gregg into the corner. The crowd were going berserk, but we got through on aggregate in the end, and after surviving there, we thought we could definitely win the cup.'

The accident the following day changed all that. On the way back from Belgrade, United's chartered Elisabethan stopped to refuel in Munich. At the third attempt at take-off, the plane failed to lift sufficiently because of slush on the runway. Instead it continued through the boundary fence and split in half, the port wing and part of the tail section hitting a house.

Seven players died instantly: Byrne and his deputy Geoff Bent, Colman, Jones, Pegg, Taylor and Whelan. Despite the efforts of the staff at the Rechts der Isar hospital in the city, 15 days later Edwards was dead. In addition Berry and Blanchflower received injuries which prevented them playing football again.

There were other fatalities. United's secretary Walter Crickmer, trainer Tom Curry and coach Bert Whalley lost their lives, and Busby himself was thought at first to have little chance of survival. Of the reporters who travelled with the team, only one, Frank Taylor, survived, and the unhappy death toll included the former England goalkeeper Frank Swift.

Details of the accident and its aftermath, as well as the effects on those who survived, have been recorded elsewhere. In all, 23 people died at Munich, and a great side, perhaps one of the finest English teams of all time, lay in ruins. The disaster attracted sympathy from clubs all over Europe, not least in Italy where the memory of the Superga crash in 1949, which wiped out the entire playing staff of the national champions Torino, was still fresh.

Ironically, United's opponents in the semi-final of the European Cup were to be AC Milan, the present Italian title holders. They had beaten Rapid Vienna after three matches and also exposed the frailties of Glasgow Rangers. At Ibrox, the Scottish champions took the lead against Milan with a goal by Murray in the first half. With 15 minutes left Rangers still led, until they were caught by a series of classic counter-attacks. Grillo, the Argentine, equalised, then Baruffi put Milan ahead.

Still the Scots pushed forward, only to find that height and weight offered little protection against an opponent with an advantage in speed and firepower. Grillo scored again and Bean completed the rout. The return match, on a dismal day in Milan, attracted only 2,000 spectators. Rangers lost again 2–0.

There was rather more interest in Milan's semi-final against Manchester United. Since Munich the fortunes of the club had been guided by Jimmy Murphy, who had missed the match in Belgrade to fulfil his duties as Welsh team manager. Incredibly, he took United to the FA Cup final, in the space of an emotional, and at times hysterical, few weeks.

His Wembley side contained the Munich survivors Gregg, Foulkes and Charlton, together with Viollet, though he was far from match fit. Murphy had added two signings, Ernie Taylor from Blackpool, and Stan Crowther from Aston Villa. The remainder were young reserves.

Perhaps understandably, United failed to make much impression on Bolton. They lost the final 2–0, and the sense of anti-climax was still apparent when United met Milan at Old Trafford the following week. Moreover, Murphy was forced to make do without Bobby Charlton, required by England for an international against Portugal. Ken Morgans came back into the side.

Dennis Viollet, a survivor of the Munich air crash, scores Manchester United's first goal in the 1958 semi-final against AC Milan. The reshaped United won 2–1 but were beaten 0–4 in the second leg at San Siro. (*Associated Press*)

Nevertheless, United won the match 2–1 with a goal by Viollet and a penalty by Taylor. It never looked like being enough in Milan, particularly as Charlton was again on England duty in Belgrade – an unfortunate choice. United lost 4–0, with Schiaffino getting two goals to add to the one he scored in the first leg. Said Harry Gregg:

'They were really a class above us. I was impressed with Schiaffino of course, and with the Swede Liedholm. What I didn't like was what happened before the game in Milan. We had travelled overland this time, and I remember coming from the hotel to the stadium for the match and getting more and more angry as the bus was turned away from different entrances to the ground.

'Eventually we got in about 25 minutes before kick-off. I think it was part
of a plan to unsettle us. Of course they were very emotional days, almost too
emotional at times. And in the circumstances some of the young lads did
remarkably well, particularly Ronnie Cope at centre half who had started the
season in the third team. But there were players lost to the game whom no
one could replace. I had only known them a few weeks, which in a way
might make me more objective in looking back at the team.

'I thought Roger Byrne was a great captain, not afraid to remind the
manager of his obligations to the players. Since he died I don't think there
has been a captain like him at Old Trafford. Eddie Colman and Duncan
Edwards could both attack, and both defend if need be. Duncan was modest,
just a really nice lad, embarrassed by all the praise heaped upon him.

'Digger Berry was for me the best winger in the country after Matthews
and Finney, and might have won his place back but for the crash. And
Tommy Taylor in attack was so unselfish and worked so well with
Dennis Viollet. Dennis was a marvellous finisher. He looked thin but when
you saw him stripped you saw the power of the man. He was like a
racehorse.

'Bobby Charlton was just coming into the side. He stood out because of
the grace with which he did everything, but he was by no means certain of
his place. That's how good a side they were.'

The accident cast a shadow across the competition, but at least the
final lived up to expectations. Milan, having disposed of the new
United, pushed Real to their very limits. The 1958 final was played in
Brussels – a neutral venue at last – where the Italians scored the first
goal, engineered by Liedholm, and put away by Schiaffino. Di
Stefano equalised, and though Grillo put the Italians back in front,
Hector Rial took the final into extra time.

There the match was decided by Gento. 'I remember the goal very
well. I shot once and when the ball rebounded to me I shot again.
This time the ball passed by three or four defenders into the corner,
where the goalkeeper could not see it. Once again we had won, but
again it was a hard match. Everyone now wanted to beat the name of
Real Madrid. Winning the European Cup was now more difficult.
Three or four teams were capable of taking the trophy, including
Manchester.'

It would be 10 years before United did win the European Cup, 10
years in which Busby, who survived appalling injury to take over the
club again, patiently built up a side to secure the trophy denied to the
Babes. For him as for the others who survived, it is difficult to assess
the brilliant team of the 1950s, without letting sentiment intrude. 'But
I honestly felt they had reached the stage when I could nearly have
sat in my office for about 10 years, and just gone out to see the
match. They had reached that stage of experience, power, skill and
everything else, and there were prizes to be won, many many prizes
to be won, and I felt they would have done wonderful things for a
number of years.'

United's next attempt to enter the European Cup, however,
provoked a constitutional crisis in England's football hierarchy, and
ended shabbily. In the aftermath of Munich, UEFA invited the club
to take part in the 1958–59 tournament, along with the English
League champions Wolverhampton Wanderers. The FA again raised
no objection, but the Football League, fearing the precedent of entry
by invitation, opposed United's bid.

Joe Richards, the League president, claimed many clubs objected
to United's entry, though Wolves were not among them. United now

appealed to a joint FA/League committee, which met in August 1958. They ruled that the League did not have the power to forbid clubs to enter the competition, but made no specific ruling on United. Hence the matter was referred to the FA's Consultative Committee, who, in a bureaucratic about-face, decided United could not enter, because they were not national champions.

United accepted the decision with understandable reluctance, and promptly organised home and away friendlies with the team they were to have met, Young Boys of Berne. Their withdrawal left English hopes in the hands of Wolves, whose various teams had won everything they had entered for in the 1957–58 season, apart from the FA Cup. Such strength in depth augured well for an assault on Europe, and in Billy Wright they had a captain of vast international experience. In the summer he was part of England's World Cup half-back line, along with club-mates Eddie Clamp and Bill Slater. In the group play-off against the Soviet Union, Wolves' inside forward Peter Broadbent had won his first cap.

In addition, Wolves had twice tested themselves in friendlies against Real Madrid during the season, drawing 2–2 away, after beating the Spaniards 3–2 in another epic match under the lights at Molineux. The installation of floodlights had been personally supervised by Stan Cullis, a manager of principle and foresight. He was anxious to see Molineux become an all-purpose sports stadium, on the lines of Real Madrid. He also realised, at an early stage, the appeal of foreign matches, yet in some respects his horizons remained obstinately insular.

'My ambition as a manager was to win the first division championship, not the European Cup. Until I became manager Wolves had never won the League. We won it in 1954, and again four years later, by playing attacking football, which was my whole philosophy. In the late 1950s we scored more than 100 goals for three or four years in succession.

'Of course that made us more vulnerable at the back, but that was our style. To win the European Cup required a different style. It required players to go against their natural game, and this I was not prepared to do.'

Cullis' ideals were tested in the first round by the German champions Schalke '04, who had struggled to overcome the Danish part-timers Boldklub Copenhagen in a preliminary round play-off. Yet at Molineux, in November 1958, the Germans led Wolves 1–0 at half-time with a goal by Siebert. In the second half Broadbent scored twice, but Koslowski gave Schalke the draw.

In the second leg, Wolves were without Bill Slater, a lecturer at Birmingham University, who was unable to obtain his release. And they were forced to retain the inexperienced Allan Jackson at centre-forward because Jimmy Murray was still injured.

Jackson, in fact, scored Wolves' goal in Gelsenkirchen, but by that time Kordel and Siebert had put Schalke two up. Wolves, therefore, went out of the European Cup at the first attempt on a 4–3 aggregate, and there was criticism in the German press of their tactics. One paper claimed that wing-halves Clamp and Ron Flowers 'had overstepped the limits of robustness'. In turn, Wolves accused the Germans of wasting time near the end; contrasting complaints which would become all too familiar when British and continental sides met. Cullis consoled himself by winning the League championship again.

The memorable victories by Wolves in friendlies in the 1950s seemed to bode well for their assault on the European Cup. But in their first match of the 1958–59 tournament they could manage only a 2–2 draw at Molineux with the German champions Schalke, and later went out on a 4–3 aggregate.

The Scottish champions, Heart of Midlothian, fared even worse, for all their promise. They had won the title by a convincing 13 points, scoring 132 goals in 34 matches. Jimmy Wardaugh and Jimmy Murray scored 28 apiece, while a young fair-haired centre-forward, Alex Young, managed 24. Behind this prolific trio was wing half Dave Mackay, a born competitor who, like Young, would later make his mark in England.

Hearts' opponents were Standard Liège from Belgium, who included the exquisitely named Bonga-Bonga in attack. He came from the Congo, the former Belgian colony, and scored in Standard's 5–1 home win in the first leg. At Tynecastle, Hearts could manage only a 2–1 victory and, like Rangers, had found Europe a bewildering experience.

So, too, had Juventus, whom many observers expected to reach the final, in succession to Fiorentina and Milan. Backed by the millionare Agnelli family, the Turin club had spent boldly in 1957 on two forwards: Welshman John Charles from Leeds United for £65,000, and Enrique Omar Sivori from River Plate in Argentina, for a then world record fee of £91,000. Both became idols in Italy, though in temperament they were worlds apart. Charles could play with equal facility at centre-forward or centre half, and his calmness in the face of provocation puzzled opponents. So too did his strength in the air. Sivori was more likely to invite an engagement than resist one, but his close control and balance were remarkable. The short, dark haired Argentine was named Europe's Footballer of the Year in 1961.

Sivori scored all three goals in Juventus' first European Cup match, a 3–1 win over the Austrians Wiener Sportklub in Turin. The return in Vienna, however, was a disaster as the Italians conceded seven goals without reply. They were to do rather better at their next attempt, and in 1973 reached the final; but like Glasgow Rangers, Juventus' success in the competition bears no relation to the number of times they took part.

More successful were Reims, whom Batteux had again taken to the championship in 1958, adding a cup win for good measure. Since the departure of Kopa in 1956, he had recruited not only Just Fontaine, but Jean Vincent from Lille and later Roger Piantoni from Nancy. Not surprisingly, Reims easily won the French title, with Fontaine scoring 34 goals in 26 games. In the summer, with his two Reims colleagues alongside, and Kopa prompting from behind, he scored a record 13 goals, as France took third place in the 1958 World Cup.

After beating Ards of Northern Ireland and Finnish champions Palloseura, Reims were drawn against Standard Liège in the quarter-final. With Fontaine out through injury, the French lost the first leg in Belgium 2–0, which prompted Standard's coach, the Hungarian Kalocsai, to claim that Reims were past their best, and pursuing old fashioned methods.

At the Parc des Princes in the second leg, he was made to pay for his boldness. In a festive atmosphere – the Parisians again adopting Reims as their own – the French champions drew level, and Fontaine got the winner 10 minutes from time. The semi-final against Young Boys of Berne was a less dramatic affair. Reims, trailing 1–0 from the first leg, again scored three times without reply at home, to reach the final for the second time in four years. For a club of modest resources, it was no mean achievement.

The 1959 final in Stuttgart pitted Real Madrid against Stade de Reims for the second time in four years. This time Kopa was appearing for the Spanish side against his old colleagues. Though Puskas appeared in the programme, he was not considered fit enough to play and was replaced by Rial.

Amtliches Programm des DFB

Endspiel um den Europa-Pokal der Landesmeister
Real Madrid - Stade Reims

am 3. Juni 1959 im Neckar-Stadion in Stuttgart · Spiel-Beginn um 18 Uhr

Real Madrid, however, were still the yardstick by which any progress was judged. While Reims and the rest of Europe struggled to close the gap on the Spanish pacemakers, Real, like a great athlete, kicked again. This time the added ingredient was the Hungarian Ferenc Puskas, who arrived in Madrid in the summer of 1958, aged 31. His transfer, unlike those of Di Stefano, Kopa and Santamaria, was something of a gamble, but one which others clubs could easily have taken.

Puskas, of course, would still have been a legend if he had never kicked a ball in Spain. His career as captain of Honved and Hungary made certain of that. He was the dominant personality in a team of stars, though his deficiencies made some teachers of the game despair. He was weak on his right side, headed the ball poorly, and was a little too heavy. Yet his record as a goalscorer in all competitions was outstanding. Years later when told of Pele's 1,000th goal, Puskas claimed to have left that total far behind.

Until Real arrived in his life, in the person of Emil Osterreicher – a Hungarian now working for Bernabeu – it seemed Puskas had scored his last. Since the revolution he had lounged about Europe playing friendlies and fighting a suspension by the Hungarian FA, as well as a thickening waistline. Under the Spanish sun, however, the pounds dropped from him. Though he looked short of pace in his early games, the goals began to flow: 21 in 24 league games in 1958–59, second only to Di Stefano.

The story goes that Puskas allowed Di Stefano to beat him to the title, as a means of appeasing the imperious Argentine. Puskas has neither confirmed nor denied the story, but his Real colleague Gento is clear about one thing.

'There was never any trouble between Puskas and Di Stefano. Nobody could fail to get on with Pancho – he was almost too good a person. He was the only player I used to stay and watch after training, and I wish I had seen him when he was younger. His shooting was unbelievable and his left foot was like a hand, he could do anything with it. In the showers he would even juggle with the soap.

'And the people who came to see him . . . wherever we played in Europe, there would be a little group of Hungarians waiting for him. I never knew there were so many Hungarians! He would always give them something – a souvenir or perhaps some money. I'm sure he has no medals left.'

Puskas played his part in Real's passage to the 1959 European Cup final, but a leg injury meant he missed the match against Reims. Carniglia, perhaps recalling that a half-fit Puskas had cost Hungary dear in the 1954 World Cup final, decided not to risk him.

Earlier Real had disposed of the Turkish champions Besiktas, despite having Di Stefano sent off in Madrid. In the next round, Puskas himself was dismissed for retaliating against the Wiener defender Barschandt. He greeted his tormentor with flowers at the airport before the second leg in Madrid, but missed the match. Real still managed seven goals against the Austrians, four of them from Di Stefano.

Now in the semi-final, Real were drawn against their rivals from across the city, Atletico Madrid. They had entered the European Cup as runners-up to Real in the Spanish championship, and their supporters welcomed a chance to settle old scores.

Atletico were then the poor relations in Madrid; their stadium on the south side a shambles compared to Chamartin, but their team was not to be taken lightly. Like their wealthy neighbours, they blended nations in attack, teaming the Portuguese Mendonca with Joaquim Peiro, a Spaniard who later won the European Cup with Internazionale in Italy. In addition, they had signed the celebrated Brazilian Vava, scorer of two goals in the 1958 World Cup final.

They had reached the semi-final by beating Drumcondra, CDNA Sofia and Schalke '04, the conquerors of Wolves. When the German team arrived in Madrid, they found that the game was to be played at Chamartin because of its greater capacity. Bernabeu himself showed the players round Real's trophy room, but Schalke came no nearer to the European Cup, losing to Atletico by 3–0. The second leg was drawn 1–1.

Real craftily offered to play both legs of the semi-final in their own stadium, but for Atletico there was pride at stake, as well as gate money. The first leg, however, did take place at Chamartin, where Chuzo scored first for Atletico. Rial equalised, and the game then turned on the award of a penalty to each side. Puskas scored for Real, but Vava's spot kick was saved by Dominguez, the Argentine who had replaced Alonso in goal.

For the second leg at the Metropolitano, Real left out Puskas, but restored Kopa who had missed the first match through injury. Atletico won the game with a goal by their winger Enrique Collar before half-time, and the semi-final went to a third match in Zaragoza. Puskas now returned in place of Rial, and had the satisfaction of scoring the goal which put his side in the final. After Collar had cancelled out an early goal by Di Stefano, the tubby Hungarian took his chance well in the 40th minute, sliding his shot wide of Pazos' right hand.

The final was held in Stuttgart where Real, even without Puskas, were the overwhelming favourites. Batteux's defenders still had three world class forwards to contain, including their former colleague Kopa. The French manager argued against setting a man on Di Stefano. 'To ask a man to mark him, is to ask him to commit suicide . . . it is better to mark the others tightly, and let the artist play.'

His theory, like many others put forward against Real, was soon in shreds. Mateos scored a soft goal with less than two minutes gone, and would have scored again had not Colonna made a magnificent save from his penalty kick. Di Stefano scored in the second half to maintain his record of a goal in every final, but Real did not extend themselves, particularly after Kopa was injured during the match. 'I was savagely and deliberately fouled by Jean Vincent', wrote Kopa later, 'and when he came to apologise after the match I did not accept his excuses.'

Both Batteux and his team were criticised for their poor performance, and although with Kopa back, Reims were to qualify for the European Cup again, the Stuttgart final began a period of failure for French football. Their next finalist in the competition would be St Etienne, 17 years later.

It is true they failed to show any sort of form, a fact which Fontaine himself emphasised while watching Malmo labour against Nottingham Forest in 1979: 'We did not play well against Real Madrid, but at least we tried to attack them. When we were playing there was more space on the field, and when you face world class players, you cannot stop every one of them. We were by no means a bad side, but Real were the best I ever saw, apart from Brazil.'

More than two decades after that final, it is difficult to fault the assessment of Fontaine. No club since has dominated the continent to the extent of Real in the later 1950s. The European Cup advanced in four years to an event of immense profit and prestige, and the Spanish club marched with it. Their players were in demand all over Europe. Real grew richer through a programme of friendly matches, and used the receipts to acquire still more famous names.

Their next major signing, however, was less successful. As Kopa departed, Real made overtures to Botafago of Brazil for their brilliant inside forward Didi. He arrived in Madrid, along with fellow countryman Canario, with his reputation secured by his displays in the 1958 World Cup, but Di Stefano was far from impressed. 'I hear you are my successor', he was reported to have told Didi, who at 30 was three years younger than Di Stefano. 'Well you are too old and you are not good enough.'

Real used the Brazilian sparingly in the League, but paraded him in exhibition matches. These included a sparkling evening at Old Trafford in October 1959 when, with three immortals – Didi, Di Stefano and Puskas – at inside forward, Real beat Manchester United by 6–1. Canario also played on the wing, but he took time to settle. He remained, however, to figure in Real's greatest European final in 1960, by which time Didi had returned to Brazil.

Gento recalled that the Brazilian star had problems adjusting to the pace of Spanish football. But more damaging was his failure to combine with Di Stefano, the centre of Real's universe. Their pattern of play was determined by the more gifted players, an arrangement underlined by the promotion of Miguel Muñoz to team manager during the 1959–60 season. Said Gento:

'He was of course an old friend, and we respected each other. In a sense it was easy for him. He did not need to talk a lot, because we played the same way all the time, going out to win the game. We never had a blackboard, and hardly ever talked about our opponents, and this attitude helped us to turn games our way.

'When I became a manager, I learned it was sometimes better to know about the team you were playing. But when we played, we had men who did not need to be taught. Later on I remember that we sent three spies to look at Benfica. We lost to them by five goals to one. In the days of Di Stefano, we just came to the stadium, put on our shirts, and played.'

Such confidence and simplicity of style took Real beyond the reach of their rivals in Europe. But, in Spain, admiration for what they had achieved was tinged with envy. Nowhere was this more true than in Barcelona, whose proud people were resentful of authority of most kinds, particularly after the excesses which flowed from Madrid after the Civil War. To the delight of the whole of Catalonia, CF Barcelona beat Real into second place in the 1959 Spanish championship, with a team which also boasted a galaxy of international stars.

They included Puskas' old Honved colleagues, Kocsis and Czibor, but the crowd's favourite was Ladislav Kubala, an inside forward of vast experience and ability, who had been capped for three European nations. He had also represented FIFA against England in 1953 at Wembley, where he dictated the course of the match. His apprentice in attack was a young Spaniard, Luis Suarez, signed from RCD Coruna, soon after making a sensational début for them against Barcelona. Slim and elusive, he quickly became a power in his own right, and in 1960 was named European Footballer of the Year. Later he would move to Internazionale in Italy for a world record fee.

Not content with the élite of the old world, Barcelona had also recruited a Brazilian forward Evaristo, a 'naturalised' Paraguayan in Martinez, and a Uruguayan winger Villaverde. In defence there was a sprinkling of Spanish internationals, starting with Ramallets in goal, a consistent choice for his country since the 1950 World Cup. In March 1960, he was one of seven Barcelona players in the Spanish side which beat Italy 3–1. The others were Olivella, Gracia, Segarra, Gensana, Martinez and Suarez. The ringmaster of this talented circus was the charismatic Helenio Herrera, born in Buenos Aires in 1916. At an early age, his family moved to Casablanca. After a moderate career as a player, Herrera became a coach, first in France, later in Spain and Portugal.

In his first season at Barcelona, 1958–59, he led them to a league and cup double, with a mixture of devilry and attention to detail. Players bowed before his personality and propaganda, which included the pinning of slogans to the walls of the dressing-room. The press were encouraged to prey on the nerves of forthcoming opponents, while the fans could be incited to fever pitch by his appearance on the touchline. But Herrera was also a coach of some standing, a shrewd dissector of a team's strengths and weaknesses. Domestically he had shrugged aside the might of Real. Now, a mortal with the temerity to challenge a god, he attempted to loosen their grip on the European Cup.

Victory over CDNA Sofia was followed by home and away wins against the formidable Italians, AC Milan. Now in the quarter-final, Herrera's team drew Wolverhampton Wanderers, winners of the League championship for the second year running. Stan Cullis had lost his captain Billy Wright, who retired at the start of the 1959–60 season. Cullis simply switched Slater to centre half which enabled Wolves to accommodate both Clamp and Flowers alongside him. Murray was back to his best, while Broadbent's unhurried excellence in midfield belied Cullis' supposed reliance on power. 'Peter was a classic. The kind of player you allowed to express himself and entertain the public. Above all, he had balance and you cannot be a really good player without that. Perhaps he lacked a little determination, I don't know. I do know he was a natural, and the £7,500 I paid for him was one of the best things I ever did.'

Broadbent scored Wolves' first goal of their new European Cup campaign against Vorwaerts of East Germany. Wolves lost 2–1 in Berlin, but had a comfortable 2–0 win at Molineux. In Belgrade, against Red Star in their next match, Wolves were involved in another rough encounter, but managed to draw the first leg 1–1. On Armistice Day, some of the tackling seemed wholly inappropriate, and once again local journalists complained of 'the incorrect play of the guests which spoiled the match'. At home in the second leg, Wolves won 3–0, with two late goals from Bobby Mason.

Two newspaper articles set the scene for Wolves' quarter-final tie with Barcelona. In the first, Di Stefano advised the English champions how to beat the Spaniards, and was greeted by banners recalling his treachery when Real next visited the Gran Estadio. More prophetically, Dennis Viollet wrote in his weekly column: 'I don't fancy Wolves to win the European Cup. Their power football may get them through another round, but I cannot see them winning the trophy.' His remarks brought him a reprimand from the League, but his thoughts were given credence by what followed.

The first leg was played in Barcelona, where with a little more fortune, Wolves might have scored first. But as they pushed forward in search of an early goal, the Spaniards' counter was crisp and clinical. Villaverde and Kubala scored in the first quarter of an hour, and Wolves finally lost 4–0. The Spanish press found praise only for Ron Flowers. Most echoed the words of the reporter who wrote: 'Wolves, like all English teams, continue to play football that is 20 years behind the times.'

At Molineux the pitch, heavy after rain, and the packed crowd seemed to recreate the conditions of Wolves' epic friendlies, but this time it was the visitors who were inspired. Barcelona won 5–2, with Kocsis, replacing Kubala, the tormentor-in-chief and scorer of four of the goals. Cullis said afterwards: 'If we had to be beaten, I'm glad it was by a team like this.' And once again the Englishmen, novices in Europe, showed themselves to be masters of their own kingdom. Wolves won the FA Cup in May 1960, and missed the first League and Cup double of the century by a single point.

The stage was now set for the meeting which Herrera had relished. Barcelona would meet Real Madrid for a place in the final. In Madrid, there was a hint of crisis in the air. Real were unhappy with their new coach, Fleitas Solich, who replaced Carniglia. A month before the semi-final he was paid off, and Muñoz was promoted and became his successor. His appointment was well received by the players, but Muñoz knew the team needed strengthening if Real were to reach the final.

From Osasuna, therefore, came full back Enrique Pachin, while from Betis of Seville Luis Del Sol arrived, to add his industry to the Real midfield. Neither were eligible to play in the Spanish championship until the following season, but UEFA's three-month qualification rule was passed too late to prevent them playing in the European Cup.

Barcelona's chances of winning the first leg of the semi-final in Madrid were now set back by a row between Herrera and Kubala. He objected to the system of bonuses offered by the club, and Czibor supported him. Herrera left them both out of the side, a decision which was to have a large bearing on the tie, not to mention the manager's own future.

If Real were thought to be slipping, they found a foothold in the match with a 3–1 win. Di Stefano, at his most majestic, scored twice. Puskas scored the other, then added two more in the second leg, which Real also won 3–1.

The two emphatic wins for Madrid precipitated the fall of Herrera. Flying too near the sun, he had been badly burned, and the crowd could not forgive the exclusion of Kubala. Besides, like Real in an earlier decade, Barcelona had the financial burden of a new stadium to shoulder, and failure in Europe closed one of the roads to solvency. Herrera left for Inter, and yet another episode in his chequered career. Barcelona held on to win the Spanish league, and earn themselves the chance of revenge against Real.

The other semi-final offered plainer fare: the rugged organisation of Glasgow Rangers, playing in the European Cup for the third time in four years, against the West German champions Eintracht Frankfurt. The Germans, as Rangers were soon to discover, were not to be taken lightly. Indeed until the hat trick of wins by Bayern Munich in the 1970s, Eintracht were the only German side to reach the final of the European Cup. Their performances owed much to the wisdom of two forwards in their 30s, Alfred Pfaff and winger Richard Kress; and in centre-forward Erwin Stein, they possessed a youngster of true promise, outshone in Germany only by the brilliance of the Hamburg forward Uwe Seeler. Eintracht had beaten Young Boys of Berne, semi-finalists the previous year, and Wiener Sportklub, en route to the semi-final against Rangers.

The Scots had the incentive of knowing that the final would be played at Hampden Park, but in terms of coping with the special demands of Europe, they remained unprepared. Their wing half Willie Stevenson, later to reach another European Cup semi-final with Liverpool, said:

'When you look back at that year, our lack of knowledge was laughable. We had some skill in the side as well as just strength, but it was all chanelled into specific areas of the field. My job at left half was to get the ball out to the left winger, and woe betide me if I then loitered about in the penalty area. I had to get straight back.

'Alex Scott, for instance, had tremendous ability to beat a man, but he was not allowed to stray from his touchline, and intrude on other people's territory. And the training. All that running we did. No wonder they encouraged the big men. The dressing-room was built for them – we used to laugh because little Willie Henderson had to jump up to reach his peg. When I was there the defenders were men like Bobby Shearer, who was built like a tree trunk. Up front there was Jimmy Millar, a hard man who would chase anything. The exception was Ian McMillan, a really skilful inside right who had come to Ibrox late in his career. Too late to change him.

'Our first match that season was against Anderlecht, which was a battle. At one stage I remember their forward Jurion, who played in glasses, kicked Harold Davis, which was not a very sensible thing to do. He knew it as well, because as soon as Harold moved towards him, he ran off behind the back of the goal.

'We won the home match 5–2 after their goalkeeper had a bit of concussion. We knew there would be trouble in the return, and there was. It was a small ground with a wall around the side close to the pitch, and sure enough someone slid Alex Scott into it. He came back with his head all bandaged, but played on and we won the match 2–0.'

The Czech champions, Red Star Bratislava, now visited Ibrox, and lost 4–3 after having goalkeeper Hlavaty stretchered off, and Matlak sent off. Rangers' Millar was sent off in the return, which was drawn 1–1.

Their quarter-final opponents were Sparta Rotterdam, who included the Irish international Johnny Crossan, later to return to Britain after suspension to help Sunderland and then Manchester City reach the first division. Rangers beat Sparta 3–2 in the first leg in the Netherlands (for once the match was free from incident) but then lost 1–0 at Ibrox. The Dutch part-timers agreed to play the third match at Highbury – it was to be London's first European Cup game – where the Scots squeezed through by 3–2 to reach the semi-final.

'At that stage', recalled Stevenson, 'we fancied our chances of getting to Hampden Park. But that thought lasted about five minutes into the first leg against Eintracht in Germany. They were so quick, and they killed us at our own game, which was wingers. At half-time it was one each, and they had missed a penalty, but in the second half we didn't know whether we were coming or going.

The first goal of the 1960 final – Kress nips in front of Santamaria, Zarraga and Dominguez to put Eintracht ahead. *(Press Association)*

'They had a wing half called Stinka, who would just float the ball out to either wing, and we couldn't get near them. We were like the straight man to the comic – I didn't really feel I had been in a game because I only touched the ball about 20 times in the match. We lost 6–1 but honestly it could have been 10.'

At Ibrox, Rangers were forced to go forward, and were beaten again 6–3. Stevenson, refusing to believe a team which had put 12 goals past his side could possibly lose, immediately put five pounds on Eintracht to beat Real at Hampden.

The 1960 European Cup final has already gone down in the annals of sporting excellence. As a contest, it was all over by half-time, but as a display of the highest skills the game of football can offer, the match has become a collector's piece. Indeed the English FA has retained the film of the match as a coaching aid. But its effect on the viewer goes beyond mere instruction for, 20 years later, the artistry of the Spaniards can still delight and amaze. Not that Eintracht did not play a part in the classic. For a while Stevenson's bet looked safe, particularly when Kress, arriving quickly at the near post, put the Germans ahead after 20 minutes. But soon Real were level when Zarraga found Canario, whose cross was turned instantly past Loy by Di Stefano.

Alfredo Di Stefano, perfectly balanced, equalises for Real Madrid in the 1960 final against Eintracht Frankfurt. He went on to complete a hat trick as Real won 7–3. *(Keystone)*

After half an hour Real were ahead when the goalkeeper failed to hold Canario's shot and Di Stefano reacted sharply to force the ball in. Then a poor clearance was seized on by Puskas, who hit a fierce left footed shot into the net from near the byline. At half-time Real led 3–1. Still there was more as the conjurors reached deep into their repertoire of tricks, to the delight of the 127,000 crowd: Di Stefano was everywhere, every arrogant flick destined for a colleague; Gento's pace was bewildering, his understanding with Puskas total; behind them Del Sol tidied the loose ends, rarely wasting a ball.

A penalty, harshly awarded for obstruction on Gento gave Puskas his second goal. Soon he had four: with a header from Gento's cross; and then, as he stretched to kill a ball he had no right to reach, he drove it under the angle of post and bar. All power and class.

Stein's left footed shot made the score 6–2 after 72 minutes, but Di

Stefano's answer was immediate. From the restart, he received the ball from Puskas, accelerated towards goal and drove the ball past Loy for Real's seventh. A poor back pass let in Stein near the end to make the final score 7–3.

Real's Ferenc Puskas completes his hat trick against Eintracht in the 1960 final. Puskas scored four goals in Real's 7–3 victory. (*Press Association*)

The spectators rose to acclaim the Spanish masters, who were soon doing a lap of honour round Hampden with the trophy. Real's fifth final had seen them at their most fluent. Said Gento:

'We were aware that the day was something special, even for us. I don't think any of us wanted the referee to end the match, and I think that was true of the crowd also. I think it was our best display, because of the quality of the goals. But you must also remember that Eintracht played very correctly, and that it was a friendly game.'

In subsequent years, the Glasgow final became a symbol of a more innocent age, when teams like Real were allowed to perform unmolested. Later, their stars would collide with more brutal forms of play. For the moment, their challengers could only relax and bask in reflected glory. The Spaniards were, unquestionably, one of the greatest teams of all time and the European Cup was fortunate that its formative years coincided with, and provided a platform for, Real at their peak. For they gave status to the competition, which in turn gave the others who entered prestige also, not to mention a fortune in gate receipts. UEFA allowed the original trophy to stay in Madrid. It seemed the very least they could do.

CHAPTER THREE

THE FLIGHT OF THE EAGLES
(Benfica, 1961–63)

The man chiefly responsible for ending Real Madrid's momentous European Cup reign came to an untimely end himself in the hot summer of 1979. When Sandor Kocsis, aged 51, fell to his death from the fourth floor window of a clinic in Barcelona, it was an unworthy exit for the man the Hungarians called 'Golden Head'. But then, despite his halcyon days in international and European club football, Kocsis had quite often found his luck taking a wrong turning. The memory of an illustrious career could not compensate for unhappiness brought about by domestic problems and illness – first a serious leg operation, then a stomach complaint for which he was being treated in the hospital where he died.

Kocsis will be remembered as the top scorer in the 1954 World Cup; for his average of more than one goal a game in 68 internationals for Hungary; for the devastation of Wolves in the 1959–60 European Cup; and, perhaps, above all else, by the Spanish football fraternity, for the part he played in unseating Real as European champions.

Having imperiously ruled a continent with their five consecutive titles, Real proceeded in the summer of 1960 to make themselves undisputed kings of world club football. They played Penarol of Montevideo, the club champions of South America, in a then unofficial world club championship. Real drew 0–0 in Uruguay in July, then swamped Penarol 5–1 in Madrid in September, with Puskas scoring twice.

Unaware of the unholy rows this same championship would provoke in the future, Real had no difficulty either in winning, or in fitting in the two matches. They were given a bye in the opening round of the 1960–61 European Cup. But when the draw was made for the round of the last 16, it brought together again, with waspish irony, the two Spanish protagonists – Real and Barcelona.

Although their defeat in the previous season's semi-final had led to the immediate departure of Helenio Herrera, Barcelona hung on to win the Spanish league on fractional goal average from Real. Now, under their new Yugoslav coach Ljubisa Brocic, the Catalans were doubly determined to exact revenge. Barcelona had strengthened their defence by signing Jesus Garay, the commanding Bilbao centre half who had played against Manchester United in the European Cup in 1957. Saporta, inevitably, had again been shopping. Real now had a new goalkeeper, José Vicente from Espanol, preferred to Dominguez. But ironically, they were unable to use their latest expensive import against Barcelona. Real had signed the talented Swedish centre-forward, Agne Simonsson, who scored against Brazil in the 1958 World Cup final and got two of the goals when Sweden beat England at Wembley in 1959. But a new European Cup rule, brought in at the start of the 1960–61 season, now meant that players had to be registered with their club for three months before they could take part in the competition. Simonsson would not be eligible until December. Real Madrid and Barcelona were to meet in November.

Real were also without the injured Santamaria for the first leg in Madrid, although their reshuffled team made a splendid start when Mateos, recalled at inside right, scored with a fine shot after two minutes. But Luis Saurez, who was a month away from being voted European Footballer of the Year, equalised for Barcelona from a free kick, as he flighted the ball cunningly past Vicente. Still in the first half, Gento restored Real's lead at 2–1. And that's how it stood until three minutes from the end, with Real below their best but believing their one goal advantage would be sufficient, at least, to earn a third match when they played the return in Barcelona.

The man who ruined their plans and threw the packed Bernabeu Stadium into uproar was Sandor Kocsis. As the ball was put through the defence by Evaristo, the Hungarian sped into Real's penalty area with the defenders appealing for offside and then, a second or two later, sending Kocsis sprawling. The arguments which followed hinged on which offence the linesman had flagged first. Offside *against* Kocsis, or the trip *on* Kocsis? English referee Arthur Ellis had no doubts. He gave Barcelona a penalty. Suarez coolly scored his second goal of the game from the spot, squaring the first leg at 2–2. It was the first time in 17 ties that Real had failed to win a home leg in the European Cup.

Barcelona's £1½ million Gran Estadio was stretched to bursting point with 112,000 spectators, for the second leg a fortnight later. If anything, the atmosphere was more intense than it had been in Madrid, and the referee with the task of keeping the frenzy under control was another Englishman, Reg Leafe. He disallowed a goal by both sides, before Barcelona took the lead. Again it was Kocsis who was the thorn in Real's flesh, crossing for Verges to shoot, and then dancing in delight as Pachin unluckily deflected the ball past Vicente. For the first time in four European Cup matches against Real, the Catalans held the aggregate lead.

Real Madrid responded with the pride of wounded champions. Pachin, indeed, spent the second half limping in the forward line. His was one of three 'goals' disallowed much to Barcelona's relief, by referee Leafe. Di Stefano was twice unlucky. He had one effort ruled out for offside, then appealed in vain as Ramallets turned his shot against the post and a defender scrambled the ball off the line. But even Real were not immune to the most telling tactic in European football – the swift counter-attack. Nine minutes from time,

The goal which ended an era – Evaristo heads Barcelona's second goal at the Gran Estadio. Real Madrid are on their way out of the European Cup.

Barcelona suddenly broke out and Evaristo headed the goal that put them two up on aggregate and out of reach.

Near the end Canario did score for Real, but their domination of the competition was over and with it the European Cup's first and perhaps finest era. Fireworks lit up the Gran Estadio in Barcelona as Leafe signalled the end of an epic struggle.

News of Barcelona's 4–3 aggregate victory made the wires hum across Europe. The tie may have belonged exclusively to Spain, but its consequences affected pretenders everywhere. Real were beaten at last. Their own players bemoaned the Kocsis incident in the first leg which the deposed champions felt was the turning point in the tie. Barcelona's huge gamble of well over £2 million appeared to have paid off. They assumed they were the natural heirs to Real's throne; their gigantic stadium and gifted team ready to assume their places in the vanguard of European football.

If the Catalans' celebrations would be proved premature, Barcelona for the moment made a splendid contrast with Burnley, who had won the English championship in 1960 with average home crowds of under 27,000. They had paid a mere £8,000 for their most expensive player, Irish inside forward Jimmy McIlroy. Yet Burnley, too, were through to the quarter-final of the European Cup, despite McIlroy's pre-season foreboding. He said publicly he was not looking forward to playing in the competition, which he believed had become the province of the greedy and the violent. But McIlroy was to change his mind. His modest, home-grown club received a bye in the opening round, then started their European Cup journey with a 2–0 victory at Turf Moor over Reims, twice beaten finalists. Jimmy Robson scored for Burnley in the first minute, and McIlroy got a second before half-time.

Reims' prolific goalscorer, Just Fontaine, missed the match through injury. He returned for the second leg in France, but now a bad ankle kept out his partner and veteran of four European Cup finals, Raymond Kopa. Without him, the French champions won the second leg but lost the tie. Burnley's 4–3 aggregate victory was marred, however, by a second half incident which typified a now disturbing trend in the spirit of the competition. The Spanish referee allowed Reims to take undisguised liberties at free kicks, sometimes moving the ball 20 yards forward from where the offence took place. Burnley's manager Harry Potts, unable to control himself any longer, took the law into his own hands. He ran from his seat on the touchline on to the pitch, remonstrated with opposition and referee, and moved the ball back to where the latest kick should have been taken. He was later fined by the English Football Association and ordered to sit in the stand for the rest of the season.

But Burnley were through to the quarter-finals, where they were drawn against the West German champions, Hamburger Sport-Verein. Although Hamburg, as they became known, had won the end of season 'play-off', they were still playing in the North German regional league. The formation of the national Bundesliga was still three years away.

A change in the English football structure was more imminent. This 1960–61 season was the last under the stricture of a maximum wage for players, and some of the results Burnley produced suggest that before the wage ruling was lifted and the stakes soared, the game was more entertaining for the spectator. Between September and March, Burnley won 6–2 at Chelsea, 5–2 at Arsenal and 5–3 at Bolton. At Turf Moor they thrashed Preston and Fulham each 5–0, and defeated Wolves, Manchester United and Newcastle all by 5–3. Three days after the European Cup match in Reims, they had staged a memorable recovery at Tottenham from 4–0 down to draw 4–4.

So Hamburg seemed to be going the way of many English clubs when they trailed 3–0 at Turf Moor in the first leg of the quarter-final. Two goals from Brian Pilkington and one from Robson put Burnley in control, and a late goal by Hamburg's outside left, Dorfel, seemed only a mild inconvenience to 46,000 Burnley fans packed inside the ground. 'Looking back, that is what beat us', recalled Burnley's captain, Jimmy Adamson. 'Together with the number of games we had to play, and a fellow called Uwe Seeler.'

Certainly Burnley experienced one of the worst fixture congestions yet to affect a British club. Besides making progress in Europe, they reached the semi-finals of both the FA Cup and the Football League Cup, 1960–61 being the latter's first season. They were forced to play five matches in 14 days, and for a League game against Chelsea on 11 March – four days before the second leg in Hamburg – Burnley took the field at Turf Moor with 10 reserves in their team.

Harris (left, dark shirt) scores Burnley's only goal in Hamburg. The English champions lost 4–1 and went out of the competition on a 5–4 aggregate.

The Football League Management Committee were not sympathetic. They fined Burnley £1,000. Incidentally, the match against Chelsea ended in another 4–4 draw! The following Wednesday, Burnley's first choice defence conceded four goals – two of them to Uwe Seeler. The stocky centre forward, who became the most admired German footballer of his time, led Adamson and Burnley a merry dance, and the English champions saw their lead whittled away. Hamburg's 4–1 victory gave them an aggregate win of 5–4.

Burnley's brave venture from the Lancashire hills was over. The lessons they learned from playing in Europe were of no use to a club who have never appeared in the champions' cup since, but Jimmy McIlroy's thoughts were not lost on English clubs who followed them. 'We attacked too much in the second leg, instead of concentrating on holding the Germans for a period. They took advantage of the gaps we left. I remember suffering from cramp and nervous exhaustion.'

So Hamburg went on to face Barcelona in the 1961 semi-final. The Spanish champions had followed their victory over Real Madrid with a rather less eventful defeat of Spartak Kralove, from Czechoslovakia. But Barcelona's league form was poor, and it cost coach Brocic his job. His assistant and successor, Enrique Orizaola, had to manage without the injured Kocsis for the first leg of the European Cup semi-final.

In their own stadium, Barcelona had to be content with a single, second half goal from Evaristo. Hamburg, having defended well, had the home leg to come, and when they led 2–0 in Germany it seemed as though Spain's hold on the European Cup had been broken. But with less than a minute left, the recovered Kocsis, with his piquant sense of drama, intervened again. His golden head turned a hopeful cross into Barcelona's salvation, and forced a third match. Hamburg's spirit was broken. In the play-off in Brussels, they fell to another goal from Evaristo. One need hardly add that Kocsis helped to make it.

Barcelona, nervous where Real would have been nonchalant, were in their first European Cup final. But it was the impression made by a club in the other half of the draw which was to be their undoing, and which was to bring colour to the next phase of the competition. If the success of Real and Barcelona was essentially due to outstanding players – coaches came and went but the budget enabled all of them to work with internationals of high quality – the relatively sudden rise of the Portuguese champions, Benfica of Lisbon, brought to the European Cup the advent of the great manager.

Bela Guttmann, born in Hungary at the turn of the century and a member of the national team in the 1924 Olympic Games, first felt the coaching urge during a visit to Hugo Meisl's developing football scene in Austria. His experiences in the Netherlands and the United States gave Guttmann a thorough grounding in world football, and when he returned home to Hungary he coached the Ujpest side which won the Mitropa Cup in 1939. During the war, Guttmann was imprisoned in a concentration camp, but resumed his job afterwards and led Ujpest to the league championship and the Hungarian Cup. He also spent some time at Kispest, the club in a Budapest suburb where Puskas started, and which later became known as Honved. But before the players he coached there started their triumphant march across Europe with the national team, Guttmann was on his travels again – this time to Italy.

If the directors of AC Milan had been a little more patient, their club might have prevented Real Madrid taking such an emphatic early hold on the European Cup. For in the 1954–55 season, Milan sacked Guttmann while they were top of the Italian League. They won the championship without him, but the little Hungarian got his hands on the European Cup before they did. Guttmann's period of unemployment ended with the Hungarian Revolution in 1956. He joined the mass exodus, and early the following year accompanied the Honved 'rebels' on a tour of South America.

When the Hungarian party returned to Europe, Guttmann stayed behind in Brazil. Here, he led Sao Paulo to the national championship in 1958, and his 4-2-4 system was adopted so successfully by Vicente Feola, the national coach, that with these tactics Brazil won the World Cup in Sweden in the same year. The following season, Guttmann returned to Europe. FC Porto employed him when they were five points behind leaders Benfica in the Portuguese first division. By the end of that 1958–59 season, Porto were champions. For Benfica, founder members of the Portuguese first division in 1934 and winners of nine championships since, it was too much to take. They promptly hired Guttmann themselves. Now the small Hungarian was poised to make an international reputation.

'The first thing I did when I took over at Benfica was to sack 20 players and gradually rebuild the staff. I was handicapped by two things – players who were not good enough, and the club rule which stipulated that Benfica would never sign players from outside Portugal or her colonies. I started to push the best young players through from the youth team to the first team. Cruz and Neto, the two wing halves, were the first. I also made two important signings early on. One was Germano, the centre half, from Atletico of Lisbon. The other was José Augusto, from Barreirense, who we converted from centre-forward to outside right.

'Although I had been one of the prime movers in the shift towards a 4-2-4 formation I decided to alternate that at Benfica with the old English W-M pattern with five forwards. It suited my belief about football. I always wanted to give the public their money's worth. I believed in defending only if my team were ahead with five minutes to go. I never subscribed to the Italian approach of stopping other teams from playing. In my time at Benfica, I think we only ever had one goalless draw. We nearly always scored first, and I never minded that much if the opposition scored, because I always felt we could score one more than them.

'My coaching was based on the two simple things: passing and shooting. I spent hours working on the quick return ball, what some called the one-two or wall-pass, because I discovered in Brazil it was the best way of opening up any defence on the edge of their penalty area.'

With these progressive tactics, Guttmann won the championship in his first season at Benfica – they lost only one match – and got his first taste of the European Cup by coming to Britain. Heart of Midlothian were again champions of Scotland, their attack still led by Alex Young and strengthened by the signing from neighbours Hibernian of Gordon Smith, whose skill on the right wing had helped Hibs reach the semi-final of the first European Cup. 'Although Hearts had a team that was doing well in Scotland, we were absolutely outclassed by Benfica in both matches. They were streets ahead of us in style, technique and set play. We were running about hoping. They beat us 2–1 in Edinburgh and 3–0 in Lisbon, but frankly the score should have been much bigger.'

Portugal's African colonies had proved a rich hunting ground for Benfica. From Angola came the lively centre-forward and captain, José Aguas, and the little inside right, Joaquim Santana, with his deft control and sharp eye for an opening. Mozambique produced their most influential player, not Eusebio, who came later, but Mario Coluna, a dominating figure in defence and attack. Under Guttmann, he developed into one of the first complete midfield players in the modern game.

In their awesome Estadio da Luz (Stadium of Light), another Iberian edifice with vast open-air seating, Benfica were to prove impregnable in the European Cup for six years. The Eagles, as they were called after the bird on the club emblem, were about to take flight. Their next prey were the Hungarians, Ujpest Dozsa, who found themselves five goals down at half-time in Lisbon. Augusto and Aguas, who each scored in both legs against Hearts, were on target again in Benfica's 6–2 win. An unkind way for Guttmann to treat one of his former clubs.

Aarhus of Denmark were easily defeated in the quarter-final, but in the 1961 semi-final between Benfica and Rapid Vienna came the first riot in the European Cup, posing questions about the control and behaviour of partisan crowds which were to tax UEFA for many years to come.

The first leg, in Lisbon, passed without incident, apart from the three goals which Coluna, Aguas and winger Cavem put past the Rapid defence without reply. The Viennese had a reputation for stirring recoveries, but found Benfica's defence in mean mood in the second leg. It was Benfica who scored first, through Aguas after 66 minutes, and although Rapid equalised they were still 4–1 behind on aggregate.

When they had a penalty appeal turned down with two minutes to go by referee Reg Leafe – the Englishman who presided over the last rites to Real – Rapid's players and supporters lost their heads. Fighting broke out on the pitch, and fans came leaping over the barriers to join in. Police hustled Leafe and the players back to the dressing-room, and UEFA went through the formality of awarding the unfinished match to Benfica. But Rapid's real punishment was a three-year ban on European ties in their own stadium.

So the sixth European Cup final – and the first without Real Madrid – was played in the Wankdorf Stadium in Berne on 31 May 1961, between Benfica and Barcelona. Before the match, Bela Guttmann was pessimistic: I was afraid of their forward line. Nearly 20 years later, mention of those five names still scared me: Kubala, Kocsis, Evaristo, Suarez and Czibor – we did not have players like that. But what we lacked in class, we made up for in stamina and determination. I suppose you would call us a team of fighters at that time.'

And fight was exactly what Benfica had to do, especially after Kocsis put Barcelona in front with a typical diving header from a Suarez cross after 19 minutes. It could have been 2–0 or even 3–0. Costa Pereira, Benfica's capable goalkeeper from Portuguese East Africa, saved superbly from Kocsis; and when he was beaten by Czibor, the balding, moustachioed Germano got the ball away.

Then the course of the match turned almost in the twinkle of an eye. Benfica scored twice within a minute, and Barcelona's veteran goalkeeper and captain, Antonio Ramallets, was widely blamed for both goals. A careful look at the film of the match suggests he was only partly at fault. For the first goal, Coluna had already bisected the Spanish defence with a searching through pass inside the full back to winger Cavem, who was able to make an angled but unchallenged run on goal. Ramallets had to come out, but he did so impetuously, rather than just narrowing the angle. All Cavem had to do was push the ball square to the right, and Aguas trundled in his 11th goal of the competition.

Straight from the kick-off, Benfica attacked again, and a chip from Neto was headed back towards his own goal by Barcelona's Gensana. Some said Ramallets lost the flight of the ball in the early evening sun, because he knocked it against the inside of his left hand post, high up near the angle with the crossbar. As the goalkeeper turned, the ball dropped to the ground – *behind* the line, said referee Dienst of Switzerland – and in spite of Ramallets' attempt to scoop it out and play on, Benfica were 2–1 ahead.

Barcelona still had more of the play – Suarez was keen to impress in his last match before rejoining Helenio Herrera at Internazionale in Milan – but none of the luck. Ten minutes into the second half, the Spaniards fell further behind by a goal from Coluna. He picked up the ball in the centre circle, fed Cavem on the left touchline, and continued his run through the middle. When Cavem's cross was headed away from a crowded penalty area, it was Coluna's unerring right foot volley which sped low into the corner of the net to make it 3–1 to Benfica.

Now Barcelona lashed out like a drowning man. The huge mortgage on their stadium, the £500-a-man bonus for winning, their place in the next European Cup; all hinged on the success they had anticipated in Berne. Kocsis headed against a post from no more than a yard out, then used his head again to set up a chance for Kubala. The shot hit the left hand post, then the right hand post, then came out.

It was Czibor who reduced the lead, with a wonderful left-foot shot 15 minutes from the end. Then he became the third Barcelona forward to hit the post, at the end of a dazzling eight-man move. But Benfica still led 3–2. When the final whistle went, Czibor and Kocsis left the field in tears. No wonder. Seven years earlier, they had been in the Hungarian side so unexpectedly beaten on this same pitch, and by the same score, in the World Cup final against West Germany. Cruelly deprived at the last minute of the two highest honours in the game, both Hungarians settled in Barcelona after their retirement. And it was there that Kocsis died 18 years later.

Among those who saw him play in that 1961 European Cup final – the crowd of 33,000 in Berne was the lowest for the event – was Bill Nicholson, manager of the new English champions, Tottenham Hotspur. What he saw as he made his plans for the following season's assault on the European Cup was one expensive team in decline – Barcelona's stars broke up at the end of the season – and one collective team still to reach their peak.

Bela Guttmann knew Benfica would be better still with the introduction of a natural goalscorer to help Aguas. Coluna was being asked to do one job too many, and the side as it stood might not retain the European Cup. A week after the final in Berne, in Benfica's last league match at Belenenses, Guttmann showed off his new player from Mozambique; and 19-year-old Eusebio da Silva Ferreira scored on his début. Seven days later, in the final of the Paris Tournament against Santos of Brazil, Eusebio came on as substitute when Benfica were 4–0 down and scored a second half hat trick to make the final score 6–3 to Santos – whose side included Pele. He was only 20 himself, but Eusebio was being described as his European heir.

Guttmann only heard of Eusebio by chance. He met one of his old Sao Paulo players, Carlos Bauer, in a barber's shop in Lisbon. Bauer was taking a Brazilian team on a tour of the Portuguese colonies in Africa, and Guttmann asked him to keep his eyes open for new talent.

'I forgot about the conversation entirely, then five weeks later I was in the same barber's shop and Bauer walked in again. He said "Mister" (he always called me that), "I saw a player we wanted but he was too expensive for us. His name is Eusebio." I phoned up the president of Eusebio's club in Lourenco Marques, and they sent him over two days later. We kept him hidden from our great rivals Sporting, who also wanted him, and we bought him for US $20,000.

'By signing Eusebio, I was able to play Coluna deeper, more as a wing half than as an inside forward. He did not like it at first because he did not score as many goals, but he became my best player. He had everything.'

Benfica lost the World Club Championship to Penarol in a play-off, but started the defence of their European title by comfortably accounting for FK Austria. For the first leg of the quarter-final in Nuremburg, they were without the injured Eusebio. Guttmann pushed Coluna forward into his old position, pulled Cavem back to wing half, and introduced at outside left 17-year-old Antonio Simoes, whose speed and skill in both feet, made him one of Europe's most dangerous wingers.

Benfica lost 3–1 in Germany, and lesser sides might have relinquished their hold on the trophy. But with Eusebio back, and Simoes retained, they turned on a blinding display in the Stadium of Light. Bill Nicholson watched transfixed as Benfica wiped out the two-goal deficit in four minutes and went on to win 6–0. It was compelling football. This time the Tottenham manager had a more specific reason for watching Benfica. His own club, having become the first this century to carry off the English League and Cup double, had reached the semi-final of the European Cup at the first attempt and were drawn to meet the winners of the Benfica-Nuremburg tie.

Spurs' devastating side was the best in England since the demise of the Busby Babes and arguably the most artistic of the post-war period. Much of their elegance stemmed from the intelligence of the right half and captain, Danny Blanchflower, and the vision of the slender Scottish inside forward, John White. But their embroidery was balanced by the blistering power of Dave Mackay, a dashing, daunting competitor at left half who never knew the meaning of defeat, and the scorching attacking prowess of the Welsh international winger Cliff Jones, who was equally dangerous on the ground or in the air. Super Spurs, as they were joyfully christened by the headline writers, revolved around these four players. But they had an international goalkeeper in Bill Brown, a solid centre half in the tall Maurice Norman, and a lethal attacking tandem of Bobby Smith and Les Allen.

Tottenham fairly cruised to the first division championship – winning 31 of their 42 games, and securing exactly half their 66 points away from home. After winning their first 11 matches, they never looked like being caught. But Europe was different, as Nicholson quickly discovered when he went to watch Spurs' first opponents, the Polish Champions Gornik Zabrze. His trip to Katowice, deep in the mining belt in the south of the country, was an experience he never forgot.

'The first thing that struck me was a great sense of mystery. I made a four-hour train journey from Warsaw to Katowice, and was met at the end of the line by three men in long coats. They took me to the Orbis Hotel, and told me that was where Tottenham would be staying. It was very poor, and I told them so. Quite a scene developed, and they started showing me into the bedrooms one after the other, even though some of them were occupied.

'I told them Gornik would stay in the best hotel when they came to London, so I wanted Spurs to be in the best hotel in Katowice. They said this *was* the best hotel. I said we would stay in Chorzow instead. They said there were no decent hotels in Chorzow. Well, we would stay in Warsaw then. Warsaw was much too far away, they said.'

And in the end, the immovable East Europeans had their way. Even though the Orbis Hotel was decorated and spring-cleaned between Nicholson's visit and Spurs' arrival, several players were bitten in bed by fleas. But not as fiercely as they were attacked the following day by Gornik, who adapted swiftly to the magnificent pitch in the Slaski

Stadium and romped to a 4–0 lead within an hour. Nicholson was horrified.

'I was bloody upset with our players. We did not show enough determination or discipline. Mind you, I was partly to blame. We were treating it too much like an ordinary League match and taking far too many chances. Gornik relaxed a little, and we got two goals back through Cliff Jones and Terry Dyson. I remember a little group of Spurs supporters, with their Union Jacks, almost hidden in one corner of the stadium among a vast crowd of 70,000 Polish miners.'

But if Gornik could draw strength from a partisan following, so too could Tottenham. The return match at White Hart Lane on 20 September 1961, the first of the great European nights in north London, generated an atmosphere which shook even the stolid Nicholson. 'I had never experienced anything like it. It was frightening. It was such an emotional night that I couldn't tell you how the game went.' In fact, it went entirely Tottenham's way. Lifted by an early penalty from Blanchflower, galvanised by a hat trick from Jones, they ravaged the Poles to the tune of 8–1. Nicholson and his team were learning fast.

'Gornik complained we were too rough, and they did sustain a couple of injuries. But we overwhelmed them with the physical side to the game. I told our players not to stand back and admire the opposition, but to frighten them with the aggressive style we knew best. And that was my attitude towards every home game in Europe. I think the British have paid the continentals a damn sight too much respect sometimes. We talk about their skill so much, that we find ourselves playing right into their hands.
'The truth is no overseas side ever looked forward to playing on an English ground. Even years later they were still afraid. You only have to look at the way Liverpool made the most of their matches at Anfield. The high cross into the penalty area was often scoffed at as being too predictable, but heading is a skill, and so is crossing the ball accurately. At Tottenham, we were good at those things. We had John White who could chip a ball on to a sixpence, and we had Bobby Smith who was good in the air and used to frighten the life out of goalkeepers.
'When we realised how much we had going for us at White Hart Lane, we wanted to be drawn away first every time. It wasn't just that we knew how many goals we needed, it was the fact that you spent half the first leg getting to know the opposition. By the time you had done that, more than half the first match had gone.'

Spurs were drawn away first in the next round and beat Feyenoord 3–1 in the Netherlands. The Dutch had only started paying their players six years earlier and their impact on the European Cup was still to come. Four days after the second leg, drawn 1–1 at White Hart Lane, Nicholson followed Guttmann's example and bought himself a forward of rare pedigree. Jimmy Greaves arrived at Tottenham.
An East Londoner from Dagenham, the son of a tube train driver, Greaves was signed, perversely, from the Italian club AC Milan. Here, he had spent five unhappy months under the tutelage of Milan's strict coach, Nereo Rocco. Part of an exodus to Italy in the summer of 1961 which also included Denis Law, Joe Baker and Gerry Hitchens, the unsettled Greaves was the first to come home. His old club Chelsea wanted him back, but Nicholson outbid them

with a fee of £99,999, thereby relieving Greaves of the pressure of being the first six-figure footballer in Britain.

Greaves was ineligible for Tottenham's quarter-final against Dukla Prague. Again the away leg came first, and Nicholson found out a few more home-truths about European football.

'The mid-winter break was only just over in Czechoslovakia. Dukla made various promises about training facilities, but they did not come up with much. It was wet and mucky where we trained. I learned from visiting Iron Curtain countries that you had to be very specific about what you wanted. You had to say well in advance if it was lemon tea, or minerals or whatever, at half-time.

'Anyway we trained in the rain in these brand new white tracksuit tops. Dave Mackay was fooling around in goal and got his absolutely filthy. It showed why he always had mud down the front of his shirt. What a fantastic fellow he was. We played Tony Marchi as a sweeper in Prague, and they beat us 1–0. At Tottenham, I pushed Mackay into the attack, and he scored twice in our 4–1 win.'

So Spurs were through to the semi-final, and it so happened that when the draw was made, pairing them with Benfica or Nuremburg, this was one of two other quarter-finals still outstanding; hence Nicholson's trip to Lisbon for Benfica's six-goal extravaganza in the second leg.

'In those early years, UEFA would set a time limit by which ties had to be played, but actual dates were agreed between the clubs. Consequently, not everybody played on the same night. Fixing dates for European matches was my biggest headache. We had so many commitments, with League games, cup ties, and a lot of our players being required for internationals. Don't forget the home internationals were fitted in during the season in those days.

'I used to go to the European Cup draw and show the other team our fixture list, and they just would not believe me. Eventually UEFA fixed specific dates and these were incorporated into the programme in England. It was the best thing that ever happened for our clubs in Europe.

'On my way to Portugal to see Benfica play Nuremburg, I stopped in Madrid to see Real play the second leg of their quarter-final against Juventus. They were not the side they had been, and I came back thinking that if we could get past Benfica, we would beat Real in the final.'

Real had qualified for the 1961–62 European Cup as Spanish champions, and set about trying to recapture their old crown by beating Vasas of Hungary, and Odense of Denmark. Their quarter-final against Juventus, with the first leg in Turin, brought them face to face with John Charles, until then by far the most successful of the British exports. Charles' immense dignity on the field, as much as his massive ability, made him an idol of the critical Italian fans. They called him *Il Gigante Buono*, the Gentle Giant.

Juventus chose to play Charles in defence against Real, but their attack looked ineffective without him. When Di Stefano scored the only goal of the first leg in the second half, Turin's Stadio Communale fell silent. Nicholson was among an 80,000 crowd for the second leg in Madrid, and far from being a formality for Real, it produced a shock result. Omar Sivori, the master craftsman of Juventus who always wore his socks down around his ankles, now scored the only goal of the match.

This was the first time Real had lost a European Cup match in the Bernabeu Stadium, but they beat Juventus 3–1 in a play-off in Paris. They also singled out John Charles for special attention. 'Yes, Real were a truly great team, make no mistake about that. But they could dish out the hard stuff too, especially Santamaria. People gloat about them and say they never kicked anybody. Well, they certainly kicked me', Charles said later.

The French referee took a lenient view towards Real's treatment of the big Welshman, but Arthur Ellis, watching the match on television at his home in Halifax, saw the sequence of fouls on Charles as a torrid turning point in the European Cup: 'When I saw the most honoured club team in Europe chopping Charles down so brutally, I realised the convictions I had about the European Cup when I was refereeing in it myself were being proved correct. The competition was getting out of hand. The will to win had become the predominant factor and the financial incentives for players were almost making it a matter of life and death.'

There was also a political edge creeping in, as Glasgow Rangers discovered. Scottish champions again in 1961, they beat the French club Monaco in their first European Cup engagement, then drew the East German champions, ASK Vorwaerts. Rangers won the first leg in East Berlin 2–1, but when the East Germans were refused visas to come to Glasgow, the second leg was switched to Malmo, in Sweden. Here, Rangers were leading 1–0 at half-time, and 3–1 on aggregate, when fog came down and the Swedish referee abandoned the match. The East Germans cheekily suggested deciding the tie by tossing a coin, then wanted to play the following (Thursday) afternoon.

With a Scottish League match looming up on Saturday, Rangers could not risk fog delaying their return to Glasgow. So the match was replayed at 10 o'clock on the Thursday morning, Rangers winning 4–1 before a crowd of fewer than 2,000. But in the quarter-final, Rangers were beaten by the Belgian champions, Standard Liège. A 2–0 win in the second leg at Ibrox Park was not quite enough to atone for Rangers' 4–1 defeat in Belgium, where two of the Liège goals came from Irish exile Johnny Crossan, who had played against Rangers in the European Cup two years earlier for Sparta Rotterdam.

So the 1962 semi-final battle was joined. Standard Liège would play Real Madrid, and Benfica would meet Tottenham Hotspur. In the first leg in Lisbon, Nicholson again used a defensive strategy, with Marchi as sweeper and Blanchflower wearing the number 10 shirt. Greaves made his European Cup début at number seven, playing in a three-man attack with Bobby Smith and Cliff Jones. Smith was to play a considerable part in a memorable semi-final, but only after Spurs got off to the worst possible start in the Stadium of Light. Their defence crumbled in the first 20 minutes, allowing Aguas and Augusto to score for Benfica.

In the second half, with Tottenham recovering their poise, Smith headed a good goal. He also had one disallowed for offside. 'It was close, and on another night it might have been allowed', reflected Nicholson. As it was the rampant Augusto was a sword in Spurs' left side with his speed and shooting power. He had not lost the ability in the air which he once used as a centre-forward, and came in from the right to head Cavem's cross past Brown. Benfica won the first leg 3–1.

The European Cup holders' arrival in London for the return at White Hart Lane a fortnight later captured the imagination of press and public as much as any visit from an overseas team since the

Two views of Spurs' equaliser against Benfica in the highly charged second leg at White Hart Lane: Bobby Smith swings his right foot. . . and watches his shot fly past Germano and Costa Pereira. (*Popperfoto and Keystone*)

Hungarians had appeared nine years earlier. Had Spurs not made a two-goal deficit look commonplace before their enraptured night crowds with their 'Glory, Glory Hallelujahs'? And was an English club not just one step away from the untrodden ground of a European Cup final?

Nobody was more acutely aware of the local feeling than Bela Guttmann, who played his part with a marvellous sense of occasion. Not for nothing was he nicknamed by his contemporaries, 'the Old Fox'.

'The match at Tottenham was a fantastic experience, the highlight of my career with Benfica. Nicholson later became a good friend of mine, but European games were a war of nerves, and I played three little tricks on him. When we arrived in London, it was raining slightly, but I was surprised to discover the pitch at White Hart Lane was virtually under water. What's more, Nicholson suggested we trained on the pitch itself.

'They were trying to frighten us with the heavy going, but I called their bluff. I told my players to run round the pitch, and offered to pour more water on it myself if Spurs wanted it that muddy.

'What did worry me more at the time was the physical side to the game, because Smith and Mackay could be very fierce especially at home. So I told the journalists that I expected a bloodbath and they, in turn, went to Poulsen, the Danish referee, and told him Guttmann did not think he was strong enough to handle the match. It was an old ploy, but it worked. Poulsen kept a close check on those two players, and we got more than our fair share of free kicks.

'On the night of the match, I was concerned about the effect the Spurs crowd might have on the nerves of my players. They are much closer on English grounds than on the continent. So I locked the dressing-room door and only let Benfica go out at the last minute, with the referee and linesman. The game started before the crowd got at us.'

Guttmann's little manoeuvres will come as no surprise to those who have been involved in European football, but he was one of the original thinkers when it came to gamesmanship within the rules. Benfica were ideally prepared for their toughest test. They displayed an icy nerve as Spurs made the predictable boisterous start, rode their luck when Greaves had an early goal dubiously disallowed for offside, then broke smoothly away to steal a shock lead after 15 minutes. Aguas was the scorer in a breakaway, and Spurs were now 4–1 down on aggregate. But a goal by Smith before half-time, and a penalty calmly converted by the phlegmatic Blanchflower three minutes afterwards, turned an impossible position into a launching pad for one of the great European recoveries. If only Tottenham could score one more goal.

That they failed was due partly to bad luck – three shots hit the posts – partly to Benfica's immense composure staunchly led by Germano and Costa Pereira, and partly, some critics insisted later, to Spurs' frantic anxiety forcing them to do things too quickly for their own good.

Looking back over 18 years, using analysis when, at the time, he felt only a numbing emotion, Nicholson refused to accept that Spurs should have played any other way.

'Yes, people said we should have slowed the game down, controlled it more. How do you control opposition like Benfica unless you go at them like we did? If we had played the clever way, we would have created only 25 per cent of the chances we did make. We felt the pace of the game was very important to us. We could have scored five or six. I lost count of the near misses, but the one I remember most is when Mackay hit the bar right at the end.

'It was a storming game, and the attitude of our players was tremendous. If it was 1962 again, I would want Tottenham to play exactly the same way. We were 4–1 down, and we only just failed.'

Nicholson and Spurs only had to wait 12 months for the European title they deserved. In 1963 they won the Cup Winners' Cup – the first British club to collect a European trophy. But their brilliant team, like the Busby Babes before them, was denied longevity by fate: John White was killed by lightning, and Dave Mackay twice broke a leg. Spurs have been in the UEFA Cup final twice since, but never played again in the champions cup.

While the embers were still glowing at White Hart Lane in spring 1962, Real Madrid eased comfortably through to their sixth European Cup final in seven years. They beat Standard Liège 4–0 in Spain, 2–0 in Belgium. So the final brought the old masters into conflict with the new. Real against Benfica. But the Portuguese holders had a battle to fight off the field, too. Bela Guttmann was on the point of leaving them.

'When I joined Benfica in 1959, I signed a two-year contract which made no provision for a bonus if we won the European Cup. It seemed so far fetched at the time, that we even laughed about it during our negotiations. So when we won the trophy in 1961, I received $4,000 less for that, than I did for winning the Portuguese championship. No attempt was made by the directors to change the situation, so I began to think about moving on again.'

But Guttmann's dilemma was not apparent when the teams lined up in Amsterdam's Olympic Stadium for the 1962 final. Benfica looked relaxed with Germano smiling broadly during the national anthems, while Real Madrid, wearing unfamiliar blue, looked old and strained by comparison. The match became known as 'the night of the long shots', because so many goals were scored from distance, but its greater significance was as the last European Cup final to be played in the old, open style, with both teams committed to attack.

How else can one explain a half-time score of Real Madrid 3, Benfica 2? Puskas, feeding on the supplies from Di Stefano and Del Sol, scored all Real's goals, the first player to record a hat trick in two European Cup finals. No wonder one of Real's coaches embraced the tubby Hungarian as he left the field at half-time. But in the Benfica dressing-room, Guttmann was far from down-hearted. 'I had told my players we would win even if we were two goals behind at half-time. Real were getting old. Di Stefano was 35, still an

Araquistain lies beaten by Eusebio's free kick in the 1962 final in Amsterdam. Benfica now lead 5–3 and Real have failed to regain the European Cup. (*Presse Sports*)

Inset: The architects of Benfica's victory over Real in Amsterdam (left to right): Eusebio, Guttmann and Coluna. (*Presse Sports*)

influence only because he dropped so deep to start Real moving. We told Cavem to follow him in the second half, and put him under pressure. This was the vital factor.'

Guttmann's tactical switch negated not only Di Stefano, but also Puskas. Now a lonely figure upfield on his own, with the first half service a mere memory, the Hungarian came back to look for the ball and was robbed in possession. Coluna snapped up the loose ball and fired a 30-yard shot past José Araquistain, Real's new goalkeeper. Now, at 3–3, Eusebio took over. He outpaced the weary Di Stefano on the right, and was brought down by a desperate Pachin. Eusebio took the penalty himself, and after 63 minutes Benfica were in the lead for the first time.

Five minutes more, and it was all over. From a free kick given for hands against a tiring Santamaria, the ball was tapped by Coluna to Eusebio, and Eusebio's deflected shot made the final score 5–3 to Benfica. Television viewers in 17 countries saw him chaired off the field by delighted Portuguese supporters. The European Cup had a new hero – and a bigger audience than ever. At the winners' banquet, 500 invited guests beseeched Guttmann to stay with Benfica and steer them to a third European title. But it was too late. The little magician had decided to cast his spell elsewhere.

While Guttmann went to Uruguay, where he spent the next two years coaching Penarol in Montevideo, Benfica chose a South American to replace him. Fernando Riera, from Chile, took over in Lisbon. He had a turbulent start. Benfica lost heavily to Santos in the

World Club Championship, and after beating Norrköping of Sweden to reach the quarter-finals of the next European Cup, they lost the inspiring figure of Germano, ruled out for the rest of the season with a knee injury.

There was also a sad farewell to José Aguas, captain of Benfica in their two winning European Cup finals. Slowed down by injury, he joined FK Austria in Vienna, and was replaced in Lisbon by the towering figure of José Torres. Eusebio still provided sufficient thrust and enough goals to power Benfica to their third consecutive European final. Their experience was enough to overcome Dukla Prague and Feyenoord; in each case the champions held their opponents away and won in the Stadium of Light.

But just as Eusebio had assumed the mantle of Puskas a year earlier, he, too, was overshadowed in the 1963 European Cup by an opportunist of Brazilian stock. Not Pele, whose contract with Santos enabled him to resist the lucrative lure of Europe, but José Altafini, who joined AC Milan from Palmeiras of Sao Paulo after playing for Brazil in the 1958 World Cup. Altafini helped the likes of Liedholm and Schiaffino win the Italian championship in 1959, but failure in the European Cup the following year meant Milan's team of stars broke up, and only Altafini and centre half Cesare Maldini survived the purge.

Now the unsmiling disciplinarian, Nereo Rocco, coached a new, grimly determined Milan, replacing the departed *enfant terrible* Greaves with the balding Dino Sani, a Brazilian born of Italian parents but signed from Boca Juniors in Argentina.

The touch of genius in the Milan team which won the Italian title in 1962 was provided by the 'Golden Boy' himself – Gianni Rivera. The handsome inside forward with the face of a filmstar and the prodigious talent to flower even in Calcio, was signed from his home town club, Alessandria, in 1960. Rivera was only 19 when Milan began their European Cup campaign, but marked his début in the competition with a goal against Union Luxembourg in the opening round.

Altafini was the perfect target for Rivera's willowy, stroked passes, ideally suited as well to making poor opposition suffer. He scored eight times against the Luxembourg champions, five at San Siro where Milan won 8–0, and three of their six in the return match. But Milan's opening salvo of 14 goals was matched by the improbable English champions, Ipswich Town. Having defeated the Maltese team Floriana 4–1 in Valletta, Ipswich scored 10 without reply at Portman Road.

Here in Suffolk, manager Alf Ramsey had worked something of a modern miracle the previous winter. He brought an Ipswich team with no established stars into the first division for the first time, and won the championship at the first attempt. Ipswich relied heavily on the double-barrelled attack of Ted Phillips, a local find with a fierce shot, and Ray Crawford, who was capped by England and scored seven goals in the two matches against Floriana. The centre half and captain, Andy Nelson, had reason to remember the match in Malta. He had his nose broken by his own goalkeeper, Roy Bailey, as both went for a cross. Bailey's son, Gary, was later to play for Manchester United.

Now Ipswich travelled to Milan, and were given a rude introduction to the harsher side of European football. They played the first leg at San Siro without Phillips and their left half John Elsworthy, who were both injured, but Nelson said they contributed to their own downfall:

'We were Babes in the Wood compared to the Italians. They were up to all the cynical stuff, pulling your hair, spitting, treading on your toes. We were naïve to all that. We used to go forward with a cavalier spirit and not bother about the cautious side. The pitch was a quagmire. It had been raining for two days and the crowd was down to 12,000. They beat us 3–0, and their big outside left, Barison, got two of the goals.

'Altafini was one of the worst offenders in the Milan team, up to all the tricks in the book. But when they came to Ipswich for the second leg, he kept himself hidden deep in his own half.'

Ipswich won the second leg 2–1, but never looked like saving the tie. Again Milan's scorer was Paulo Barison, who died in a car crash in 1979 at the age of 42.

A few months later, Ramsey left Ipswich to take on the England manager's job. He would soon discover a great deal more about the pragmatic approach of overseas teams, but he would also devise a way of beating them. If Ipswich did not last long in elevated company, the audacious exploits of the Scottish champions, Dundee, in the 1962–63 European Cup, were highly unexpected from newcomers to the competition.

The remarkable Gordon Smith now made history at the age of 38 by becoming the first man to play for three different clubs in the European Cup. He was transferred to Dundee from Hearts in 1961, and in his first season at Dens Park helped the Tayside club win their first championship.

'My main contribution was to give the other players belief in themselves. After a few games I could see Dundee were capable of doing well, but they were an unfashionable provincial team living in the shadow of the big Glasgow and Edinburgh clubs. They had an inferiority complex.

'Our manager, Bob Shankly, was quite the opposite to his brother Bill. He was reserved and never said much. People said beneath it all he was very clever, but he never gave very much away. I do know he had a super blend in his team at that time. We had some good young players on the one hand, like Ian Ure at centre half, Alan Gilzean in the attack and Andy Penman at inside forward; and plenty of experience as well, with Bobby Seith and Bob Wishart at wing half and me on the right wing.

'Before our first European Cup tie against Cologne, we went through a bad patch. They even had a spy at one of our training sessions when we were trying out new tactics which just weren't working.

'We decided to go back to our normal pattern and on the night everything went right. We beat the Germans 8–1, and although their goalkeeper was taken off after a collision with our centre-forward, Alan Cousin, we were already five goals up by then.'

The result sent shock waves through Germany, because Cologne were regarded as an experienced and resourceful team. For the second leg they welcomed back, after injury, their blond defender Karl-Heinz Schnellinger, then the German Footballer of the Year and later to win a European Cup medal with Milan.

But Gordon Smith remembers the trip to Germany for other reasons.

'When we arrived in Cologne, we found we were the victims of a hate campaign. The German press claimed we deliberately fouled their goalkeeper at Dundee, and Cologne dished out some rough treatment in the second match. This time our goalkeeper, Bert Slater, went off injured for a spell, and we lost 4–0. We were all over the place, and it was a good job we had a seven-goal lead.'

Smith was enjoying an unexpected Indian summer at the end of a majestic career. In the next round against Sporting Lisbon, his teasing crosses set up a hat trick for Alan Gilzean as Dundee won 4–1 at Dens Park after losing 1–0 in Portugal. Then, Smith himself scored in both quarter-final matches against Anderlecht, in which Dundee rose to even greater heights. The Belgian champions had knocked out Real Madrid, but Dundee went to Brussels and won 4–1. 'It was an incredible result when you bear in mind the plaudits Liverpool were to receive when they went there and beat Anderlecht 1–0 only two years later', Smith pointed out.

But this fairy tale had an unhappy ending. Dundee's refreshing charge was repelled in the semi-final by AC Milan, who won the first leg in San Siro 5–1. Again the Italians were accused of using the hostile environment to unfair advantage. Dundee's goalkeeper, Slater, found himself almost blinded by the flashbulbs of photographers when he went up to take crosses. Although Gilzean's goal at Dens Park gave Dundee a consolation victory in the second leg, he was sent off for retaliation near the end. For the sixth time in the first eight years of the European Cup, a British team had gone out in the semi-final. But at least there was a chance to see the final at first hand, even if it was still the private province of the Latins. Milan and Benfica met at Wembley on the Wednesday afternoon of 22 May 1963, watched by a disappointing crowd of 45,000.

The mood was set for an uneasy final when Rocco announced his team. Barison, despite scoring twice against Dundee in the semi-final, was dropped. Bruno Mora, Italy's international winger, was switched from the right to the left flank, and defender Pivatelli was given the number seven shirt with a brief to stay in midfield and mark Coluna. It was a tight, rigorous match compared with the finals of previous years. Symptomatic, perhaps, of the dangerous path European football was treading now that the penalty for failure was starting to match the thirst for success. The game is remembered largely for the new European Cup goalscoring record set by Altafini, whose opportunism brought two of the three moments of impressive play to an otherwise tense game. The first goal came after 18 minutes from Eusebio. Milan's skilful left-half, Giovanni Trapattoni, had a short pass to Rivera intercepted in midfield by Torres. The big centre-forward gave Eusebio a clear run at Milan's goal. Trapattoni pursued the galloping Eusebio for at least 60 yards, but he was always a couple of paces behind. Milan's goalkeeper Ghezzi seemed reluctant to leave his line, and Eusebio beat him with a shot which went in off the far post.

Milan dominated the rest of the first half. Rivera orchestrated the midfield, sending swift, searching passes forward. For once, Altafini's finishing let him down, otherwise Benfica would not still have led at half-time. The match turned in the first 15 minutes of the second half. First, Torres got past Maldini and missed the target. A second goal then, and Benfica might have made it three European Cups in a row. Instead, Milan equalised after 58 minutes. Benfica gave Rivera too much space, Altafini swivelled on his pass on the 18-yard line, and in the same movement scored with a low shot.

It was Altafini's 13th goal of the 1962–63 tournament, beating the previous best total of 12 set by Puskas three years earlier. Strangely, Altafini had failed to score in two rounds – against Ipswich and Dundee – but had collected 12 goals in four matches against weak opposition.

Now, the Brazilian went off the field for treatment, but his injury was not nearly as bad as that sustained by Benfica's Coluna a minute after the goal. He was tripped deliberately by his marker Pivatelli, and limped through the rest of the game. Ironically, it was from a corner by Coluna that Milan broke away to score the winning goal a few minutes later. The ball was cleared upfield and Benfica's central defenders were caught in possession. Humberto tried to pass to Raul, whose hurried clearance hit Rivera and rebounded to Altafini, at that moment just crossing the halfway line. It was debatable whether Altafini was still in his own half, and therefore onside, when the ball came off Rivera, but English referee Arthur Holland gave the Italians the benefit of the doubt and the television film suggests he was right.

The winning goal of the 1963 final scored by José Altafina of AC Milan (white shirt) after his first shot had rebounded from the Benfica goalkeeper Costa Pereira. It was Altafini's 14th goal of the 1962–63 competition, a record for any European Cup season. (*Central Press Photos*)

The Cup changes hands again. Milan's coach Nereo Rocco (left) and captain Cesare Maldini celebrate victory over Benfica at Wembley. (*Keystone*)

There were no defenders in sight as Altafini set off towards Costa Pereira in the distance. His first shot rebounded off the Benfica goalkeeper to Altafini's feet. He simply could not miss again, and set the new scoring record at 14.

So Milan's 2–1 victory meant the European Cup changed hands for a second time, and simultaneously the spirit of the competition underwent a marked change. Gone were the adventurous ideals of Real Madrid and Benfica, to be replaced by the sterner, systematic approach of the money-conscious Italians. Although Nereo Rocco left Milan at once to coach Torino, he had started the trend towards *catenaccio* – a preoccupation with defensive tactics – which was to keep the European Cup in Italy for two more years, but was to have a cancerous effect on the shape of world football.

Romance was out. Big business was in.

CHAPTER FOUR

THE MIGHTY MEN OF MILAN
(Internazionale 1964, 1965; Real Madrid 1966)

In the summer of 1961, while Europe was digesting the first of
Benfica's victories, England's centre-forward, Gerry Hitchens, was
jogging in the hills above Milan. With him was Luis Suarez, like
Hitchens a recent recruit to Internazionale, and behind them,
breathing heavily, was Inter's winger Mario Corso. Said Hitchens:
'We were at our pre-season training camp, and we had just finished
for the day. We had a short run back to the coach, and though the
rest of the team moved off smartly, I decided to stick with the other
new boy, and Corso, who as usual was idling away at the back. We
got to within 100 yards of the coach, and suddenly saw it move off.
The three of us including Suarez, then the most expensive player in
the world, were left stranded. We were forced to make the six miles
back to base on our own, just for being a few seconds late. That's
when I realised the kind of man we were working for.'

The man with the built-in stopwatch was Helenio Herrera, who had
preceded Suarez from Barcelona, and who would create, at Inter, the
most formidable footballing corps of the decade. Off the field, he ran
the club like a martinet, backed by the oil millionaire Angelo Moratti.
On the field, he imposed a tactical discipline which won him and
Inter few friends, but which, in the clinical climate of European
football, proved wholly successful. Under his aegis, Inter won three
Italian championships, took the European Cup twice, and secured the
world club title in successive years.

Though Hitchens, later a successful businessman in North Wales,
left Inter a few months before the first of these trophies was won, he
played his part in Herrera's progress, and retains an admiration for
the man who signed him.

Gerry Hitchens (right) is
welcomed to Internazionale by
coach Helenio Herrera. Between
the two men is earlier recruit to
Italian football from Britain,
Eddie Firmani. (*Associated
Press*)

'Herrera first approached me just after I got into the England side against Mexico in May 1961. At the time I was with Aston Villa, but they knew nothing about it. Herrera believed in consulting the player first, and the club second. By the time England went on tour I had agreed to sign. Ironically we played Italy in one of the matches and won 3–2. I got two and Jimmy Greaves,who had signed for AC Milan, got the other so that helped a bit.

'I then went on holiday but later that summer, Herrera contacted me about playing in a friendly against Santos, who included Pele of course. I hadn't trained for about a month, but he was insistent. I made my début against the Brazilians in about 90° of heat, but I didn't do too badly. I remember the Inter fans gave me a great reception.'

The pre-season training took place at Appiano Gentile, Inter's luxury headquarters in the mountains above Milan. As with most of the larger Italian clubs, their players were taken away from their families on the Friday before a Sunday game, returning on Monday lunchtime. Hitchens had to get used to the habit.

'At the camp we would be woken about 8.00 with tea or some light rolls, and be on the pitch by 9.30. Herrera would already be there, and there were fines if you were late. We would do about two hours speed and ballwork, which did wonders for me after the dull stuff we used to do in England. In fact I remember Herrera came to watch England train during the 1962 World Cup in Chile. He laughed at the methods we used, and the place we were staying in. We didn't even have a doctor there, which nearly cost poor Peter Swan his life, whereas at Inter every facility was laid on.

Mind you, the supervision was intense. At lunch, Herrera would dictate what you ate, and then he would take us for a walk as a team – always in club tracksuits, never in our own clothes. We'd then have to sleep, and then perhaps there would be a film, before going to bed about 10.00. At 10.30 he would come round the rooms, as if he hadn't seen enough of us already. I used to drive him mad, because I would occasionally have a cigarette, and he would be in the corridor sniffing the smoke, and trying to work out where it was coming from.

'If it sounds strict, it was. But it got results, and nobody really rebelled against it. On his salary – it was supposed to be more than £50,000 a year – he *had* to get results. But he was a great coach, and he certainly improved me as a player.'

In Hitchens' first season, 1961–62, Inter threw away a lead in the Italian championship, which was won by their arch rivals AC Milan. There had never been much love lost between the two camps since the March day in 1908, when Inter were founded by 43 rebel members of the Milan club. The upstarts won titles in the 1930s, when they were forced by the Fascists to amalgamate with another local club as Ambrosiana-Inter. Their star at the time was Guiseppe Meazza, who helped Italy win two World Cups, and later managed the Inter youth teams.

In May 1955, with the double-barrelled name now a memory, Moratti became president. Though Inter had won the championship in 1953 and 1954, his early years in office were spent envying the success of Inter's city neighbours, and of the Turin club Juventus. Coaches came and went until Herrera arrived in May 1960. With the taunts of the Barcelona fans still ringing in his ears, he proceeded to make his message clear. The idol of the Inter fans was the Argentine, Antonio Angelillo, who had scored a remarkable 33 goals in 1959. Herrera, however, was not impressed. He resented his forward's choice of friends outside the club, and soon Angelillo departed for Roma, to be replaced by Hitchens.

'I sooned learned how different things could be compared with England. You had to get used to the politics of the club, and the constant attention. I know Jimmy Greaves had a rough time in Milan, but in all honesty I enjoyed it. It opened up my whole life and I only wish I could have gone to Italy when I was 21 instead of 25.

'There was no doubt Inter were going to be a good side. When I was there young players like Giacinto Facchetti, who was a first-class full back, were just establishing themselves in the team. And there was also Sandro Mazzola, whose father, of course, had been a famous Italian international. We had Aristide Guaneri at the back, who was a really hard man to play against – I learnt that myself later – and Armando Picchi, the sweeper and captain, respected by everyone in the club.

'But above all there was Suarez, who was a lovely fellow, great with our kids, as well as being an unbelievable player. He was like a gazelle, he would just float over the ground, and then bang – he would hit a 30-yard ball into someone's path to open up the game.

'When I was in Italy there were three famous midfield players, Sivori, Rivera and Suarez. Rivera I didn't rate as highly, because I felt he could get a bit lost. Sivori had sensational skill, could beat you again and again, but had a terrible temper. He hated Herrera. For instance, I once saw him beat a man near the touchline, look up and drive the ball at Herrera on the bench. For me, Suarez was the best of the three.

'Herrera sold me to Torino in November 1962, and got Di Giacomo as part of the deal. The first I heard of it was in the press, and when I saw Herrera I think he thought I was going to punch him for not telling me. But he told me that he wanted the Brazilian winger Jair, who was like greased lightning, and couldn't use three foreigners in the championship. To be honest I didn't blame him. I would do the same to strengthen a side, and his record proves that he was right.

'We were given a big party when we left, and my wife was given a lovely gold bracelet. We had been doing well in the 1962–63 championship, and when Inter did win it, the club sent me the medal, which I still wear round my neck.'

The title put Inter into the European Cup draw for the first time. Their rivals, the holders AC Milan, drew a bye in the opening round, but Inter were paired with the English champions Everton. They, too, were new to the tournament, but, on paper at least, had a talented side. Their manager Harry Catterick had inherited a nucleus of good players from his predecessor, Johnny Carey. They included Brian Labone, capped by England for the first time in 1962, and two proven forwards in Roy Vernon, a slim confident Welshman who captained the side, and his partner in attack, Alex Young.

For the Goodison faithful, Young remains a cult figure, almost beyond criticism. Carey had bought him from Hearts, where he had played two seasons in the European Cup, and at Everton the fairhaired Scot gave free rein to his considerable skills. There was an air of grace about him – a rival forward once said he played as if on tiptoe – and his touch in front of goal was sure. He scored 22 goals to Vernon's 24, as Everton won the championship in 1963. No one else reached double figures.

Catterick had strengthened his side with signings of his own. Gordon West came from Blackpool at a record fee for a goalkeeper and Dennis Stevens arrived from Bolton, which released Bobby Collins to start a new and influential chapter in the history of Leeds United. En route to the title, Catterick added Alex Scott, who also had European experience with Rangers, while from the manager's old club, Sheffield Wednesday, Catterick signed a vigorous and talented

wing half, Tony Kay. He made his England début in the summer of
1963, and scored against Switzerland, but it remained his only cap. In
January 1965 Kay went to prison after being convicted of 'fixing' one
of Wednesday's matches, and received a life ban from the Football
Association.

Like Catterick, Herrera, too, had been busy in the transfer market.
Following Inter's league win, he exchanged two of his players with
Fiorentina, receiving goalkeeper Sarti and centre-forward Milani, in
return for Buffon and the naturalised Argentinian Maschio. What is
more, he signed another foreigner, the German Horst Szymaniak,
merely to take part in the European Cup. A wing half with the
discipline purely to carry out a marking detail, Szymaniak would be
used by Herrera chiefly away from home, being replaced by a more
attacking player at San Siro.

Such sophistication was beyond the scope of Everton, who were
enmeshed in the defensive web of *catenaccio* in the first leg at
Goodison. Herrera always maintained that the system was forced
upon him by the success of less gifted sides in the Italian league. But
like all converts, he became its most consistent advocate.

At Everton, Burgnich and Facchetti, two full backs of supreme
temperament, marked the opposing wingers, while Tagnin and
Guaneri blocked the centre to Young and Vernon. Behind them
patrolled the sweeper Picchi, alert to any problems. Szymaniak,
wearing number 11, rarely ventured into Everton's half, but instead
lined up alongside Suarez and a withdrawn Mazzola in midfield,
leaving Di Giacomo and Jair up front. Inter were rarely in
difficulties, and gave way only once in the match, when Parker's long
chip was headed on by Stevens for Vernon to slide the ball in. The
offside decision seemed harsh at the time, but BBC film shows that
Young was beyond the last defender as the ball was headed forward.

The crowd, themselves bewitched by Inter, applauded the Italians
at the end. But Brian Labone was less than impressed.

'Quite honestly, having heard so much about them, I expected a bit more
from Suarez and Mazzola. There was no doubt they were happy to draw 0–0.
Right from the start Szymaniak dropped back, which meant that Alec Parker
was free to go forward from full back. Poor Alec had never seen so much of
the ball. The trouble was, he wasn't the best person in the world at using it.

'In Milan, things were entirely different. We stayed at Monza near the
racetrack, and spent a sleepless night listening to Italian fans screeching their
tyres half the night. I'm sure it was all intentional. Also I remember the
coach brought us to the stadium far too early, and Harry Catterick had to tell
the driver to go round the block a few more times. There were just little
things which upset us.

'Jimmy Gabriel, our right half, couldn't play at San Siro, so Colin Harvey
made his début in the match. He nearly gave a goal away in the first 30
seconds after his back pass dropped short, but Di Giacomo missed a simple
goal. After that we might have scored ourselves, but Taffy Vernon missed a
good chance. The only goal of the match was a bit fortunate. Their winger
Jair got down near the byline, hit the ball across, and it swerved straight in.'

Inter repeated their 1–0 winning margin in their next home leg
against the French champions Monaco. Afterwards Herrera did his
best to dampen French optimism about the return. 'Monaco have left
all their strength here. We shall qualify easily in the second leg.'

Monaco's Yvon Douis was in no mood to argue, and spoke for
forwards everywhere.

'If I had to play against Tagnin every week', he said later, 'I would give up the game.' The French chose to play the second leg in Marseilles rather than in their own small stadium, and conceded three goals to Suarez and Mazzola.

Home and away victories over Partizan Belgrade took the Italians into the last four. They were drawn against Borussia Dortmund, who had beaten Benfica on their way to the semi-final. Benfica had earlier shown signs of distress against Distillery, in a tie remembered for the European Cup début of Tom Finney. The great English forward was lured out of retirement for one match by manager George Eastham, and, at 41, helped the Ulstermen draw 3–3 with the Portuguese champions in Belfast. Without him, however, Distillery went down 5–0 in Lisbon, with Eusebio scoring twice.

Benfica then beat Borussia 2–1 at home, only to be swamped in the return match. The Portuguese were forced to take the field in Germany without Costa Pereira, Germano and Eusebio, and were beaten 5–0, Brungs getting a hat trick. He scored two more in the first leg of the semi-final against Inter, which was drawn 2–2. The Germans, who also included two men – goalkeeper Hans Tilkowski and winger Lothar Emmerich – who would later oppose England in the World Cup final, were then beaten 2–0 in Milan. That match, however, has since become the subject of some controversy after the Yugoslavian referee Tesanic was later found holidaying on the Italian coast allegedly at Inter's expense. (The record of involvement with match officials by some Italian clubs is to say the least suspicious, and is discussed further in Chapter Seven.)

As the Italians notoriety and seeming lack of conscience grew, so the legend of Real Madrid gained strength also. Their all-white strip and devotion to the game's attacking skills cast them in the role of Europe's deity. But, although Real won the Spanish championship by 12 points in 1963, their leading players were finding they were increasingly short of breath. Puskas was 36 in April and Di Stefano nine months older.

Miguel Muñoz, Real's manager, had started to rebuild after the defeat by Benfica in the 1962 European Cup final. Dominguez had returned to Argentina, while Del Sol, whose relationship with some of his older colleagues was uneasy, departed to make his fortune with Juventus. Saporta had courted Pele as a replacement, but Santos refused to let him go; besides, the memory of Didi's unhappy stay in Madrid was still fresh. Real did sign a defender, Ignacio Zoco from Osasuna, while Lucien Muller arrived from Reims to help organise the midfield. Then, in La Coruna, the northern province where Suarez was born, the Spanish champions found a true bargain. For £35,000 Real secured the services of Amancio Amaro, who would develop into one of the most talented and penetrative forwards in Europe. After a slow start at inside forward, Muñoz moved him on to the wing, diplomatically explaining that it would be easier there for him to win a Spanish cap. That proved prophetic, for Amancio was an integral part of Spain's European Nations victory in June 1964.

All three newcomers had played in the disappointing defeat by Anderlecht in the autumn of 1962. Now, a year later, they faced Glasgow Rangers at Ibrox, as Real resumed their romance with the European Cup. Rangers had recently completed the double in Scotland, and in Jim Baxter, Willie Henderson, and Dave Wilson they possessed a much coveted attacking trio. All three had conspired to beat England at Wembley in May 1963, and thrash Spain in Madrid a month later. But, in Glasgow, in the first leg, Rangers' tactics were all too familiar. Frustrated by the composure of Santamaria at the back, they were caught by a breakaway goal near the end of the match. Real's scorer, almost inevitably, was Puskas, who added a hat trick in Madrid, where Real won as they pleased.

Victory over Dinamo Bucharest brought Real a quarter-final draw against the holders AC Milan. The Italians had put out Norrköping – and their young forward Ove Kindvall – with something to spare, but more taxing had been their three games against Santos for the World Club Championship. In Milan, the home side paraded their latest signing from Botafago, Amarildo, who deputised for Pele in the 1962 World Cup. Both scored twice in a match which Milan won 4–2. A month later Santos, without Pele this time, triumphed by the same score. The play-off, which was also held in Rio, was an ill-tempered affair, in which Maldini and the Santos full back, Ismael, were dismissed. The match was won by the Brazilians with a disputed penalty.

Maldini was injured in the first half against Real in the first leg in Madrid, and soon both sides were down to 10 men when Ruiz broke a collar bone. Milan were also without Trapattoni and Dino Sani, and not surprisingly looked hesitant. Rivera and Altafini were given a lesson by their elders Di Stefano and Puskas, who each scored in Real's 4–1 win. Milan's cause was not helped by a row between Maldini and coach Viani – successor to Rocco – about the extent of the injury. The tall sweeper did not play in the second leg and nor, as it turned out did Rivera, who failed a fitness test.

Nevertheless Real, toying feebly with defensive tactics, found themselves two goals down just before half-time at San Siro, with 80,000 fans bellowing for a third. Although they held on to win 4–3 on aggregate, Real's play lacked any sort of system, and consisted merely of getting players behind the ball, and passing it to Di Stefano. Such simplicity proved capable of despatching Zurich in the semi-final, but Inter in the 1964 final were an altogether different matter.

Herrera, a master of propaganda, made public his fears about coping with Di Stefano and Puskas, knowing Inter had the edge in stamina. Di Stefano, for one, was taken in. Later *France Football* would blame his selfishness for Real's defeat in Vienna. Yet in their seventh final the Spaniards were only one goal down at half-time – Mazzola having guided his shot past Vicente from 20 yards – and still looked dangerous. Puskas proceeded to underline the fact by beating Sarti shortly after the break, only to see his shot come back off a post.

But in midfield Suarez and Corso jealously kept possession, and the game slowly slipped away from the former holders. They were undone finally by defensive errors. First Milani, preferred as Mazzola's partner, watched his shot bounce awkwardly past Vicente. Then, after Felo had scored acrobatically for Real, a clearance by Santamaria struck Mazzola on the shoulder, and allowed the Inter forward to run on and make the final score 3–1. Herrera now rose from his seat on the touchline, and faced the crowd with arms aloft. There would be a new name on the European Cup.

The match billed as a contest between the romantics and the cynics was ultimately decided by seniority. It proved to be Di Stefano's last

Two goals by Mazzola, seen here rising above Real's Santamaria, helped decide the 1964 final in Vienna. Inter had youth on their side, and won 3–1.

European Cup match, and the last final for Puskas and Santamaria. As Gento, Real's captain in the final, explained.

'When you have class, it does not matter about the age of your team. But if both teams have class, the younger will triumph. Our players were older, and Inter waited for our mistakes and punished us. Suarez was a great organiser – only Beckenbauer compared with him in this respect – and he made sure the ball was played out to the wing, where Jair was too good for us. Against Benfica in Amsterdam, I thought we should have won the match. But in Vienna there was no doubt Inter deserved to win. It was a sad occasion, but sometimes you have to lose.'

Internazionale, the team which Herrera built and which dominated Europe in the mid-1960s (left to right, standing): Sarti, Guaneri, Facchetti, Tagnin, Burgnich, Picchi, (kneeling): Jair, Mazzola, Suarez, Corso, Milani.

It was difficult to resist the conclusion that in 1962 Real had been beaten at their own game, whereas here in 1964, they had been defeated by a style which was foreign to them. Real's commitment to attack wielded no authority against a team which conceded only five goals in seven matches, one of which was a penalty. Inter's success was built on allowing sides to outreach themselves before breaking quickly to score. By killing the rhythm of the game, Inter tested the patience of spectators as well as opponents; but their methods proved horribly effective.

Others might copy *catenaccio*; few had the ammunition available to Herrera to exploit it to the full. In Suarez, Inter possessed a general of supreme vision, in Jair a winger of immense pace, and in Mazzola a finisher of the highest quality. Even if they fell below form, Inter were capable of forcing a goalless draw. The two-legged system seemed designed for them, for a single goal would suffice to settle a tie. Inter, by reducing risk to a bare minimum, became the first team to win the European Cup without losing a match.

To add insult to injury, the Italians went on to emulate Real by winning the World Club Championship – in Madrid. The contest with Independiente went to a third match, played at Chamartin, where Inter once again played defensive football after Corso had scored. If the derisory chanting of the crowd reached Italian ears, they showed no sign of it.

Of more significance to the Madrid faithful was the departure of Di Stefano, freed by Real in the summer of 1964, after scoring a record 49 goals in the European Cup. It was an uneasy exit. Muñoz, caught between friendship and the facts of life, found explanation difficult. Di Stefano, ruler in Madrid for more than a decade, refused to go quietly. In the end Bernabeu would not agree to the Argentinian's request for a new contract and Di Stefano departed to the relatively unknown Espanol. Later he would enter the European Cup again – as coach to Valencia.

Muñoz continued to make changes, adding a forward José Martinez Sanchez (Pirri) to his squad, and giving Ramon Grosso, from Real's nursery club, Plus Ultra, the chance to succeed Di Stefano. Victories over Odense and Dukla Prague in the autumn of 1964 took Real into the quarter-final of the European Cup and gave them a chance of revenge against Benfica. But the tie confirmed what Muñoz already knew: there was still much work to be done.

The Portuguese had again won the double, after welcoming Eusebio back from military service, and Germano after two knee operations. Torres, too, had found his touch as Benfica scored 103 goals in their 26 league matches, the first century in Portugal for 25 years. Their assault on Europe was led by a new manager, Elek Schwartz, whose team took Real apart in Lisbon. Benfica won 5–1, Eusebio scoring twice, and he might easily have had more. The spirit of the competition, once the responsibility of Real, had passed to the Portuguese. In Madrid, Puskas, now clearly fallible, missed a penalty, though he did score Real's irrelevant winner.

Benfica went on to reach their fourth final in five years, by beating the unfancied Hungarians, Vasas Gyor, in the semi-final. Gyor's main attraction was the reputation of their manager Nandor Hidegkuti, who had played in the first European Cup tournament with Voros Lobogo. Gyor had beaten the more glamorous Ferencvaros to the Hungarian title on goal average, and proceeded to remove Chemie Leipzig, Lokomotiv Sofia and DWS Amsterdam from the European Cup. But even Hidegkuti's experience was no match for Benfica, who beat Gyor in Hungary with a goal by Augusto, and thrashed them 4–0 in Lisbon.

The other semi-final proved less predictable and far more controversial. Once again Inter's victory was marred by a doubtful decision by the referee.

This time their victims were Liverpool, who had succeeded neighbours Everton as English champions. 'At that time', Liverpool's manager Bill Shankly once claimed, 'I had the best 12 players there had been in Britain since the war.' Though a man rarely given to understatement, Shankly's boast contained a good deal of truth. Liverpool came agonisingly close in 1965 to becoming the first British side to reach the final of the European Cup, and in doing so prepared the way, tactically and administratively, for the club's successes in the 1970s.

Yet until Shankly's arrival in December 1959, Liverpool had had problems getting out of the second division, let alone menacing Europe. The remarkable Scotsman changed all that. Brisk and to the point, his emotional appeal to players rivalled that of Herrera. Mention of defeat was forbidden, opponents' skills and achievements dismissed with scorn during team talks. His confidence was virtually unquenchable. Behind the bluster, however, lay a keen footballing brain, and an inspired notion of value for money. In 1961, he bought for little more than £75,000 the backbone of his team – a giant centre half, Ron Yeats from Dundee United, and centre-forward Ian St John who, like Alex Young, is still revered on Merseyside.

Shankly had spotted them playing against each other in a featureless match at Falkirk. 'Of all the hundreds of matches I have watched in my career', said Shankly later, 'this was the most historic.' St John recalled:

'I was with Motherwell at the time, where I played in a really good forward line with Willie Hunter, Pat Quinn, and Andy Weir. We grew up together and I remember all of us going over to watch Real Madrid train before the Hampden final in 1960, and then practising what we saw. In those days we played a number of friendlies against foreign clubs like Bilbao, and Flamengo of Brazil, whom we beat 9–1. We had a quick and accurate style, we didn't rely on strength like some of the other Scottish teams.

'I got into the Scottish side, but, of course, in those days we were on about £16 a week, which was just ridiculous. There was a lot of talk about English clubs coming for me, including Newcastle. I certainly wasn't thinking about Liverpool, because they were still in the second division. But when Shankly came to see me in May 1961, he sold the club to me. My wife and I went down with him in the car and for the whole six-hour drive he talked about football. I think he fell asleep for about 10 minutes, and as soon as he woke up, he started off again about what a good player I was, and what we would achieve together. When it came to signing, I really had no choice.

'A few days after I joined, I played against Everton in the Liverpool Senior Cup final. It didn't mean a lot to me at first – to be honest I didn't actually know Everton was part of Liverpool - but I soon found out it was serious. Fortunately we won 4–3, and I got a hat trick and we just went on from there.'

At the end of St John's first season, Liverpool were promoted. Two years later, in 1964, they were first division champions, with a comfortable blend of strength and skill.

In defence the solidity of goalkeeper Tommy Lawrence, and Yeats the captain, was offset by the industry of right half Gordon Milne, and the measured passing of Willie Stevenson. Milne was signed from Preston, where Shankly himself had been a tireless wing half, while Stevenson, who had fallen out with Glasgow Rangers and tried his luck for a time in Australia, was recruited in November 1962 for a mere £20,000. In attack, Ian Callaghan's boundless energy on one flank was matched by the peerless dribbling of Peter Thompson on the other. The foil for St John was Roger Hunt, whose international rivalry with Jimmy Greaves recalled the old arguments about genius being one per cent inspiration and 99 per cent perspiration. The Liverpool fans made it clear where they stood. Hunt's refusal to spare himself in the interests of his side was a byword at Anfield. His goalscoring records for the club still stand and in 1966 he was to play in the England match which mattered most of all.

'By the time we entered the European Cup', said St John, 'everything was falling into place. The only changes in the side were to accommodate Chris Lawler at right back, and replace Alf Arrowsmith, who had suffered a bad injury. I felt sorry for Alf, because he never established himself again. He was a great lad and used to love scoring goals. He would count them all, even the ones in the five-a-sides. Shanks would ask him "How many this week, son?" and Alf would say quite seriously, "27, boss".

'Without him we tried a couple of reserve forwards against Reykjavik in the first round, and then before we played Anderlecht, Shanks asked Ron Yeats and I about bringing in Tommy Smith at the back. Everyone knew Tommy would get into the first team sooner or later. He was a man the day he arrived. When he was an apprentice you never saw him sweeping the terraces or anything like that. I think the staff were too afraid to ask him.

'Anyway he came in wearing a number 10 shirt, to do a marking job on Van Himst, who hardly got a kick at the ball. We pushed Milne and Stevenson a little further forward, and that became our regular pattern. Anderlecht were a good side – they had beaten Real Madrid a year or so earlier – but we thrashed them at home, and won away as well.'

Earlier Anderlecht had triumphed by the toss of a coin against Bologna, the first of three ties in the 1964–65 competition to be settled in this way. Bologna had won the Italian championship in a play-off with Inter, and faced another against Anderlecht after the teams had drawn 2–2 on aggregate. When that proved goalless, the coin put Bologna, and their famous German forward Helmut Haller, out of the European Cup. If the method seemed arbitrary, it permitted no appeal. Gornik came through in similar fashion against Dukla Prague, and in the quarter-final, Liverpool themselves were to benefit.

After two 0–0 draws, their tie with the German champions Cologne went to a third match in Rotterdam. There, the German wing half Wolfgang Weber cracked a shinbone in a tackle with Milne, and was forced to carry on in pain at centre forward. While he was still limping, Hunt's determined run to the byline set up a simple goal for St John, the first goal of the tie after more than 200 minutes of football. Soon there was another, when Hunt's header from Callaghan's cross hit the bar and dropped behind the line, where Milne made sure it was a goal.

Now Overath, who with Weber was to face England in the next World Cup final the following year, took a hold on the match. His midfield industry was rewarded when Thielen headed Hornig's free kick past Lawrence, and again in the second half, when Lohr's low drive beat the goalkeeper from outside the area. Löhr had the ball in the net again before the 90 minutes were up, but although Weber forgot his pain for a moment to leap high in the air, the goal was disallowed for an earlier foul on Lawrence.

Extra time proved fruitless, and at the end the referee spun the red and white disc twice. The first time it landed tantalisingly on edge in the mud; the second with Liverpool's red uppermost. An English team had reached the semi-final again, though it was difficult in the circumstances to feel anything but sorrow for Cologne.

Weber's bravery was equalled by that of Gerry Byrne, Liverpool's full back, in the FA Cup final against Leeds a few weeks later. He concealed a broken collar bone as Liverpool took the cup in a poor match, remembered mainly for the exuberance of their supporters, who brought to Wembley the fierce loyalty and ready humour of Merseyside. Indeed, at a time when an ear for a lyric and a Liverpool accent guaranteed a fortune for some, Anfield's terrace fans became fashionable overnight, courted by writers and makers of documentaries. On occasions, it seemed, there were more cameras trained on the Kop than the playing area.

Three days after the Wembley final, Inter discovered the power of the Mersey sound for themselves in the first leg of the European Cup semi-final. The holders had previously put out those hardy annuals Glasgow Rangers, though not without some difficulty. The Scots' chances of beating Inter had been seriously impaired by the absence of Baxter, who had earlier broken his right leg against Rapid on an icy pitch in Vienna. His skill had illuminated Rangers' path to the quarter-final, and some feel the accident marked the turning point in his career. Though Baxter was fit to resume playing after three months, he perhaps never quite regained his former fluency. Without him, Rangers battered away at Inter without becoming a truly positive threat. Having lost the first leg in Milan 3–1, the Scots took an early lead at Ibrox through Jim Forrest. But at that point Inter simply closed ranks, deaf to the outrage of an 80,000 crowd, and went through on a 3–2 aggregate. Herrera later shrugged: 'It is not the fans who score goals.' But he was about to be converted by the Kop.

At Anfield for the first leg, the gates were opened at three in the afternoon, and most closed by six. When at last kick-off time grew near, Byrne emerged from the tunnel first, his jacket slung over his injured shoulder, and paraded the FA Cup around the pitch with Milne, who had missed the Wembley match through injury. The crowd, presented with the spoils of war, clamoured for more. Any thoughts Inter might have had of playing themselves into the match were wrecked in the third minute, when Callaghan's cross dropped near the penalty spot and Hunt struck it instantly – against the flight – past Sarti.

The first leg of Liverpool's semi-final with Inter at Anfield. Lawler's shot is on its way past Sarti into the net, but Suarez (white shirt) appeals successfully; Strong is offside. (*Keystone*)

The BBC recording of the controversial second goal scored by Peiro for Inter against Liverpool. It shows that the ball was not kicked from Lawrence's hands, but forced away from him as he bounced the ball. The goal put Inter level on aggregate and their third, scored by Facchetti, ended Liverpool's hopes of a place in the final. (*BBC*)

Next, a long kick downfield by Facchetti was fumbled by Yeats, who allowed Peiro, the former Atletico Madrid and Torino forward, to rob him and make a run towards Lawrence. As the defence closed, he squared the ball to Mazzola who made the finish look easy. Those who had come expecting attrition had now witnessed two goals in 10 minutes.

Liverpool made light of the loss, and after half an hour of the match scored again. Callaghan ran over the ball at a free kick on the edge of the area, Stevenson played it to Hunt, who touched it first time into the path of the still sprinting Callaghan. His low shot beat Sarti again – practice made perfect.

There was almost a third goal when Lawler ran from the half way line, took a return from Smith and thumped the ball in. As the ground erupted again, the goal was disallowed for offside, almost certainly against Geoff Strong. Liverpool had to wait until the second half for the goal by St John which made the final score 3–1. The move began with Thompson near his own left corner flag, and the ball travelled via Callaghan and Smith to Hunt, whose shot was beaten down by Sarti. St John slid the ball over the line. Almost unbelievably, Inter had conceded three goals, all of great quality. At the end, the Liverpool players stood in the centre circle to acknowledge their fans' contribution to a memorable Anfield occasion. Herrera told Shankly afterwards: 'We have been beaten before, but never defeated. Tonight we were defeated.'

For St John, the evening stands out in a career of many highlights, heightened perhaps by the misfortune which was to befall Liverpool in the second leg.

'Quite honestly we would have tackled a bear that night at Anfield. We were so worked up, the Italians later claimed we had been drugged. They couldn't cope with us, or the Kop who were singing "Go back to Italy" to the tune of *Santa Lucia*. But when we got to Milan, there was a really hostile reception. Their fans had been worked up, and they tried everything to stop us getting some sleep. As if that wasn't enough, our hotel close to Lake Como was near a church, and the bells kept us awake as well. Shanks tried to get them bandaged up!

'At the stadium there were rockets and firecrackers, and an overpowering noise. But what affected us more was the Spanish referee Ortiz de Mendibil. In the first 10 minutes, he gave an indirect free kick on the edge of the area, Corso shot straight in, and de Mendibil awarded a goal.

'Then Peiro came up behind Tommy Lawrence, as he was bouncing the ball, and kicked it away from him into the net. He didn't actually kick it out of his hands, and I suppose in a way you must blame Tommy for dreaming a bit, but in England it would definitely have been disallowed for dangerous play.

'The referee was stopping the game all the time. We just couldn't get going. We ended up just trying to stem the tide, and in the second half Facchetti scored a brilliant goal. He must have run about 70 yards and just hit the ball first time past Tommy. It was a heartbreak, because we had a real chance that year. But at least we learned something. We learned about the travel, and the waiting around, and the little things that can go wrong, like bad roads, and poor training pitches. If you like, we learned the lessons which later helped Liverpool win the European Cup.'

By the time that happened, St John had long since left the club, and Shankly too had departed, after a further nine years of success at Anfield. Although Liverpool, were to enter the European Cup twice more under his management, they never went as far as on this first attempt. For Shankly, the memory of defeat in Milan still rankles.

'It was just like a war, like the Battle of the Bulge, with us in the centre of it. Really and truly Inter, who were a good side, didn't play well. The atmosphere affected their players as well. So the game was nothing. I had the feeling that something was wrong politically, and I believe there were some investigations later about Inter and Liverpool. We can't really prove anything, but I remember being told before the game that whatever happened, we would not win.'

There was more political manoeuvring before the 1965 final, as Benfica sought to reverse UEFA's decision to play the match in Inter's own stadium in Milan. There were precedents of course. Real's first final was in Paris, where Reims had played most of their home matches, and their second on their own ground at Chamartin. Still Benfica threatened to withdraw, or send their youth team, if the venue was not changed. But UEFA made it clear that they would be liable for a fine, on top of compensation to Inter for the loss of gate receipts.

Finally the game went ahead at San Siro, though as a contest it proved as absurd as the negotiations which preceded it. Heavy rain produced large pools on the playing surface, killing any hopes of a rhythm to the match. More important, Benfica were forced to play

An unhappy Costa Pereira tries in vain to make up for his error, but the shot from Inter's Jair (white shirt) has slipped through his grasp and across the line. It was the only goal of the 1965 final.

much of the second half with 10 men, after Costa Pereira hurt his leg, and was replaced in goal by an already limping Germano. By that time Inter were one up, after Jair's far from powerful low shot skidded through the hands of the crouching Costa Pereira, and beyond him into the net. It was a goal to match the character of the occasion, and a mistake which recalled the way Benfica had first won the trophy – against Barcelona and poor Ramallets – four years earlier.

Towards the end, Inter were content to play out time. A goal in front against weakened opponents induced in Herrera's men no obligation to excite or entertain. Though Peiro hit a post late on, the Italians largely chose to protect their one goal lead. The result was inevitable.

Looking back, the assessment of the Benfica winger José Augusto, bordered on the generous:

'It made no difference for me to play on their pitch. And though the conditions were bad, they were the same for both sides. What made me sad was to see Latin players perform like Inter. We Latins are different from the English or German players. We need to create things, to lift the mood of the game. Inter had a system, which they played very well, especially Suarez. But really good players impose their own system. When we saw Italy in the 1978 World Cup, they had players who had created a different way of playing.'

That particular road to Damascus lay some way ahead for the Italians. For the moment, the game in Europe was in danger of stagnating, as teams sought to copy the vices of the victors. The European Cup stood accused of encouraging a system where the result, however shabbily achieved, was paramount. The stifling approach to away matches, perfected in Europe, was being applied equally at home.

Not all the signs were gloomy, however. At Wembley, a week before the final at San Siro, West Ham United and TSV Munich 1860 produced a European Cup Winners' Cup final to delight the connoisseur. And, elsewhere in Europe, three men in particular were prepared to challenge the hegemony of Milan.

In Spain, Real were champions yet again, with Muñoz patiently grooming a younger side to meet the obligations of the past. Also back in the European Cup were Benfica, who now recalled Bela Guttman, in a bid to recapture the formula which had twice won them the trophy. And in England, in May 1965, Matt Busby celebrated his fourth league title with Manchester United, another club where the players were aware of their inheritance. Recalled Bobby Charlton: 'By the time we got back into the European Cup, we realised how much the previous side, many of whom had been killed, had left a legacy for us. The mystique of Manchester United and the European Cup had grown, and nothing was ever going to satisfy the players, the manager, or the supporters until we had won it. No one could say we were really back again until we'd done that.'

Charlton, of course, was one of the players around whom Busby had started to rebuild his side. United finished runners-up in the first season after Munich, but the process of full recovery was to take somewhat longer. Gregg and Foulkes also remained, but gradually the other survivors of the crash left Old Trafford: Morgans and Scanlon, goalkeeper Wood and eventually Dennis Viollet. Busby looked to the youngsters again, but though many showed promise, few retained a permanent place in the side. The gaps left by the disaster meant players were often elevated ahead of schedule, and it showed.

Busby papered over the cracks with a series of expensive buys. Albert Quixall arrived in September 1958 for a then record £45,000, and later came Maurice Setters, David Herd and Noel Cantwell. More significantly, at a time of transition, Busby shrewdly kept United's name alive in Europe with a series of friendlies. Both Real and Benfica were among those who accepted invitations to Old Trafford.

In May 1963, despite a struggle throughout the season against relegation, United won the FA Cup by beating Leicester City in a one-sided final. Their victory owed much to the performance of Busby's most recent signings, Pat Crerand and Denis Law, two Scots who combined for the first goal. Law was to prove one of the finest inside forwards Britain has ever produced, not least by his display for the Rest of the World side at Wembley in October 1963, when he moved with ease among the master forwards of Europe: Kopa, Puskas, Gento and Di Stefano. Busby had admired him for years, ever since he watched him inspire a Huddersfield Town youth team against United, after which he offered the Yorkshire club £10,000 – a fortune for a 15-year-old.

Busby, in fact, gave Law his first Scottish cap, but when eventually Huddersfield did sell him in 1960, it was to United's rivals, Manchester City. After little more than a season at Maine Road, Law was wooed by the big Italian combines. Herrera wanted him for Inter, but though terms were discussed, the fair haired Scotsman moved to Torino. There he spent an unhappy season of club discipline and close marking, which nevertheless sharpened his considerable skill. He returned to England in 1962 as the complete inside forward, his awareness and industry an asset to any side.

At Old Trafford, Busby, desperate for goals, was forced to use him almost entirely in a striking role. Law's astonishing reflexes and agility were ideal for the job, and there is no doubt that his 23 League goals helped preserve United's first division status in 1963. But some have argued, including one or two of his former team-mates, that a confined role was a cruel waste of his talents. Said Harry Gregg:

'I honestly thought Denis was in the class of Di Stefano, because he could do everything, organise a side and score goals. His close control was not as good perhaps, but he beat people by his speed of thought. If you asked him to dribble round a man he could struggle, but if you said play the ball against a wall and then beat him, he would succeed every time.

'He was a man's man who could look after himself on the field, and off it he was a good professional, who stood up for what he thought was right. Busby knew how important he was. When Denis was doubtful the boss would practically be on his hands and knees, hoping he could play.'

In 1964, after a crop of goals in the Cup Winners' Cup, Law was named European Footballer of the Year. The following season, despite a lengthy suspension – not the first or last of his career – his 28 League goals helped United win the championship. The title was a personal triumph for Busby, who had overcome not only injury, but the infinite mental anguish of Munich, to take up the reins of office again. Though the family atmosphere of the club in the 1950s could never quite be repeated – there were too many egos at Old Trafford now – Busby continued to adhere to a style of management in which good players could thrive.

He could be hard at times – Pat Crerand called his method the iron fist in the velvet glove - but on the whole, he earned the respect of his players by respecting them. When in 1966, the much-prized Law delivered an ultimatum over a proposed pay rise, Busby placed him on the transfer list. Law soon climbed down and was welcomed back without a hint of a grudge.

On the field Busby encouraged players to express themselves, and in doing so invested United with a glamour no other English side could match. The opposition were not ignored – the manager's mispronunciation of the names of the foreign players he had watched was a standing joke at Old Trafford – but for Busby, tactics were more a matter of establishing a framework, than a detailed analysis of strengths and weaknesses. This attitude filled grounds up and down the country, but it remained to be seen if it would prove totally adequate in Europe.

Nevertheless, Busby had again assembled a considerable side. If the forward line could at times take the breath away, the defence too had performed well on the way to the championship, conceding less than a goal a game, despite the occasional lapses of Eire international Pat Dunne in goal. In front of him was Shay Brennan, who as a third team winger had been drafted into United's first match after Munich and scored twice. He had now settled at full back and, like his goalkeeper, had won an Irish cap. So too had the other Dunne, Tony, a stocky figure with the speed of a sprinter, who arrived from Shelbourne for a bargain £5,000.

Bill Foulkes had been converted by Busby to centre half. If he was sometimes embarrassed by a forward with close control, and had the reputation as something of a loner, he remained a fierce competitor, powerful in the air. Alongside him was Nobby Stiles, who had seen off the challenge of Setters and won his first England cap against Scotland in April 1965. He, too, could look clumsy at times, and his tackle on the French forward Simon in the 1966 World Cup would create a diplomatic incident. But his positional play was uncanny, and his commitment to United and England never less than absolute. Said Gregg: 'Quite frankly there were times when Nobby should have drawn the wages of some of the people he played with. He not only did his job, he made sure everyone else did theirs. As a young player he had to fight for every chance he got at Old Trafford. I remember watching him in a reserve match and hearing someone say that Stiles was just a good utility player. I told him he was watching the best wing half in the club.'

The bite of Stiles was complemented by the gentle prompting of Pat Crerand, whose ability to propel a football with precision over 20 yards or more reminded older observers of Busby himself. Critics pointed out his poor tackling and almost funereal pace. Colleagues preferred to admire his passing skills and assured sense of timing. Like all good players, Crerand, at his best, made the game look easy. In the forward line, David Herd, signed from Arsenal, was the foil for Law, a willing target for defenders forced to part hurriedly with the ball. If he lacked Law's real sharpness in front of goal, there was a fearsome power to his shooting.

On the wings, John Connelly's direct approach balanced the precocious skill of George Best. Busby bought Connelly from neighbouring Burnley, and at United he not only scored his share of goals – none more vital than that which beat Leeds in April and helped decide the championship – but was capped again by England in the summer of 1965. Best, in his first full season in the first division, was simply irrepressible. His frail appearance encouraged full backs to engage him at close quarters, where the young Irishman would outwit them with his extraordinary array of feints and fierce acceleration.

The newspapers were already aware of his attraction for both sexes, but it all seemed good-natured. For Best, these months were still the age of innocence. He owned an Austin 1100, though he did not drive, spent his money on snooker and horror comics, and lived contentedly in digs with David Sadler. Even so, Danny Blanchflower, with a prescience perhaps granted only to the Irish, sounded a warning. 'It is hard to believe', he wrote at the time, 'that one boy can be blessed with so much talent, and that fate will not take some sort of quick revenge upon him.'

The emergence of Best had enabled Busby to experiment again
with Bobby Charlton. His form in the seasons following the aircrash –
he had been thrown out into the snow still strapped to his seat – was
erratic. Some thought his shy personality prevented him exploiting his
talent to the full. United for a time played him on the wing and
England followed suit, though Charlton himself cared little for the
position. For the championship season Busby moved him back to
inside forward, where he gradually forged a link with Crerand in the
middle of the field. Now, in the autumn of 1965, Charlton wore
number nine, though his role remained that of provider.

Alf Ramsey soon chose him to perform the same role for England,
a decision which paved the way for success in the summer of 1966. At
Old Trafford, Charlton's enthusiasm and elegance, not to mention his
level of sportsmanship, were a positive joy, and his shooting could
still bring a crowd instantly to its feet. On the whole, however, he
commanded the respect rather than the worship of United's
followers. They preferred the combustible presence of Law, whose
theatrical gestures and sense of anarchy endeared him to the
Stretford End. Charlton's appeal was to the sportswriters and
schoolmasters in the stands.

United's assault on the 1966 European Cup began in Helsinki,
where they scraped an uneasy 3–2 victory over the Finnish
part-timers, HJK. The second leg was won 6–0, however, with a hat
trick from Connelly.

Dunne and David Gaskell each played a game in goal, but the
position remained a problem for Busby. For a League match at
Blackpool, he now turned to Gregg, out of favour at Old Trafford
following an injury to his shoulder.

'I hadn't played in the first team for about 18 months', he recalled. 'I wasn't
even on the club photograph. What is more, there were some people at Old
Trafford who thought the injury was a sham, and I felt I was being ignored.
But I still felt I was the best goalkeeper in the club. It was a hard time, but I
am not a man to go asking for favours. I think it was my stubbornness which
kept me going all that time.'

The recall proved popular, and Gregg, who in 1979 joined the
coaching staff at Old Trafford, had an outstanding match in East
Berlin against ASK Vorwaerts. Goals by Law and Connelly won the
match, remembered by Pat Crerand for two things: 'It was so cold
even the Germans wore woollen vests under their jerseys, and the
food afterwards was awful.'

In the return match, Herd scored all three goals in a comfortable
win and United now found themselves drawn against Guttman's
Benfica in the quarter-final. The Portuguese had set up a European
Cup record in their first tie of the 1965–66 season, by beating Stade
Dudelange 18–0 on aggregate.

Manchester was now alive again to the European Cup. A capacity
crowd of 63,000 – more than twice the number which had watched
Vorwaerts – packed Old Trafford, drawn by the prospect of a
dramatic match. Benfica scored first, when Augusto headed in from a
corner. But soon United were in control, their intricate patterns
testing the patience of Germano and his fellow defenders. Herd
equalised, and by half-time United were ahead when Law's reflexes
enabled him to reach, and convert, Charlton's cross.

Foulkes, pushed forward at a free kick, got the third goal –

George Best, dubbed El Beatle after his performance for Manchester United in the 5–1 win over Benfica, returns in triumph from Lisbon. (*Press Association*)

In Benfica's Stadium of Light Manchester United produced one of their most thrilling performances. Here George Best scores his second goal in United's 5–1 win, a result which made their subsequent semi-final defeat by Partizan all the more baffling.

his first, but not his last in the European Cup. But with 10 minutes left, Gregg could not hold Eusebio's wicked drive, and Torres made it 3–2. Said Gregg: 'Eusebio was almost on the byline, and I had come a little way off my line expecting the orthodox centre. Instead he swerved the ball fiercely between me and the near post. All I could do was dive backwards and push the ball out. It hit Torres on the knee and went in. Few people would have spotted the opening, only Eusebio could have created a goal from it.'

A one-goal margin scarcely seemed enough for United against a team which had never lost a European Cup tie in Lisbon. The sense of foreboding was not improved when United were kept waiting before the kick-off for the second leg, while Eusebio was presented with his European Footballer of the Year trophy. Nor when Crerand broke a mirror in the dressing-room while he was nervously juggling a ball. Such omens were cast aside in the first 15 minutes, in which United scored three times, and went on to produce one of the most majestic performances in the history of the competition. In the Estadio da Luz, their own stadium of light, Benfica were snuffed out.

Busby had asked Best and Connelly to drop deep for the early part of the match, but the Irishman clearly had not listened. In Crerand's words, 'Besty just went daft'.

First he headed in Dunne's free kick after six minutes, then after Gregg's long shot was headed on by Herd, Best accelerated away from Germano and beat Costa Pereira again. He made scoring look simple against one of the most feared sides in Europe. Soon there was another goal from Connelly, and though Brennan put through his goal in the second half, United, in total command, added two more. Law sent Crerand sprinting in to score United's fourth with a typically exaggerated sidefoot pass. Soon it was 5–1 as Charlton took the ball round the goalkeeper with a nonchalant swerve and rolled it over the line.

The extent of United's victory startled Europe. In Italy one paper claimed: 'The myth of Benfica collapsed in 15 minutes, destroyed by the powerful, irresistible Manchester, who showed themselves as the great stars of European soccer, worthy rivals to Internazionale for the European Cup.'

More concisely, Busby claimed: 'This was our finest hour.'

United chose to stay an extra day in Portugal, as the tributes poured in. When they did return to England – where Best was endlessly photographed in an enormous sombrero – they were beaten in a

League match by Chelsea. United's first division title was slipping away, but such was the mood at Old Trafford that its loss was not mourned deeply. There were more weighty matters to be considered. Benfica's season simply fell apart. The championship passed to Sporting, and Guttman, of whom so much had been expected, departed for Switzerland.

United's opponents in the semi-final were the relatively unknown Partizan Belgrade. They seemed an easier option than the other two clubs which had reached the last four: the holders, Inter, and Real Madrid. Real had put out Feyenoord in the preliminary round, with Puskas scoring four goals in the 5–0 win in Madrid. The Hungarian also played – along with the veteran Santamaria - against the new Scottish champions Kilmarnock. But their modest Rugby Park pitch was to provide the somewhat inappropriate setting for the end of two famous careers. For both the Madrid players the 2–2 draw was their last appearance in the European Cup; from now on they would follow Real's progress from the stands.

De Felipe, who had come through the junior ranks, took the place of Santamaria in the 5–1 win over the Scots in Madrid. Later, Velasquez would emerge to claim a place in the forward line, vacated by Puskas. Real's youth policy had to some extent been forced upon them, following the Spanish FA's decision that henceforth only foreigners of proven Spanish parentage would be allowed to play. Real, in fact, would reach the 1966 European Cup final with an all-Spanish side, containing only two players, Pachin and Gento, who already owned winners' medals.

The Spaniard's quarter-final opponents were Anderlecht, who had earlier beaten Derry City 9–0. The Irish side agreed to play only one leg of the tie – perhaps just as well – after UEFA had ruled their own ground unsuitable. Against Real, in Brussels, Anderlecht repeated their famous 1–0 victory of three seasons earlier, but this time were beaten comfortably 4–2 in Madrid.

Inter reached the semi-final again after wins over Dinamo Bucharest and Ferencvaros. Now, in Madrid, their tactics were depressingly familiar. Eight of Herrera's team had confounded Real in the 1964 final. This time they restricted the home side to a single goal, scored by Pirri in the first half. In San Siro, however, Inter's prospects of a third successive final, and a dynasty to match that of Real, were destroyed by a goal made by Gento, and scored by Amancio. The Italians were now two down on aggregate.

Although they pressed forward incessantly, Inter found that the new Madrid could defend also, that *catenaccio* was no longer their own preserve. Sanchis, the full back, subdued Jair and Araquistain was inspired in goal. Inter could manage only a single goal, scored by Facchetti 12 minutes from time. Real's 2–1 aggregate win, applauded across Europe, meant they would play in their eighth final. Said Gento:

'Before the match, there was a lot of talk in the newspapers about revenge for the final in Vienna. But for me, the match against Inter was played for its own sake. But the mood of our team was different now. There was less freedom, and also we were more nervous. As captain, I was nervous also, which I never used to be. I realised I had to help Velazquez, Grosso and Pirri, as people had once helped me.

'The new players were not in the same category as some of the great names of the past. They could not expect to be. But they were younger and fitter, and in the shirt of Real they grew up quickly. In some ways we tried to play like the old side. Grosso played deeper in the manner of Di Stefano, but he did not score the same number of goals. Amancio switched like Kopa between the wings and inside, while I played the same way, although I was older.'

If the eclipse of Inter was a surprise, the defeat of Manchester United by Partizan was bewildering, and continues to defy explanation. The Yugoslavs, in their first semi-final, were a talented side. Soskic, who had played for the Rest of the World against England in 1963, was a goalkeeper of great competence, Jusufi a most dependable full back, while Vasovic was an adaptable defender who would later play in two European Cup finals for Ajax. But their attack scarcely rated comparison with that of United. Their best forward, Milan Galic, was even forced to miss both legs of the 1966 semi-final because of military service, though he was able to contest the final against Real. He was available also for Partizan's first match of the campaign against Nantes of France, and scored in a 2–0 win in the first leg. The second leg was drawn, and the Slavs then disposed of Werder Bremen, winning 3–0 at home and losing 1–0 away in a match in which three players were sent off.

Sparta Prague then overwhelmed Partizan in the first leg of the quarter-final, winning 4–1 in Czechoslovakia. But in Belgrade Kovacevic scored early on and goals came at regular intervals. By half-time Partizan were ahead on aggregate, and eventually won 5–0. This remarkable victory was noted by the more discerning followers of United, who remembered a similar recovery by Sporting in Lisbon two years earlier in the Cup Winners' Cup. But the United party left Manchester in good spirits for the first leg of the semi-final, their only concern being a cartilage injury to Best. He had been hurt against Preston in the FA Cup – where United had also reached the semi-final – and the club decided to postpone an operation. Best was rested for a League game against Aston Villa, then survived a match against Leicester. Busby decided he would play in Belgrade. It was a gamble which failed. The Irishman broke down in the first half, and though he was able to complete the match, the injury clearly affected United. But at half-time with the score 0–0, Law having earlier missed a simple chance, the match seemed well in hand. Said Crerand: 'I remember coming off at the end of the first half, and Noel Cantwell, who had been watching, said we had no problem. But I was worried that we weren't winning, because they had started the match frightened to death of us. Sure enough we went out and gave away a bad goal after we left a man unmarked at a throw in. We eventually lost 2–0, but I still felt we could do it at Old Trafford.'

There United, with Willie Anderson replacing Best, dominated possession, but were frustated by a compact and well organised Partizan. The Yugoslavs, marshalled by Jusufi and the stopper Rasovic, conceded just one goal – Stiles' low cross from the byline being turned into his own net by Soskic. United's intuitive skills were not enough. In their third attempt at the European Cup, they had lost their third semi-final.

Disappointment at their exit did not deflect criticism of Busby or his methods. He was accused of being too soft with his players, and of pursuing tactics which made few concessions to the modern game. In football politics the United manager was considered something of a reactionary. Said Gregg:

'The thing about Matt Busby was that he never changed his ideas on the game. His team talks were always on the same lines – "get hold of the game first, and then start to play". He was never a man to go out and try and get a 0–0 draw. With the sort of players we had, we could not have done it anyway. And in a sense you have to admire him for that.

'But I felt, at the time, that Partizan were not as good a side as we were led to believe they were. The manager and chairman had been over to see them, and Busby came back talking about the strengths of their players. The truth is they were not a good side. In fact they were terrified of us. But their goals gave them confidence, and at Old Trafford they proved they could change their game to suit the occasion, which we never seemed to do.

'I suppose it upset me not winning the European Cup that year, because I wasn't around when United did win it. But we were a better side than the one which eventually won the cup, and there is no doubt in my mind that we threw it away.'

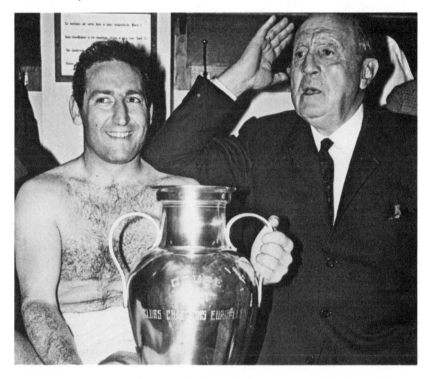

The architects of Real's 1966 triumph, Francisco Gento (holding cup), who received his sixth winner's medal, and Santiago Bernabeu, who realised his ambition to win the European Cup with an all-Spanish team. (*Presse Sport*)

There were rumours that Busby, his European dream fading, might retire. As Crerand recalled, the mood of the dressing-room afterwards was not encouraging:

'The match at Old Trafford had been a niggly affair, and I had been sent off near the end with a fellow called Miladinovic. Actually, it was Nobby Stiles who had got at him. After the others had changed and gone out, I was sitting in the dressing-room, and Matt was the only other person there. He was in a bad state, and kept mumbling about never winning the European Cup. But I said "You hold on here, because in two years we will win this cup". I really believed it.'

Busby's melancholy was not improved by defeat by Everton in the FA Cup semi-final three days later. He said:

'I remember coming to the ground on the following Monday, and I thought the whole world was upside down. I was fed up and everything else, but as I was driving along, I stopped at the crossing near the blind school, and saw

The team which brought Real Madrid their sixth success (left to right, standing): Araquistain, Pachin, De Felipe, Sanchis, Muñoz (trainer), Pirri, Zoco, Betancourt; (kneeling): Serena, Amancio, Grosso, Velasquez, Gento.

seven little children with sticks being led across the road. I just sat in the car and thought "Matt what problems have you got? You've got no problems". 'And in a way that did me a lot of good.'

United's failure meant that Real Madrid would play Partizan in the 1966 final in Brussels. There the young Spaniards, mindful of the club's epic traditions, seemed nervous and hasty in the first half, despite the efforts of Gento to steady them. It was Partizan who went ahead early in the second half when Vasovic headed in from a corner. Galic then missed a chance to make the game safe for the Yugoslavs, before Amancio, reacting quickly to Grosso's pass, slid his shot past Soskic for the equaliser.

There were just six minutes left when Serena, Real's right winger, received the ball just outside the area, turned and drove a left foot shot wide of the goalkeeper. Said Gento later: 'We could not believe it, because he hardly ever kicked the ball with his left foot. For me, winning the final was a proud moment. The team was young but they had struggled well. The game was no longer so easy to play, and it was a great achievement to bring the European Cup back to our club.'

It was a final of suspense, rather than good football. Gento's men, though talented, could not be expected to compare with the team which had won at Hampden Park six years earlier. But their win seemed to symbolise a change of emphasis in the European game. The iron grip of Inter, though still strong, had to some extent been relaxed. And the challenge to Herrera would now materialise from a most unexpected source.

CHAPTER FIVE

THE IMMORTALITY OF JOCK STEIN
(Celtic 1967)

The first meeting of Helenio Herrera and Jock Stein was scarcely a momentous occasion. It took place at Inter's training camp in November 1963 but attracted few headlines, save in the Scottish newspaper which had laid on Stein's visit to Italy.

Four years later in Lisbon the two men would meet again in more competitive circumstances, not to mention a blaze of publicity, in the final of the European Cup. But at the time of his Italian trip, Stein was unaware that he would one day manage Celtic, still less that he would pit his knowledge against the wily Herrera for the greatest club prize in Europe.

'I was the manager of Dunfermline then, and I went out with Willie Waddell of Kilmarnock on a tour organised by the Scottish *Daily Express*. It was a bit of a publicity exercise to give two provincial managers a taste of the big time. We spoke briefly to Herrera through an interpreter, but we were more observers than anything else. I noticed a few things about his methods, the amount of work they did with the ball for instance, and also that he concerned himself only with the first team. He didn't seem to bother with anyone else.'

Later, Stein would learn much more about him, after moving to Celtic and embarking on the club's first European Cup campaign.

The Scots were not expected to make much impact. Their previous experience had been in the Fairs Cup and the Cup Winners' Cup, where they had reached two semi-finals, only to lose them both after leading from the first leg. The second of these was at Anfield in April 1966, where Liverpool won the battle of the British champions-elect 2–0. They, rather than the Scots, seemed better equipped for the assault on the champions' cup. That claim was underlined by the events of the summer, when England won the World Cup, not necessarily because they had the best players, but because they employed a system where each man performed to his personal maximum. The same could be said of Shankly's men, and, as with the world champions, there was no doubting their stamina.

Yet it was Celtic, at their initial attempt, who became the first British side to win the European Cup, while the English champions faltered. It was Stein who embraced the trophy, though typically, as Celtic triumphed in Lisbon, Shankly was the one British manager present to add his congratulations. 'John', said the Liverpool boss, 'you'll be immortal now'.

If the prospect of immortality now beckoned Stein, it offered a marked contrast to his early career as a player. Born into the mining community of Blantyre in Lanarkshire in 1923, he had played for the local junior side, and then for Albion Rovers, but seemed to be drifting into obscurity after his move to the Welsh non-league side Llanelli.

At that point came a most unexpected approach from Celtic. They signed him in 1951 to nurse a number of promising reserves, but soon Stein was in the first team, forming a stylish half-back line with Bobby Evans and the Irishman Bertie Peacock. In 1954, with Stein

Jock Stein, whose sense of adventure and attention to detail helped Celtic become the first British team to win the European Cup. (*Sportapics*)

now captain, Celtic won both Cup and League. It was the last time they were to win either trophy until he became manager. An ankle injury eventually ended his career, but as club coach he encouraged a series of fine young players. Among them were Pat Crerand, who helped to transform Manchester United, and Billy McNeill, who in turn would become captain and manager at Parkhead.

In 1960, Dunfermline offered Stein the post of manager. He promptly led the little Fife club to a Cup final victory over Celtic, and later to a tactical triumph against Everton in the Fairs Cup. His achievements opened the way for a move to Hibernian in May 1964, but his stay at Easter Road was short. Early in 1965, it was announced at a press conference that Stein was leaving to join Celtic, an event of immense significance in Glasgow. First because Bob Kelly, the vigorous and influential chairman of the club, stressed that the new man would have total control of the team and its affairs. Second because Stein was, and indeed remains, a Protestant.

In a city divided by the explosive and interacting elements of football and religion, the appointment was a giant step, reflected in front page headlines. Celtic were then, and have always been, identified with the Catholic faith, ever since the club was founded by Marist Brothers at the turn of the century.

The idea of Brother Walfrid, when he formed Celtic Football and Athletic Club on 6 November 1887, was to organise a team to play for Catholic charities. Chief of these were the so-called 'penny dinners', provided for the children of Irish immigrants in the mean streets of Glasgow's East End. The first year, according to club records, raised £421 16s 9d, and even today Celtic donate money to charity. Yet the area has remained deprived: a few miles from Parkhead lie some of the worst housing conditions in Britain.

Celtic's earliest match, in May 1888, was against Glasgow Rangers, which began a century of rivalry, not all of it peaceful. It took place at the club's first pitch near a cemetery – the move to Parkhead came four years later – and was won by Celtic 5–2. Their team included Willy Maley, who later became their first manager. Stein was, in fact, only Celtic's fourth, testament to a policy of appointments made without haste. It should also be added, without prejudice – a course made clear early in the club's history when in 1895, a motion to limit Protestant players in the team to three was defeated in committee.

Nevertheless, Celtic's image, and the majority of its support, remained staunchly Catholic. And as with their Protestant rivals Rangers, that support included a sprinkling of extremists, for whom the selection of Stein was a sign of weakness, even heresy. In fact his appointment ushered in a period of unprecedented strength. Soon after he took charge, Celtic won the Scottish FA Cup for the first time in 11 years, to begin a decade of achievement. As if to emphasise Celtic's working relationship with religion, the arrival of Stein was announced on a Sunday. 'I was fortunate, because I had been there as a player and a coach. I knew the set-up. But I suppose there was always a doubt whether I could become manager because of the religious thing. The appointment was a surprise to many people, but really religion has never been a problem at Celtic. And I knew that if the club made up their mind, they would keep to their decision.'

On his return to Parkhead, Stein found a nucleus of players with whom to work. As well as McNeill, there was another half-back John

Clark, whom Stein converted to a defensive role alongside the tall centre half. There was also an extrovert character in full back Tommy Gemmell, whose attacking style was reminiscent of Facchetti. Up front there was Bobby Lennox, whose pace and stamina would last into the 1980s, a willing servant in Steve Chalmers, and a persistent and powerful forward in John Hughes, nicknamed Yogi by the fans, after the bear in a television cartoon.

Stein's major changes were the signing of Joe McBride, an unsophisticated striker who had failed to make the grade in England but scored freely north of the border, and the reshaping of the midfield.

'When I got there Bobby Murdoch was playing inside forward. But I moved him from number eight to a number four, and there was no better wing half than him. He had a bit of a weight problem, but he was a natural passer of the ball, and had an outstanding match in the European Cup final.'

'Then there was Bertie Auld, another good passer of the ball, and a fellow who could look after himself on the field. He arrived from Birmingham just before me, for his second spell at the club. He was then a left winger, but towards the end of the championship season in 1966 I moved him inside. That became more definite when we toured America that summer.'

It proved an inspired switch and one which Auld, maturing as a player after a stormy spell in his career, was quick to accept. 'It was hard to break the habits of a lifetime', he said later, 'but in the new set-up there was only going to be one winger, and that was Jimmy Johnstone.' The little man himself was, and is still, something of an enigma. Johnstone was a shy man who could erupt into violence, a player who admitted feeling inferior to the likes of Law and Baxter on occasions, but whose close skills even they could not match. Others might probe an opponent's weakness, searching for an opening, Johnstone would simply demoralise defenders with his dribbling. Like Best at Manchester United, he could, at times, bring training to a standstill by his reluctance to part with the ball. Like Best, he could often baffle his employers with his disregard for discipline.

Stein, in fact, dropped him in favour of Chalmers for the 1965 Cup win, but there was no greater admirer of the red-haired winger's ability. In the European Cup final against Inter, Johnstone was instructed to roam at will early on, and his tormenting of the Italians set the tone for the whole match.

The most remarkable story of all at Celtic concerned Ronnie Simpson, who at five feet 10 inches was a few inches taller than Johnstone, but still on the short side for a goalkeeper. He had played for Queen's Park as a 14-year-old amateur in 1945, and three years later played for the British team in the Olympic Games. Matt Busby, the team manager, tried to sign him for Manchester United, but when Simpson did turn professional, it was for the Scottish club Third Lanark.

In 1951, he was transferred to Newcastle United, where he won two FA Cup winners medals, before being transferred to Hibernian in 1960, where it was thought he would play out the last few years of his career. At Easter Road he was encouraged by manager Hugh Shaw, who had helped to pioneer Hibernian's entry into the European Cup, and who had maintained his enthusiasm for continental competition. Said Simpson:

'I remember us beating Barcelona in the Fairs Cup, soon after I joined Hibs. They were on their way to the European Cup final that season, but we drew in Spain and then beat them 3–2 at home. Our winner was a penalty which the Spaniards disputed. At the end of the match one of their players punched the referee, and even when they got down the tunnel, they were trying to break down the door to his dressing-room.'

Shaw's resignation, at the age of 65, spelled the end of Simpson's ambitions at Easter Road. When Jock Stein arrived as manager, the veteran goalkeeper was out of the first team, and in dispute over wages. In his own words:

'Not so much drifting, as rushing headlong out of the game. By then I was 33, and frankly I wasn't too bothered whether I played again or not, because I'd had a good career. I was working as a rep for an oil company, and enjoying my golf. I was still getting about seven pounds a week from Hibs, and the only time I went there was to pick up my wage. I used to see Jock there, and he would ask me to come back and start training again. But I didn't pay any attention.

'The season started without me, and then one day, in September 1964, a friend of mine, Ian Spence, who was manager of Berwick Rangers, came to my house to ask if I would play for them. I told him that I wasn't interested in playing any more, but while he was there I got a phone call from Jock. He told me to come down to the ground immediately. When I got there, he said Sean Fallon of Celtic had rung to ask if I wanted to go to Parkhead. It seemed ridiculous. I hadn't kicked a ball for months, and this man wanted me to sign for Celtic. Well of course I had to say yes.'

So Simpson, son of a former Rangers and Scotland defender, found himself sold by Stein to Celtic. His brief was to help in the reserves, but like Stein a decade earlier, Simpson soon made his presence felt. 'I worked really hard, and Neilly Mochan the trainer helped me a lot. Luckily I don't put on a lot of weight. I got into the first team for a European match in Spain – in Barcelona of all places – and made about 10 appearances. Jock arrived about halfway through the 1964–65 season, and though I wasn't in the cup final team in May, he picked me the following September for a league match against Aberdeen. I honestly did not believe it, but I was determined that I would not let him down.'

The team which Stein built (left to right, standing): Craig, Gemmell, Simpson, Murdoch, McNeill, Clark; (sitting): Johnstone, Chalmers, Auld, Lennox, Wallace.

From then on Simpson remained first choice, winning his first
League championship medal in May 1966. His haul the following year
defied belief. In 1966–67 he won League, League Cup and FA Cup
winners' medals. In April he won his first Scottish cap against the
world champions at Wembley, and a month later, at the age of 36
and seven months, he had his hands around the European Cup.

Celtic's first match in search of this last trophy was against Zurich
at Parkhead, where McBride scored the first goal. Gemmell added a
second against the Swiss champions with a 35-yard shot.

The Scottish players expected Zurich to throw men forward in the
return match. But Stein, celebrating his 44th birthday on the day of
the second leg, proved wiser. He explained to his team that the Swiss
would be happy to keep the score down, and not for the first time
was proved correct. Stein could even afford to rest McBride, and
replace him with Lennox. But the goals came easily enough, with
Gemmell getting two more – one a penalty – and Chalmers one.
Celtic won the tie 5–0 on aggregate.

Remarkably, the Zurich manager, Ladislav Kubala chose to play in
the second leg. It was more than five years since he had played for
Barcelona in the 1961 European Cup final, and, at 39, could hardly
be expected to trouble the Scots. The Celtic defender, John Clark,
recalled, 'Just in flashes you could see he had been a great player,
but really he was gone'.

Celtic's next opponents were Nantes, who had won the French
championship for the second year in a row. They had signed Vladimir
Kovacevic, the Partizan midfield player, who had helped to knock
them out of the European Cup the previous season. But it was his
team-mate Magny who put Nantes ahead in the first leg in France.

One down on a heavy pitch away from home, Celtic shrugged off
any thought of containment. McBride, whom the French
photographers decided bore a resemblance to Marlon Brando,
equalised before half-time, and Lennox and Chalmers made the game
safe in the second half. Celtic's recovery was largely the work of
Jimmy Johnstone, who had an inspired night, his artistry a throwback
to an old Scottish heritage – skills first perfected with a small ball on
a cobbled street.

Johnstone himself scored at Parkhead, after Kovacevic had
troubled Simpson with a shot which hit the woodwork. In the second
half the little winger made goals for Chalmers and Lennox. The
French press, with a certain lack of respect, dubbed Johnstone *la
puce volante*, the flying flea.

Just before Christmas Celtic's top scorer Joe McBride suffered a
knee injury which meant he would miss the rest of the European Cup
campaign. So prolific had he been, that his total of 38 goals in 30
matches would not be overtaken in the second half of the season.
Stein found himself another forward in Willie Wallace from Hearts,
but a mix-up over European deadlines meant he was unable to play
in Celtic's quarter-final tie with Vojvodina.

John Hughes, who had played against the Swiss, but not the
French, came back into the side. There was also a change at full
back, where Jim Craig had by now replaced Willie O'Neill. Craig had
signed for Celtic in 1965 while still at Glasgow University. At first he
was reluctant to turn professional, preferring to concentrate on his
career as a dentist. He was a gifted all-round athlete and had
established himself in the first team in January, his solid qualities

proving a perfect foil for the attacking flair of Gemmell.

Vojvodina, champions of Yugoslavia, had eliminated the Spanish champions Atletico Madrid in the previous round after a play-off. Goalkeeper Pantelic had scored from a penalty in the first leg in Yugoslavia, which the home side won 3–1. That lead was wiped out in Madrid and a third match was held at Chamartin, home of Real. There Vojvodina found themselves two goals down in 10 minutes, but improbably came back to win the match in extra time, despite having two players sent off.

Sorcery of this kind might well have bewitched Celtic in the first leg, played in the town of Novi Sad on the River Danube. But the Scots played calmly throughout, and conceded only one goal, when Gemmell's backpass fell short of Simpson and Stanic put the ball away in an instant.

The second leg of the quarter-final at Parkhead was a match of high drama played before a capacity crowd of 75,000. At half-time Celtic were still one down on aggregate, but Stein encouraged his players to compress their opponents deep in their own half. On the hour came an equaliser from Chalmers, but a third match still seemed imminent. Then in the very last minute, Celtic were awarded yet another corner. Charlie Gallagher – standing in for Auld – took it, and McNeill got his head to the ball, which dipped under the bar to send Celtic into the semi-final.

'Quite honestly', said John Clark, 'I have never known an atmosphere to compare with that night. Vojvodina were a very good side, well organised like all the Yugoslav teams. For me, that game was the hardest of the European Cup season, more difficult than the final. Pantelic, the goalkeeper, was absolutely brilliant. Some people think he might have had our first goal, but over the two legs he made a string of saves which were out of this world. And they had a defender Radovic, who was murder. Hard, but some skill I can tell you.

'After we beat them, we thought we might go all the way. We knew we had a good squad, and could bring in players who didn't upset the pattern. We also had great confidence in our own ability. There were some quiet men – like Jimmy Johnstone – who were cocky on the field. Bertie Auld would swagger around, putting his foot on the ball to show how easy it all was. And we were confident in our own style, so that if things did go a bit wrong, or we got a goal down, we kept our heads. Nobody panicked, or tried to change what we were doing. That was the real strength of that team.'

Celtic were now in the last four, which had proved a graveyard for British hopes in the past. Since the competition began, English or Scottish teams had reached the semi-final in eight of the previous 11 seasons. None had reached the final. The barrier to Celtic's further progress was Dukla Prague, whose performance in the quarter-final had earned them a certain respect in Britain, not least on Merseyside. For the Czechs had put out Ajax of Amsterdam, the conquerors of Liverpool.

In retrospect the emergence of the Dutch, and Johan Cruyff in particular, was to make Liverpool's defeat a shade more credible. But at the time it was a real blow for a team of their experience and collective strength. The 1966 League championship had been won with only 14 players, of whom Arrowsmith played in only three matches, and Graham one. Shankly's 12 good men and true enabled him to boast to the press each week that the team would be 'the same as last season'.

Yet even the Rumanians, Petrolul Ploesti, found a few chinks in the Anfield armour. Shankly picked an attacking team for the first leg, but the margin on Merseyside was only 2–0. In Rumania, the lights went out in the English dressing-room at one point, easing the task of the headline writers at home, after Liverpool lost 3–1. Only in the play-off did the English champions find their true form. First half goals by St John and Thompson in Brussels took them through to meet Ajax.

The Amsterdam club had recently won the Dutch championship for the first time since 1960. That year they had lost feebly in the European Cup to Frederikstad of Norway, but now, under manager Rinus Michels, they were a more talented, if still inexperienced side. The new star was their coltish centre-forward Cruyff, who in time would create a style in Europe, much envied, but seldom matched. He had won his first cap for the Netherlands in September 1966, but in his second international, against the Czechs in Amsterdam, he was sent off for arguing with the referee, and suspended for 12 months by the national association. The ban, later commuted to six months, did not affect the European Cup. In November, Cruyff lined up with his Ajax colleagues in Amsterdam's Olympic stadium, for the first leg against Liverpool.

Hopes of a classic confrontation disappeared in the thick mist, which persisted throughout the match. The game had a dreamlike quality, but for the English champions the result was only too real. Liverpool were four goals down at half-time, including one by Cruyff. In the second half, Ajax scored again, before Chris Lawler pulled one back just before the end. 'The whole game', said St John, 'was a farce. We could hardly see each other, let alone the goals. They must have played well to beat us 5–1, but I honestly could not tell you what they were like. The main thing I remember is Shanks coming on to the pitch, and yelling at Bobby Graham to stop hiding.'

Shankly's post-match assessment was just as startling. He called Ajax a defensive side, and prophesied a Liverpool landslide in the return. Such was his messianic quality that no one on Merseyside dared to discourage him. The Anfield faithful turned up in their thousands to hail the destruction of the Dutch, only to find their own heroes deflated. Ajax cleverly kept Liverpool at arm's length, and scored two good goals in the match, both put away by Cruyff. A goal by Hunt near the end salvaged a 2–2 draw for Shankly's men, but the aggregate was a salutary 7–3. The Dutch had found signs of deterioration in the Mersey machine.

No Liverpool player, however, was as old as Josef Masopust, who at 36 now helped Dukla Prague defeat Ajax and reach the semi-final. In the first leg in Amsterdam, he had a hand in the Czech goal, but his colleague Ivo Viktor in goal was the main reason why Cruyff and company could manage only a 1–1 draw. In Prague, Ajax actually led for a short time in the second half, with a goal by Jackie Swart. But they were undone by a cruel combination: a penalty and an own goal. Dukla would play Celtic for a place in the final.

The first leg, at Parkhead on 12 April, was a triumph for Willie Wallace, who scored twice on his European Cup début. The final margin was 3–1, but Dukla troubled the Scots until they tired badly in the last 30 minutes. Masopust gave the Czechs a touch of elegance in the middle of the field, and Dukla might have gone ahead before Johnstone scored after 28 minutes. But at half-time the scores were

Willie Wallace (right) scores the first of his two goals past Dukla's Ivo Viktor in the semi-final at Parkhead. Celtic won 3–1 to become the first British team to reach the European Cup final. (*Rod McLeod*)

level, after Nederost and Masopust had engineered a goal for the tall winger Strunc. Celtic's second was an old-fashioned affair. On the hour, a long kick downfield by Gemmell was pursued, and met decisively, by Wallace. Six minutes later, with the Czechs obviously tired, Wallace scored again. This time the guileful Auld held centre stage at a free kick. As he ran to take it, he suddenly stopped and bent down as if to check the position of the ball. Dukla relaxed, Auld played the ball to his right, and Wallace thumped it past Viktor.

To cap a memorable week, Wallace was selected for the Scotland side to meet England the following Saturday. Bobby Brown had originally selected Johnstone, but he was injured against Dukla, and was replaced by his club colleague. Wallace, along with Simpson, Gemmell and Lennox, helped Scotland beat the world champions 3–2 at Wembley.

In a less majestic setting at the small Juliska stadium in Prague, the same foursome helped Celtic become the first British side to reach the final of the European Cup. For once Stein, with the prize so close, counselled caution. Celtic drew the match 0–0, but the defensive strategy took its toll of Scottish nerves. Said John Clark:

'Jock asked us to play a game which was foreign to us, and I think it was the worst thing we ever did. With Masopust pulling the strings, they made a number of chances in the first half, mainly because we were so edgy. Remember they only needed one goal, and then the whole game would have turned upside down. At one point they nearly had a penalty, when Bobby Murdoch went down in a heap with one of their forwards, but the referee waved play on. Steve Chalmers ran his heart out by himself up front, and gradually, as the game wore on, we became more composed. But afterwards Jock admitted that he'd never ask us to do it again.'

Celtic, having flirted with *catenaccio*, learned a few days later that they would meet its finest exponents. For in Bologna on 3 May, a goal by Renato Cappellini gave Inter victory in a semi-final play-off against CSKA Sofia. The Italians, playing in their third final in four years, would start favourites in Lisbon.

Inter's attempt to regain the trophy had begun with a dismal tie against Moscow Torpedo. In the two matches, there was only one goal, scored against his own side by the Torpedo defender Valeri Voronin. For the first leg, Herrera paraded his latest recruit, the Brazilian Vinicio, from Lanerossi Vicenza. His record of a goal in every two Italian league games seemed recommendation enough, but Vinicio was now 35 and found life under Herrera hard going. He was replaced at centre-forward by Angelo Domenghini for the second leg, and never established himself again.

Domenghini had made his league début with Atalanta in 1961 when still a few months short of his 20th birthday. He moved to Inter in 1964, where he was forced to compete with Jair for a place on the right wing. But when Milani, scorer of one of Inter's goals in the 1964 final, was forced to retire early because of sciatica, Domenghini was used in the centre for league matches, with the Spaniard Peiro replacing him in the European games. But in the autumn of 1966, with Peiro having left for Roma, and Vinicio struggling, Domenghini played both matches against Vasas Budapest. The Hungarians included Janos Farkas – scorer of a famous volley at Goodison in the World Cup match against Brazil – but were beaten home and away by the Italians. That victory gave Inter a quarter-final tie with Real Madrid, a repeat of the previous year's semi-final, which Real had won.

But restoring the European Cup to Madrid had not eased the life of Real's coach Miguel Muñoz, who was forced to endure pointless comparisons between the present and the past. As if to underline his predicament, Real's opponents in the World Club Championship were Peñarol of Uruguay, whom Di Stefano and friends had demolished in 1960. This time the South Americans won comfortably, home and away.

The holders squeezed through in the European Cup against TSV 1860 Munich, and now braced themselves for the first leg of the quarter-final against Inter in Milan. At San Siro, Herrera threw in another centre-forward, 23-year-old Cappellini, who had returned to Inter after a spell on loan to Genoa. He scored the only goal of the match and in the second leg in Madrid put Inter ahead again, effectively settling the tie. Domenghini took Jair's place on the wing, but the inspiration behind their win was Suarez, who scored Inter's second, his shot being deflected in by Zoco.

Muñoz was left to bemoan an injury to De Felipe which had caused a reshuffle, but Real's 3–0 aggregate defeat gave fresh ammunition to the press. There were even rumours that Muñoz might be replaced by Herrera. Inter's semi-final opponents were the Bulgarian Army side CSKA, who had been made to struggle in the previous round by a gallant Linfield, champions of Northern Ireland. Their player manager was Tommy Leishman, once of Hibernian and Liverpool, while in goal in the early rounds they fielded Iam McFaul, later to win a Fairs Cup medal with Newcastle United. The Irish held the Bulgarians to a 2–2 draw in Belfast but in the second leg of the quarter-final went down 1–0, the goal being scored by the World Cup player, Dimiter Yakimov. No Irish side went further in the European Cup in its first 25 years.

CSKA now held Inter 1–1 in Milan, despite having Rajkov sent off for punching Suarez. Facchetti scored Inter's goal, then added another in Sofia, before the Bulgarians equalised late in the game. The play-off, first scheduled for Graz in Austria, was switched to Bologna after Inter offered three-quarters of the gate receipts to their opponents. Cappellini's goal put Inter in the final. Facchetti's performance, however, was of equal significance. Tall and dignified, with the speed of a sprinter, his goals were an asset to any side, and in defence he was rarely extended. He formed a barrier of experience with Burgnich and Guaneri, which was supplemented by the intelligent sweeper Picchi, and the veteran Sarti in goal. All five had played in Inter's first European Cup match at Goodison four years earlier.

So, too, had Mazzola for whom the forthcoming final in Lisbon was particularly poignant. For it was while returning from the Portuguese capital that his father Valentino, and the entire Torino team, had died in the Superga air disaster of 1949. Sandro was then six years old, but despite some family reluctance, both he and his younger brother Ferruccio chose to become professionals, though in Milan rather than Turin. It was the elder boy who showed more promise, encouraged first by the former Inter forward Guiseppe Meazza; then, when he made the first team, by Herrera himself. He made his international début in 1963 and scored against Brazil. Later he would move into midfield to begin a long, and often bitter, rivalry with Gianni Rivera in the Italian team. For the moment his goals made him a forward of world class, a player who numbered Jock Stein among his admirers.

Mazzola's form helped hide the fact that Jair had struggled for much of the season and would now be ruled out of the final with injury. More serious for Herrera: Suarez would also miss the match with a thigh strain. Moreover, Inter had been unable to coast in the Italian championship, where Juventus had pressed them hard for months.

By contrast Celtic arrived in Estoril – the plush resort outside Lisbon – with their domestic chores done. Stein sensed the confidence in the camp.

'After the season we'd had, we thought we could do anything. And the thing in our favour was that we saw the European Cup as an adventure. Other teams had been over the course before, and knew the pitfalls. But we didn't, so we were afraid of nothing. Also I was pleased we were playing Inter in just the one game. I didn't think we had any chance over two games against an Italian side, and events since have proved, I think, that you're better off meeting them just the once.

'There was no doubt they were worried about us. I remember that they waited behind to watch us train on the pitch in Lisbon. I looked at my team, all home-bred players, and looked at their star names, and I thought it was a great compliment to have them stay on to watch us. Herrera, of course, had been to watch us play in Glasgow. It was the match against Rangers which clinched the championship. It was played in thick mud at about 100mph, and finished 2–2. I think it frightened him to death, because he knew they could not match us for strength and stamina.'

The Scot's belief in themselves was given a further boost by the arrival at their hotel of a deputation from Real Madrid. They wanted Celtic to provide the opposition for Di Stefano's testimonial. It seemed a mark of respect for Europe's latest royalty, but Stein was anxious that his players should not be undersold. 'Real's first offer of a guarantee was a joke. Bob Kelly, the chairman, was saying never mind the fee, it's an honour to be asked to play. But I said we had arrived in Europe now, and this was a matter of business. Eventually Real increased the fee substantially, and we agreed to play, even though the match would extend the season by 10 days or so.'

Stein had earned the total respect of his side by his attention to detail. It extended even to his strict instruction that the players were to keep out of the heat at all times. Reserve goalkeeper John Fallon earned a reprimand for allowing the sun to catch the back of his head through a gap in the curtains in his room. Only the unfortunate McBride, who had no chance of playing, was allowed in the hotel pool. On the afternoon of the final, the players spent two hours resting in their rooms. Simpson read a golf magazine. A short loosen up session on the lawn was followed by a meal of steaks – brought over from Glasgow – and the ride to the stadium. The coach driver, perplexed by the heavy traffic, or perhaps by the exuberant singing of the players, managed to reach the Estadio Nacional only 35 minutes before kick-off. Simpson immediately took a cold shower. The temperature would be in the 80s.

The marbled stadium, a symbol of Portugal's Fascist past, was already alive to the sound of Scottish anthems. For days Celtic fans had poured into Lisbon, many of them having made the long trek overland. Their sense of humour and outrageous dress appealed to the locals – one Scot entirely kitted out in Celtic's green and white particularly caught their eye. They were not to know the costume was his bus conductor's uniform, which he had failed to remove before leaving for the match. In all, it was estimated, some 12,000 Scots made the long journey south, some of whom took weeks to come home. 'Every time we opened a cupboard', said one hard-pressed British consulate official later, 'a Celtic supporter fell out'.

Their loyalty ensured Celtic a massive advantage in support as the teams emerged. Stein, following his players out into the early evening sun, was immediately faced with an example of Italian gamesmanship, of which Shankly had warned him. 'I'd had a word with the Shank beforehand, and he said they would try anything. When we went on to the field, we found Herrera had sent out some of his men to claim our bench. I had my trainers with me, and we just pushed them out of the way. We won that one, and in a sense that went a long way towards winning the match.'

Nevertheless the first few minutes belonged to Inter. Mazzola had a downward header parried by Simpson, and then, after Johnstone had almost put Celtic ahead, the elusive Italian sent a long ball

Cappellini falls, Craig looks horrified and Inter are awarded a penalty in the opening minutes of the 1967 final in Lisbon. Mazzola scored from the spot but Celtic came back to win the match. (*Associated Press*)

forward for Cappellini to chase. As he reached it, he was tackled by Craig in the penalty area and fell awkwardly. Mazzola sent Simpson the wrong way from the penalty. Inter were ahead with just seven minutes gone.

Far from discouraged, Celtic immediately attacked, with Johnstone wandering at will, his role having been made clear to him by Stein.

'People think we won the match with wingers, but in fact we didn't play Johnstone and Lennox on the wings. I wanted them to take people on in the centre, and leave the sidelines free for Gemmell and Craig to get forward. The wee man put the fear of God into Burgnich. He must have beaten him three or four times in the opening minutes. That can help to lift a team, and it also won over the Portuguese in the crowd. There was not much sympathy for Inter that day. The other thing that helped us was that Corso chose to play very deep on his own left hand side. That gave Bobby Murdoch so much room, and we just channelled everything through him.'

While Murdoch and Auld wrested control of midfield from Corso, Bedin and Bicicli – the replacement for Suarez – Celtic pushed men forward from the back, keeping the Italians in their own half for long periods. As fast as the overworked Picchi stifled one threat, another sprang up, as the Inter players were hustled and harried out of possession. The hurt showed on their faces; few teams had treated Herrera's men with such a lack of respect. Facchetti, troubled with the pace of Lennox, said later: 'Many times I tried to get forward in the match, but when I played the ball and ran, I did not get it back. Really we were five men against 11.'

Celtic's other problem, of course, was to guard against a second swift counter. Just before half-time, after Sarti had brilliantly saved Gemmell's volley, the ball was hacked downfield towards Simpson. The goalkeeper came out of his area, but was then forced by the approach of Domenghini to backheel the ball to Clark. If it seemed an act of nonchalance, it strained the nerves on the Celtic bench. Said Clark:

'It was our only moment of danger. We had so much of the ball it was unbelievable. When they scored so early, I thought, God Almighty what chance have we got now. But the thing was, we were back in the game at once. They were content to be pushed back.

'At half-time we were still one down, but Jock told us to keep playing the way we were. But he told us to cut the ball back in front of their defence more, instead of playing it into them. When we came out of the dressing-room, some of the lads were singing, which must have astonished the Italians. But we were still confident, and in the second half had all the game again.'

The second 45 minutes were even more one-sided than the first. Simpson's one moment of discomfort was when he had to punch away a lob from Mazzola. For the rest he was largely a spectator. At the other end, Sarti saved Inter time after time, leaping backwards to hold Gemmell's drive with one hand on the line itself, then plunging into a group of players to hold the ball near the foot of his post. Even he could not prevent Celtic's equaliser after 62 minutes. Gemmell began the move down the left, before Murdoch switched play to Craig on the opposite flank. He delayed his pass until Gemmell came further forward, then rolled the ball – as Stein had insisted – in front of the line of defenders. Gemmell's shot flew past Sarti from 25 yards.

Inter's goalkeeper Sarti, beaten by Gemmell's equaliser, was aware that two Celtic forwards might have been ruled offside. His protest, however, went unheard and the Scots went on to a richly deserved win. (*Associated Press*)

Inset: The BBC recording of Gemmell's equaliser against Inter shows that at least two Celtic players *were* offside as the shot was struck. There was no further protest from the Italians who later conceded the winning goal to Chalmers. (*BBC*)

The Italians seemed stunned. It seemed a goal to end all argument. But the BBC film reveals that two Celtic players were offside when Gemmell struck his shot. The incident is similar to the one from which Leeds United suffered in the 1975 final. Then Lorimer's volley beat the goalkeeper easily, only for the goal to be disallowed because Bremner was offside. The Leeds player, unlike those of Celtic, was judged to have been interfering with play. After Gemmell's effort, the siege of Sarti's goal continued. If anything, Celtic quickened their pace even more. Gemmell hit the bar with a long cross, then Murdoch had a header saved at point blank range from a free kick after Johnstone was fouled. Said Clark: 'That was probably the best save I have ever seen. Sarti had started to commit himself one way, but somehow reacted quick enough to change direction and reach the ball one-handed. None of us could believe it.'

Chalmers (right, hooped shirt) turns away after deflecting Murdoch's drive into the net for Celtic's winner in the 1967 final in Lisbon. (*Central Press*)

The winning goal came just five minutes from time, when Gemmell again made ground on the left, and passed the ball back to Murdoch. His shot – his umpteenth of the match – might have slid wide had not Chalmers got his foot to the ball. The goal was Celtic's 200th of the season. With the game in his grasp, Stein's nerves for once got the better of him. For a few moments he left the bench and walked up the touchline with his back to the play, before returning for the final whistle. 'In the end I remember Inter raised a wee bit of a gallop, but they didn't have very much to offer, because we had run the legs off them in the match. I felt then it was only carelessness which would cost us the European Cup.'

When the game ended there was pure pandemonium as Celtic fans poured on to the pitch. Simpson, embracing Stein and Fallon, saw Lennox racing towards the goal he had just left, and immediately turned to join him. Both players were anxious to claim their false teeth from the net, before they were stolen as souvenirs. Clark was lifted on to the shoulders of supporters and lost a boot in the process; other fans knelt to kiss, and in some cases remove, the stadium turf. Gemmell, in Mazzola's shirt, stood with his arms aloft, surrounded by Scottish faces. The BBC's Scottish football correspondent, Archie MacPherson, recalled pursuing two hopeless causes: 'I was asked to get down from our commentary position and try to interview Jock Stein. It was mission impossible. All I got for my pains was a shirt ripped in two. Then the stadium officials asked me to broadcast a request to the fans to clear the pitch for the presentation. I doubt if anyone heard it, let alone took any notice.'

The sea of supporters would have taxed the resources of Canute. A lap of honour was out of the question, the mere collection of the trophy fraught with danger. McNeill lost his jersey on his way back to the dressing-room, but grabbed another, and set out again to collect the European Cup. Simpson went with him, but was soon pushed back by the crowd. His captain finally crossed the pitch for the presentation and was then sensibly ferried out of the stadium by car, and round to the sanctuary of the dressing-room on the other side. The scenes inside the dressing-room were a shambles also, as players attempted to change among the throng of officials and well-wishers. Only later could Stein, after Shankly's salute, reflect on the enormity of Celtic's achievement.

The homecoming – Glasgow Celtic players parade the European Cup at Parkhead after their return from Lisbon. (*Press Association*)

'The fact that a Scottish side had become the first British winners of the European Cup was a marvellous thing for us. We felt the British game moved up a level at that time, because in the past so many teams had got so far and failed. We won because we were afraid of nothing in the match. We had great confidence, and the day they came to watch us train was an important boost for us.

'We thought we were better than perhaps we really were. I think later on some teams might have beaten us, if they had thought the same way and had a go at us. But on that occasion I don't think Celtic would have lost to anyone. We felt everything was going our way. Even when we lost the first goal, we came back to score two goals in the match. All in all it was Celtic's day and nothing could take that away from us.'

The victory of the Scots, or more truly the manner of it, was welcomed around Europe. But those who claimed it meant the end of the defensive era were somewhat premature. It was only Inter's star which was, for the moment, eclipsed. A few days later, they lost the Italian championship to Juventus, whose coach Heriberto Herrera – no relation to the Inter coach – explained: 'The collective and athletic type of football as displayed by Celtic is my model. A player must show no weakness in 90 minutes.'

That kind of transformation, particularly in Italy, would take time. There was little doubt, however, that Inter's authority was diminished. In the summer Guaneri, Picchi and Jair left the club. Within a year Angelo Moratti had resigned, and Helenio Herrera, sensing that the wind of change might affect him also, went south to Roma. Celtic had breathed life into the European Cup, recalling the spirit of its founding fathers. So it was fitting that their final appearance of the season should be against Real Madrid, in the match for Di Stefano. Celtic, tired but still inspired, won a competitive and entertaining game with a goal by Bobby Lennox. Said Clark:

'It was a great way to finish, because the scenes in Lisbon meant we could not collect our medals, and we felt cheated in a way. At the banquet afterwards, they were just given to Billy McNeill in a box, and he had to hand them out to us. It was all a bit shabby. But when we returned to Glasgow, there was the most amazing reception at Parkhead. And again in Madrid, where we really felt we were European champions.

'Di Stefano actually played for about 15 minutes of the first half, and suddenly the lights went out. Then a single spotlight picked him out in the centre circle. He stood there like a god with the crowd going mad. Then he turned and trotted off, leaving the stage to us. Somehow that seemed to sum up what we had achieved.'

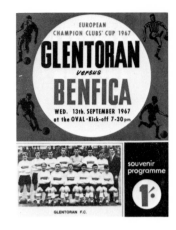

Glentoran almost caused a sensation at the start of the 1967–68 season against Benfica. The Portuguese could manage only a 1–1 draw in Belfast and a 0–0 draw in Lisbon. They therefore eliminated the Irish on the away goals rule, and went on to reach the final.

CHAPTER SIX

THE BEST OF MANCHESTER UNITED
(Manchester United 1968)

There was an air of expectancy at London's Upton Park on
6 May 1967. Matt Busby's Manchester United were in town, chasing
their fifth post-war League championship. Since Christmas, United
had adhered to the classic European pattern of winning their home
games and drawing away. Now they needed a single point against
West Ham, to be certain of entering the European Cup again the
following year. The situation seemed to favour a prudent approach.
Instead, Busby's team reverted to type. Said George Best: 'I can
think of plenty of teams at that time who would have settled for a
0–0 draw. But there was a great confidence in the side. We had
Matt's usual team talk, and just went out and played. Bobby
Charlton scored in two minutes, we were four up at half-time, and
eventually beat West Ham 6–1.'

Busby himself was late leaving the dressing-room, and was taking
his seat as the third goal went in. For a few minutes he suffered while
the Hammers swarmed round the United goal, seeking what he
thought would be the equaliser. Only when Best scored United's
fourth did he discover the true disparity between the teams.

Busby, almost 58, would be making another attempt at the
European Cup. If the mood of his players that afternoon gave him
heart, his resolve was further strengthened by the events in Lisbon
three weeks later. For Celtic's win against Internazionale was an
enormous breakthrough, a massive example to United. In the football
capitals of Europe that summer, all the talk was of Jock Stein's team.
They were upstarts in an ordered society. Their sense of adventure
was both admired, and envied. Like the man who attends a formal
dinner in fancy dress, and proceeds to make the best speech. Yet
Celtics' reign as champions was to last less than five months. The
team which toppled Inter were themselves deposed by Dynamo Kiev.

The breathless style of the Scots, so effective against the Italians,
failed to subdue the Soviet team, who upset the new masters of
Europe by winning 2–1 in Glasgow, effectively settling the tie. Celtic
could manage only a 1–1 draw in Kiev, and became the first holders
of the European Cup to depart in the first round. In a sense they
were unfortunate to meet an emerging power so early, for the draw
had been seeded by UEFA for the first time. They based their
predictions, somewhat obscurely, on which clubs had reached the
final before, and then on which countries had previously supplied
finalists.

St Etienne were, therefore, seeded because Reims had twice
reached the last stage of the tournament. There were other
anomalies. Real Madrid, for instance, were forced to play the
promising Ajax of Amsterdam in the first round. UEFA made a still
more controversial change in the rules for the 1967–68 season. In an
attempt to encourage teams to attack more away from home, and to
cut down the number of play-offs, they coined the now established

away goals rule. This meant that if teams were level on aggregate after 90 minutes of the second leg, goals scored away from home were said to count double. Only if the aggregate still remained equal was extra time to take place. If that failed to produce a winner the result would be decided by the toss of a coin. However, UEFA specified that the new ruling only applied until the last eight of the competition. At that stage, a third match could take place, but two years later the play-offs disappeared, to be replaced first by the toss of a coin, then by the nerve-wracking system of penalty kicks. Such administrative chicanery was not thought to concern Celtic, when they faced Kiev in Glasgow on 20 September 1967. The Scots fielded the team which had won the final, and there was a further link with the happy occasion in Lisbon, in the presence of the West German referee, Tschenscher.

But the feeling of ease among the large crowd was dispelled as early as the third minute, when the Soviet champions scored after a classic counter-attack. Auld's corner was swept away from Gemmell by Bychevets, who drove the ball down the right hand touchline to the swift moving Sabo. His cross was turned in at the near post by Pusach. After half an hour, Kiev went two up, when Rudakov's long shot downfield was misread by McNeill, whose clearance hit Bychevets, allowing him to run on and score a second goal. The Celtic skipper stood alone for a moment, his head in his hands, while the visitors celebrated.

The second half was a continuous Celtic assault in which Lennox finally scored after a pass from Chalmers, and Auld hit the bar with the goalkeeper beaten. Not surprisingly, tempers ran high: after Sabo hacked down Gemmell, the Scottish full back butted his assailant as he tried to get up, and was fortunate to stay on the field. Celtic's 2–1 defeat meant that, under the new rules, they had to score at least twice in Kiev and keep their opponents out. It seemed a tall order for the holders, more so when Murdoch was sent off early in the second half for a piece of petulance at a free kick.

Lennox, however, put Celtic ahead in the match, but in another fierce encounter – with Johnstone coming in for some special attention – the second goal would not come. Indeed, in the final minute, Bychevets scored, to put Celtic out on a 3–2 aggregate. The Scots had been beaten by a side which man for man was less skilful, but which had matched them for effort and endeavour. Said John Clark: 'They were a hard side, there's no doubt about that. Sabo must be one of the hardest men I ever played against. And Bychevets was a good finisher. We still felt we should have beaten them, but two bad errors at home cost us the tie. After that we were always struggling to catch up.'

Although they had been dismissed from Europe, Celtic still had the World Club Championship to play for; but their three matches against Racing Club from Argentina were to produce new lows in sportsmanship. A fortnight after the draw in Kiev, Celtic beat Racing with a goal by McNeill, the match being played at Hampden because of the ground improvements taking place at Parkhead. It was played in poor spirit, but that was nothing compared to the atmosphere in Buenos Aires on 1 November.

There, Celtic's goalkeeper Simpson was hit on the head by a bottle during the kick-in, and had to be replaced by Fallon. The incident set the tone for another unpleasant skirmish between the teams. Gemmell put the Scots ahead with a penalty, but goals by Raffo – which was almost certainly offside – and Cardenas meant the clubs would have to meet again. The play-off was fixed for Montevideo three days later, too soon for the frustrations of both teams to be forgotten. Celtic's sense of injustice was already aflame; Racing's suspect temper by now at boiling point. The result was a match from which neither side emerged with the slightest credit.

In all six players were sent off – two from Racing and four from Celtic – one of whom, Bertie Auld, refused to leave the field. The tackling on both sides was deplorable, and Johnstone in particular was persecuted in unsavoury fashion. At half-time he had to wash the saliva out of his hair, and at one stage, when he was lying injured on the touchline, Cejas, the Racing keeper, ran yards out of his goal to kick him. But the traffic in fouls was by no means one way. Gemmell was clearly seen by the millions who watched the game on television to lash out at an opponent while his back was turned. Too many of the Celtic players seemed to conduct savage, if pardonable, vendettas during the game.

To be fair Celtic officials made no attempt to excuse the excesses of their players. On their return, the staff were assembled at Parkhead, and told they would lose their promised £250 bonus. It was an unhappy end to what had been an exceptional year.

Their achievements in Europe, though, were not forgotten, least of all in Manchester, where Busby still sought the immortality accorded by Shankly to Stein. United were back for a fourth attempt at the European Cup, their mission as ever to help erase the memories of Munich by winning the trophy. As if to fuel their enterprise, UEFA announced that the 1968 final would take place at Wembley.

Busby had despaired in the dressing-room after the 1966 defeat by Partizan, but now there was a fresh impetus to his ambition. The team which won the championship in 1967 had shown itself capable of tightening up considerably away from home, while still retaining the flair and creative bias which had characterised his earlier teams. But there were a number of changes in personnel. In goal, Alex Stepney arrived from Chelsea in September 1966, and made his début against Manchester City in United's 1–0 win. His handling that day, and for the rest of the season, helped steady the defence – later Busby would claim that the title would not have been won without him. At full back, the former youth team captain, Bobby Noble had also forced his way into the side and kept his place until he was badly hurt in a car crash as he returned from a match in Sunderland. Unfortunately the head injuries he received in the crash were to mean the end of his career in football. Said Pat Crerand: 'Bobby would have played for England, no question about it, and he would have been a captain round whom the club might have rebuilt later. He wasn't tall, but he was quick, with a real hardness about him on the field. Off it, he was a popular lad, and everyone at Old Trafford was upset when he had to give up the game.'

David Herd too had been injured on the run-in to the title; he broke a leg as he scored a goal against Leicester. He never regained a permanent place, though he was to figure prominently in United's European Cup match in Poland.

It was as well for Busby's peace of mind that David Sadler at last arrived as a first team regular. He came to Old Trafford in November

1962 as a centre-forward, who had won youth and amateur caps for England, but failed to hold a place up front. In the 1966–67 season United used him just behind the front line, which gave the team a certain flexibility. Sadler also deputised successfully for Stiles and Foulkes in defence on occasions, and in November 1967 was capped for England at centre half.

'It took me a long while to settle at Old Trafford. As a youngster I had always been a goalscorer, which is why Jimmy Murphy followed me round for so long, but I could never get enough goals in the first team. It wasn't easy with all the big stars at the club. I can remember the crowd used to go very quiet when they announced my name, when Law or someone was injured. I was part of the squad for the earlier European campaigns, but one minute I'd be in Lisbon, the next with the reserves at Chesterfield. One day I came on as substitute for Bill Foulkes and played at the back. It worked fine, and though in the European Cup final I played mainly in midfield, my best position was in the back four, alongside the centre half.'

United's left winger, John Aston, son of United's coach, also knew what it was like to battle for a place among the leading players at Old Trafford. He took his chance after the departure of John Connelly to Blackburn, but was taunted cruelly at times by the crowd. His short haircut and unsophisticated style were a sharp contrast to the flights of fancy on United's other flank, but Aston had plenty of pace, a fact which the Benfica full back would endorse, after the winger's finest game for United in the final at Wembley.

United's European Cup winning season began in bizarre fashion in the Charity Shield match at Old Trafford. A long kick by the Spurs' goalkeeper Pat Jennings deceived both Foulkes and Stepney, who allowed the ball to bounce over them into the net. United came back to draw a thrilling match 3–3, with two tremendous drives from Charlton, and a typically poached effort by Law. United's brilliant Scot, however, was troubled by a knee injury, which defied diagnosis. His appearances during the 1967–68 season would be erratic, and to his lasting regret, Law would miss the European Cup final, watching the match on television from his hospital bed. Surgery revealed what he had maintained in the face of some scepticism from the Old Trafford staff, that the joint had been damaged. The operation removed a piece of bone found floating behind the knee.

Without him, there was no doubt United were a less potent force. Certainly Busby feared Law's absence would cost the club dearly, as they prepared to tackle the best in Europe again. 'To be truthful, I wasn't as confident as I had been the time before. Law's injury was a great blow at this time, because he was a mercurial player, and you don't just pick up players of his kind. Bobby and George were doing their stuff, so was Nobby Stiles, but I felt we would have been stronger if Denis had been there.'

Later in the campaign, Busby would offer a British record fee of £200,000 for West Ham's Geoff Hurst, only to be turned down by Ron Greenwood. United had to rely on their own resources: of their nine matches in Europe, Law would play in only three. Two of those were in the first round against the Maltese champions, the part-timers Hibernian. Law scored twice in a 4–0 win in the first leg at Old Trafford. There were also two goals from David Sadler, while two more youngsters, Francis Burns and Brian Kidd, made their European Cup débuts. Both had been taken on United's tour of

Australia in the summer, though Burns had returned early for a cartilage operation. The young Scot recovered to make his first division bow in United's fourth League match at West Ham. He held his place until late in the season, when he was replaced by the veteran Shay Brennan for the semi-final in Madrid, and for the final itself.

Kidd was more fortunate. His performance in the Charity Shield match had critics drooling over yet another Busby Babe, and in the absence of Law during the season, he would share the burden up front. Tall and slim, with a natural bodyswerve, he would end the season in style, scoring against Benfica on his 19th birthday.

In Malta, however, neither he nor his colleagues could manage a single goal, much to the disappointment of the local crowd, many of whom cheered for United. The appeal of Old Trafford throughout Europe was amply illustrated on the sunny island, which still boasts a thriving branch of the United supporters club. The players were fêted wherever they went, but on the hard sandy pitch there was little sign of a carnival spirit, and the match was drawn 0–0.

United had survived without serious problems, which was more than could be said for the Portuguese champions, Benfica. They seemed to have an easy task, when they were drawn against the Northern Ireland side, Glentoran. The Irish player-manager was John Colrain – Pat Crerand of United had been his best man. Colrain did his best to remove a barrier from his friend's path. At home, he put his side ahead with a penalty, and the Portuguese looked highly uncomfortable, hounded as they were in midfield by Tommy Jackson, who was later to make an impression in the English first division.

Eusebio equalised, and his goal was to prove still more precious when Glentoran, against all odds, held Benfica to a goalless draw in Lisbon. Benfica were, therefore, among the first to proceed on the away goals rule, and from such a chastening start would reach the final.

Elsewhere there were few surprises, though Real needed a goal from Veloso in extra time to dispose of Ajax. Juventus, who had by now shed Sivori, but still had Del Sol in midfield, beat the unfancied Olympiakos, while another minnow, Tirana of Albania, simply refused to play at all, conceding their tie to the new West German champions, Eintracht Brunswick. The second round took Manchester United to Sarajevo, where the players posed happily on the bridge on which in 1914, the Archduke Ferdinand had been shot dead by a local student, precipitating the first world war.

United were forced to leave out Stiles, who needed a cartilage operation, and Law who had been suspended for six weeks after being sent off in a League match against Arsenal. Sadler moved in alongside Foulkes, while the shaggy-haired John Fitzpatrick strengthened the midfield. The result was a 0–0 draw, which was far from amicable: Sarajevo were unfortunate when a shot by Musemic appeared to cross the line, only to be ruled out; and when their winger Prodanovic had to leave the field with an old injury, leaving the Slavs to play two-thirds of the match with 10 men. Though substitute goalkeepers were now allowed in the competition, no outfield player could yet be replaced.

Sarajevo's approach to the match, however, scarcely deserved more. Said Crerand: 'They were a vicious side, they really did kick lumps out of us. Our trainer Jack Crompton was on the field so often, I bet half the crowd thought he was playing. When they did play properly, they looked a good side. They had an international full back Fazlagic who was a very good player. But some of them just wanted to fight.'

At Old Trafford in the second leg, the willing Aston scored the first goal after 11 minutes, forcing the ball home after Best's header had been parried. But the game exploded in the second half: first when Best aimed a punch at goalkeeper Muftic, then when the United player was himself hacked down by Prljaca, who was immediately sent off. The Slavs sense of grievance was magnified by United's second goal. The ball seemed to be over the byline, before being pulled back for Best to score. The home side had a late scare when Delalic scored with a header. Another goal would have ended Busby's hopes, but United held on to win. Some of the Sarajevo team, however, were anxious to prolong the discussion. Said Best:

'Some of the things they did in the match were ridiculous. I remember colliding with the goalkeeper, and, as he reached over to pick me up, he dug his nails right into me which hurt. That's why I had a swing at him. It must have looked bad to the crowd, because they thought he was just helping me get up. But everytime I went near him after that, I could see him pointing his finger at me. At the end I sensed he was looking for me, so I picked out the biggest lunatic in our side – Paddy Crerand – and said this fellow is going to hit me. Sure enough there was a bit of a scuffle in the tunnel.'

Added Crerand: 'I know they were upset about the goal, perhaps rightly. But I thought George was joking about the goalkeeper. But as we reached the dressing-room, I was aware of this fellow behind us. I just turned and gave him such a clout. I nearly broke my hand. Then the boss appeared and sorted the whole thing out in his usual diplomatic fashion. He wasn't too pleased with us.'

United were again in the quarter-final of the European Cup and were also League leaders. As the year turned, they were beaten at Tottenham in an FA Cup replay, but returned a few days later to reverse the result in a League match, and stretch their lead at the top of the first division to five points.

United's winning goal at White Hart Lane was a magnificent solo effort by Charlton, who with Crerand was still responsible for keeping United ticking over in the centre of the field. The other goal that afternoon came from Best, who, even by his own magnificient standards, was enjoying a vintage season. At the end his 28 League goals made him the first division's joint leading scorer, and helped him win the Footballer of the Year trophy by a mile. Furthermore his displays in Europe would gain him the European version also, following the earlier awards to Law in 1964, and Charlton in 1966. Brave and quick, with a total absence of nerves, Best was simply a natural footballer, whose skill lit up many a winter's afternoon. And as Crerand emphasised, at United, he was encouraged to express it.

'That was the thing about Matt. He had confidence in you, and he didn't expect you to conform to a set pattern. If Best wore 11, it was a waste of time asking him to stay near the touchline. If you weren't getting the ball, it made sense to go and get it. People said we had a free hand. Well we did, but we were bound by commonsense as well. When we played away in Europe, we used to start by playing a 4–4–2 formation on occasions, until we saw the way the game was going.

'But we had players who could change things, the special players you need to win trophies in Europe, as opposed to League titles. When Denis was fit, his sharpness in the box made him special, Bobby Charlton's passing and shooting were out of the ordinary, while George could alter the course of a match with a single dribble.'

By now, Best was attracting the sort of publicity hitherto reserved for film and pop stars, his presence was enough to double the police force in some instances away from home. And at Old Trafford, for the young females pressed against the touchline fence, the handsome Irishman was a figure of fantasy, evoking squeals of anticipation from them whenever he moved near. His performance against Gornik Zabrze in the first leg of a quarter-final of the European Cup also delighted the purists. United won a sporting contest 2–0, after which Dr Kalocsai, coach to the Polish champions, said of Best: 'If there is a better winger in the world, I have not seen him, He could have played at any time in the great teams of the past.'

Gornik arrived at Old Trafford having beaten Celtic's conquerors, Dynamo Kiev, in the previous round. That victory was largely engineered in the away leg, which the Poles won 2–1, despite conceding an early own goal. Their winning goal came from a rising star, Wlodimierz Lubanski, capped at 16, who would celebrate his 21st birthday during the first leg against United.

At Old Trafford, at the end of February, he and Gornik looked sharp and skilful, despite the fact that their winter break meant they were short of match practice. Stepney made two good saves in the first half, the first being a marvellous piece of anticipation to foil Lubanski, after he was left unmarked 12 yards out. At the other end of the pitch, Kostka, who had saved a Sabo penalty in Kiev, was also inspired; while in front of him Gornik depended on the worthy Oslizlo, a survivor of the side humiliated by Spurs six years earlier.

Law had failed a fitness test on his swollen knee on the morning of the match, and been replaced by Jimmy Ryan. In his absence, Best merely moved up a gear, troubling Gornik through the centre as well as on the wing. It was he who broke the deadlock in the second half, reaching Crerand's chipped pass in the right hand corner of the area, instantly slipping past two defenders, and seeing his low drive deflected into the net by the Polish defender Florenki.

As the game moved into the final minute, United's 1–0 margin scarcely seemed sufficient. Then they were awarded a free kick outside the area. Crerand took it, and saw Kostka punch the ball away. Ryan returned it immediately towards goal, and the ball, touched on by Kidd, rolled into the corner of the net. It was no more than United deserved, but the whole match, in fact, had been a credit to the competition. The United players lined up near the tunnel to applaud their opponents off the field. Kostka received a standing ovation.

The return, on 13 March was to be played in Chorzow, between Zabrze and Katowice, where the stadium held 100,000. United arrived to find the ground, and the surrounding countryside, still in the grip of the Polish winter, as Crerand emphasised, European Cup campaigns were not always glamorous.

'These trips were all right if you won well. But very often you arrived after a long journey by coach from the airport, and you just felt awful. The chief problem was boredom. You usually had about an hour's training, and for the rest of the time you were just sitting around. You couldn't read the paper, you couldn't watch the telly. All you could do was to sit and wait for the game.

'I had been to Poland before with Scotland, and the food was awful. So this time Alex Stepney and I filled this battered old suitcase with tins of food, and tea and a little stove. But to be honest, the food had improved a lot, so that by the end we were left with having to finish everything on the last night. We didn't want to take it all the way back.'

United's manager was less concerned with catering, than with trying to get the game called off. The day before the match was spent in a vain attempt to contact the Italian referee, Concetto Lo Bello. After a decade of saving hard for the European Cup, Busby was not about to risk his stock in a winter lottery. In the end, overnight work by the home club produced a pitch which was just about playable, though it was still very hard, and the lines soon obliterated by snow. Much of the match took place in a light blizzard.

In the circumstances, United fielded a very different team to the one at Old Trafford. Sadler continued at centre half, with Stiles alongside, but the middle of the field was reinforced by Fitzpatrick. With Law still absent, Busby recalled the faithful Herd to share the hustling up front with Best and Kidd, and left out Aston. The game was hardly spectacular, though it was again played in a good spirit. Gornik, despite an injury to Wilczek early on, pressed incessantly, only to be repulsed each time by a United whose discipline would have delighted Herrera.

Only once did Gornik break through, when Stepney was penalised for delaying his clearance. From the free kick the ball was swept out to the right, then returned for Lubanski to score. In the final 20 minutes, Tony Dunne, too, was reduced to a limp, but United held on to reach the semi-final on a 2–1 aggregate.

Busby's relief was obvious, and he celebrated by treating his players to his own version of 'I belong to Glasgow' after a few drinks at the hotel. His fellow Scot, Pat Crerand, recalled the spirit of the side: 'Honestly, these little parties were part of the reason why we were a good side. I know it sounds corny, but having a big sing-song and a few drinks after a game was important to us. There was a great cameraderie in those days. You'd even get the directors joining in the parties on those long away trips.'

The following day Benfica reached the semi-final with a 3–0 win in Lisbon against Vasas Budapest. And within a week, United learned the last four would be completed by Juventus and Real Madrid. UEFA had reason to be satisfied by the way the seedings had worked out. Benfica, however, were an old team, rather than the team of old. Defenders Humberto and Cruz were now the wrong side of 30, while Coluna and José Augusto formed a somewhat veteran midfield. Much of the labour fell to Jaime Graca, recruited from Setubal after the 1966 World Cup. In December that year, his quick thinking had helped prevent a more serious accident at the club, when some whirlpool equipment failed. Graca, a former electrician, managed to turn off the current, but not before Luciano, an occasional first team defender, had died.

There had also been an upheaval at the top, where the Chilean Fernando Riera resigned between the two legs of Benfica's tie with St Etienne. After a short while, Otto Gloria, who had taken Portugal to third place in the 1966 World Cup finals, arrived from Atletico Madrid for his second spell with Benfica. After beating the French, and Vasas Budapest, the Portuguese were drawn against Juventus, whose progress owed much to the Swedish forward Roger

Magnusson, reserved by the Italians for European matches only.

In Lisbon, even he could not crack Benfica, who won 2–0 with second half goals by Eusebio and Torres. In Turin, Eusebio scored again, driving in a free kick from 35 yards for the only goal of the game. Benfica were through to their fifth European Cup final in eight years. Eusebio, however, was nursing a knee injury, which would require an operation in the close season. For the moment, his manager preferred to keep it secret, and intensive treatment allowed him to field his precious forward against both Juventus and Manchester United. Eusebio recalled: 'I thought I would not be able to play against Juventus in the second leg. But Otto Gloria said I would play on crutches if necessary. So I played at half pace, and all I did really was take free kicks. From one of them I gave it all I had, and the ball flashed past the goalkeeper. I laughed – there I was playing on one leg and scoring a goal.'

There was no doubting Eusebio's value. Despite the injury, he scored 42 goals in 26 league matches as Benfica won the title again, and in the European Cup scored six of their 10 goals, to take his current total in the competition to 36, the same as Puskas. Meanwhile in Madrid, the days of the tubby Hungarian and his partner Di Stefano were only a memory; but the patient Muñoz had guided his side to the semi-final again, dismissing the Danish part-timers Hvidovre Boldklub, then Sparta Prague in the quarter-final.

Amancio scored a hat trick in eight minutes against the Czechs, midway through the second half, to give Real a 3–0 lead in the first leg. In the return match, however, he was sent off, but the Spaniards lost only 2–1, their goal coming from Gento.

On a sunny April evening in Manchester, it was Gento, now 34, who led Real out to face Manchester United in the first leg of the semi-final. He was the only survivor in the Spanish side from the semi-final at Old Trafford 11 years earlier. Of the United team, only Charlton remained, though Foulkes was to make a spectacular return in Madrid. Real, their traditions and beliefs long admired by Busby, needed little introduction. The match was a complete sell-out, and attracted maximum exposure. The television audience, who were watching the two most popular teams in Europe, was estimated at 150 million. Sadly, the game failed to live up to expectations. Real, without the suspended Amancio, played calmly enough, and had the best player on the field in Pirri. But United, for whom Law returned as captain, though he was far from 100 per cent fit, were largely uninspired. Early in the match, Aston had a point-blank header saved at the foot of the post, and Crerand hit a post following a corner.

Then Perez, freed by Gento who had dropped into midfield, put the ball past Stepney, only to be given offside by the Soviet referee Bakhramov.

Eight minutes from half-time, United went ahead when Aston's persistence took him to the byline, and his low cross reached Best. The Irishman instantly struck a left foot shot past Betancourt. On the whole, however, Best was well marked by Sanchis, and United's four-man forward line made little impression. The best chance in the second half fell to Perez after an error by Sadler, but the winger delayed his shot long enough for the defender to recover, and tackle him from behind. The game ended with the home side still attacking, but unable to add to their single goal. It was hard to dispel a feeling of anti-climax, or that United, after a long season, increasingly were

not playing their best. A series of home defeats had already cost
them their first division lead. On the last day of the season,
11 May, they lost at home to Sunderland, while their neighbours
Manchester City were winning in thrilling style at Newcastle to
become the new champions.

Four days later Bobby Charlton led United up the steep steps and
on to the pitch in Madrid, knowing his team had to survive, then win
the final, if they were to qualify for the next European Cup. The
place was packed. Every tier of the Bernabeu stadium filled with
supporters of Real, save for a small section of fans who had paid £20
or more for a return flight from Manchester. Their scarves seemed
lost among the hundreds of white flags which welcomed the home
side. It was one of the highlights of the European Cup.

For Busby the ground held a mixture of memories. It was here that
his Babes had succumbed to Di Stefano in 1957. Five years later, in a
friendly, he had watched Denis Law inspire a rebuilt side to a 2–0
win, the first by an English club on Real's ground. Now Law was out,
and the game was infinitely more competitive. Real would test how
far Busby and United had come. His tactics and choice of players
were largely decided for him. Foulkes came back at centre half,
allowing Sadler to slip in alongside him, and Stiles to keep an eye on
both. Brennan also returned at full back. United's two wingers, Best
and Aston, were asked to drop into midfield early on. For 30
minutes, with Real tense and over-anxious, United held on. Then, in
Busby's words, 'the world came tumbling down again'.

First Pirri scored with a header from a free kick, and then 10
minutes later Brennan allowed a long ball to escape him, and Gento
went away like the wind to score unopposed. A minute later,
Dunne's forward lob was badly sliced by Real's Zoco, and the ball
dropped past his goalkeeper. The vast crowd fell silent, but on the
stroke of half-time erupted again, when Amancio shot through a
crowd of players to make the score 3–1. Half-time was greeted with
the sound of firecrackers as the Madrid fans celebrated. United, as
Crerand recalled all too vividly, were on the way out.

'We hadn't played well. In fact we had played terribly. It could have been
five or six. In the dressing-room, no one said anything for about a couple of
minutes. Then the boss said "you are not doing too well defensively. So let's
have a go and attack them". Well, honestly, some of the lads were smiling by
then. Here we were, having been outplayed, our only goal a joke, and this
man was telling us to attack them.

'But he kept reminding us that we were only 3–2 down on aggregate. With
all the noise out there, it was difficult to remember what the score was. He
said their players were just strutting about thinking the match was over. We
must keep hold of the ball, don't give it away, and go at them. The amazing
thing was, when we did this, they started to look a poor side.'

What happened in the second half has become part of the folklore of
the competition. United, revived by Busby's words and the traditions
which had inspired them, came back to draw the match 3–3 in startling fashion. The change was more psychological than tactical, a
triumph of spirit as well as skill. Certainly the goals had an air of
unreality about them. With 20 minutes left Foulkes headed Crerand's
free kick across goal, where it was flicked in by Sadler. He said: 'It
was a strange goal, because the game seemed to stop as the ball came
towards me. I had gone too far forward, and all I could do was catch
the ball with my heel as it dropped.'

The goal which completed Manchester United's sensational recovery in Madrid. It was sidefooted past Real goalkeeper Betancourt by centre half Bill Foulkes (arm raised).

Eight minutes later, Best won the ball on the right from a throw-in and scampered past Sanchis towards the byline. At the same time, Foulkes started to move from his defensive position, as if drawn by a magnet. Ignoring the shouts of his colleagues to get back, he continued to the edge of the area where he met Best's pass with the sweetest of sidefoot kicks. The ball slid past Betancourt to put United into the final. Said Best:

'I hadn't played well in the match. I was feeling disappointed with myself. Sanchis marked me well. He wasn't physical, but he was the kind of player whom you thought you had beaten, and then he was back in front of you again. This time I didn't so much beat him, as stumble past him. Then I saw this red shirt to my left and just pushed the ball inside. When I saw Bill Foulkes, I wished I'd hung on to it. I thought he would just lash at the ball. Instead he was really calm and just placed it past the keeper.

'Suddenly I started to panic. I thought we had scored too soon, and they could get at us again. But everyone was running like mad by then, and we were not in much trouble. Afterwards I was completely shattered. David Sadler and I just stood under the showers with our kit still on. The old man was crying a little I think. Some of the older players would also have some deep thoughts. For myself, I was thinking of the people back in Manchester, people like my landlady, who would be so pleased we had reached the final at last, and she could see us at Wembley.'

Added Crerand:

'It was simply unbelievable. When David Sadler scored, no one thought the ball was actually in, until he ran behind the goal with his arm up. Then Bill Foulkes of all people. Goodness knows what he was doing there. I know people have talked since about providence being involved. About fate evening things out for what happened to the club 10 years earlier.

'You cannot know about things like that. What I do know is that Nobby Stiles put a big note in the collection when we went to Mass on the morning of the match! Maybe he sold his soul. Or maybe someone decided we should win.'

Gento, Real's skipper, is also at a loss to explain the miracle in Madrid.

'It was a strange game and it is difficult to say why we lost. Our goalkeeper let us down for one of the goals. But our performance proved we were not the same as our old team. They would not have lost a lead like that. But we remained friends with Manchester. I admired Charlton very much, and also Best until he wanted to play on many fields at the same time. We knew about the history of the club, and we were happy that if we could not win the Cup, that they would do it.'

There were few people in Britain who begrudged United their place in the final. They had, after all, been trying for some time. This put pressure on the team. They would start favourites against Benfica, but Busby was aware that the match would not be won on sympathy, or because the club were a deserving case. He took his players away from Manchester early, to a hotel near Egham in Surrey, where United were left in peace. Recalled Crerand:

'It was an old Tudor mansion really, with drapes on the walls and four poster beds. We were lucky to get in actually, because Matt had left it to the last moment. He didn't want to book hotels and travel, until he knew we were in the final. The mood was very confident. We'd beaten Benfica home and away two years ago, although they had beaten us in a friendly in Los Angeles the previous summer. We knew their players and how they would play. We were well prepared. We had a pleasant few days there. The only bother was with Brian Kidd, who was playing with a frog one day near one of those mossy pools you get in old places. Of course he fell in, and came back to the room covered in green slime.'

The incident served as a reminder that Kidd was only a youngster – he would be 19 on the day of the match. Like Eusebio six years earlier, he was attempting to win a European Cup winners medal at the end of his first season in the side. He and the other United players trained briefly at Wembley the day before the match. With Law confined to a hospital bed, the team would be the one which had played in Madrid.

The Benfica team beaten in the 1968 final by Manchester United (left to right, standing): Adolfo, Humberto, Graca, Jacinto, Cruz, Henrique; (kneeling): Augusto, Torres, Eusebio, Coluna, Simoes. It was the Portuguese team's fifth final in eight years. (*Press Association*)

All of them knew what to expect: Best that he would be shadowed by Cruz. Foulkes that he must compete with the giant Torres in the air; Stiles would again police Eusebio; while Charlton and Crerand would pit their experience against Coluna and Augusto, who, like Cruz, were appearing in their fifth European Cup final. The referee would be the Italian, Lo Bello, who had been in charge of United's memorable 5–1 win in Lisbon two years earlier. If that seemed a good omen, Busby was more concerned with clarifying the official's position on the four-step rule. Stepney had been penalised in Poland by Lo Bello, and it had cost United a goal.

A further omen came on the day of the match, when the heavily backed Derby favourite Sir Ivor, ridden by Lestor Piggott, came safely home in front of the field.

Though seven of Benfica's players had been to Wembley before, United's home advantage seemed of immense benefit, more so as the ground filled with fans, arriving in the afternoon by coach and train. The stadium was awash with red and white banners almost two hours before the kick-off, many of them proclaiming the candidacy of United's manager for high political and religious office. None of them seemed perturbed that both teams would be forced to change their normal colours. Benifica would wear white, while United would appear in all-blue, the colour they had worn in a Wembley FA Cup final 20 years earlier.

The first part of the match was dominated by United. Aston indicated that his pace might prove too much for Adolfo, while Cruz imposed his presence with a couple of fouls on Best. In fact the first half was an untidy affair, fussily refereed by Lo Bello, who booked Humberto for a foul on Best, and warned Stiles for arriving late on Eusebio. Sadler had two chances for United, but Benfica came closer to scoring. Best lost the ball in midfield where Graca and Torres set Eusebio in space. He evaded Stiles and hit the ball, with scarcely any backlift, against Stepney's bar. The goalkeeper, capped by England on the same pitch a week earlier, was beaten, but the ball bounced safely down for Brennan to clear.

The first goal came after 52 minutes, and from a somewhat unexpected source. Dunne pushed the ball to Sadler from a United throw-in on the left. Sadler's cross was touched into the corner of Henrique's goal by the head of Charlton. From the restart, Best had the ball past the keeper again, but was clearly offside. United, however, should have added to their lead, particularly when Best, wheeling past three tackles, had his shot parried. Sadler hit the rebound tamely, and Henrique saved with his foot as he fell backwards.

With 20 minutes to play United faced a difficult decision. Though still more dangerous they were increasingly tired, and tempted to settle for what they had; and they allowed Benfica back in the match. Eusebio wasted a good chance, and then, with 11 minutes left, came the equaliser by Graca. He started the move by passing the ball to Augusto whose soaring cross was headed down by Torres, too far in front of Eusebio. But Graca had continued his run and met the ball near the byline to beat Stepney's right hand.

With the game poised at 1–1, Eusebio now had chances to win the match. First, forced wide by Sadler, he saw his shot saved easily by Stepney. Then, after a Charlton shot was charged down at one end, Simoes passed the dusky striker a fine ball down the middle. As Dunne and Foulkes converged, Eusebio chose to hit the ball from 18 yards rather than place it. Stepney, who had started to advance and then stopped, felt the ball crash against him like the recoil of a rifle, but hung on. The sporting Eusebio at once congratulated him, but it was an expensive miss: with hindsight, the turning point of the match. Recalled Sadler:

'It was a magnificent save at a time when we had all just gone. I felt terrible because I'd had chances to win the match. I'd have been ready to take the blame if we had lost. At the end of 90 minutes we just sat on the ground, while the manager and Jimmy Murphy moved quietly round us. One or two

Matt Busby, Jimmy Murphy and John Aston Sr attempt to revive tired limbs and worried minds before the start of extra time in the 1968 final against Benfica. The players responded with three goals in the first seven minutes after the restart. (*Press Association*)

of the lads had a rub. The boss said we should play as more of a unit, that we shouldn't get too stretched. And that we would win comfortably in extra time.'

As in Madrid, the United players now drew deep on mental, as well as physical, reserves. After the reprieve by Stepney, the side as a whole gained strength during those precious moments. Busby's patience was rewarded by three goals in seven minutes; the match was settled.

The first was scored by Best, after Stepney's kick was headed on by Kidd. Faced with Jacinto, he touched the ball past him, rounded Henrique, and from a narrow angle rolled the ball towards goal. For a moment it seemed the goalkeeper, might reach the ball as he launched himself backwards, but when he did it was in the depths of his own net. Said Best:

'I knew exactly what I was doing. Paddy said to me afterwards, "I thought you were never going to put it in", but I knew, as soon as the centre half came at me, that I would score. I just nicked it past him, and waited for the goalkeeper to make his move before I beat him. I knew there was no one

George Best (dark shirt) turns away. Despite Henrique's attempt to recover, the ball is already over the line for Manchester United's second goal against Benfica in the 1968 final at Wembley. (*Popperfoto*)

Bobby Charlton (half hidden by the Benfica goalkeeper Henrique) chips the ball into the net for Manchester United's final goal in the 4–1 win over Benfica at Wembley. (*Press Association*)

else near, and I remember thinking this is too easy, something will go wrong. I saw the goalkeeper jump back at the ball, but he couldn't have reached it. I had turned away before the ball crossed the line.

I was so pleased to score because I hadn't done well. Because it was Wembley, I wanted to win in style. I was trying to overdo it, to score great goals, instead of playing simply. But when extra time came, I wasn't tired at all. I just thought this is a second chance for us to win it well.'

That particular wish soon became reality. From the kick-off United won a corner, after Aston had again sped past Adolfo. The kick was touched on by Sadler to Kidd. Kidd's first header was parried by Henrique, but the second looped over Henrique into the net. Now Charlton won the ball again deep in his own half, and sent Kidd sprinting down the right. Hurdling Cruz's tackle, the youngster knocked the ball towards the near post, where Charlton met it perfectly and sent it soaring in an elegant curve over the goalkeeper. At 4–1, United were quite beyond reach.

Indeed their only worry now was whether their supporters might try to invade the pitch, as the Celtic fans had done a year earlier. But at the whistle, the first man on to the field was Busby, to congratulate the Benfica side, then unashamedly to hug Bobby Charlton. He refused, however, a request from some of the senior players to collect the trophy himself. So it was Charlton who received the European Cup at last, though, as the Wembley spotlight picked him out on the lap of honour, he handed the huge trophy to his team-mates. The United captain was physically and mentally exhausted. 'I knew what it meant to the club, and to some of us who had been trying for so long. That's why, as I looked around me, I was pleased that Bill Foulkes, Shay Brennan and Nobby Stiles were there. They'd been at the club when the accident happened, and now they were there at the end.'

Foulkes and Charlton, of course, were actual survivors of the disaster 10 years earlier. As if to help exorcise that particular spirit,

The moment of triumph – Matt Busby congratulates Crerand, Stepney and Aston after Manchester United's 4–1 win over Benfica at Wembley. (*Press Association*)

United had invited the relatives of those who died, and the other survivors, to watch the final. One of them was Johnny Berry. 'I was living not far from London, and when United sent me a ticket, I went along. I saw some of the old faces, and I was glad that United won. But that was as far as it went for me. I was pleased they won, that was all.'

His thoughts were echoed by David Sadler. 'People were talking about Munich, and I know some of the older players were affected by it. But Matt Busby told us before the match that we were professionals first and foremost, and playing for the present, not for anything that had gone before.' All United's friends, however, were delighted for Busby, who later paid generous tribute to his players, and expressed the hope that the European victory marked the beginning rather than the end of an era.

Yet 12 months later, with United having been knocked out of a European Cup semi-final by AC Milan, Busby himself closed a particular chapter in the history of the club by announcing his retirement. The following few years were not kind to Busby, or

Manchester United fans jam the city's Albert Square as their favourites return with the European Cup. It was United's first success at their fourth attempt. (*Press Association*)

United. A succession of managers failed to keep the club out of the second division in 1974, just six years after the famous evening at Wembley. There are some who felt that Busby should have started to rebuild the side, even before the European Cup had been won. Others that he allowed his influence to pervade the dressing-room, long after his elevation to the board of directors, which cut the lines of communication between manager and players.

George Best, whose subsequent disenchantment with football was both a cause and an effect of United's decline, said:

'Frankly I think there was a feeling of relief when we won the European Cup, instead of a feeling that we should go on from there. The club had been trying for so long that it was understandable, but for me it was disappointing. They talk about old players in the side, but there were also a lot of youngsters. I was 22, Brian Kidd 19. We were nowhere near our peak, and I felt cheated later, because we struggled for so long with players who weren't really United calibre. We could have been better covered. With a bit of foresight, 1968 could have been the start of three or four years domination in Europe.

'For me, personally, the later years when we were out of Europe were depressing. I hear people say the League championship is the most important thing to win. It was only important to me because it meant we were in the European Cup the following year. There was so much atmosphere at those games. For one thing they were usually night matches, which I loved. They were one-offs, and I missed them terribly. After we were out of Europe, there was just an empty feeling.'

Chapter Seven

DOUBLE DUTCH
(Ajax, Feyenoord 1969–1973)

The Arabian sheik sitting in the foyer of the Hilton Hotel in Istanbul could not understand what all the fuss was about. The boisterous behaviour of 500 Dutchmen who seemed to fill the building intrigued, rather than annoyed him, but the cause for their high spirits left him baffled. For this was 1968, and football missionaries from the west had still to reach the oil fields of Arabia. The sheik had never heard of soccer, let alone seen it.

When it was explained to him that Ajax, the champions of the Netherlands, were in Istanbul to play Fenerbahce, the best team in Turkey, he began to understand that an event of some importance was taking place. The sheik sought out the Ajax players, who were staying in the hotel, and offered his solid gold wrist watch, together with $200 in cash, to the first player to score a goal that day. It was won by Piet Keizer, the clever Ajax outside left, who wore the watch for years afterwards.

Keizer's goal put Ajax on the way to a comfortable 2–0 victory – the same score as in the first leg in Amsterdam. The Dutch champions were through to the quarter-finals, and a new epoch was about to start in the European Cup.

Strangely, Ajax would never have been in Istanbul at all, had it not been for the unexpected behaviour of two British champions: Manchester City, who lost to opponents they should have beaten, and Celtic, who at one point simply refused to play at all.

Tuesday 20 August 1968 will be remembered not for anything as mundane as the start of a new football season, but as the day Soviet troops invaded Czechoslovakia to bury, with a ruthless demonstration of Communist force, the liberal régime of Alexander Dubcek. Celtic made a political protest by withdrawing from their first round European Cup tie against the Hungarian champions, Ferencvaros. Other West European teams drawn against sides from the Eastern bloc threatened to pull out of the competition.

UEFA's reaction was to scrap the original draw and make new first round pairings, keeping east and west apart. Now the Iron Curtain countries protested, and the champions of Bulgaria, East Germany, Hungary, Poland, and the Soviet Union withdrew. Such unpleasant scuffling would have saddened Gabriel Hanot, who died that year and whose European Cup patently had been marred by political influences.

Celtic, having made their point, now played the French champions St Etienne, guided by the experienced hand of the former Reims boss, Albert Batteux. The Scots lost 2–0 in France but with Tommy Gemmell and Bobby Murdoch returning from injury, and Jimmy Johnstone rampant, they won the second leg 4–0 in Glasgow. There was no such joy for the English champions Manchester City, who had won the first division title for only the second time in their history while their neighbours Manchester United had clinched the European Cup. Malcolm Allison, City's coach, teamed up with whimsical Joe

CITY LEAGUE CHAMPIONS
WEDNESDAY
SEPTEMBER 18th 1968
Kick-off 7-45 p.m.
VERSUS
FENERBAHCE S.K. Champions of Turkey

MANCHESTER CITY FOOTBALL CLUB LTD.
European Champion Clubs' Cup
OFFICIAL PROGRAMME ONE SHILLING
>

'We shall frighten the cowards of Europe', announced Manchester City's coach Malcolm Allison before the 1968–69 tournament. But City could manage only a 0–0 draw at home to Fenerbahce of Turkey and went out in the first round.

Mercer to create a bold team which played in huge, attacking waves. Exciting forwards like Francis Lee, Mike Summerbee and Colin Bell led the extrovert Allison to predict: 'We shall frighten the cowards of Europe'. But City's flamboyance was muted at Maine Road by the obstinate Turkish side, Fenerbahce. There was no score in the first leg. City's injured captain, Tony Book, went with the team to Istanbul for the return: 'We stayed in the Hilton Hotel (where Ajax would soon follow) which is situated on a hill overlooking the stadium where the match was to be played. People started going in at six o'clock in the morning, and by lunchtime the ground was full.'

Even in this hostile atmosphere – Mercer said it was like going to your execution – City managed to score first through outside left Tony Coleman. But Fenerbahce got the benefit of two soft goals which cost City's keeper, Ken Mulhearn, his place in the team. One of them was scored by Abdullah, who had been brought on as substitute by Fenerbahce in accordance with a new UEFA rule. From the start of the 1968–69 season, two substitutes were permitted at any time, and for any reason, in the European Cup. Allison's words had been thrown back sharply in his face, but he and his team were smart enough to learn quickly, and the following season they won the European Cup Winners' Cup in style.

City's elimination left the way clear for Ajax to announce their arrival not only in Istanbul, but near the forefront of European football. Their European Cup victory over Liverpool two years earlier had been merely a taste of what was to come. The Dutch club was formed in 1900 by a group of businessmen who met in top hats one Sunday morning at the Café East India in Amsterdam's Kalverstraat. The Dutch, like the rest of the world, learned the game from the British. Pim Mulier founded the Haarlem club in the Netherlands in 1879 after seeing football played in England, and Ajax were one of several Dutch clubs to employ British coaches.

Jack Reynolds built a fine Ajax team between the wars, when they won the Dutch championship five times in nine years. But football in the Netherlands remained strictly amateur until 1954, when semi-professionalism was introduced. Now the Dutch began to apply their minds to the game with intelligence and zeal. In 1964, when the top players became full-time professionals, Ajax appointed a Dutchman Rinus Michels, to succeed Englishman Vic Buckingham as coach.

Piet Keizer was then 21, but he had been in the first team for four years, and had been connected with Ajax since he was 12. On the continent, schoolboys were legitimately linked with top clubs much earlier than in England.

'I was one of a nucleus of Ajax players who grew up together as kids in the same part of Amsterdam. There was Jackie Swart, Benny Muller, Tony Pronk and myself. But when Michels took over, he changed the playing staff considerably. And he changed the training schedule even more. His was the hardest physical preparation I ever had. We sometimes had four sessions a day.

'He also introduced the Italian system of taking the players away for a period of concentrated training before a big match. We would start work in the morning, and carry on until the evening. It was a holiday under Buckingham by comparison. Michels was by no means a miserable man, but he was very strict with players and there were lots of arguments about discipline. The message was pretty clear. Those who did not like it would have to leave.'

Michels' first task was to save Ajax from relegation, but he then won three championships in a row. He assembled a team based on what became known across Europe as the 'squad system', with 16 or 17 players working together as a first team pool. In front of goalkeeper Gert Bals, whom he signed from PSV Eindhoven, Michels had four versatile defenders. The full backs, Wim Suurbier and Theo van Duivenbode, were encouraged to attack, while in the centre the strong stopper Barry Hulshoff struck an ideal balance with the Yugoslav sweeper, Velibor Vasovic, signed from Partizan Belgrade.

Tony Pronk's partner in midfield was Henk Groot, another who grew up with Ajax but who was allowed to move to their fierce Rotterdam rivals, Feyenoord, before Michels brought him back. Keizer's aides in attack were Jackie Swart on the right wing; Inge Danielsson, a lively opportunist from Sweden; and the ubiquitous Johan Cruyff, who made his début for Ajax at the age of 17 in the year that Michels took over.

But Ajax were not merely on the verge of uncovering a great team. They were to trigger a football explosion in the Netherlands which was to have telling repercussions across the continent, and which first caught the public imagination when they played Benfica in the 1969 European Cup quarter-final. Having beaten Fenerbahce so comfortably, Ajax were confident of making further progress, despite the fact that Benfica had reached the previous final against Manchester United. Keizer felt the Dutch were too cocky.

'The first leg in Amsterdam was played in snow, and we didn't think Benfica would perform in those conditions. As it turned out, they were better prepared than us. Their players wore gloves and tights, and they were 3–0 up before we got a goal back. We went to Lisbon two goals behind, and with our pride hurt. Before the match, our dressing-room was quiet, which was unusual. Even Cruyff was nervous. We did not have our usual team talk. Michels spoke about two sentences. We all knew what had to be done.'

And Ajax did it. Just like Benfica in Amsterdam, they surged into a three-goal lead, only allowing their opponents a late goal. So the tie was squared, and a third match fixed in Paris. Keizer said: 'Years later, after Dutch teams had won four European Cups and played in two World Cup Finals, it seemed fantastic to think of 40,000 supporters travelling from the Netherlands to watch that play-off in France. But they did. It was at that precise moment that football took off in our country – we never had such a big following for an overseas match before or since'.

There was no score after 90 minutes, but in extra time Ajax rapped in three goals. Danielsson got two, Cruyff the other, and to the delight of their massed supporters the Dutch were through to the semi-final. So, too, were the holders, Manchester United, who since their triumph at Wembley had strengthed their attack by signing Willie Morgan, the Scottish international winger from Burnley, and tested their nerve against the South American club champions, Estudiantes de la Plata of Argentina.

This latest version of the World Club Championship was as full of acrimony as that between Celtic and Racing Club a year earlier. In Buenos Aires, United were victims of a hate campaign before the match and then subjected to intolerable provocation on the field. The Argentine target was Nobby Stiles, who was eventually sent off for making a gesture at a linesman. In the infamous Bombonera

Stadium, United were glad to come away in one piece, even though they lost the first leg 1–0.

In the return match at Old Trafford, George Best and the Estudiantes defender Medina were sent off for fighting, and a 1–1 draw meant the South Americans again won what had now become a thoroughly discredited event. Denis Law was back in the Manchester United team now, to the joy of the Stretford End. Although he went off injured in the second leg against Estudiantes, his knee was standing up to the strain of top class competition and Law seemed doubly determined, after missing the final against Benfica, to make his mark on the European Cup.

Law scored seven goals in two lighthearted matches against Waterford, the Republic of Ireland champions. Then he got two more in a 3–0 win over Anderlecht at Old Trafford, after missing a penalty. United were without the suspended Best both for this match and for the return in Brussels. Carlo Sartori, an Italian born winger, took his place and put United further ahead in the second leg, but Anderlecht replied with three goals and United scraped through on a 4–3 aggregate.

It was the returning Best who, in the quarter-final against Rapid Vienna, suggested United might still have enough class to retain the trophy. He scored twice in a 3–0 win in Manchester – his second goal being a breathtaking individual effort – then performed heroically with Bobby Charlton in Austria, where Busby's team forced a 0–0 draw. But now came the acid test. United's semi-final opponents were the revitalised AC Milan, who had marked Nereo Rocco's return as coach the previous season by winning both the Italian championship – their first since he had left four years earlier – and the European Cup Winners' Cup.

There were only two survivors from the Milan team which had won the European Cup under Rocco in 1963: Gianni Rivera, soon to be voted European Footballer of the Year, and Giovanni Trapattoni, who would later become a successful coach himself and lead Juventus into the European Cup. In a furious attempt to wrest their national and European standing back from Internazionale, with whom they shared the San Siro Stadium, AC Milan had again spent extravagantly.

Karl-Heinz Schnellinger, the blond German full back who played against England in the 1966 World Cup final, was a tower of strength in their defence. The attack, led by the Brazilian Sormani, relied also on 34-year-old Kurt Hamrin, the little Swedish winger who had first entered Italian football with Juventus in 1956, then won a European Cup Winners' Cup medal with Fiorentina. Milan still played with classic Italian connivance, luring the opposition into their intricate defensive net, then striking when the enemy's guard was down. Even Celtic, conquerors of *catenaccio* less than two years earlier, fell into the trap in the 1969 quarter-final.

The Scots defended resolutely in San Siro, forcing a 0–0 draw and understandably fancying their chances before a 75,000 crowd at Parkhead, where in the previous round they had put five goals past Red Star Belgrade. But the only goal this time came from Milan's 22-year-old left winger Pierino Prati, who cashed in on a mistake by Billy McNeill which came, unluckily for Celtic, in the 13th minute. It was a victory which gave Milan confidence for their semi-final against Manchester United.

The holders proved such a huge attraction that Milan's crowd paid a record 206 million lire to watch the first leg. They got the result they wanted, largely because United were a team in decline rather than a team in the making. Alex Stepney had lost form, so reserve goalkeeper Jimmy Rimmer was selected. At 37, Bill Foulkes was called back to replace the young Steve James at centre half. In other words, United were not at full strength. They appealed for handball when Sormani gave Milan the lead, and fell further behind when Hamrin scored in the second half. United's John Fitzpatrick was sent off for retaliating against Hamrin; this completed an unhappy night for Busby. Could his ailing champions make up a two goal margin at Old Trafford?

There are those who insist to this day that they did. United got one goal back through Charlton, and near the end Law seemed to have forced Crerand's cross over Milan's line before substitute Santin hooked the ball away. The French referee, Machin, waved play on, and Law still insisted years later that it was a goal: 'The referee was only a few yards away, and had one of the best views of the incident. Yet he seemed the only person inside Old Trafford who did not think it was a goal. It was a travesty of justice which I believe cost Manchester United the European Cup.'

In fairness, Milan, too, had a goal disallowed, when Hamrin was given offside. Also their goalkeeper, Fabio Cudicini, was knocked down by a missile thrown from the Stretford End. The delay while he was treated may well have checked United's rhythm, but a more sober reason for their defeat was the way Milan contained Best by Anquilletti's excellent marking.

So Milan had put out the two previous winners of the European Cup, Manchester United and Celtic; but the omens were even stronger than that for Rocco. When his team had last won the trophy in 1963, they numbered among their victims two British champions, Ipswich Town and Dundee! Milan's opponents in the 1969 final would be Ajax, who accounted for Spartak Trnava after a semi-final scare. The Czechs were beaten by three goals in Amsterdam, and Keizer, who scored the third, said they wanted revenge at any price in the return match.

'They finished Cruyff in 15 minutes and I hardly got a kick. They were the most physical side we had played, and Bals saved us with an amazing display in goal. They managed to beat him twice, but we squeezed through by one goal. When it came to the final, our lack of experience told against us. I don't just mean in the way we played, because there is no doubt Milan were the better side, but in the build up to the match in Madrid. You had the uneasy feeling that there were things going on behind the scenes. Our directors were very naïve about what went on at this level, but the Italians seemed to be up to all sorts of little schemes.'

Keizer's hints at malpractice would be taken up more forcibly in years to come, when Italian clubs were frequently accused, and sometimes proved guilty, of overstepping the rules. For the moment, Milan marched on to a convincing victory.

Two first half goals by Prati shook what little confidence Ajax could muster. The first, after seven minutes, was made by Sormani; the second, six minutes before half-time, was designed by Rivera. When Keizer was fouled on the hour, Vasovic scored for Ajax from a penalty – thus becoming the only man in the first 25 years of the European Cup to score in the final for different clubs. He had been

Milan's Pierino Prati scores his third goal in the 1969 final against Ajax. He and Puskas are the only men to claim a hat trick in the European Cup final.

Partizan's marksman in the 1966 final against Real Madrid. But he earned Ajax only a stay of execution. Five minutes later, Sormani made it 3–1, and eight minutes after that, Prati got his third to become the first man since Puskas to score a hat trick in the final.

Milan's 4–1 victory meant they, like Inter, could now point to two European titles. It also emphasised the close partnership between Rocco and Rivera, the strategy of the first and the style of the second significantly contributing to both triumphs. But the losers in 1969 would, ultimately, be the winners. Not twice, but three times. Ajax were learning quickly, and the example of Vasovic made a lasting impression on Michels.

He made the strong Yugoslav his new captain in place of Bals, despite having five other players in the side who had spent their whole career with Ajax. Michels was never afraid to make changes: after the 1969 final came the departure of left back Theo van Duivenbode, to make way for another young player emerging through the Ajax ranks – Ruud Krol. But van Duivenbode had no complaints: 'I had been a winger, so when Michels said he wanted a tougher left back I could see his point. I was not a physical player and the slide tackle was not my style.'

So van Duivenbode moved to Feyenoord, who had just beaten Ajax to the Dutch championship under coach Ernst Happel, a defender in the fine Austrian national team of the early 1950s, and scorer of a European Cup hat trick against Real Madrid in 1957. Michels and Happel, the one in Amsterdam, the other in Rotterdam, were contemporaries who did more than other coaches to improve Dutch football and thus win the Netherlands so many admirers. Van Duivenbode was the only senior player of his time given the opportunity to compare the two men at first hand.

'Michels was an expert in planning the tactics before the match and preparing players physically and mentally, but Happel was a superb dissector of the game. He saw things so quickly that he would make changes from the bench after only a few minutes play.

'Happel did not have at Feyenoord the outstanding individual players that Michels had at Ajax, so he went into greater tactical detail and produced more of a co-operative team. Not so much flair, perhaps, but very thorough teamwork. Happel also preferred the zonal marking system, with defenders responsible for certain areas, to the man-for-man method that Michels used at Ajax.'

Van Duivenbode's views are obviously relative, because Feyenoord possessed a team of skilful, intuitive players. Their sweeper, Rinus

Israel, patrolled the defence, but came through to score important
goals. In midfield the chief architect was the arrogant Dutch
international Wim Van Hanegem, with his invaluable foresight,
cunning distribution and model left foot. He was ably supported by the
Austrian Franz Hasil, who had had previous European Cup
experience with Rapid Vienna, and the young, shy Wim Jansen, later
to play splendidly for the Netherlands in two World Cups.

Feyenoord's attack was notable for its width and speed. Coen
Moulijn, on the left, won 40 caps for the Netherlands, thanks to his
fierce acceleration; Henk Wery, on the right, had one of the hardest
shots in the Dutch game; in the middle, the Swedish international,
Ove Kindvall, was a natural, consistent matchwinner.

Heartened by the appearance of Ajax in the 1969 final, Feyenoord
began the following European Cup by crushing the Icelandic
amateurs, Reykjavik, 12–2 and 4–0. Both matches were played in
Rotterdam. As it turned out, they were not the only side to score 16
goals in the first round in 1969–70. Leeds United, the new English
champions making their bow in Europe's senior competition, did so
without a goal against them when they played the Norwegians, Lyn
Oslo.

Leeds were undoubtedly a formidable side, built from raw
foundations by their former player, Don Revie. He took over as
manager in 1961, when the club was threatened with relegation to the
third division and the city's rugby league club was attracting more
attention. One of Revie's first decisions was to change Leeds' strip
from blue and gold to all white, his standards set on the then
transcendant Real Madrid. But his team's approach was not as
untarnished. Leeds' physical indiscretions and elastic conscience
earned them a bad reputation as they were promoted from the
second division in 1964, and a year later finished runners-up both in
the first division and in the FA Cup. But their fearless ambition,
mixed with a family pride and developing skills, served Leeds well in
Europe. There were some blazing nights, especially when their
pocket general, Bobby Collins, had his thigh bone broken in Turin,
but Leeds were runners-up in the Fairs Cup in 1967, and winners a
year later when they beat Ferencvaros in the final.

By the time Leeds won the Football League championship for the
first time in 1969, setting records with 67 points and a mere two
defeats in 42 games, they had shifted the emphasis in their game.
Their once desperate desire to succeed had been channelled by Revie
into a controlled but irresistible force. His team were capable of
football of the highest order. But there were times in his career at
Elland Road when Revie was accused not just of gamesmanship, but
also of acute pessimism. For all the excellence in his side, he often
feared the worst, and Leeds, for all their consistency, finished second
more often than first.

Later, as England manager, Revie would be accused of being
obsessed with the opposition, and how to counter them. But part of
Leeds' success was the attention to detail of his backroom team, men
like Tony Collins, Maurice Lindley and Syd Owen, who would report
meticulously on teams Leeds were to meet. On the training field,
Revie's chief aide was the gritty little trainer, Les Cocker, who died
suddenly in 1979. The two men shared an unashamed, compulsive
desire to win, and worked assiduously with a Leeds squad which at
one time included 14 internationals.

Gary Sprake, the Welsh goalkeeper, was a Jekyll and Hyde figure, capable of brilliance one day, plagued by quirkish error the next. But he was protected by four defenders who all served England – the full backs, Paul Reaney on the right and Terry Cooper on the left; centre half Jack Charlton, Bobby's elder brother and 1966 World Cup colleague; and Norman Hunter, whose fierce tackling and fine left foot were a constant inspiration to the rest of the team.

The style and invention in the Leeds side stemmed from a midfield which delighted Revie and which Leeds have never replaced. The combustible Scot, Billy Bremner, a tireless captain who never admitted that a game was lost, and Irishman Johnny Giles, whose exquisite passing sometimes masked his hard streak. Giles, at five feet seven inches, gave the team its direction; Bremner, at five feet five and a half inches gave the team its desire. And there were two more Scots: Peter Lorimer, with his explosive shooting, on the right; and Eddie Gray, with his masterful dribbling, on the left. In the centre, Mick Jones dutifully sacrificed himself for the cause without ever getting the credit his wholesome contribution deserved.

It was to provide the fitting partner for Jones that Revie preceded Leeds' entry into the European Cup by buying Allan Clarke from Leicester City. He was essentially an individualist, his skills finely tuned and his finishing clinical, but Clarke became a team player in a Leeds squad which also included future internationals such as Paul Madeley, Terry Yorath and David Harvey. Leeds' capacity for coping with injuries, the replacements conforming to the team's established pattern, enabled them to keep winning. They played both matches against Ferencvaros in the second round of the 1970 European Cup without Clarke, and one without Cooper, but still won handsomely at Elland Road and in Budapest.

The Hungarians – Leeds' old adversaries from the Fairs Cup – could point to the absence of Florian Albert, their international centre-forward. But a 3–0 defeat at home, as well as away, made the excuse look poor and made Leeds' chances of winning the cup look very good, especially as two of the favourites, the holders Milan and the still worthy Real Madrid, fell in the same round.

Happel took Feyenoord to San Siro for the first leg well aware of what Milan had done to Ajax in the final a few months earlier. He played a careful 4–4–2 formation, denying Rivera the space he sought, and restricting the Italians to a single goal from one of their summer signings, the Argentine Nestor Combin, from Torino. Milan looked tired after winning another violent World Club championship encounter with the infamous Estudiantes, and they succumbed to Feyenoord in Rotterdam. Jansen levelled the aggregate after only five minutes with one of his rare goals, a swirling effort from the right wing which Cudicini thought was going wide until the ball hit the far post and went in.

Eight minutes from time, Van Hanegem scored Feyenoord's winner. It was sweet revenge for Dutch flair over Italian pragmatism. Neither of the Milanese clubs would win the cup in the next decade. Nor would Real Madrid, who had been beaten both home and away by the Belgian champions, Standard Liège. The second leg in Madrid, which Real lost 3–2, marked the 88th and last European Cup appearance of Francisco Gento. No player could match his total, and before retiring the famous winger went on to play against Chelsea in the 1971 Cup Winners' Cup final.

Now, in the quarter-final, Standard Liège faced Leeds. The Belgians had a cosmopolitan team, including Louis Pilot, the captain of Luxembourg, and Milan Galic, the Yugoslav forward who had played for Partizan Belgrade in the 1966 final in Brussels. But Leeds again won both home and away games, taking their European Cup record to six wins in six matches. A second half goal by Lorimer clinched the first leg in Liège, where Leeds adapted well to the freezing conditions, and a penalty by Giles decided the return at Elland Road.

Leeds' opponents in the semi-final were Celtic, whose team included seven survivors from the 'Lisbon Lions' who had won the trophy three years earlier. Stein's side had dealt efficiently with Basle in the first round, and impressively with Italy's Fiorentina in the quarter-final. But in their second round tie, against Benfica, the Scots had won only on the toss of a coin. It was an historic moment when, after Benfica had repeated in Lisbon the 3–0 victory Celtic had recorded at Parkhead, the referee spun the disc in the Stadium of Light to see who went through.

Never again was this arbitrary, unsatisfactory method used to determine a European Cup tie. From next season onwards, extra time in the second leg would be followed by a penalty competition. For now, Celtic marched on, and their semi-final with Leeds was justifiably labelled 'the Battle of Britain'.

The first leg was played at Elland Road on the Wednesday after Easter, and it was Leeds' eighth match in 14 days. So hard had Leeds pressed towards a treble of championship, FA Cup and European Cup, that fixture congestion had left them complaining they were mentally and physically drained. Two days earlier, Revie had fielded a complete reserve side in an Easter Monday League match at Derby, where Leeds' 4–1 defeat virtually handed the championship to Everton. Now, against Celtic, he was still without the injured Hunter.

If Revie had a reputation for sharp practice, Jock Stein's experiences with the likes of Herrera had made him nobody's stooge. When Celtic arrived at Leeds for the first leg, the French referee told the two managers he was unhappy with both teams wearing white stockings. Somebody had to change, and Stein was on his guard.

'Don very kindly offered us a set of blue stockings. That would have been sacrilege, of course, for Celtic to wear anything blue. I thought we had already agreed beforehand that Leeds would change, but Don now insisted we did. It was his way of trying to upset us before the match. In the end we wore orange stockings, but we settled down a lot quicker than Leeds. We got on with things and scored an early goal that made all the difference.'

The scorer, with a deflected shot after only 90 seconds, was George Connelly, a versatile player who was to retire prematurely when he had an international future. His influence on the match did not end there. The midfield trio of Connelly, Murdoch and Auld enabled Celtic to keep a grip on the designs of Bremner and Giles. When Bremner went off with concussion in the second half, with Celtic still leading, the Leeds engine spluttered and failed. Eddie Gray came closest to scoring when he hit the bar with Celtic's goalkeeper, Evan Williams, beaten. But with David Hay prominent at right back the Scots defence never faltered again.

Four days before the second leg, Leeds drew 2–2 at Wembley with Chelsea in the FA Cup final. Now with that replay delayed, they went to Hampden Park to face Celtic in a match which made history even before a ball was kicked. Celtic had switched their home tie from Parkhead, where the capacity was 80,000, knowing they could fill Hampden, where the official limit was normally 134,000. The attendance on the night of Wednesday, 15 April 1970 was later confirmed at 136,505, the biggest crowd in the history of the European Cup.

David Harvey, the replacement in goal for Gary Sprake, is beaten by Bobby Murdoch's shot which put Celtic 2–1 ahead in the second leg of the semi-final at Hampden Park. (*Syndication International*)

They saw a thrilling match in which Leeds, briefly, mounted a revival. After 14 minutes, Bremner beat Williams, with a fierce, swerving shot from well outside the penalty area, to level the aggregate. But it was a Sassenach thrust quickly repelled. Celtic swarmed over Leeds in much the same way as they had over Inter in the 1967 final, and again the key figure was Jimmy Johnstone.

In the first leg at Elland Road, his very presence had curtailed the attacking forays of Cooper. Now the boot was on the other foot, with Johnstone attacking and the England defender back-pedalling furiously. Both Celtic's goals, which came in a five-minute spell early in the second half, emanated from this right flank. The first was courageously headed by John Hughes, thus restoring the Scots' lead, and moments later, when he threatened to score again, Sprake was injured at Hughes' feet and replaced by Harvey.

The first time the substitute goalkeeper touched the ball was to pick it out of the net. The shot came from Murdoch, the cross, inevitably, from Johnstone. Celtic were two goals in front and through to their second European Cup final. Leeds trudged wearily on to lose the FA Cup final replay to Chelsea, and had to wait five years to play in another European Cup final. By then, Revie would have left, and fate, once more, would appear to have a grudge against them.

Celtic's momentum and experience made them favourites to win the 1970 final in Milan against Feyenoord, whose progress since they knocked out AC Milan had been solid if unspectacular. They beat Vorwaerts of East Germany in the quarter-final, and Legia Warsaw, the Polish champions, in the semi-final. In each case, a disciplined display in Eastern Europe was followed by a decisive victory in Rotterdam.

When the British press had understandably called the Leeds-Celtic epic the real final, Jock Stein had tried unconvincingly to remind them there were still two other teams left in the competition. Now, his side were caught in the trap of over-confidence. 'I think we believed we had done the hardest part, beating Leeds. We had watched Feyenoord and had not seen much to frighten us. I think we would have won the final with a wee bit more care, but we got even more complacent after scoring the first goal.'

Tommy Gemmell blasts a free kick through the Feyenoord wall to put Celtic ahead in the 1970 final. The Dutch came back to win the match, but Gemmell remains the only Briton to score in two European Cup finals. (*Keystone*)

The man who gave Celtic their 29th-minute lead was Tommy Gemmell, firing in Murdoch's short free kick to score in a European Cup final for the second time. But Celtic were still mentally congratulating themselves when their defence lost concentration at a Feyenoord free kick two minutes later, and Israel headed the equaliser when the ball should have been cleared. Feyenoord had the better of a lively second half, as the Dutch supporters honked their horns incessantly to match the fanaticism of the travelling Scottish hordes. Van Hanegem and Hasil helped keep the match tantalisingly beyond Celtic's reach, and four minutes from the end of extra time, Feyenoord scored a dramatic winning goal.

Israel's long pass was misjudged by Billy McNeil, who handled the ball as he lost his balance. The Italian referee, Lo Bello, correctly

Feyenoord's Ove Kindvall lifts the ball over Celtic's goalkeeper Williams to score the winning goal in the 1970 final. The other Celtic player is McNeill who, seconds earlier, had handled the ball in an attempt to prevent it reaching Kindvall. (*Associated Press*)

allowed Kindvall to run on, and he beat Williams comfortably. Van Duivenbode, a loser a year earlier, now had a winners' medal.

'I think maybe Celtic tried to play too fast. Happel told us to keep cool and just play at an easy pace, to take the sting out of them. The key to our victory was in how quickly we cancelled out Celtic's lead. Rotterdam went football crazy when we brought the European Cup home. After all, it was the first time a Dutch team had won it. About 200,000 people were in the streets to welcome us. You could have walked over the heads.'

The start of the 1970s marked a watershed in the European Cup; not just because the Dutch took the ascendancy from the previously dominant Latins and British, but because the football they played offered something new and exciting. Ajax, champions again in the Netherlands in 1970, resumed where Feyenoord left off and accentuated the trend towards 'total football' – the label coaches attached to a concept which allowed players to move freely round the field as the game developed, improvising where before they had been restricted. This individual expression made light of specific roles for attackers, defenders and midfield players. The modern footballer would now adapt to the demands of the team according to how the game was going.

Years earlier, in his book *Soccer Revolution*, Willy Meisl, brother of the great football pioneer Hugo, had advanced such a theory which he called 'the whirl'. Players would rotate, as complete all-rounders, each one able to do the others' jobs, temporarily and when necessary, without more ado. Meisl was writing in 1955, the year the European Cup started. Now, in 1970–71, Ajax were on the point of coming closest to what he envisaged.

They disposed of Nendori Tirana, the champions of Albania, and Basle of Switzerland, to earn a quarter-final against Celtic, who themselves had an easy passage against Kokkolan of Finland, and the Republic of Ireland champions, Waterford. In the first leg in Amsterdam, the Scots held out until 15 minutes from the end. Then Johan Cruyff took over with the scintillating skills which were now his stock in trade. He scored one goal himself and made others for Hulshoff and Keizer.

Although Celtic won the return match in Glasgow with a goal from Johnstone, they never looked like saving the tie. This match, watched at Hampden by a crowd of 83,000, is the one which convinced Keizer of the chasm which had opened between Dutch and British football:

'We were confident about our technique, but the English and Scottish teams relied on other things. They were predictable, rather like a machine, not prepared, like us, to rely on their individual skills. I think we had a better football education than the British. They could perhaps have played like us, but their crowds would never have stood for it. They wanted excitement all the time, hence the stereotyped target man in the English attack, to whom they played the high balls constantly.

'The Dutch were not as formalised. At times we played without a centre-forward. We left it to the other players to use that space when they felt the time was right, and we were not influenced by the demands of the crowd. Our experience in Europe taught us how to slow the game down, especially in the away legs. If the crowd went quiet, we knew we were doing well. I think, eventually, the public appreciated what we were doing.'

Such was the independence of the new, assured Ajax, that the players frequently flouted authority, and there were many arguments with the coach, Michels; thus one of the popular football phrases of the 1970s – 'player power' – came into being.

After Ajax lost 1–0 to Atletico Madrid in the first leg of their 1971 semi-final in Spain, Michels was so disgusted with their performance that he banned the players' wives from the hotel on the night after the match. Keizer and company resented this imposition. 'There was a storming row at the hotel between Michels and the players. We stayed up all night in protest, emptying many bottles from behind the bar. We would always stick together to make a point. Vasovic and I were the main leaders at that time. Cruyff assumed the role later.'

There was another argument after the second leg against Atletico, which Ajax won 3–0 with goals by Keizer, full back Suurbier and their emerging midfield discovery, Johan Neeskens. Players and directors argued over bonuses, but a compromise eventually was reached. Ajax were setting new standards not just on the field, but also in the finances of professional footballers in the Netherlands. The Ajax team which reached the European Cup final in 1971 included six members of the side beaten two years earlier in the final by Milan. Three of them were in defence: Suurbier with his speed and brilliant tackling; Hulshoff, the bearded stopper rarely beaten in the air; and Vasovic, whose leadership was based on resistance to misfortune with which not all Yugoslavs were blessed.

The three others were in attack: Jackie Swart, the loyal servant, on the right wing; Keizer, swift and unpredictable, on the left; Cruyff leading from the front, but given, as Keizer explained, flexible instructions by Michels. 'Johan would often drift to outside left, and I was at liberty to wander across the front line. If we found ourselves followed by defenders, we would drop back and take our markers with us, allowing our midfield players and full backs to make runs from deep positions into the space we had left.'

The newcomers in the Ajax team included two players who revelled in that sort of opening – Johan Neeskens and Ruud Krol. Both were blessed with that classic Dutch mixture of power and poise, Neeskens physical condition enabling him to win tackles which it seemed almost impossible to do, and Krol attacking splendidly down the left wing, though he was stronger on his right foot.

The team was completed by Heinz Stuy in goal, successor to Gert Bals; the defensive midfield player Nico Rijnders; and Gerrie Muhren, who had a compendium of endless tricks and a stamina to match. The only surprise was the team Ajax had to play in the final at Wembley. Panathinaikos of Greece were unlikely contenders, but they were managed by the redoubtable Ferenc Puskas, and they prospered in a season which had more than its fair share of shocks. The biggest brought down the holders, Feyenoord, who stumbled in the first round against the unknown Rumanians, UT Arad, who beat them on the away goals rule. The Dutch had just beaten Estudiantes in another unpleasant World Club championship match.

It was also the first year that penalties were to decide drawn ties, and the first club to benefit were the English champions, Everton. The Merseyside club, beaten in the first round by Internazionale in 1963, were still managed by the private, purposeful Harry Catterick, their directors still motivated by a thirst for success which stemmed from the controlling figure of John Moores and the fortune his family had amassed in Littlewoods Pools. Catterick won his second League title with cultured football in the best Everton tradition. His midfield of Alan Ball, Howard Kendall and Colin Harvey were artists whose work was still ardently admired years later. The next decade would bring nothing to Evertonians to match the memory of that midfield trio.

But Everton made an unsteady start to the 1970–71 season. After beating Keflavik of Iceland in the first round of the European Cup, they faced the West German champions Borussia Moenchengladbach, whose team included the international trio of Bertie Vogts, Günter Netzer and Jupp Heynckes. Everton's Howard Kendall had good reason to remember what happened.

'We were not playing well, and when Harry Catterick bought Henry Newton, a midfield player from Nottingham Forest, a lot of people said I would lose my place. Especially when we lost 4–0 at Arsenal only four days before the first leg in Germany. Bertie Vogts put Borussia ahead in the first half, but the playing surface was beautiful, just right for us, and I equalised with one of my best goals for Everton. I hit a shot from 25 yards and it fell away from the keeper into the corner. After that, they played Henry Newton at full back.'

In the second leg at Goodison Park, outside left John Morrissey put Everton ahead in the first minute, but Laumen equalised for the Germans and extra time produced no further scoring. So, with both matches drawn 1–1, Kendall and his team waited for the penalty 'shoot out'. 'The atmosphere was unbearable. Half our lot did not want to look. Tommy Wright, our full back who had played in the World Cup for England in Mexico the year before, was so scared of being asked to take one of the penalties that he kept looking at the bench and pointing to his groin, making out he was injured.' Joe Royle, Everton's prolific centre-forward at the time, added to the tension by driving the first penalty straight at Borussia's goalkeeper, Wolfgang Kleff. But Laumen shot wide for the Germans and with Everton's four other kicks being converted by Ball, Morrissey, Kendall and substitute Sandy Brown, the fifth Borussia penalty from Ludwig Muller was crucial, with Everton leading 4–3.

Andy Rankin, who had just taken over as Everton's goalkeeper from Gordon West, flung himself to his right to save Muller's shot. The English champions were through to a quarter-final against Panathinaikos. This time the first leg was at Goodison Park, but it was a woeful night for Everton. They attacked repeatedly without reward, lost a goal on a breakaway to the tall Greek striker Antoniadis, and only equalised with the last kick of the match from their 19-year-old substitute, David Johnson.

Kendall remembered that during the game some of the Greek players were muttering 'Athens, Athens' to their English opponents. When Everton went to Greece for the second leg, he realised why.

'It was a frightening experience. The Greek fans kept up a barrage of noise outside our hotel throughout the night before the game. They would stop for half an hour, then start again so that we could not sleep. When we got to the ground the following afternoon, there were people stopping us outside the players' entrance, pulling back their jackets and revealing guns.

The crowd were caged in behind fences but they spat at us when we went over to take a throw-in. John Hurst ran into the Greek penalty area for a corner and one of their players stuck two fingers like a fork straight into his eye. Even our internationals, who had been to Mexico for the World Cup, were surprised how hostile it was. We managed a 0–0 draw, but they won on away goals. Three days later, we lost the FA Cup semi-final to Liverpool at Old Trafford. It was a terrible week, and there were some people who never recovered. For me, that fine Everton era ended in those few days.'

The stakes in the European Cup were now so high that Everton were not alone in finding it something of a battle ground. In another quarter-final, between Red Star Belgrade and Carl Zeiss Jena of East Germany, the famous Yugoslav outside left, Dragan Dzajic, was sent off after a brawl and suspended by UEFA for four matches.

Even without him, Red Star romped to a 4–1 victory in the first leg of the semi-final against Panathinaikos. But, incredibly, they too were beaten in the afternoon sun in Athens. Antoniadis scored twice as the Greeks won 3–0, and became the first club to win both the quarter-final and semi-final on the away goals rule.

Ajax line up before the 1971 final at Wembley (left to right, standing): Hulshoff, Stuy, Suurbier, Van Dijk, Muhren; (sitting): Keizer, Swart, Rijnders, Vasovic, Cruyff, Neeskens. (*Press Association*)

Puskas now was fêted in Athens in the way he had once been in Budapest and Madrid. His side drew much of its belief from Mimis Domazos, the tricky Greek international inside forward. But they were no match for Ajax at Wembley, where a 90,000 crowd largely composed of Dutchmen gave the 1971 final a convivial atmosphere. There was never much doubt about the result after the fifth minute when Keizer – playing thanks to pain-killing injections – laid on a

Dick Van Dijk head the first of Ajax's two goals in the 1971 final against Panathinaikos. (*Popperfoto*)

goal for Dick Van Dijk, himself only in the side because Krol had broken a leg before the final.

Rijnders, who always suffered from a high pulse rate, blacked out at half-time and was replaced by the German, Horst Blankenburg. Six years later, Rijnders died of a heart attack. In a second Ajax substitution, Swart was replaced by Arie Haan, then 22 years old and a product of the club's youth scheme. In midfield and in defence, this highly mobile, intelligent player went on to win an unequalled string of medals with Ajax, Anderlecht and the Netherlands.

Haan it was who put the 1971 final beyond doubt three minutes from the end. Cruyff began the move with one of his many dazzling runs, and Haan's shot was deflected into the net by Kapsis. The score of 2–0 was kind to Panathinaikos. So Ajax won the European Cup for the first time, with a team clearly destined to go much further. But not under Rinus Michels, who accepted a lucrative offer from Barcelona and was succeeded in Amsterdam by the little Rumanian coach, Stefan Kovacs.

Also departing was Velibor Vasovic, the captain. When he discussed a new contract, he told Ajax he was thinking of quitting; they called his bluff, and did not renew his contract. Keizer was not surprised. 'He had lost interest in league matches and was saving himself for big cup games. It was so obvious, that after one league match I asked him why he was bothering to take a shower!'

Blankenburg was the ready-made replacement in defence, now the only non-international among the Ajax outfield players. Keizer was appointed captain and found a significant change at the club in the 1971–72 season. 'Whereas Michels had Ajax deep at heart, involving himself right down to the youth team, Kovacs was one of the modern international coaches, widely-travelled, accustomed to working on short contracts, and concerning themselves only with the first team.'

Kovacs, despite his difficulty with the language, made himself very much at home in the Netherlands after a cool reception from the Ajax players and from the Dutch press. He used the situation to his own advantage. He did not train the players as hard as Michels had done, neither was he worried about the star system creeping in. Rather, he was happy to allow Cruyff and Keizer a strong influence in a team that was virtually capable of running itself. 'He recognised the value of getting support from the better players. Our reputation now went before us, and some teams were beaten even before we played them. Kovacs never put much emphasis on marking opponents. With a midfield trio of Haan, Neeskens and Gerrie Muhren, Ajax were built to go forward.'

And so they did, accounting for Dynamo Dresden and the French champions, Marseille, in the opening rounds of the 1972 tournament. But Arsenal, playing in the European Cup for the first time, were a tough proposition in the quarter-final, especially as Ajax had lost to the London club in the semi-final of the Fairs Cup two years earlier.

Arsenal had used their success in that competition as the springboard for a momentous season in 1970–71. Under the manager-coach partnership of Bertie Mee and Don Howe, the club revived memories of the Chapman era by winning the double – the League championship and FA Cup – something even the pre-war Arsenal never achieved. Their style was not as attractive as that of Tottenham's double team 10 years earlier, but their organisation and discipline overpowered most teams, who never quite contained the attacking thrust of John Radford and the young Ray Kennedy.

Arsenal owed much to the experience in defence of two senior players: centre half and captain Frank McLintock, and goalkeeper Bob Wilson. Both were disturbed when Howe left Highbury in the summer of 1971 to manage West Bromwich Albion. But the legacy his coaching had left, coupled with Mee's expert management, made Arsenal genuine European Cup contenders. They beat Stromgodset Drammen, of Norway, and Grasshoppers of Switzerland, winning all four matches and scoring 12 goals against one.

In December, Mee paid a British transfer record of £220,000 to Everton for Alan Ball, who alas was not signed in time to play in the quarter-finals of the European Cup. Without him, Arsenal performed heroically in the first leg of the quarter-final in Amsterdam. The match was played in the Olympic Stadium, where the capacity of 65,000 was double that of the Ajax ground. When Ray Kennedy put Arsenal ahead after 14 minutes, it meant he had scored in four of his club's five European Cup matches, and it put the holders a goal behind in front of their own crowd. But Ajax, and Cruyff in particular, responded with a stunning exhibition of crisp, cohesive football. Kovacs said later he never saw them play better.

Wilson had one of his best games for Arsenal, stopping everything that was driven at him apart from a deflected shot and a disputed penalty – both coming from Gerrie Muhren. The Arsenal goalkeeper was applauded off the field at the end of the match. 'Frankly, we thought we had got Ajax cornered. We had only lost the first leg 2–1, which meant a 1–0 win at Highbury would be good enough. There was a lot of confidence in the team after winning the double.'

But before the second leg, John Radford was given a three-week suspension for being sent off in a reserve match. His replacement against Ajax at Highbury was the expensive teenager, Peter Marinello, who was being given his first senior game for six months. It was unfortunate for Arsenal that their best chance should fall to him in the first minute. Blankenburg failed to control a throw from his goalkeeper, and Marinello was through with only Stuy to beat. His shot hit the right leg of the falling goalkeeper and Kennedy blazed the rebound high and wide.

Worse befell Arsenal soon after. After 14 minutes Cruyff, in his familiar number 14 shirt, took a throw-in on the Ajax left. Krol chipped the ball forward for the advancing Haan, and Arsenal's George Graham, unaware that Wilson was on his way out, headed past his own goalkeeper. The English champions were now two goals behind and Ajax were too practised to let that sort of lead slip. Cruyff, barely fit to play, operated fitfully on the left wing, but his presence was enough to count.

Dutch hopes of getting both their former winners to the 1972 final were spoiled when Feyenoord, entering this year as champions of the Netherlands, lost in one of the other quarter-finals to Benfica. The Portuguese champions were now managed by an Englishman, Jimmy Hagan, who had once been in charge of West Bromwich Albion. Benfica lost 1–0 in Rotterdam, but swamped Feyenoord 5–1 in Lisbon, with Eusebio among the scorers and the young Portuguese prodigy, Nene, scoring a hat trick.

The semi-final between Ajax and Benfica was a repeat of the memorable quarter-final three years earlier, when Dutch football had really taken off. This time, after Swart's goal had won the first leg in

Amsterdam, supporters made the news again, but for different reasons. The second leg in Lisbon was a tense affair refereed by an Englishman, Norman Burtenshaw. When he turned down Benfica's appeals for a penalty, the crowd showered the pitch with bottles, cushions and fruit. A policeman ran on to the pitch waving a baton and was held back by his colleagues. Burtenshaw reported Benfica to UEFA, whose secretary Hans Bangerter had earlier that season warned clubs that violence on or off the field would be 'mercilessly punished' by the disciplinary committee. Benfica received a nominal fine, but the goalless draw in Lisbon meant Ajax were again in the final.

This was a minor incident compared to the one earlier in the 1971–72 tournament involving the side who eventually came through to play Ajax in the final – the remodelled Internazionale. There were only five survivors from Herrera's team which had been beaten in the final by Celtic five years earlier. They were the full backs, Tarcisio Burgnich and Giacinto Facchetti; in midfield Sandro Mazzola, playing deeper as he approached his 30th birthday, and Gianfranco Bedin; and in attack Mario Corso, whose controversial reputation would mean he missed the chance to play in his fourth European Cup final.

Burgnich, Facchetti and Mazzola were three of five Inter players in Italy's team beaten 4–1 by Brazil in the 1970 World Cup final in Mexico. The others were the centre-forward, Roberto Boninsegna, who had come from Cagliari in 1969, and the defensive midfield player Mario Bertini, signed from Fiorentina.

It was Bertini who got Inter's renewed European Cup challenge off to an unseemly start. He was sent off for fighting in the first round against AEK Athens, and it set the tone for what followed. Inter were drawn against Borussia Moenchengladbach, West German champions for the second year running under the wise tutorship of coach Hennes Weisweiler. Their blond, elegant midfield schemer Günter Netzer was at the peak of his powers. Later that season he would humiliate Ramsey's fading England side in the European Championship quarter-final at Wembley, and inspire the West Germans to win the title for the first time.

Netzer stamped his early control on the first leg against Inter. Borussia were leading 2–1 when a soft drink can was thrown from the German crowd striking Boninsegna – who had scored Inter's goal – on the head. The Italian forward was carried off, substituted by Ghio, and Inter fell apart. They were 4–1 down at half-time, when they replaced goalkeeper Lido Vieri with his substitute, Ivano Bordon. So, when Jair was hurt in the second half, Inter had already used both their permitted substitutes. Then they had Corso sent off for pushing the referee. They finished with nine men and lost the match 7–1; Netzer and Jupp Heynckes both scored twice.

Inter demanded that, in the light of the Boninsegna incident, they should be awarded the match 3–0, since this was the punishment UEFA had threatened for clubs whose crowds threw fireworks on to the pitch. Furthermore, Inter contended, had the missile been thrown in the Italian league, the match would have been awarded 2–0 to the afflicted team. UEFA's disciplinary committee declared the result null and void, and ordered the match to be replayed on a neutral ground. Before then the teams had to meet in Milan for what now, effectively, became the first leg. Corso was suspended by UEFA from all European matches for a year, and would therefore miss the final, but without him Inter beat Borussia 4–2 in Milan. Boninsegna was among the scorers, and Mazzola eclipsed Netzer in midfield.

The replayed match, now the second leg, took place in Berlin and ended in a goalless draw. As though the fates favoured Inter, Bordon saved a penalty and Borussia's Ludwig Muller was carried off with a broken leg after tackling . . . yes, Boninsegna! Thus, unruly crowd behaviour robbed the Germans of their chance to make an impression on club football in Europe in 1972. Their time was to come, but Borussia remain the one team in the competition's history to win a match 7–1 and still lose the tie.

Inter's luck held. In the quarter-final they beat Standard Liège, but only thanks to Mazzola's away goal counting double when the aggregate scores finished level. And in the semi-final, the Italians exacted some revenge for their defeat in Lisbon in 1967 when they beat Celtic on penalty kicks. The two teams fenced with each other with the cautious discretion of old enemies, and both matches were drawn without a goal being scored. Celtic defended stoutly in the first leg in San Siro, and Inter did likewise at Parkhead.

In the second leg in Glasgow, Stein took off 21-year-old Kenny Dalglish, who had made his European Cup début that season, and replaced him with John 'Dixie' Deans, who had the misfortune to miss Celtic's first kick in the penalty competition which followed extra time. All the other penalties were converted, so Inter became the first side to qualify for the final by this hair-raising method. It summed up their bumpy ride in the 1972 tournament.

The final in Rotterdam was Inter's fourth, but the third for Ajax in only four years. The Dutch were in no mood to be checked by the Italians' dreary defensive trap, and Piet Keizer singled out this match as the finest Dutch club performance of all: 'We were a bit worried before the final about the reaction of the crowd, because Ajax were playing in the stadium of our biggest rivals, Feyenoord. But the fans were on our side from the start, and you could not find a flaw in the way we played that night.'

The Italians, simply turned inside out by a really thrilling demonstration of 'total football', seemed to have stood still tactically since 1967. The Dutch had a verve and imagination which a flaccid Inter simply could not counter. The Italians survived in the first half by keeping everybody behind the ball apart from Boninsegna, who was left isolated up the field and rarely got the ball. Mazzola and Gabriele Oriali worked overtime in midfield as Inter grimly hung on.

Kovacs made a slight adjustment at half-time, pushing Suurbier further forward for Ajax. Three minutes into the second half, the full back's cross from the right was dropped by goalkeeper Bordon and Cruyff forced the ball in at the far post. Thirteen minutes from the end, with Inter showing no sign of recovery, Cruyff completed the execution when he applied a majestic header to Keizer's cross from the left.

His two goals in the final highlighted another vintage year for Cruyff. He had been voted European Footballer of the Year the previous December, and lived up to his reputation by extending his huge influence beyond and behind the Ajax attack. Keizer saw the significance in such maturity. 'It was at this time that Johan got fed up with being constantly kicked by defenders, and dropped deeper to become the organiser of the team. He had avoided injury by his

Johan Cruyff taps in the first of his two goals in the 1972 final against Inter. The goalkeeper is Bordon. (*Presse Sports*)

tremendous acceleration over the first 10 to 15 yards. He looked to have a slender frame, but it was deceptive really, because he had fantastic power in his body.'

One of the matches in which Cruyff suffered from ruthless marking was the first leg of the World Club Championship against Independiente in Buenos Aires in September 1972. A year earlier, after their first European Cup triumph, Ajax had refused to play the South American champions, and runners-up Panathinaikos had taken their place. But with their fame spreading across a world in which televised football had taken a firm hold, the Dutch were persuaded to take part.

Cruyff scored in a 1–1 draw in the first leg in Argentina, but then left the field with his legs raw and bleeding and his ankle badly damaged. His replacement was Arnold Muhren, Gerrie's younger brother, who was an Ajax substitute in two European Cup finals and later played with distinction for Ipswich Town in England. Cruyff returned with a flourish for the second leg against Independiente in Amsterdam. But the man who stole the headlines that night was a handsome 20-year-old called Johnny Rep, who came on as substitute for Swart and scored twice in a 3–0 win.

Disillusioned by the spirit in which these games were played, Ajax proposed to UEFA that the European champions should take no further part in the world club matches, and that they should meet the holders of the European Cup Winners' Cup instead. The holders of that trophy at the time were Glasgow Rangers, and Ajax set an example by playing the Scots over two legs and beating them. The following year, UEFA officially launched the 'Super Cup', which became an annual event. But the World Club Championship still existed, if often in a diluted form.

So, in 1972, Ajax were World Club champions, European champions for the second year running, Dutch champions for the 15th time, and Dutch Cup winners for the third consecutive season. No wonder Europe gasped for breath and wondered who could stop them. Certainly there was no shortage of big names in the European

Cup for 1972–73. Real Madrid were back after an absence of two seasons; former winners Benfica and Celtic both qualified again; Juventus and Bayern Munich added class to the field.

Nobody on the continent knew what to make of a fresh English name – Derby County. They became more perplexed when they saw the vast exposure given in his own country to Derby's volatile, outspoken manager, Brian Clough. Derby had been founder members of the Football League in 1888, but until Clough arrived they had never won the championship and had even had a spell in the third division in the 1950s. Apart from winning the FA Cup in 1946, they had given the industrial town in the East Midlands little to cheer about. Derby's Baseball Ground, cramped among pinched and sooty streets, was a legacy from the Victorian age.

Into this depressed setting in 1967 strode the forthright Mr Clough and his assistant Peter Taylor. They had struck up a fierce friendship from their playing days together at Middlesbrough, where Taylor was a goalkeeper and Clough a devastating centre-forward. His career was cruelly ended by a knee injury in 1964, soon after he joined nearby Sunderland. But Clough scored a total of 251 goals in 274 league appearances for the two north-east clubs.

As a manager, Clough adopted the same brave, direct approach he showed as a player. He was brash and self-assured, stopping for nobody when he believed he was on the right lines. Taylor joined him in management at Hartlepool in 1965, starting an improbable journey in the fourth division which eventually led to one of football's most coveted trophies – the European Cup – in 1979. It took Clough and Taylor only two years to get Derby back into the first division, thanks largely to the inspired signing of Dave Mackay, the former Tottenham captain and European warrior.

Three years later, in 1972, Derby won the first division title. Having completed their programme, Derby went on holiday to Majorca leaving their two rivals, Liverpool and Leeds, to play their final matches. Neither won, so Derby finished one point in front.

Far from feeling daunted about mixing with Europe's élite, Clough and Taylor attacked the prospect with relish. They were of the humble opinion that the continent should be worrying about them. And not without cause. Derby's team had been carefully assembled, the astute signing of players from clubs lower in the League was an early guide to how Clough and Taylor became the smartest team builders of their time.

Roy McFarland cost just £25,000 from Tranmere and was to become England's best centre half. Alongside him, Colin Todd was a more expensive purchase from Sunderland, but £170,000 soon became commonplace with transfer fees escalating in England. The quick, compact defender was an ideal successor to the now departed Mackay. In midfield, the energetic little Scot, Archie Gemmill, came for £60,000 from Preston, and the obedient John McGovern for a pittance from Hartlepool. They were to give Clough's team its heart, as they would do again later at Nottingham Forest.

Derby played swift, controlled football, the ball delivered right to a player's feet whenever possible. The attacking partnership of Kevin Hector, a natural goalscorer, and John O'Hare, a broad-shouldered target man, was well served by the left winger Alan Hinton, who could cross with uncanny accuracy using either foot. Alan Durban, a Welsh international half back, was one of those already at Derby when Clough arrived. Durban put the rapid improvement down to a new professionalism which ran through the club, and he remembered the reaction to Derby's first European match. 'We went to Yugoslavia to play Zeljeznicar Sarajevo, and we got no co-operation at all. There were no proper training facilities, no balls, and when the match started some awful tackling.'

But Derby won both legs comfortably, and in the second round showed how quickly they were adjusting to European football by defeating Benfica 3–0 at Derby. The Portuguese champions fielded six survivors from the Wembley final against Manchester United, including Eusebio, but even he could not match John McGovern's 25-yard shot which brought Derby's third goal. Before the second leg in Lisbon, Derby's players trained on the beach, drank a few beers by the hotel pool, and generally relaxed before holding Benfica to a 0–0 draw. It was an approach for which Clough and Taylor became renowned.

In the same round, Celtic were beaten by the Hungarians, Ujpest Dozsa. It was only the second time in seven seasons that Stein's side failed to make the last eight. But Derby were there, giving British football a fillip it badly needed in what had been a dismal year. The failure of England and Scotland in the European Championship was the prelude to England's elimination by Poland in the qualifying tournament for the 1974 World Cup. Alf Ramsey was later sacked, having been conveniently blamed for the sterile state of the domestic game. English football had done a backward somersault since 1966 and was festering in the grip of shady, negative thinking.

Clough was not slow to make the point, either in person, through his increasing television appearances, or in the shape of his Derby team, who stuck to clean attacking principles which Durban, among others, found refreshing. 'Peter Taylor used to go and watch the opposition before European games, but he would always come back and play them down. He and Cloughie believed the way to beat the continentals was at our game, pulling their defenders out of position with our front men and then getting midfield players into the spaces they left.'

Durban was finding it hard to keep his place. Clough had never been his greatest admirer, preferring the more physical style of Terry Hennessey, a Welsh international he bought from Nottingham Forest. When Hennessey was injured, Derby brought O'Hare back into midfield and gave the tall, lean Roger Davies his chance at centre-forward. He was signed from Southern League Worcester City, one of several attacking players who Taylor cannily spotted outside the Football League. But Derby were not afraid to spend at the other end of the market. They broke the British transfer record when they bought full back David Nish from Leicester for £240,000, and he became eligible for the European Cup when Derby travelled to Czechoslovakia for the first leg of their quarter-final against Spartak Trnava.

A 1–0 defeat was reversed in the second leg at the Baseball Ground, where two goals by Hector – that unassuming opportunist – shot Derby into the semi-final. The crowd of under 37,000 crammed into the Baseball Ground played their part, although earlier in the season Clough had called them 'a disgraceful lot' and Derby's chairman, Sam Longson, had disassociated himself from the manager's remarks.

In the other quarter-finals Real Madrid disposed of Dynamo Kiev; Juventus scraped through on away goals against Ujpest Dozsa; and Ajax confirmed their position as champions by putting out the emerging threat from West Germany, Bayern Munich. Such was the international interest in the first leg in Amsterdam, that a party of British managers chartered a private plane to the Netherlands. An appreciation of what the Dutch were doing, coupled with a curiosity about how the Germans were shaping at club level after their European Championship success, had made pupils of those who were once the masters. Ajax did not let them down. Bayern held them for nearly an hour, but mistakes by goalkeeper Sepp Maier, and the lack of fitness of centre-forward Gerd Muller, contributed to the Germans' collapse.

Even Franz Beckenbauer could not stem the tide as the holders, with Cruyff omnipotent, struck four goals without reply. Although Ajax were still playing brilliantly, there was discontent in the dressing-room. Cruyff was unsettled, in Keizer's view using a slight knee injury as an excuse to miss the second leg in Munich. 'A lot of people thought we might be in trouble without Johan, even though we had a four-goal start. But I scored another after 15 minutes, and we were so superior that the Germans got angry. The two goals they scored later made no difference to the result. Most of all, we enjoyed taunting Beckenbauer.'

It was the turn of the old maestros, Real Madrid, to be taunted by Ajax in the semi-final. The Dutch won both matches, emphasising how completely they had assumed Real's mantle when Gerrie Muhren ridiculed the Spanish players by juggling the ball during the second leg in the Bernabeu Stadium.

Dutch football advanced so quickly that in March 1973 a party of English managers chartered an aircraft to visit the Netherlands for the European Cup quarter-final between Ajax and Bayern Munich. The front page of the programme suggests Ajax were confident; they went on to win the match 4–0 and completed a hat trick of European Cup wins in consecutive years.

Barry Hulshoff (left, light shirt) fires Ajax ahead in the first leg of the 1973 semi-final against Real Madrid. The other Ajax player is Johnny Rep. (*Presse Sports*)

The pairing of Derby and Juventus in the other semi-final said much about the development of European football: both before the match, when the striking contrast between the two clubs was irresistible, and afterwards, when an enormous scandal blew up about alleged attempts to bribe a referee. If Derby represented the grass roots of English football, with its long and proud tradition, the Italian champions from Turin symbolised the hold football had taken among wealthy aristocrats in major cities on the continent. Juventus, backed by the Agnelli family and their giant Fiat motor company, had already failed in four attempts on the European Cup. That was bad business in a country where supporters paid more to watch football than almost anywhere else in the world, in a city where arch rivals Torino shared the same stadium, and for a club who now had the most expensive player in the world in centre-forward Pietro Anastasi. His unlikely partner in attack was none other than José Altafini, now 35 but still holder of the European Cup record of 14 goals in one season, which he had set exactly 10 years earlier with AC Milan.

The Juventus side also included six players who would be chosen by Italy for the 1974 World Cup finals: goalkeeper Dino Zoff, full back Luciano Spinosi, centre half Francesco Morini, the skilful midfield schemer Fabio Capello, and forwards Anastasi and Franco Causio. But their followers still sighed for their great idol of a decade and more ago, John Charles, and it was with a shrewd sense of public relations that Derby took the genial Welshman in their official party to Turin for the first leg. Charles was fêted everywhere he went. Alan Durban said he had never seen hero worship like it. But Durban had other things on his mind, such as being told by Clough that he was being left out of the Derby team.

'On the day before the match, he told me he was giving my position to a young coloured boy called Tony Parry, who was signed from Hartlepool and had only played two full matches in the first team at Derby. The following day, we got to the stadium early, and I went on the pitch with the other players. As I came off I remarked to Clough what a great playing surface it was. He replied: "OK, you had better put the number four on". I never knew whether it was an instinctive decision or whether he had it planned. It was typical of how unpredictable he could be. Even the other players were telling me I had the wrong shirt on, while we were getting changed.'

But it was in another dressing-room down the corridor – that of the West German referee Schulenburg – that the first act unfolded in drama that was to smack of conspiracy, complaint and corruption. Helmut Haller, one of the Juventus substitutes and a West German international, was spotted in the referee's room before the match. Derby's suspicions were aroused further when the match started and Schulenburg booked McFarland and Gemmill in the first half. It was the second time they had been cautioned in the competition, and meant both would miss the second leg at Derby.

The English champions stayed cool under great provocation. Although Anastasi laid on a superb opening goal for Altafini, Derby equalised with a fine opportunist effort by Hector, and were level when Schulenburg blew his whistle for half-time. Now, Peter Taylor became convinced there was some sort of conspiracy afoot.

'Haller was sitting with the other substitutes on the Juventus bench to my left, and when the whistle went for half-time he went straight across to the referee and was talking earnestly to him in German as they walked off the pitch and down the track together. I got within earshot and tried to intercept them, to let them know I was aware something was going on. At that moment I suddenly found my path barred by a group of tough looking Italians.

'There was an unpleasant scuffle and in the end word was sent in to the dressing-room, and I gather the Juventus president, or one of their other directors was told of what had happened. Anyway, when I finally got through and down the tunnel, we were told that Haller was in with the referee again. Nothing can ever be proved, but I believe it was corrupt and dirty. It brought us on a ton in learning about Europe and put us on our mettle for the future.'

Clough added: 'In any other industry, there would have been a full scale inquiry into the behaviour of Juventus. But UEFA just looked the other way.'

If there were doubts about the ethics of Juventus, there could be no argument over their finishing. In the second half, Causio and Altafini beat Derby's goalkeeper, Colin Boulton, with shots that took the breath away. The veteran Brazilian had, it seemed, lost none of his effectiveness in the penalty area. So Derby lost the first leg 3–1, though Durban had missed a presentable chance to make the score 2–2 before Altafini made the game safe. 'The bookings morally shattered us. We felt we had been cheated. But we knew we could still reach the final. We had to beat Juventus 2–0 at Derby.'

Durban was among the substitutes for the second leg, but with no score at half-time he was sent on in place of 17-year-old Steve Powell, and he soon provided the pass which sent Alan Hinton through. When Hinton was pulled down by desperate Juventus defenders, he got up to take the penalty himself. He was normally utterly reliable from the penalty spot, but on this occasion put his kick wide of the goal and threw away Derby's last chance of reaching the final.

The tackling now was wild, with the Juventus captain Giuseppe Furino especially guilty. Eventually Roger Davies lost his temper, swung a punch in retaliation, and was sent off by the Portuguese referee, Francisco Lobo. And it was Lobo who exposed the biggest scandal yet to emerge within the European Cup. He told his football federation in Portugal that before taking charge of the match at Derby, he was approached by a man named Solti and asked to favour Juventus.

The Portuguese reported the alleged bribery attempt to UEFA, who appointed a disciplinary sub-committee to investigate. They recommended that Juventus be exonerated and Solti banned from European football. Dezso Solti was a Hungarian Jew domiciled in Milan but holding Argentine citizenship. He worked for Internazionale as an agent during their successful European Cup days of the 1960s, then followed Inter's general manager, Italo Allodi, to Juventus. Brian Glanville, the eminent English football writer with strong European connections, was unhappy with UEFA's handling of the affair. With Keith Botsford, his colleague on the sports staff of *The Sunday Times*, he persuaded the European body to re-open their file on the case in April 1974. UEFA failed to establish any official connection between Juventus and Solti, but later Glanville and Botsford produced a letter signed by him on the club's notepaper.

UEFA took no action against the Italian club. They said Solti was an independent agent, and eventually satisfied their conscience by declaring him *persona non grata* in December 1974. Solti went back to Milan, but Glanville believed the UEFA investigation to be superficial.

'There were suspicions of pressures being applied to referees many years earlier. Real Madrid were never accused openly, but the reign of Inter was littered with allegations of referees being bribed. One of the strongest concerned the referee who took charge of a semi-final between Inter and Borussia Dortmund in 1964. He allowed Suarez to remain on the field when most people thought he should have sent him off.

'A few weeks later, the same referee was found enjoying a luxury holiday with his wife, allegedly, at Inter's expense. One of the most common ways of currying favour was to give the referee and linesmen presents before the match. One famous European club used to give the referee a beer tankard, professing it to be a mere souvenir. Inside the tankard, there was a gold watch.

'There was so much money and prestige at stake in the European Cup that I had no doubt at all that a number of referees were got at over the years. But it was very hard to prove, especially when UEFA were reluctant to bring rumours out into the open.'

It was a further five years before UEFA took action against an Italian club. Then, they fined AC Milan £8,000 for taking three Scottish officials, including World Cup referee John Gordon, on a shopping expedition 'beyond the accepted limits of hospitality', before a UEFA Cup tie against Levski Spartak in 1978.

One thing that should be made clear, before we leave an embittered Derby, is that *their* complaints revolved only around the *German* referee's handling of the first leg against Juventus in Turin. No blame was attached in hindsight to Lobo, who reported the alleged bribery attempt to his superiors and competently handled the second leg. After all, he did award Derby a penalty, and Clough backed his decision to send off Davies by fining his centre-forward. But Derby were out, and Clough and Taylor were forced to wait six more years before they could fulfil their dream of winning the European Cup. Juventus would face Ajax in the 1973 final in Belgrade.

The Dutch had four players – Cruyff, Keizer, Suurbier and Hulshoff – playing in their fourth final; five more – Neeskens, Gerrie Muhren, Stuy, Haan and Blankenburg – were appearing in their third; yet it was the one man in the team not to have been there before, Johnny Rep, who scored the only goal. It came after just four minutes, a far post header from a cross by Blankenburg which settled one of the most forgettable European Cup finals. Juventus, having spent 18 years and millions of pounds in getting there, were a complete disappointment. If anything, they were even more negative than Inter had been a year earlier. Despite being only one goal behind, they were suffocated not only by the bewildering assurance of the Dutch, but by the lack of ambition which has stifled Italian teams before and since.

Italian clubs, winners of the European Cup four times in the 1960s, had finished a poor second in two consecutive finals. There was some truth in the argument that after the ban on importing players was imposed in January 1965, the Italians' national team improved but their club sides lacked imagination. This was something Ajax had in abundance, and the initiative of their players extended to an awareness of their market potential. The team that had completed a hat trick of European Cup victories was on the point of breaking up, and Keizer found it inevitable.

'The personal interests of the players had taken over by the time we won for the third time. There was not quite the same incentive once we had done that. Several players knew they could earn bigger money outside, but remember the wages and bonuses we received at Ajax were far higher than had been dreamed of before in Dutch football. Our success set standards for the players of the future.'

Cruyff left in the autumn to rejoin Rinus Michels at Barcelona, later to be followed to Spain by Neeskens, Rep and Gerrie Muhren. Haan would go to Anderlecht in Belgium, and Keizer would soon retire, but not before sharing with the nucleus of the old Ajax team the thrill of the Netherland's contribution to the 1974 World Cup, when Michels and Cruyff led the Dutch to second place. Their final season together had seen a clash of personalities between Cruyff and Keizer, who had grown up together at Ajax. Both took a turn as captain, and when the choice was put to the other players, Keizer was preferred.

It was advanced as one reason why Cruyff left, but at 26 he was the most marketable product in the commercially conscious football world of 1973. As Michels said when Barcelona paid over £900,000 for the man again voted European Footballer of the Year: 'Football is a business. And business is business.' It was a suitable slogan for the European Cup itself. Even the Americans were taking an interest.

At the time of the Ajax-Juventus final, *Time* magazine devoted six pages to the sociological impact of the match on the city of Belgrade, and of modern football on the world in general. A dozen European correspondents were used on the story, and they wrote:

'They began converging on Belgrade days before the big game. By sea, by air and by land – by hitchhiker's thumb, barefoot, and, who knows, maybe even on hands and knees like pleading pilgrims to Lourdes – they flocked by the tens of thousands and they pushed and they shoved and they gouged and swore and spat their way into town.

'They were muscular young hard-hats from Amsterdam's east side, long-haired knapsackers in flight from the chilly spring in Vondel Park, respectable burghers from the elegant board rooms on the Keizersgracht. They were assembly line workers from Turin, Italian deputies and pushers and peasants, and starlets fresh out of their warm Lambretta saddles on the Via Veneto.

'All of them – the 40,000 Italians and the 10,000 Dutch and the rest – had one thing in common. They were *tifosi*, victims of the most menacing disease known to Europe – *il tifo* (football fever).

'The great football matches like the European Cup final radiate a special, almost hysterical aura, they fuse national and personal passions, draw massive, cross-border migrations of celebrators, and play to near global audiences. As the besieged citizens of Belgrade discovered this year, they bring ordinary life to a standstill.

'It is not likely that this brutal but stirring ritual will fade for some time to come. Not while the likes of Johan Cruyff are born to the game, and millions of people – whatever their complexes – are ready to cheer them on.'

CHAPTER EIGHT

BAYERN, BECKENBAUER AND DER BOMBER
(Bayern Munich 1974–76)

The transfer of Johan Cruyff proved protracted, expensive, and for Ajax, ultimately crippling.

The delay, however, had nothing to do with Barcelona's desire, or ability, to pay the asking fee. There were few men in the world capable of transforming the fortunes of a club but Cruyff, unquestionably, was one of them. When the time came, the Spanish plutocrats would part with almost a million pounds without a murmur.

The immediate problem was more personal. Cruyff's mother-in-law was said to be unhappy about her daughter and grandchildren living beyond her reach in Spain. At one stage, the deal was called off. But money has a way of transcending family ties. Particularly when the agent concluding the transfer, Cor Coster, was also the player's father-in-law. The final fee was £922,300, of which almost half went to the man born in one of the poorest quarters of Amsterdam. What is more, Cruyff's earnings from sources outside the game were enormously enhanced. In a single week, soon after his arrival in Spain in the autumn of 1973, he was said to have made more than £9,000 from endorsements and interviews.

The relaxation of the ban on foreigners by the Spanish FA had again ushered in a golden age for the players, of which Cruyff was both the symbol and the principle beneficiary. Hailed as Di Stefano's successor, his income dwarfed that of the celebrated Argentine. For Cruyff was a truly cosmopolitan figure. To hear him converse easily in four or five different tongues during the 1974 World Cup was to realise that a new breed of player was at large – intelligent, confident, and aware of his own market potential. The Dutch were the brand leaders and their training camp at times resembled an international bazaar to which agents and journalists came bearing gifts.

This was only the culmination of a process which had its roots in earlier events: the removal of the maximum wage in England; the growth of professionalism in Europe; and the contractual freedom for employees, laid down by the Treaty of Rome. Furthermore, this new found wealth and emancipation encouraged players to voice opinions within their own clubs, widening the influence of 'player power' which was already evident at Ajax. The term was as ill-defined as its antithesis 'soccer slavery', but its effect was to loosen further the grip of the manager, and lead to a series of stormy incidents at some of Europe's premier football institutions.

Cruyff himself would later find fault with his mentor, Rinus Michels, paving the way for a new face at Barcelona. But not before the costly import had at least delivered the goods. After a shaky start, the Catalans won the Spanish championship in 1974, for the first time since the days of Kocsis and Kubala.

Without Cruyff, however, Ajax struggled to find the right blend. For a friendly in October 1973 against Manchester United, they included Jan Mulder, a striker who numbered Malcolm Allison among his admirers, but who had struggled with injury since arriving from Anderlecht. Curiously United were also attempting to resurrect a famous name. The match – a testimonial for Denis Law – marked the beginning of George Best's final, fruitless comeback at Old Trafford. At the end of the month, in Amsterdam, Ajax faced CSKA Sofia in the second round of the European Cup, having had a bye in the first. They had beaten the Bulgarians home and away the previous season, en route to the final in Belgrade, but things were no longer so straightforward for the holders.

New manager Georg Knobel watched Ajax win 1–0 with a goal from Mulder, but the same player also missed a penalty, which proved vital. In Sofia, a goal by Maraschliev took the tie into extra time, where Mikhailov got the winner. The demise of Ajax was sudden, if not entirely unexpected. The club had for some time shown signs of decline. By the end of the season, the championship had been conceded to Feyenoord, Knobel had left, complaining of intrigue and ill discipline, and half the team were in contact with foreign clubs.

But Ajax were not the only major casualties of the early rounds of the 1973–74 campaign. Among the debris were Juventus, runners-up the previous season, who went out to Dynamo Dresden in the first round. Benfica and Liverpool both failed to reach the quarter-final, while Celtic survived – but only just – after being held at home by the Danish part-timers Vejle. A goal by one of Lisbon Lions, Bobby Lennox, spared Celtic's blushes, but they were clearly a team in transit, no longer to be feared, even at Parkhead. The field indeed seemed wide open, the European Cup within the range of any team which could find a semblance of real quality.

No club was more aware of this than Bayern Munich who were still smarting from their humiliation at the hands of Ajax the previous spring. They won the Bundesliga title again in 1973, but in September almost went out in the first round of the European Cup to Atvidaberg of Sweden. After Gerd Müller had scored inside two minutes, Bayern won comfortably at home 3–1. But in the return match, they were two goals down after a quarter of an hour, and when Atvidaberg's Conny Torstensson scored his second goal of the match in the 72nd minute, the Swedes led 4–3 on aggregate. Uli Hoeness scored for Bayern to take the teams into extra time, and when that failed to produce a winner, the tie was decided on penalty kicks. The Germans immediately fell behind when Gersdorff missed, but were rescued by Maier's marvellous save from Karlsson. In the final round of kicks, Beckenbauer scored, Franzen missed for the Swedes, and Bayern squeezed through.

From such an inauspicious start, Bayern would advance steadily to their first European Cup final. Their coach Udo Lattek called the game 'a walk on a razor's edge', and promptly opened negotiations which brought Torstensson to Munich.

Bayern's second round tie was against the East Germans, Dynamo Dresden, who actually led at half-time in Munich, but finally lost this first leg 4–3. The return was another seesaw affair, in which Bayern at one time led 2–0, then conceded three goals. With half an hour left, Dresden were therefore ahead in the tie on away goals, but Bayern's third goal took the West Germans through on a 7–6 aggregate. The scorer, almost inevitably, was Müller, the most consistent striker in Europe.

Although he was now being fêted for his ability to score goals, Müller's early career was marked by doubts, and at times outright hostility. When he first arrived at Bayern – from nearby TSV Nordlingen in 1963 – the stocky centre-forward was taunted about his weight. Müller then seemed a donkey among thoroughbreds, but his scoring feats soon silenced his critics. Though he never became an elegant footballer, his surefootedness in the penalty area – at a time when defences were better organised than ever – was unequalled. By the time he left Munich to play in Florida in 1979, Müller had scored a record 365 goals in the Bundesliga; for Germany his total was an astounding 68 goals in 62 internationals.

Müller was capable of spectacular efforts – the fans called him *der Bomber* – but his stock in trade were the ordinary goals, the low shots and rebounds from inside the area. Even with his back to the goal he could be deadly, his strong thighs enabling him to withstand the fiercest challenge, and his speed off the mark giving him the yard he needed in which to get in a shot. In the summer of 1973, Barcelona tried to sign him, but their interest cooled when he signed a new contract with Bayern. The Spaniards turned their attention back to Cruyff, a decision which helped shape the next phase of the European Cup. The Dutchman left for Spain, while Müller remained to help Bayern emulate Ajax by winning three consecutive finals.

Such an achievement would have been beyond belief for the Bavarian club in the early 1960s. They were then a regional club, with an antiquated stadium in the Grunwald district of Munich. When the German league became national in 1963, Bayern were not even among the 18 clubs which formed the first Bundesliga. Two men in particular helped Bayern abandon their provincial outlook. The first was Wilhelm Neudecker, their powerful president, and the second, the club's technical director, Robert Schwan. Neudecker promoted the club's interests at national level, while Schwan, like Raimondo Saporta at Real, handled the business side. His facility with the small print permitted Bayern to secure good players, and having acquired them, to make money for them and himself. This was particularly true of the club's greatest signing, Franz Beckenbauer, though in his case fortune also had a hand in his arrival.

'I was playing for a local junior club, and at that time we all wanted to play for TSV Munich 1860, which was then the more famous club in Munich. One day we played against their junior team, and in the match, one of their players hit me in the face without warning. I was so angry that I decided I would not go to their club. My friends went to 1860, but I signed for Bayern.'

Schwan became the young star's agent – Beckenbauer even married his secretary – and encouraged him to invest in insurance and property. They proved a successful and much envied partnership. It was not financial necessity which drove Beckenbauer to New York in 1977, though naturally, when he did leave Bayern, Schwan set up the deal. His role in the transfer, which Schwan kept secret until negotiations with the Cosmos were complete, attracted intense criticism in Germany, and virtually compelled Neudecker to sack him.

For Beckenbauer had become a national institution, an immense asset to Bayern, where his aristocratic bearing on and off the field had earned him the nickname *der Kaiser*. For his club he had begun life as a defender, though for a while the West German team manager, Helmut Schoen, preferred to employ him in midfield. Said Beckenbauer:

'It was very difficult for me at the end of the 1960s. I was always the sweeper for Bayern, but Willie Schulz was established there in the national team, so I was used further forward. Sometimes we had an international game on the Wednesday, and a league game a few days later, and it was hard for me to keep changing. Only during the 1966 and 1970 World Cups, when we had time to prepare, did it become easier.'

But this ambiguity in his early career helped Beckenbauer create a new role for both club and country in the 1970s – that of the attacking sweeper. His ability to read the game, as well as his coolness under pressure, made him the ideal defender; but he was also confident and skilful enough to bring the ball out of the back four and give his side an added option in midfield. Only rarely did opposing forwards drop back to challenge him, and even when confronted, Beckenbauer was rarely caught out. A softly struck chip to the wing, or a sharply played 'one-two' with a colleague, and he was free to glide forward again. At times he seemed able to dictate the course of a match without effort.

With Beckenbauer and Müller prominent, and coached by the Yugoslav Tschik Cajkovski, Bayern were promoted to the Bundesliga in 1965. The following season they took third place, still overshadowed by their Munich neighbours 1860, who won the title. But Bayern did win the cup which enabled them to enter, and win, the European Cup Winners' Cup in 1967.

The regular goalkeeper was Josef 'Sepp' Maier, an awkward looking athlete, whose lumbering walk and large gloves gave him an almost comic appearance. There were some who doubted his consistency, particularly in the air, but his record of 442 consecutive appearances for Bayern may never be beaten. A humorous man, with a passion for tennis, he remained first choice for club and country until his career was ended by a road accident in 1979.

Maier, Müller and Beckenbauer were in the West German side which eliminated England in the 1970 World Cup match at Leon. Two years later, in April 1972, all three faced England at Wembley in the quarter-final of the European Championship. But this time they were joined by three more Bayern colleagues: the stopper Georg Schwarzenbeck, another local find, and two 20-year-olds, Uli Hoeness and Paul Breitner. The two youngsters had been brought to the club by Udo Lattek – now coach in succession to Cajkovski and another Yugoslav Branco Zebec – who had first learned of their ability while coach to the national youth team. Despite their relative lack of experience, Schoen was not afraid to risk playing them at Wembley, and was rewarded by two brilliant displays. Breitner shuttled easily between defence and midfield; while Hoeness, still technically an amateur, scored the first goal.

West Germany's 3–1 win confirmed that their football had progressed since 1970. They were more flexible in technique and approach, while England offered the same rigid formula. The Bavarian sextet were now worthy of a major setting. As if to underline the club's international standing, Bayern – winners of the Bundesliga for the second time in 1972 – moved out of their old ground in the Grunwaldstrasse. From September, they would play their home matches in the new Olympic stadium on Munich's west side, where five consecutive seasons in the European Cup would yield a small fortune in receipts.

In March 1974, for instance, more than 70,000 people paid to see Bayern face CSKA Sofia in the first leg of the European Cup quarter-final. They were out of sorts against Atvidaberg, and a trifle fortunate against Dresden, but Bayern now delighted their supporters by thrashing the conquerors of Ajax 4–1. Two of the goals came from Torstensson – there was nothing in UEFA's rules to prevent a player representing two clubs in the same tournament – while the others came from Beckenbauer and Müller. The latter even missed a much disputed penalty and the Bulgarians had a man sent off near the end.

The return of Breitner restored the Germans' fluency. He had been forced to miss the Dresden tie after being injured by a stone thrown during the match in Sweden. In the second leg in Sofia, his penalty put Bayern even further ahead on aggregate, and, although CSKA came back to win the match, the Germans' place in the semi-final was never in doubt. Bayern's composure in a hostile atmosphere was particularly satisfying for Lattek, who had been roughly handled by police while trying to leave his seat during the match.

In Budapest on 10 April his side virtually assured themselves of going a stage further, when they drew 1–1 with Ujpest Dosza. Torstensson scored again, and in Munich added another in Bayern's 3–0 win. The Germans were now the toast of Europe, their six brightest stars heading for an unprecedented set of honours: league championship, European Cup and World Cup winners' medals. In the acclaim which greeted their football in the spring of 1974, it was easy to overlook that Bayern were only the second German team to reach the final of the European Cup, and the first for 14 years.

Such reminders were of little solace to English supporters, who in November 1973 saw their League champions Liverpool knocked out of Europe by Red Star Belgrade, and the national team removed from the World Cup by Poland. Twenty years after England's defeat by Hungary, the superiority of foreign football was being debated all over again. Liverpool's loss was easier to comprehend. Shankly's rebuilt side was beaten by a team which matched them for attacking commitment, even at Anfield. Red Star's football recalled that of Ajax seven years earlier, though the calibre of the home side was perhaps not as high.

Shankly had begun to prepare for the future, even while St John and company were still capable of first division football. He had sought replacements from the lower divisions: Ray Clemence of Scunthorpe, Larry Lloyd of Bristol Rovers and Alec Lindsay of Bury were all recruited; then converted to Liverpool's exacting way of life in the reserve team. Shankly also found two forwards in unlikely surroundings: Brian Hall and Steve Heighway, both university graduates, surprised even the most seasoned first division defenders in 1970. Their new teammates, masters of wit if not academic wisdom, instantly named them Little Bamber and Big Bamber, after the host of the university TV quiz game.

Liverpool's reshaped side, with Tommy Smith now captain, and an earlier signing, Emlyn Hughes from Blackpool, in midfield, earned its stripes by reaching the 1971 FA Cup final. The 2–1 defeat by Arsenal was watched by Shankly's latest bargain, Kevin Keegan, also from Scunthorpe. At a mere £35,000, the little Yorkshireman was not expected to make an immediate impact. But at the start of the following season he caught the eye of a senior professional, Ian St John.

'We were doing the pre-season routines, things we'd done a hundred times before, and I suddenly realised this new fellow Keegan was winning everything. He lacked a bit of touch, but he had a fantastic enthusiasm for whatever we did. I talked to Ian Ross about him after a practice match, and he told me what a nuisance he was to mark, because he never stopped still.

'At the time Alun Evans was a regular first team choice up front. But he had put on a bit of weight in the summer, and when the first teamsheet went up, Keegan was in, and he stayed in.'

In 1973 the combination of Keegan's energy and the aerial power of Welshman John Toshack helped Liverpool defeat Borussia Moenchengladbach in the UEFA Cup, and win the club's first European trophy. Shankly had also won his third League title, and another crack at the champions cup. In September against Jeunesse Esch, Liverpool had to work hard for a 1–1 draw in Luxembourg, while at home they needed an own goal to help them win the match 2–0.

They now faced Red Star – managed since 1966 by the shrewd multilingual figure, Miljan Miljanic. He was also coach to the national side, which included Red Star's midfield players Acimovic and Karasi, and the sweeper Bogicevic, who was later to earn a good living alongside Beckenbauer in New York.

The first leg in Belgrade was won 2–1 by the Yugoslavs with a late goal by Chris Lawler raising Liverpool's hopes of an aggregate win. But on arrival at Anfield, Miljanic announced he would attack, and kept to his word. Red Star produced a marvellous display, and even Clemence was powerless to prevent Lazarevic scoring with a long, swerving shot after an hour. Lawler scored again to level the match, but the Yugoslavs became only the second continental side to win a European leg at Anfield in 10 seasons, when Jankovic scored from a free kick near the end. The final aggregate was 4–2.

It was Shankly's last match in Europe. But even in defeat it was clear that he had assembled a side with the potential to match the performance of his earlier team. When he resigned in the summer of 1974, he left the club in impressive shape, with an FA Cup win, and an important new signing in Arsenal's Ray Kennedy. Furthermore, Anfield boasted a faithful and far sighted backroom team, which would provide a successor to Shankly, and give the club its character and continuity.

Miljanic, too, was on the move. Red Star lost their quarter-final tie to the Spanish champions Atletico Madrid, which hastened his departure. After the 1974 World Cup finals, Miljanic would move to the Spanish capital to become the coach to Real. Atletico's change of direction came earlier, following their 1973 championship win. Their coach then was the Austrian Max Merkel, but he was sacked in the summer for criticising the club's directors in a foreign magazine.

Into the breach stepped a controversial figure, Juan Carlos Lorenzo, manager of the 1966 Argentine World Cup team, condemned for their conduct against England at Wembley. In 1970, Lorenzo was himself involved in a street brawl with Arsenal players, while manager of the Italian club Lazio. This time a British side fell foul of him again. Atletico came to Glasgow, in April 1974, to play Celtic in the first leg of the semi-final. But the match was ruined as a spectacle by the tactics of Lorenzo's team. Their persistent disregard for the laws mocked the spirit of international competition. In the city where Real Madrid lit a torch for the European Cup, Atletico did their best to extinguish it.

In the seventh minute of the match, Ruben Ayala, Atletico's Argentine forward, had his name taken, to begin a dreary succession of bookings by Babacan, the Turkish referee. In all he cautioned nine players – two from Celtic and seven from Atletico – and sent three of the Spanish team, Ayala, Diaz and Quique, off the field. Diaz in particular produced a series of shameful fouls on Jimmy Johnstone, which revived memories of the two players' previous meeting. Diaz had played for Racing in the infamous World Club Championship matches of 1967.

The Scots, who had struggled to beat Basle in the quarter-final, were unable to manage a single goal, even against a depleted side. The Spaniards showed little interest in attack, and the game finished 0–0. Celtic's manager Jock Stein was understandably sickened by what he saw.

'It was never a match. It was just a shambles. They used people to try and take players out of the game, particularly Johnstone. They didn't care if some of their players got taken off, as long as Johnstone and one or two others were involved with them.

'Actually they were a good side, and if they'd gone out to play properly, they could have showed the people something. They didn't need to be afraid of us, because at that time we weren't as strong as we had been. Over there they showed us that they could play, and in the final against Bayern they showed it as well.

'Actually, I was keen to try and get the second leg moved. I was worried about the safety of the players, I still think UEFA should have made us play on a neutral ground. There was some talk at the time of Celtic not travelling to Madrid. But the club were worried about being fined, or even banned in the future, if we refused to play the match.'

In the event the tie went ahead normally, though six Atletico players were suspended from it. Goals by Garate and Adelardo in the second half gave the Spaniards a 2–0 win. The Parkhead fiasco was symptomatic of a growing trend in European football. Earlier in the 1973–74 season, the UEFA Cup match between Lazio and Ipswich Town in Rome had produced dreadful scenes. At one time the crowd attempted to invade the pitch, and at the end some of the Ipswich players were assaulted in the tunnel. UEFA banned Lazio from European competition for a year, a sentence which was given further emphasis when Lazio went on to win the Italian championship, and were forced to withdraw from the European Cup.

But in a sense the ban underlined the limits to UEFA's authority. They could penalise clubs for failing to control their own crowd, as with Lazio, and the unfortunate Moenchengladbach after the Boninsegna affair. But they seemed powerless to prevent offences against the spirit of the game, to punish violence which was confined to areas within the touchlines. Atletico thus escaped with half a dozen suspensions, rather than dismissal from European competition. In the event their misdemeanours were punished in almost poetic fashion in the final, where, having behaved impeccably and having scored a good goal in extra time to lead Bayern Munich 1–0, their hopes were dashed in the last seconds of the match.

The Spaniards' scorer in Brussels was their 36-year-old midfield

general Luis, who curved a free kick round the wall past
Maier. Atletico seemed to have survived comfortably until
Schwarzenbeck struck a right foot shot in desperation from 30 yards
out, and the ball dipped past Reina's dive. Bayern, as Beckenbauer
acknowledged, had had their share of good fortune.

'That year we were out of the European Cup two or three times, and each
time came back to win. Against Atvidaberg we were lucky, and against
Dresden we were losing on away goals, until Gerd Müller scored. Then in
the final it was the same. And it was more remarkable because this time the
goal came from Schwarzenbeck.

'We played badly, because we were nervous. It was the same for Ajax in
their first final. But afterwards we knew we would win the cup, because we
could not be so bad again.'

Bayern celebrate after winning
the replayed final against
Atletico Madrid in 1974.
The goalscorers Gerd Müller and
Uli Hoeness are standing either
side of captain Franz
Beckenbauer – the trio are on
the right hand side of the back
row. (*Presse Sports*)

The replay, on the same pitch two days later, was the first in the
history of the competition. Atletico took the field without the
suspended Irureta, an important midfield player who was booked
against Bayern for the second time in the tournament, the first being
at Parkhead. The Bayern team was unchanged, though this time
Lattek instructed Müller to drop deeper and drag his marker out of
the centre, to allow Hoeness to use his pace further forward. The
tactical change helped to produce Bayern's first goal, when Breitner's
long forward pass found Hoeness already in full stride, and he went
on to beat Reina.

In the second half, Müller made it 2–0 after 56 minutes, when he
allowed Jupp Kapellmann's cross to bounce at the far post, then
volleyed the ball emphatically past the keeper. With 20 minutes left,
Müller put the game beyond reach. This time a chip from Hoeness
found him onside as the defence moved out, and he reacted instantly
to lob the ball over Reina's head. Hoeness capped a brilliant display
by running from the halfway line to score the fourth, beating
Adelardo, Eusebio and Reina in succession, before shooting high into
an empty goal.

Bayern had made the most of their reprieve, as Lorenzo was quick
to appreciate: 'Two days ago the Bavarians were dead. Today they
played like young gods'. Hoeness was less romantic.

'Obviously we played much better, but I think the main reason for the change was that they had some older players in the team, and two matches in three days was too much. The day after the final, we also had to play a match, against Borussia Moenchengladbach. At one time it seemed the game would decide the Bundesliga, but in fact we had already won the title. We still had to play of course, and it was very funny. We were full of whisky and champagne, and the crowd were laughing at us. We lost 5–0, but it did not matter!'

The atmosphere in Munich off the field, however, was less light-hearted. There were divisions within the club, and accusations of preferential treatment. The chief critic was the free thinking Breitner, a player of pronounced left wing opinions, who made a living from the game, while resenting its lack of democracy. Though Hoeness remained a friend, Breitner was an uneasy companion, who preferred to avoid alliances within the club.

At Bayern, it was said, Breitner was invariably last to arrive for training and first to leave, often with his thick bushy hair still wet from a shower. For him Bayern Munich was a club built on the class system, with Neudecker, a self-made man of extreme conservative views, at its apex. Then came the Beckenbauer-Schwan axis, then Müller, who also had the ear of the management, then everyone else.

The influence of Beckenbauer was undeniable, and also extended to the national side. In the 1974 World Cup finals, it was widely believed that he was responsible for dropping his clubmate Hoeness from the team for the match against Yugoslavia. But the strong, fair haired forward soon returned, and all six Bayern stars helped West Germany beat the Netherlands 2–1 in the final. The match was further confirmation that the balance of power in Europe had shifted: for the Dutch, captained by Cruyff, bore the unmistakable imprint of Ajax.

Breitner, scorer of the Germans' equaliser – the winner, naturally, was the work of Müller – was by then negotiating his transfer to Real Madrid, for whom he would later perform in the European Cup. Four years later, after the departure of Schwan and Beckenbauer, he returned to Bayern, richer and somewhat wiser. His influence on a young side was enormous and prompted Hoeness, who became Bayern's general manager, to comment in 1980:

'Paul was always the aggressive one, but he has become calmer. He is a fine captain for our team. The club is different now. There were problems of personality earlier, as with any team which contains great stars. Because we were so successful, there were always stories about us, some of which were invented.

'For instance, Franz Beckenbauer was always under pressure from people. They wanted to know things about his private life. I think it helped him to go to New York where he has become more of a gentleman, a more easy going person.'

With hindsight, the summer of 1974 may be seen as Bayern's high watermark: though they were to win two more European Cups, the departure of Breitner, and later the injuries to Hoeness and Müller, made them a less confident and enterprising side. Weariness too played a part. Some of Bayern's stars played more than 100 matches during the 1973–74 season, yet the club insisted on a backbreaking series of friendlies before the next one began. Schwan, who arranged them, explained it was the only way to finance the players' high salaries.

The programme took its toll. Bayern conceded six goals in their first match of the season against Offenbach Kickers, and at the end of September were beaten at home for the first time in four years. Already there was a hint of crisis in the air. Neudecker's new signing, Klaus Wunder from Duisburg, failed to find his true form, and injuries gave the side an unsettled appearance.

At the end of the year, the storm broke. After a defeat at Bochum, Neudecker called a meeting of the management at his penthouse. Significantly, Müller and Beckenbauer were also invited. After three hours it was announced that Lattek, manager since March 1970 and under contract until the end of the 1975–76 season, would leave the club a year early. In the event Lattek, aware of where the wind was blowing, resigned in January 1975. Beckenbauer now took a hand in the appointment of his successor: a small, balding FIFA coach called Dettmar Cramer. Known as the 'little professor', Cramer had had little experience in the Bundesliga, but had coached all over the world, and influenced Beckenbauer's early career, when he was assigned to the German youth team. Before joining Bayern, Cramer had been coach to the United States FA, who were not impressed by his sudden departure, and threatened to sue. Cramer's arrival in Munich was made still less comfortable by three defeats. There were shouts of support for his predecessor from the seats in the Olympic stadium.

The league title was now virtually out of reach, but Bayern were still in the European Cup, by virtue of a 5–3 aggregate win over FC Magdeburg in October 1974. The tie was given added poignance by the fact that the East Germans included Jurgen Sparwasser, scorer of the goal in Hamburg which inflicted on West Germany their only defeat of the World Cup finals.

In Munich, in the first leg, Bayern were a goal down in less than a minute, when Hoffmann's cross hit Hansen in the back and beat Maier. Before half-time Magdeburg, holders of the Cup Winners' Cup, went two up, when Sparwasser scored. But in the second half, Müller again rescued Bayern with a hat trick. The first was a penalty for a foul on Hoeness, his second a shot on the turn, and his third came 20 minutes from time, when his effort was deflected past Schulze in the East German goal.

The old resentment between the two nations surfaced before the start of the second leg. The previous year, Neudecker had upset Dresden officials by staying on the west side of the German border on the night before the match. Now Bayern made headlines again by announcing their intention to eat all their meals aboard their luxury coach, rather than in the hotels reserved for tourists in East Germany. Eventually the president bowed to his hosts' request, but his hardline stance won Bayern few friends.

It was as well for them that Müller was again at his sharpest, scoring two more goals, before Sparwasser pulled a goal back for Magdeburg in the 56th minute. Soon afterwards, Maier was hit in the jaw by an elbow, and was forced to remove his own tooth and continue the match with a bandage in his mouth. But Magdeburg failed to inconvenience him further; their frantic endeavour a contrast to the calmness born of experience which the holders displayed.

By the quarter-final, Lattek had departed, though Bayern's league form remained patchy. Their opponents were Ararat Erevan, champions of the Soviet Union, who had recently emerged from their winter break. At half-time in the first leg in Munich the match was scoreless, but Cramer then gambled by sending on Hoeness. He was still recovering from a knee injury, and playing with injections in his foot, as well as a special pad to protect a recently gashed ankle.

Even in this condition Hoeness was sprightly enough to score – with his injured foot – with 12 minutes left, and there was an added bonus for Bayern, when Torstensson aimed a cross at Müller's head and watched the ball float directly into the net. The return was won by Ararat with a goal by Andriassian, but Bayern, winners by 2–1 on aggregate, had again reached the last four.

Their semi-final opponents would be St Etienne, champions of France, whose football was emerging from the doldrums of the 1960s. The other tie would be fought out between Barcelona and Leeds United, who, like Bayern, had survived internal troubles to reach this stage. Since Leeds' European Cup defeat by Celtic in 1970, they had continued – under Don Revie – to dominate English football, without having the trophies to show for it. Though they won the Fairs Cup in 1971, and the FA Cup a year later, two League championships had eluded them in the final match of the season. And in May 1973 they lost two cup finals: to Sunderland at Wembley, and to AC Milan in the Cup Winners' Cup in Greece.

Some felt their failures no more than just reward for some uncompromising football in the 1960s. Others that the pressure of Revie's own personality, his obsession and superstition, encouraged his players to 'choke' at vital moments. But in the 1973–74 season, Leeds deservedly won the League championship again. Bremner and Giles continued to dominate opponents from the middle of the field; David Harvey had proved an admirable replacement for Sprake, while Joe Jordan's power and unselfish running helped fill the gap left by an injury to Mick Jones. Moreover, Revie seemed to have solved the problem of Jack Charlton's retirement by introducing a young Scot, Gordon McQueen from St Mirren, at centre half. Peter Lorimer was aware of a change of mood at Elland Road.

'We knew we had been unpopular in the past, and frankly it did not bother us. If anything it made us more determined. But that season I think Don's attitude changed a bit. After all, we had been together a long time, and he knew how well we could play. We were a good side, and even better with the reins off.

'Maybe we could have done it earlier, I don't know. But everything went right that season. The club was well organised – we never went on without knowing everything about the opposition. Syd Owen and Maurice Lindley saw to that. So there was great confidence about the European Cup.'

But in the summer of 1974, Lorimer and the Leeds family were stunned by the departure of Revie. The man who had been their godfather was tempted away by an offer to manage England. He continued to live in Leeds, where his presence, like that of Busby at Old Trafford, could not help but pervade the club, and influence its personnel. But even Revie could not determine his successor. The board, a little perversely, chose a man with a known antipathy to Revie and Leeds, the former Derby manager Brian Clough.

He and his assistant Peter Taylor had undergone a change in fortunes since taking Derby to the European Cup semi-final in 1973. Both had resigned in October of that year, after a bitter row with chairman Sam Longson, who felt Clough's television performances and outspoken personality were interfering with the primary job of managing the club. Clough's answer was to point out his successful record: like Revie he had rescued the club from the anonymity of the second division, a fact which at least the Derby players recognised. After hearing of the resignation, they barricaded themselves in the dressing-room, in a sincere, if vain attempt, to provoke Longson into climbing down and asking Clough back.

The manager's next move was equally impulsive. Clough and Taylor were persuaded by an ambitious chairman, Mike Bamber, to join Brighton, then languishing in the third division. But the sea air never suited Clough, who kept his home in Derby. When Leeds approached him in July 1974, he reacted with typical dash, interrupting a family holiday to talk to the board, and flying back to the beach after shaking hands on the deal.

Taylor, however, preferred to complete his contract at Brighton, and without him, Clough ran into problems at Elland Road. His criticism of the club – once when speaking at a dinner in Peter Lorimer's honour – had been noted by the players. They were further unsettled by his signing of two Derby men, John McGovern and John O'Hare, and the spending of a quarter of a million pounds on a clever, but erratic forward in Duncan McKenzie. For men like Lorimer, reared on Revie's more paternal approach, Clough's insensitive style bred insecurity and suspicion.

'I know he has a brilliant record as a manager, but in those circumstances, he was not the right man. Actually, I quite liked him in some ways, but he made his feelings for Don Revie quite clear, and the players just could not accept his methods. Besides, it was not as though we were doing well. We had an awful start, and slipped down to the foot of the table. The way things were going, we could forget all about the European Cup.'

In the face of serious unrest, the Leeds board lost their nerve. They sacked Clough only 44 days after his arrival, softening the blow to his ego with compensation estimated at almost £100,000. After a short delay, they appointed the Bolton manager Jimmy Armfield – whose image as one of football's diplomats was a massive contrast to Clough's.

'When I arrived at Leeds, so much had happened so quickly that I made it my policy to keep in the background as it were, and take the heat out of the situation. At that time, I was definitely the right man for the job. I remember meeting the players for the first time at a hotel before they were due to play Arsenal. I can even remember what I wore – a light brown suit, a green shirt, and a tie in the club colours blue and yellow. I thought that might help.

'I had heard all the stories about the players and Clough. But I can honestly say I had no problems with any of them. I told them I admired them as players, which was true, and besides, I don't like falling out with people. I think I helped them, because they were more bewildered than anything else, having lost Don Revie, and then had all the upheavals with Brian Clough. I helped to steady things down. And of course they helped me. For one thing their experience of Europe was greater than mine, and I would have been foolish to ignore the knowledge of men like Bremner and Giles.'

The statesmanlike Armfield had missed the first round of the European Cup, in which Leeds, for all their problems, had disposed of FC Zurich. That was more than could be said for Glasgow Celtic, who went out at this early stage to Olympiakos of Greece.

Leeds' next opponents seemed to offer a sterner test. Ujpest Dosza had been semi-finalists the previous season, but the English champions, with Armfield learning fast, beat them home and away, despite having McKenzie sent off in the first leg in Hungary.

'We had been forced to reshape the side in any case, because of an injury to Billy Bremner which kept him out for a few weeks. When Duncan was sent off for retaliating, we just left Jordan and Lorimer up front, while Norman Hunter and Terry Yorath played in midfield with Giles.

'We played with bags of character, but my own feeling was that the Hungarians made a mistake in moving the match to the Nep stadium in Budapest. There would have been more atmosphere in their own little ground. We won 2–1, with Peter Lorimer scoring a brilliant goal. I think it was the best performance by a Leeds team in all the time I was there. When they came off at the end, I sent them back out to acknowledge the applause.'

At Elland Road, Bremner was able to play and helped his side win 3–0. McQueen scored with a header, as he had in the first leg, Bremner himself added a second, and the third fell to Yorath. Another 3–0 home win – this time against Anderlecht – in fog so dense that the referee took the players off for 15 minutes in the first half – set up Leeds for the semi-final.

'I could not see Anderlecht getting four against us on their own ground, even if they had the whole of Belgium turn out. It was a wet, heavy pitch, and they played much better. They had one or two class players like Rensenbrink and Van Himst, and for some reason had the band playing throughout the match.

'But I had the feeling that night, that our players really wanted to win the European Cup, and in the end we won the match with another brilliant goal. This time Billy Bremner pulled the ball down on the edge of the area, and chipped the 'keeper from about 25 yards. Really, it was worth going just to see that. Mind you, I was glad it was Anderlecht we were playing, and not Ararat. Before the quarter-final draw was made, I looked at a map of the Soviet Union, and could not even find the place. Besides we were also in the middle of FA Cup ties, and there was no way we could afford two or three days travelling.

'The team that concerned me most, though, were Bayern. I was sorry Ararat did not beat them, because I sensed the holders were getting better as the season wore on.'

Armfield would later test these observations first hand. For the moment his obstacle was Barcelona, who had also suffered a mixed reaction after winning their domestic championship.

The arrival of Johan Neeskens from Ajax, after the 1974 World Cup finals, had complicated the issue of foreign players on the staff. The Spaniards now had three: Neeskens, Cruyff, and the Peruvian Hugo Sotil, a skilful forward popular with the crowd. The rules of the Spanish FA allowed the club to register only two, and Rinus Michels, not unnaturally, plumped for his fellow countrymen. Sotil was left to sulk on the sidelines, sentenced to a season of inactivity while waiting to become a 'naturalised' Spaniard.

Michels made a further signing, the Brazilian international defender Mario Marinho, who had established his Spanish ancestry. But the team took time to absorb the changes. Cruyff clashed with Michels repeatedly, and was accused of giving less than his best away from home. Neeskens failed to reproduce his true form, while doubts lingered about the veteran goalkeeper Sadurni.

It was as well that the Catalans had a relatively easy passage to the semi-final. Only Feyenoord – defeated by a Carlos Rexach hat trick in Spain – caused problems, while the Swedes Atvidaberg made life easier by electing to play both legs of their quarter-final in Barcelona.

At Elland Road, in the first leg of the semi-final, the Spaniards fell behind to a splendid Leeds goal after only 10 minutes. Giles crossed from the left, Jordan headed the ball sideways, and Bremner came striding through to shoot high past Sadurni into the right hand corner of the goal. The home side continued to dominate, but Cruyff remained dangerous in bursts. Midway through the second half he sent Heredia down the centre, where he was stopped by what seemed an innocuous tackle by Reaney. The BBC television replay later showed it to have been a foul, and Asensi scored from the free kick. Reaney then made amends with a run down the right which led to Clarke's winning goal, but most observers felt Leeds' margin was too slender to ensure a place in the final. They did not, however, include Armfield.

'There were times in the match when Barcelona had looked a poor side, and I felt our 2–1 win might well be enough. On the morning of the second leg, I went down to their vast stadium on my own. I looked around, and thought to myself that this was as good a place as any to reach the final.

'When the teams came out in the evening, and stood for the anthems, I looked at my lads, and thought there was no way they were going to lick us. I brought back Peter Lorimer for this match. He had number 11 on his back, and I told him to go and stand on the left wing for the first 10 minutes, and then to his normal place on the right.

'I knew what would happen when he moved. Sure enough, the right back went back with him, and was forced to mark Peter on his weaker side. That was the best game I saw Lorimer play. He was tremendous – making runs, taking men on, and giving us the breathing space we needed. He also scored our goal after about seven minutes, after Joe Jordan flicked the ball on. We were so much in control in the first half, that when the interval came and we were still leading 1–0, I lit my pipe.'

Needing two goals to force extra time, Cruyff and company raised the tempo of the match. Leeds, with the reward for years of striving so close, were pushed back, and David Stewart, deputy for the injured Harvey in goal, pulled off a number of fine saves. He was beaten, however, by a Clares header with 25 minutes to go, the signal for a frenzied last period of the match. Leeds' cause was not helped by having McQueen sent off, a few minutes after the goal, for an unnecessary piece of retaliation.

'Gordon was in a terrible state, because he knew he had lost out either way. Either he cost us the match or, if we won, he would miss the final through suspension. I had to get up and leave the 99, as it were, and go with the one, because he was so upset. When I got back to my seat, it was still 1–1. When the whistle went, I'm afraid I wasn't my usual calm self. I just ran on to the pitch to see the players. In my whole career it was the first time I had reached the final of anything.

'I looked around for Don Revie who I knew was there, but I couldn't see him. It must have been a difficult moment for him. He'd have been pleased that his old pros had reached the final, sorry that he wasn't still with them.'

Leeds had become only the second English team to reach the final, and celebrated accordingly that evening. In contrast the mood in the Barcelona camp was savage, recalling the search for a scapegoat which followed their exit from the European Cup in 1960. Then Herrera had been cast out. This time, Rinus Michels would leave at the end of the season.

In the other semi-final Dettmar Cramer had taken Bayern to the final, at the expense of St Etienne. The French had beaten Bayern 3–2 on aggregate, in the Germans' first European Cup tie in 1969–70. They were then managed by former Reims coach Albert Batteux, but since then he had been succeeded by Robert Herbin, already an idol from his playing days with St Etienne. He had assembled a talented, improving side, built round the Revelli brothers, Hervé and Patrick, the captain Jean Michel Larqué, and two foreign defenders in goalkeeper Ivan Curkovic from Yugoslavia, and the Argentine sweeper Osvaldo Piazza.

In the first round of the 1974–75 competition, St Etienne put out Sporting Lisbon who were still dismayed by the sudden departure of coach Alfredo Di Stefano after only a few weeks in charge. Then, after losing the first leg 4–1, the French had recovered to beat Hadjuk Split 6–5 on aggregate, after extra time.

St Etienne were at one time three goals down in the tie against Ruch Chorzow in the quarter-final, but with a stirring sense of occasion had again come back to win. Bayern Munich in the semi-final proved a different proposition. Snow fell throughout the first leg at St Etienne's Geoffroy Guichard stadium, and Bayern, with Müller playing in midfield and Beckenbauer limiting his forward movement, yielded little. The game was drawn 0–0.

In Munich, the Bayern captain scored the first goal after only two minutes, squeezing his shot in at the near post from the corner of the six-yard line. Durnberger made the game safe after a solo run 20 minutes from time, but Beckenbauer knew the hard part of the campaign was to come: 'When we learned it was Leeds we had to play in the final we were worried. We would rather have played Barcelona, because against the Latin teams you can perform more easily. The British do not let you settle the game. However Dettmar Cramer had watched Leeds and everyday in training he told us how they would play. I felt I knew Jordan and Lorimer better than my own colleagues.'

Bayern's team to play Leeds showed only two changes, both enforced, from the one which had beaten Atletico Madrid a year earlier. The Swedish international Bjorn Andersson filled Breitner's position, while an injury to the other full back, Johnny Hansen, meant a place for Bernd Durnberger. He was formerly a winger, who had played with Brietner for a local team, Freilassig, and had been recommended to Bayern by Breitner's father. Durnberger's ability to play in a number of positions was vital to Bayern, as was the presence of another utility player, Franz 'Bulle' Roth, son of a local farmer.

He had made his début at the start of the 1966–67 season, and ended it by scoring the winning goal against Glasgow Rangers in the final of the Cup Winners' Cup. Powerful and thickset, Roth was an uncomplicated, uncomplaining player, happy to fill any role among the more illustrious names in the Bayern line-up. In the final he would play in midfield, along with Torstensson, Zobel, and Kapellmann, another German international, signed by Bayern from Cologne.

Leeds chose to leave out Eddie Gray and McKenzie for the final, while Madeley dropped back to centre half to replace the suspended McQueen. Stewart continued in goal for the injured Harvey.

Otherwise the side was very much the Leeds' old guard, a fact which struck a chord in the heart of Bobby Charlton. Before the final, he commented: 'It's unlikely I suppose that Johnny Giles, Billy Bremner, and Norman Hunter will reach the final of the European Cup again. And I shall feel for them, because the situation is similar to the one we experienced in 1968. They have given a lot to the club, and as a club player, there is nothing better you can top your career with than to win the European Cup. I only hope none of them miss out.'

The 1975 final was the competition's 20th, and UEFA marked the anniversary by playing it at the Parc des Princes in Paris, where the first final was held.

On the morning of the match a plaque was unveiled in the room at the Ambassador Hotel where the original rules of the European Cup were drawn up. *L'Equipe*'s director-general, Jacques Goddet, was joined by some of his fellow pioneers: Sebes, Germain, Piazzalunga, Steppe and Bernabeu. There were reunions, too, for some of the great players of Europe. Di Stefano, Puskas and Gento spent Cup final eve at one of the French capital's famous nightspots, and were endlessly photographed at cocktail parties with Raymond Kopa.

Sadly, the feeling of goodwill in Paris was destroyed after four minutes of the final, when Yorath caught Bayern's defender Andersson with a late tackle, which put the full back out of the match. Said Uli Hoeness: 'It was the most brutal foul I think I have ever seen. His leg was a mess, and it was eight or nine months before he could play again.' Hoeness was less than 100 per cent fit himself, and had to be replaced in the first half, after aggravating his suspect knee. Bayern's tactics became merely those of survival, until they came back to win the match with two late goals.

Leeds, who had by far the majority of the play, failed to make their possession count, and had what seemed a good goal disallowed at a crucial stage in the match. The performance of the French referee Kitabdjian was sharply criticised afterwards, and to complete an unhappy birthday party, a section of the Leeds support rioted behind one goal. *L'Equipe*, as usual made the telling comment: 'It was Bayern's day' ran their headline, 'but Leeds and football deserved something better'.

The first half contained two substitutions and two appeals for penalties, both against Beckenbauer. Andersson was replaced by Sepp Weiss, who now snapped at Bremner's heels, while Wunder, left out of the original team, came on for Hoeness. Later Dettmar Cramer would blame Bayern's defensive posture on the enforced reshuffle. The first penalty appeal came after a handball seemed to prevent Lorimer going through. The second, when Clarke was tripped in the area, appeared a more legitimate case. Said Beckenbauer: 'I suppose this was a penalty, because I did foul him. But the referee was in a bad position, and he could not see what happened. I think he gave me the benefit of the doubt. To be honest, Leeds were unlucky, because they were the better team on the day.'

This incident apart, Beckenbauer's contribution in the match was immense. Without his leadership and his flair for making light of defensive burdens, Bayern could not have survived, let alone been in a position to win the match. The game turned in a seven-minute spell midway through the second half. After 64 minutes Maier made an instinctive save from Bremner. Two minutes later, following a Giles

The genius of Gerd Müller: (a) he is on the far side of Madeley as Kapellmann bursts down the right . . . (b) but as the cross comes in Müller has cut in to the near post . . . (c) and neither Madeley nor Stewart can stop his shot . . . (d) which puts Bayern 2–0 ahead and beyond the reach of Leeds. (*BBC*)

free kick, Lorimer volleyed past the Bayern 'keeper, only for Kitabdjian to disallow the goal. Television replays confirmed that Bremner was standing offside, though whether he was interfering with play seemed open to doubt.

Five minutes later, with a hail of missiles coming from the Leeds fans behind Maier's goal, Bayern went ahead. Müller, who once again had played in a withdrawn role, set Torstensson on his way, and Roth reached his pass a split second before Madeley to strike the ball wide of Stewart. For the supporters of the English team, the sense of injustice, inflamed by years of near misses, proved too much. Some of them began to break up seats and hurl them on to the pitch. Others, still more foolish, attempted to scale the wall and moat surrounding the playing area. One man who managed it was simply set on by the French riot police, and thrown back over the wall.

Seven minutes from time, with Eddie Gray substituted for Yorath, the holders scored again. This time Kapellmann got away down the right and crossed for Müller, arriving at the near post, to tuck away one of his 'little goals'.

Beckenbauer received the trophy again, but Bayern's attempt at a proper lap of honour had to be abandoned, because of further examples of the 'English disease' at the Leeds end. For Armfield, the activities of the supporters made the post match assessment more difficult.

'Afterwards everyone wanted to talk about the riot. Nobody seemed interested in how defensively Bayern had played. The fans took the pressure off them, and the referee. I never criticised him publicly. But I can do it now. He was diabolical. Even some of the French officials apologised to me later.

'I remember when Hoeness was injured that I went out to help Cramer with him. I saw the referee's eyes and they were all glassy. The occasion was too much for him. We should definitely have had a penalty, never mind about the Lorimer goal which was disallowed. And Jordan was pushed and shoved throughout the game. People criticised us afterwards for playing so much to Jordan's head, but the fact was that it caused them real problems.

'The scene in the dressing-room afterwards was awful. The lads came in and just tossed their losers' medals to one side. I told them to put them on the table, because they would want them later. Then, as they sat down, I suddenly realised that I didn't know what to say to them. For the first time in my life I was lost for words. I started to tell them how well they had done after the terrible beginning to the season. Then I saw Billy Bremner just staring at me, and I knew I should have kept my mouth shut.

'At that moment some of them knew that it was the end. That the side would break up sooner, rather than later. They had gone through years of trying to win trophies together, and they had wanted to win this European Cup. At that moment, I was proud to be associated with them.'

The final act of a notorious final was held in Zurich in the summer, when Leeds were banned from Europe for four years by UEFA. Armfield complained he was not allowed to give evidence at the hearing, but he did speak at the appeal, where his commonsense helped reduce the ban by half.

'None of the board came with me. I had to prepare the case myself, with a barrister to advise me, and I was on my feet for about an hour at the appeal. I pointed out one or two things about the organisation at the final, which were not right. For instance they took alcohol away from the Leeds fans at the turnstiles, but sold some drink inside. The police were all inside the perimeter fence, there were none with the crowd. And the loudspeaker

Angry Leeds fans during the 1975 final against Bayern in Paris. The English club was later banned from Europe because of the behaviour of a section of their supporters who rioted during the second half.

announcements were all in French.

'But actually I was impressed with the UEFA people. I think they sympathised with the club, and realised how difficult it was to be responsible for the fans especially away from home. But as their secretary Hans Bangerter said, "Every year we seem to have trouble with British supporters. Why can't you live with other people? We are fed up with the hooligans, and we have to do something."

'To be honest, it was hard not to agree with him.'

The record of British fans in Europe was certainly worthy of censure. There had been problems with Glasgow Rangers followers at the 1972 Cup Winners' Cup final, and with those of Tottenham at the 1974 UEFA final. Manchester United supporters had not let the lack of competitive matches in Europe upset their rampaging. They had recently run riot during a friendly in Belgium. Though the proportion of troublemakers was small in relation to the total number of travellers, their influence was far reaching. UEFA were naturally determined to spell out the consequences of crowd violence. Clubs who offended risked the penalties accorded to Leeds.

Even Real Madrid found they were not immune to a moment's madness. They, too, were banned for a year after an incident in their 1976 semi-final with Bayern in Madrid, when a fan attacked both referee Linemayr and Gerd Müller. The ban was later commuted to an order that Real should play a number of home legs away from their own stadium. Earlier, Real's displays in the 1975–76 tournament gave rise to hopes that the trophy might return to Madrid. The remarkable Miljanic had won the Spanish championship at his first attempt, with a young side shaped around the two Germans in midfield: Günter Netzer from Borussia Moenchengladbach, and Paul Breitner from Bayern Munich.

Moreover, the popular Amancio, whose career seemed finished when his thigh was split open in a domestic cup match, had recovered to add his craft to a fresh assault on the European Cup. His comeback symbolised the rejuvenation of the whole club. Netzer's form, after his arrival in 1973, had been uncertain, and the comparisons with Cruyff at Barcelona embarrassing. His house hunting problems seemed to emphasise that the man from

Moenchengladbach was merely passing through. But the arrival of Breitner in Madrid refurbished his ambitions. Each would play against his former club in the European Cup.

Netzer scored in Real's 4–1 win over Dinamo Bucharest in their first match. The strong Santillana scored twice, and the other goal came from Roberto Martinez, still allowed to play for Real despite a scandal over his naturalisation papers. A 1–0 defeat in Rumania meant that Real qualified comfortably, and would meet the new English champions, Derby County, in the next round.

The Midlands club was now managed by Dave Mackay, their former captain. When Brian Clough left in 1973, the directors appointed Mackay from nearby Nottingham Forest, thereby starting the chain of events which would lead Clough and Taylor into the European Cup with Forest.

Mackay at first found the spirit of his predecessor difficult to dislodge. Many of the players still felt unhappy about the way Clough had resigned, and there were meetings in the town aimed at his restoration. But an influx of fresh blood helped to settle allegiances in the dressing-room.

Rod Thomas, a Welsh international full back, arrived from Swindon, where Mackay had also been manager. He bought a stylish wing half, Bruce Rioch from Aston Villa, and persuaded Manchester City to part with Francis Lee. For £100,000, the ebullient little striker was a bargain, his goals an essential contribution to the 1975 League title. Derby, however, had won the first division with only 53 points, and were clearly not infallible. But for the European Cup campaign, Mackay welcomed back Roy McFarland at centre half, after a long lay off, and signed another forward, the artful Charlie George, who had played for Arsenal in the 1972 European Cup.

After beating Slovan Bratislava 3–1 on aggregate, Derby seemed to have established a winning lead against Real at the Baseball Ground, only to be undone in Madrid. In the first leg Derby won 4–1, with a hat trick from George. Two of them were penalties, but his opening goal was an instinctive first-time drive with his left foot, which gave Miguel Angel not a hope. David Nish scored the other goal, while Real replied through Pirri, who controversially had another effort disallowed.

At the Bernabeu stadium Derby were forced to leave out the injured Rioch and the suspended Lee, and fell behind to a goal by Martinez after only three minutes. But at half-time the English still

Santillana launches himself through the air to score against Derby in Madrid, despite the mass of defenders covering the goal. Real won 6–5 on aggregate after extra time.

led by two goals on aggregate. Martinez scored again after the interval, and then Santillana launched himself through the air to level the tie. George restored Derby's advantage, only for Pirri to send the teams into extra time from the penalty spot. Now a weary Derby, with several players limping, conceded a further goal to Santillana, and went out of the competition. Their tactics had been puzzling, though Real's attacking display recalled their glorious past.

The Spaniards now faced Borussia Moenchengladbach, in the tournament for the first time since the unfortunate affair with Internazionale four years earlier. The Germans won the first of three successive championships in 1975 – as well as the UEFA Cup – but the real significance of the tie lay in the return of Günter Netzer to his old club. The accomplished blond forward had helped build Borussia's reputation in the early 1970s, under the guidance of Hennes Weisweiler, whose methods had attracted deep interest from the English coach, Dave Sexton.

'I used to travel to Germany and watch Borussia quite a bit. Weisweiler was an interesting man, because he had come into the professional game late, and was not encumbered with the attitudes of the past. He was always looking to try new things, and would constantly find ways of getting men forward. In that respect his teams were very different from say, those at Bayern Munich, who were much slower to build attacks, and could be quite dull at times.

'Borussia combined the best continental techniques with the more direct approach of the British game.'

The Germans, however, were forced to find a new coach for the European Cup. Weisweiler, having left his mark on the club, spent a short while at Barcelona, in succession to Michels. His place at Borussia was taken by the former Bayern coach, Udo Lattek. Lattek inherited a fine side, including the German internationals Wimmer, Heynckes and Vogts, and a tough little Danish forward in Allan Simonsen, who scored in both legs as Borussia put out Juventus. In the first leg of the quarter-final against Real, it was another Dane, Henning Jensen, who put the Germans ahead. Wittkamp added another, but Netzer inspired a rally, and the game in Germany was drawn 2–2.

In Madrid, Borussia were a shade unfortunate. Heynckes put them ahead in the first half, only for Santillana to level the score just after the interval. Late in the game the Germans had two goals disallowed for offside – both marginal decisions – and the 1–1 draw meant that they went out of the European Cup on the away goals rule.

Having disposed of one German team, Real now drew the other, Bayern Munich in the semi-final. The holders were again showing signs of wear. They took part in the Supercup – against the holders of the Cup Winners' Cup, Dynamo Kiev – but were beaten home and away. Oleg Blokhin, European Footballer of the Year in 1975, scored all three goals in the tie.

Worse still, Müller had limped off with a muscle injury, which later needed surgery, in Bayern's easy 5–0 win over Jeunesse Esch in the European Cup. The bearded striker would miss many months of the season. Hoeness too was having problems with his knee, and Neudecker's attempts to find replacements in Britain – Leeds' Joe Jordan and Motherwell's Willie Pettigrew were among those mentioned – came to nothing.

Without their two main strikers, Bayern went down 1–0 to the

Swedish champions Malmo in the first leg of the second round, and there was a whiff of scandal about the way the holders eventually got through. In Munich, the second leg was scoreless for almost an hour, until Kapellmann, chasing Beckenbauer's through pass, fell spectacularly in the penalty area. The Bulgarian referee Staneff gave a penalty from which Durnberger scored, and the winner came from a Swede – Conny Torstensson!

Malmo officials were incensed after the match, and not for the first time in the competition, there were rumours of expensive presents reaching referees and linesmen. Malmo's manager, the Englishman Bob Houghton, recalled:

'There was some talk of an investigation afterwards, but nothing came of it, and I suppose it does not matter now. But there was no way the penalty should have been awarded. That was just a gift. Over the two legs we were unlucky not to win, and if we had put out the holders, we would have been on the map long before we played Nottingham Forest in the final three years later.'

The spring of 1976 brought some relief for the oppressed Dettmar Cramer. Hoeness and Müller both returned for the quarter-final with Benfica. Bayern drew 0–0 in the Stadium of Light, then swamped the Portuguese 5–1 in Munich. A further bright spot was the form of young Karl-Heinz Rummenigge on the wing. Now came the semi-final against Real Madrid. The first leg was played at Chamartin, where unfortunately Breitner was not fit to face his former colleagues. The game, drawn 1–1, ended in more disappointment after a fan tried to assault the referee and some of the Bayern players, after the final whistle. Said Hoeness:

'We were just leaving the field, pleased because we had drawn a difficult match. Suddenly one of the spectators was with us, and he ran at Herr Linemayr the referee. Then he hit Gerd Müller, who had scored our goal. By that time Sepp Maier and I had arrived to grab him, and give him to the police.

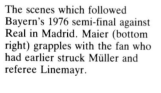

The scenes which followed Bayern's 1976 semi-final against Real in Madrid. Maier (bottom right) grapples with the fan who had earlier struck Müller and referee Linemayr.

'In Munich we played one of our best games. Gerd Müller scored both of our goals. Breitner played this time, and of course was booed all through the match by the crowd. But Real were a good side, and we felt after beating them that we would win the European Cup again.'

The sending off of Amancio two minutes from time, for kicking the ball away at a free kick, completed a miserable tie for Madrid.

On the same night, a few hundred miles to the north-west, St Etienne became the first French club to reach the final of the

European Cup since 1959. Their victory over the Dutch champions
PSV Eindhoven – who had at last, broken the monopoly of Ajax and
Feyenoord in the Netherlands – was something of a surprise. For the
Dutch included the Van der Kerkhof twins, and the Swedish
international Ralf Edstroem. But the French won the first leg 1–0,
with a goal by Larqué, and defended stoutly in the Netherlands to
gain a goalless draw.

St Etienne had earlier dismissed Glasgow Rangers, another side to
end a sequence of championships: the nine successive titles won by
Celtic; but Rangers' hopes of emulating their rivals' European
successes met a setback in France. The Scots lost 2–0, and then found
themselves a further two goals down at Ibrox before MacDonald
scored a late goal.

Kiev and Blokhin were next, hampered somewhat by a lack of
match practice. That did not prevent them gaining a 2–0 lead over St
Etienne in Kiev, but amid scenes of intense excitement, the French
levelled the scores in their own stadium, with goals by Hervé Revelli
and Larqué. The winner, in extra time, came from St Etienne's
outstanding discovery, 20-year-old Dominique Rocheteau. A brilliant
winger, with the looks of a pop singer, he had been spotted by St
Etienne in a youth competition in Paris. His family, however, had
been oyster catchers for generations and it was only with some
difficulty that they were persuaded to let him make a career in
football.

During the 1975–76 season Rocheteau had established a place in
the French national side, but now St Etienne were forced to manage
without him, at the moment when their need was greatest. Rocheteau
was injured during the semi-final against Eindhoven, and was able to
play only a few minutes as substitute in the final against Bayern.
Compared with the emerging Rocheteau, the German players were
old hands. Only Rummenigge, and the young full back Horsmann
were playing their first European Cup final. Bayern's experience was
to be an important factor in the match.

The Germans arrived somewhat grudgingly in Glasgow. The prickly
Neudecker, who feared the Scotland v England match at Hampden a
few days hence would affect the attendance at the European Cup

The only goal of the 1976 final at
Hampden Park – St Etienne's
Curkovic is beaten by Roth's free
kick, and Bayern win their third
successive European Cup.
(*Syndication International*)

final, had attempted to change the venue. At one stage he even offered to play in Paris, where a capacity crowd would be guaranteed, but succeeded only in upsetting UEFA officials as well as his Scottish hosts. Bayern's preparations were hampered by rumours of terrorist threats, after Ulrike Meinhof, a member of the notorious anarchist group, was found hanging in her cell. Later, the club would cite these threats as their reason for leaving Glasgow in the early hours of the morning after the match. One newspaper claimed: 'Bayern won the cup like thieves, and carried it away like fugitives'.

That verdict seemed a little harsh. Bayern's margin was a single goal, but it might have been doubled had Müller's early effort not been ruled out for offside. Television replays suggested he was onside, when Durnberger threaded the ball through to him. The French hit the woodwork twice in the first half, but against that, Bayern could point to a shot from Roth which Curkovic fumbled, and turned to grasp uneasily on the line. The only goal came after 57 minutes, when Piazza pushed Müller, and Roth scored from a simply taken free kick. Once again the less famous Franz had scored a goal in a European final.

With less than 10 minutes left, Rocheteau replaced Sarramagna, who had failed to repeat his form of the first half. Twice in the closing moments the winger almost saved his side with his skilful dribbling, but it was a case of too little too late. Beckenbauer held the Cup for the third successive season. Said Hoeness: 'The only time I was worried was when Rocheteau came on. It was fortunate for us that he was not fit enough to play any longer. But I still think we were the better side, even though they were more experienced than when we beat them in the semi-final.'

St Etienne's Argentine defender Piazza commented: 'In my philosophy there is no such thing as bad luck. People were complaining afterwards that if the posts had been round, some of our shots would have gone in. But I think that is rubbish.' In Italy, *Corriere dello Sport* said simply: 'Professional skill triumphed over amateur enthusiasm'.

Though the final was disappointing, the appeal of the European Cup showed no sign of diminishing. Attendances for the 61 matches were almost a million up on the previous year, at an average of more than 38,000 a match. For all the concern with violence on and off the field, the champions Cup provided the gala occasions in the European calendar. But Bayern, despite emulating the achievements of Ajax, had not quite equalled the enterprise or the invention of the Dutch. For one thing, the Germans lacked a midfield player of world class: a Neeskens, a Netzer, or even a Giles. They were forced to improvise. Many of their really telling moves began with Beckenbauer moving forward, or Müller dropping deep. Perhaps if Breitner had stayed he might have provided the extra element.

His departure, and the injuries to key players, meant Bayern never consistently recaptured the form they showed in beating Atletico Madrid in 1974. It was Cramer's achievement that he was able twice to retain the trophy with a team that was possibly past its peak. Said Hoeness:

'In a way Lattek was lucky. He had grown up with the team and taken us to the top of the mountain. Cramer had to try and keep us there. It was difficult for him, because playing in the European Cup means you cannot experiment easily. I think Ajax found this out also. And the spectators are impatient. They do not want to wait a few years while a new side is built up.

'For me, we played best in 1974. After that we had problems, and I had the knee injury which later meant I had to retire early. Our triumphs after that, particularly against Leeds, were a triumph of character.'

Nevertheless the early 1970s were vintage years for the Germans. They had two powerful club sides in Munich and Moenchengladbach, and a national team which won a European Championship in style, and a World Cup with character. But their era, also, was coming to a close. In the summer of 1976, Hoeness missed a penalty in Belgrade which helped Czechoslovakia become the new European champions, and in the autumn, Bayern would stumble also. After Spain and Portugal, Italy, the Netherlands and West Germany, it was now the turn of England to dominate the European Cup.

CHAPTER NINE

THE KOP CONQUERS A CONTINENT
(Liverpool 1977, 1978)

The crippling severity of the Russian winter, which halted the march of Emperor Napoleon Bonaparte in 1812 and froze the advance of Führer Adolf Hitler in 1943, was largely responsible in 1977 for ending the European reign of Kaiser Franz Beckenbauer. The flame Bayern Munich had carried across the continent for three years was finally extinguished in the bitter cold of the Ukraine.

The Germans began convincingly their attempt to surpass their predecessors as champions, Ajax, and win the European Cup for a fourth consecutive time. They brushed aside the Danish champions, Koge, then defeated Banik Ostrava 5–0 in Munich after losing the first leg 2–1 in Czechoslovakia. Gerd Müller was still the most potent attacker in Europe. He scored five goals in those four games to take his total in the European Cup to 37 – only Di Stefano and Eusebio had done better and both played more games – and it was *der Bomber's* absence through injury that was to prove crucial to Bayern in their quarter-final against Dynamo Kiev in March 1977.

The Soviet champions were such a well integrated side that two years earlier, when they won the European Cup Winners' Cup, they were selected *en masse* to represent the international team, and Oleg Blokhin, their left-sided striker, was voted European Footballer of the Year. They reached the European Cup quarter-final without conceding a goal, disposing of the Yugoslav champions, Partizan Belgrade, and the Greeks from Salonika.

It was Müller's deputy, Rainer Künkel, who first breached Kiev's defence, scoring for Bayern two minutes before half-time in the first leg in Munich. But it was the only goal of the match, and Bayern arrived in the Ukraine without Müller and Durnberger, to find their slender lead further threatened by sub-zero temperatures. Yet the aplomb of Beckenbauer and the acrobatics of Sepp Maier, who saved a Blokhin penalty, kept the champions' defence intact against a barrage of Dynamo attacks backed by a frantic 100,000 crowd in the Republic Stadium in Kiev. With seven minutes to go in the second leg, there was no score and Bayern still held their aggregate lead.

Then Kiev were awarded a second penalty. Bayern hotly contested the decision of the Austrian referee, Erich Linemayr, that Kapellman had fouled Konkov. Burjak scored from the spot, and the tie was squared. But extra time was not required. With three minutes to go, substitute Slobodjan forced Kiev's winner past Maier, and inflicted on Bayern their first European Cup defeat for four years – since they had lost to Ajax in the 1973 quarter-final.

Dettmar Cramer, Bayern's coach, blamed the fall of the champions on the poor form of individual players. But the snow and ice in the Ukraine did more than just divert the course of the European Cup. It eroded the pillar of West German football. Only a month after Bayern were knocked out, Franz Beckenbauer announced he was going to the United States to play for New York Cosmos. Previously, only players past their prime had responded to the lure of the dollar, but now the current European Footballer of the Year, unsettled domestically, went to join the circus in the North American Soccer League.

It meant the end of an illustrious international career in which Beckenbauer won 103 caps in 12 years, playing in three World Cups for West Germany and collecting the trophy on their behalf in 1974. At club level, his departure left Bayern without their cornerstone. Temporarily, anyway, West German interest in the European Cup was still strong. Bundesliga champions Borussia Moenchengladbach, still coached by Lattek and steered by the versatile World Cup star Rainer Bonhof, were through to the semi-final.

Their attack still included the experienced Jupp Heynckes, as well as the now much-coveted Allan Simonsen. The hardness in the side came from the aptly named Uli Stielike; and in the stout little full back, Berti Vogts, they had a captain as respected as Beckenbauer. It was Vogts who scored one of Borussia's goals in a splendid 2–1 win in Turin in the second round. But when the Italian champions came to Germany for the second leg in Dusseldorf – Borussia usually switched their big European games to the spacious Rheinstadion – pandemonium broke out. Three Torino players were sent off in an ugly 0–0 draw, reviving memories of Celtic's unpleasant semi-final against Atletico Madrid in 1974. This time the offenders did not prosper; Moenchengladbach's first leg victory in Italy effectively took them into the quarter-finals.

Here, they met a Bruges side who had already put out Real Madrid and who included Roger Davies, the Derby centre-forward sent off in the semi-final against Juventus four years earlier. Coached by the brooding Ernst Happel of Feyenoord fame, the Belgians played resourcefully in the first leg in Dusseldorf and were delighted with a 2–2 draw. A low-scoring draw in the home leg would have taken Bruges through, but Lattek matched Happel in what was becoming more and more like a game of poker. Borussia's trump card was substitute Wilfried Hannes, who scored eight minutes from time to give the Germans an unexpected victory.

Now Moenchengladbach followed Bayern's progress to the Ukraine, losing the first leg of the semi-final against Dynamo Kiev to a goal by Onishenko. But the Soviet champions proved less formidable when required to play away in the second match, and in Dusseldorf a penalty by Bonhof and a goal by Jurgen Wittkamp deprived Kiev of the chance to become the first side from the Soviet Union to reach the champions' Cup final.

Instead West Germany had a team there for the fourth year running, but paradoxically the 1977 European Cup final in Rome was to be a platform for a little man soon to invade their football from a quite unexpected background. Kevin Keegan, unlike the prototype international footballer, never played for his country at schoolboy or youth level. The son of a Yorkshire miner, he even had a job getting in the team at Peglers, the Doncaster brass factory where he worked before he was spotted by Scunthorpe United. Since his first, brief taste of the European Cup with Liverpool in 1973, when they were beaten by Red Star, Keegan had been part of a side which won the UEFA Cup and the first division championship in 1976 – the second time the Merseyside club had achieved this particular double.

Now, as an established member of Don Revie's England side, Keegan wanted a fresh challenge. His natural appetite for self-improvement, the urge of his restless nature, made him look towards the continent. Real Madrid were ready with an offer of at least £650,000. John Smith, Liverpool's ambitious chairman, talked Keegan into staying at Anfield for one season more, to add his infectious style to the club's fourth attempt to win the European Cup. In return, Smith promised Keegan, in an unwritten gentlemen's agreement, that he could leave to join a European club at the end of the 1976–77 season.

Liverpool were not to know then how perfectly the arrangement would work out. But then, as a club who firmly believed in conformity and continuity, they had a sound record when it came to making big decisions. There was none bigger than appointing Bill Shankly's successor when the inimitable Scot, who created the modern Liverpool, unexpectedly announced his retirement in the summer of 1974. Anfield without Shankly seemed at the time utterly inconceivable. The man was an institution, unique in his passion for the game and the mutual affection he shared with those in and around it, besides injecting the Liverpool team with so much of his own unbridled enthusiasm.

But part of Shankly's strength was the loyalty of his staff, and Liverpool made a selection which may have seemed obvious but was in fact inspired. They chose as Shankly's successor his second-in-command, Bob Paisley.

'I have to admit that at the time of Bill's resignation, certain other well-known names were discussed in the boardroom', recalled Peter Robinson, Liverpool's general secretary. 'But only one man was ever approached about the job, and that was Bob. Even though he tried to turn it down at first, and insisted for years afterwards that he had not wanted to become manager.'

Paisley had been on the Anfield staff since he was 19, a former colliery worker and bricklayer who came to Merseyside from his native County Durham just before war broke out in 1939. He served Liverpool as player, reserve team trainer, first team trainer, first team coach, then assistant manager, before stepping gently into Shankly's shoes at the start of the 1974–75 season.

Emlyn Hughes, then Liverpool's captain, pointed out that Leeds United, who had just beaten them to the championship, were looking for a new manager at the same time. Don Revie had resigned to take the England job.

'The difference was, that while Leeds brought in Brian Clough whose appointment caused upheaval and lasted only 44 days, Liverpool kept the ship stable by letting Bob Paisley get on with things in his own quiet way. Nothing changed much at Anfield. This policy of keeping it in the family was probably the biggest secret, if there was a secret, of Liverpool's success. It was started by Bill Shankly, and it's an attitude which was handed down among staff and players over the years.'

'When I went to Liverpool in 1967, I wanted to be as devoted to the cause as the established players I admired, blokes like Ron Yeats and Ian St John. And I suppose in the next generation of players, somebody like Phil Thompson might have taken his example from me. But attitude was only half of it. The other part was ability, because Liverpool just went on buying good players. That sounds easy, but actually they could also afford to buy the odd one or two who were not a success.'

'There were more of those than you think if you look back over the years, but the club used to get their money back simply because the lad had been a Liverpool player. The club was built on secure habits. The 1976–77 season

was the climax of everything Liverpool had attempted since Shanks invested
the club with good players prepared to give everything. Suddenly in that
season it all came right, but the players who wore the shirts that year were
only a reflection of those who wore them before. Remember, Liverpool had
been trying to win the European Cup for 12 years. It took them that long to
perfect the continental style of play. At first, we lost a lot of tactical battles,
but we gradually learned how to get results by being patient and keeping
possession.'

Hughes' reference to Liverpool's tactical maturity touched a nerve in
the Anfield system which possibly defined a subtle difference between
the policies of the two great mentors, Shankly and Paisley.

   In the early years, Liverpool's common fault in European football
was their galvanised style. So successful at overpowering their
opponents in the English first division with their burning belief and
supreme fitness, they found continental teams catching them in a
spider's web and countering them with the sudden sting of a wasp.
Paisley felt it keenly.

'Our approach was a bit frantic. We treated every match like a war. The
strength of British football lay in our challenge for the ball, but the
continentals took that away from us by learning how to intercept. We
discovered it was no use winning the ball if you finished up on your backside
in a desperate position.
   'The top European teams showed us how to break out of defence
effectively. The pace of their movement was dictated by the first pass. We
had to learn how to be patient like that, and think about the next two or
three moves ahead when we had the ball.
   'Of course, it didn't happen overnight. The crowd still wanted the faster,
more aggressive English style. When we first tried to slow it down, we used
to be a bit negative, just passing square balls across the field. The key to the
change was actually found in our five-a-side practice matches.'

These small sided games, for many professional teams the most
enjoyable form of training, were a staple diet most days of the week
at Liverpool's training ground at Melwood. Those preoccupied with a
more functional type of coaching would often click their tongues and
shake their heads when they discussed Liverpool's training schedule.
'All they do is play five-a-sides.'
   But it was here, on an unmarked patch of grass with makeshift
goalposts, that Paisley and his staff, notably assistant manager Joe
Fagan and coach Ronnie Moran, persuaded a team that had been
reared on relentless attack that the secret of European football lay in
tight control, intelligent movement and most of all, in careful passing.
   Liverpool had achieved everything the domestic game had to offer,
but they still yearned for the European Cup. Paisley, on a personal
level, emerged as a manager in his own right away from the shadow
of Shankly.

'One of the most satisfying things I did, and one of the reasons why we
changed styles so successfully, was to convert Ray Kennedy from a forward
into a midfield player. I got crucified for that decision at the time.
Experienced first division managers said it would never work, but I felt Ray's
control and passing could become a vital factor in our new type of build-up.
   'He had been in Arsenal's double winning side when he was only 19, and
so much happened to him so young that he had never really been a boy. He
had a tendency to put on weight, but I think in the football sense he lost
rather than improved his appetite. He grew weary of playing up front, and
lost his place in the side.

'I knew he had good vision, he was strong on the ball, and although nobody agreed with me at the time, I had this feeling he would be the steadying influence we needed in the middle of the field. So I chatted to him about it, and we tried it in the reserves.'

In January 1976, Kennedy succeeded Peter Cormack in the Liverpool number five shirt, by now traditionally worn by the left-sided midfield player. He was to keep it for the best five years he or the club ever had.

At the end of that season, Kennedy scored one of the goals in Liverpool's UEFA Cup final victory over Bruges. But more significantly, he got the last goal in their last League game at Wolverhampton, where victory clinched the first division title. Liverpool were back in the European Cup.

Their team now was a menacing mixture of old and new. Shankly's stalwarts were still there. Ian Callaghan, selfless and reliable in midfield, had made his début as an outside right in Shankly's first season, 1959–60, and played in all Liverpool's European campaigns. So too had Tommy Smith, although by now the durable defender was finding it hard to gain a regular place. Joey Jones, an enthusiastic signing from Wrexham, was partnering Phil Neal at full back, while the centre of the defence was occupied by the captain Emlyn Hughes, successfully converted from midfield, and Shankly's young protégé Phil Thompson, a local lad from Kirkby who used to support the team from the Kop.

Shankly's eye for potential had been ably backed by a shrewd scouting staff led by former Liverpool player, Geoff Twentyman and Reuben Bennett. Players were never recommended hurriedly, and those who were signed often served a long apprenticeship in the reserves. One of them was goalkeeper Ray Clemence, who had preceded Keegan from Scunthorpe to Liverpool. His long clearances were a simple but effective Liverpool manoeuvre when they won the championship in 1976. His huge kicks with his left foot were aimed at the head of John Toshack, the Welsh international, whose understanding with the elusive Keegan was almost telepathic.

But Paisley knew simplicity was not enough, and added his own signings. The first two, full back Phil Neal from Northampton Town and the energetic midfield forager Terry McDermott from Newcastle United, made their Liverpool débuts together in a Merseyside derby against Everton soon after Paisley took over. In time, they developed a fine understanding on the right flank with Jimmy Case, who came from the local club South Liverpool and won a championship medal in his first season. Case's fierce shooting would bring many valuable European goals, but he somehow captured in his undemonstrative style the very essence of what Liverpool wanted a good footballer to be – utterly subject to the demands of the team.

Another non-League discovery was Steve Heighway, whose pace on Liverpool's left flank made him an orthodox winger in League matches, but who widened his game in Europe to join Keegan as a two-man attack, the ideal foil for rigid man-to-man marking. Said Keegan: 'When we went for the treble in 1977, it was essentially a typical team effort by Liverpool, but if there was one player who shone above the rest that season, it was Steve Heighway. He was so good at taking on defenders, that he ought really to have done what I did and played abroad. He would have been a certainty to do well in German football.'

So perfectly did the Keegan-Heighway tandem suit Liverpool's preferred 4–4–2 formation for European games once Toshack was injured, that their £200,000 pre-season signing from Ipswich, David Johnson, could not command a regular place. A Liverpudlian who made his European début with Everton in 1971, Johnson won three England caps while with Ipswich and played for them in the UEFA Cup, before returning to Merseyside in August 1976. He scored twice in Belfast as Liverpool won 5–0 in the first round of the European Cup against the Northern Ireland champions Crusaders, who had done well in the first leg at Anfield to keep the score down to two.

In the second round, Johnson scored again. This time, against the Turkish side Trabzonspor, who succumbed 3–0 at Liverpool after winning the home leg by a penalty goal. Coming back home one goal down never unduly worried Liverpool in their European campaigns. If their togetherness as a team was their forte, then it extended as it had in the 1960s to the heaving mass of humanity on the Kop – a passionate crowd whose original wit matched their considerable contribution to the cause.

This stunning noise barrier was an enormous psychological advantage to Liverpool. Overseas teams, even their international players, could turn numb once they sensed the sheer volume and proximity of the 20,000 loyalists who packed behind the goal. Phil Thompson experienced the Kop's unique influence from three different points of view: first as spectator, then as player, and once as an invalid. As a terrace supporter at Anfield, he played a part in Liverpool's first European adventure.

'The most memorable match I ever saw as a Liverpool supporter was the European Cup semi-final against Inter at Anfield in 1965. My mum and her twin sister had been to Wembley the previous Saturday to see Liverpool beat Leeds in the FA Cup final, but they couldn't get tickets for Owen, my brother, and me.

'Instead, they made sure we had tickets for the Inter game on the Wednesday. It's history how Liverpool won 3–1 but the Italians froze because the atmosphere was so fantastic. The Kop were at them all the time, singing "Go Back to Italy". They were frightened to death. When it came to my turn to play for Liverpool, I appreciated just how important the crowd were. Owen still stood where we used to go, so when we ran out for a home match I always gave him a wave.

'By the time I played in the European Cup in 1976, I realised something else, and that was just how much the earlier Liverpool teams had passed on about how to play against the continentals. The attitude away from home was to get men behind the ball, and not to panic if we conceded a goal. We always felt we could wipe that out with the crowd behind us in the second leg.'

That was what happened against Trabzonspor, and it happened again, in circumstances far more dramatic, in the quarter-final in March 1977, against St Etienne. The French champions had a growing reputation after their appearance in the previous year's final, and Liverpool's training session on the morning of the first leg in France revealed what they feared – Keegan was unfit to play. Already his imminent move to Europe was being widely discussed, and it was in the Geoffroy Guichard Stadium – where the French supporters with their cry of 'Allez Les Verts' gave St Etienne every encouragement – that Liverpool proved conclusively they were no one-man team.

They attacked the French early on, and Thompson should have scored when he put a free header over the bar. Then they defended resolutely, controlling the pace of St Etienne's attack and snuffing out its chief source of inspiration – Dominique Rocheteau. The French broke through following a corner in the second half, when Dominique Bathenay volleyed past Clemence. But late in the match Heighway hit a post in one of several incisive Liverpool breaks.

A week later, Thompson tore a cartilage. When St Etienne came to Anfield for the second leg, he was lying in Park House nursing home, in the Liverpool suburb of Crosby, listening to the match on the radio. But Keegan was fit to return, and after only three minutes his intended cross from the left swirled inwards, deceived goalkeeper Curkovic, and put Liverpool level on aggregate. If the capacity crowd of 55,000 anticipated an easy ride for Liverpool after that, they forgot St Etienne's defensive record in the European Cup. In six previous away matches over two seasons, they had conceded just three goals.

So when Bathenay scored with a swerving, dipping shot from 30 yards in the second half, giving the French not only the aggregate lead but also an away goal, it meant Liverpool had to get two goals to win. As he lay in his hospital bed, Thompson thought it was all over.

'There were less than 20 minutes to go, and the radio commentator was saying that Liverpool were out of the European Cup. I thought so too. But suddenly Ray Kennedy scored. Then David Fairclough, who had come on as substitute for John Toshack, got another.'

'I was sitting in bed screaming my head off. I could hardly believe we had done it. I made so much noise that two nurses came rushing into the room to find out what had happened.'

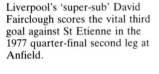

Liverpool's 'super-sub' David Fairclough scores the vital third goal against St Etienne in the 1977 quarter-final second leg at Anfield.

For the Liverpool players who took part in the match, it was one of the most emotional of many great Anfield nights. Phil Neal had experienced nothing like it.

'For sheer atmosphere, that night surpassed all the Cup finals I played in, even the experience of playing for England in South America. When Ray Kennedy scored, the whole place was shaking, but we knew we would go out on away goals if we didn't score again. Then Davie Fairclough stuck in another, and I looked up at the Kop and they were all jumping up and down like jack-in-the-boxes. It was amazing.'

Fairclough, a likeable Liverpool boy with red hair and pale skin, was making a name for himself as a useful substitute, able to come on in the last 20 minutes and strike goals from the most unlikely positions. But his effort against St Etienne was his most important. It took Liverpool into the semi-final, equalling their best European Cup performance in 1965. But whereas then they had to trade punches with the mighty Internazionale, their 1977 opponents were the comparatively modest Swiss champions, FC Zurich.

After beating Glasgow Rangers in the first round, Zurich progressed thanks to the opportunism of Franco Cucinotta, who scored in five of their six matches. But he was suspended for the first leg against Liverpool in Switzerland, and Emlyn Hughes found Zurich an undistinguished side. 'We were finding by now that some of the continental teams just did not deserve the reputation they had. We went to Zurich expecting to meet something special. In fact, they were terrible.'

So bad, that Liverpool could have won more easily than 3–1. Both sides scored from a penalty, Phil Neal adding another goal to the one he got from the spot. Liverpool's other scorer was Steve Heighway, who tortured the Swiss defence with his positive running.

Although the return at Anfield was a formality, over 50,000 saw Liverpool reach the European Cup final for the first time. They did so in style, with two goals from Case and one from Keegan. Three goals in each leg of the semi-final was a fitting performance, because Liverpool were chasing trophies on three fronts. They were near to a record 10th Football League championship, and after a semi-final scare against neighbours Everton, they were due to play Manchester United in the FA Cup final at Wembley.

Anfield in May 1977 was chaotic – and not only on match days. The commercial, as well as the sporting world, was alive to the fact that Liverpool were on the threshold of football immortality in England. When they were not being asked to win matches, the players were being invited to make records, wear the latest fashions, put their names to every feasible product or competition, and appear in a wide variety of radio and television programmes.

Keegan was an international target. Reporters from abroad were almost as regular visitors at Anfield as those from the *Liverpool Daily Post*. The French, the Germans, the Dutch and the Spanish all wondered if one of their clubs would sign Keegan a few weeks hence.

'Although I had said at the start of the season that I would be leaving, and had made my deal with the chairman, some of the other players and quite a lot of the supporters did not seem to believe me. It was an unsettling time, because although I knew I was going, I had no ideas where I would finish up. I suppose this led to a bit of unrest on my part, and on that of the fans.'

It was not until the last week of the domestic season that the West German club, Hamburg, came in with a firm offer of £500,000 for Keegan. Valencia of Spain put in a late bid, and would doubtless have topped Hamburg's price, but Liverpool did business with Dr Peter Krohn, the German club's general manager, and Keegan's future was settled. Thus John Smith kept his promise to the player, just as Keegan had kept his. Now it was a question of how many of the three trophies he would help Liverpool win before he left.

For he was still Liverpool's trump card, still the player most likely to turn a tight game their way. His headed goal gave them two points in a Cup final rehearsal against Manchester United, and at Anfield on 14 May Liverpool clinched the championship with a subdued 0–0 draw against West Ham.

One down, two to go. But at Wembley a week later, four days before the European Cup final in Rome, the treble bid was halted by Manchester United in a curious but entertaining FA Cup final. Liverpool had nearly all the game, but lost 2–1. Bob Paisley later questioned his own decision to play a 4–3–3 formation, with Johnson playing instead of Callaghan. Joe Fagan said the team were not as 'psyched up' for the domestic final as they would normally be. John Toshack, whose injury kept him out of both finals, summed up: 'Manchester United did not beat us. They just scored more goals than us.'

The big fear was whether reaction to the Wembley defeat would tell against Borussia Moenchengladbach the following Wednesday. But Liverpool's players got it out of their system quickly, preparing the way for the greatest day in the life of the club and their supporters. Many Liverpool fans left Wembley and started the trek to Rome straight away. It was a mass migration by every possible means of transport. The club secretary, Peter Robinson, knew from the demand for tickets just how many 'Scousers' and 'Koppites' wanted to follow their team to the Eternal City.

'At first, we were allocated only 20,000 tickets for the final. The demand was so strong that I flew to Rome and pleaded with the Italian FA to increase our allowance. In the end, we got 27,000. Every travel agent on Merseyside was doing good business, but we felt a real responsibility for the good name of Liverpool Football Club. We vetted every travelling supporter ourselves to make sure there were none from the black list we had compiled from previous trips.

'We also checked the booking arrangements made by the various agents, to ensure all the fans had hotel rooms. One firm wanted to sleep people in tents on the way to Rome by road. The club would not accept that.'

Added Phil Thompson: 'Some of them made the journey in vile conditions. They were hours going across Europe on trains with no toilets. Yet they would go through it all again. It said a lot about the spirit of Liverpool.'

Phil Neal remembered:

'There was a lot of unemployment on Merseyside at the time, and many of the fans were broke. They had been to Wembley on the Saturday and they sold everything bar the kitchen sink to get to Rome. A lot of them had brought their flags and banners on poles, but the police confiscated these when the fans arrived at the Olympic Stadium. So they bought these chequered flags instead.

'It made for a fantastic sight when we went out. There were twice as many Liverpool supporters in the ground as we expected. Before the match started, my body was tingling with emotion. I thought we couldn't let people like this down.'

Nor did they in a European Cup final which Liverpool commanded for all but 20 minutes. Paisley reverted to his trusted 4–4–2 formation, with the dependable Callaghan restored to midfield and Johnson on the substitutes' bench. Callaghan started the move which led to Liverpool scoring first after 27 minutes. He won the ball from Bonhof and fed Highway just inside the German half, moving off outside him down the right wing.

Also making a run off the ball was Kevin Keegan. He drew his

A move typical of the modern Liverpool ends with Terry McDermott scoring the first goal in the 1977 final against Borussia Moenchengladbach. Vogts and Kneib are the German players. (*Harry Ormesher*)

marker, the devoted Vogts, away to the left. Into the space in the inside right channel, with the sort of timed run from a deep position which was becoming his trademark, went Terry McDermott. Taking Heighway's pass in his stride, he struck a low shot unerringly past Kneib. Bob Paisley saw it as a vindication of the new Liverpool.

'Vogts might as well have been selling programmes when the goal went in. He was told to follow Keegan, and by the time he left him, it was too late to intercept the move. We had done our work from midfield. It was the strategy we worked on for our European games. Getting the front players to pull their markers away, and leaving space for our midfield men to come through.'

But Moenchengladbach were a team of pedigree and heart. Although Heynckes was not fully fit and Liverpool's respect for Bonhof was obvious, Lattek had in Allan Simonsen a sprightly finisher who could be every bit as deadly as Keegan. Six minutes after half-time, the little Dane pounced on a ball lost in transit between Case and Neal, and beat Clemence with a brilliant, swerving shot with his left foot from the corner of the penalty area. The England goalkeeper said later he had never been beaten by a better strike.

The fact that he was not beaten again, five minutes later, was one of the reasons Liverpool won. A fast move across the field by the Germans put Stielike through the middle, but Clemence made a magnificent save as he came out. It was the turning point in the

The old warhorse himself, Tommy Smith, heads Liverpool 2–1 ahead in Rome. (*Harry Ormesher*)

match. At the time, nobody would have put much money on Liverpool surviving Borussia's 10-minute spell in the ascendancy; still less on who would play the hero's role.

As Heighway took a left-wing corner in the 65th minute, a Liverpool player ran towards the near post to smack an emphatic header high into the net. It took a second or two to realise it was Tommy Smith. The old Anfield warhorse was only in the side because Thompson had still not recovered from his operation, and Smith had announced he would retire after the final. The fact that he changed his mind had something to do with the way he changed the course of the match.

Now the Germans were torn between all-out attack and retaining enough discipline to stop Liverpool scoring again. Keegan was leading a tired Vogts a merry dance, and twice managed to lose him. 'The first time, I tried to pass to Ian Callaghan. I thought when I got behind their sweeper the second time, I would go it alone but the keeper was slow in coming out. I took the ball on another step and Bertie Vogts chopped me down from behind.'

Phil Neal had already scored from 10 penalties for Liverpool that season, including one against Zurich in the semi-final. Now, with seven minutes left and Liverpool leading 2–1, his accuracy was put to the ultimate test.

'I knew all the goals were shown on television around Europe, so I assumed the goalkeeper had done his homework. I picked the opposite corner to the one I used against Zurich, and sure enough he went the wrong way. It wasn't until I watched it again on television afterwards, that I noticed Ian Callaghan standing on the edge of the penalty area with his hands clasped together, praying for me to score.

'I think it was only then that I realised just how much winning the European Cup meant to Liverpool. I had only come to the club three years before, and I was not from Merseyside, but Cally was, and he had been with the club nearly 20 years. He had been through it all, and he was praying nothing would go wrong at the last minute.'

And nothing did go wrong. When the final whistle went with the score 3–1 to Liverpool, the scenes of jubilation among players, staff and supporters as Emlyn Hughes received the huge trophy were akin to those enjoyed nine years earlier by Manchester United, the only other English club to win the European Cup.

The Olympic Stadium in Rome, where England's World Cup hopes had been blown sky high by Italy six months earlier, was now an English stronghold, as 27,000 Merseysiders with their red and white favours celebrated the fact that Liverpool were champions of Europe. The Kop had conquered the continent. But for their departing talisman, the once idolised Keegan, there was an element of strange anti-climax.

'At the end I just felt flat. It was the end of my Liverpool career, and already it was in the past. The fans had given me a bit of stick about going, but I had tried to be honest. I only half did the lap of honour. Everybody said my battle with Vogts was the key to Liverpool's victory, but frankly I wouldn't put the European Cup final among my best 10 games for Liverpool.

'The thing I remember most was Bertie coming to sit with me at the reception afterwards. He came along to congratulate us. I said to Jean, my wife, what a gesture that was. I don't think I could have done it.'

But Vogts and Keegan, locked in their mutual respect, with the little

Englishman now on his way to play in German football, were out of
step with everybody else at the party thrown by Liverpool at their
city hotel. It did not go strictly according to Peter Robinson's plans.

'We had arranged a private reception for 200 people – players, officials, staff,
wives, press and guests. But in the nicest possible way, it got out of hand.
Hundreds of our fans turned up outside asking if they could see the Cup. It
was the night of their lives, and we had always said they were part and parcel
of Liverpool Football Club, so there was nothing else we could do but let
them in.

   'We admitted about 20 at a time, so that they could have a glass of wine
and have their photograph taken with the European Cup. They had backed
us so well, and behaved so correctly, it was the least we could do. It was an
emotional occasion for all of us. I tried to stay calm, but I finished up
embracing Tommy Smith. I didn't do that too often.'

Robinson's recollection of a party that went on until dawn is
significant for another reason. If Liverpool's team were the best in
Europe, so was their organisation off the field. The fact that there
was rarely a flaw in their arrangements, at home or abroad, was due
in no small measure to the urbane Robinson, who joined them from
Brighton and Hove Albion in 1965.

'We learned so many lessons in the early years. We used to leave for a
European game on a Monday, and return on a Thursday. It used to take
almost a week to go, play the match, and get back. So we decided it was
better for the players to spend as little time as possible in foreign
surroundings. We devised a system of chartering an aircraft, flying out the
day before the match, and returning when possible immediately after the
game. That meant only one night away and it was a much tidier operation.

   'Again with hotels, it used to be the accepted thing to stay out in the
country where it was quiet, but we found that city hotels were more
convenient and more comfortable on the continent, especially in winter. Our
routine became commonplace for other clubs travelling in Europe, but in
many of these habits Liverpool were pioneers. In the early days some of the
players suffered while we learned from experience, and one press reporter
once slept on the landing in a hotel in Bucharest.

   'We found East European countries gave us the biggest headaches, but we
never believed in shouting our heads off. I think over the years Liverpool
were involved in fewer incidents than most clubs. We were also among the
first clubs to take a special adviser on food when we travelled to certain
countries, and we always looked after the press when it came to meals and so
on. They were part of the party, and we openly cultivated our relationship
with them because it was the best avenue to reach our supporters.'

Liverpool's red army descended
on Rome with their enthusiasm
undimmed by defeat in the FA
Cup final. Their loyalty made a
lasting impression on the
Liverpool players. (*Harry
Ormesher*)

Robinson's attention to detail could be applied to any successful commercial concern, rather than just to a football club. As John Smith, the chairman, often said: 'Liverpool are in business – the business of winning trophies. If we finish second, that's failure.'

This tight triumvirate, Smith in the boardroom, Robinson at the administrative helm, and Paisley on the training ground, headed an Anfield staff which worked as efficiently and unselfishly as the team.

Tom Saunders, a former headmaster and coach to England schoolboys, would usually be the first to fly out on Paisley's behalf and assess forthcoming European opponents. For solid professionals like this, the euphoria of Rome was a dizzy climax to the unpretentious groundwork which had been done at Anfield for the last 13 years, and which would go on being done afterwards. Even Paisley, with his homespun Geordie philosophy and dry sense of humour, had a mischievious twinkle in his eye when he recounted the story of his previous visit to Rome.

'I was a gunner with the Royal Artillery's anti-tank regiment towards the end of the war, and when we arrived in Rome the fighting had stopped. We were conquerors then, too. As for our fans when we won the European Cup, my favourite tale was the one about the two Liverpool supporters who had tickets at opposite ends of the ground. "I'll meet you at the Vatican afterwards", said one. "Where?" asked the other, "in the bar or in the lounge?"

'But within a matter of days the champagne of the Via Veneto was cast aside for the bottled beer of the famous bootroom under the Anfield stand, where Paisley and his training staff did their thinking. Liverpool had won the European Cup, but they had lost Kevin Keegan, and he needed replacing.'

Liverpool's homework was again sound, their decision unequivocal. They paid Celtic £440,000 for their Scottish international forward, Kenny Dalglish, who cost £60,000 less than Hamburg paid for Keegan and, more saliently, just one quarter of what English clubs would be paying for a player in little more than two years.

Dalglish, a teetotaller with a baby face and broad accent, was at 26 a mature player. He had already played 20 European Cup matches for Celtic, including the semi-finals of 1972 and 1974, and would shortly pass Denis Law's all-time record of 55 caps for Scotland. His first match for Liverpool was in the FA Charity Shield at Wembley, against Manchester United. Phil Neal spoke for the whole Liverpool team when he said:

'There had been a lot of discussion about how we would manage without Kevin, but after about half an hour of his first game we saw what a team player Kenny was. He was always available, wanting the ball played in to his feet while he had his back to the goal. It meant a change of style as far as our attacking play was concerned, but if anything our build-up became even more controlled. Kenny had this terrific ability to bring all our other players into the game because he laid the ball off so accurately.'

While Dalglish settled in by scoring six goals in his first seven matches, Liverpool had a little breathing space before starting their defence of the European Cup. A bye in the first round enabled the holders to assess the field for the 1977–78 tournament. Borussia Moenchengladbach were there again, qualifying as Bundesliga champions despite their defeat by Liverpool in the final. And Ajax, whose European Cup victory over Liverpool 11 years before had started the Anfield brains thinking anew, were back after an absence of three seasons.

There was a strong fancy for Juventus, whose experienced team formed the nucleus of Italy's World Cup squad for Argentina, and whose scorers in the first round against Omonia of Cyprus included Roberto Boninsegna, the former Inter star. In the second round, the Italians brought a touch of romance to the competition when they took their £2 million team to Belfast to play Glentoran. Franco Causio's goal was enough to win the first leg, and the Irish were not disgraced when they lost 5–0 in Turin.

But the Scots lost their champions at the same hurdle when Celtic were beaten by the Austrians of Innsbruck, a defeat which dashed Jock Stein's hopes of leading Celtic to a third European final in what was his last season at Parkhead. Roger Davies was still scoring goals for Bruges, three in the first round against Kuopian Palloseura of Finland, and a penalty in the second round victory over Panathinaikos of Greece.

But Liverpool's entry at this stage sounded a warning to all these pretenders. They crushed Dynamo Dresden 5–1 at Anfield, one of their scorers being the tall defender Alan Hansen, whose arrival at Anfield from Partick Thistle at the end of the previous season was overshadowed by Rome, Keegan and latterly Dalglish.

In Dresden, Liverpool were outplayed for long periods in the second leg, but stemmed the tide when Fairclough came on as substitute. Heighway was their scorer in a 2–1 defeat.

The champions bridged the four-month gap between second round and quarter-finals by meeting Hamburg home and away in the Super Cup. The German club had won the Cup Winners' Cup prior to Keegan's arrival, but his appearance in their side added obvious spice to the matches against Liverpool.

After a 1–1 draw in Germany, Liverpool turned on an almost faultless display under the Anfield floodlights and beat Hamburg 6–0, with Terry McDermott scoring three. That night, as Keegan joined in the applause for his former club, Liverpool with Dalglish fitting their system like a glove, seemed to have the better of the bargain.

Keegan's first few months in Germany were traumatic. The other Hamburg players resented his presence and that of the other summer signing, Ivan Buljan from Yugoslavia, taking their dislike to the point of not even passing the pair the ball. To make matters worse, Keegan lost his temper under provocation in a match late in 1977. He was sent off for punching an opponent, and automatically suspended for eight weeks.

The blow was softened by his election as runner-up to Simonsen in the European Footballer of the Year poll, and by the fact that Hamburg struggled without him. Events there were later to turn dramatically.

Meanwhile another Englishman abroad, John Mortimore, was puzzling out how to check Liverpool. The former Chelsea half back and Southampton coach was in charge at Benfica, champions again in Portugal, though not the force they were in Eusebio's prime. After scraping through on penalties against Moscow Torpedo of the Soviet Union, then putting out the moderate Danish champions, BK Copenhagen, the Eagles of Lisbon were drawn against Liverpool in the quarter-final.

Benfica's chances of building a lead in the first leg in Lisbon were weakened by the absence for disciplinary reasons of Vitor Batista, their controversial striker, and of the injured Chalana, who

Mortimore rated his best forward. His attack depended almost entirely now on Nene, at 28 the most consistent marksman in the Portuguese national team, and he it was who caught Liverpool square to give Benfica the lead. The match was played in pouring rain, the Stadium of Light a plethora of umbrellas. Benfica could not capitalise on their lead, simply because Liverpool's teamwork, even in these conditions, was absolute.

Case equalised from a free kick, and in the second half Hughes scored Liverpool's winner with a curling effort from the left wing. 'Benfica were another false reputation team,' said the Liverpool captain.

Certainly there seemed little hope for them at Anfield, where they started a goal down. Things got worse when their goalkeeper, Bento, sliced Callaghan's cross into his own net in Liverpool's first attack, and then a mistake between Mortimore's two most experienced players, Humberto and Toni, allowed Dalglish a chance he took with his accustomed, unfussy efficiency.

Nene scored again for Benfica, but it was academic. McDermott and Neal added further goals in the second half to give Liverpool a 4–1 win, and Mortimore was left to moan about the riotous inconsistency of continental goalkeepers. 'Bento was brilliant all season, then he let me down like that.'

Mortimore wished he had a Ray Clemence, or even a Dino Zoff. The veteran Italian goalkeeper, who at 36 was soon to play in the World Cup in Argentina, played a vital part in the quarter-final between Juventus and Ajax. Both matches were drawn 1–1, and the tie went to penalties. Zoff saved two of the first three Dutch kicks, and the other went wide, so Juventus, like Liverpool, went through to the semi-final.

So too did Bruges, although by now Roger Davies had gone back to England to play for Leicester City. Without him, the Belgian champions won a thrilling tie against Atletico Madrid, winning 2–0 in Bruges and losing 3–2 in Spain.

The last four was completed by Liverpool's old adversaries Moenchengladbach, who trailed 3–0 in the first leg in Innsbruck. But then Heynckes scored an away goal. That proved conclusive when Borussia beat the Austrians 2–0 in Dusseldorf, with Heynckes scoring again after Bonhof had converted a penalty. Bonhof's accuracy at set-piece kicks was now deadly. Playing for West Germany against England in a friendly international in Munich, he bent a free kick round Ray Clemence's wall for the winning goal, and a month later, in the European Cup semi-final, he haunted the Liverpool goalkeeper again.

Borussia were without two of the forwards who had faced Liverpool in the final a year earlier. Stielike had moved on to Real Madrid, and Simonsen was injured, although he too would soon be leaving Germany – to join Barcelona. In the first leg in Dusseldorf, Liverpool played to their predictable pattern, containing the threat of Heynckes and restricting Moenchengladbach to a goal by defender Hannes in the first half.

Paisley made two substitutions, giving Graeme Souness his first taste of the European Cup in place of Heighway, and replacing McDermott with David Johnson, who marked his first European appearance for a year by forcing in an equaliser late in the game. But two minutes from the end, Bonhof struck a vicious free kick which bounced in front of the crouching Clemence, reared up to hit him on the shoulder, and flew into the net. It gave the Germans a 2–1 lead, but Bob Paisley was philosophical. 'Borussia were better than they were in the final in Rome. We were worse. It will be a great return game.'

But Bonhof hardly made his presence felt in the second leg at Anfield, and was probably to blame when the unmarked Kennedy headed in Dalglish's cross to level the aggregate after only seven minutes. Dalglish put Liverpool ahead after 34 minutes, and Case confirmed their place in the final with a goal in the second half. Bertie Vogts was disappointed with the Germans' attitude in their 3–0 defeat. 'We had some players in our team, internationals even, who were petrified of playing at Anfield. They know they are good players, but they were frightened of Liverpool.'

Souness, signed for £325,000 from Middlesbrough, played his first full match for Liverpool in Europe and showed in his tailored passing that the holders had found a creative successor to Callaghan, now sitting on the substitutes bench.

With the World Cup finals imminent, Souness was pressing his claim to a place in the Scotland team, and in the other European Cup semi-final the presence of no fewer than nine of Italy's team for Argentina made Juventus favourites to beat Bruges. But Ernst Happel, the taciturn tactician, got it right again. In Turin, the Belgians kept Juventus down to a single goal by Roberto Bettega, and Happel, soon to coach the Dutch national side in the World Cup, planned how to crack the Italian defence in the return match.

The man who did it, not surprisingly, came from a deep position. Alfons Bastijns, the experienced Bruges captain and right back, popped up in the Juventus penalty area after just three minutes and squeezed a shot past Zoff. It was only the third goal the Italians had conceded in the competition. Even then, the tie went into extra time, but the suspect Italian temperament cracked. Full back Claudio Gentile was sent off six minutes from time for a second cautionable offence, and a minute later, with penalties looking likely, Rene Vandereycken scored from Jan Sorensen's cross.

So Club Brugge KV, to give them their full title, became the first Belgian side to reach the final of the European Cup. The fact that they made little impression on that final, they blamed on the absence through injury of their veteran centre-forward, Raoul Lambert, and their most imaginative midfield player, Paul Courant. But the side as a whole seemed weakened mentally by the memory of the 1976 UEFA final, when Liverpool had won after Bruges led 2–0 at Anfield, and by this time having to face the formidable English club at Wembley.

Liverpool's general secretary Peter Robinson found a 'home' final still had its headaches. 'We were furious when we found our allocation was only 20,000 tickets out of a Wembley capacity of 92,000. It meant fewer Liverpool fans saw this final than the previous one in Rome. I am convinced such a situation would never have happened anywhere else in Europe. The effect was the biggest black market in my experience.'

Those Liverpool supporters who paid a small fortune for tickets were rewarded with the result they wanted, but with a disappointing match. Bruges were tentative and unprepared to take chances, even though their team included seven internationals. Liverpool dominated

In these few seconds Liverpool retained the European Cup. Kenny Dalglish (dark strip) lifts the ball over the diving Bruges goalkeeper, Birger Jensen, to score the only goal of a disappointing 1978 final at Wembley. 'It was the sort of goal not many players would have scored, but it summed up Kenny Dalglish,' said his team mate Ray Clemence.

a dour match and it became a matter of time before they scored. Bruges held out for 65 minutes thanks to some brave goalkeeping by the Dane, Birger Jensen, but finally gave way just after Heighway came on as substitute for Case.

It was Heighway, who had lost his place in the side to Fairclough, who began with McDermott the move which brought the goal. But it was made and scored by Liverpool's two major signings of that season – emphasising how quickly the right players fitted the system. Souness chipped his pass through a square Bruges defence to the

right hand side of the penalty area, and Dalglish waited for Jensen to make a move before raising the ball over the goalkeeper into the far side of the net. Nobody appreciated the cheekiness of the finish more than Ray Clemence, watching from the other end. 'It was the sort of goal not many players would have scored, but it summed up Kenny Dalglish. He sensed what the goalkeeper would do, waited for him to dive, and created a gap which was not there while Jensen was standing upright.'

If this final was an anti-climax for those who had played on that emotional night in Rome a year earlier, it had a special meaning for Phil Thompson, who had missed the first game through injury.

'I prayed after the 1977 final that Liverpool would get there again, and that I would play. I was probably more desperate to beat Bruges than the other lads, and a few minutes from the end, when we were leading 1–0, I think it showed. They had hardly attacked all night, then suddenly Alan Hansen made a faulty back pass and their fellow, Simoen, dribbled round Ray Clemence and tried to cut the ball back into the empty net.

'I remember running back and thinking I had to reach the ball before it went inside the post. I was at full stretch when I got there, and just managed to knock it away for a corner. That made it for me.'

A year earlier, it had been Thompson and Toshack's turn to miss the thrill of playing in the final. Now, at the final whistle, another injured pair joined in the Liverpool lap of honour: David Johnson, on crutches after an operation, and Tommy Smith, whose Liverpool career really was over this time.

There was sentiment too, for Ian Callaghan, like Smith a survivor of Liverpool's first European campaign 14 years earlier, but now on the substitutes' bench in what was his final hour with the club. The following season, both men joined their former colleague, John Toshack, at Swansea City. But the legacy they left was there for all to see. Liverpool became the first British club to retain the European Cup and with five changes from the side which had won in Rome. So assured was Paisley's pattern that there was no evident weakness as Thompson, Hansen, Souness, Dalglish and Fairclough replaced Smith, Jones, Callaghan, Keegan and Heighway.

But the Liverpool manager knew the 1978 final was an anti-climax. 'Bruges came to Wembley determined to keep the score down. It takes two to tango, and it would have been a better final if it had been played in a neutral country.'

Emlyn Hughes, who had switched to the left back position during the season to replace Jones and accommodate Hansen, received the trophy for the second time and tried to explain Liverpool's invincibility. 'Continental teams were frightened to death of us. They were scared of our record and the fact that we played 70 games a season. They expected us to be super-fit, every one of us a man-mountain. They did not dare go forward in case we crushed them.'

Liverpool played 62 competitive matches in the 1977–78 season, and lost only 12. But that was enough to concede their first division title to Nottingham Forest, who also beat them in the final of the Football League Cup. Forest would have a surprising say in whether Liverpool equalled their predecessors as European champions, Bayern Munich and Ajax, in winning the cup three years running. But for the moment, in that summer of 1978, Bob Paisley took quiet

McDermott, Dalglish and Hansen celebrate Liverpool's victory over Bruges. Dalglish and Hansen were two of the five changes from the team which won the trophy in Rome a year earlier. (*Harry Ormesher*)

satisfaction from the two goals which stood out in Liverpool's two European Cup finals.

McDermott's opening goal in the 1977 final, and Dalglish's delicate winner in 1978, were telling examples of how Liverpool added a thoughtful vein to their full-blooded qualities of fitness and persistence. And, as Paisley said, such moments of priceless skill also explained why his team suffered less than their fair share of injuries.

'If you are patient enough when you have the ball to give yourself thinking time, the pass you eventually make will be a better one. And the next two or three passes will be better still. Careless passing is the most common cause of injury. Seven injuries out of 10 could be avoided if the man stretching to receive the ball had been given a more comfortable pass to his feet.'

But how did Liverpool manage to keep their feet, even those of established internationals, so firmly on the ground? Phil Neal explained the simple way of life which kept the players heads out of the clouds and the club so stable.

'Joe Fagan and Ronnie Moran may often have stayed in the background, but they had this saying: "Look after the little things and the big things will look after themselves".

'There was nothing special about the way Liverpool lived, even when we were European champions. When we travelled, we ate a sensible set meal, not off the à la carte menu like some clubs. The tracksuits we trained in had short sleeves and ridiculous baggy trousers, but we went on wearing them and nobody gave it another thought. There were no airs and graces at Anfield.'

No airs and graces. Just a group of good players in red shirts knowing how and when to pass the ball to each other, and a cabinet full of trophies in the boardroom.

CHAPTER TEN

ROBIN HOOD AND PETER TAYLOR
(Nottingham Forest 1979)

On 30 October 1976, just as Liverpool were changing into top gear ready for their first European Cup win, Nottingham Forest were backpedalling in the second division. They dropped from fifth position to eighth after a 1–0 defeat at Oldham.

Forest's manager, Brian Clough, did not go to the game. Neither was he present at their reserve match that day, at home to Liverpool. As Clough said later: 'To think then that we would be European Champions in less than three years was too daft even to laugh at.' But it was on that crisp October afternoon, as the wind cut a sharp chill across the East Midlands, that two humdrum matches watched by a handful of people produced two forwards who helped to turn the joke on to the rest of Europe.

Clough drove that day from his home in Derby, where he was still living after his adventures at Brighton and Leeds, to the George Street ground in Enderby – a village on the outskirts of Leicester, almost hidden between two motorways. There, he saw Enderby Town play Long Eaton United, from neighbouring Nottinghamshire, in the first qualifying round of the FA Trophy – the senior cup competition for English clubs outside the Football League. As he hugged his shoulders inside his overcoat and drank Oxo to keep warm, Clough's attention was focused on Long Eaton's inside left, a slim 20-year-old called Garry Birtles. Forest had been told, wrongly as it turned out, that the player was being watched by Manchester United.

Clough saw nothing to support such interest. Although Long Eaton won the match 1–0, he left Enderby unimpressed by Birtles, who at the time was earning his living as a floor-layer.

Peter Taylor, who had rejoined Clough the previous July, returned from Oldham to hear his partner's reaction with mixed feelings. They had disagreed before about the potential of non-League players. 'The classic case was Peter Ward, when he was playing for Burton Albion', said Clough. 'I had him watched 24 times by one of our Forest scouts, and I was told he could not play. Peter Taylor watched him twice, then signed him for Brighton where he became a first division player.'

Taylor added:

'In Birtles' case, we had to let Long Eaton know if we wanted him, so I did a deal to take him on trial for a month. If we liked him, we would pay them £2,000 for him.

'He didn't show much in that month, but one night I watched him in a reserve match at Coventry. He produced one flash of skill, when he turned quickly to get in a shot, which convinced me he could make it.

'I had taken my wife to the match and paid to get in. As soon as I saw Birtles do that, we got up and walked out. The following day, we told Long Eaton we would pay the £2,000.'

Clough continued: 'Even then, he was kicking around in our reserves for a while and I was on the point several times of throwing him out. One of the things that kept him at Forest was that he made me a useful squash partner.'

On the Monday morning following his visit to Enderby, Clough sat in his office at the City Ground in Nottingham and listened tolerantly to a report on the Central League match against Liverpool from the late Jack Levey, then a member of Forest's nine-man committee. Clough still had scant time for directors – Forest's were called committee men because the club was not a limited company – and Levey was the only one who could keep the manager in conversation for anything more than a brief exchange.

Now, he was praising the performance of a pale-faced, tousle-haired forward called Tony Woodcock, who had scored a goal in the reserves' 3–3 draw against Liverpool. Nottingham-born Woodcock had joined Forest straight from school, but had been on loan to Lincoln City, and more recently Doncaster Rovers who could have signed him had they wanted to pay Clough's price of around £15,000. But Woodcock was eventually recalled from Doncaster because Forest's staff was weakened by injuries.

Clough's account:

'Tony had been playing mostly at outside left, but we tried him in midfield in the reserves and even at left back. He kept telling us he wanted to play off the centre-forward. We had an Anglo-Scottish Cup tie at Ayr United on the Wednesday, so more to get Jack Levey out of my office than anything else, I told him I would put Tony in the team for that.'

Woodcock played and scored at Ayr, kept his place as Forest won promotion from the second division, then added a first division championship medal, two Football League Cup winners' medals, six England caps and a European Cup winners' medal to his collection, before leaving Forest in 1979 to play for Cologne in West Germany.

It was a remarkable story in which accident played a bigger part than design, yet no more so than in the case of Birtles, who scored six goals in his first seven European Cup games and struck up a partnership with Woodcock that made these two left-footed players the scourge of the continent.

But then, Clough and Taylor had proved at Derby that with their incongruous, non-conformist approach to management, they were perfectly capable of developing the skills of young players. Their methods were so highly individual, their decisions so rapidly taken, that no other managerial team could match them for snap or style. And had anybody tried to copy them, it is doubtful whether he would have found the courage to do so. Who else but Clough would leave the ground to play squash an hour before his team were to start a vital match? What other manager went on holiday with his family in the middle of the season? Or gave the players four days off training and told them not to turn up until the next match?

The captivating force of the man lay in his unpredictable personality. Polite and considerate one minute, Clough could be brusque and abrupt the next. This penchant for keeping those around him guessing was one reason why his players were always nicely on edge, never likely to give anything below their best. Ruling by fear his critics called it, but Clough said sarcastically:

'The Forest players were so afraid, that they expressed themselves freely enough to win the first division championship and the European Cup. Of course I laid down the law heavily when I had to. When things needed saying to players, they got it straight to their faces, there in the dressing-room, in front of the others. And it didn't matter a damn whether they were internationals or not.'

Such a headstrong approach towards men who had been around in the game, effectively got Clough the sack after 44 days at Leeds, after which he had four months out of work and seriously considered giving up football. He took over at Forest in January 1975.

'But when I arrived I knew straight away I couldn't change. Decisions needed making, and I would do the job the way I had always done it, only a little more quietly if you like. My wife, Barbara, told me to concentrate on my family and my job, and not to get involved in all the other things I had done at Derby. Soon after joining Forest, I stopped appearing on television and stayed off the box for three years.'

Clough's rehabilitation was helped by the fact that Forest were not a club hungry for headlines. They had made their name more in the last century, when they were responsible for such innovations as shinguards, crossbars, and the referee's whistle. They celebrated their move to the City Ground, in 1898, by winning the FA Cup, but had to wait until 1959 before they won it again. Their best performance in the League had come in 1967, when they finished second to Manchester United and in the same season reached the FA Cup semi-final.

Those highlights apart, there was not much to disturb the tranquility of a pleasant, compact club whose ground was built on the banks of the River Trent. Nottingham was a prosperous City, involved in light industry with no reputation as a football hotbed. Even Clough's former captain at Derby, Dave Mackay, failed to inspire Forest when he took the manager's job in 1972. In a game of musical chairs he later followed his old boss into the Derby job, while Mackay's successor at Forest, Allan Brown, eventually gave way to Clough at the City Ground.

Forest were 13th in the second division when he arrived, and marked his first match by winning an FA Cup replay at Tottenham. But Clough inherited an unexceptional playing staff which included, at best, four players of unfulfilled promise. There was Martin O'Neill, an Irish international and potential goalscorer; Ian Bowyer, who had played in a European final for Manchester City but drifted to Forest after a spell with Orient; John Robertson, a skilful Scottish player whose weight raised doubts about his application; and Viv Anderson, a black boy born in Nottingham. One of Clough's first decisions was to give him a run at right back.

The new manager's first major signings were the former Derby pair, John McGovern and John O'Hare, who had followed him to Leeds. When Clough left Elland Road neither remained in the first team, but both had proved their worth in Derby's 1973 European Cup run. McGovern, who started with Clough at Hartlepool and became his captain at Forest, seemed to epitomise what a professional footballer, in Clough's eyes, should look like. He was always immaculately dressed, his hair short and tidy. And if he was not the most ornate of players, he made up in example and industry what he lacked in flair. His sensible passing was the backbone of Forest's possession game.

At the end of the 1974–75 season, with Forest finishing 16th in the second division, Clough gave further evidence of the type of character he admired by signing 31-year-old Frank Clark, surprisingly given a free transfer by Newcastle United. 'Here was a smashing lad, solid, dependable, and talented. He told me he was going to retire at

33, but he finished up winning a European Cup medal at nearly 36. He became football's original fairy tale.' Said Clark:

'When Newcastle gave me the sack, which was virtually what it was, I nearly went somewhere like Northampton or Doncaster. Then Brian Clough offered me a chance at Forest. The next four years made me a better player than I had ever been, dragged more out of me than I ever thought was there. What I learned from Clough about managing a football club and motivating people was experience you could not buy.'

With Clark ever-present at left back, Forest improved to eighth in the second division the following season. Clough strengthened the defence further by buying Colin Barrett from Manchester City. But it was the signing he made in the summer of 1976 – when he persuaded Peter Taylor to leave Brighton and join him at Forest as assistant manager – that enabled Clough to work something just short of a miracle in the next three years.

He did not have to twist Taylor's arm very far. Brighton had just missed out on promotion, and Taylor was Nottingham born and bred. Before the war, he watched Forest play from behind the goal, running on to the pitch with other small boys at the end of the game to pat Percy Ashton, Forest's goalkeeper, on the back as he left the field.

'Brian and I believed from our Derby days that management was a two-man job. We were both impetuous by nature, and when we went our separate ways at Leeds and Brighton, I think we both wanted things to happen too quickly. We wanted to run before we could walk. As a partnership, we disagreed about a lot of things, sometimes quite violently, but we could restrain each other when we had to. But above all else, we saw ourselves as builders, as good judges of players.'

This was essentially Taylor's forte, his ability to comb the market inside and outside the Football League to assess, sometimes in the face of conflicting opinion from other experienced managers, whether certain players would fit the Forest pattern.

An early example was Larry Lloyd, the tall centre half who played for Liverpool in the European Cup, but whose obstinate nature led to a disagreement with Shankly and finally to a transfer to Coventry City. Lloyd arrived at Forest on loan, but even when he signed permanently there were arguments. Clough once fined him for not wearing his club blazer on a European trip, but Lloyd responded the way he knew best – playing as an orthodox, blood and guts centre half.

Taylor also put his faith in Peter Withe. Withe had travelled as far as South Africa playing football; and his exceptional heading made him a fearless centre-forward. His partnership with Woodcock, before Birtles took over, helped Forest win the first division championship.

John Robertson was a player Taylor greatly admired, but there were problems of position and discipline. Once he was moved to the left wing, and forced to go on a diet, he developed into the most effective provider of his type in British football.

So Clough and Taylor's new team was beginning to take shape. But events in February 1977 could have meant that Nottingham Forest remained merely another second division club, with no thoughts of European glory. Derby County, just 16 miles down the road, were looking for a new manager. Their ambitious chairman, George Hardy, had sacked Dave Mackay, and when he offered their old jobs back to Clough and Taylor, they intimated they would accept.

Nobody was terribly surprised. Forest's promotion bid seemed on the wane now they had slipped again to seventh place. With Liverpool setting the football world alight with their assault on the treble, it was natural that Clough and Taylor – still revered in Derby – should be tempted by the thought of a quick return to the first division. Not for the first or the last time in his colourful career, Clough was unpredictable. Only a few hours after the morning newspapers made his return to Derby a formality, he arrived in person at the Baseball Ground to announce he was turning the job down.

The reason was never satisfactorily explained. Hardy said later he thought the continued presence in the Derby corridors of former chairman Sam Longson, who by now was club president, was a salient factor. Instead Derby, like Leeds, were left to wonder what might have happened had Clough not left in the first place. Clough and Taylor showed no outward regret over the episode, not even when Forest, having climbed back into the promotion race, lost consecutive matches to Chelsea and Cardiff in April. Their chance of first division football seemed to have gone.

But a slip by Bolton enabled Forest, by taking seven points out of the last eight, to squeeze into third place behind Wolves and Chelsea. The Cardiff defeat would be their last at home for 50 matches. Clough was back in the big time.

'As soon as we got into the first division, we decided which players we wanted to strengthen the team and went out and got them. One of our strengths has always been making decisions. Not all of them have been right, but if you know a bit about the game and you are brave enough to make 10 decisions in a week, there's a good chance you'll make seven correct ones.

'Some managers don't make enough decisions in the first place, and that's why they are not successful. People said we were lucky in the transfer market, but we made our own luck. We took players other managers wouldn't touch, because we backed our judgement and knew we could get the best out of them. Kenny Burns from Birmingham was a good example. Everybody said he was a man you could not control. We had to curb his tackling a bit, but off the field he never gave us any trouble.

'As for Peter Shilton, it was disgraceful that a goalkeeper supposedly at the top of his profession should be starting the season at Mansfield, which is where he was playing with Stoke on the day we opened our first division season at Everton. He was on big wages at Stoke, which stopped some managers coming in for him. We paid those, but we told him it was scandalous that he had been in the game all those years and got no medals to show for it.'

Clough and Taylor had tried to buy Shilton when they were at Derby and he was at Leicester, offering a then considerable £170,000. Given the chance to join Forest, Shilton did not hesitate. 'I was a positive person myself, and I saw in Brian Clough a man I knew I would respect, who would do the job the right way. We had a good team for a while at Stoke, but things went on there which were not totally professional. There was never any danger of that happening under Clough. I read him as a born winner.'

Shilton even tried to get a clause inserted in his contract, allowing him immediate release if Clough ever left Forest. 'With all due respect to them as a club, it was only Brian Clough and Peter Taylor who made Forest what they became. They put us in the big time, which suited me. I had not had the opportunity of playing for a really successful club before.'

Shilton's arrival in September 1977 meant Forest's England Under-21 international goalkeeper, John Middleton, moved down the road to Derby. And for a further £100,000 in the same deal, Clough secured again the services of Archie Gemmill, the indefatigable Scottish midfield player who had given his Derby team its inspiration. 'Whether it was Archie Gemmill, Peter Shilton, or a young apprentice, the first thing we looked for when we signed a player was skill. It blinded us to everything else. Peter and I used to think if a player had skill, we could improve the other things.'

Forest, with their team now assembled, went to the top of the first division on 8 October, and stayed there for the rest of the season. They lost only three League matches out of 42, and their defeat at Leeds on 19 November would be their last in the League for over a year. In the replayed final of the Football League Cup, they beat European champions Liverpool without Shilton and Gemmill, both cup-tied; and McGovern and Barrett, both injured; but Forest won thanks to Robertson's disputed penalty.

Just to emphasise their arrival, Forest finished seven points clear of Liverpool in the 1978 championship race, completing their programme, fittingly, with a 0–0 draw at Anfield. It was essentially a co-operative effort by a team whose defence kept a clean sheet in 25 matches. Shilton was defiant but generally protected by Anderson, Lloyd, Burns and Barrett; with Clark and David Needham, signed from Queens Park Rangers, filling in when required. The midfield of McGovern, Gemmill and O'Neill had a Derby look about it, with the ball moved quickly and accurately by the three players. Bowyer, too, when he came in, was expected to work hard and appear in both penalty areas. The outlet on the left, where Derby had used Hinton so effectively, was Robertson, whose steady supply of crosses with either foot gave regular and varied service to Withe and Woodcock.

At the end of Forest's championship season, Burns was voted Footballer of the Year by the football writers; Shilton elected Player of the Year and Woodcock the Young Player of the Year by their fellow professionals; and Brian Clough, the first manager since Herbert Chapman to win the first division championship with different clubs, was made Manager of the Year. This, in spite of Liverpool winning the European Cup for the second time under Bob Paisley. Now, two English clubs were able to enter the competition for the first time since 1968–69, but anticipation turned to dismay when the draw for the first round paired them together.

Ironically, it was Liverpool who, along with Juventus, pressed UEFA into introducing a seeding system in the first round draw in 1965–66, when the English and Italian Cup winners found themselves drawn together in the first round of the Cup Winners' Cup. Now, the system had worked against the English, although there were good reasons why Forest were not seeded. They were, after all, newcomers to the European Cup, with only two Fairs Cup appearances in the 1960s to give them any European identity at all.

Not that Liverpool, with their record, should have had anything to fear from Forest, Juventus, or any other club among the field for the 1978–79 European Cup. The holders were starting their 15th consecutive season in European football, and it was 10 years since Liverpool had lost in the first round. If those statistics were not daunting enough, the start the two clubs made to the new domestic season suggested only one result. Liverpool won their first five League games, scoring 19 goals and conceding two. Forest won only one of *their* five, drawing the other four and failing to score in three of them. The sudden departure of Peter Withe, transferred to Newcastle after the first League match, had left Forest without a partner for Woodcock, who had been capped for England during the summer.

Steve Elliott was given his chance at centre-forward but failed to score. So for a home match against Arsenal, just four days before Liverpool were due at the City Ground for the first leg of the European tie, Clough backed Taylor's judgement and threw in Garry Birtles. At the start of the season, Birtles was simply a poor third choice. He was not even on the photograph the club had taken of the first team squad, and when he was left out of the pre-season tour party he felt, not for the first time, his days at Forest were numbered. Liverpool did not even know who he was, as Ray Clemence admitted later. 'We had never seen him before, and all they told us about him was that he was good at squash. By the time the match at Nottingham was over, we realised he knew a bit about football as well.'

Birtles took Liverpool, and everybody else, by surprise. He stabbed in Woodcock's pass for the opening goal in the first half, then made the crucial second three minutes from time. He intercepted a bad pass on Liverpool's right flank, evaded a challenge by Phil Thompson, and crossed from the outside left position. Woodcock headed the ball down and Colin Barrett, appearing unexpectedly from left back, volleyed fiercely past Clemence to give Forest a 2–0 lead. Liverpool, as Emlyn Hughes said, blamed only themselves.

'We treated it like a League match, instead of a European Cup tie. Because we were playing an English team, we attacked far more than we would have done in say, Germany or Spain. I don't think we would have got caught out twice over there, like we were at Nottingham.'

The very familiarity of English opponents had made Liverpool's 15 years experience in Europe of little consequence. Clough's team had played resourcefully, but Taylor was furious when the experts predicted Liverpool would erase the deficit at Anfield. 'Only three first division managers out of 22 said we would survive. I ask you, with our record they still doubted us. It was this that made Brian and I absolutely determined to get our tactics right for the second leg.'

Those tactics were to eliminate the power of Liverpool's midfield. Gemmill played on the right to mark Ray Kennedy; on the Forest left, Robertson dropped back to counter Case; McGovern's job was to stop Souness; and Bowyer, who played in place of O'Neill, had to check the runs of McDermott. 'If we had had just one goal to make up', reflected Bob Paisley afterwards, 'we might have done it. But to get two, you need a little bit of a break early on, because after that time is always against you.'

In an atmosphere most European clubs would envy, Forest were chillingly competent before a packed Anfield house of 52,000. When Dalglish beat Shilton with a header from a corner in the first half, the watchful Anderson cleared off the line. In the second half, Shilton saved magnificently from Dalglish. For the fifth time in six meetings,

Forest stopped Liverpool from scoring. And in doing so, ended their two-year reign as European champions. Phil Thompson left the field in tears.

But there was no sign of euphoria in the Forest dressing-room. The new European pretenders dressed quietly as Taylor sipped a mug of tea and snapped: 'We came to do a job, and we did a job'.

Clough gave a typically sharp television interview: 'perhaps now you people will realise that we are quite a good side'; but cautioned his players about celebrations: 'We *might* have a few beers on the coach home'.

So Nottingham Forest, having changed the course of the European Cup, were not allowed to revel in one of its cutest performances. The players filed dutifully out of Anfield in their club blazers, and desperate newspaper reporters were left short of that spicy essential – the after-match quote. Clough's insistence on a quiet approach was, said Shilton, one of the reasons why he and Taylor extracted so many maximum performances from their players.

'They tended to play up the small games, so that we took nothing for granted, and play down the big ones, so we didn't get too tense. They never did anything special or different before or after European games than on normal match days. Once the game was over, there was no hanging around, no celebrations. It was a case of let's get straight back to our families.'

Clough's firmness over players' behaviour, his control of what they were allowed to do or say, was often criticised as dictatorial management. He made no apology for keeping it that way. 'We had definite opinions on how professional footballers should conduct themselves off the field, in order to give a peak performance on it.'

As for Liverpool, the rest of the season seemed empty; their only European involvement now being the Super Cup against Anderlecht. Liverpool lost this as well, going down 3–1 in Brussels and managing only a 2–1 win in the fog at Anfield. But the holders were not the only celebrated team to fall in the first round of the 1979 European Cup. Much to the satisfaction of Forest's former Derby contingent, for whom the memory of the 1973 semi-final still rankled, Juventus also went out.

The Italian champions, nine of their players weary from the World Cup finals in Argentina, had to start their European Cup matches before the league programme in Italy got underway. But that did not detract from the performance of the team who beat them – Glasgow Rangers. The Scottish champions were under new management. John Greig, whose playing career at Ibrox Park had spanned 16 years of European competition, had ended his time as captain on a high note and now began his career as a manager in a winning key.

Rangers lost to a single goal in Turin, scored early in the game by Virdis, but Greig's tactics worked a treat in the return in Glasgow, especially when it came to free kicks, where he believed Juventus were susceptible. They proved doubly so. Alex MacDonald headed Rangers level after 18 minutes, and Gordon Smith beat Zoff with an emphatic header from Robert Russell's free kick after 68 minutes. It was a winning goal of which his old Hibernian namesake would have been proud.

Rangers reward was tougher opposition still. Their second round opponents, Dutch champions PSV Eindhoven, were holders of the UEFA Cup and included six members of the Dutch squad which had finished in second place in Argentina.

René Van der Kerkhof missed the first leg at Ibrox Park, but the presence of his twin brother Willy, with the likes of Ernie Brandts and Jan Poortvliet, was sufficient to earn the Dutch a goalless draw. So when René returned in Eindhoven, and Harry Lubse struck a brilliant goal for the Dutch in the first minute, Rangers' cause looked lost. But the Scots recovered to produce what Greig described as 'Rangers greatest ever display in over 100 European games'.

Twelve minutes after half-time, MacDonald headed in a cross from Tommy McLean to put Rangers in front on away goals. But within three minutes PSV led 2–1 with a goal by Gerrie Deyckers. It was another of Rangers' free kicks that turned the game, although the goal had an element of luck about it. McLean pushed the ball short to Kenny Watson. Watson's shot was then diverted past goalkeeper van Engelen by the head of Derek Johnstone, who had come up from centre half. Now Rangers were again technically in front at 2–2, but they made sure of a memorable victory when, after surviving immense Dutch pressure, they broke through for Russell to score from McLean's pass.

It was exciting stuff from the Scottish champions, who had now beaten two excellent teams. The favourites were going down like skittles, it seemed; the second round also saw the demise of Real Madrid. Their executioner was a young Swiss law student called Claudio Sulser, who motored 60 miles every morning from Zurich to St Gallen to attend lectures, then drove back for afternoon training with Grasshoppers, the sports club patronised by the wealthy élite of Zurich.

Sulser's first appearance in the European Cup put even the débuts of Di Stefano and Eusebio in the shade. He scored five times in 24 minutes as Grasshoppers cruised to an 8–0 victory against Valletta of Malta. In the second leg, he got another goal as the Swiss won 5–3. But it was the three goals he scored against Real that brought the broad, curly-haired Sulser to European prominence. At Chamartin, where Real won the first leg 3–1, he scored for Grasshoppers the 'away goal' that was to prove decisive.

Real played both matches without Uli Stielike, the combative West German who joined them after playing for Borussia Moenchengladbach in the 1977 final against Liverpool. In Zurich, where Real defended a two-goal lead, his presence would have given them protection. As it was, Sulser scored after eight minutes and delivered the *coup de grâce* just four minutes from the end of normal time. His winning goal, joyfully greeted by 30,000 Swiss fans in the tidy Hardturm Stadium, meant Sulser now had nine goals in just four European Cup matches. Altafini's record of 14, which had stood since 1963, was suddenly threatened.

So, too, was Real Madrid's plan to stage a four-club European tournament in memory of their late president, Santiago Bernabeu. The man who had pioneered, with the likes of Hanot, the organisation of European football, as well as making Real its finest advertisement, died in the summer of 1978 at the age of 83.

After their defeat by Grasshoppers, the Spanish champions wanted to use the remaining European dates in the 1978–79 season to stage a round-robin competition against three other former European Cup winners not otherwise involved in Europe. But UEFA's reaction was firm. 'Only UEFA can authorise the start of a European League, and we believe it is too early to introduce such a competition.' Football historians recalled Hanot and Levy's original plan for a European league nearly half a century earlier; but UEFA's attitude was more aptly compared with their own slow acceptance of the European Cup itself in 1955.

One of the men whose exploits on the field did much to break down the original insularity, Ferenc Puskas, cropped up yet again in the 1979 tournament. This time, as manager of the Greek champions, AEK Athens. The tubby Hungarian was still idolised across Europe, and his team did him proud in their first match when they defeated FC Porto, the champions of Portugal, 6–1 in Athens. Two of their goals came from Dusan Bajevic, the tall centre-forward who played for Yugoslavia in the 1974 World Cup finals.

Bajevic scored again in the second leg in Oporto, putting AEK 7–1 ahead on aggregate, but Porto then scored four times in the last 27 minutes. It was not enough to prevent Puskas and his men going through, but it suggested the Greek defence would give way under stress. There was no side left in the competition better equipped to exploit this than Nottingham Forest, buoyant after beating Liverpool and undefeated in the English first division for a year. 'As soon as we arrive in Athens, I am taking the players on the beach to get some sun', announced a brazen Brian Clough, as Forest set off on what would now become customary charter flights from the nearby East Midlands airport at Castle Donington.

But Clough's opposite number, Puskas, had more pressing things on his mind. Mimis Domazos, the 36-year-old midfield general who had played for Puskas and Panathinaikos in the 1971 European Cup final at Wembley, had a blazing row with his manager before the first leg against Forest. Puskas dropped Domazos, and replaced him at the last minute with the tough Uruguayan, Milton Viera. It was an expensive decision.

From the Forest point of view, the match was a personal triumph for 35-year-old Frank Clark, who came back into the side when Barrett was injured, played calmly in the second leg at Liverpool, and now had a hand in both Forest goals in Athens. After nine minutes, his quick free kick to Robertson was moved down the left to Woodcock. The England forward, who had a splendid match against the cynical marking of Ravousis, turned his man and crossed to the far post, where McGovern forced the ball in.

The Greeks were shaken by the way Forest attacked and their frustration soon spilled over. After 21 minutes, a scuffle near the touchline ended with Viera punching Burns and being sent off, while Burns was booked. Then, a minute before half-time, Clark moved forward to beat the Greeks' offside game. He ran the ball half the length of the field before squaring it to Birtles, who made the score 2–0. Forest had two further goals disallowed in the second half, and Shilton was beaten only by a penalty. Burns was harshly penalised for a tackle on AEK's best forward, Thomas Mavros.

It was Mavros who missed an early chance to level the aggregate in the second leg at Nottingham, but after that Forest had little difficulty. Robertson led the Greek defence astray on the left, Birtles scored twice, and the best goal of the night came from Viv Anderson, who four weeks later became the first black player to represent England at full international level.

But as Anderson and Forest faced an exciting future, poor Puskas was left to enjoy the past. His stay in Nottingham included a poignant reunion with Billy Wright, his old international adversary, but AEK's defeat was the prelude to his departure from Athens at the end of the season.

If Puskas was on his way, Brian Clough and Peter Taylor were staying put. On the morning after the second leg against the Greeks, Clough announced he would not be accepting the manager's job at Sunderland. If Forest had to live with their management team being in constant demand, with the possibility of Clough growing unsettled at any time, there were more than adequate compensations. Forest were in the quarter-final of the European Cup, less than two years after being in the second division.

As Forest's then chairman, Stuart Dryden, said in 1979: 'I knew we would make progress under Brian Clough, because he was a genius. But the cost to us was sometimes putting up with the ructions he caused. But then you looked at what he had achieved, and you knew he was a bargain.'

A bargain was what Clough, in turn, called Trevor Francis. On 9 February 1979, while Forest were waiting for the European Cup to get underway again after its customary mid-winter break, they made history by breaking the £1 million transfer barrier. At the age of 24, but with eight years first team experience behind him, Francis was the most natural, unfulfilled talent in the British game. His perennial struggle against relegation with Birmingham City had blunted his edge and restricted his international exposure. Clough and Taylor believed they were the right men to give him full rein, even though Francis would not be eligible for the European Cup until the final.

Forest's committee were frightened by the fee. The club was still the only one in the Football League not to be made a limited company. Their 200 members wondered what return they would get on their investment. It was certainly not coming through the turnstiles. Forest's support continued to be unworthy of a championship side. Less than 32,000 turned out to watch them play Grasshoppers in the first leg of the European Cup quarter-final. Clough even banned live radio coverage of the match in an attempt to prise the Nottingham public out of their armchairs.

Those who did go saw a compelling contest, in which Sulser lived up to his reputation. He put the Swiss champions ahead after 10 minutes with a fine goal, brushing his way down the centre past Larry Lloyd and beating the advancing Shilton by shooting early with the outside of his left foot. It was a bad start for Forest, but the way they recovered typified their high morale. It would be unfair to say they broke down the continental man-for-man marking by using Liverpool's method, because Taylor had said in their Derby days just how it could be done. 'If our midfield players carried the ball at the opposition enough, it destroyed their defensive system. If their defenders came at the man with the ball, we had somebody free; if they followed our front men, there were spaces there for the midfield players to use.'

Forest went in front with a goal either side of half-time. The first was made by Woodcock for Birtles, the second a penalty by Robertson awarded for hands. But the turning point came 15 minutes from the end, when Sulser broke clear again and was this time foiled by a superb save from Shilton.

Gemmill was now at his busiest, covering every yard of the heavy pitch with those urgent, pumping strides. It was fitting he should score Forest's third goal three minutes from the end; and fitting too that the man who made it, Larry Lloyd should himself head the fourth, from the last of Forest's 28 corners, in the last minute. 'We would have been happy to go back to Zurich losing 2–1', said Grasshopper's coach, Helmut Johanneson, 'but by scoring twice in the last three minutes, Forest put the tie beyond our reach. They taught us that a match lasts 90 minutes.'

Further evidence of Clough's motivating powers, and Forest's capacity for shaking off a setback, was displayed in the Football League Cup Final at Wembley. A goal down to Southampton, they won 3–2 and became the first club to retain the trophy. Again Garry Birtles performed well, scoring two of the goals, but his squash partner, the indomitable Mr Clough, saw no reason for a special celebration. 'I got hold of the Cup when we got off the bus at Nottingham, bought some fish and chips to take home, and watched *Match of the Day* with my family, with the cup standing on top of the telly.'

A consistent streak in Clough's otherwise inconsistent nature was his feeling for a close family life. He often confessed that his wife, Barbara, was the most influential figure in their household, and he jealously guarded time spent with his three children. His simple Saturday night after the emotion of a Wembley occasion may have seemed a contradiction, when you consider he spent the night before the game pouring his players champagne. But not when you remember what Shilton said – Clough had ways of playing things down. And ways of shattering any complacency in the Forest camp.

He demanded a thoroughly professional performance in Zurich, where Forest took a 4–1 lead into the second leg against Grasshoppers. Martin O'Neill equalised a penalty by Sulser, and Forest were in the semi-final. Sulser finished with a total of 11 goals, the best individual performance in the champions Cup since Gerd Muller scored that number in the 1972–73 season, and a figure bettered only by Altafini and Puskas.

It was Müller who ended Glasgow Rangers' interest in the competition at this same quarter-final stage. Not the original article – *der Bomber* was now in the United States with Fort Lauderdale Strikers – but Dieter Müller, his namesake playing for the West German champions, 1 FC Köln. The club from the cathedral city of Cologne were in the European Cup for the first time since 1965, when they lost that three-match marathon to Bill Shankly's first Liverpool side.

Now Cologne were guided by Hennes Weisweiler, nearly 60 years of age but still admired by his contemporaries across the continent after his days at Borussia Moenchengladbach and Barcelona. His team dismissed weak opposition from Iceland and Bulgaria to reach the last eight. If Dieter Müller was a lethal finisher, the finesse was provided by Heinz Flohe, the West German international midfield player who modelled his game on Bobby Charlton.

Rangers were ravaged by injuries before the first leg in Cologne's Mungersdorfer Stadium: Derek Johnstone missed the match; while Tom Forsyth, Tommy McLean and Alex MacDonald all played below full fitness.

The Germans squandered a number of chances before scoring after nearly an hour: Flohe crossed from the right, and Müller poked a foot between the defenders to score at the far post.

Extra police on duty in case the Scottish fans misbehaved were not extended. The Rangers supporters, believing a 1–0 defeat could be a moral victory, were described as 'drunk but happy'. But there was no Caledonian carnival at Ibrox Park. Müller scored again in the second half to put the Germans further ahead, and McLean's goal came too late to save Rangers. The Scots went out rueing the absence of a fully-fit Johnstone, used in the second leg only as a substitute. Rangers, despite winning the Cup Winners' Cup in 1972, still had to improve on their champions Cup performance of 1960, when they reached the semi-final.

So for the sixth year running, a West German club were in the last four of the European Cup. Cologne would now meet Nottingham Forest, a match better suited to the final itself, especially as the two teams in the other semi-final, Malmo of Sweden and Austria/WAC, were clearly inferior.

There was lively English interest in Malmo because their coach, 32-year-old Bob Houghton, was a player at Fulham and Brighton, coached the youth team at Ipswich Town, and once had the dubious distinction of being sacked by Southern League Maidstone. Since moving to Sweden in January 1974 Houghton had steered Malmo to the championship three times. They gave Bayern Munich a fright in the 1975–76 European Cup, and lost by the odd goal to Torino the following year.

This time, a carefully schooled defence had stood Malmo in good stead. They beat Monaco, the French champions, and the stern Soviet side, Dynamo Kiev, without conceding a goal. In the quarter-final, Houghton's side lost 2–1 in Poland to Wisla Krakow, but won 4–1 in the return match when a hat trick by their international midfield player, Anders Ljungberg, included two penalties.

The Viennese club, Austria/WAC, had been beaten finalists in the Cup Winners' Cup a year earlier, but even with the Austrian World Cup star, Walter Schachner, in their attack, they could not break down Malmo in the semi-final. The first leg in Vienna ended 0–0, with Houghton's defence doing their job to perfection. There were great celebrations when Tommy Hansson headed the only goal of the second leg: it was the first time a Swedish club had reached a European final.

But the rest of Europe noted Malmo's achievement with barely a second glance, so taken were they with the drama of the other semi-final between Nottingham Forest and Cologne.

Forest were without Anderson for the first leg played on a heavy, churned pitch at the City Ground. He had been suspended after receiving two yellow cards in the quarter-final; and Burns was injured. Forest's back four of Barrett, Lloyd, Needham and Bowyer started sluggishly against the speedy German attack, but neither they nor the 40,000 packed inside the ground were prepared for a below par performance from Peter Shilton.

Cologne, themselves without the injured Flohe, took the lead after six minutes. Jurgen Glowacz made an opening for the Belgian Van Gool, whose shot sneaked low past Shilton's right side and in off the post. Although he took the blame, the Forest goalkeeper said later: 'Looking back, it was not a bad shot. He hit it well, and I did get a hand to it. The ball actually hit both posts before going in, and that made it look worse really.'

What made it worse for the English champions was that the Germans scored a second goal after 19 minutes. It was an easy tap-in for Dieter Muller after Neumann and Van Gool had sliced open the Forest defence. Two goals down at home in the first leg, Forest should have rightfully been on their way out of the European Cup. But now, despite losing Gemmill with an injury, they played with the obsessive motivation which only Clough can inspire, and Cologne revealed weaknesses which Taylor, in fairness, had stressed in his pre-match briefing.

With Bowyer pushed into midfield for Gemmill and Clark coming on at left back, Forest turned a hopeless position into a winning one. Goals by Birtles, Bowyer and Robertson – a rare header this – put them 3–2 up with 27 minutes left. Cologne's defence was creaking, the ground almost shaking with excitement, as Forest pinned their hopes on a storming finish. But 10 minutes from the end, Shilton stumbled again.

Yasuhiko Okudera, the little Japanese forward sent on by Weisweiler as substitute, with only his second touch tried a hopeful shot from 25 yards. The ball squirmed under the body of the diving Shilton.

'The pitch was tacky and I expected the ball to come up at me off the surface. But when it bounced just in front of me, it stayed low and went under my hands. It was possibly the first major error I had made since joining Forest, and I remember the feeling of utter disgust that came over me, anger really that it should happen in a European Cup semi-final of all things. I did something I never normally would, and just kicked the ball furiously back into the net. Then I just sank to my knees.'

The first leg score of 3–3 meant, quite simply, that Forest would have to win in Cologne to reach the final. But the temptation to write them off was immediately challenged by Clough and Taylor.

'People thought I was putting a brave face on it when I predicted, straight after the game, that we would win over there', Taylor said. 'I knew our mistakes in the first leg were down to lack of application by our players. Doncaster Butchers would have taken advantage, never mind Cologne.

'Nothing made me change my mind about the Germans. I had watched them carefully, and I knew they were not a good side. That is why I forecast they would not score against us in Cologne. For Brian and myself, the European Cup was us against other managers. I did my homework on Weisweiler. My niece's husband had been a student of his in Germany, and told me that deep down he was a conservative man, who lacked courage and would try to protect what he had.'

It was a significant character reference. Weisweiler, knowing that a 0–0 result at home would put Cologne into the final, had to decide whether to play for a win or a draw. Clough and Taylor, confident of keeping a clean sheet, knew that Forest had to score. It was now that they proved beyond all doubt that they were tacticians when the occasion demanded, even though Clough's absences from the ground irked his critics.

'Because I wasn't on the training ground every five minutes, I was accused of not doing any coaching. Well, I was there enough, and I coached every time I opened my mouth.

'We told our lot how to play by breaking the game down into simple terms. Larry Lloyd and Kenny Burns would get worried about how the opposition would play and who they should mark. I told them to get on with their normal jobs. I would work out the opposition from the bench in the first five minutes.'

Brian Clough and Peter Taylor won the battle of wits with Hennes Weisweiler during Forest's semi-final second leg in Cologne. Forest won 1–0 with a goal by Bowyer to reach the final. (*Bob Thomas*)

Such a practical approach to what some modern coaches could make sound horribly complicated, only reiterated that Clough and Taylor's acumen lay in their mental approach. Now, as Forest prepared for their 55th competitive match of the season and their most important, they brought the players to peak performance in Cologne. 'People who knocked us asked why we took holidays during the season', said Clough. 'The answer was the other way round – we were successful because we took holidays. We stayed fresh, and we kept the players fresh.

'Some weeks we hardly trained at all,' said Shilton. 'Jimmy Gordon would just keep us ticking over, but Brian Clough and Peter Taylor relied on this fantastic motivation, on getting every player to give 110 per cent effort and concentration in every match. When you did that you were drained, so they wanted you to rest a lot before the next game.

'I think our attitude in Cologne was summed up at the kick-off. As soon as the ball was in motion, Tony Woodcock, Garry Birtles and Martin O'Neill rushed over the halfway line at their defence. It showed just how determined we were for what I think was the biggest test of character I had faced in my career.'

Shilton had Anderson and Burns back in front of him, and although Forest were without Gemmill, their concentration was total. Muller missed a rare chance early on, but later went off injured and was replaced by Flohe. Neither man was fit enough to play at his best.

With 65 minutes gone, there was no score and Cologne remained in front on away goals. Then, from Robertson's corner on the left, Birtles flicked the ball on from the near post and Bowyer, unmarked in the six-yard area, headed the ball past Schumacher. It was a simple goal, but its impact was profound. In that moment Weisweiler lost the battle of wits to Clough and Taylor, and Forest laid at least one hand on the European Cup.

It needed one magnificent, last-minute save by Shilton from Cologne's full back, Konopka, to secure their place in the final. 'Although I say it myself, it was a terrific shot. It swerved and did everything. I saved it going to my left and I remember thinking then that I had balanced the scales after what had happened in the first leg.'

When the final whistle went, Clough and Taylor shared a moment of private, mutual congratulation, then the manager grabbed his two sons, Nigel and Simon, as they came out of the crowd. Together, the three of them walked hand in hand round the running track, savouring Clough's finest hour. It was just two years, almost to the day, since Forest had lost at home to Cardiff in the second division and almost conceded their chance of promotion. Now they were in the final of the European Cup. No English club had ever come so far in such a short time.

'And it is all down to Brian Clough', admitted John McGovern when Forest arrived home in the early hours of the morning. 'I have been with him longer than any other player, but don't ask me to define his success. I can only say he makes you want to play for him.' A model character like McGovern could, perhaps, have been persuaded to play for a number of managers. But the men who went about Forest's business in the European Cup included a hothead in Lloyd, a discard in Clark, a rebel in Burns, a reject in Bowyer, and a once overweight and disinterested Robertson. Not to mention the men who got into the team by accident: Tony Woodcock, who might have gone to Lincoln or Doncaster; and Garry Birtles, who might still have been playing for Long Eaton.

Compared to some of the European giants of the past, Forest's team was a motley collection of characters who had lost their way, but found a common path under a managerial team whose ego was so big that no player was allowed any licence with his own. Not even Trevor Francis, the one million pound man who was now eligible for the European Cup final, having completed UEFA's three-month qualification. But would he be chosen? And in place of whom?

This propensity for keeping everybody on their toes, alternating the rows with the reassurance, was part of Clough's patented psychology. Nobody was allowed to take anything for granted, not even established internationals like Archie Gemmill and Martin O'Neill. Both insisted they were fully recovered from injury in time for the final in Munich, but Clough did not think so. He named both as substitutes, keeping Bowyer in Gemmill's position and giving Francis his début in European club football in O'Neill's role on the right hand side of the attack.

Later Clough said: 'No way would Francis have played if the others had been fully fit. He won a medal by a freak.'

Bob Houghton, with his soft speech and bright blue eyes maintaining a quiet dignity as manager of underdogs Malmo, could be excused for casting an envious glance towards the Forest reserves' bench when the teams came out in the Olympic Stadium. Both his central defenders, experienced internationals Bo Larsson and Roy Andersson, were ruled out of the final by injury. And in light training on the pitch the evening before the match, his captain and midfield general, Staffan Tapper, broke a toe. 'We were heavily criticised after the match for adopting negative tactics', said Houghton, 'but what were we supposed to do? Let Forest walk all over us? We knew they had better players than us, and our only chance was to try and stop them scoring.'

It was a similar attitude to that adopted by Happel and Bruges in the previous year's final against Liverpool, and the effect was identical in that the English champions were given a marked psychological advantage. Even though Peter Shilton was not looking forward to the final.

'I knew it would be a match in which I wouldn't have a lot to do, and those are always worrying for goalkeepers. I kept wondering if I could keep my concentration. Actually, I saw more of the ball than I expected, but my only worrying moment came early in the game. Kenny Burns misjudged a back pass as I came out, and their fellow Kinvall had a hell of a chance. If he had lobbed the ball over me, it was a goal, but he lost his confidence and mishit the shot, so I was able to jump and catch it.'

It was the only cause for concern for Forest and their 20,000 supporters, who did their best to give the final the special red and white flavour Liverpool had enjoyed in Rome two years earlier. Even so, the crowd of 57,000 was some 18,000 short of capacity, and the match never had the same distinction because it was so one-sided.

The decisive moment of the 1979 final – Trevor Francis, in his first European Cup match, hurls himself at Robertson's cross to head the winning goal.

Forest dominated the first half, with Francis on the right easily the most dangerous forward on the pitch. When he scored on the stroke of half-time, the move portrayed perfectly Forest's playing pattern. Robertson on the left wing, with his deceptive, hunched stride, had been drifting inside on his right foot until then. He suddenly beat Malmo's defenders on the outside, and whipped over a fierce cross from the dead ball line with his left foot. As the ball flew across the face of the Malmo goal, niether goalkeeper Moller nor his defenders could intercept. Francis, coming in at the far post, hurled himself forward to head high into the net. The goal actually came in time added on at the end of the half for stoppages, one of which was Malmo's substitution of Malmberg for Tapper, who managed to play in pain for 35 minutes.

In the second half, the lively Francis returned Robertson's compliment with a cross which the little Scot struck against the base of the post. But it was evident by then, that one goal would be enough. Malmo's attack was so lightweight, with Cervin ineffective and the anonymous Hansson taken off before the end, that Shilton and his defence had one of their easiest nights of the season. 'I suppose there was a sense of anti-climax at the end because we had been such hot favourites, and we would have liked to score more goals. The elation really hit me two days later, when I got home and it sunk in that we were European champions.'

Peter Taylor agreed: 'As a final it was a non-event. We won, and that was that. But what else could you expect after what happened in Cologne in the semi-final? We were never going to get the players psyched up like that again.' This time, Taylor and Clough responded to the final whistle with a perfunctory handshake, before running across the track to acknowledge the contribution made by Forest's supporters.

Clough went into the dressing-room only briefly to congratulate his players, then hurried off to Crete to resume a family holiday. 'How do you celebrate winning?' he asked later, 'my way was to get my feet up as soon as possible with the wife and kids. That was our 76th game of a very long season.'

There was no celebration banquet, Liverpool style. Forest would have flown back to Nottingham that night if they could. Instead they had to re-book their hotel, where some of the players went with their wives into the discotheque for a spontaneous champagne party. But the general mood in Munich was felt to be an anti-climax. The European press found the final a bore, condemning Malmo for their monotonous offside tactics. One writer suggested the European Cup, as a spectacle, was finished.

Forest celebrate victory over Malmo in Munich. Clough's team were virtually unknown in Europe when the season began but, like Internazionale and Celtic before them, won the famous trophy at the first attempt. (Left to right, back row): McGovern, Bowyer, Francis; (front): Lloyd, Robertson and Woodcock.

Maybe Forest did themselves a disservice by beating two of the best sides earlier in the competition, but there was no challenging their achievement; they were only the third club to win the European Cup at their first attempt, following Internazionale and Celtic, and the first English club to do so.

In the same season, Forest retained the Football League Cup, set a new Football League record of 42 consecutive games without defeat, and finished second in the first division to Liverpool.

Over two extraordinary seasons, Clough and Taylor's team had played 119 competitive matches in English and European football, and lost only eight. Not even Revie's Leeds in their prime, nor even Liverpool at their most consistent, could quote figures like those. Peter Shilton, whose arrival marked the start of the run, put it into perspective.

'I had never played for one of the big clubs like Liverpool, Manchester United or Spurs, where you don't have to build anything to get recognition. That really is the measure of what Brian Clough achieved at Forest – the fact that the club was never geared for his sort of success.

'In a funny way, though, I think it suited him and Peter Taylor to manage that sort of club. They are builders essentially, and I think their style of management demands they are in charge of absolutely everything. At a less fashionable club they could be. In terms of his personality and his ambition, Brian Clough was a total one-off. He was such a winner, so involved with what he was doing, that he would sometimes lose sight of the fact that other people had a job to do, and that could make him very intolerant.

'The key to how he survived was his double act with Peter Taylor, who was very much half the partnership. They bounced off each other superbly. When one was in a bad mood, the other would lift things. If one criticised a player, the other would soften it. They controlled us this way.'

His rival managers applauded Clough's success but still shook their heads at his outrageous methods. There was a lot of deep respect, too, for the loyal Jimmy Gordon, the silver-haired trainer who kept the Forest players in physical shape.

But as the football world went on trying to analyse something which seemed to defy analysis, Clough and Taylor revelled in a record at Derby and Forest unmatched by any of their counterparts. 'If you want the secret in two words' said Taylor, 'it's man management. You either have it or you haven't.'

'If you want it in one word', interjected Clough, 'it's talent'.

Before coming to England for the first leg of the European Cup quarter-final against Forest, Roger Berbig, genial goalkeeper of Swiss champions Grasshoppers, admitted with a smile: 'All I know about Nottingham is the story of Robin Hood'.

In 1979, the city had a footballing legend to savour.

CHAPTER ELEVEN

SILVER JUBILEE
(1980)

On the eve of the 25th anniversary of the European Cup. Bela Guttmann could be found addressing a small, attentive audience in the corner of a hotel lounge in Vienna. The little Hungarian itinerant, nearly 80 years old and domiciled in Austria, had a simple message after a lifetime in football all over the world. 'Please let us remember', he implored, hands held out in a solemn gesture, his eyes moving anxiously behind his dark glasses, 'the European Cup stands for great teams. And it should be about great players.'

Guttmann's concern for the stature of the competition he once ruled with Benfica, reflected a mood of disenchantment which spread across the continent after the 1979 final between Nottingham Forest and Malmo. The anglophile in Guttmann refused to blame Forest for an undistinguished match, neither would he criticise Liverpool for an equally mundane final against Bruges, a year earlier. But the fact that a Belgian side with no great ambition, and a Swedish team whose main weapon was a well-rehearsed offside trap, had in turn made drab a cup final which was supposed to be an international showpiece, led Guttmann to fear for the reputation of tournament he loved.

His foreboding was partially lifted by the field for the European Cup's silver jubilee. Although Guttmann's beloved Benfica had been squeezed out by FC Porto, by now their fiercest rivals in Portugal, fortune fittingly conspired to ensure that the big names the little coach demanded were in the draw for the 1979–80 competition. The presence of Real Madrid, Ajax, AC Milan, Liverpool, Celtic and Nottingham Forest, meant that six former winners were among the 33 starters; and between them, those six clubs had won the trophy in 15 of its 24 completed seasons.

Neither did the impressive parade of champions end there. Sitting in another corner of the same hotel, talking in German while Guttmann spoke in English, was Kevin Keegan, the European Footballer of the Year. To see Keegan fêted across a continent as an international celebrity, was ruefully to recall how awkwardly England had first responded to the call for competitive club football in Europe a quarter of a century earlier. How churlish and hesitant they had been, in the motherland of the game, to recognise the ideals and potential unveiled by Hanot and his pioneers. How proud they were now, not just in producing Keegan, but in having won the European Cup three years running – twice with Liverpool and once with Nottingham Forest. England, indeed, were the only country to have spawned three different winners of the trophy, Manchester United having put their name on the cup in 1968.

Keegan's club, Hamburg, were among the new pretenders for Europe's top prize. He had led them to their first Bundesliga championship, and to their first appearance among Europe's élite for 19 years. For Racing Club de Strasbourg, the new champions of France, it was a first appearance in the European Cup; and the draw also included hardened campaigners like Ujpest Dozsa, from Hungary, and Dukla Prague, champions again in Czechoslovakia.

So the ambitious and the established were busy preparing themselves for the 25th tournament, when UEFA decided to take a lead and marked their own anniversary by announcing a partial amnesty for over one hundred players who were under suspension at the start of the 1979–80 season. In reducing the length of bans carried over from the previous season, the European Union said their gesture should not be seen as a sign of weakness but as an act of encouragement for a higher standard of fairness and sportsmanship. They made a specific appeal to fans across the continent for the maintenance of law and order in stadiums. The age of the football hooligan had caused wanton damage far and wide, but it was violence of a political significance which gave the Silver Jubilee of the European Cup a sour start.

When Dundalk, the Republic of Ireland champions, were paired with their Northern Ireland counterparts, Linfield, in a preliminary round tie, it was only the second time in the competition's history that two Irish clubs had been drawn together. Waterford had defeated Glentoran in 1970. Linfield's home is Belfast, centre of the political strife in the province of Ulster which has caused some 2,000 deaths in Northern Ireland over the past decade. Sectarian killings between Catholics and Protestants had become horribly commonplace, but there was a renewed sense of shock and outrage when two days before Dundalk and Linfield were due to meet for the first time, Lord Mountbatten and three of his companions were murdered when the Provisional IRA blew up his fishing boat off the west coast of Ireland. Later the same day 18 soldiers were killed in an ambush at Warrenpoint on the Irish border.

A football match at Dundalk's Oriel Park barely 48 hours later was an obvious battle ground. Fighting broke out before the match between rival sets of supporters, and it had very little to do with any strong feelings for the football clubs of Dundalk and Linfield. English referee Pat Partridge tried to keep his concentration and that of the players on the match, which was drawn 1–1. But demonstrators clashed repeatedly with police on the terraces and in the stand. A third of the 100 people injured were policemen.

UEFA had no alternative but to prohibit Linfield from staging the second leg in Belfast a week later. So Haarlem, where football in the Netherlands began exactly 100 years earlier, offered their ground as a neutral venue for Linfield's 'home' match. Fewer than one thousand people saw Dundalk win 2–0 – one of the smallest crowds in the history of the European Cup. It was the start of a handy run for the Republic of Ireland champions. Their opponents in the first round proper were the moderate Maltese team, Hibernians, who lost 2–0 in Ireland and could only halve the deficit in the return. Later, Dundalk were to give some uncomfortable moments to Celtic, but the Scottish champions, managed now by their former European Cup winning captain Billy McNeill, found their problems started the moment the draw was made.

Albania were now back in the European Cup after being absent between 1971 and 1978, and their government acted obstructively when their champions, Partizani Tirana, were drawn at home to Celtic in the first leg. They took to extremes the common ploy by countries from the eastern bloc to delay issuing sufficient visas for travelling football parties from the west. The Albanians at first refused not only to admit supporters and journalists for the Celtic match, but would not even clear the full Scottish playing party. A number of deadlines went by, with Celtic at one point threatening to withdraw, before UEFA cleared the way for all their players and officials. But they could not persuade the Albanians to admit any fans or reporters.

Thankfully, Celtic won the tie after an uneasy start. They lost 1–0 in Tirana, and went further behind when Alan Sneddon put through his own goal early in the second leg at Parkhead. But then Davie Provan, later to be voted Player of the Year by his fellow professionals in Scotland, tore the Albanian defence asunder down the flanks. Celtic scored four goals from crosses, and could even afford to miss a penalty.

Liverpool, too, had visa problems in facing a journey into the unknown. In 99 European matches they had never played a team from the Soviet Union, but it was Tblisi in Georgia where they would fall in the first round of the European Cup – for the second year running. Anybody watching Liverpool regain their first division crown from Nottingham Forest, winning the championship for the 11th time with a record 68 points and conceding only 16 goals, would have placed long odds against an early exit in Liverpool's 16th consecutive season in European football. Dynamo Tblisi were something of an unknown quantity, but it was not the most encouraging time for Soviet football. The national team had just been ignominiously knocked out of the European Championship by Greece, and 17

Liverpool's three wise men – Ronnie Moran, Joe Fagan and Bob Paisley – stroll round the Tbilisi stadium before the first round match in September 1979. (*Harry Ormesher*)

players and officials of the Pakhtakor club, from Tashkent, were killed when their aeroplane crashed in the Ukraine on the way to a match in Minsk.

Pakhtakor recruited players from other clubs, and promptly defeated Liverpool's opponents Tblisi in a league match. The champions looked stale after playing 10 games in 27 days, including the Soviet cup final which they won on penalties against Moscow Dynamo. So when Tblisi's coach, Nodari Akhalkatsi, arrived in Liverpool to watch them play Coventry in early September, his task looked awesome. He added to the mystique of Soviet behaviour by booking into one of the city's least salubrious hotels – he was later rescued by Liverpool's general secretary Peter Robinson – and taking up his seat in the Anfield directors' box a full two hours before kick-off.

Liverpool rewarded his patience by beating Coventry 4–0, but the champions were not at their best. They failed to maintain the momentum of an outstanding display against Arsenal in the FA Charity Shield at Wembley, and dropped seven points in their first seven league games. Emlyn Hughes, having collected over £100,000 from his testimonial, had been sold to Wolves. He was suffering from a nagging knee injury which meant Liverpool no longer saw him as an automatic choice. But the additions Bob Paisley had made to his squad were not ready to face first division football, let alone the European Cup.

Avi Cohen, the Israeli international defender signed from the Maccabi club of Tel Aviv, was as yet unused to the pace of the English game. While Frank McGarvey, a 23-year-old winger signed for £300,000 from St Mirren and capped by Scotland during the summer, failed to earn a single first team game at Anfield. He was sold to Celtic seven months later for £275,000. So when Alan Hansen and Ray Kennedy both went down with untimely thigh injuries on the eve of the first leg against Tblisi at Anfield, Paisley called in defender Colin Irwin, a loyal reserve, and picked a 4–4–3 formation which included David Fairclough in attack with Kenny Dalglish and David Johnson. 'We definitely lost the tie in the first leg', Ray Clemence said later. 'We didn't take the initiative as we normally would at home, but you have to give Tblisi credit for that. They were a better side than we expected.'

The Soviet champions' cool temperament was quite unruffled by the proximity of the boisterous Anfield crowd. They showed a precision in their passing and a purpose in their running which shook Liverpool from the start. Attacking the Kop end in the first half, Tblisi were inspired by their midfield general, David Kipiani, and the Soviet player of the year, Ramaz Shengelia. The Georgians made and missed three good chances to the one Johnson took at the other end for Liverpool.

Tblisi equalised after 33 minutes with a fine goal from their sweeper, Chivadze. He began the move in his own half, took a return pass from Shengelia, and shot low under the left arm of Clemence as the goalkeeper came out. Jimmy Case restored Liverpool's lead with a fierce free kick on the stroke of half-time, but the former European Cup holders failed to score again when they played towards the Kop in the second half. Tblisi's goalkeeper, Gabelia, predictably rose to the occasion.

It was now debatable whether even Liverpool's vast European

experience would ensure survival with just a 2–1 lead. Trouble over
visas did not augur well, neither did a 1–0 defeat at Nottingham
Forest two days before Liverpool set off on the 3,000-mile journey to
Georgia for the second leg. An injury sustained at Nottingham now
ruled out Alan Kennedy, so although his namesake Ray and Alan
Hansen were both back, Liverpool were forced to play Irwin at left
back.

A student demonstration in their hotel at 4.00 am on the morning
of the match ensured that Liverpool's players did not get a good
night's sleep. 'It was obviously done deliberately. You need special
permission for that sort of thing over there', said Clemence ruefully.
But the England goalkeeper made three splendid saves in the first
half in Tblisi's Lenin Stadium, where the match was played on an
afternoon of pouring rain. There were those who felt Liverpool might
survive then, but they cracked under Tblisi's relentless pressure in the
second half. Clemence could only touch Kipiani's driven cross from
the right, and Vladimir Gutsaev bundled the ball in to put the
Georgians ahead on away goals. They did not need that technicality.
After 74 minutes, defender Chileya set off on what Clemence
described as 'the greatest run in the history of Liverpool Football
Club'.

'He must have covered 60 yards by the time he went past the fourth of our
defenders. Then he just pushed the ball to one side of me to Shengelia, who
only had to tap it into the net.'

Eight minutes from the end, when Phil Thompson was harshly judged
to have fouled Gutsaev, Tblisi made it 3–0 with Chivadze's penalty.
Liverpool's misery was complete. It was their heaviest defeat in
Europe since Ajax beat them 5–1 in 1966, and it was greeted by
78,000 delirious Georgians, who made torches out of lighted
newspapers to signal Tblisi's triumph.

Elimination from the European Cup in the first round for the
second time running hit Liverpool's pocket as well as their pride. To
a club whose running costs were now around £2 million a year, a
good run in the competition could have grossed £500,000. Said Peter
Robinson:

'Our normal income from domestic matches, advertising, television and
commercial activities would cover our expenditure, but it was from Europe
that we expected to make our profit.'

Ironically, the defeat in Tblisi was the low point of another otherwise
successful Liverpool season. They promptly went 19 matches without
defeat, won the first division championship for the 12th time, and
reached the semi-finals of both the Football League Cup and the FA
Cup.

Liverpool's was not the only famous scalp to be taken in the first
round of the 25th European Cup. AC Milan also discovered that
winning the trophy twice was no insurance against being toppled by
an unseeded team. Italy had been the scene of much political
manoeuvring since the end of the previous season. Nils Liedholm, the
57-year-old Swede whose love affair with Milan had begun 30 years
earlier when he was part of the Grenoli trio, had led the club to their
first Italian league title for 11 years. But although Liedholm was
hugely popular with the supporters, he refused a new contract –
accusing the club's directors of trying to line up his successor during

the championship season, with a view to moving him upstairs into a more general capacity.

Like all Italian clubs, Milan could be a political minefield as well as a football team. Gianni Rivera, having announced his retirement as a player at the age of 35, was one of the most influential figures in the boardroom, but he had been shocked earlier in the year by the death of his great mentor, Milan's old coach Nereo Rocco. As though there was some spiritual foreboding about the place, Liedholm's assistant, Alvaro Gasparini, also unexpectedly died; he suffered a heart attack in Buenos Aires while Milan were on a summer tour of South America. When the players returned, Liedholm was installed as the new coach at Roma and Milan's new boss was Massimo Giacomini, one of their former players who had made his name as a manager by bringing unfashionable Udinese from the third division of *Calcio* to the first. His first competitive exercise was the Santiago Bernabeu tournament in Madrid, UEFA having now given Real permission to stage a pre-season competition between four former European Cup winners in memory of their late president.

The tournament was won by Bayern Munich, but Milan lost their opening match against Ajax on penalties. Giacomini publicly rebuked two of his Italian stars, Roberto Antonelli and Walter Novellino, for ignoring his tactical instructions. Both players had been substituted. It was not a harmonious start for the new coach, especially as Milan's opponents in the first round of the European Cup, FC Porto, were among the dark horses. The Portuguese champions had lost only one league match the previous season, and two years earlier they had reached the quarter finals of the Cup Winners' Cup after an eventful victory over Manchester United.

A crowd of 55,000 paid record receipts of £130,000 to watch the first leg in Oporto, and they saw Milan achieve a predictable 0–0 draw thanks to practised defence. It was a familiar story and Italy assumed the second leg in Milan would be a formality. It might have been, had Milan's sweeper Franco Baresi not gone down sick just before the match. Giacomini had to replace him, besides gambling on the fitness of captain Albertino Bigon in midfield, and on the temperament of the relatively untried 19-year-old Francesco Romano. With an hour gone, there was still no score in the tie, but then Porto were awarded a free kick 25 yards out. Duda, the 32-year-old Brazilian dead ball specialist, bent his shot round an inadequate wall and saw another veteran, Milan's 39-year-old goalkeeper Enrico Albertosi, drop the ball from his chest against the post, whence it rebounded into the net.

Gianni Rivera, who had toyed with the idea of extending his 700-match career in order to play once more in the European Cup, must have regretted his decision to retire. Milan had no natural leader and their defeat was a bitter blow to Italian football in a season when they were to host the European Championship for national teams. Worse was to follow. In March 1980 Milan's president, Felice Colombo, was arrested together with 12 leading players on allegations of 'fixing' matches in a betting coup. Albertosi was among the first division stars whisked straight out of the dressing-room one Sunday and into waiting police cars. Even before the 'Totonero' scandal came to court, Colombo and Albertosi were banned for life by the Italian Football Federation; and Milan were relegated to Serie B, the Italian second division, despite finishing third in the 1979–80 championship. For a club which had twice won Europe's greatest prize, it was the ultimate indignity.

Meanwhile Milan's conquerors Porto threatened to spring another surprise. Their next opponents were more illustrious still, the second round draw coupling them with Real Madrid in a classic Iberian confrontation. The result was settled by the somewhat unlikely presence of a young West Indian from England. Real had lived up to their early European tradition by spending more on one player than ever before, but at the time of his transfer in the summer of 1979 he was largely unknown on the continent. Laurie Cunningham, born in London of Jamaican parents, had been playing on the wing just over two years earlier for Orient, one of the less fashionable second division clubs. Even when Johnny Giles signed him for West Bromwich Albion, Cunningham's obvious natural gifts of bewildering pace, sinuous ball skills and deadly finishing were subject to spells of brooding uncertainty. He became the first black player to represent England at under-21 level, and when Ron Greenwood capped him against Wales at the age of 23 in the 1979 Home Internationals, Cunningham had still to convince his critics.

Real signed him as replacement for the Danish international Henning Jensen, who had moved on to Ajax, and Cunningham now had to produce, in front of the critical Spanish public, the form he had shown for West Brom against Valencia in the previous season's UEFA Cup – the performance which first made Real aware of his potential. Fittingly, Valencia were the opposition in Cunningham's first Spanish league match for Real, and he seized the opportunity by scoring twice and making a third goal. Then, before a 110,000 crowd paying record receipts for the Bernabeu Stadium, he scored the winner against Real's oldest foe, Barcelona. The fans nicknamed him *El Negrito*, the little black one, as Cunningham and his girlfriend settled down to the Spanish lifestyle.

Injury prevented Cunningham playing in Real's opening European Cup match in Sofia, where they beat Levski Spartak 1–0. But he was back for the return at Chamartin, scoring from a penalty in a 2–0 win over the Bulgarian champions. Cunningham's early impact enabled Real's new coach, the Yugoslav Vujadin Boskov, to make light the loss of Juanito, the Spanish international forward banned from playing in European games after manhandling the referee when Real were knocked out of the previous season's tournament by Grasshoppers of Zurich. Even with the benefit of the amnesty, Juanito would not be available until the quarter-finals. But Cunningham was linking well with the strong Spanish international centre-forward, Santillana, and in midfield there was the combative Uli Stielike, who later that season was to help West Germany win the European Championship in Rome.

Real were led from the back by their captain Pirri, now 34 and a survivor of the team which had last taken the Cup to Madrid in 1966. His link with the days of Gento meant the chain of tradition was unbroken, and his influence from the sweeper's position was a vital ingredient in Real's new mixture of youth and experience. Pirri's absence from the first leg in Oporto nearly cost them dear. At half-time Real trailed 2–0 to a Porto side high on morale after the conquest of Milan; without their injured captain, they looked a confused and fragile side. But four minutes into the second half Porto's inconsistent goalkeeper Fonseca was penalised for taking more than four steps with the ball. Stielike pushed the indirect free kick to Cunningham, and his shot meant Real escaped with merely a 2–1 defeat. So when Cunningham supplied the cross from a corner for Benito to head the only goal of the second leg in Madrid, it meant Real were through on the 'away goals' rule, and that he had produced the two most telling moments in the tie.

If Cunningham was beginning to woo the Spaniards under their own sunshine, then another England international, Kevin Keegan, had already captured the admiration and imagination not just of one country, but of a whole continent. While piloting Hamburg to the Bundesliga title, the infectious character the Germans nicknamed 'Mighty Mouse' had been voted 1978 European Footballer of the Year. Could this be the same Keegan who, exactly one year earlier, had been at an all-time low? On the last day of 1977 Keegan played for Hamburg in a friendly match at Lubeck. Early in the game he was punched and kicked several times by a defender called Erhard Preuss, and eventually all the frustration of Keegan's first, unhappy months in Germany came to the boil. Keegan hit Preuss on the jaw with a perfect left hook, and knocked him unconscious with the right which followed. Then, without waiting for the red card, he walked off to face an automatic eight-week suspension.

'When I left Liverpool after helping them to win the European Cup in 1977, Hamburg looked exactly the kind of challenge I was after. But it proved a lot bigger than I expected. My first five months were terrible, especially as I did not know the language then. The other players shunned me, because there was jealousy over money. I had cost nearly twice as much as any other player in Germany, and having just won the Cup Winners' Cup themselves I suppose the Hamburg team saw me as an unnecessary luxury.'

The man who signed him, Hamburg's extrovert business manager Dr Peter Krohn, left during his first season. So too did the coach, Rudi Gutendorf. Word had it that Keegan too would be on his way. But when he returned from his two-month suspension, the atmosphere had softened. Hamburg had not played well in Keegan's absence, and he was to strike up an immediate rapport with the new general manager, Günter Netzer, the former West German international who had graced the European Cup with Borussia Moenchengladbach and Real Madrid. Hamburg's new coach, Branko Zebec, also had considerable experience in European football: the former Yugoslav international had played in the very first European Cup tie for Partizan Belgrade in 1955, and his demanding training methods took Hamburg to the Bundesliga championship in his first season in charge. Keegan scored 17 goals from midfield.

'I have never known such a transformation. Players who had snubbed me only a few months earlier were suddenly as friendly and as keen to help as the Liverpool lads had been. Zebec trained us harder than I had ever seen a coach work players before, but it got results.'

Zebec marked Hamburg's opening European Cup match by taking his wife, Dusica, to watch an important game for the first time in their 26 years of married life. The venue, of all places, was Iceland! Hamburg beat Reykjavik 3–0, thus removing all interest in the second leg. Only 5,000 Germans bothered to turn up and Keegan made both goals as Hamburg won, almost apologetically, 2–1.

But it was the goals he scored in the next round which underlined Keegan's claim for a second successive European player of the year award, and stamped Hamburg's credentials as possible European Cup winners. Their opponents now were Dynamo Tblisi, conquerors of Liverpool, and appropriately Keegan went a long way towards avenging the defeat of his old club. Hamburg won both legs – 3–1 in Germany and 3–2 in Georgia – but the Soviet side again acquitted themselves well, and Keegan's goals proved to be the turning point in both matches.

His re-election by correspondents of *France Football* as the 1979 European Footballer of the Year was virtually unopposed. As captain of a revitalised England team, Keegan had also led his country to the finals of the European Championship – their first significant achievement since reaching the quarter-finals of the 1970 World Cup. But even his admirers and associates at home were astonished when, in February 1980, Keegan suddenly announced he was coming back to England to play for Southampton. It was widely known that Keegan had negotiated the right to arrange his own transfer when his contract with Hamburg finished in the summer of 1980, but he had supported the popular belief that he would then go to increase his considerable fortune either in Italy, where Juventus were favourites to sign him, or in Spain. But Southampton's remarkable manager, Lawrie McMenemy, produced Keegan from behind a door at an incredulous press conference rather like a magician pulling a rabbit out of a hat. It was a master stroke which even the redoubtable Brian Clough was forced to applaud.

Clough and Nottingham Forest, meantime, had been forced to start their defence of the European Cup without the man whose goal enabled them to win it. Under a deal signed with the North American Soccer League Club, Detroit Express, while he was still with Birmingham City, Trevor Francis had spent the summer of 1979 playing in the United States and was not back at Forest in time to be registered for the first two rounds of the 1979–80 European Cup. It was an incongruous situation which Clough was forced to accept with some reluctance. When Francis came into the Forest side for his first League match of the season after recovering from a groin injury received in America, Clough told the press sarcastically: 'We are flying in some cheer leaders, and Trevor can have a hamburger with his cup of tea at half-time if it makes him feel at home.'

Forest began their second European Cup campaign at home, but the City Ground looked very different. A new £2½ million stand was being erected on one side, keeping the capacity down to 30,000 until it was completed in December, and keeping Forest's committee on edge about the extent of their financial outlay under Clough's ambitious control. Clough and Peter Taylor were determined to improve their team. Frank Gray was bought from Leeds United for £400,000 to replace the retired Frank Clark at left back, and Asa Hartford was signed for a similar fee from Manchester City, to fill the gap on the left side of midfield caused by Archie Gemmill's departure to Birmingham City. But Hartford only lasted 63 days. He played in three League matches, all of which Forest won, but was then transferred to Everton. The explanation was that Hartford did not fit the Forest pattern, and was not the right man to blend with Gray and John Robertson.

So the faithful Ian Bowyer, who had been on the point of leaving, stayed with a new contract and revived memories of Cologne by scoring both goals against the Swedish champions, Osters, who held

Forest until half-time in the first leg at Nottingham. It was when Forest arrived in Sweden for the second leg that the English press carried, under banner headlines, a withering outburst from Clough. This time, his target was the Forest committee.

'If they have the slightest doubt that Peter Taylor and I are handling their affairs to the best of our ability, I suggest they get someone else. Some football directors are a bunch of nobodies trying to be somebody through football. They are welcome to do so, but not off my back. Let them earn their own corn.'

It was typical of Clough, never one to bow to diplomacy, that he should choose to throw down the gauntlet at a time when the options for Forest and their committee were so clearly defined: either to continue to pursue domestic and European success under the expensive, expansive Clough-Taylor regime; or else to withdraw into what might otherwise be anonymity. Although Clough later apologised publicly for his remarks, it was clear there was a running battle on policy, and especially on how Forest's money was being spent, between management and committee.

But those members who travelled with the Forest party to the second leg in Sweden might have reminded themselves just how far Forest had been removed from any sort of European trip only three years earlier. This one was fairly uneventful, although Forest went a goal down to Osters and three of their players – Anderson, Birtles and Woodcock – were shown the yellow card. Woodcock scored the equaliser, heading in a cross from 17-year-old Gary Mills, who was playing in place of the ineligible Francis.

The holders now found themselves drawn against Arges Pitesti of Rumania, who had the sort of reputation one might expect from a team based in Dracula country. In the first round the Transylvanians had put out AEK Athens, and so incensed the Greek fans in the second leg that the windows of the referee's dressing-room were smashed after the game. The incident earned AEK a ban from the next European competition for which they qualified. The Rumanians were certainly not particular about their behaviour when they played at Nottingham in the first leg of the second round. Defender Zamfir was sent off after a series of blatant fouls, but they managed to keep Forest down to two goals. These came in the opening quarter of an hour from Woodcock and Birtles, and when Forest travelled to Rumania to play the second leg in the shadow of the Caucasian mountains, they killed off Pitesti's hopes by again scoring twice early in the game – this time through Bowyer and Birtles.

The Rumanians thus found themselves four goals down, and managed only a second half penalty in reply. Forest were now unbeaten in 13 European Cup matches, and in six away legs had conceded only four goals, three of them penalties.

One of the drawbacks of whetting the appetite of their players for European football was the departure of Tony Woodcock. He was the only member of Forest's squad not to sign a new three-year contract in the autumn of 1979; his eyes were fastened instead on the financial security acquired on the continent by Keegan and Cunningham. Woodcock signed, in November, for the West German club Cologne, whose European Cup ambitions he and Forest had punctured in the semi-final only seven months earlier. Forest received a fee of £650,000, only half the money they could have commanded from another English club now that players in the Football League were changing hands for up to £1½ million. But it was still more than the statutory limit of £500,000 which, under UEFA rules, would have been the maximum payable to Forest by a continental club when Woodcock's contract finished at the end of the season. Forest had no option but to cut their losses. Rewards for top players on the continent had now far outgrown what English clubs could afford. It was estimated that Woodcock would earn £250,000 in two years in Germany, and even that would not put him in the millionaire bracket to which Keegan now belonged.

The movement of players between European countries had now become so commonplace that the acquisition of one man with star quality could make the difference between a good and an outstanding side. One transfer could tip the scales sufficiently to change the course of the European Cup. Hence Cologne's anxiety to strengthen their side with Woodcock in an attempt to prise the Bundesliga title away from Hamburg, and out of the reach of the improving Bayern Munich. Even though their coach, Hennes Weisweiler, was on his way to New York Cosmos.

When a player of rare pedigree became available at the end of his contract, there was no shortage of takers. Such was the case with the Ajax captain, Ruud Krol, the only survivor from their European Cup winning team of the early 1970s. Krol led the Dutch club to a league and cup double in 1978–79, but there were many in the Netherlands who thought his departure, with his contract having expired, was inevitable.

'Real Madrid and Arsenal were both interested in signing me, but Ajax offered me such a good new contract that I decided to stay in the Netherlands for another year. But comparing the Ajax team of 1979 with the side we had when Cruyff was here, I did not think we had a chance of winning the European Cup again.'

And 12 days before they started their campaign, Ajax sacked the coach who had guided them to the double, Dutchman Cor Brom. His dismissal followed a protracted rift in his relationship with the forceful Ajax president Ton Harmsen. Brom was succeeded by 37-year-old Leo Beenhakker, promoted from his post as youth team manager at Ajax. He had previously managed three less celebrated clubs in the Netherlands.

The team Beenhakker inherited included two Danish inter-nationals, Soren Lerby and Frank Arnesen, in midfield. A third Dane, Henning Jensen from Real Madrid, had been bought as a replacement for top scorer Ray Clarke, the Englishman who went to Bruges but was soon to move back home to Brighton. Jensen wrote his name in European Cup history, alongside that of Scotsman Gordon Smith, when he made his first Ajax appearance in the competition. He had previously played for Borussia Moenchengladbach and Real, and thus equalled Smith's record of appearing in the competition with three different clubs. But it was 19-year-old Ton Blanker, promoted by Beenhakker from the youth team he had groomed, who made his name in the opening rounds. Ajax, against pitifully weak opposition, created a record by scoring 26 times in their first three matches.

They beat the Finnish champions, HJK Helsinki, by the same 8–1 margin home and away; then crushed Omonia Nicosia, of Cyprus,

10–0 in the first leg in Amsterdam. Blanker scored four goals in the second leg against Helsinki – in his first full European match – and added a hat trick against the Cypriots. Lerby scored five in this match, equalling the highest individual total for a single game in the competition. But Ajax fined their players for a strolling, casual approach to the second leg, which they lost 4–0 in Nicosia. With their champions in the quarter-finals of the European Cup and their national team winning in East Germany to qualify for the European Championship finals, the Dutch were buoyant again despite the defection to the United States of Cruyff, Neeskens and Wim Jansen. Ajax were strong in attack down both flanks thanks to the control and speed of Tscheu La Ling, a player of Chinese descent who played on the right, and Simon Tahamata, the South Moluccan, who preferred to play on the left.

With Ajax, Forest, Real Madrid and Hamburg all safely through to the quarter-finals, the tournament was assuming the type of quality Guttmann had called for. A touch of romance was provided by the part-time Irishmen from Dundalk, whose victories over Linfield and Hibernians of Malta earned them a crack at Celtic in the second round.

On the night before the first leg in Glasgow, Dundalk's genial manager Jimmy McLaughlin encouraged his players to go into the city and have a few drinks. 'I don't want you lying in bed worrying about Celtic', he said. 'Stay out until two o'clock in the morning if you feel better for it.' Any misgivings McLaughlin might have had when his team trailed 3–1 at half-time were more than forgotten when substitute Mick Lawlor – one of two brothers in the Dundalk team – scored in the second half. His goal meant that Celtic would go out of the competition if they lost 1–0 in Ireland.

Dundalk resisted the temptation to make a financial killing and switch the second leg to Dublin. Instead, they crammed 16,500 into their own Oriel Park ground, but there were no repeats of the Linfield riots. Celtic, as a club of Catholic origin, were popular visitors to the Republic. Sanity also prevailed on the field. The Scottish champions obeyed to the letter manager Billy McNeill's instructions to play sensibly, and they secured the goalless draw they needed. Celtic were in the last eight of the European Cup for the first time in six years.

Also there, but in their case at the first attempt, were the French champions Racing Club de Strasbourg. Their achievement confirmed the growing regard for their 38-year-old coach Gilbert Gress, whose long hair and spectacles made him look, at first sight, more like a poet or a musician than a football manager. Gress was born in Strasbourg, signed for them as a young professional, and later moved to Stuttgart in West Germany. His exile was one reason why he won only three caps for France, but when he returned home he played for Olympique Marseille and scored against Ajax in the European Cup in the 1971–72 season. Now Gress would grapple with the Dutch again, in the 1980 quarter-finals, but not before his aspiring young team overcame the challenge of the Norwegian champions, Start Kristiansand, and the experienced Czechs, Dukla Prague.

Strasbourg had won their first French title on average home gates of 14,000 and with a first team squad of only 14 players. Gress knew the team had to be increased in scope, and made two new signings – the Swiss midfield schemer Michel Decastel, and the most consistent goalscorer in French football, the Argentine Carlos Bianchi. Now 31, Bianchi had made himself something of a legend on two continents. For six years he had scored regularly for the Velez Sarsfield club in Buenos Aires, and retained the habit when Reims brought him to France in 1973. From there he moved to Paris St Germain, and twice finished runner-up in the 'Golden Boot' award for the top scorer in Europe. His career total at the beginning of the 1979–80 season was 292 goals in 12 seasons.

Had it not been for the prolific form of the home-based Leopoldo Luque, Argentina's coach Cesar Luis Menotti would have considered Bianchi as a member of his 1978 World Cup squad. As it was, Carlos was given a belated chance to leave his mark on the European Cup. He did so in the first round, scoring a hat-trick against the Norwegians whom Strasbourg beat 6–1 on aggregate. But Bianchi's overall contribution to a game was something Gress questioned, which was why he was left out when they played Dukla Prague in the second round.

The Czechs, who had already beaten Ujpest Dozsa, gave the French defence a thorough examination in the first leg in Prague. But all they had to show for their possession was a penalty goal by Vizek. The Alsacians fell over themselves to get tickets for the return in Strasbourg's compact Meinau Stadium. It was packed to its 35,000 capacity, and Gress took the tension out of the occasion with a prescient team talk. 'Do not be impatient', he implored his players. 'You have 90 minutes to equalise, and two further periods of 15 minutes to qualify for the quarter-finals.'

Halfway through the second half Strasbourg had still not breached the Czech defence, and the crowd were beseeching Gress to bring Bianchi off the substitutes bench. So he did, and three minutes later the popular Argentine had a hand in the goal scored by Francis Piasecki which levelled the aggregate and sent the tie into the predicted extra time. With only three minutes left, and penalties imminent, Strasbourg's other summer signing, Decastel, popped up with a dramatic winning goal. It was a famous victory, confirming that Gress was a coach capable of drawing every ounce from the players at his disposal.

But against Ajax in the quarter-final, that was not enough. This time Strasbourg played the home leg first, the onus on them to break down a disciplined Dutch defence superbly marshalled by Krol. Bianchi was absent through injury, and Strasbourg's hopes of a breakthrough were further dashed when an injury to Roland Wagner, their striker who played on the right, led to him being replaced after an hour. Piasecki, thrust into the centre-forward position, was not as effective, and the first leg ended in a goalless draw.

The second leg, watched by a 48,000 crowd in the Olympic Stadium in Amsterdam, was a personal triumph for Krol, who made three of the four Ajax goals. Strasbourg held out until he initiated a fine move after 33 minutes, to which Dick Schoenaker – the midfield player the Dutch called 'The Metronome' – applied the finishing touch with a header at the far post. Three minutes later Arnesen got the second; the powerful running of Lerby and La Ling, who each added a further goal in the second half, left their French markers a yard or more behind.

The three other quarter-finals were very much in the control of the English: Nottingham Forest provided one of the great away

performances of the European Cup after losing the first leg at home
to Dynamo Berlin; while exiled internationals Keegan and
Cunningham played a significant part in the further progress of
Hamburg and Real Madrid. The Germans were involved in a
three-way tussle with Cologne and Bayern Munich in an attempt to
retain their Bundesliga title, a cause not helped when Ivan Buljan,
valuable in defence or midfield, contacted hepatitis. Günter Netzer,
resigned now to losing Keegan at the end of the season, paid Hertha
Berlin £200,000 for Jurgen Milewski, a 22-year-old who could cover
the midfield or forward positions. Neither Buljan nor Milewski were
in the Hamburg team for the first leg of the quarter-final against
Hajduk Split. The Yugoslav champions, who had sold Buljan to
Hamburg, had reached the last eight by beating their counterparts
from Turkey and Denmark, Trabzonspor and Vejle.

Tomislav Ivic, the Hajduk coach, had been in charge at Ajax for
two years from 1976 to 1978, leading them to a European Cup
quarter-final in his second season in Amsterdam. Now he had taken
the Yugoslav champions the same distance with a team which
included nine internationals. Among them were two survivors from
the 1974 World Cup finals in West Germany: the striker Ivo Surjak
and the dependable defender, Drazen Muzinic.

Their return to West Germany for the first leg of the quarter-final
in Hamburg was a mixed one. Split were confident after thrashing
Manchester United 6–0 in a friendly, and could feel satisfied with
restricting Keegan and company to a single goal. But it was the
manner in which it was scored which upset the Yugoslavs. It came
when Keegan made a run down the left just before half-time, and
centre-forward Horst Hrubesch, in trying to reach the ball, appeared
to foul the Split goalkeeper, Pudar. The ball ran on to Willi
Reimann, but as he scored his colleague Hrubesch now appeared to
be offside. The Scottish referee, Ian Foote, gave neither a foul nor
offside and it proved to be the only goal of the game.

Hrubesch played a crucial part too in the second leg in Split, for
which Hamburg had Buljan and Milewski fit again. After only two
minutes, Hrubesch seized on a defensive error to increase Hamburg's
lead, but Zlatko Vujovic, one of the 21-year-old twins in the Hajduk
side, got a goal back after 21 minutes. Two minutes later Manfred
Kaltz, Hamburg's accomplished international defender, brought down
Borisav Djordjevic and Hajduk's Boro Primorac had the chance to
level the aggregate with a penalty. But Hamburg's goalkeeper Rudi
Kargus made a save which proved to be the turning point in the
match. Two minutes later Holger Hieronymus, a 20-year-old making
an impact at left back, scored a stunning goal to restore Hamburg's
two-goal advantage. Although Hajduk wiped that out with second
half goals by Djordjevic and Primorac, their 3–2 victory merely
meant that the Germans went through thanks to their away goals.

Keegan had a fine match, and so on the same night did Laurie
Cunningham, as Real Madrid turned round a two-goal deficit against
Celtic. Both Celtic's goals in the first leg had come in the second half
from crosses by Alan Sneddon. The first was scored by George
McCluskey after a mistake by Real goalkeeper Garcia Remon; the
second by Johnny Doyle, who beat two Real defenders to head a
goal which the 67,000-strong Parkhead crowd felt would be enough to
see the Scottish champions through to the next round.

With Pirri returning from injury and Stielike released to play in midfield, Real were a different proposition before 110,000 Spaniards in the Bernabeu Stadium a fortnight later. It was Cunningham's night; but before he had time to get going, Celtic could have put the tie beyond Real's reach. Doyle missed a good chance after five minutes, and McCluskey hit the bar. A minute before half-time, with Celtic's two-goal advantage still intact, Cunningham hit one of his now famous inswinging corners with the outside of his right foot. Santillana appeared to impede goalkeeper Peter Latchford before forcing the ball over the line, but the goal was allowed.

Real drew level 11 minutes into the second half. Cunningham worked his passage down the left, and his cross was meticulously headed down by Santillana for Stielike to score. Four minutes from the end, Cunningham switched to the right again and put Angel away behind the defence. As three Celtic players were drawn towards the ball, his cross to the far post was joyfully headed in by Juanito. So Real, motivated by high bonuses and the knowledge that the 1980 final would be played in their own stadium, were through to the semi-finals; and this was after trailing by two goals in the last two rounds.

Even their recovery rate, however, could not be compared with that of Nottingham Forest. The holders contrived to lose at home to Dynamo Berlin in the first leg of the quarter-final, yet went to East Germany and won handsomely against all the odds. Forest's form since they defeated Arges Pitesti in the second round four months earlier had been decidedly inconsistent by their standards. Having lost only six first division matches in the previous two seasons, they now lost six away games in succession. Woodcock's departure to Cologne left Clough and Taylor bemoaning the lack of a first-class forward to play alongside Birtles. They still needed convincing that this was the right position in which to use Francis, who frequently found himself playing from the right side of midfield.

That would have been a permanent move had Forest managed to swap Martin O'Neill for Coventry's burly striker Mick Ferguson. The deal fell through after the clubs had agreed terms, so O'Neill stayed with the European Cup holders. Forest also flirted with the idea of buying Charlie George, whose immense natural talent had been seen in the European Cup with Arsenal and Derby. Now, at Southampton, George nursed a nagging knee injury, and Clough decided not to buy him after his month's loan at Forest. But while he was there, George played a significant part in helping Forest win another European trophy. His goal in the first leg of the Super Cup against Barcelona gave the European Cup holders a lead to take to Spain, where they drew 1–1 thanks to a headed goal by Burns.

So when Forest finally resumed their defence of the champions Cup, the only new face in their side was that of Stan Bowles, like George a player of acknowledged gifts which had too often been marred by inconsistency. Bowles made his Forest début two days before his 31st birthday. Forest used him largely on the left hand side of midfield, but if he possessed the pure skill which made £200,000 seem a modest price, his application was sufficiently arguable for Clough to prefer the more pedestrian Ian Bowyer in tough away matches. That was the pattern in the quarter-final against Dynamo Berlin. The East Germans were playing in the competition for the first time, and sprang a double surprise when they came to Nottingham for the first leg.

Hans-Jurgen Riediger, their blond 24-year-old striker, had been out of the team for months with a broken ankle, and Forest were surprised to see him take the field. Still more by his 73rd-minute goal which threatened to knock them out of the competition. Having survived against a toothless Forest attack, Dynamo suddenly swarmed out of their own half and their captain Frank Terletzki pitched a brilliant crossfield pass at Riediger's feet. Already goal-side of Frank Gray, he brushed past Burns and shot wide of Shilton in the same movement. It was the only goal of the first leg. Forest created only two chances, missed by Birtles and Francis, and Burns collected his second yellow card of the tournament. Now he would miss the trip to Berlin.

Comparisons with the previous season's semi-final against Cologne were now inevitable. Then Forest had drawn 3–3 at home and gone to West Germany needing to win. Now they had to win again, but this time behind the Berlin Wall, and by more than one goal. The weekend before the second leg there was a classic illustration of how misleading domestic form can be. While Dynamo put 10 goals past Chemie Leipzig in the East German Oberliga, League Cup holders Forest went to Wembley for the third year running in that competition and lost 1–0 to Wolves. Although Forest had more of the play, scoring a goal was again beyond them. So when Shilton and Needham collided to present Andy Gray with an easy winner for Wolves, it meant another Wembley win for Emlyn Hughes. 'At the moment I couldn't even lift a glass of champagne', was Clough's reply when asked whether he could raise his side's morale in time for the return in Berlin four days later.

But by the time the Forest party assembled at East Midlands airport on the Monday morning the mood was already rising. Clough gave Trevor Francis a typical blast on the sports pages, while Taylor insisted that most of the writers had got it wrong anyway – Forest, he said, had played well at Wembley without scoring. The only change they made was to bring back Larry Lloyd, who missed the League Cup final through suspension, in place of Burns, now missing for that very reason. Bowyer was preferred on the left hand side of midfield to Bowles, who had not been eligible for Wembley. But where would Francis play? Having decided to move him back to the right wing where he played in the previous year's final against Malmo, Clough took his £1 million matador on to the pitch in Berlin to sample the atmosphere.

'When I asked him where he wanted to play, he looked at me with those lovely eyes of his and said he felt like performing up front. So we took him to get changed and told Martin O'Neill he was back on the right.'

It was another instinctive, brash decision by the Forest management and again their bravado paid huge dividends. Francis scored after 15 minutes to level the tie, then turned swiftly to strike the goal which put Forest ahead after 35 minutes. Three minutes later, they were in dreamland. Robertson was brought down by Noack and scored from the penalty. The holders were three goals up – and two ahead on aggregate – with seven minutes left in the first half. Clearly, Dynamo were uncertain how to approach a home match when they already held the aggregate lead. But more than that, they were outwitted by Clough and Taylor, outgunned by Francis.

The East Germans came to life when Terletzki scored from a

Trevor Francis, restored as a striker by Brian Clough, scores Nottingham Forest's second goal in Berlin, despite the challenge of Dynamo's Rainer Troppa. Forest won 3–1 to reach the semi-final in thrilling fashion. (*UPI*)

penalty early in the second half, but with Shilton and McGovern at their best, Forest held on to win 3–1, 3–2 on aggregate. Clough and Taylor, having worked a miracle again in front of Europe's football sophisticates, went home muttering about still needing a striker and a midfield player. As for Francis, he went to Spain with England a week later and scored again – playing up front!

UEFA departed with tradition and held the semi-final draw on Saturday night, so that it could be screened live across the continent by Swiss television. It brought Forest out of the vase first, to be paired with Ajax, and gave England's two exiled competitors, Kevin Keegan and Laurie Cunningham, the chance to shine in a match which brought together Hamburg and Real Madrid. Real were drawn at home in the first leg, their players and 110,000 supporters hoping it would be a prelude to their appearance in the final in the Bernabeu Stadium seven weeks later. They were not alone in considering that the biggest obstacle to their ambitions was Kevin Keegan. By now the England captain was widely regarded as one of the best three players in the world, and with his immediate future settled he was playing for club and country at the peak of his form. But even the man-to-man marking which Keegan was used to overcoming in the Bundesliga had not shackled him as effectively as did the virtually unknown teenager Perez Garcia, who Real appointed to shadow him in the first leg. It was only Garcia's fourth senior match for Real.

Hamburg elected to play defensively and spent most of the match trying to keep the Spaniards at bay. The fact that they did so until well into the second half was due partly to goals by Santillana and Cunningham being disallowed, and Cunningham's header being cleared off the line with Kargus beaten. But Cunningham and Santillana would not be stopped. The strong centre-forward scored twice in 13 minutes in the second half: the first when Hamburg left a gap in the centre of their defence; the second from a move started by Cunningham but really engineered by Stielike, who beat everybody including the goalkeeper before Santillana applied the finishing touch.

Had Cunningham's crashing volley gone in, rather than hitting the bar, Real would have had a three-goal lead. As it was, they finished the first leg leading 2–0 and Keegan said optimistically: 'I am certain we can score enough goals in Hamburg to win the tie.' He was not to know how accurate his prediction would be, still less the drama which was to unfold in Hamburg's Volkparkstadion, where the second leg of the 1980 semi-final was a match worthy of comparison with the most memorable in the history of the European Cup. Again it was played before a capacity crowd, but 61,000 was but half the attendance in Madrid. This time, Hamburg had Buljan back in their defence, but their midfield player Jimmy Hartwig was in hospital for a cartilage operation.

Real, with Benito back in their defence, again appointed Perez Garcia to shadow Keegan, but this time the youngster was overawed by the task and the occasion. After 11 minutes he brought the Englishman crashing down in the penalty area, and Manny Kaltz scored from the penalty. Six minutes later, Hamburg levelled the tie. Their impressive blond centre-forward Horst Hrubesch beat Garcia Remon with a flying header. Soon afterwards Real took off their goalkeeper and brought on substitute Miguel Angel. They blamed an injury to Remon, but he came off with eyes glazed; his team were in grave danger of being obliterated by the German onslaught. Yet, incredibly, Real regained the initiative. Hamburg's goalkeeper, Rudi Kargus, left his line and failed to gather the ball. Cunningham took advantage of his mistake with a precise lob. Hamburg attacked again, but the away goal meant they now needed two more to go in front: the first came from Kaltz, a blistering drive from 25 yards; the second was another header by Hrubesch. At half-time Hamburg led 4–1, 4–3 on aggregate.

They did not falter again. Keegan led Real such a dance that young Garcia was taken away from his marking job, and when the experienced Vicente Del Bosque took over, he lost his temper and hit Keegan in the face. Del Bosque was sent off. In the last seconds of the match Hrubesch set up a fifth and final goal for Caspar Memering and Real came off the pitch bewildered at losing 5–1.

So Hamburg were through to the final and Keegan heard in the dressing-room that their opponents were to be Brian Clough's Nottingham Forest. It was clear in the first leg at Nottingham that Ajax, with the distinguished exception of Krol, were nothing like the side they had once been. The Danes Lerby and Arnesen were talented, their forwards La Ling and Tahamata were fast, but they did not have the presence of Neeskens, the brains of Haan, the ingenuity of Keizer, still less the omnipotence of Cruyff.

Forest's own natural matchwinner, Trevor Francis, gave the Dutch a harrowing night. He struck twice, first when Ajax made a mess of a Robertson corner after 33 minutes, then in the second half when he retrieved a loose ball and hooked in a cross which defender Cees Zwamborn handled. John Robertson scored from the penalty – his 13th successful kick of the season – and Forest finished the first leg 2–0 ahead. But for Ajax goalkeeper Piet Schrijvers making two good saves from O'Neill, it would have been more.

For the second leg in Amsterdam's Olympic Stadium, Ajax dropped the ineffective Tahamata and instead played Karel Bonsink, who had come on as substitute at Nottingham. Forest again selected Bowyer ahead of Bowles. And again Clough's team had the resources to cope before a capacity crowd of 67,000. Indeed, Francis might have scored from a header. As it was Ajax set up a sustained attack. Burns and Lloyd rose to the occasion, and behind them Shilton produced three excellent saves when they were needed. Two of these came from free kicks, but apart from set pieces the Dutch could not get through. Their only goal came from a corner after 63 minutes, when Forest left Lerby unmarked on the far post, enabling him to score with a header.

The only scare in the closing minutes came when Henning Jensen stole in unmarked at the far post, but he placed his header straight into Shilton's arms. Forest were through to their second consecutive final on a 2–1 aggregate.

It was the end of the European road for Ruud Krol. The great defender was outstanding in both matches against Forest, his presence enabling Ajax to retain their domestic championship and qualify again for the European Cup. But Krol – briefly having been linked with Forest – left for Vancouver Whitecaps, joining the trail of Dutch internationals now making their living in the North American League.

So the 25th European Cup final would be between Nottingham Forest, the holders, and Hamburg, still striving to retain their Bundesliga title in the face of a furious challenge from Bayern Munich. Kevin Keegan found time to lead England to victory over the world champions, Argentina, in a friendly at Wembley, and when asked whether he saw the final in Madrid as a personal conflict between himself and Brian Clough, replied coyly: 'Not really. From where I am, I might just be able to score a goal. From where he is sitting, he will find that very difficult.' But before deciding how to combat Keegan, Clough was stunned by a serious injury to his own England player, Trevor Francis. The Forest management pair were actually away spying on Hamburg when their £1 million forward severely tore an achilles tendon during a home match against Crystal Palace. An operation the following day ruled Francis out of football for months. He would miss not only the European Cup final, but also the European Championship finals in Italy. It was a cruel blow for the man whose goal had won the European Cup a year earlier. Sharply critical of Francis at times during the season, Clough now seemed to feel the blow as keenly as the player. Since the tactical switch in Berlin, Francis had been playing the best football of his short Forest career.

In their remaining matches before the final Forest tried a number of permutations to discover the most suitable support for Garry Birtles, himself an international after coming on as a substitute for England against Argentina. Clough withdrew all his players bar one for the Home Internationals which followed. The exception was Larry Lloyd, recalled by England after an absence of eight years to cap a season in which he was voted Player of the Year by Forest's supporters. Lloyd was injured during England's unhappy 4–1 defeat by Wales at Wrexham but his ankle mended in time for the European Cup final. The absentee on the plane to Madrid, apart from Francis, was the enigmatic Stan Bowles.

Apparently piqued by being left out of certain matches, Bowles walked out of the Forest ground before John Robertson's testimonial match. Then he failed to turn up for the team's trip to Majorca the week before the final. It was not the first time in his wayward career that Bowles had gone missing, but by acting in haste he deprived himself of an opportunity to right a number of wrongs. He would almost certainly have played in Madrid, and by going absent without leave became one of the few men to turn down the opportunity of playing in a European Cup final.

Thus Forest became the first club to go into such an important match a player short! They took a squad of only 15 to Spain, leaving themselves one substitute less than the permitted five; even more important, four of the men who at one time could have worn the number 10 shirt, were absent: the departed Woodcock, the injured Francis, the rejected Charlie George, and the unhappy Bowles.

If Clough and Taylor were to be tested once more, the strain of management at top level had taken its toll on Hamburg's Branko Zebec. During one league match he had to be carried to the team bus after collapsing on the touchline bench, suffering from a stomach complaint. His recovery was hardly hastened when, four days before the Madrid final, Hamburg lost their Bundesliga championship. They were beaten 2–1 at Leverkusen in their penultimate league match which enabled Bayern Munich, under the general management of their former European Cup star Uli Hoeness, to clinch the title by beating Stuttgart.

To make things worse, Hamburg's centre-forward and semi-final hero, Horst Hrubesch, suffered an ankle injury which meant he was unlikely to be available for the final. With midfield player Jimmy Hartwig already ruled out after a cartilage operation, Hrubesch's absence would, according to Günter Netzer, be as big a setback to Hamburg as the Francis injury was to Forest. After Keegan, the tall, blond Hrubesch was Hamburg's most expensive player. He had cost £325,000 from Rot-Weiss Essen, and at 29 was suddenly attracting international attention. Nicknamed by the fans *das Ungeheur* ('the monster'), he would later prove West Germany's match winner in the European Championship final in Rome.

So Forest and Hamburg went into the final with three things in common: both had a key forward injured; neither would play in the European Cup the following season if they lost; and neither could easily afford the financial loss which such an absence would cause.

The Germans, thanks to sponsorship by British Petroleum and earlier by Hitachi, had been generous with their team. And if transfer fees were not as high as in England, wages were certainly higher. Furthermore, the impending departure of Keegan and defender Peter Nogly meant there would be a period of change before Hamburg had such a good chance again of winning the Cup.

For Forest, defeat would carry a heavier penalty still. They would be out of Europe in 1980–81, having missed the UEFA Cup by losing the League Cup and finishing fifth in the first division. As Peter Taylor said when Forest left Nottingham on the Monday before the final: 'Depending on the result on Wednesday, a minor or major rebuilding job will be necessary.'

And then we were in Madrid: the city of wide, tree-lined avenues where 25 years earlier Di Stefano and Gento had given the European Cup its early impetus, its unique identity. It was appropriate that the huge bowl at Chamartin, to which the endearing Santiago Bernabeu had given his name, should stage the Silver Jubilee final. Were he or his fellow pioneer Gabriel Hanot still alive, they might have been startled to find an English team in the final for the fourth year running. They would have recalled how 25 years earlier the Football League had baulked Chelsea's entry in the first tournament, then remembered how Matt Busby and his babes had left a legacy which Liverpool and Nottingham Forest now inherited.

Forest trained at the Bernabeu Stadium the day before the game. One was struck by the tanned, relaxed faces, the disarming mood produced by the tune-up in Majorca. Eight of the team had played the year before against Malmö, and Martin O'Neill, whose disappointment at being an unused substitute that night almost led to him leaving the club, made nine survivors from the 1979 squad. The newcomers were each making history: at left back Frank Gray became the first player to appear in the European Cup final for two English clubs, having been a member of the Leeds team beaten by Bayern Munich in Paris five years earlier; and 18-year-old Gary Mills, selected to wear the Forest number 10 shirt, was the youngest-ever British finalist. 'It's not Mills who has something to prove as much as Garry Birtles', was Clough's pre-match conclusion. 'Sometimes he plays like an amateur. How well he leads our line against Hamburg will be vital to how we get on.'

Peter Taylor, true to the style of the two men, was less effusive and more succinct. 'If you're a betting man', he advised, 'I should get your money on us to win 1–0.' We remembered what he had said before the match in Cologne: 'we will win and they will not score'; what he had said in East Berlin: 'the East Germans were so terrified when we came out that if there had been a betting shop on the ground I'd put my house on us', and we remembered too what he had said nearly two years earlier, when Forest played their first away match in the competition at Liverpool: 'Fancy other managers doubting our ability to keep a clean sheet'.

Forest, then, seemed confident about their task and certain of their tactics. Not so Hamburg, who delayed announcing their team until the day of the match. Zebec finally had to accept that Hrubesch was fit enough only to be among the substitutes. Keegan would lead the attack, with Reimann to his right and Milewski just behind him.

Enthusiasts expecting a day of festivities to mark the 25th European Cup final were disappointed. Madrid was quiet, with both sets of supporters arriving later than usual, and UEFA choosing not to stage the reunion of old friends and adversaries which had marked the 20th anniversary in Paris in 1975. Added to which, the match was shown live on Spanish television, persuading many locals to stay home rather than risk the mixture of rain and pale sunshine along the Avenida del Generalisimo.

Inside the Bernabeu Stadium, soon to have a new roof in readiness for the 1982 World Cup, the scene was like a film set. Hamburg's supporters were grouped, closely and deliberately, at the south end of the stadium, while Forest's army of 8,000 made a bold red barrier at the north end. But with only 51,000 in all, the open spaces in the vast upper tiers gave the impression of a final only half as compelling as it ought to be. So it would prove, but at least there was no quarrelling with the size of the stage, the merit of the occasion.

As though to underline the point, the sweep of packed press benches down the stadium's east side presented a vivid picture of Europe's football media at work: the official count was 358 writers and 113 photographers from 29 counties; plus 52 commentators broadcasting the match to television and radio networks in 26

The Nottingham Forest fans'
reaction to the German
opposition in Madrid in May
1980. (*All-Sport*)

countries. Among those whose views were sought was Alfredo Di
Stefano, fresh from coaching Valencia to victory in the Cup Winners'
Cup. His presence was a reminder not just of the champagne days at
Chamartin, but of how 20 years earlier millions had marvelled at the
televised final from Hampden Park, where Real had crushed
Eintracht Frankfurt 7–3 in the greatest European showpiece of all. As
Bela Guttmann had seen fit to remind us at the beginning of the
season, such balmy days had gone. We realised how right he was
within seconds of the start of the 1980 final, when Forest pulled back
all their players – apart from Birtles – into their own half.

The Germans' early play was promising. With Caspar Memering
well forward on the left and Manny Kaltz predictably joining every
attack down the right, they forced a series of corners and free kicks.
Kenny Burns settled into the job of marking Keegan with two
obvious fouls – he was later booked for a third – and from one free
kick Hamburg's midfield international Felix Magath brought Shilton
springing to his left to turn the ball round the post.

Clough and Taylor, rewarded only hours before the match with
improved three-year contracts, were seen in animated conversation
on the touchline. Now that Hamburg's formation was clear, signals
went out to various Forest players; Mills moved from right to left;
O'Neill from the centre towards the right; Birtles remained isolated,
doggedly shadowed by Ivan Buljan. It was 18 minutes before Forest
attacked. Then Viv Anderson, winning the ball in his own half,
carried it 40 yards and freed Birtles to run at the German defence
and shoot wide of the right hand post.

Then Forest built up the play down their left, with the precocious
Mills and the confident Gray combining to put Robertson in
possession at inside left. The hunched winger attempted to work a
return move with Birtles, and when the ball ran loose from an

John Robertson scores for Forest and for the third year in succession a single goal decides the final. (*Syndication International Ltd*)

intervening Hamburg foot, Robertson struck it with his right foot from just outside the penalty area. The shot flew across Kargus, hit the inside of the far post, and rebounded into the net.

Hamburg went straight into attack: Kaltz unleashed a fierce shot to which Keegan got a deflection, and Shilton made a stupendous save. As the ball came out, Reimann sent it back into the Forest goal, only for an alert linesman to flag the stranded Keegan offside. The 1980 European Cup final was decided in those two minutes. For Shilton, who earlier in the day had been treated for a calf injury, had shown that this was to be one of those occasions when he was unbeatable. The German players held their heads in disbelief after 35 minutes, when Shilton threw himself half the width of the goal to turn away a drive from Milewski. The chance was set up by a deft flick from Keegan.

Forest forced their first corner after 37 minutes. Lloyd and Burns took a few seconds break from their defensive duty but they were quickly back, protected by a screen of five midfield players. As Keegan said later: 'Forest are uncanny in the way they make you play to *their* strengths. They block off the middle with so many players that they force you to go wide. Then they have two central defenders and a goalkeeper who are outstanding at dealing with crosses.' Zebec made changes at half-time. He took off Hieronymus, who had been playing in midfield, pulled Keegan further back, and gambled on the half-fit Hrubesch in his attack. Milewski moved more to the left,

Kevin Keegan wheels away in triumph but the Hamburg 'goal' is disallowed. (*All-Sport*)

Kaltz if anything even further forward on the right. Forest, unperturbed, remained exactly where they were.

Neither did the flow of the game change. The Germans called on their high technical skills to thread passes towards the Forest goal; the holders repelled every Hamburg attack. Burns, after his bad start, was now the man of the match – Shilton apart. Together they made the Nottingham defence utterly impregnable.

Halfway through the second half, Forest removed the tiring Mills. His replacement was John O'Hare, once a centre-forward with Derby in the European Cup. He was brought on to reinforce the midfield, which was smothering Hamburg's attack. The Germans released Nogly from defence to join the throng on the edge of the Forest penalty area, and after 73 minutes, shortly after receiving the yellow card for fouling O'Neill, the Hamburg sweeper was foiled twice: Nogly's first shot was cleanly struck, heading directly for the bottom corner of the net, when Shilton flung himself to his left to turn it round the post with his left hand. From the corner, Nogly tried again from the edge of the penalty area. This time the drive was deflected. O'Neill, trying to clear hurriedly to his right, hit the ball straight into the legs of Buljan, and it rebounded gently past the post. Even Shilton could not have saved that.

The introduction of Hrubesch had not had the desired effect: Lloyd and Burns were more than his equals in the air; and the tall centre-forward was too slow to turn on the ground. Keegan, who was making less impact as the game progressed, screamed at the Portuguese referee, Garrido, for a penalty in one of the countless scrambles near the Forest goal. But Clough's men still survived. Seven minutes from time they had to replace the injured Gray with Bryn Gunn, but it was too late for Hamburg to test the substitute's nerve. Instead the marauding Kaltz had to scamper back to his own penalty area to make a saving tackle on Birtles, who ran on alone from the halfway line. It was the climax of a memorably selfless performance by the centre-forward.

Five minutes later the match was all over. As Clough and Taylor clasped each other in celebration, the Forest players simply collapsed into each other's arms, most of them mentally and physically exhausted. Nobody more so than Garry Birtles, whose final run near the end had brought him to his knees. He had responded with a vengeance to his manager's pre-match exhortation and afterwards drew from Clough the ultimate compliment 'When your centre-forward doesn't have the energy to take off his shin pads 30 seconds from time, it's got to be a great reflection on Forest and English football'. The Germans, meanwhile, shuffled disconsolately to the middle of the pitch. There were generous exchanges between Keegan and a number of Forest players.

John McGovern went forward to receive the cup from Jacques George, the vice-president of UEFA. The most prized trophy in international club football would remain in England for a fourth consecutive year. It was fitting that Robertson, the goalscorer, should be one of the most prominent Forest players as they began their lap of honour. He had exuded confidence when he gave the fans a clenched fist salute as the team walked on to the pitch before the game. After the players, came the men whose words had encouraged them. As Clough and Taylor greeted the Forest supporters, the stadium lights went out. Only the popping photographers' flashbulbs lit up the delighted pair. Even in this hour of victory, Clough was unpredictable. Having sparred with the European press, he whisked the Forest players back to their mountain retreat some 30 miles outside the city, leaving a party of bewildered wives, dressed for a celebration, to their own devices. The following day, Forest flew home to a magnificent reception. They were warmly welcomed at East Midlands airport, driven round the city with the Cup, and given a civic greeting by the Mayor of Nottingham.

Such euphoria was natural and understandable; but the achievement of Forest in winning the European Cup for the second time, and of England in making it four consecutive years, left the rest of the continent harbouring decidedly mixed feelings. The only recent parallel was the performance of Feyenoord and Ajax in keeping the Cup in the Netherlands between 1970 and 1973; and the only country to surpass this achievement was Spain in the competition's formative years: Real Madrid's illustrious reign was perhaps the main reason why the Spanish capital did not share the English rejoicing. The Spanish headlines were sober. 'Football compact and strong, but without soul', complained one. 'One goal from Robertson and the saves of Shilton – that was all', said another. 'Nottingham defend their title by building a wall', explained a third. From a country bred on the deeds of Di Stefano and Del Sol, the panache of Puskas, such sentiments were justified. They only echoed, after all, the words of Bela Guttmann a year earlier.

Cast alongside Real Madrid, Benfica and Ajax, then Forest were certainly not a great team. And despite the rightful indignance at being regarded as 'a rag bag outfit inspired by Clough', the likes of McGovern, Bowyer and O'Neill would not stand individual comparison with men of the calibre of Coluna, Rivera or Keizer. Still less did the English double champions boast players like Beckenbauer, Cruyff, or Eusebio. But as Clough countered, they did have in Shilton a goalkeeper who had surely performed better than his European predecessors; in Robertson a player of deceptive thrift who had created the winning goal in one European Cup final, scored it himself in a second.

Three years earlier Forest had been a second division club; that was the size of their achievement. If Forest were to be blamed for the way in which they had beaten the best team the continent had to offer, what did that say for the continent? Until Germany, Italy, the Netherlands or Spain could produce a side whose class could overturn Forest's commitment, whose individuals could undermine the English team's collective effort, whose mentor could outwit the motivating powers of Clough and Taylor, then Europe had no grounds for complaint. They were forced to pay respect, however uneasily, to the most effective team of the time.

The small town of Palencia lies to the north east of Madrid, some three hours' drive across the dry plateau of central Spain. Though it contains a fine mediaeval church, its features are not on the whole remarkable: a cluster of shops and offices around the market place and two comfortable hotels. There is also a bull ring and a tiny stadium where the local football club performs, without great distinction, in the Spanish second division.

They have a link, however, with a more famous past. Until the summer of 1980 their manager was Francisco Gento, whose dazzling skills helped Real Madrid dominate Europe for almost a decade. No one has played more matches in the European Cup; his total of 88 includes eight finals, of which six were won. A man of some modesty, he can recall Real's salad days without regret. Gento is aware of the past, but not awed by it. 'You still have another life to lead when you stop playing. The most difficult thing is to know when to stop.'

As we spoke a small crowd gathered patiently outside the steps of the hotel, their purpose underlining the point he had made. For they were waiting not for Gento, whose presence in Palencia is now a commonplace, but for the bullfighter El Cordobes, attempting a comeback, at the age of 43, in the sport where he was already a legend. Gento senses his predicament – the one which haunts all athletes:

'El Cordobes is now a very rich man who does not need to fight. But I think he was bored on his farms. After seven years away he wanted to return, and for that I admire him. This afternoon he finished with two good kills, but at first he was not good and the crowd were scornful. Yet he risks that, and of course a bad injury, because he feels excited again.'

Such intensity of feeling cannot be recaptured outside the playing areas of professional sport. Even those who choose, like Gento, the precarious pleasures of football management cannot quite attain it – though we may be sure Brian Clough, for one, has found there some consolation for a playing career cruelly cut short. Clough now stands on the brink of a unique achievement in the European Cup. No man in the first 25 years of the competition has managed three winning sides, in succession. Real Madrid's nap hand was achieved by three coaches – Villalonga, Carniglia, and Muñoz – while the hat tricks by Ajax and Bayern Munich in the 1970s were the work of Michels and Kovacs on the one hand, and Lattek and Cramer on the other.

Ironically, all three clubs – Real, Ajax and Bayern – would be represented in the 26th tournament. All were again national champions, in Bayern's case after an absence of six years. Their return was inspired by captain Paul Breitner, and also by Uli Hoeness whose career, like Clough's, was ended by injury, and who is now the club's general manager.

In Italy Sandro Mazzola, who played in four finals, holds a similar post at his *alma mater* Internazionale. Their presence in the 1980–81 competition offered a stark contrast to the fate of their neighbours AC Milan. To the list of former winners taking part must be added that of Liverpool, champions in England yet again. Their duel with another of Europe's darlings, Mamchester United, provided the highlights in an otherwise predictable first division campaign, and in the end Paisley's men clinched the title in their 41st match.

These five great clubs, like El Cordobes, will be sampling the excitement of the early rounds, attempting to emulate, and therefore in a sense to obliterate, the past. None more so than Real, where the monuments built to their achievements in Madrid have sometimes acted as millstones. Their performance in the 1960 final is still the example by which the teams of the 1980s will be judged, even though the tournament has created a catalogue of fresh heroes. Says Gento simply:

'When we first played in the European Cup, nobody thought it would be important. Now when I think of all the great names who have taken part, it makes me proud. To have been a part of the story of the European Cup, that is something to tell your children.'

———————————————

APPENDICES

Ties played at ground of home club unless otherwise stated.

The appendices which follow are intended to serve as an accurate work of reference covering the first 25 years of the European Cup. In the case of Appendix One, where we have produced a classified list of every match result and goalscorer, the authors would like to make it clear that considerable checking and research with a large number of individual clubs and players has revealed a number of errors in previous lists of this kind published in Britain and Europe over the years. UEFA themselves have not kept a tabulated list of goalscorers, and our investigations revealed that a number of goals from time to time have been wrongly credited to players by books, magazines and newspapers. We hope therefore that the list which follows will clarify various ambiguities.

Appendix Two is designed to provide easy reference to the first 25 finals. Appendix Three is a list of leading goalscorers in the competition over the period 1955–80; Appendix Four reveals which clubs have been most successful in the European Cup; Appendix Five deals with the annual European Footballer of the Year award.

Any queries concerning the statistics which follow will be gladly dealt with by the authors, who can be contacted through the publishers.

APPENDIX ONE
RESULTS AND GOALSCORERS 1955–80
First season – 1955–56

FIRST ROUND

14 September 1955

Rot-Weiss Essen 0
Hibernian 4 (Turnbull 2, Reilly, Ormond)

Rot-Weiss: Herkenrath, Jaenisch, Sastrau, Köchling, Wewers, Roettger, Röhrig, Vordenbaumen, Arbotmeit, Sauer, Steffens.

Hibernian: Younger, Higgins, Paterson, Thomson, Plenderleith, Preston, Smith, Combe, Reilly, Turnbull, Ormond.

12 October 1955

Hibernian 1 (J. Buchanan)
Rot-Weiss Essen 1 (Arbotmeit)

Hibernian: Adams, Macfarlane, Paterson, Thomson, Plenderleith, Preston, J. Buchanan, Combe, Mulkerrin, Turnbull, Ormond.

Rot-Weiss: Herkenrath, Grewer, Köchling, Vordenbaumen, Wewers, Jahnel, Arbotmeit, Sauer, Seemann, Islacker, Röhrig.

4 September 1955

Sporting Lisbon 3 (Martins, Quim 2)
Partizan Belgrade 3 (Pajeric, Passos og, Bobek)

12 October 1955

Partizan Belgrade 5 (Milutinovic 4, Jovic)
Sporting Lisbon 2 (Walter 2)

7 September 1955

Vörös Lobogo 6 (Szimczak, Palotas 3, Hidegkuti, Sandor)
Anderlecht 3 (Van der Wilt, H. Van den Bosch, J. Van den Bosch)

19 October 1955

Anderlecht 1 (H. Van den Bosch)
Vörös Lobogo 4 (Hidegkuti, Lantos, Palotas, Kovacs I)

8 September 1955

Servette (Geneva) 0
Real Madrid 2 (Muñoz, Rial)

12 October 1955

Real Madrid 5 (Molowny, Di Stefano 2, Joseito, Rial)
Servette (Geneva) 0

20 September 1955

Djurgarden 0
Gwardia Warsaw 0

12 October 1955

Gwardia Warsaw 1 (Baszkiewicz)
Djurgarden 4 (Eriksson 3, Sandberg)
(Gwardia Warsaw replaced Chelsea, who withdrew after the draw was made)

21 September 1955
Copenhagen

Aarhus GF 0
Stade de Reims 2 (Glovacki, 2)

26 October 1955

Stade de Reims 2 (Glovacki, Bliard)
Aarhus GF 2 (E. Jensen , Bjeregaard)

21 September 1955

Rapid Vienna 6 (Körner II 3, Mehsarosch, Hanappi, Probst)
PSV Eindhoven 1 (Fransen)

1 November 1955

PSV Eindhoven 1 (Fransen)
Rapid Vienna 0

1 November 1955

AC Milan 3 (Frignani, Schiaffino, Dal Monte)
Saarbrücken 4 (Krieger, Philippi, Schirra, Martin)

23 November 1955

Saarbrücken 1 (Binkert)
AC Milan 4 (Valli 2, Nordahl, Beraldo)

QUARTER-FINALS

23 November 1955
Glasgow

Djurgarden 1 (Edlund)
Hibernian 3 (Combe, Mulkerrin, Olsson og)

Djurgarden: Arvidsson, Forsberg, Gustafsson, Holmstrom, Olsson, Parling, Andersson, Grybb, Eriksson, Edlund, Sandberg.

Hibernian: Younger, Macfarlane, Paterson, Thomson, Plenderleith, Preston, Smith, Combe, Mulkerrin, Turnbull, Ormond.

28 November 1955

Hibernian 1 (Turnbull pen)
Djurgarden 0

Hibernian: Younger, Macfarlane, Paterson, Thomson, Plenderleith, Preston, Smith, Combe, Mulkerrin, Turnbull, Ormond.

Djurgarden: Arvidsson, Forsberg, Gustafsson, Edlund, Olsson, Parling, Andersson, Tvilling, Eriksson, Eklund, Sandberg.

14 December 1955

Stade de Reims 4 (Glovacki, Leblond 2, Bliard)
Vörös Lobogo 2 (Szolnok, Lantos pen)

28 December 1955

Vörös Lobogo 4 (Lantos 2 pens, Palotas, Giraudo og)
Stade de Reims 4 (Glovacki, Bliard 2, Templin)
(*Vörös Lobogo ('Red Banner') later appear as MTK Budapest*)

25 December 1955	**Real Madrid 4** (Castano 2, Gento, Di Stefano) **Partizan Belgrade 0**
29 January 1956	**Partizan Belgrade 3** (Herceg, Milutinovic 2) **Real Madrid 0**
18 January 1956	**Rapid Vienna 1** (Körner 1 pen) **AC Milan 1** (Nordahl)
12 February 1956	**AC Milan 7** (Mariani, Nordahl 2, Ricagni 2, Frignani, Schiaffino) **Rapid Vienna 2** (Golobic, Körner 1)

SEMI-FINALS

4 April 1956

Stade de Reims 2 (Leblond, Bliard)
Hibernian 0

Reims: Jacquet, Zimny, Giraudo, Siatka, Jonquet, Cicci, Hidalgo, Glovacki, Kopa, Leblond, Bliard.
Hibernian: Younger, Macfarlane, Paterson, A. Buchanan, Grant, Thomson, Smith, Combe, Reilly, Turnbull, Ormond.

18 April 1956

Hibernian 0
Stades de Reims 1 (Glovacki)

Hibernian: Younger, Macfarlane, Paterson, A. Buchanan, Grant, Thomson, Smith, Combe, Reilly, Turnbull, Ormond.
Reims: Jacquet, Zimny, Giraudo, Leblond, Jonquet, Siatka, Hidalgo, Glovacki, Kopa, Bliard, Templin.

19 April 1956

Real Madrid 4 (Rial, Joseito, Olsen, Di Stefano)
AC Milan 2 (Nordahl, Schiaffino)

1 May 1956

AC Milan 2 (Dal Monte 2 pens)
Real Madrid 1 (Joseito)

FINAL

13 June 1956
Paris

Real Madrid 4 (Di Stefano, Rial 2, Marquitos)
Stade de Reims 3 (Leblond, Hidalgo, Templin)

Real Madrid: Alonso, Atienza, Lesmes, Muñoz, Marquitos, Zarraga, Joseito, Marsal, Di Stefano, Rial, Gento.
Reims: Jacquet, Zimny, Giraudo, Leblond, Jonquet, Siatka, Hidalgo, Glovacki, Kopa, Bliard, Templin.
Referee: Ellis (Eng)
Attendance: 38,000.

Second season – 1956–57

PRELIMINARY ROUND

Byes: Real Madrid, Rapid Vienna, Glasgow Rangers, Honved, CDNA Sofia, Red Star Belgrade, Rapid Heerlen, Grasshoppers, IFK Norrköping, Fiorentina.

12 September 1956

Anderlecht 0
Manchester.United 2 (Viollet, T. Taylor)

Anderlecht: Week, Matthys, Culot, Lippens, De Koster, Van der Wilt, De Driver, Jurion, Dewael, Mermans, J. Van den Bosch.
Manchester United: Wood, Foulkes, Byrne, Colman, Jones, Blanchflower, Berry, Whelan, T. Taylor, Viollet, Pegg.

26 September 1956

Manchester United 10 (Viollet 4, T. Taylor 3, Whelan 2, Berry)
Anderlecht 0

Manchester United: Wood, Foulkes, Byrne, Colman, Jones, Edwards, Berry, Whelan, T. Taylor, Viollet, Pegg.
Anderlecht: Week, Gettemans, Culot, Van der Wilt, De Koster, Hanon, De Driver, H. Van den Bosch, Mermans, Dewael, Jurion.

1 August 1956

Borussia Dortmund 4 (Bracht, Niepieklo, Preissler 2)
Spora Luxembourg 3 (Boreux 3)

6 September 1956

Spora Luxembourg 2 (Fiedler, Letsch)
Borussia Dortmund 1 (Preissler)

16 September 1956
Dortmund

Borussia Dortmund 7 (Peters 2, Preissler 2, Kapitulski 2, Bracht)
Spora Luxembourg 0

26 August 1956

Dinamo Bucharest 3 (Voica 2, Ene)
Galatasaray 1 (Metin II)

30 September 1956

Galatasaray 2 (Kadri, Metin II)
Dinamo Bucharest 1 (Suru)

12 September 1956	**Slovan Bratislava 4** (Pazicky 2, Moravcik, Kovacs pen) **CWKS Warsaw 0**
19 September 1956	**CWKS Warsaw 2** (Kowal, Brychczy) **Slovan Bratislava 0** *(CWKS later appear as Legia Warsaw)*
19 September 1956 Copenhagen	**Aarhus GF 1** (E. Jensen) **OGC Nice 1** (Foix)
27 September 1956	**OGC Nice 5** (Foix, Milazzo 2, Faivre 2) **Aarhus GF 1** (E. Jensen)
20 September 1956	**FC Porto 1** (Jose Maria) **Atletico Bilbao 2** (Maguregui, Gainza)
26 September 1956	**Atletico Bilbao 3** (Arteche 3 – 1 pen) **FC Porto 2** (Hernani, Jaburu)

FIRST ROUND

17 October 1956	**Manchester United 3** (Viollet 2, Burgsmüller og) **Borussia Dortmund 2** (Kapitulski, Preissler) *Manchester United:* Wood, Foulkes, Byrne, Colman, Jones, Edwards, Berry, Whelan, T. Taylor, Viollet, Pegg. *Dortmund:* Kwiatkowski, Burgsmüller, Sandmann, Schlebrowski, Michallek, Bracht, Peters, Preissler, Kelbassa, Schmidt, Kapitulski.
21 November 1956	**Borussia Dortmund 0** **Manchester United 0** *Dortmund:* Kwiatkowski, Burgsmüller, Sandmann, Schlebrowski, Michallek, Bracht, Peters, Preissler, Kelbassa, Schmidt, Niepieklo. *Manchester United:* Wood, Foulkes, Byrne, Colman, Jones, McGuinness, Berry, Whelan, T. Taylor, Edwards, Pegg.
24 October 1956	**Glasgow Rangers 2** (Murray, Simpson) **OGC Nice 1** (Faivre) *Rangers:* Niven, Shearer, Caldow, McColl, Young, Logie, Scott, Simpson, Murray, Baird, Hubbard. *Nice:* Colonna, Bonvin, Nani, Ferry, Gonzales, Nuremberg, Foix, Muro, Bravo, Diratz, Faivre.
14 November 1956	**OGC Nice 2** (Bravo, Foix) **Glasgow Rangers 1** (Hubbard pen) *Nice:* Colonna, Bonvin, Martinez, Ferry, Gonzales, Nuremberg, Foix, Ujlaki, Bravo, Muro, Faivre. *Rangers:* Niven, Shearer, Caldow, McColl, Young, Logie, Scott, Simpson, Murray, Baird, Hubbard.
28 November 1956 Paris	**Glasgow Rangers 1** (Bonvin og) **OGC Nice 3** (Foix, Muro, Faivre) *Rangers:* Niven, Shearer, Caldow, McColl, Davis, Logie, Scott, Simpson, Murray, Baird, Hubbard. *Nice:* Colonna, Bonvin, Martinez, Ferry, Gonzales, Nuremberg, Foix, Ujlaki, Bravo, Muro, Faivre.
24 October 1956	**Slovan Bratislava 1** (Kovacs pen) **Grasshoppers 0**
12 December 1956	**Grasshoppers 2** (Vuko, Duret) **Slovan Bratislava 0**
1 November 1956	**Real Madrid 4** (Di Stefano 2, Marsal 2) **Rapid Vienna 2** (Dienst, Giesser)
14 November 1956	**Rapid Vienna 3** (Happel 3 – 1 pen) **Real Madrid 1** (Di Stefano)
13 December 1956 Madrid	**Real Madrid 2** (Joseito, Kopa) **Rapid Vienna 0**
3 November 1956	**Rapid Heerlen 3** (Jansen, Bisschops, Tasic og) **Red Star Belgrade 4** (Kostic 2, Toplak, Rudinski)
8 November 1956	**Red Star Belgrade 2** (Toplak, Kostic) **Rapid Heerlen 0**
21 November 1956	**Fiorentina 1** (Bizzarri) **IFK Norrköping 1** (Bild)
28 November 1956 Rome	**IFK Norrköping 0** **Fiorentina 1** (Virgili)
21 October 1956	**CDNA Sofia 8** (Kolev 4, Panayotov 2, Milanov, Dimitrov) **Dinamo Bucharest 1** (Bacutz I pen)
30 December 1956	**Dinamo Bucharest 3** (Nicolae pen, Lazar II, Neagu) **CDNA Sofia 2** (Stoyanov, Yanev)

22 November 1956	**Atletico Bilbao 3** (Arteche, Marcaida, Arieta)
	Honved 2 (Budai, Kocsis)
20 December 1956	**Honved 3** (Kocsis 2, Puskas)
Brussels	**Atletico Bilbao 3** (Merodio 2, Arieta)

QUARTER-FINALS

16 January 1957

Atletico Bilbao 5 (Arteche, Uribe 2, Marcaida, Merodio)
Manchester United 3 (T. Taylor, Viollet, Whelan)

Bilbao: Carmelo, Orue, Canito, Mauri, Garay, Etura, Arteche, Marcaida, Merodio, Gainza, Uribe.

Manchester United: Wood, Foulkes, Byrne, Colman, Jones, Edwards, Berry, Whelan, T. Taylor, Viollet, Pegg.

6 February 1957

Manchester United 3 (Viollet, T. Taylor, Berry)
Atletico Bilbao 0

Manchester United: Wood, Foulkes, Byrne, Colman, Jones, Edwards, Berry, Whelan, T. Taylor, Viollet, Pegg.

Bilbao: Carmelo, Orue, Canito, Mauri, Garay, Maguregui, Arteche, Marcaida, Etura, Merodio, Gainza.

6 February 1957

Fiorentina 3 (Taccaola 2, Segato)
Grasshoppers 1 (Ballaman)

27 February 1957

Grasshoppers 2 (Ballaman, Vuko)
Fiorentina 2 (Julinho, Montuori)

14 February 1957

Real Madrid 3 (Mateos 2, Joseito)
OGC Nice 0

14 March 1957

OGC Nice 2 (Foix, Ferry pen)
Real Madrid 3 (Di Stefano 2, Joseito)

17 February 1957

Red Star Belgrade 3 (Kostic 2, V. Popovic)
CDNA Sofia 1 (Yanev)

24 February 1957

CDNA Sofia 2 (Boskov pen, Panayotov)
Red Star Belgrade 1 (Tasic pen)

SEMI-FINALS

11 April 1957

Real Madrid 3 (Rial, Di Stefano, Mateos)
Manchester United 1 (T. Taylor)

Real Madrid: Alonso, Becerril, Lesmes, Muñoz, Marquitos, Zarraga, Kopa, Mateos, Di Stefano, Rial, Gento.

Manchester United: Wood, Foulkes, Byrne, Colman, Blanchflower, Edwards, Berry, Whelan, T. Taylor, Viollet, Pegg.

25 April 1957

Manchester United 2 (T. Taylor, Charlton)
Real Madrid 2 (Kopa, Rial)

Manchester United: Wood, Foulkes, Byrne, Colman, Blanchflower, Edwards, Berry, Whelan, T. Taylor, Charlton, Pegg.

Real Madrid: Alonso, Torres, Lesmes, Muñoz, Marquitos, Zarraga, Kopa, Mateos, Di Stefano, Rial, Gento.

3 April 1957.

Red Star Belgrade 0
Fiorentina 1 (Prini)

18 April 1957

Fiorentina 0
Red Star Belgrade 0

FINAL

30 May 1957
Madrid

Real Madrid 2 (Di Stefano pen, Gento)
Fiorentina 0

Real Madrid: Alonso, Torres, Lesmes, Muñoz, Marquitos, Zarraga, Kopa, Mateos, Di Stefano, Rial, Gento.

Fiorentina: Sarti, Magnini, Cervato, Scaramucci, Orzan, Segato, Julinho, Gratton, Virgili, Montuori, Bizzarri.

Referee: Horn (Nth)

Attendance: 124,000

Third season – 1957–58

PRELIMINARY ROUND

Byes: Real Madrid, IFK Norrköping, Antwerp, Ajax, Young Boys Berne, Borussia Dortmund, CCA Bucharest, Dukla Prague.

25 September 1957

Shamrock Rovers 0
Manchester United 6 (Whelan 2, T. Taylor 2, Berry, Pegg)

Shamrock: D'Arcy, Burke, Mackay, Nolan, Keogh, Hennessy, Peyton, Ambrose, Hamilton, Coad, Tuohy.

Manchester United: Wood, Foulkes, Byrne, Goodwin, Blanchflower, Edwards, Berry, Whelan, T. Taylor, Viollet, Pegg.

2 October 1957	**Manchester United 3** (Viollet 2, Pegg) **Shamrock Rovers 2** (McCann, Hamilton)

Manchester United: Wood, Foulkes, Byrne, Colman, Jones, McGuinness, Berry, Webster, T. Taylor, Viollet, Pegg.

Shamrock: D'Arcy, Burke, Mackay, Nolan, Keogh, Coad, McCann, Peyton, Hamilton, Ambrose, Tuohy.

4 September 1957	**Glasgow Rangers 3** (Kichenbrand, Scott, Simpson) **Saint Etienne 1** (Mekloufi)

Rangers: Niven, Shearer, Caldow, McColl, Davis, Baird, Scott, Simpson, Kichenbrand, Murray, Hubbard.

Saint Etienne: Abbès, R. Tylinski, Wicart, Domingo, M. Tylinski, Bordas, Njo Léa, Mekloufi, Fevrier, Goujon, Lefèvre.

25 September 1957	**Saint Etienne 2** (Oleksiak, Fevrier) **Glasgow Rangers 1** (Wilson)

Saint Etienne: Abbès, M. Tylinski, Wicart, Domingo, R. Tylinski, Fevrier, Njo Léa, Mekloufi, Goujon, Oleksiak, Lefèvre.

Rangers: Ritchie, Shearer, Caldow, McColl, Valentine, Millar, Scott, Simpson, Murray, Baird, Wilson.

11 September 1957	**Aarhus GF 0** **Glenavon 0**

Aarhus: From, Greguson, Gundlev, Andersen, Nielsen, Olesen, Christensen, J. Jensen, E. Jensen, A. Jensen, Kjär-Andersen.

Glenavon: Rea, Armstrong, Lyske, Corr, Davis, Cush, Wilson, McVeigh, Jones, Campbell, Elwood.

25 September 1957	**Glenavon 0** **Aarhus GF 3** (Kjär-Andersen 2, J. Jensen)

Glenavon: Rea, Armstrong, Lyske, Corr, Davis, Cush, Wilson, McVeigh, Jones, Campbell, Elwood.

Aarhus: From, Greguson, Gundlev, Andersen, Nielsen, Olesen, Christensen, Madsen, J. Jensen, A. Jensen, Kjär-Andersen.

4 September 1957	**CDNA Sofia 2** (Milanov 2) **Vasas Budapest 1** (Berendhi)
3 October 1957	**Vasas Budapest 6** (Csordas 3, Berendhi, Bundszak, Szilagy I) **CDNA Sofia 1** (Panayotov)
5 September 1957	**Stade Dudelange 0** **Red Star Belgrade 5** (Kostic 2, Toplak 2, V. Popovic)
2 October 1957	**Red Star Belgrade 9** (Cokic 2, Mitic 2, Kostic 4, Toplak) **Stade Dudelange 1** (Rongoni)
11 September 1957	**Gwardia Warsaw 3** (Baszkiewicz, Lewandowski, Gawronski) **SC Wismut 1** (S. Kaiser)
13 October 1957	**SC Wismut 3** (S. Kaiser 2, M. Kaiser) **Gwardia Warsaw 1** (Baszkiewicz)
15 October 1957 East Berlin	**SC Wismut 1** (Tröger) **Gwardia Warsaw 1** (Baszkiewicz)

SC Wismut won on toss after extra time.

19 September 1957	**Seville 3** (Pauet, Antoniet, Pepillo) **Benfica 1** (Palmeiro)
26 September 1957	**Benefica 0** **Seville 0**
2 October 1957	**AC Milan 4** (Grillo, Bean, Holtl og, Mariani) **Rapid Vienna 1** (Dienst)
9 October 1957	**Rapid Vienna 5** (Körner II, Dienst, Bertalan, Riegler, Hanappi) **AC Milan 2** (Grillo, Bean)
30 October 1957 Zurich	**AC Milan 4** (Bean 2, Bergamaschi, Schiaffino) **Rapid Vienna 2** (Happel pen, Bertalan)

FIRST ROUND

20 November 1957	**Manchester United 3** (Webster, T. Taylor, Whelan) **Dukla Prague 0**

Manchester United: Wood, Foulkes, Byrne, Colman, Blanchflower, Edwards, Berry, Whelan, T. Taylor, Webster, Pegg.

Dukla Prague: Pavlis, Jecny, L. Novak, Pluskal, Cadek, Masopust, Vacenovsky, Dvorak, Borovicka, Safranek, Dobai.

4 December 1957

Dukla Prague 1 (Dvorak)
Manchester United 0

Dukla Prague: Pavlis, Jecny, L. Novak, Pluskal, Cadek, Masopust, Safranek, Dvorak, Urban, Borovicka, Vacenovsky.

Manchester United: Wood, Foulkes, Byrne, Colman, Jones, Edwards, Scanlon, Whelan, T. Taylor, Webster, Pegg.

27 November 1957

Glasgow Rangers 1 (Murray)
AC Milan 4 (Grillo 2, Baruffi, Bean)

Rangers: Ritchie, Little, Caldow, McColl, Telfer, Millar, Scott, Simpson, Murray, Baird, Hubbard.

AC Milan: Buffon, Maldini, Zagatti, Bergamaschi, Bean, Zannier, Fontana, Beraldo, Schiaffino, Grillo, Baruffi.

11 December 1957

AC Milan 2 (Baruffi, Galli)
Glasgow Rangers 0

AC Milan: Buffon, Maldini, Zagatti, Fontana, Zannier, Beraldo, Galli, Liedholm, Bean, Grillo, Baruffi.

Rangers: Niven, Shearer, Caldow, McColl, Telfer, Baird, Scott, Millar, Kichenbrand, Wilson, Hubbard.

31 October 1957

Antwerp 1 (De Backker)
Real Madrid 2 (Di Stefano 2)

28 November 1957

Real Madrid 6 (Rial 3, Marsal, Kopa, Gento)
Antwerp 0

2 November 1957

IFK Norrköping 2 (Hakansson, Källgren)
Red Star Belgrade 2 (Kostic, Toplak)

23 November 1957

Red Star Belgrade 2 (Spajic 2)
IFK Norrköping 1 (Blackman)

20 November 1957
Geneva

Young Boys Berne 1 (Allemann)
Vasas Budapest 1 (Csordas)

30 November 1957

Vasas Budapest 2 (Csordas 2)
Young Boys Berne 1 (Schneider)

20 November 1957

SC Wismut 1 (Muller)
Ajax 3 (van der Kuil 2, Bleyenburg)

27 November 1957

Ajax 1 (Ouderland)
SC Wismut 0

27 November 1957

Seville 4 (Antoniet 2, Loren, 2)
Aarhus GF 0

4 December 1957

Aarhus GF 2 (E. Jensen 2)
Seville 0

27 November 1957

Borussia Dortmund 4 (Preissler, Peters 2, Niepieklo)
CCA Bucharest 2 (Zavoda, Bone)

8 December 1957

CCA Bucharest 3 (Tataru 2, Constantin)
Borussia Dortmund 1 (Preissler)

29 December 1957
Bologna

Borussia Dortmund 3 (Dulz, Kelbassa, Preissler)
CCA Bucharest 1 (Cacoveanu)

QUARTER-FINALS

14 January 1958

Manchester United 2 (Charlton, Colman)
Red Star Belgrade 1 (Tasic)

Manchester United: Gregg, Foulkes, Byrne, Colman, Jones, Edwards, Morgans, Charlton, T. Taylor, Viollet, Scanlon.

Red Star: Beara, Tomic, Zekovic, Mitic, Spajic, V. Popovic, Borozan, Sekularac, Toplak, Tasic, Kostic.

5 February 1958

Red Star Belgrade 3 (Kostic 2, Tasic pen)
Manchester United 3 (Viollet, Charlton 2)

Red Star: Beara, Tomic, Zekovic, Mitic, Spajic, V. Popovic, Borozan, Sekularac, Tasic, Kostic, Cokic.

Manchester United: Gregg, Foulkes, Byrne, Colman, Jones, Edwards, Morgans, Charlton, T. Taylor, Viollet, Scanlon.

23 January 1958

Real Madrid 8 (Di Stefano 4 – 1 pen, Kopa 2, Marsal, Gento)
Seville 0

23 February 1958

Seville 2 (Paya, Pauet)
Real Madrid 2 (Pereda 2)

5 February 1958	**Ajax 2** (Ouderland 2) **Vasas Budapest 2** (Bundszak 2)
26 February 1958	**Vasas Budapest 4** (Bundszak, Szilagy 2, Csordas) **Ajax 0**
12 February 1958	**Borussia Dortmund 1** (Bergamaschi og) **AC Milan 1** (Galli)
26 March 1958	**AC Milan 4** (Cucchiaroni, Liedholm, Galli, Grillo) **Borussia Dortmund 1** (Preissler)

SEMI-FINALS

8 May 1958

Manchester United 2 (Viollet, E. Taylor pen)
AC Milan 1 (Schiaffino)

Manchester United: Gregg, Foulkes, Greaves, Goodwin, Cope, Crowther, Morgans, E. Taylor, Webster, Viollet, Pearson.

AC Milan: Buffon, Fontana, Beraldo, Bergamaschi, Maldini, Radice, Mariani, Bredesen, Schiaffino, Liedholm, Cucchiaroni.

14 May 1958

AC Milan 4 (Schiaffino 2, Liedholm, Danova)
Manchester United 0

AC Milan: Buffon, Fontana, Beraldo, Bergamaschi, Zannier, Radice, Danova, Bredesen, Schiaffino, Liedholm, Cucchiaroni.

Manchester United: Gregg, Foulkes, Greaves, Goodwin, Cope, Crowther, Morgans, E. Taylor, Webster, Viollet, Pearson.

2 April 1958	**Real Madrid 4** (Di Stefano 3, Marsal) **Vasas Budapest 0**
14 April 1958	**Vasas Budapest 2** (Bundszak, Csordas) **Real Madrid 0**

FINAL

28 May 1958
Brussels

Real Madrid 3 (Di Stefano, Rial, Gento)
AC Milan 2 (Schiaffino, Grillo)

After extra time. Score at 90 minutes 2–2.

Real Madrid: Alonso, Atienza, Lesmes, Santisteban, Santamaria, Zarraga, Kopa, Joseito, Di Stefano, Rial, Gento.

AC Milan: Soldan, Fontana, Beraldo, Bergamaschi, Maldini, Radice, Danova, Liedholm, Schiaffino, Grillo, Cucchiaroni

Referee: Alsteen (Belgium)

Attendance: 67,000

Fourth season – 1958–59

PRELIMINARY ROUND

Byes: Wolverhampton Wanderers, Real Madrid, CDNA Sofia, Helsinki Palloseura.

3 September 1958

Standard Liège 5 (Jadot 2, Piters, Bonga-Bonga, Houf)
Heart of Midlothian 1 (Crawford)

Standard Liège: Nicolay, Happart, Thellin, Bolsée, Marnett, Mathonet, Piters, Jadot, Bonga-Bonga, Houf, Paeschen

Heart of Midlothian: Marshall, Kirk, Thompson, Cumming, Glidden, Bowman, Blackwood, Mackay, Bauld, Wardaugh, Crawford

9 September 1958

Heart of Midlothian 2 (Bauld 2)
Standard Liège 1 (Givard)

Heart of Midlothian: Marshall, Kirk, Thompson, Mackay, Glidden, Cumming, Blackwood, Murray, Bauld. Crawford, Hamilton

Standard Liège: Nicolay, Happart, Thellin, Bolsée, Marnett, Anoul, Piters, Givard, Bonga-Bonga, Houf, Paeschen

17 September 1958

Ards 1 (Lowry)
Stade de Reims 4 (Fontaine 4)

Ards: Moffat, Hunter, McGuickan, Giffen, Forde, Fletcher, Humphries, Conkey, Lawther, Lowry, Boyd

Reims: Colonna, Rodzik, Giraudo, Penverne, Jonquet, Siatka, Bliard, Leblond, Fontaine, Piantoni, Vincent

8 October 1958

Stade de Reims 6 (Piantoni 2, Fontaine 2, Bliard 2)
Ards 2 (Lawther, Quee)

Reims: Colonna, Rodzik, Gouttes, Penverne, Siatka, Leblond, Lamartine, Bliard, Fontaine, Piantoni, Vincent.

Ards: Moffat, Hunter, McGuickan, Giffen, Forde, Fletcher, Boyd, Richardson, Lawther, Quee, Lockhart.

10 September 1958

Dynamo Zagreb 2 (Liposinovic 2)
Dukla Prague 2 (Borovicka, Kordula)

1 October 1958

Dukla Prague 2 (Dvorak, Vacenovsky)
Dynamo Zagreb 1 (Gaspert)

14 September 1958

Jeunesse Esch 1 (May)
IFK Gothenburg 2 (N. Johansson, B. Johansson)

30 September 1958

IFK Gothenburg 0
Jeunesse Esch 1 (May)

15 October 1958
Gothenburg

IFK Gothenburg 5 (Andersson, Berndtsson 2, B. Johansson, N. Johansson)
Jeunesse Esch 1 (Meurisse)

17 September 1958

SC Wismut 4 (Tröger, Viertel 2, S. Kaiser)
Petrolul Ploesti 2 (M. Dridea 2)

28 September 1958

Petrolul Ploesti 2 (Fronea, Marinescu)
SC Wismut 0

12 October 1958
Kiev

SC Wismut 4 (Zink, Tröger 2, K. Wolf)
Petrolul Ploesti 0

17 September 1958

Schalke 04 5 (Klodt 2, Sadlowski, Nowak, Brocker)
KB Copenhagen 2 (Andersen 2)

26 September 1958

KB Copenhagen 3 (Birkeland 2, Krog)
Schalke 04 0

1 October 1958
Enschede

KB Copenhagen 1 (J. Sörensen)
Schalke 04 3 (Siebert, Nowak, Klodt)

17 September 1958

Atletico Madrid 8 (Peiro 2, Vava 2, Collar 2, Mendonça 2)
Drumcondra 0

1 October 1958

Drumcondra 1 (Fullam pen)
Atletico Madrid 5 (Peiro 2, Csoka, Collar, Vava)

17 September 1958

Polonia Bytom 0
MTK Budapest 3 (Sandor, Palotas 2 – 1 pen)

1 October 1958

MTK Budapest 3 (Molnar, Palotas 2 – 1 pen)
Polonia Bytom 0

(MTK Budapest formerly appeared as Vörös Lobogo)

24 September 1958

Juventus 3 (Sivori 3)
Wiener Sportklub 1 (Horak)

1 October 1958

Wiener Sportklub 7 (Skerlan, Hammerl 4, Hof 2 – 1 pen)
Juventus 0

1 October 1958

DOS Utrecht 3 (Temming pen, Krommert 2)
Sporting Lisbon 4 (Ivson 2, Hugo, Martins)

8 October 1958

Sporting Lisbon 2 (Ivson, Carabello)
DOS Utrecht 1 (van der Linden)

Besktas Walkover
Olympiakos Withdrew

Young Boys Berne Walkover
Manchester United Withdrew

FIRST ROUND

12 November 1958

Wolverhampton Wanderers 2 (Broadbent 2)
Schalke 04 2 (Siebert, Koslowski)

Wolverhampton Wanderers: Sidebottom, Stuart, Harris, Slater, Wright, Flowers, Deeley, Broadbent, Jackson, Mason, Mullen.

Schalke: Loweg, Brocker, Laszig, Borutta, Kreuz, Karnhof, Koslowski, Kördel, Siebert, Jagielski, Klodt.

18 November 1958

Schalke 04 2 (Siebert, Kördel)
Wolverhampton Wanderers 1 (Jackson)

Schalke: Loweg, Brocker, Laszig, Karnhof, Kreuz, Borutta, Koslowski, Kördel, Siebert, Jagielski, Klodt.

Wolverhampton Wanderers: Finlayson, Stuart, Harris, Clamp, Wright, Flowers, Deeley, Broadbent, Jackson, Mason, Mullen.

29 October 1958

Sporting Lisbon 2 (Bolsée og, Mendes)
Standard Liège 3 (Paeschen, Jadot, Mallants)

12 November 1958

Standard Liège 3 (Paeschen, Houf, Mallants)
Sporting Lisbon 0

5 November 1958	**Wiener Sportklub 3** (Hof, Hammerl, Knoll) **Dukla Prague 1** (Pluskal)
26 November 1958	**Dukla Prague 1** (Masopust) **Wiener Sportklub 0**
5 November 1958	**MTK Budapest 1** (Molnar) **Young Boys Berne 2** (Wechselberger, Zahnd)
26 November 1958	**Young Boys Berne 4** (Wechselberger 2, Meier, Alleman) **MTK Budapest 1** (Molnar)
5 November 1958	**Atletico Madrid 2** (Vava, Peiro) **CDNA Sofia 1** (Milanov)
26 November 1958	**CDNA Sofia 1** (Panayotov) **Atletico Madrid 0**
18 December 1958 Geneva	**Atletico Madrid 3** (Callejo, Vava 2 – 1 pen) **CDNA Sofia 1** (Dimitrov) After extra time.
9 November 1958	**IFK Gothenburg 2** (Olsson, Andersson) **SC Wismut 2** (Siefert, Zink)
15 November 1958	**SC Wismut 4** (Zink 2, S. Kaiser 2) **IFK Gothenburg 0**
13 November 1958	**Real Madrid 2** (Santisteban, Kopa) **Besiktas 0**
27 November 1958	**Besiktas 1** (Kaya) **Real Madrid 1** (Santisteban)
26 November 1958	**Stade de Reims 4** (Vincent 3, Siatka) **Helsinki Palloseura 0**
3 December 1958 Rouen	**Helsinki Palloseura 0** **Stade de Reims 3** (Fontaine 2, Lintamo og)

QUARTER-FINALS

4 February 1959	**Standard Liège 2** (Jadot, Givard pen) **Stade de Reims 0**
18 February 1959	**Stade de Reims 3** (Piantoni, Fontaine 2) **Standard Liège 0**
4 March 1959	**Atletico Madrid 3** (Vava, Miguel, Peiro pen) **Schalke 04 0**
18 March 1959	**Schalke 04 1** (Nowak) **Atletico Madrid 1** (Vava)
4 March 1959	**Wiener Sportklub 0** **Real Madrid 0**
18 March 1959	**Real Madrid 7** (Mateos, Di Stefano 4, Rial, Gento) **Wiener Sportklub 1** (Horak)
11 March 1959	**Young Boys Berne 2** (Meier, Rey) **SC Wismut 2** (Wagner, Zink)
18 March 1959	**SC Wismut 0** **Young Boys Berne 0**
1 April 1959 Amsterdam	**Young Boys Berne 2** (Meier, Wechselberger) **SC Wismut 1** (Erler pen)

SEMI-FINALS

15 April 1959	**Young Boys Berne 1** (Meier) **Stade de Reims 0**
13 May 1959	**Stade de Reims 3** (Piantoni 2, Penverne) **Young Boys Berne 0**
23 April 1959	**Real Madrid 2** (Rial, Puskas pen) **Atletico Madrid 1** (Chuzo)
7 May 1959	**Atletico Madrid 1** (Collar) **Real Madrid 0**
13 May 1959 Zaragoza	**Real Madrid 2** (Di Stefano, Puskas) **Atletico Madrid 1** (Collar)

FINAL

3 June 1959 Stuttgart	**Real Madrid 2** (Mateos, Di Stefano) **Stade de Reims 0**

Real Madrid: Dominguez, Marquitos, Zarraga, Santisteban, Santamaria, Ruiz, Kopa, Mateos, Di Stefano, Rial, Gento.
Reims: Colonna, Rodzik, Giraudo, Penverne, Jonquet, Leblond, Lamartine, Bliard, Fontaine, Piantoni, Vincent.
Referee: Dusch (GFR)
Attendance: 80,000

Fifth season – 1959–60

PRELIMINARY ROUND

Byes: Real Madrid, Sparta Rotterdam, Red Star Belgrade, Young Boys Berne, BK 09 Odense.

30 September 1959

ASK Vorwaerts 2 (Nöldner, Kohle)
Wolverhampton Wanderers 1 (Broadbent)
Vorwaerts: Spickenagel, Kalinke, Krampe, Unger, Kiupel, Reichelt, Wirth, Riese, Meyer, Nöldner, Kohle.
Wolverhampton Wanderers: Finlayson, Stuart, Harris, Flowers, Showell, Clamp, Lill, Mason, Murray, Broadbent, Deeley.

7 October 1959

Wolverhampton Wanderers 2 (Broadbent, Mason)
ASK Vorwaerts 0
Wolverhampton Wanderers: Finlayson, Stuart, Harris, Slater, Showell, Flowers, Lill, Mason, Murray, Broadbent, Deeley.
Vorwaerts: Spickenagel, Kalinke, Krampe, Reichelt, Kiupel, Unger, Riese, Meyer, Vogt, Nöldner, Kohle.

16 September 1959

Glasgow Rangers 5 (Millar, Scott, Matthew, Baird 2 – 1 pen)
Anderlecht 2 (Stockman, Dewaele)
Rangers: Niven, Shearer, Little, Davis, Telfer, Stevenson, Scott, McMillan, Millar, Baird, Matthew.
Anderlecht: Meert, Devolelaere, Culot, Hanon, De Koster, Van Wilden, Dewaele, Jurion, Stockman, Vandenboer, J. Van den Bosch.

23 September 1959

Anderlecht 0
Glasgow Rangers 2 (Matthew, McMillan)
Anderlecht: Meert, Devolelaere, Culot, Hanon, De Koster, Van Wilden, Lippens, Jurion, Stockman, Vandenboer, J. Van den Bosch.
Rangers: Niven, Shearer, Little, Davis, Telfer, Stevenson, Scott, McMillan, Wilson, Baird, Matthew.

9 September 1959

Linfield 2 (Milburn 2)
IFK Gothenburg 1 (Ohlsson)
Linfield: Irvine, Gilliland, Parke, Nixon, Hamill, Wilson, Stewart, Ervine, Milburn, Dickson, Ferguson.
Gothenburg: Lars Andersson, Johnsson, Ekeroth, A. Johansson, Nilsson, Noren, Berndtsson, N. Johansson, Ohlsson, B. Johansson, Lennart Andersson.

23 September 1959

IFK Gothenburg 6 (Ohlsson 5, B. Johansson)
Linfield 1 (Dickson)
Gothenburg: Lars Andersson, Johnsson, Noren, A. Johansson, Nilsson, Hansson, Berndtsson, N. Johansson, Ohlsson, B. Johansson, Lennart Andersson.
Linfield: Irvine, Gilliland, Graham, Nixon, Hamill, Wilson, Milburn, Ervine, Parke, Dickson, Braithwaite.

26 August 1959

OGC Nice 3 (Nuremburg pen, Foix 2)
Shamrock Rovers 2 (Hamilton, Tuohy)

23 September 1959

Shamrock Rovers 1 (Hennessy)
OGC Nice 1 (Faivre)

3 September 1959

CDNA Sofia 2 (Rakarov, Kolev)
Barcelona 2 (Segarra, Martinez)

23 September 1959

Barcelona 6 (Kubala 3 – 2 pens, Evaristo 3)
CDNA Sofia 2 (Milanov, Martinov)

9 September 1959

Jeunesse Esch 5 (Theis, May, Schaak, Meurisse 2)
LKS Lodz 0

23 September 1959

LKS Lodz 2 (Szymborski 2 – 1 pen)
Jeunesse Esch 1 (Jann)

9 September 1959

Wiener Sportklub 0
Petrolul Ploesti 0

16 September 1959

Petrolul Ploesti 1 (Badulescu)
Wiener Sportklub 2 (Horak 2)

11 September 1959	**Red Star Bratislava 2** (Gajdos, Scherer)
	FC Porto 1 (Teixeira)
29 September 1959	**FC Porto 0**
	Red Star Bratislava 2 (Costa og, Dolinsky)
13 September 1959	**Olympiakos 2** (Papazoglou, Ifantis)
	AC Milan 2 (Altafini 2)
23 September 1959	**AC Milan 3** (Danova 3)
	Olympiakos 1 (Ifantis)
13 September 1959	**Fenerbahce 1** (Can)
	Csepel Budapest 1 (Kisuczki)
23 September 1959	**Csepel Budapest 2** (Ughy, Nemeth)
	Fenerbahce 3 (Lefter, Seref, Avni)
	Eintracht Frankfurt Walkover
	Kuopion Palloseura Withdrew

FIRST ROUND

11 November 1959

Red Star Belgrade 1 (Kostic)
Wolverhampton Wanderers 1 (Deeley)

Red Star; Beara, Durkovic, Stojanovic, Tasic, Spajic, V. Popovic, Sekularac, Zebec, I. Popovic, Kostic, Rudinski.

Wolverhampton Wanderers: Finlayson, Stuart, Harris, Clamp, Showell, Flowers, Deeley, Mason, Murray, Broadbent, Horne.

24 November 1959

Wolverhampton Wanderers 3 (Murray, Mason 2)
Red Star Belgrade 0

Wolverhampton Wanderers: Finlayson, Stuart, Harris, Clamp, Showell, Flowers, Deeley, Mason, Murray, Broadbent, Horne.

Red Star: Beara, Durkovic, Stojanovic, Tasic, Spajic, V. Popovic, Stipic, Maravic, Sekularac, Zebec, Kostic.

11 November 1959

Glasgow Rangers 4 (McMillan, Scott, Wilson, Millar)
Red Star Bratislava 3 (Scherer 2, Dolinsky)

Rangers: Niven, Caldow, Little, Davis, Telfer, Stevenson, Scott, McMillan, Millar, Baird, Wilson.

Red Star: Hlavaty, Hlozek, Weis, Matlak, Tichy, Rias, Gajdos, Scherer, Cimra, Kacani, Dolinsky.

18 November 1959

Red Star Bratislava 1 (Tichy)
Glasgow Rangers 1 (Scott)

Red Star: Hlavaty, Hlozek, Weis, Bubernik, Tichy, Rias, Gajdos, Scherer, Cimra, Kacani, Dolinsky.

Rangers: Niven, Shearer, Little, Davis, Telfer, Stevenson, Scott, McMillan, Millar, Baird, Wilson.

21 October 1959	**Real Madrid 7** (Di Stefano, Puskas 3, Herrera 2, Mateos)
	Jeunesse Esch 0
4 November 1959	**Jeunesse Esch 2** (May, Schaak)
	Real Madrid 5 (Vidal, Mateos 2, Di Stefano, Puskas)
21 October 1959	**BK 09 Odense 0**
	Wiener Sportklub 3 (Knoll 2, Horak)
4 November 1959	**Wiener Sportklub 2** (Hof 2)
	BK 09 Odense 2 (Basset, Berg)
25 October 1959	**Sparta Rotterdam 3** (Daniels 3)
	IFK Gothenburg 1 (N. Johansson)
5 November 1959	**IFK Gothenburg 3** (Ohlsson, Helmer, Lennart Andersson)
	Sparta Rotterdam 1 (Schilder)
25 November 1959 Bremen	**Sparta Rotterdam 3** (van Ede, Bosselaar, Crossan)
	IFK Gothenburg 1 (B. Johansson)
4 November 1959	**AC Milan 0**
	Barcelona 2 (Verges, Suarez)
25 November 1959	**Barcelona 5** (Martinez, Segarra, Kubala 2, Czibor)
	AC Milan 1 (Ferrario)
4 November 1959	**Young Boys Berne 1** (Meier)
	Eintracht Frankfurt 4 (Weilbächer, Stein, Bäumler pen, Meier)
25 November 1959	**Eintracht Frankfurt 1** (Bäumler pen)
	Young Boys Berne 1 (Schneider)
19 November 1959	**Fenerbahce 2** (Can, Seref)
	OGC Nice 1 (Milazzo)
3 December 1959	**OGC Nice 2** (Foix, Faivre)
	Fenerbahce 1 (Lefter pen)

23 December 1959 Geneva	**OGC Nice 5** (Foix 2, Milazzo, Faivre, De Bourgoing) **Fenerbahce 1** (Seref)

QUARTER-FINALS

10 February 1960

Barcelona 4 (Villaverde 2, Kubala, Evaristo)
Wolverhampton Wanderers 0

Barcelona: Ramallets, Flotats, Gensana, Gracia, Segarra, Verges, Martinez, Kubala, Evaristo, Suarez, Villaverde.

Wolverhampton Wanderers: Finlayson, Stuart, Harris, Clamp, Showell, Flowers, Deeley, Mason, Murray, Broadbent, Horne.

2 March 1960

Wolverhampton Wanderers 2 (Murray, Mason)
Barcelona 5 (Kocsis 4, Villaverde)

Wolverhampton Wanderers: Sidebottom, Showell, Harris, Clamp, Slater, Flowers, Deeley, Broadbent, Mason, Murray, Horne.

Barcelona: Ramallets, Olivella, Rodri, Gracia, Segarra, Gensana, Coll, Kocsis, Martinez, Suarez, Villaverde.

9 March 1960

Sparta Rotterdam 2 (de Vries 2)
Glasgow Rangers 3 (Wilson, Baird, Murray)

Sparta: van Dijk, Visser, van der Lee, Villerius, Schilder, de Koining, van Ede, Crossan, Fitzgerald, de Vries, Bosselaar.

Rangers: Niven, Caldow, Little, Davis, Paterson, Stevenson, Scott, McMillan, Murray, Baird, Wilson.

16 March 1960

Glasgow Rangers 0
Sparta Rotterdam 1 (van Ede)

Rangers: Ritchie, Caldow, Little, Davis, Paterson, Stevenson, Scott, Baird, Millar, Brand, Wilson.

Sparta: van Dijk, Visser, van der Lee, Verhoeven, Villerius, de Koning, van Ede, Crossan, Fitzgerald, de Vries, Bosselaar.

30 March 1960
Highbury, London

Glasgow Rangers 3 (Baird, Wilson, van der Lee og)
Sparta Rotterdam 2 (Verhoeven, Bosselaar pen)

Rangers: Niven, Caldow, Little, Davis, Paterson, Stevenson, Scott, McMillan, Millar, Baird, Wilson.

Sparta: van Dijk, Visser, van der Lee, Verhoeven, Villerius, de Koning, van Ede, Crossan, Fitzgerald, de Vries, Bosselaar.

4 February 1960

OGC Nice 3 (Nuremberg 3 – 1 pen)
Real Madrid 2 (Herrera, Rial)

2 March 1960

Real Madrid 4 (Pepillo, Gento, Di Stefano, Puskas)
OGC Nice 0

3 March 1960

Eintracht Frankfurt 2 (Lindner, Meier)
Wiener Sportklub 1 (Skerlan)

16 March 1960

Wiener Sportklub 1 (Hof)
Eintracht Frankfurt 1 (Stein)

SEMI-FINALS

13 April 1960

Eintracht Frankfurt 6 (Stinka, Pfaff 2, Lindner 2, Stein)
Glasgow Rangers 1 (Caldow pen)

Eintracht: Loy, Lütz, Höfer, Weilbächer, Eigenbrodt, Stinka, Kress, Lindner, Stein, Pfaff, Meier.

Rangers: Niven, Caldow, Little, Baird, Paterson, Stevenson, Scott, McMillan, Murray, Millar, Wilson.

5 May 1960

Glasgow Rangers 3 (McMillan 2, Wilson)
Eintracht Frankfurt 6 (Lindner 2, Pfaff 2, Meier 2)

Rangers: Niven, Caldow, Little, Davis, Paterson, Stevenson, Scott, McMillan, Millar, Baird, Wilson.

Eintracht: Loy, Lütz, Höfer, Weilbächer, Eigenbrodt, Stinka, Kress, Lindner, Stein, Pfaff, Meier.

21 April 1960

Real Madrid 3 (Di Stefano 2, Puskas)
Barcelona 1 (Martinez)

27 April 1960

Barcelona 1 (Kocsis)
Real Madrid 3 (Puskas 2, Gento)

FINAL

18 May 1960
Glasgow

Real Madrid 7 (Di Stefano 3, Puskas 4 – 1 pen)
Eintracht Frankfurt 3 (Kress, Stein 2)

Real Madrid: Dominguez, Marquitos, Pachin, Vidal, Santamaria, Zarraga, Canario, Del Sol, Di Stefano, Puskas, Gento.

Eintracht: Loy, Lütz, Höfer, Weilbächer, Eigenbrodt, Stinka, Kress, Lindner, Stein, Pfaff, Meier.

Referee: Mowat (Sco)

Attendance: 127,621.

Sixth season – 1960–61

PRELIMINARY ROUND

Byes: Real Madrid, Burnley, Panathinaikos, Hamburg.

29 September 1960

Heart of Midlothian 1 (Young)
Benfica 2 (Aguas, Augusto)

Heart of Midlothian: Marshall, Kirk, Thomson, Cumming, Milne, Bowman, Young, Murray, Bauld, Blackwood, Smith.

Benfica: Costa Pereira, Joao, Cruz, Saraiva, Germano, Neto, Augusto, Santana, Aguas, Coluna, Cavem.

5 October 1960

Benfica 3 (Aguas 2, Augusto)
Heart of Midlothian 0

Benfica: Costa Pereira, Angelo, Cruz, Saraiva, Germano, Neto, Augusto, Santana, Aguas, Coluna, Cavem.

Heart of Midlothian: Marshall, Kirk, Thomson, Cumming, Milne, Bowman, Smith, Murray, Young, Blackwood, Crawford.

31 August 1960

Fredrikstad 4 (Pedersen 2, Borgen, Olsen)
Ajax 3 (Swart, Groot, Muller)

7 September 1960

Ajax 0
Fredrikstad 0

31 August 1960

Limerick 0
Young Boys Berne 5 (Wechselberger 2, Schneider, Dürr, Meier)

5 October 1960

Young Boys Berne 4 (Alleman, Schneider 2, Dürr)
Limerick 2 (Lynam, O'Reilly)

1 September 1960

HIFK Helsinki 1 (Kankkonen)
IFK Malmo 3 (Olofsson 2, Borg)

28 September 1960

IFK Malmo 2 (Lundquist, Ljung)
HIFK Helsinki 1 (Kivela)

7 September 1960

Stade de Reims 6 (Dubaele 3, Piantoni, Rustichelli, Vincent)
Jeunesse Esch 1 (Meurisse)

5 October 1960

Jeunesse Esch 0
Stade de Reims 5 (Vincent, Moreau, Heinen og, Rustichelli 2)

14 September 1960

Rapid Vienna 4 (Dienst, Glechner pen, Bertalan, Oktay og)
Besiktas 0

28 September 1960

Besiktas 1 (Ahmet)
Rapid Vienna 0

21 September 1960

Aarhus GF 3 (Amidsen, Kjär-Andersen, J. Jensen)
Legia Warsaw 0

5 October 1960

Legia Warsaw 1 (Nowak)
Aarhus GF 0

(Legia Warsaw previously appeared as CWKS Warsaw)

21 September 1960

Juventus 2 (Lojodice, Sivori)
CDNA Sofia 0

12 October 1960

CDNA Sofia 4 (Rakarov, Zanev, Panayotov, Kovatchev)
Juventus 1 (Nicole)

28 September 1960

Barcelona 2 (Czibor, Suarez)
Lierse SK 0

5 October 1960

Lierse SK 0
Barcelona 3 (Villaverde 2, Evaristo)

28 September 1960

Red Star Belgrade 1 (Kostic)
Ujpest Dozsa 2 (Göröcs, Kuharszki)

12 October 1960

Ujpest Dozsa 3 (Borsanyi, Pataki, Göröcs)
Red Star Belgrade 0

Spartak Kralove Walkover
CCA Bucharest Withdrew

SC Wismut Walkover
Glenavon Withdrew

FIRST ROUND

16 November 1960

Burnley 2 (Robson, McIlroy)
Stade de Reims 0

Burnley: Blacklaw, Angus, Elder, Joyce, Adamson, Miller, Connelly, McIlroy, Pointer, Robson, Pilkington.

Reims: Jacquet, Wendling, Rodzik, Leblond, Siatka, Moreau, Rustichelli, Muller, Kopa, Piantoni, Vincent.

30 November 1960	**Stade de Reims 3** (Rodzik 2, Piantoni) **Burnley 2** (Robson, Connelly)

Reims: Jacquet, Wendling, Rodzik, Leblond, Siatka, Moreau, Glovacki, Muller, Fontaine, Piantoni, Vincent.

Burnley: Blacklaw, Angus, Elder, Joyce, Adamson, Miller, Connelly, McIlroy, Pointer, Robson, Pilkington.

19 October 1960
Aarhus GF 3 (A. Jensen 2, Overby)
Fredrikstad 0

26 October 1960
Fredrickstad 0
Aarhus GF 1 (J. Hansen)

2 November 1960
IFK Malmo 1 (Karlsson)
CDNA Sofia 0

13 November 1960
CDNA Sofia 1 (Zanev)
IFK Malmo 1 (Olofsson)

2 November 1960
Young Boys Berne 0
Hamburg 5 (Stürmer 2, U. Seeler 2, Neisner)

27 November 1960
Hamburg 3 (U. Seeler 2, Dorfel)
Young Boys Berne 3 (Bigler pen, Meier, Schneider)

6 November 1960
Spartak Kralove 1 (Sonka)
Panathinaikos 0

7 December 1960
Panathinaikos 0
Spartak Kralove 0

6 November 1960
Benfica 6 (Coluna, Aguas 2, Augusto 2, Santana)
Ujpest Dozsa 2 (Göröcs 2)

30 November 1960
Ujpest Dozsa 2 (Halapi, Szusza)
Benfica 1 (Santana)

9 November 1960
Real Madrid 2 (Mateos, Gento)
Barcelona 2 (Suarez 2 – 1 pen)

25 November 1960
Barcelona 2 (Verges, Evaristo)
Real Madrid 1 (Canario)

9 November 1960
Rapid Vienna 3 (Dienst, Milanovic, Hanappi)
SC Wismut 1 (Wagner)

23 November 1960
SC Wismut 2 (Bamberger, Zink)
Rapid Vienna 0

21 December 1960
Basle
Rapid Vienna 1 (Flögel)
SC Wismut 0

QUARTER-FINALS

18 January 1961
Burnley 3 (Pilkington 2, Robson)
Hamburg 1 (Dörfel)

Burnley: Blacklaw, Angus, Elder, Joyce, Adamson, Miller, Connelly, McIlroy, Pointer, Robson, Pilkington.

Hamburg: Schnoor, Krug, Kurbjuhn, Werner, Meinke, D. Seeler, Neisner, Dehn, U. Seeler, Stürmer, Dörfel.

15 March 1961
Hamburg 4 (Stürmer, U. Seeler 2, Dörfel)
Burnley 1 (Harris)

Hamburg: Schnoor, Krug, Kurbjuhn, Werner, Meinke, D. Seeler, Neisner, Dehn, U. Seeler, Stürmer, Dörfel.

Burnley: Blacklaw, Angus, Elder, Joyce, Adamson, Miller, Connelly, McIlroy, Pointer, Robson, Harris.

8 March 1961
Barcelona 4 (Tejada 2, Evaristo, Kubala pen)
Spartak Kralove 0

15 March 1961
Spartak Kralove 1 (Zikan)
Barcelona 1 (Suarez)

8 March 1961
Benfica 3 (Aguas 2, Augusto pen)
Aarhus GF 1 (Amidsen)

30 March 1961
Aarhus GF 1 (Germano og)
Benfica 4 (Augusto 2, Aguas, Santana)

22 March 1961	**Rapid Vienna 2** (Dienst, Bertalan) **IFK Malmo 0**
3 April 1961	**IFK Malmo 0** **Rapid Vienna 2** (Bertalan, Flögel)

SEMI-FINALS

12 April 1961	**Barcelona 1** (Evaristo) **Hamburg 0**
26 April 1961	**Hamburg 2** (Wulf, U. Seeler) **Barcelona 1** (Kocsis)
3 May 1961 Brussels	**Barcelona 1** (Evaristo) **Hamburg 0**
26 April 1961	**Benfica 3** (Coluna, Aguas, Cavem) **Rapid Vienna 0**
4 May 1961	**Rapid Vienna 1** (Skocik) **Benfica 1** (Aguas)

This match in Vienna was awarded to Benfica, after being abandoned in the last few minutes when the crowd invaded the pitch (see chapter three).

FINAL

31 May 1961 Berne	**Benfica 3** (Aguas, Gensana og, Coluna) **Barcelona 2** (Kocsis, Czibor)

Benfica: Costa Pereira, Joao, Angelo, Neto, Germano, Cruz, Augusto, Santana, Aguas, Coluna, Cavem.

Barcelona: Ramallets, Foncho, Gracia, Verges, Garay, Gensana, Kubala, Kocsis, Evaristo, Suarez, Czibor.

Referee: Dienst (Swi).

Attendance: 33,000

Seventh season – 1961–62

PRELIMINARY ROUND

Byes: Benfica, Fenerbahce, Valkeakosken Haka.

13 September 1961	**Gornik Zabrze 4** (Norman og, Musialek 2, Pol) **Tottenham Hotspur 2** (Jones, Dyson)

Gornik: Kostka, Franosz, Olszowska, Florenki, Oslizlo, Kowalksi, Wilczek, Pol, Musialek, Jankowski, Lentner.

Tottenham Hotspur: Brown, Baker, Henry, Blanchflower, Norman, Mackay, Jones, White, Smith, Allen, Dyson.

20 September 1961	**Tottenham Hotspur 8** (Blanchflower pen, Jones 3, Smith 2, Dyson, White) **Gornik Zabrze 1** (Pol)

Tottenham Hotspur: Brown, Baker, Henry, Blanchflower, Norman, Mackay, Jones, White, Smith, Allen, Dyson.

Gornik: Kostka, Franosz, Olzowska, Gawlik, Oslizlo, Oleiznik, Florenki, Pol, Jankowski, Wilczek, Lentner.

5 September 1961	**AS Monaco 2** (Douis, Carlier pen) **Glasgow Rangers 3** (Baxter, Scott 2)

Monaco: Hernandez, Novak, Artelesa, Biancheri, Ludo, Hidalgo, Djibrill, Hess, Douis, Theo, Carlier.

Rangers: Ritchie, Shearer, Caldow, Davis, Paterson, Baxter, Scott, McMillan, Millar, Brand, Wilson.

12 September 1961	**Glasgow Rangers 3** (Christie 2, Scott) **AS Monaco 2** (Hess 2)

Rangers: Ritchie, Shearer, Caldow, Davis, Paterson, Baxter, Scott, McMillan, Christie, Brand, Wilson.

Monaco: Garafalo, Novak, Thomas, Artelesa, Ludo, Biancheri, Djibrill, Hess, Douis, Hidalgo, Carlier

30 August 1961	**ASK Vorwaerts 3** (Kohle 2, Wirth) **Linfield 0**

Vorwaerts: Spickenagel, Kalinke, Kiupel, Krampe, Vogt, Körner, Hoge, Riese, Meyer, Kohle, Wirth.
Linfield: Irvine, Gilliland, Parke, Andrews, Hatton, Gough, Stewart, Barr, Reid, Dickson, Braithwaite.

The second leg of this tie was not played. Linfield conceded the match when Vorwaerts were refused visas to come to Ireland.

23 August 1961	**Nuremberg 5** (Strehl 2, Gettinger 2, Muller) **Drumcondra 0**
13 September 1961	**Drumcondra 1** (Fullam) **Nuremberg 4** (S. Smyth og, Strehl 2, Prole og)
6 September 1961	**IFK Gothenburg 0** **Feyenoord 3** (Bouwmeester, Temming, Bennaers)
13 September 1961	**Feyenoord 8** (Bouwmeester 4, Temming 2, Bennaers, Schouten) **IFK Gothenburg 2** (Danielsson, Svensson)
6 September 1961	**CDNA Sofia 4** (Rankov, Rakarov, Romanov, Yakimov) **Dukla Prague 4** (Kucera, Adamec, Borovicka, Manolov og)
13 September 1961	**Dukla Prague 2** (Kucera, Safranek) **CDNA Sofia 1** (Rankov)
6 September 1961	**Vasas Budapest 0** **Real Madrid 2** (Tejada 2)
20 September 1961	**Real Madrid 3** (Di Stefano 2, Tejada) **Vasas Budapest 1** (Machos)
6 September 1961	**Servette (Geneva) 5** (Robbiani 2, Georgy 2, Nemeth) **Hibernians (Malta) 0**
20 September 1961	**Hibernians (Malta) 1** (Sultana) **Servette (Geneva) 2** (Robbiani, Wüthrich)
6 September 1961	**Standard Liège 2** (Dierendonck, Paeschen) **Fredrikstad 1** (Bergersen)
20 September 1961	**Fredrikstad 0** **Standard Liège 2** (Claessen 2)
7 September 1961	**Spora Luxembourg 0** **BK 1913 Odense 6** (Lofquist, Brunn, Remy og, Hansen, Rasmussen 2)
13 September 1961	**BK 1913 Odense 9** (Lofquist 5, O. Andersen 3, Rasmussen) **Spora Luxembourg 2** (Scheer, Leer)
13 September 1961	**Sporting Lisbon 1** (Lucio) **Partizan Belgrade 1** (Vukelic)
20 September 1961	**Partizan Belgrade 2** (Radovic, Vislavski) **Sporting Lisbon 0**
20 September 1961	**Panathinaikos 1** (Papaemanouil) **Juventus 1** (Mora)
27 September 1961	**Juventus 2** (Nicole, Rossano) **Panathinaikos 1** (Kolevas)
21 September 1961	**CCA Bucharest 0** **FK Austria 0**
28 September 1961	**FK Austria 2** (Stotz pen, Nemec) **CCA Bucharest 0** *(CCA Bucharest later appear as Steaua Bucharest)*

FIRST ROUND

1 November 1961	**Feyenoord 1** (Kreyermaat) **Tottenham Hotspur 3** (Dyson, Saul 2) *Feyenoord:* Pieters-Graafland, Kerkum, Veldhoven, Kreyermaat, Kraay, Klaasens, Schouten, Bennaers, van der Gijp, Bouwmeester, Moulijn. *Tottenham Hotspur:* Brown, Baker, Henry, Blanchflower, Norman, Marchi, Jones, White, Saul, Clayton, Dyson.
15 November 1961	**Tottenham Hotspur 1** (Dyson) **Feyenoord 1** (Bennaers) *Tottenham Hotspur:* Brown, Baker, Henry, Blanchflower, Norman, Marchi, Jones, White, Saul, Mackay, Dyson. *Feyenoord:* Pieters-Graafland, Kerkum, Veldhoven, Kreyermaat, Kraay, Klaasens, Bergholtz, Bennaers, van der Gijp, Schouten, Moulijn.
15 November 1961	**ASK Vorwaerts 1** (Kohle) **Glasgow Rangers 2** (Caldow pen, Brand) *Vorwaerts:* Spickenagel, Kalinke, Krampe, Prüfke, Kiupel, Körner, Hoge, Kohle, Vogt, Nöldner, Wirth. *Rangers:* Ritchie, Shearer, Caldow, Davis, Paterson, Baxter, Scott, McMillan, Millar, Brand, Wilson.
22 November 1961	*ASK Vorwaerts were refused visas to travel to Glasgow, so the second leg was played in Malmo, Sweden. The game on this date was abandoned after 45 minutes due to fog, with Rangers leading 1–0 (Henderson). The match was replayed the next day with the following result:*

23 November 1961

Glasgow Rangers 4 (Kalinke og, McMillan 2, Henderson)
ASK Vorwaerts 1 (Caldow og)

Rangers: Ritchie, Shearer, Caldow, Davis, Paterson, Baxter, Henderson, McMillan, Millar, Brand, Wilson.

Vorwaerts: Spickenagel, Kalinke, Krampe, Unger, Kiupel, Körner, Hoge, Karrow, Vogt, Nöldner, Wirth.

18 October 1961

BK 1913 Odense 0
Real Madrid 3 (Puskas 2, Tejada)

25 October 1961

Real Madrid 9 (Di Stefano 3, Del Sol 2, Gento 2, Puskas, Isidro)
BK 1913 Odense 0

18 October 1961

Fenerbahce 1 (Can)
Nuremberg 2 (Strehl, Flackeneker)

3 December 1961

Nuremberg 1 (Wild)
Fenerbahce 0

24 October 1961

Standard Liège 5 (Claessen 3, Paeschen, Dierendonck)
Valkeakosken Haka 1 (Kumpulampi)

2 November 1961

Valkeakosken Haka 0
Standard Liège 2 (Semmeling, Nyttymaeki og)

31 October 1961

FK Austria 1 (Stark)
Benfica 1 (Augusto)

8 November 1961

Benfica 5 (Aguas 2, Santana 2, Eusebio)
FK Austria 1 (Humberto og)

5 November 1961

Servette (Geneva) 4 (Fatton 3, Robbiani)
Dukla Prague 3 (Adamec 2, Vacenovsky)

22 November 1961

Dukla Prague 2 (Kucera 2)
Servette (Geneva) 0

8 November 1961

Partizan Belgrade 1 (Vasovic)
Juventus 2 (Nicole, Rosa)

15 November 1961

Juventus 5 (Nicole, Mora 2, Rosa, Stacchini)
Partizan Belgrade 0

QUARTER-FINALS

14 February 1962

Dukla Prague 1 (Kucera)
Tottenham Hotspur 0

Dukla: Kouba, Safranek, L. Novak, Pluskal, Cadek, Masopust, Brumovsky, Kucera, Borovicka, Adamec, Jelinek.

Tottenham Hotspur: Brown, Baker, Henry, Marchi, Norman, Mackay, Medwin, White, Smith, Blanchflower, Jones.

26 February 1962

Tottenham Hotspur 4 (Smith 2, Mackay 2)
Dukla Prague 1 (Jelinek)

Tottenham Hotspur: Brown, Baker, Henry, Blanchflower, Norman, Marchi, Medwin, White, Smith, Mackay, Jones.

Dukla: Kouba, Safranek, L. Novak, Pluskal, Cadek, Masopust, Brumovsky, Kucera, Borovicka, Adamec, Jelinek.

7 February 1962

Standard Liège 4 (Claessen, Crossan 2, Vliers)
Glasgow Rangers 1 (Wilson)

Standard Liège: Nicolay, Vliers, Marchal, Bonga-Bonga, Spronck, Houf, Semmeling, Sztani, Claessen, Crossan, Paeschen.

Rangers: Ritchie, Shearer, King, Davis, Paterson, Baxter, Henderson, Greig, Millar, Brand, Wilson.

14 February 1962

Glasgow Rangers 2 (Brand, Caldow pen)
Standard Liège 0

Rangers: Ritchie, Shearer, Caldow, Davis, Baillie, Baxter, Scott, McMillan, Millar, Brand, Wilson.

Standard Liège: Nicolay, Vliers, Thellin, Bonga-Bonga, Marchal, Houf, Semmeling, Sztani, Claessen, Crossan, Paeschen.

1 February 1962

Nuremberg 3 (Flackeneker 2, Strehl)
Benfica 1 (Cavem)

22 February 1962

Benfica 6 (Aguas, Augusto 2, Coluna, Eusebio 2)
Nuremberg 0

14 February 1962

Juventus 0
Real Madrid 1 (Di Stefano)

21 February 1962

Real Madrid 0
Juventus 1 (Sivori)

28 February 1962
Paris

Real Madrid 3 (Felo, Tejada, Del Sol)
Juventus 1 (Sivori)

SEMI-FINALS

21 March 1962

Benfica 3 (Aguas, Augusto 2)
Tottenham Hotspur 1 (Smith)

Benfica: Costa Pereira, Joao, Angelo, Cavem, Germano, Cruz, Augusto, Eusebio, Aguas, Coluna, Simoes.

Tottenham Hotspur: Brown, Baker, Henry, Marchi, Norman, Mackay, Greaves, White, Smith, Blanchflower, Jones.

5 April 1962

Tottenham Hotspur 2 (Smith, Blanchflower pen)
Benfica 1 (Aguas)

Tottenham Hotspur: Brown, Baker, Henry, Blanchflower, Norman, Mackay, Medwin, White, Smith, Greaves, Jones.

Benfica: Costa Pereira, Joao, Angelo, Cavem, Germano, Cruz, Augusto, Eusebio, Aguas, Coluna, Simoes.

22 March 1962

Real Madrid 4 (Di Stefano, Tejada 2, Casado)
Standard Liège 0

12 April 1962

Standard Liège 0
Real Madrid 2 (Puskas, Del Sol)

FINAL

2 May 1962
Amsterdam

Benfica 5 (Eusebio 2 – 1 pen, Aguas, Cavem, Coluna)
Real Madrid 3 (Puskas 3)

Benfica: Costa Pereira, Joao, Angelo, Cavem, Germano, Cruz, Augusto, Eusebio, Aguas, Coluna, Simoes.

Real Madrid: Araquistain, Casado, Miera, Felo, Santamaria, Pachin, Tejada, Del Sol, Di Stefano, Puskas, Gento.

Referee: Horn (Nth)

Attendance: 68,000.

Eighth season – 1962–63

PRELIMINARY ROUND

Byes: Benfica, Stade de Reims

18 September 1962

Floriana (Malta) 1 (Borg)
Ipswich Town 4 (Crawford 2, Phillips 2)

Floriana: Mizzi, de Batista, McKay, de Grima, Azzopardi, Vella-James, Borg, Dalli, Cauchi, Bennetti, Demanuele.

Ipswich Town: Bailey, Malcolm, Compton, Baxter, Nelson, Elsworthy, Stephenson, Moran, Crawford, Phillips, Blackwood.

25 September 1962

Ipswich Town 10 (Crawford 5, Moran 2, Phillips 2 – 1 pen, Elsworthy)
Floriana 0

Ipswich Town: Bailey, Malcolm, Compton, Baxter, Laurel, Elsworthy, Stephenson, Moran, Crawford, Phillips, Blackwood.

Floriana: Mizzi, de Batista, Farrugia, de Grima, Azzopardi, Vella-James, Borg, Dalli, Cauchi, Bennetti, Demanuele.

5 September 1962

Dundee 8 (Gilzean 3, Wishart, Smith, Penman, Robertson, Hemmersbach og)
Cologne 1 (Hamilton og)

Dundee: Slater, Hamilton, Cox, Seith, Ure, Wishart, Smith, Penman, Cousin, Gilzean, Robertson.

Cologne: Ewert, Regh, Sturm, Hemmersbach, Wilden, Benthaus, Thielen, Schäfer, Müller, Habig, Hornig.

26 September 1962

Cologne 4 (Habig, Müller, Schäfer, Ure og)
Dundee 0

Cologne: Schumacher, Pott, Regh, Schnellinger, Wilden, Benthaus, Thielen, Habig, Müller, Schäfer, Hornig.

Dundee: Slater, Hamilton, Cox, Seith, Ure, Wishart, Smith, Penman, Cousin, Gilzean, Robertson.

5 September 1962

Linfield 1 (Dickson)
Esbjerg BK 2 (Berthelsen 2)

Linfield: Irvine, Gilliland, Graham, Andrews, Hatton, Parke, Stewart, Ferguson, Reid, Dickson, Braithwaite.

Esbjerg: Gaardhoeje, J. Hansen, P. Jensen, E. Jensen, Madsen, J. Petersen, K. Petersen, Christiansen, Berthelsen, Frandsen, Andersen.

19 September 1962

Esbjerg BK 0
Linfield 0

Esbjerg: Gaardhoeje, J. Hansen, P. Jensen, E. Jensen, Madsen, J. Petersen, K. Petersen, Christiansen, Berthelsen, Frandsen, P. Hansen.

Linfield: Irvine, Gilliland, Graham, Andrews, Hatton, Parke, Stewart, Ferguson, Reid, Dickson, Braithwaite.

26 August 1962

IFK Norrköping 2 (Bild, Rosander)
Partizan Tirana 0

12 September 1962

Partizan Tirana 1 (Pano)
IFK Norrköping 1 (Kindvall)

5 September 1962

Real Madrid 3 (Hellens og, Gento, Di Stefano)
Anderlecht 3 (van Himst, Janssens, Stockman)

26 September 1962

Anderlecht 1 (Jurion)
Real Madrid 0

5 September 1962

Fredrikstad 1 (Aas)
Vasas Budapest 4 (Pal I 3, Machos)

19 September 1962

Vasas Budapest 7 (Farkas 3, Pal I 2, Pal II 2)
Fredrikstad 0

5 September 1962

FK Austria 5 (Nemec 3, Hirnschrodt, Schleger)
HIFK Helsinki 3 (Ekman, Wilk, Kankkonen)

26 September 1962

HIFK Helsinki 0
FK Austria 2 (Nemec, Jacare)

9 September 1962

Dinamo Bucharest 1 (Pircalab pen)
Galatasaray 1 (Metin)

16 September 1962

Galatasaray 3 (Tarik 2, Metin)
Dinamo Bucharest 0

12 September 1962

Servette 1 (Mekloufi)
Feyenoord 3 (Kruiver 2, Bennaers)

19 September 1962

Feyenoord 1 (Kerkum pen)
Servette 3 (Mekloufi 2, Henry)

17 October 1962
Dusseldorf

Servette 1 (Nemeth)
Feyenoord 3 (Kruiver, Bouwmeester, van der Gijp)

After extra time.

12 September 1962

Polonia Bytom 2 (Pogrzeba, Liberda)
Panathinaikos 1 (Theophanis)

19 September 1962

Panathinaikos 1 (Panakis)
Polonia Bytom 4 (Liberda, Kempny 2, Pogrzeba)

12 September 1962

AC Milan 8 (Altafini 5, Germano 2, Rivera)
US Luxembourg 0

19 September 1962

US Luxembourg 0
AC Milan 6 (Altafini 3, Rossano 2, Pivatelli)

19 September 1962

CDNA Sofia 2 (Zanev, Kolev)
Partizan Belgrade 1 (Kovacevic pen)

3 October 1962

Partizan Belgrade 1 (Galic)
CDNA Sofia 4 (Zanev, Yakimov, Kovacevic pen, Panayotov)

19 September 1962

Shelbourne 0
Sporting Lisbon 2 (Morais, Geo)

26 September 1962

Sporting Lisbon 5 (Lucio, Mascarenhas 2, Carlos, Morais)
Shelbourne 1 (Hennessy)

26 September 1962

ASK Vorwaerts 0
Dukla Prague 3 (Adamec 3)

3 October 1962

Dukla Prague 1 (Adamec)
ASK Vorwaerts 0

FIRST ROUND

19 November 1962

AC Milan 3 (Barison 2, Dino Sani)
Ipswich Town 0

Milan: Liberalato, David, Radice, Pivatelli, Maldini, Trapattoni, Germano, Dino Sani, Altafini, Rivera, Barison.

Ipswich Town: Bailey, Carberry, Malcolm, Baxter, Nelson, Pickett, Stephenson, Moran, Crawford, Blackwood, Leadbetter.

28 November 1962

Ipswich Town 2 (Crawford, Blackwood)
AC Milan 1 (Barison)

Ipswich Town: Bailey, Carberry, Compton, Baxter, Nelson, Elsworthy, Stephenson, Moran, Crawford, Phillips, Blackwood.

Milan: Ghezzi, David, Trebbi, Trapattoni, Maldini, Radice, Pelagalli, Rivera, Altafini, Dino Sani, Barison.

24 October 1962	**Sporting Lisbon 1** (Geo) **Dundee 0** *Sporting:* Carvalho, Carlos, Hilario, Perides, Lucio, Julio, Hugo, Osvaldo, Mascarenhas, Geo, Morais. *Dundee:* Slater, Hamilton, Cox, Seith, Ure, Wishart, Smith, Penman, Cousin, Gilzean, Houston.
31 October 1962	**Dundee 4** (Gilzean 3, Cousin) **Sporting Lisbon 1** (Figeuiredo) *Dundee:* Slater, Hamilton, Cox, Seith, Ure, Wishart, Smith, Penman, Cousin, Gilzean, Robertson. *Sporting:* Carvalho, Lino, Hilario, Carlos, Lucio, Julio, Figeuiredo , Osvaldo, Mascarenhas, Geo, Morais.
18 October 1962	**FK Austria 3** (Jacare, Hirnschrodt, Fiala pen) **Stade de Reims 2** (Sauvage 2 – 1 pen)
14 November 1962	**Stade de Reims 5** (Kopa 2, Siatka, Dubaele, Akesbi) **FK Austria 0**
24 October 1962	**CDNA Sofia 2** (Kolev, Yakimov) **Anderlecht 2** (Jurion 2)
14 November 1962	**Anderlecht 2** (Lippens 2 – 1 pen) **CDNA Sofia 0** *(CDNA Sofia later appear as CSKA Sofia)*
31 October 1962	**IFK Norrköping 1** (Björklund) **Benfica 1** (Eusebio)
22 November 1962	**Benfica 5** (Aguas, Eusebio 3, Coluna) **IFK Norrköping 1** (Björklund)
7 November 1962	**Galatasaray 4** (Meint 3 – 1 pen, Suat) **Polonia Bytom 1** (Kempny)
18 November 1962	**Polonia Bytom 1** (Jozwiak) **Galatasaray 0**
7 November 1962	**Esbjerg BK 0** **Dukla Prague 0**
14 November 1962	**Dukla Prague 5** (Vacenovsky 2, Masopust, Brumovsky, Hansen og) **Esbjerg BK 0**
14 November 1962	**Feyenoord 1** (van der Gijp) **Vasas Budapest 1** (Pal I)
28 November 1962	**Vasas Budapest 2** (Machos 2 pens) **Feyenoord 2** (Kruiver, Kerkum pen)
12 December 1962 Anvers	**Feyenoord 1** (Bennaers) **Vasas Budapest 0**

QUARTER-FINALS

6 March 1963	**Anderlecht 1** (Lippens pen) **Dundee 4** (Gilzean 2, Cousin, Smith) *Anderlecht:* Fazekas, Heylens, Cornelis, Hanon, Verbiest, Lippens, Janssens, Jurion, Stockman, van Himst, Puis. *Dundee:* Slater, Hamilton, Cox, Seith, Ure, Wishart, Smith, Penman, Cousin, Gilzean, Robertson.
13 March 1963	**Dundee 2** (Smith, Cousin) **Anderlecht 1** (Stockman) *Dundee:* Slater, Hamilton, Cox, Seith, Ure, Wishart, Smith, Penman, Cousin, Gilzean, Robertson. *Anderlecht:* Trappeniers, Plaskie, Cornelis, Hanon, Verbiest, Lippens, Janssens, Jurion, Stockman, van Himst, Puis.
23 January 1963	**Galatasaray 1** (Ugur) **AC Milan 3** (Mora pen, Altafini, Barison)
13 March 1963	**AC Milan 5** (Pivatelli 2, Altafini 3) **Galatasaray 0**
6 February 1963	**Stade de Reims 0** **Feyenoord 1** (Kreyermaat)
13 March 1963	**Feyenoord 1** (Kruiver) **Stade de Reims 1** (Akesbi)
6 March 1963	**Benfica 2** (Coluna 2) **Dukla Prague 1** (Brumovsky)
13 March 1963	**Dukla Prague 0** **Benfica 0**

SEMI-FINALS

24 April 1963

AC Milan 5 (Dino Sani, Barison 2, Mora 2)
Dundee 1 (Cousin)

Milan: Ghezzi, David, Trebbi, Benitez, Maldini, Trapattoni, Mora, Dino Sani, Altafini, Rivera, Barison.

Dundee: Slater, Hamilton, Stuart, Seith, Ure, Wishart, Smith, Penman, Cousin, Gilzean, Houston.

1 May 1963

Dundee 1 (Gilzean)
AC Milan 0

Dundee: Slater, Hamilton, Stuart, Seith, Ure, Wishart, Smith, Penman, Cousin, Gilzean, Houston.

Milan: Ghezzi, David, Trebbi, Benitez, Maldini, Trapattoni, Mora, Pivatelli, Altafini, Rivera, Barison.

10 April 1963

Feyenoord 0
Benfica 0

8 May 1963

Benfica 3 (Eusebio, Augusto, Santana)
Feyenoord 1 (Bouwmeester)

FINAL

22 May 1963
Wembley

AC Milan 2 (Altafini 2)
Benfica 1 (Eusebio)

Milan: Ghezzi, David, Trebbi, Benitez, Maldini, Trapattoni, Pivatelli, Dino Sani, Altafini, Rivera, Mora.

Benfica: Costa Pereira, Cavem, Cruz, Humberto, Raul, Coluna, Augusto, Santana, Torres, Eusebio, Simoes.

Referee: Holland (Eng)

Attendance: 45,000.

Ninth season 1963–64

PRELIMINARY ROUND

Bye: AC Milan

18 September 1963

Everton 0
Internazionale 0

Everton: West, Parker, Harris, Gabriel, Labone, Kay, Scott, Stevens, Young, Vernon, Temple.

Inter: Sarti, Burgnich, Facchetti, Tagnin, Guarneri, Picchi, Jair, Mazzola, Di Giacomo, Suarez, Szymaniak.

25 September 1963

Internazionale 1 (Jair)
Everton 0

Inter: Sarti, Burgnich, Facchetti, Tagnin, Guarneri, Picchi, Jair, Mazzola, Di Giacomo, Suarez, Corso.

Everton: West, Parker, Harris, Stevens, Labone, Kay, Scott, Harvey, Young, Vernon, Temple.

25 September 1963

Glasgow Rangers 0
Real Madrid 1 (Puskas)

Rangers: Ritchie, Shearer, Provan, Greig, McKinnon, Baxter, Henderson, McLean, Forrest, Brand, Wilson.

Real Madrid: Araquistain, Casado, Isidro, Muller, Santamaria, Zoco, Amancio, F. Ruiz, Di Stefano, Puskas, Gento.

9 October 1963

Real Madrid 6 (Puskas 3, Evaristo, Gento, F. Ruiz)
Glasgow Rangers 0

Real Madrid: Araquistain, Casado, Isidro, Muller, Santamaria, Zoco, Evaristo, F. Ruiz, Di Stefano, Puskas, Gento.

Rangers: Ritchie, Shearer, Provan, Greig, McKinnon, Baxter, Henderson, McLean, Forrest, Willoughby, Watson.

25 September 1963

Distillery 3 (John Kennedy, Hamilton, Ellison)
Benfica 3 (Serafim 2, Eusebio)

Distillery: Jack Kennedy, D. Meldrum, Patterson, John Kennedy, Gregg, Ellison, Anderson, Campbell, Tom Finney, J. Meldrum, Hamilton.

Benfica: Costa Pereira, Cavem, Raul, Cruz, Germano, Humberto, Yauco, Eusebio, Coluna, Serafim, Simoes.

2 October 1963

Benfica 5 (Eusebio 2, Simoes, Yauca, Serafim)
Distillery 0

Benfica: Costa Pereira, Luciano, Humberto, Cruz, Raul, Cavem, Augusto, Yauca, Eusebio, Serafim, Simoes.

Distillery: Jack Kennedy, D. Meldrum, Ellison, Patterson, Gregg, John Kennedy, J. Meldrum, Anderson, Campbell, White, Hamilton.

11 September 1963	**Lyn Oslo 2** (Berg, Stavrum) **Borussia Dortmund 4** (Emmerich 3, Wosab)
2 October 1963	**Borussia Dortmund 3** (Konietzka 2, Cyliax) **Lyn Oslo 1** (Stavrum)
11 September 1963	**Partizan Tirana 1** (Pano) **Spartak Plovdiv 0**
2 October 1963	**Spartak Plovdiv 3** (Stoinov, Dichkov, Diev) **Partizan Tirana 1** (Pano)
11 September 1963	**Partizan Belgrade 3** (Kovacevic 2 – 1 pen, Galic) **Anorthosis Nicosia 0**
1 October 1963	**Anorthosis Nicosia 1** (Kostalis) **Partizan Belgrade 3** (Galic, Bagic, Kovacevic)
11 September 1963	**Dundalk 0** **FC Zurich 3** (Feller 2, von Burg)
25 September 1963	**FC Zurich 1** (Feller) **Dundalk 2** (Cross, Hasty)
11 September 1963	**Galatasaray 4** (Bahri, Metin 2 – 1 pen, Tarik) **Ferencvaros 0**
12 October 1963	**Ferencvaros 2** (Albert 2) **Galatasaray 0**
15 September 1963	**Dukla Prague 6** (Kucera 3, Safranek, Brumovsky, Jelinek) **Valletta (Malta) 0**
29 September 1963	**Valletta (Malta) 0** **Dukla Prague 2** (Geleta, Jelinek)
18 September 1963	**Dinamo Bucharest 2** (Petru, Pircalab) **Carl Zeiss Jena 0**
25 September 1963	**Carl Zeiss Jena 0** **Dinamo Bucharest 1** (Tircovnicu)
18 September 1963	**AS Monaco 7** (Cossou 4, Douis 2, Djibrill) **AEK Athens 2** (Nestoridis, Tassinos)
2 October 1963	**AEK Athens 1** (Theophanidis) **AS Monaco 1** (Theo pen)
18 September 1963	**Gornik Zabrze 1** (Lentner) **FK Austria 0**
2 October 1963	**FK Austria 1** (Buzek) **Gornik Zabrze 0**
9 October 1963 Vienna	**Gornik Zabrze 2** (Pol, Szoltysik) **FK Austria 1** (Geyer)
25 September 1963	**Valkeakosken Haka 4** (Peltonen 2, Kumpulampi 2) **Jeunesse Esch 1** (Theis)
9 October 1963	**Jeunesse Esch 4** (Theis 2, Niemen og, May) **Valkeakoksen Haka 0**
25 September 1963	**Esbjerg BK 3** (Christiansen, Berthelsen, Frandsen) **PSV Eindhoven 4** (Theunissen , Kerkoffs 2, Brusselers)
9 October 1963	**PSV Eindhoven 7** (Kerkoffs 2, Theunissen 3, Giesen 2) **Esbjerg BK 1** (Berthelsen)
25 September 1963	**Standard Liège 1** (Pilot) **IFK Norrköping 0**
3 October 1963	**IFK Norrköping 2** (Kindvall, Martinsson) **Standard Liège 0**

FIRST ROUND

6 November 1963	**Benfica 2** (Simoes, Eusebio) **Borussia Dortmund 1** (Wosab)
4 December 1963	**Borussia Dortmund 5** (Konietzka, Brungs 3, Wosab) **Benfica 0**
13 November 1963	**Spartak Plovdiv 0** **PSV Eindhoven 1** (Kerkoffs)
27 November 1963	**PSV Eindhoven 0** **Spartak Plovdiv 0**

13 November 1963	**Dinamo Bucharest 1** (Tircovnicu) **Real Madrid 3** (F. Ruiz, Di Stefano, Gento)
18 December 1963	**Real Madrid 5** (F. Ruiz, Di Stefano, Amancio, Zoco, Puskas pen) **Dinamo Bucharest 3** (L. Nunweiller, Fratila, Pircalab)
13 November 1963	**Gornick Zabrze 2** (Musialek, Lubanski) **Dukla Prague 0**
20 November 1963	**Dukla Prague 4** (Kucera 2, Masopust, Jelinek) **Gornik Zabrze 1** (Lubanski)
14 November 1963	**FC Zurich 2** (Martinelli, Stürmer) **Galatasaray 0**
27 November 1963	**Galatasaray 2** (Metin 2 pens) **FC Zurich 0**
11 December 1963 Rome	**FC Zurich 2** (von Burg, Leimgruber) **Galatasaray 2** (Metin, Ugur) *Zurich won on toss after extra time.*
20 November 1963	**Jeunesse Esch 2** (May, Theis) **Partizan Belgrade 1** (Galic)
27 November 1963	**Partizan Belgrade 6** (Kovacevic 4, Cebinac, Galic) **Jeunesse Esch 2** (Langer, Bach)
27 November 1963	**IFK Norrköping 1** (Nordquist) **AC Milan 1** (Fortunato)
4 December 1963	**AC Milan 5** (Altafini 3, Nordquist og, Rivera) **IFK Norrköping 2** (Martinsson, Dino Sani og)
27 November 1963	**Internazionale 1** (Ciccolo) **AS Monaco 0**
4 December 1963	**AS Monaco 1** (Theo pen) **Internazionale 3** (Mazzola 2, Suarez)

QUARTER-FINALS

29 January 1964	**Real Madrid 4** (Amancio, Puskas, Di Stefano, Gento) **AC Milan 1** (Lodetti)
13 February 1964	**AC Milan 2** (Lodetti, Altafini) **Real Madrid 0**
26 February 1964	**Partizan Belgrade 0** **Internazionale 2** (Jair, Mazzola)
4 March 1964	**Internazionale 2** (Corso, Jair) **Partizan Belgrade 1** (Bagic)
4 March 1964	**PSV Eindhoven 1** (Theunissen) **FC Zurich 0**
11 March 1964	**FC Zurich 3** (Stürmer, Brizzi, Rufli) **PSV Eindhoven 1** (Verdonck)
4 March 1964	**Dukla Prague 0** **Borussia Dortmund 4** (Brungs, Konietzka, Wosab 2 – 1 pen)
18 March 1964	**Borussia Dortmund 1** (Rylewicz) **Dukla Prague 3** (Röder, Jelinek 2)

SEMI-FINALS

15 April 1964	**Borussia Dortmund 2** (Brungs 2) **Internazionale 2** (Mazzola, Corso)
29 April 1964	**Internazionale 2** (Mazzola, Jair) **Borussia Dortmund 0**
22 April 1964	**FC Zurich 1** (Brizzi) **Real Madrid 2** (Di Stefano, Zoco)
7 May 1964	**Real Madrid 6** (Zoco, Felo, Muller, Puskas, Di Stefano, Amancio) **FC Zurich 0**

FINAL

27 May 1964 Vienna	**Internazionale 3** (Mazzola 2, Milani) **Real Madrid 1** (Felo) *Internazionale:* Sarti, Burgnich, Facchetti, Tagnin, Guarneri, Picchi, Jair, Mazzola, Milani, Suarez, Corso.

Real Madrid: Vicente, Isidro, Pachin, Muller, Santamaria, Zoco, Amancio, Felo, Di Stefano, Puskas, Gento.

Referee: Stoll (Aus)

Attendance: 72,000

Tenth season – 1964–65

PRELIMINARY ROUND

Bye: Internazionale

17 August 1964

KR Reykjavik 0
Liverpool 5 (Wallace 2, Hunt 2, Chisnall)

Reykjavik: Thorkelsson Arsaelsson, B. Felixson, T. Jonsson, H. Felixson, T. Gundmundsson, G. Gundmundsson, S. Jonsson, G. Felixson, Schram, Jakobsson.

Liverpool: Lawrence, Byrne, Moran, Milne, Yeats, Stevenson, Callaghan, Hunt, Chisnall, Wallace, Thompson.

14 September 1964

Liverpool 6 (Byrne, St John 2, Hunt, Graham, Stevenson)
KR Reykjavik 1 (G. Felixson)

Liverpool: Lawrence, Byrne, Moran, Milne, Yeats, Stevenson, Callaghan, Hunt, St John, Graham, A'Court.

Reykjavik: Guddjonsson, Arsaelsson, B. Felixson, T. Jonsson, H. Felixson, Jartsson, T. Gundmundsson, S. Jonsson, G. Felixson, Schram, G. Gundmundsson.

2 September 1964

Glasgow Rangers 3 (Brand 2, Forrest)
Red Star Belgrade 1 (Kostic)

Rangers: Ritchie, Hynd, Provan, Greig, McKinnon, Baxter, Henderson, McLean, Forrest, Brand, Wilson.

Red Star: Dujkovic, Durkovic, Jeftic, Melic, Cop, Popovic, Cebinac, Skrbic, Milosevic, Kostic, Djajic.

9 September 1964

Red Star Belgrade 4 (Kostic, Brlincevic 2, Melic)
Glasgow Rangers 2 (Greig, McKinnon)

Red Star: Dujkovic, Durkovic, Jeftic, Skrbic, Cop, Popovic, Cebinac, Melic, Kostic, Brlincevic, Djajic.

Rangers: Ritchie, Shearer, Provan, Greig, McKinnon, Baxter, Henderson, Millar, Forrest, Brand, Wilson.

4 November 1964
Highbury, London

Glasgow Rangers 3 (Forrest 2, Brand)
Red Star Belgrade 1 (Cop)

Rangers: Ritchie, Provan, Caldow, Greig, McKinnon, Wood, Brand, Millar, Forrest, Baxter, Johnston.

Red Star: Dujkovic, Durkovic, Jeftic, Skrbic, Cop, Popovic, Cebinac, Melic, Brlincevic, Kostic, Djajic.

16 September 1964

Glentoran 2 (Turner pen, Thompson)
Panathinaikos 2 (Yanakopoulos, Papoutsakis)

Glentoran: Finlay, Creighton, Borne, Stewart, McCullough, Bruce, Warbuton, Turner, Thompson, Brannigan, Davis.

Panathinaikos: Oekonomopoulis, Kamaras, Andreou, Loukanidis, Papoulidis, Sourbis, Papamaenouil, Domazos, Yanakopoulis, Pitixetis, Papoutsakis.

30 September 1964

Panathinaikos 3 (Loukanidis 2 – 1 pen, Papoutsakis)
Glentoran 2 (Turner, Davis)

Panathinaikos: Peconomides, Kamaras, Andreou, Loukanidis, Papoulidis, Sourbis, Panayotidis, Domazos, Komanidis, Papamaenouil, Papoutsakis.

Glentoran: Finlay, Creighton, Borne, Stewart, McCullough, Bruce, Warburton, Turner, Thompson, Brannigan, Davis.

2 September 1964

Chemie Leipzig 0
Vasas Györ 2 (Keglovitch, Korsos)

9 September 1964

Vasas Györ 4 (Palotai, Keglovitch 2, Orosz)
Chemie Leipzig 2 (Scherbarth, Slaby)

6 September 1964

Dukla Prague 4 (Vacenovsky, Nedorost 2, Masopust)
Gornik Zabrze 1 (Lubanski)

20 September 1964

Gornik Zabrze 3 (Pol 2, Musialek)
Dukla Prague 0

14 October 1964
Duisberg

Dukla Prague 0
Gornik Zabrze 0

Dukla Prague won on toss after extra time.

9 September 1964

Lahden Reipas 2 (Kaukkonen, Talsi)
Lyn Oslo 1 (Stavrum)

7 October 1964	**Lyn Oslo 3** (Seemann 2, J. Berg) **Lahden Reipas 0**
9 September 1964	**Saint Etienne 2** (Mekloufi, Guy) **La Chaux-De-Fonds 2** (Bertschi 2)
16 September 1964	**La Chaux-De-Fonds 2** (Vuilleumier, Trivellin) **Saint Etienne 1** (Guy)
9 September 1964	**Anderlecht 1** (Van Himst) **Bologna 0**
7 October 1964	**Bologna 2** (Pascutti, Nielsen) **Anderlecht 1** (Stockman)
14 October 1964 Barcelona	**Anderlecht 0** **Bologna 0** *Anderlecht won on toss after extra time.*
9 September 1964	**Partizan Tirana 0** **Cologne 0**
23 September 1964	**Cologne 2** (Sturm, Overath) **Partizan Tirana 0**
10 September 1964	**Lokomotiv Sofia 8** (Kotkov 5, Debarszki 2, Milev) **Malmo FF 3** (Eskstrom, Larsson 2)
30 September 1964	**Malmo FF 2** (Larsson 2 – 1 pen) **Lokomotiv Sofia 0**
13 September 1964	**Sliema Wanderers 0** **Dinamo Bucharest 2** (Fratela, Pircalab)
19 September 1964	**Dinamo Bucharest 5** (Dinu 2, Popescu, Dumitrache 2 – 1 pen) **Sliema Wanderers 0**
16 September 1964	**Rapid Vienna 3** (Wolny, Glechner 2) **Shamrock Rovers 0**
30 September 1964	**Shamrock Rovers 0** **Rapid Vienna 2** (Wolny, Flögel)
16 September 1964	**Aris Bonnevoie 1** (Hoffman) **Benfica 5** (Torres 4, Eusebio)
30 September 1964	**Benfica 5** (Eusebio 2, Simoes, Torres, Augusto) **Aris Bonnevoie 1** (Schreiner)
16 September 1964	**DWS Amsterdam 3** (Guertsen 2, Hollander) **Fenerbahce 1** (Ogun)
7 October 1964	**Fenerbahce 0** **DWS Amsterdam 1** (Temming)
23 September 1964	**BK 09 Odense 2** (Richter, Betancort og) **Real Madrid 5** (Grosso, Gento 3, Puskas)
14 October 1964	**Real Madrid 4** (Gento 2, Grosso, Suarez) **BK 09 Odense 0**

FIRST ROUND

25 November 1964	**Liverpool 3** (St John, Hunt, Yeats) **Anderlecht 0** *Liverpool:* Lawrence, Lawler, Byrne, Milne, Yeats, Stevenson, Callaghan, Hunt, St John, Smith, Thompson. *Anderlecht:* Trappeniers, Heylens, Cornelis, Hanon, Verbiest, Plaskie, Cayuela, Stockman, Jurion, Van Himst, Puis.
16 December 1964	**Anderlecht 0** **Liverpool 1** (Hunt) *Anderlecht:* Trappeniers, Heylens, Cornelis, Hanon, Verbiest, Plaskie, Jurion, Stockman, Van Himst, Devrindt, Puis. *Liverpool:* Lawrence, Lawler, Byrne, Milne, Yeats, Stevenson, Callaghan, Hunt, St John, Smith, Thompson.
18 November 1964	**Glasgow Rangers 1** (Wilson) **Rapid Vienna 0** *Rangers:* Ritchie, Provan, Caldow, Greig, McKinnon, Wood, Wilson, Millar, Forrest, Baxter, Johnston. *Rapid:* Veres, Halla, Höltl, Skocik, Glechner, Hasil, Schmidt, Wolny, Grausam, Flögel, Seitl.
8 December 1964	**Rapid Vienna 0** **Glasgow Rangers 2** (Forrest, Wilson)

Rapid: Veres, Zaglitsch, Höltl, Skocik, Glechner, Hasil, Schmidt, Wolny, Grausam, Flögel, Seitl.

Rangers: Ritchie, Provan, Caldow, Greig, McKinnon, Wood, Johnston, Millar, Forrest, Baxter, Wilson.

4 November 1964	**DWS Amsterdam 5** (Temming 2, Lenz, Israel, Burgers) **Lyn Oslo 0**
18 November 1964	**Lyn Oslo 1** (Seemann) **DWS Amsterdam 3** (Guertsen, Temming, Hollander)
4 November 1964	**La Chaux-De-Fonds 1** (Antenen) **Benfica 1** (Torres)
9 December 1964	**Benfica 5** (Coluna, Augusto 2, Eusebio, Torres) **La Chaux-De-Fonds 0**
11 November 1964	**Panathinaikos 1** (Papoutsakis) **Cologne 1** (Müller)
25 November 1964	**Cologne 2** (Thielen, Müller) **Panathinaikos 1** (Komanidis)
11 November 1964	**Internazionale 6** (Jair 2, Mazzola 2, Suarez, Milani) **Dinamo Bucharest 0**
3 December 1964	**Dinamo Bucharest 0** **Internazionale 1** (Domenghini)
18 November 1964	**Real Madrid 4** (Amancio 3, Grosso) **Dukla Prague 0**
2 December 1964	**Dukla Prague 2** (Geleta 2) **Real Madrid 2** (Felo, Amancio)
18 November 1964	**Vasas Györ 5** (Korsos, Györfi 2, Povazsai 2) **Lokomotiv Sofia 3** (Kotkov 2, Debarszki)
6 December 1964	**Lokomotiv Sofia 4** (Debarszki 2, Kirilov, Milev) **Vasas Györ 3** (Györfi, Povazsai, Keglovitch)

QUARTER-FINALS

10 February 1965

Cologne 0
Liverpool 0

Cologne: Schumacher, Pott, Regh, Benthaus, Wilden, Weber, Thielen, Stürm, Müller, Overath, Löhr.

Liverpool: Lawrence, Lawler, Byrne, Milne, Yeats, Stevenson, Callaghan, Hunt, St John, Smith, Thompson.

17 March 1965

Liverpool 0
Cologne 0

Liverpool: Lawrence, Lawler, Byrne, Milne, Yeats, Stevenson, Callaghan, Hunt, St John, Smith, Thompson.

Cologne: Schumacher, Pott, Regh, Stürm, Hemmersbach, Weber, Thielen, Zeze, Löhr, Overath, Hornig.

24 March 1965
Rotterdam

Liverpool 2 (St John, Hunt)
Cologne 2 (Thielen, Löhr)

Liverpool: Lawrence, Lawler, Byrne, Milne, Yeats, Stevenson, Callaghan, Hunt, St John, Smith, Thompson.

Cologne: Schumacher, Pott, Regh, Weber, Hemmersbach, Stürm, Thielen, Löhr, Müller, Overath, Hornig.

Liverpool won on toss after extra time.

17 February 1965

Internazionale 3 (Suarez, Peiro 2)
Glasgow Rangers 1 (Forrest)

Internazionale: Sarti, Burgnich, Facchetti, Tagnin, Guarneri, Malatrasai, Domenghini, Peiro, Mazzola, Suarez, Corso.

Rangers: Ritchie, Provan, Caldow, Wood, McKinnon, Greig, Henderson, Millar, Forrest, Brand, Wilson.

3 March 1965

Glasgow Rangers 1 (Forrest)
Internazionale 0

Rangers: Ritchie, Provan, Caldow, Greig, McKinnon, Hynd, Henderson, Millar, Forrest, McLean, Johnston.

Internazionale: Sarti, Burgnich, Facchetti, Tagnin, Guarneri, Picchi, Jair, Mazzola, Peiro, Suarez, Domenghini.

24 February 1965

Benfica 5 (Augusto, Eusebio 2, Simoes, Coluna)
Real Madrid 1 (Amancio)

17 March 1965

Real Madrid 2 (Grosso, Puskas)
Benfica 1 (Sanchis og)

24 February 1965	**DWS Amsterdam 1** (Schrijvers pen) **Vasas Györ 1** (Korsos)
10 March 1965	**Vasas Györ 1** (Povazsai) **DWS Amsterdam 0**

SEMI-FINALS

4 May 1965

Liverpool 3 (Hunt, Callaghan, St John)
Internazionale 1 (Mazzola)

Liverpool: Lawrence, Lawler, Moran, Strong, Yeats, Stevenson, Callaghan, Hunt, St John, Smith, Thompson.

Internazionale: Sarti, Burgnich, Facchetti, Tagnin, Guarneri, Picchi, Jair, Mazzola, Peiro, Suarez, Corso.

12 May 1965

Internazionale 3 (Corso, Peiro, Facchetti)
Liverpool 0

Internazionale: Sarti, Burgnich, Facchetti, Bedin, Guarneri, Picchi, Jair, Mazzola, Peiro, Suarez, Corso.

Liverpool: Lawrence, Lawler, Moran, Strong, Yeats, Stevenson, Callaghan, Hunt, St John, Smith, Thompson.

30 April 1965

Vasas Györ 0
Benfica 1 (Augusto)

6 May 1965

Benfica 4 (Eusebio 2, Torres 2)
Vasas Györ 0

FINAL

27 May 1965
Milan

Internazionale 1 (Jair)
Benfica 0

Internazionale: Sarti, Burgnich, Facchetti, Bedin, Guarneri, Picchi, Jair, Mazzola, Peiro, Suarez, Corso.

Benfica: Costa Pereira, Cavem, Cruz, Neto, Germano, Raul, Augusto, Eusebio, Torres, Coluna, Simoes.

Referee: Dienst (Swi)

Attendance: 80,000.

Eleventh season – 1965–66

PRELIMINARY ROUND

Bye: Internazionale

22 September 1965

HJK Helsinki 2 (Pahlmann, Peltoniemi)
Manchester United 3 (Herd, Connelly, Law)

Helsinki: Heinonen, Jalava, Murtovaara, Kaupinnen, Laine, Peltoniemi, Pajo, Kaartinen, Letholainen, Pahlmann, Lindahl.

Manchester United: Gaskell, Brennan, A. Dunne, Fitzpatrick, Foulkes, Stiles, Connelly, Charlton, Herd, Law, Aston.

6 October 1965

Manchester United 6 (Connelly 3, Best 2, Charlton)
HJK Helsinki 0

Manchester United: P. Dunne, Brennan, A. Dunne, Crerand, Foulkes, Stiles, Connelly, Best, Charlton, Law, Aston.

Helsinki: Heinonen, Jalava, Murtovaara, Kokko, Laine, Peltoniemi, Rytkonens, Kaupinnen, Letholainen, Pahlmann, Lindahl.

8 September 1965

17 Nendori Tirana 0
Kilmarnock 0

Nendori: Janku, Frasheri, Halili, Kasmi, Mema, Bylyku, Xhacka, Bukoviku, Gjoka, Ishka, Hyka.

Kilmarnock: Ferguson, King, Watson, Murray, Beattie, McFadzean, McLean, McInally, Black, Sneddon, McIlroy.

29 September 1965

Kilmarnock 1 (Black)
17 Nendori Tirana 0

Kilmarnock: Ferguson, King, Watson, O'Connor, Beattie, McFadzean, McLean, McInally, Black, Sneddon, McIlroy.

Nendori: Janku, Frasheri, Halili, Kasmi, Mema, Byluku, Xhacka, Bukoviku, Hyka, Ishka, Bytyci.

31 August 1965

Lyn Oslo 5 (J. Berg 2, Stavrum, Dybwad-Olsen 2 – 1 pen)
Derry City 3 (R. Wood, Gilbert 2)

Lyn Oslo: Braathen, Rodvang, Aarnseth, Saga, A. Berg, Gulden, Ostlien, F. Berg, Stavrum, J. Berg, Dybwad-Olsen.

Derry: Connor, Blake, Cathcart, McGeough, Crossan, D. Wood, R. Wood, Doherty, Gilbert, Wilson, Webb.

9 September 1965 **Derry City 5** (Wilson 2, Crossan, R. Wood, McGeough)
Lyn Oslo 1 (Stavrum)

Derry City: Connor, Blake, Cathcart, McGeough, Crossan, D. Wood, R. Wood, Doherty, Coyle, Wilson, Webb.

Lyn Oslo: Martinsen, Rodvang, Morrisbaak, Saga, Aarnseth, Gulden, Ostlien, J. Berg, Stavrum, H. Berg, Seeman.

29 August 1965 **IBK Keflavik 1** (Julinsson)
Ferencvaros 4 (Nemeth, Karaba, Varga, Albert)

8 September 1965 **Ferencvaros 9** (Albert 5, Novak 2, Varga 2)
IBK Keflavik 1 (Johansson)

8 September 1965 **Fenerbahce 0**
Anderlecht 0

15 September 1965 **Anderlecht 5** (Stockman 3, Van Himst, Hanon)
Fenerbahce 1 (Ogun)

8 September 1965 **Feyenoord 2** (Venneker, Kruiver)
Real Madrid 1 (Puskas)

22 September 1965 **Real Madrid 5** (Puskas 4, Grosso)
Feyenoord 0

12 September 1965 **Djurgarden 2** (H. Nilsson 2)
Levski Sofia 1 (Sokolov)

3 October 1965 **Levski Sofia 6** (Asparoukhov 2, Hiev 2, Nikolov, Abadjiev)
Djurgarden 0

15 September 1965 **Drumcondra 1** (Morrissey)
ASK Vorwaerts 0

22 September 1965 **ASK Vorwaerts 3** (Vogt, Bergerad, Piepenburg)
Drumcondra 0

15 September 1965 **ASK Linz 1** (Kögelberger)
Gornik Zabrze 3 (Musialek, Wilczek 2)

22 September 1965 **Gornik Zabrze 2** (Pol, Szoltysik)
ASK Linz 1 (Liposinovic pen)

22 September 1965 **Lausanne 0**
Sparta Prague 0

29 September 1965 **Sparta Prague 4** (Mraz 3, Dyba)
Lausanne 0

26 September 1965 **Panathinaikos 4** (Sakellaridis, Lougalidis, Domazos, Kamaras)
Sliema Wanderers 1 (Cini)

10 October 1965 **Sliema Wanderers 1** (Micallef)
Panathinaikos 0

28 September 1965 **Dinamo Bucharest 4** (Ene II, Ghergheli, Fratila 2)
BK 09 Odense 0

6 October 1965 **BK 09 Odense 2** (J. Pedersen, A. Hansen)
Dinamo Bucharest 3 (Nunweiller, Pircalab, Ene II)

30 September 1965 **Stade Dudelange 0**
Benfica 8 (Pedras 3, Serafim, Jauca 2, Santana, Eusebio)

5 October 1965 **Benfica 10** (Eusebio 4, Augusto 3, Pinto, Guerreiro, Torres)
Stade Dudelange 0

Benfica's 18–0 aggregate win was a record for the first 25 years.

6 October 1965 **Apoel Nicosia 0**
Hamburg **Werder Bremen 5** (Matischak 2, Podlich, Schulz, Zebrowski)

13 October 1965 **Werder Bremen 5** (Danielsen 2, Ferner, Höttges 2– 1 pen)
Apoel Nicosia 0

22 September 1965 **Partizan Belgrade 2** (Galic, Hasanagic)
Nantes 0

13 October 1965 **Nantes 2** (Magny, Blanchet)
Partizan Belgrade 2 (Kovacevic, Galic)

FIRST ROUND

17 November 1965 **ASK Vorwaerts 0**
Manchester United 2 (Law, Connelly)

Vorwaerts: Weiss, Fräsdorf, Krampe, Kiupel, Unger, Körner, Nachtigall, Nöldner, Vogt, Bergerad, Piepenburg.

Manchester United: Gregg, A. Dunne, Cantwell, Crerand, Foulkes, Stiles, Best, Law, Charlton, Herd, Connelly.

1 December 1965

Manchester United 3 (Herd 3)
ASK Vorwaerts 1 (Piepenburg)

Manchester United: P. Dunne, A. Dunne, Cantwell, Crerand, Foulkes, Stiles, Best, Law, Charlton, Herd, Connelly.

Vorwaerts: Zulkowski, Fräsdorf, Kramp, Kiupel, Unger, Körner, Piepenburg, Kalinke, Vogt, Bergerad, Grossheim.

17 November 1965

Kilmarnock 2 (McLean pen, McInally)
Real Madrid 2 (Pirri, Amancio)

Kilmarnock: Ferguson, King, Watson, O'Connor, Murray, McFadzean, McLean, McInally, Hamilton, Sneddon, McIlroy.

Real Madrid: Betancort, Miera, Sanchis, F. Ruiz, Santamaria, Zoco, Amancio, Pirri, Grosso, Puskas, Gento.

1 December 1965

Real Madrid 5 (Grosso 2, F. Ruiz, Gento, Pirri)
Kilmarnock 1 (McIlroy)

Real Madrid: Betancort, Miera, Sanchis, Tejada, De Felipe, Zoco, Amancio, Pirri, Grosso, F. Ruiz, Gento.

Kilmarnock: Ferguson, King, Watson, O'Connor, Murray, McFadzean, McLean, McInally, Hamilton, Sneddon, McIlroy.

23 November 1965

Anderlecht 9 (Jurion, Van Himst 2, Puis 2, Mulder 3, Stockman)
Derry City 0

Anderlecht: Trappeniers, Heylens, Plaskie, Verbiest, Cornelis, Hanon, Jurion, Stockman, Mulder, Van Himst, Puis.

Derry: Connor, Blake, Cathcart, R. Wood, Crossan, D. Wood, Wright, Doherty, Coyle, Wilson, Fullerton.

The second leg of this tie was not played. UEFA decided Derry's ground was unsuitable, and when the Irish club refused to play anywhere else, Anderlecht were given a walkover.

9 November 1965

Partizan Belgrade 3 (Jusufi, Hasanagic, Pirmajer)
Werder Bremen 0

17 November 1965

Werder Bremen 1 (Schulz)
Partizan Belgrade 0

10 November 1965

Levski Sofia 2 (Asparoukhov, Nikolov)
Benfica 2 (Eusebio 2)

8 December 1965

Benfica 3 (Eusebio, Coluna, Torres)
Levski Sofia 2 (Asparoukhov 2)

10 November 1965

Ferencvaros 0
Panathinaikos 0

17 November 1965

Panathinaikos 1 (Domazos)
Ferencvaros 3 (Karaba, Fenyvesi, Albert)

24 November 1965

Sparta Prague 3 (Kvasnak pen, Jilek, Vrana)
Gornik Zabrze 0

28 November 1965

Gornik Zabrze 1 (Szoltysik)
Sparta Prague 2 (Mraz 2)

1 December 1965

Dinamo Bucharest 2 (Fratila, Haidu)
Internazionale 1 (Jair)

15 December 1965

Internazionale 2 (Mazzola pen, Facchetti)
Dinamo Bucharest 0

QUARTER-FINALS

2 February 1966

Manchester United 3 (Herd, Law, Foulkes)
Benfica 2 (Augusto, Torres)

Manchester United: Gregg, A. Dunne, Cantwell, Crerand, Foulkes, Stiles, Best, Law, Charlton, Herd, Connelly.

Benfica: Costa Pereira, Raul, Cruz, Coluna, Germano, Pinto, Silva, Eusebio, Torres, Augusto, Simoes.

9 March 1966

Benfica 1 (Brennan og)
Manchester United 5 (Best 2, Connelly, Crerand, Charlton)

Benefica: Costa Pereira, Cavem, Cruz, Coluna, Germano, Pinto, Silva, Eusebio, Torres, Augusto, Simoes.

Manchester United: Gregg, Brennan, A. Dunne, Crerand, Foulkes, Stiles, Best, Law, Charlton, Herd, Connelly.

23 February 1966	**Internazionale 4** (Jair, Corso, Peiro 2) **Ferencvaros 0**
2 March 1966	**Ferencvaros 1** (Novak pen) **Internazionale 1** (Domenghini)
23 February 1966	**Anderlecht 1** (Van Himst) **Real Madrid 0**
9 March 1966	**Real Madrid 4** (Amancio 2, Gento 2 – 1 pen) **Anderlecht 2** (Jurion, Puis)
2 March 1966	**Sparta Prague 4** (Kvasnak 3 – 1 pen, Masek) **Partizan Belgrade 1** (Hasanagic)
9 March 1966	**Partizan Belgrade 5** (Kovacevic 2, Vasovic, Hasanagic 2) **Sparta Prague 0**

SEMI-FINALS

13 April 1966

Partizan Belgrade 2 (Hasanagic, Becejac)
Manchester United 0

Partizan: Soskic, Jusufi, Mihailovic, Becejac, Rasovic, Vasovic, Bajic, Kovacevic, Hasanagic, Miladinovic, Pirmajer.

Manchester United: Gregg, Brennan, A. Dunne, Crerand, Foulkes, Stiles, Best, Law, Charlton, Herd, Connelly.

20 April 1966

Manchester United 1 (Soskic og)
Partizan Belgrade 0

Manchester United: Gregg, Brennan, A. Dunne, Crerand, Foulkes, Stiles, Anderson, Law, Charlton, Herd, Connelly.

Partizan: Soskic, Jusufi, Mihailovic, Becejac, Rasovic, Vasovic, Bajic, Davidovic, Hasanagic, Miladinovic, Pirmajer.

13 April 1966

Real Madrid 1 (Pirri)
Internazionale 0

20 April 1966

Internazionale 1 (Facchetti)
Real Madrid 1 (Amancio)

FINAL

11 May 1966
Brussels

Real Madrid 2 (Amancio, Serena)
Partizan Belgrade 1 (Vasovic)

Real Madrid: Araquistain, Pachin, Sanchis, Pirri, De Felipe, Zoco, Serena, Amancio, Grosso, Velazquez, Gento.

Partizan: Soskic, Jusufi, Mihailovic, Becejac, Rasovic, Vasovic, Bajic, Kovacevic, Hasanagic, Galic, Pirmajer.

Referee: Kreitlein (GFR)

Attendance: 55,000.

Twelfth season – 1966–67

PRELIMINARY ROUND

31 August 1966

Waterford 1 (Lynch)
ASK Vorwaerts 6 (Piepenburg 3, Nachtigall 2, Fräsdorf)

7 September 1966

ASK Vorwaerts 6 (Wruck, Müller 2, Piepenburg 2, Grossheim)
Waterford 0

7 September 1966

Sliema Wanderers 1 (Cini)
CSKA Sofia 2 (Yakimov 2 – 1 pen)

14 September 1966

CSKA Sofia 4 (Zafirov, Yakimov pen, Nikidomov, Zanev)
Sliema Wanderers 0

(CSKA Sofia formerly appeared as CDNA Sofia)

FIRST ROUND

Bye: Real Madrid

28 September 1966

Liverpool 2 (St John, Callaghan)
Petrolul Ploesti 0

Liverpool: Lawrence, Lawler, Strong, Smith, Yeats, Stevenson, Callaghan, Hunt, St John, Graham, Thompson.

Petrolul: Ionescu, Pahontu, Boc, Mocanu, Juhasz, Florea, Roman, Badea, M. Dridea, Dragomir, Moldoveanu.

12 October 1965

Petrolul Ploesti 3 (Moldoveanu, Boc, M. Dridea)
Liverpool 1 (Hunt)

Petrolul: Ionescu, Pahontu, Mocanu, Boc, Florea, Dincuta, Moldoveanu, M. Dridea, Badea, Dragomir, V. Dridea.

Liverpool: Lawrence, Lawler, Strong, Milne, Yeats, Stevenson, Callaghan, Hunt, St John, Smith Thompson.

19 October 1966
Brussels

Liverpool 2 (St John, Thompson)
Petrolul Ploesti 0

Liverpool: Lawrence, Lawler, Strong, Milne, Yeats, Stevenson, Callaghan, Hunt, St John, Smith, Thompson.

Petrolul: Ionescu, Pahontu, Boc, Mocanu, Monteanu, Dragomir, Moldoveanu, Dincuta, M. Dridea, Pal, V. Dridea.

28 September 1966

Celtic 2 (Gemmell, McBride)
FC Zurich 0

Celtic: Simpson, Gemmell, O'Neill, Murdoch, McNeill, Clark, Johnstone, McBride, Chalmers, Auld, Hughes.

Zurich: Iten, Münsch, Leimgruber, Stierli, Neumann, Brodmann, Kuhn, Martinelli, Bäni, Meyer, Künzli.

5 October 1966

FC Zurich 0
Celtic 3 (Gemmell 2 – 1 pen, Chalmers)

Zurich: Iten, Neumann, Münsch, Kyburz, Leimgruber, Stierli, Bäni, Kuhn, Kubala, Künzli, Stürmer.

Celtic: Simpson, Gemmell, O'Neill, Murdoch, McNeill, Clark, Johnstone, Auld, Lennox, Chalmers, Hughes.

7 September 1966

Aris Bonnevoie 3 (Heger, Hoffmann, Kirchens)
Linfield 3 (Hamilton, Scott, Pavis)

Aris: Stendebach, Wagner, Hoschiedt, Jeitz, Hofstetter, Hoffmann, Schreiner, Lang, Maas, Kirchens, Heger.

Linfield: McFaul, Gilliland, Patterson, Hatton, Leishman, Gregg, Ferguson, Hamilton, Pavis, Scott, Shields.

14 September 1966

Linfield 6 (Thomas 3, Scott 2, Pavis)
Aris Bonnevoie 1 (Lang)

Linfield: McFaul, Gilliland, White, Gregg, Hatton, Patterson, Ferguson, Thomas, Pavis, Scott, Shields.

Aris: Stendebach, Wagner, Hofstetter, Hoscheidt, Jeitz, Hoffmann, Schreiner, Lang, Maas, Kirchens, Heger.

7 September 1966

KR Reykjavik 2 (Schram 2 – 1 pen)
Nantes 3 (Gondet 2, Simon)

5 October 1966

Nantes 5 (Suaudeau, Simon, Magny 2, Michel)
KR Reykjavik 2 (Baldvinsson, Felixson)

7 September 1966

Admira 0
Vojvodina 1 (Sekerec)

20 September 1966

Vojvodina 0
Admira 0

14 September 1966

Valkeakosken Haka 1 (Makila)
Anderlecht 10 (Van Himst 5, Devrindt 3, Puis, Cayuela)

28 September 1966

Anderlecht 2 (Van Himst, Devrindt)
Valkeakosken Haka 0

20 September 1966

1860 Munich 8 (Konietzka 4, Kuppers 2, Kohlars 2)
Omonia Nicosia 0

25 September 1966

Omonia Nicosia 1 (Karalambos)
1860 Munich 2 (Kohlars, Brunnenmeier)

28 September 1966

Malmo FF 0
Atletico Madrid 2 (Cardona, Luis)

12 October 1966

Atletico Madrid 3 (Luis, Mendoza, Urtiaga)
Malmo FF 1 (Svahn)

28 September 1966

Internazionale 1 (Voronin og)
Torpedo Moscow 0

12 October 1966

Torpedo Moscow 0
Internazionale 0

28 September 1966

Esbjerg BK 0
Dukla Prague 2 (Enemark og, Dvorak)

4 October 1966	**Dukla Prague 4** (Strunc, Vacenovsky 2, Mraz) **Esbjerg BK 0**
28 September 1966	**Ajax 2** (Keizer, Muller) **Besiktas 0**
5 October 1966	**Besiktas 1** (Faruk) **Ajax 2** (Swart, Keizer)
28 September 1966	**CSKA Sofia 3** (Vassilev, Penev, Zanev) **Olympiakos 1** (Papazoglu)
5 October 1966	**Olympiakos 1** (Sideris) **CSKA Sofia 0**
28 September 1966	**Gornik Zabrze 2** (Pol 2 – 1 pen) **ASK Vorwaerts 1** (Fräsdorf)
12 October 1966	**ASK Vorwaerts 2** (Piepenburg, Nöldner) **Gornik Zabrze 1** (Lubanski)
26 October 1966 Budapest	**Gornik Zabrze 3** (Lubanski 2, Pol) **ASK Vorwaerts 1** (Kalinke)
5 October 1966	**Vasas Budapest 5** (Bakos, Farkas 3, L. Puskas) **Sporting Lisbon 0**
12 October 1966	**Sporting Lisbon 0** **Vasas Budapest 2** (Tibor, L. Puskas)
	Valerengens Walkover **17 Nendori Tirana** Withdrew

SECOND ROUND

7 December 1966	**Ajax 5** (De Wolff, Cruyff, Nuninga 2, Groot) **Liverpool 1** (Lawler) *Ajax:* Bals, Suurbier, Pronk, Soetekouw, Van Duivenbode, Groot, Muller, Swart, Cruyff, Nuninga, De Wolff. *Liverpool:* Lawrence, Lawler, Strong, Smith, Yeats, Stevenson, Callaghan, Hunt, St John, Graham, Thompson.
14 December 1966	**Liverpool 2** (Hunt 2) **Ajax 2** (Cruyff 2) *Liverpool:* Lawrence, Lawler, Strong, Milne, Yeats, Stevenson, Callaghan, Hunt, St John, Graham, Thompson. *Ajax:* Bals, Hulshoff, Pronk, Soetekouw, Van Duivenbode, Muller, Groot, Swart, Cruyff, Nuninga, Keizer.
30 November 1966	**Nantes 1** (Magny) **Celtic 3** (McBride, Lennox, Chalmers) *Nantes:* Castel, Le Chenadec, Budzinski, Robin, De Michele, Kovacevic, Suaudeau, Blanchet, Simon, Magny, Michel. *Celtic:* Simpson, Gemmell, O'Neill, Murdoch, McNeill, Clark, Johnstone, Auld, Chalmers, McBride, Lennox.
7 December 1966	**Celtic 3** (Johnstone, Chalmers, Lennox) **Nantes 1** (Georgin) *Celtic:* Simpson, Gemmell, O'Neill, Murdoch, McNeill, Clark, Johnstone, Auld, Gallagher, Chalmers, Lennox. *Nantes:* Castel, Le Chenadec, Budzinski, Robin, Grabowski, Kovacevic, Georgin, Blanchet, Simon, Magny, Michel.
25 October 1966	**Valerengens 1** (E. Larsen) **Linfield 4** (Scott, Pavis, Thomas pen, Shields) *Valerengens:* Sörlie, Mathisen, T. Larsen, Skjerwen, Skogli, Prestrud, Knudsen, E. Larsen, Markussen, Sörensen, Olsen. *Linfield:* McFaul, Gilliland, Gregg, Hatton, Patterson, Leishman, Hamilton, Thomas, Pavis, Scott, Shields.
8 November 1966	**Linfield 1** (Thomas) **Valerengens 1** (T. Larsen) *Linfield:* McFaul, Gilliland, Gregg, Hatton, Patterson, Leishman, Ferguson, Thomas, Pavis, Scott, Shields. *Valerengens:* Sörlie, Mathisen, T. Larsen, Syvertsen, Skogli, Jacobsen, Knudsen, E. Larsen, Sörensen, Olsen, Eriksen.
16 November 1966	**Vojvodina 3** (Takac, Pantelic, Brzic) **Atletico Madrid 1** (Luis)
14 December 1966	**Atletico Madrid 2** (Luis pen, Adelardo) **Vojvodina 0**

21 December 1966 Madrid	**Atletico Madrid 2** (Collar 2) **Vojvodina 3** (Takac 2, Radovic) *After extra time.*
16 November 1966	**Internazionale 2** (Soldo, Corso) **Vasas Budapest 1** (L. Puskas)
8 December 1966	**Vasas Budapest 0** **Internazionale 2** (Mazzola 2)
17 November 1966	**Dukla Prague 4** (Masopust, Nedorost 2, Mraz) **Anderlecht 1** (Mulder)
7 December 1966	**Anderlecht 1** (Mulder) **Dukla Prague 2** (Nederost, Mraz)
17 November 1966	**1860 Munich 1** (Küppers) **Real Madrid 0**
30 November 1966	**Real Madrid 3** (Grosso, Veloso, Pirri) **1860 Munich 1** (Brunnenmeier)
23 November 1966	**CSKA Sofia 4** (Maraschliev 2, Zanev pen, Vassilev) **Gornik Zabrze 0**
7 December 1966	**Gornik Zabrze 3** (Szoltysik, Pol 2) **CSKA Sofia 0**

QUARTER-FINALS

1 March 1967	**Vojvodina 1** (Stanic) **Celtic 0** *Vojvodina:* Pantelic, Aleksic, Radovic, Brzic, Nesticki, Daki, Sekeres, Rakic, Radosav, Dordic, Stanic. *Celtic:* Simpson, Craig, Gemmell, Murdoch, McNeill, Clark, Johnstone, Auld, Lennox, Chalmers, Hughes.
8 March 1967	**Celtic 2** (Chalmers, McNeill) **Vojvodina 0** *Celtic:* Simpson, Craig, Gemmell, Murdoch, McNeill, Clark, Johnstone, Gallagher, Lennox, Chalmers, Hughes. *Vojvodina:* Pantelic, Aleksic, Radovic, Brzic, Nesticki, Dakic, Sekeres, Rakic, Radosav, Trivic, Pusibric.
1 March 1967	**Linfield 2** (Hamilton, Shields) **CSKA Sofia 2** (Romanov 2) *Linfield:* Moffatt, Patterson, White, Andrews, Hatton, Leishman, Ferguson, Hamilton, Thomas, Scott, Shields. *CSKA:* Filipov, Vassilev, Gaganelov, Marinshev, Stankov, Penev, Rajkov, Zanev, Romanov, Yakimov, Nikodimov.
15 March 1967	**CSKA Sofia 1** (Yakimov) **Linfield 0** *CSKA:* Yordanov, Vassilev, Penev, Marinshev, Gaganelov, Stankov, Romanov, Rajkov, Zanev, Yakimov, Nikodimov. *Linfield:* Moffatt, Patterson, White, Andrews, Hatton, Leishman, Thomas, Gregg, Pavis, Scott, Shields.
15 February 1967	**Internazionale 1** (Cappellini) **Real Madrid 0**
1 March 1967	**Real Madrid 0** **Internazionale 2** (Cappellini, Zoco og)
1 March 1967	**Ajax 1** (Swart) **Dukla Prague 1** (Mraz)
8 March 1967	**Dukla Prague 2** (Strunc pen, Soetekouw og) **Ajax 1** (Swart)

SEMI-FINALS

12 April 1967	**Celtic 3** (Johnstone, Wallace 2) **Dukla Prague 1** (Strunc) *Celtic:* Simpson, Craig, Gemmell, Murdoch, McNeill, Clark, Johnstone, Auld, Wallace, Chalmers, Hughes. *Dukla:* Viktor, Cmarara, Novak, Zlocha, Taborsky, Dvorak, Masopust, Strunc, Geleta, Nedorost, Vacenovsky.
25 April 1967	**Dukla Prague 0** **Celtic 0**

Dukla: Viktor, Cmarara, Novak, Zlocha, Taborsky, Geleta, Masopust, Strunc, Knebort, Nedorost, Vacenovsky.

Celtic: Simpson, Craig, Gemmell, Murdoch, McNeill, Clark, Johnstone, Lennox, Chalmers, Wallace, Auld.

19 April 1967	**Internazionale 1** (Facchetti) **CSKA Sofia 1** (Zanev)
26 April 1967	**CSKA Sofia 1** (Radlev) **Internazionale 1** (Facchetti)
3 May 1967 Bologna	**Internazionale 1** (Cappellini) **CSKA Sofia 0**

FINAL

25 May 1967
Lisbon

Celtic 2 (Gemmell, Chalmers)
Internazionale 1 (Mazzola pen)

Celtic: Simpson, Craig, Gemmell, Murdoch, McNeill, Clark, Johnstone, Wallace, Chalmers, Auld, Lennox.

Internazionale: Sarti, Burgnich, Facchetti, Bedin, Guarneri, Picchi, Domenghini, Bicicli, Mazzola, Cappellini, Corso.

Referee: Tschenscher (GFR)

Attendance: 55,000.

Thirteenth season – 1967–68

This season marked the introduction of the 'away goals' rule. If the aggregate scores were level at the end of the two legs, the team who had scored most goals away from home were declared the winners. If 'away goals' were also equal, extra time of half an hour was played at the end of the second leg. But at first the new rule applied only to the first two rounds. From the quarter-finals onwards, a third match 'play-off' was still staged if the aggregate scores were level after two legs.

FIRST ROUND

20 September 1967

Manchester United 4 (Sadler 2, Law 2)
Hibernians (Malta) 0

Manchester United: Stepney, A. Dunne, Burns, Crerand, Foulkes, Stiles, Best, Sadler, Law, Charlton, Kidd.

Hibernians: Mizzi, Privitera, Caruana, Gatti, Mallia, Theobald, Mifaud, Scerri, Cassar, Delia, Young.

27 September 1967

Hibernians (Malta) 0
Manchester United 0

Hibernians: Mizzi, Privitera, Caruana, Gatti, Mallia, Theobald, Young, Scerri, Cassar, Delia, Attard.

Manchester United: Stepney, A. Dunne, Burns, Crerand, Foulkes, Stiles, Best, Sadler, Charlton, Law, Kidd.

20 September 1967

Celtic 1 (Lennox)
Dynamo Kiev 2 (Pusasch, Bychevetz)

Celtic: Simpson, Craig, Gemmell, Murdoch, McNeill, Clark, Johnstone, Wallace, Chalmers, Auld, Lennox.

Dynamo Kiev: Rudakov, Schegolokov, Sosnichin, Levchenko, Sabo, Kruukovski, Turianchik, Bychevetz, Medvid, Serebrianikov, Pusasch.

4 October 1967

Dynamo Kiev 1 (Bychevetz)
Celtic 1 (Lennox)

Dynamo Kiev: Bannikov, Schegolokov, Sosnichin, Levchenko, Sabo, Kruukovski, Turianchik, Bychevetz, Medvid, Serebrianikov, Pusasch.

Celtic: Simpson, Craig, Gemmell, Murdoch, McNeill, Clark, Johnstone, Lennox, Wallace, Auld, Hughes.

13 September 1967

Glentoran 1 (Colrain – pen)
Benfica 1 (Eusebio)

Glentoran: Finlay, Creighton, McKeag, Jackson, McCullough, Sinclair, Colrain, Thompson, Bruce, Weatherup, Morrow.

Benfica: Henrique, Cavem, Cruz, Jacinto, Raul, Graca, Coluna, Augusto, Eusebio, Torres, Nelson.

4 October 1967	**Benfica 0** **Glentoran 0** *Benfica:* Henrique, Cavem, Humberto, Jacinto, Cruz, Graca, Coluna, Augusto, Eusebio, Nelson, Simoes. *Glentoran:* Finlay, Creighton, McKeag, Jackson, McCullough, Sinclair, Colrain, Stewart, Johnstone, Weatherup, Morrow. *Benfica won on away goals.*
13 September 1967	**Besiktas 0** **Rapid Vienna 1** (Flögel)
19 September 1967	**Rapid Vienna 3** (Seitl, Grausam, Flögel) **Besiktas 0**
17 September 1967	**Valur (Reykjavik) 1** (Hermann) **Jeunesse Esch 1** (Di Giovanni og)
1 October 1967	**Jeunesse Esch 3** (Hnatow, Di Genova, Langer) **Valur (Reykjavik) 3** (Skulasson, Gunnarsson 2) *Valur won on away goals.*
20 September 1967	**Basle 1** (Hauser) **Hvidovre (Copenhagen) 2** (Larsen, Soerensen)
18 October 1967	**Hvidovre (Copenhagen) 3** (Soerensen, Hansen, Olsen) **Basle 3** (Hauser, Benthaus, Wenger)
20 September 1967	**Dundalk 0** **Vasas Budapest 1** (Korsos)
11 October 1967	**Vasas Budapest 8** (Vidats 2, Farkas 3, Korsos 2, Molnar) **Dundalk 1** (Hale)
20 September 1967	**Olympiakos Piraeus 0** **Juventus 0**
11 October 1967	**Juventus 2** (Zigoni, Menichelli) **Olympiakos Piraeus 0**
20 September 1967	**Wismut Karl Marx Stadt 1** (Steinmann) **Anderlecht 3** (Mulder 2, Van Himst)
18 October 1967	**Anderlecht 2** (Bergholtz, Van Himst) **Wismut Karl Marx Stadt 1** (Schuster)
20 September 1967	**Ajax 1** (Cruyff) **Real Madrid 1** (Pirri)
11 October 1967	**Real Madrid 2** (Gento, Veloso) **Ajax 1** (Groot) *After extra time.*
20 September 1967	**Gornik Zabrze 3** (Lentner, Lubanski 2) **Djurgarden 0**
4 October 1967	**Djurgarden 0** **Gornik Zabrze 1** (Musialek)
20 September 1967	**Skeid Oslo 0** **Sparta Prague 1** (Mraz)
4 October 1967	**Sparta Prague 1** (Mraz) **Skeid Oslo 1** (Sjoeberg)
20 September 1967	**Olympiakos Nicosia 2** (Katanis, Tesan og) **Sarajevo 2** (Antic 2)
18 October 1967	**Sarajevo 3** (Antic, Silijkut 2) **Olympiakos Nicosia 1** (Katanis)
20 September 1967	**Saint Etienne 2** (Herbin, Jacquet) **Kuopion Palloseura 0**
4 October 1967	**Kuopion Palloseura 0** **Saint Etienne 3** (Herbin, Bosquier, H. Revelli pen)
27 September 1967	**Trakia Plovdiv 2** (Dermendijev, Popov) **Rapid Bucharest 0**
11 October 1967	**Rapid Bucharest 3** (Codreanu 2, Ionescu) **Trakia Plovdiv 0** *After extra time.*
	Eintracht Brunswick Walkover **Dynamo Tirana** Withdrew

SECOND ROUND

15 November 1967

Sarajevo 0
Manchester United 0

Sarajevo: Muftic, Fazlagic, Blazevic, Jesenkovic, Vujovic, Bajic, Prodanovic, Silijkut, Musemic, Prijaca, Antic.

Manchester United: Stepney, A. Dunne, Burns, Crerand, Foulkes, Sadler, Fitzpatrick, Kidd, Charlton, Best, Aston.

29 November 1967

Manchester United 2 (Aston, Best)
Sarajevo 1 (Delalic)

Manchester United: Stepney, Brennan, A. Dunne, Crerand, Foulkes, Sadler, Burns, Kidd, Charlton, Best, Aston.

Sarajevo: Muftic, Fazlagic, Blazevic, Jesenkovic, Vujovic, Bajic, Delalic, Silijkut, Musemic, Prijaca, Antic

15 November 1967

Vasas Budapest 6 (Radics 3, Pal, L. Puskas, Dagsson og)
Valur 0

17 November 1967

Valur 1 (Gunnarsson)
Vasas Budapest 5 (Molnar, Pal, Mathesz, Varadi, Kovacs)

15 November 1967

Hvidovre 2 (Hansen, Petersen)
Real Madrid 2 (Pirri, Gento)

29 November 1967

Real Madrid 4 (Velazquez, Grosso 2, Gento)
Hvidovre 1 (Petersen)

15 November 1967

Rapid Vienna 1 (Hasil)
Eintracht Brunswick 0

29 November 1967

Eintracht Brunswick 2 (Grzyb, Saborowski)
Rapid Vienna 0

16 November 1967

Benfica 2 (Augusto, Eusebio pen)
Saint Etienne 0

30 November 1967

Saint Etienne 1 (Bereta)
Benfica 0

17 November 1967

Dynamo Kiev 1 (Olek og)
Gornik Zabrze 2 (Szoltysik, Lubanski)

29 November 1967

Gornik Zabrze 1 (Szoltysik)
Dynamo Kiev 1 (Turianchik)

29 November 1967

Juventus 1 (Magnusson)
Rapid Bucharest 0

13 December 1967

Rapid Bucharest 0
Juventus 0

29 November 1967

Sparta Prague 3 (Masek 3 – 1 pen)
Anderlecht 2 (Jurion, Van Himst)

6 December 1967

Anderlecht 3 (Van Himst 2, Devrindt)
Sparta Prague 3 (Masek 2, Vrana)

QUARTER-FINALS

28 February 1968

Manchester United 2 (Florenki og, Kidd)
Gornik Zabrze 0

Manchester United: Stepney, A. Dunne, Burns, Crerand, Sadler, Stiles, Best, Kidd, Charlton, Ryan, Aston.

Gornik: Kostka, Kuchta, Florenki, Oslizlo, Latocha, Wilczek, Olek, Szoltysik, Deja, Lubanski, Musialek.

13 March 1968

Gornik Zabrze 1 (Lubanski)
Manchester United 0

Gornik: Kostka, Kuchta, Florenki, Oslizlo, Latocha, Wilczek, Olek, Deja, Lubanski, Musialek, Lentner.

Manchester United: Stepney, A. Dunne, Burns, Crerand, Sadler, Stiles, Fitzpatrick, Charlton, Herd, Kidd, Best.

31 January 1968

Eintracht Brunswick 3 (Kaack, Dulz, Berg)
Juventus 2 (Kaack og, Sacchi)

28 February 1968

Juventus 1 (Bercellino pen)
Entracht Brunswick 0

20 March 1968
Berne

Juventus 1 (Magnusson)
Eintracht Brunswick 0

6 March 1968	**Real Madrid 3** (Amancio 3) **Sparta Prague 0**
20 March 1968	**Sparta Prague 2** (Kvasnak, Varna) **Real Madrid 1** (Gento)
6 March 1968	**Vasas Budapest 0** **Benfica 0**
14 March 1968	**Benfica 3** (Eusebio 2, Torres) **Vasas Budapest 0**

SEMI-FINALS

24 April 1968

Manchester United 1 (Best)
Real Madrid 0

Manchester United: Stepney, A. Dunne, Burns, Crerand, Sadler, Stiles, Best, Kidd, Charlton, Law, Aston.

Real Madrid: Betancort, Gonzales, Sanchis, Pirri, Zunzunegui, Zoco, Perez, Jose Luis, Grosso, Velazquez, Gento.

15 May 1968

Real Madrid 3 (Pirri, Gento, Amancio)
Manchester United 3 (Zoco og, Sadler, Foulkes)

Real Madrid: Betancort, Gonzales, Sanchis, Pirri, Zunzunegui, Zoco, Perez, Amancio, Grosso, Velazquez, Gento.
Manchester United: Stepney, Brennan, A. Dunne, Crerand, Foulkes, Stiles, Best, Kidd, Charlton, Sadler, Aston.

9 May 1968

Benfica 2 (Torres, Eusebio)
Juventus 0

15 May 1968

Juventus 0
Benfica 1 (Eusebio)

FINAL

29 May 1968
Wembley

Manchester United 4 (Charlton 2, Best, Kidd)
Benfica 1 (Graca)

After extra time – score at 90 minutes 1–1.

Manchester United: Stepney, Brennan, A. Dunne, Crerand, Foulkes, Stiles, Best, Kidd, Charlton, Sadler, Aston.

Benfica: Henrique, Adolfo, Humberto, Jacinto, Cruz, Graca, Coluna, Augusto, Eusebio, Torres, Simoes.

Referee: Lo Bello (Italy)
Attendance: 100,000.

Fourteenth season – 1968–69

This season marked the introduction of the common rule regarding substitutes. From 1968–69 onwards, teams were permitted to use two substitutes at any time during the match and for any reason. Up to five players were allowed to sit on the bench as nominated substitutes, but only two could be used in any one match.

FIRST ROUND

18 September 1968

Waterford 1 (Matthews)
Manchester United 3 (Law 3)

Waterford: Thomas, Bryan, Griffin, Maguire, Morley, McGeough, Casey, Hale, O'Neill, Coad, Matthews.

Manchester United: Stepney (Rimmer), A. Dunne, Burns, Crerand, Foulkes, Stiles, Best, Law Charlton, Sadler, Kidd.

2 October 1968

Manchester United 7 (Stiles, Law 4, Burns, Charlton)
Waterford 1 (Casey)

Manchester United: Stepney, A. Dunne, Burns, Crerand, Foulkes, Stiles, Best, Law, Charlton, Sadler, Kidd.

Waterford: Thomas, Bryan, Griffin, Morrissey, Morley, McGeough, Casey, Hale, O'Neill, Coad, Matthews.

18 September 1968

Manchester City 0
Fenerbahce 0

Manchester City: Mulhearn, Kennedy, Pardoe, Doyle, Heslop, Oakes, Lee, Bell, Summerbee, Young, Coleman.

Fenerbahce: Yavuz, Sukru, Ercan, Nunweiller, Levent, Selim, Ziya, Yilhaz, Abdullah, Nedim, Can.

2 October 1968
Fenerbahce 2 (Abdullah, Ogun)
Manchester City 1 (Coleman)
Fenerbahce: Yavuz, Sukru, Ercan, Nunweiller, Levent, Yilmar, Ziya, Ogun, Nedim, Fuat, Can (Abdullah).
Manchester City: Mulhearn, Connor, Pardoe, Doyle, Heslop, Oakes, Lee, Bell, Summerbee, Young, Coleman.

18 September 1968
Saint Etienne 2 (Keita, H. Revelli)
Celtic 0
Saint Etienne: Carnus, Durkovic, Mitoraj, Bosquier, Camerini, Jacquet, Herbin, Fefeu, H. Revelli, Keita, Bereta.
Celtic: Simpson, Craig, Brogan, O'Neill, McNeill, Connelly, Clark, Johnstone, Wallace, Lennox, Hughes.

2 October 1968
Celtic 4 (Gemmell pen, Craig, Chalmers, McBride)
Saint Etienne 0
Celtic: Simpson, Craig, Gemmell, Murdoch, McNeill, Brogan, Johnstone, Chalmers, Wallace, McBride, Hughes.
Saint Etienne: Carnus, Durkovic, Mitoraj, Bosquier, Camerini, Jacquet, Herbin, Fefeu, H. Revelli, Keita, Bereta.

18 September 1968
Anderlecht 3 (Bergholtz, Peeters, Nordahl)
Glentoran 0
Anderlecht: Trappeniers, Heylens, Kialunda, Plaskie, Peeters, Herbet, Martens, Bergholtz (Nordahl), Mulder, Van Himst, Puis.
Glentoran: Finlay, Stewart, Cree, Creighton, McKeag, Hill, Johnston, Young, Herron, Weatherup, Morrow.

2 October 1968
Glentoran 2 (Morrow, Johnston)
Anderlecht 2 (Devrindt, Bergholtz)
Glentoran: Finlay, Creighton, McCullough, Stewart, McKeag, Hill, Johnston, Herron (Welsh), Young, Weatherup, Morrow.
Anderlecht: Trappeniers, Heylens, Kialunda, Plaskie, Peeters, Nordahl, Herbet, Bergholtz, Devrindt (Mulder), Van Himst, Puis.

18 September 1968
Rosenborg (Trondheim) 1 (Iversen)
Rapid Vienna 3 (Bjerregaard, Kaltenbrunner, Grausam)

2 October 1968
Rapid Vienna 3 (Lindman 2, Kaltenbrunner)
Rosenborg (Trondheim) 3 (Iversen 3)

18 September 1968
FC Zurich 1 (Wiger)
KB Copenhagen 3 (Hansen, Wiberg, Petersen)

2 October 1968
KB Copenhagen 1 (Petersen)
FC Zurich 2 (Kunzli 2)

18 September 1968
Steaua Bucharest 3 (Creinceanu, Voinea, Constantin)
Spartak Trnava 1 (Kuna)

2 October 1968
Spartak Trnava 4 (Svec, Adamec 3)
Steaua Bucharest 0
(Steaua Bucharest formerly appeared as CCA Bucharest)

18 September 1968
Malmo FF 2 (Olsberg, Elmstedt)
AC Milan 1 (Rivera)

2 October 1968
AC Milan 4 (Prati 2, Sormani, Rivera pen)
Malmo FF 1 (Ljungberg)

18 September 1968
Valur 0
Benfica 0

2 October 1968
Benfica 8 (Simoes, Jacinto, Torres 3, Eusebio, Coluna, Augusto)
Valur 1 (Gunnarsson)

18 September 1968
Nuremberg 1 (Van Duivenbode og)
Ajax 1 (Cruyff)

2 October 1968
Ajax 4 (Swart 2, Groot pen, Cruyff)
Nuremberg 0

18 September 1968
AEK Athens 3 (Papageorgiu 2 – 1 pen, Karafeskos)
Jeunesse Esch 0

2 October 1968
Jeunesse Esch 3 (J. Hoffmann, Grouet, Langer)
AEK Athens 2 (Venturis 2)

18 September 1968
Floriana 1 (Galea pen)
Lahden Reipas 1 (Aalto)

2 October 1968	**Lahden Reipas 2** (Holtari 2)
	Floriana 0
18 September 1968	**Real Madrid 6** (Pirri 3, Amancio, Perez, Bueno)
	Limassol 0
26 September 1968	**Limassol 0**
	Real Madrid 6 (Velazquez 2, Jose Luis, Veloso, Ortega, Zunzunegui)

Both matches played in Madrid.

Red Star Belgrade Walkover.
Carl-Zeiss Jena Withdrew.

SECOND ROUND

Byes: Benfica, AC Milan

13 November 1968

Manchester United 3 (Kidd, Law 2)
Anderlecht 0

Manchester United: Stepney, Brennan, A. Dunne, Crerand, Sadler, Stiles, Ryan, Kidd, Charlton, Law, Sartori.

Anderlecht: Trappeniers, Heylens, Kialunda, Peeters, Cornelis, Herbet, Mulder, Bergholtz, Devrindt, Nordahl, Puis.

27 November 1968

Anderlecht 3 (Mulder, Bergholtz 2)
Manchester United 1 (Sartori)

Anderlecht: Trappeniers, Heylens, Hanon, Kialunda, Cornelis, Nordahl, Mulder, Bergholtz, Devrindt, Van Himst, Puis.

Manchester United: Stepney, Kopel, A. Dunne, Crerand, Foulkes, Stiles, Fitzpatrick, Law, Charlton, Sadler, Sartori.

13 November 1968

Celtic 5 (Murdoch, Johnstone 2, Lennox, Wallace)
Red Star Belgrade 1 (Lazarevic)

Celtic: Fallon, Craig, Gemmell, Murdoch, McNeill, Brogan, Johnstone, Wallace, Chalmers, Lennox, Hughes.

Red Star: Dujkovic, Djoric, Krivokuca, Pavlovic, Dojcinovski, Klenkovski, Antonijevic, Ostojic, Lazarevic, Acimovic, Dzajic.

27 November 1968

Red Star Belgrade 1 (Ostojic)
Celtic 1 (Wallace)

Red Star: Dujkovic, Djoric, Krivokuca, Pavlovic, Dojcinovski, Klenkovski, Antonijevic, Ostojic, Lazarevic, Acimovic, Dzajic.

Celtic: Fallon, Craig, Gemmell, Brogan, McNeill, Clark, Connelly, Murdoch, Chalmers (Wallace), Lennox, Hughes.

13 November 1968

AEK Athens 0
KB Copenhagen 0

27 November 1968

KB Copenhagen 0
AEK Athens 2 (Stanotiadis, Papoiannou)

13 November 1968

Ajax 2 (Muller, Nuninga)
Fenerbahce 0

27 November 1968

Fenerbahce 0
Ajax 2 (Keizer, Nuninga)

20 November 1968

Lahden Reipas 1 (Hyvarainen)
Spartak Trnava 9 (Hagara, Kabat 2, Svec 3, Martinkovich, Hrusecky, Adamec)

27 November 1968

Spartak Trnava 7 (Dobias 3, Hagara, Kuna, Adamec, Hrusecky)
Lahden Reipas 1 (Niskakoski)

20 November 1968

Rapid Vienna 1 (Kaltenbrunner)
Real Madrid 0

4 December 1968

Real Madrid 2 (Velazquez, Pirri)
Rapid Vienna 1 (Bjerregaard)

Rapid Vienna won on away goals.

QUARTER-FINALS

26 February 1969

Manchester United 3 (Best 2, Morgan)
Rapid Vienna 0

Manchester United: Stepney, Fitzpatrick, A. Dunne, Crerand, James, Stiles, Morgan, Kidd, Charlton, Law, Best

Rapid Vienna: Fuchsbichler, Gebhardt, Glechner, Fak, Bjerregaard, Lindman, Fritsch, Kaltenbrunner, Grausam, Flögel, Sondegaard.

5 March 1969	**Rapid Vienna 0** **Manchester United 0**

Rapid Vienna: Fuchsbichler, Gebhardt, Glechner, Fak, Bjerregaard, Lindman, Fritsch, Kaltenbrunner, Grausam, Flögel, Sondergaard.

Manchester United: Stepney, Fitzpatrick, A. Dunne, Crerand, James, Stiles, Morgan, Kidd, Charlton, Sadler, Best.

19 February 1969	**AC Milan 0** **Celtic 0**

AC Milan: Cudicini, Anquilletti, Schnellinger, Rosato, Malatrasi, Trapattoni, Hamrin, Lodetti, Sormani, Rivera, Prati.

Celtic: Fallon, Craig, Gemmell, Brogan, McNeill, Clark, Johnstone, Murdoch, Wallace, Lennox, Hughes.

12 March 1969	**Celtic 0** **AC Milan 1** (Prati)

Celtic: Fallon, Craig, Gemmell, Clark, McNeill, Brogan (Auld), Johnstone, Wallace, Chalmers, Murdoch, Hughes.

AC Milan: Cudicini, Anquilletti, Schnellinger, Maldera, Malatrasi, Rosato, Hamrin, Lodetti, Prati, Rivera, Scala.

12 February 1969	**Ajax 1** (Danielsson) **Benfica 3** (Jacinto pen, Torres, Augusto)
19 February 1969	**Benfica 1** (Torres) **Ajax 3** (Cruyff, Danielsson 2)
5 March 1969 Paris	**Ajax 3** (Danielsson, Cruyff 2) **Benfica 0** *After extra time.*
26 February 1969	**Spartak Trnava 2** (Jarabak, Kabat) **AEK Athens 1** (Sevastopolos)
12 March 1969	**AEK Athens 1** (Papaioannou) **Spartak Trnava 1** (Svec)

SEMI-FINALS *23 April 1969*	**AC Milan 2** (Sormani, Hamrin) **Manchester United 0**

AC Milan: Cudicini, Anquilletti, Schnellinger, Malatrasi, Rosato (Maldera), Trapattoni, Hamrin, Lodetti, Sormani, Rivera (Fogli), Prati.

Manchester United: Rimmer, Brennan, Fitzpatrick, Crerand, Foulkes, Stiles (Burns), Morgan, Kidd, Charlton, Law, Best.

15 May 1969	**Manchester United 1** (Charlton) **AC Milan 0**

Manchester United: Rimmer, Brennan, Burns, Crerand, Foulkes, Stiles, Morgan, Kidd, Charlton, Law, Best.

AC Milan: Cudicini, Anquilletti, Schnellinger, Malatrasi, Rosato (Santin), Maldera, Hamrin, Lodetti, Sormani, Rivera, Prati.

13 April 1969	**Ajax 3** (Cruyff, Swart, Keizer) **Spartak Trnava 0**
24 April 1969	**Spartak Trnava 2** (Kuna 2) **Ajax 0**

FINAL *28 May 1969* Madrid	**AC Milan 4** (Prati 3, Sormani) **Ajax 1** (Vasovic pen)

AC Milan: Cudicini, Anquilletti, Schnellinger, Maldera, Rosato, Trapattoni, Hamrin, Lodetti, Sormani, Rivera, Prati.

Ajax: Bals, Suurbier (Nuninga), Van Duivenbode, Vasovic, Hulshoff, Pronk, Groot, Swart, Cruyff, Danielsson, Keizer.

Referee: De Mendibil (Spn)

Attendance: 50,000.

Fifteenth season – 1969–70

PRELIMINARY ROUND

21 August 1969	**Turun Palloseura 0** **KB Copenhagen 1** (Skouborg)
28 August 1969	**KB Copenhagen 4** (Skouborg 2, Brage, Praest) **Turun Palloseura 0**

FIRST ROUND

17 September 1969

Leeds United 10 (O'Grady, Jones 3, Clarke 2, Bremner 2, Giles 2)
Lyn Oslo 0

Leeds United: Sprake, Reaney, Cooper, Bremner, Charlton, Hunter, Madeley, Clarke, Jones, Giles (Bates), O'Grady.

Lyn Oslo: S. Olsen, Rodvang, Kolle, Oestvold, Morisbak, Guilden, Boerrehaug, Christopherson, Berg, O. Olsen (Hovdan), Austnes.

1 October 1969

Lyn Oslo 0
Leeds United 6 (Belfitt 2, Hibbitt 2, Jones, Lorimer)

Lyn Oslo: S. Olsen, Rodvang, Oestvold, Boerrehaug, Christopherson, Kolle, Morisbak, Hovdan, Berg, O. Olsen, Birkeland.

Leeds United: Sprake, Reaney, Cooper, Bremner, Madeley, E. Gray, Lorimer, Belfitt, Jones, Bates, Hibbitt.

17 September 1969

Basle 0
Celtic 0

Basle: Kunz, Kiefer, Michaud, Siegenthaler, Fischli, Ramseier (Rahmen), Odermatt, Hauser, Balmer, Benthaus, Wenger.

Celtic: Fallon, Hay, Gemmell, Brogan, McNeill, Clark, Johnstone, Lennox, Chalmers (Hood), Wallace, Hughes.

1 October 1969

Celtic 2 (Hood, Gemmell)
Basle 0

Celtic: Fallon, Hay, Gemmell, Clark, McNeill, Callaghan, Johnstone, Wallace, Chalmers, Hood, Lennox.

Basle: Kunz, Kiefer, Michaud, Siegenthaler, Fischli, Ramseier, Balmer, Odermatt, Hauser (Demarmels), Benthaus, Wenger.

17 September 1969

Red Star Belgrade 8 (Lazarevic 2, Karasi 2, Klenkovski, Dzajic 2, Acimovic)
Linfield 0

Red Star: Dujkovic, Krivokuca, Jeftic (Ostojic), Pavlovic, Dojcinovsky, Klenkovski, Antonijevic, Karasi, Lazarevic, Acimovic, Dzajic.

Linfield: McGonigal, Gilliland (White), Patterson, Andrews, Hatton, Bowyer, Viollet, Millen, McGraw, Hamilton, Pavis (Feeney).

1 October 1969

Linfield 2 (McGraw 2)
Red Star Belgrade 4 (Antonijevic 4)

Linfield: McGonigal, Gilliland, White, Millen, Hatton, Bowyer, Viollet, Hamilton, McGraw, Pavis, Feeney.

Red Star: Racic, Keri, Krivokuca, Pavlovic, Dojcinovsky, Klenkovski, Antonijevic, Karasi, Aruejic, Ostojic, Lazarevic.

10 September 1969

AC Milan 5 (Prati 2, Rivera pen, Rognoni, Combin)
Avenir Beggen 0

24 September 1969

Avenir Beggen 0
AC Milan 3 (Combin, Sormani, Rivera)

17 September 1969

Hibernians (Malta) 2 (Cassar, Bonnello)
Spartak Trnava 2 (Adamec, Martinkovic)

1 October 1969

Spartak Trnava 4 (Hrusecky, Adamec 2, Azzopardi og)
Hibernians (Malta) 0

17 September 1969

Benfica 2 (Eusebio 2)
KB Copenhagen 0

1 October 1969

KB Copenhagen 2 (Skouborg 2 – 1 pen)
Benfica 3 (Eusebio, Diamantino 2)

17 September 1969

CSKA Sofia 2 (Jekov 2)
Ferencvaros 1 (Rakosi)

1 October 1969

Ferencvaros 4 (Szoeke 2 – 1 pen, Branikovic, Rakosi)
CSKA Sofia 1 (Marosliev)

17 September 1969

Fiorentina 1 (Maraschi)
Osters IF 0

1 October 1969

Osters IF 1 (Fjordestam)
Fiorentina 2 (Amarildo, Esposito)

17 September 1969

Standard Liège 3 (Kasmi og, Depireux 2)
17 Nendori Tirana 0

1 October 1969

17 Nendori Tirana 1 (Kozonska)
Standard Liège 1 (Galic)

17 September 1969

Feyenoord 12 (Kindvall, 3, Geels 4, Van Hanegem 2, Wery, Van Duivenbode, Romeyn)
KR Reykjavik 2 (Baldvinsson, Bjoernsson)

30 September 1969 Rotterdam	**KR Reykjavik 0** **Feyenoord 4** (Geels 2, Kindvall, Wery)
17 September 1969	**Bayern Munich 2** (Brenninger, Roth) **Saint Etienne 0**
1 October 1969	**Saint Etienne 3** (H. Revelli 2, Keita) **Bayern Munich 0**
17 September 1969	**FK Austria 1** (Riedl) **Dynamo Kiev 2** (Serber, Muntijan)
1 October 1969	**Dynamo Kiev 3** (Muntijan, Bychevetz, Pusasch) **FK Austria 1** (Parits)
17 September 1969	**UT Arad 1** (Domide) **Legia Warsaw 2** (Zmijewski, Gadocha)
1 October 1969	**Legia Warsaw 8** (Blaut, Gadocha 2, Brycheczy, Deyna, Sztachurski, Zmijewski, Pieszko pen) **UT Arad 0**
17 September 1969	**Galatasaray 2** (Gokman 2) **Waterford 0**
1 October 1969	**Waterford 2** (Buck, Morley) **Galatasaray 3** (Ugur, Gokman, Ayhan)
17 September 1969	**ASK Vorwaerts 2** (Piepenburg 2) **Panathinaikos 0**
1 October 1969	**Panathinaikos 1** (Antoniadis) **ASK Vorwaerts 1** (Laslop)
24 September 1969 Madrid	**Olympiakos Nicosia 0** **Real Madrid 8** (Gento 2, Grosso, Fleitas 2, Grande, Pirri, Georgiou og)
30 September 1969	**Real Madrid 6** (De Diego 2, Planelles, Grande, Fleitas, Avramides og) **Olympiakos Nicosia 1** (Kettenis)

SECOND ROUND

12 November 1969	**Leeds United 3** (Giles, Jones 2) **Ferencvaros 0** *Leeds United:* Sprake, Reaney, Madeley, Bremner, Charlton, Hunter, Lorimer, Bates, Jones, Giles, E. Gray. *Ferencvaros:* Geczi, Novak, Pancsics, Balint (Nemeth), Horvath, Megyvesi, Szucs, Branticovic, Jusasz, Szoeke, Katona.
26 November 1969	**Ferencvaros 0** **Leeds United 3** (Jones 2, Lorimer) *Ferencvaros:* Geczi, Novak, Balint, Megyvesi, Jusasz, Szucs, Szoeke, Branticovic, Horvath (Vajda), Nemeth, Katona. *Leeds United:* Sprake, Reaney, Cooper, Bremner, Charlton, Hunter, Lorimer, Madeley, Jones, Giles, E. Gray (Galvin).
12 November 1969	**Celtic 3** (Gemmell, Wallace, Hood) **Benfica 0** *Celtic:* Fallon, Craig, Gemmell, Murdoch, McNeill, Clark, Johnstone, Hood, Auld, Wallace, Hughes. *Benfica:* Henrique, Malta, C. Humberto, Graca, F. Humberto, Zeca, Simoes, Coluna, Torres, Eusebio (Augusto), Diamantino (Jorge).
26 November 1969	**Benfica 3** (Eusebio, Graca, Diamantino) **Celtic 0** *Benfica:* Henrique, DaSilva, Adolfo, Toni, Messias, Coluna, Aguas (Diamantino), Graca, Jorge, Eusebio (Martins), Simoes. *Celtic:* Fallon, Craig, Gemmell, Murdoch, McNeill, Brogan, Johnstone, Callaghan, Wallace, Auld, Hughes. *As the aggregate and away goals were equal, and play-offs at this stage of the competition had been abolished, a coin was tossed and Celtic declared the winners.*
12 November 1969	**Dynamo Kiev 1** (Serebryanikov) **Fiorentina 2** (Chiarugi, Maraschi)
26 November 1969	**Fiorentina 0** **Dynamo Kiev 0**
12 November 1969	**ASK Vorwaerts 2** (Fräsdorf, Bergerad) **Red Star Belgrade 1** (Antonijevic)
26 November 1969	**Red Star Belgrade 3** (Karasi 2, Acimovic) **ASK Vorwaerts 2** (Bergerad 2) *ASK Vorwaerts won on away goals.*

12 November 1969	**AC Milan 1** (Combin) **Feyenoord 0**
26 November 1969	**Feyenoord 2** (Jansen, Van Hanegem) **AC Milan 0**
12 November 1969	**Spartak Trnava 1** (Kabat) **Galatasaray 0**
26 November 1969	**Galatasaray 1** (Ergun) **Spartak Trnava 0** *Galatasaray won on toss – this method never used again.*
12 November 1969	**Legia Warsaw 2** (Pieszko, Deyna) **Saint Etienne 1** (H. Revelli)
26 November 1969	**Saint Etienne 0** **Legia Warsaw 1** (Deyna)
19 November 1969	**Standard Liège 1** (Kostedde) **Real Madrid 0**
3 December 1969	**Real Madrid 2** (Velazquez, Gento pen) **Standard Liège 3** (Pilot, Depireux, Galic)

QUARTER-FINALS

4 March 1970

Standard Liège 0
Leeds United 1 (Lorimer)

Standard Liège: Piot, Beurlet, Thissen, Dewalque, Jeck, Van Moer, Semmeling, Pilot, Galic, Depireux, Takac.

Leeds United: Sprake, Reaney, Cooper, Bremner, Charlton, Hunter, Lorimer, Clarke, Jones, Giles, Madeley.

18 March 1970

Leeds United 1 (Giles pen)
Standard Liège 0

Leeds United: Sprake, Reaney, Cooper, Bremner, Charlton, Hunter, Lorimer, Clarke, Jones, Giles, Madeley.

Standard Liège: Piot, Beurlet, Thissen, Dewalque, Jeck, Pilot, Semmeling, Van Moer, Galic, Depireux, Takac.

4 March 1970

Celtic 3 (Auld, Wallace, Carpenetti og)
Fiorentina 0

Celtic: Williams, Hay, Gemmell, Murdoch, McNeill, Brogan, Johnstone, Lennox, Auld, Wallace, Hughes (Hood).

Fiorentina: Superchi, Rogora, Longoni, Carpenetti, Ferrante, Brizi, Esposito. Merlo (Rizzo), Maraschi, De Sisti, Amarildo.

18 March 1970

Fiorentina 1 (Chiarugi)
Celtic 0

Fiorentina: Superchi, Rogora, Longoni, Esposito, Ferrante, Brizi, Chiarugi, Merlo, Maraschi, De Sisti, Amarildo.

Celtic: Williams, Hay, Gemmell, Murdoch, McNeill, Connelly, Johnstone, Auld, Wallace, Brogan, Lennox.

4 March 1970

Galatasaray 1 (Mihat-Pacha)
Legia Warsaw 1 (Brycheczy)

18 March 1970

Legia Warsaw 2 (Brycheczy 2)
Galatasaray 0

4 March 1970

ASK Vorwaerts 1 (Piepenburg)
Feyenoord 0

18 March 1970

Feyenoord 2 (Kindvall, Wery)
ASK Vorwaerts 0

SEMI-FINALS

1 April 1970

Leeds United 0
Celtic 1 (Connelly)

Leeds United: Sprake, Reaney, Cooper, Bremner (Bates), Charlton, Madeley, Lorimer, Clarke, Jones, Giles, E. Gray.

Celtic: Williams, Hay, Gemmell, Murdoch, McNeill, Brogan, Johnstone, Connelly (Hughes), Wallace, Lennox, Auld.

15 April 1970
Hampden Park

Celtic 2 (Hughes, Murdoch)
Leeds United 1 (Bremner)

Celtic: Williams, Hay, Gemmell, Murdoch, McNeill, Brogan, Johnstone, Connelly, Hughes, Auld, Lennox.

Leeds United: Sprake (Harvey), Madeley, Cooper, Bremner, Charlton, Hunter, Lorimer (Bates), Clarke, Jones, Giles, E. Gray.

1 April 1970

Legia Warsaw 0
Feyenoord 0

15 April 1970

Feyenoord 2 (Van Hanegem, Hasil)
Legia Warsaw 0

FINAL

6 May 1970
Milan

Feyenoord 2 (Israel, Kindvall)
Celtic 1 (Gemmell)

After extra time, score at 90 minutes 1–1.

Feyenoord: Pieters-Graafland, Romeyn (Haak), Van Duivenbode, Jansen, Israel, Hasil, Wery, Laseroms, Kindvall, Van Hanegem, Moulijn.

Celtic: Williams, Hay, Gemmell, Murdoch, McNeill, Brogan, Johnstone, Wallace, Hughes, Auld (Connelly), Lennox.

Referee: Lo Bello (Ita).

Attendance: 53,187.

Sixteenth season – 1970–71

This season marked the introduction of the 'penalty competition' method to decide drawn ties. From now on, if aggregate scores and away goals were level at the end of the second leg, and extra time still failed to determine a winner, the teams went into a penalty sequence with each taking five kicks. The team converting the most penalties was declared the winner. Thus all ties were now settled on the night of the second leg, without any further need for the toss of a coin, or for any play-offs.

PRELIMINARY ROUND

18 August 1970

Levski Spartak 3 (Mitkov, Asparoukhov 2)
FK Austria 1 (Riedl)

2 September 1970

FK Austria 3 (Riedl, Hickersberger, Foka)
Levski Spartak 0

FIRST ROUND

16 September 1970

Everton 6 (Ball 3, Kendall, Royle 2)
IBK Keflavik 2 (West og, Ragnarsson)

Everton: West, Wright, K. Newton, Kendall, Kenyon, Harvey, Husband (Whittle), Ball, Royle, Hurst, Morrissey.

Keflavik: Olafsson, Kartisson, E. Gunnarsson, Kjartansson, A. Gunnarsson, E. Magnusson, S. Johansson, Torfasson, G. Magnusson, Jonsson, Ragnarsson (subs used were Einarsson and J. Johansson).

30 September 1970

IBK Keflavik 0
Everton 3 (Royle 2, Whittle)

Keflavik: Olafsson, Ketilsson, A. Gunnarsson, E. Gunnarsson, Kjartansson, E. Magnusson, S. Johansson, G. Magnusson, Jonsson, Farfusson, Ragnarsson.

Everton: Rankin, Wright, K. Newton, Kendall, Labone, Harvey (Brown), Whittle, Ball (Jackson), Royle, Hurst, Morrissey.

16 September 1970

Celtic 9 (Hood 3, Hughes, McNeill, Johnstone, Wilson 2, Davidson)
KPV Kokkolan 0

Celtic: Williams, McGrain, Hay, Murdoch, McNeill, Brogan, Johnstone, Connelly, Hood, Lennox, Hughes (Davidson).

Kokkolan: Isofais, Korhonen, Makinen, Haultala, Makela, Pankanen, A. Lamberg, Sorvisto, Raatikainen, Kallio, H. Lamberg.

30 September 1970

KPV Kokkolan 0
Celtic 5 (Wallace 2, Callaghan, Davidson, Lennox)

Kokkolan: Isofais, Korhonen, Makinen, Haultala, Makela, Pankanen, A. Lamberg, Sorvisto, Raatikainen, Kallio, H. Lamberg.

Celtic: Fallon, Craig, Brogan, Murdoch, Cattenach, Davidson, Connelly, Wallace, Chalmers, Callaghan, Lennox.

16 September 1970	**Glentoran 1** (Hall)
	Waterford 3 (O'Neill, Bryan, Casey)

Glentoran: Finlay, Hill, McKeag, Coyle, McCullough, Stewart, Hutton, Weatherup, Hall, Cassidy, Lavery (subs used were Kirk and Morrow).

Waterford: Thomas, Bryan, McGuire, Morrissey, Brennan, McGeough, Buck, O'Neill, Casey, Hale, Matthews.

30 September 1970	**Waterford 1** (Casey)
	Glentoran 0

Waterford: Thomas, Bryan, McGuire, Morrissey, Brennan, McGeough, Buck, Casey, Hale, O'Neill, Matthews.

Glentoran: Finlay, Hill, McKeag, Coyle, McCullough, Stewart, Macken, Weatherup, Hall, McParland (Kirk), Morrow.

16 September 1970	**Feyenoord 1** (Jansen)
	UT Arad 1 (Dumitrescu)
30 September 1970	**UT Arad 0**
	Feyenoord 0

UT Arad won on away goals.

16 September 1970	**Sporting Lisbon 5**(Lourenco 3, Peres, Marinho)
	Floriana 0
30 September 1970	**Floriana 0**
	Sporting Lisbon 4 (Nelson 2, Dinis, Tome)
16 September 1970	**Jeunesse Esch 1** (Di Genova)
	Panathinaikos 2 (Antoniadis, Elefterakis)
30 September 1970	**Panathinaikos 5** (Elefterakis, Antoniadis 4)
	Jeunesse Esch 0
16 September 1970	**IFK Gothenburg 0**
	Legia Warsaw 4 (Gadocha, Pieszko, Stachurski 2)
30 September 1970	**Legia Warsaw 2** (Deyna, Gadocha)
	IFK Gothenburg 1 (Almqvist)
16 September 1970	**Ujpest Dozsa 2** (Nagy, A. Dunai)
	Red Star Belgrade 0
30 September 1970	**Red Star Belgrade 4** (Filipovic 2, Dzajic, Ostojic)
	Ujpest Dozsa 0
16 September 1970	**Spartak Moscow 3** (Ossianin 2, Papaev)
	Basle 2 (Odermatt, Benthaus)
30 September 1970	**Basle 2** (Siegenthaler, Balmer)
	Spartak Moscow 1 (Khusainov)

Basle won on away goals.

16 September 1970	**Slovan Bratislava 2** (Jan Capkovic, Zlocha pen)
	BK 1903 Copenhagen 1 (Johansen)
30 September 1970	**BK 1903 Copenhagen 2** (Thygessen, Johansen pen)
	Slovan Bratislava 2 (Josef Capkovic 2)
16 September 1970	**Rosenborg (Trondheim) 0**
	Standard Liège 2 (Kostedde, Depireux)
30 September 1970	**Standard Liège 5** (Pilot 2, Cvetler 2, Depireux)
	Rosenborg (Trondheim) 0
16 September 1970	**17 Nendori Tirana 2** (Kazanxhi, Hega)
	Ajax 2 (Suurbier 2)
30 September 1970	**Ajax 2** (Keizer, Swart)
	17 Nendori Tirana 0
16 September 1970	**Cagliari 3** (Riva 2, Nene)
	Saint Etienne 0
30 September 1970	**Saint Etienne 1** (Larqué)
	Cagliari 0
16 September 1970	**Fenerbahce 0**
	Carl Zeiss Jena 4 (Krauss, Ducke 2, Vogel)
30 September 1970	**Carl Zeiss Jena 1** (Vogel)
	Fenerbahce 0
16 September 1970	**Atletico Madrid 2** (Luis, Garate)
	FK Austria 0
30 September 1970	**FK Austria 1** (Krieger pen)
	Atletico Madrid 2 (Luis, Garate)

(FK Austria later appear as Austria/WAC)

16 September 1970

EPA Larnaca 0
Borussia Moenchengladbach 6 (Laumen 2, Koeppel 2, Netzer, Heynckes)

30 September 1970

Borussia Moenchengladbach 10 (Heynckes, Vogts, Netzer, Wimmer, Koeppel 2, Dietrich, Sieloff pen, Laumen 2)
EPA Larnaca 0

SECOND ROUND

21 October 1970

Borussia Moenchengladbach 1 (Vogts)
Everton 1 (Kendall)

Borussia Moenchengladbach: Kleff, Vogts, Muller, Sieloff, Wittmann, Dietrich, Netzer, Laumen, Le Fevre (Wimmer), Koeppel, Heynckes.

Everton: Rankin, Wright, K. Newton, Kendall, Kenyon, Harvey, Ball, Whittle, Royle, Hurst, Morrissey.

4 November 1970

Everton 1 (Morrissey)
Borussia Moenchengladbach 1 (Laumen)

After extra time. Everton won on penalties.

Everton: Rankin, Wright, K. Newton, Kendall, Kenyon, Harvey, Whittle, Ball, Royle, Hurst, Morrissey.

Borussia Moenchengladbach: Kleff, Vogts, Muller, Sieloff, Wittmann, Dietrich, Netzer, Laumen, Le Fevre, Koeppel, Heynckes.

21 October 1970

Waterford 0
Celtic 7 (Wallace 3, Murdoch 2, Macari 2)

Waterford: Thomas, Bryan, Morrissey, Brennan, McGuire, McGeough, Buck (Power), Casey, O'Neill, Hale, Matthews.

Celtic: Williams, Craig, Hay, Murdoch, McNeill, Connelly, Quinn, Macari, Wallace (Davidson), Hood (Chalmers), Lennox.

4 November 1970

Celtic 3 (Hughes, Johnstone 2)
Waterford 2 (McNeill og, Matthews)

Celtic: Williams, Craig, Gemmell, Murdoch (Brogan), McNeill, Hay, Johnstone, Lennox, Wallace (Hood), Connelly, Hughes.

Waterford: Thomas, Bryan, Brennan, McGuire, Morrissey, McGeough, Casey, Hale, Kirkby, O'Neill, Matthews.

21 October 1970

Panathinaikos 3 (Domazos, Antoniadis, Delyannis)
Slovan Bratislava 0

4 November 1970

Slovan Bratislava 2 (Medvid, Jan Capkovic)
Panathinaikos 1 (Antoniadis)

21 October 1970

Red Star Belgrade 3 (Filipovic, Acimovic, Ostojic)
UT Arad 0

4 November 1970

UT Arad 1 (Brosowski)
Red Star Belgrade 3 (Filipovic 2, Jankovic)

21 October 1970

Carl Zeiss Jena 2 (Kurbjuweit, Vogel)
Sporting Lisbon 1 (Marinho)

4 November 1970

Sporting Lisbon 1 (Goncalves)
Carl Zeiss Jena 2 (Ducke, Kurbjuweit)

21 October 1970

Standard Liège 1 (Pilot)
Legia Warsaw 0

4 November 1970

Legia Warsaw 2 (Pieszko, Zmitjewski)
Standard Liège 0

21 October 1970

Cagliari 2 (Riva, Gori)
Atletico Madrid 1 (Luis)

5 November 1970

Atletico Madrid 3 (Luis 3 – 1 pen)
Cagliari 0

21 October 1970

Ajax 3 (Keizer, Van Dijk, Hulshoff)
Basle 0

4 November 1970

Basle 1 (Odermatt pen)
Ajax 2 (Rijnders, Neeskens)

QUARTER-FINALS

9 March 1971

Everton 1 (Johnson)
Panathinaikos 1 (Antoniadis)

Everton: Rankin, Wright, K. Newton, Kendall, Kenyon, Harvey, Husband (Johnson), Ball, Royle, Hurst, Morrissey.

Panathinaikos: Oeconomopoulos, Tomaras, Vlahos, Elefterakis, Kamaras, Sourpis, Grammos, Filakouris, Antoniadis, Domazos, Kapsis

24 March 1971	**Panathinaikos 0** **Everton 0**
	Panathinaikos won on away goals.
	Panathinaikos: Oeconomopoulos, Tomaras, Vlahos, Elefterakis, Kamaras, Sourpis, Grammos, Filakouris, Antoniadis, Domazos, Kapsis.
	Everton: Rankin, Wright, K. Newton, Kendall, Labone, Harvey, Whittle, Ball, Royle, Hurst, Morrissey (Johnson).
10 March 1971	**Ajax 3** (Cruyff, Hulshoff, Keizer) **Celtic 0**
	Ajax: Stuy, Suurbier, Krol, Vasovic, Hulshoff, Rijnders, Swart (Van Dijk), Neeskens, Cruyff, Muhren, Keizer.
	Celtic: Williams, Craig, Gemmell, Hay, McNeill, Brogan, Johnstone, Connelly, Wallace, Callaghan, Lennox.
24 March 1971	**Celtic 1** (Johnstone) **Ajax 0**
	Celtic: Williams, Hay, Gemmell, Callaghan, McNeill, Brogan, Johnstone, Hood, Wallace (Davidson), Auld (Lennox), Hughes.
	Ajax: Stuy, Suurbier, Krol, Vasovic, Hulshoff, Rijnders, Neeskens, Blankenburg, Cruyff, Muhren, Keizer.
10 March 1971	**Carl Zeiss Jena 3** (Strempel, Ducke 2) **Red Star Belgrade 2** (Jankovic, Dzajic)
24 March 1971	**Red Star Belgrade 4** (Djoric pen, Filipovic, Ostojic, Karasi) **Carl Zeiss Jena 0**
10 March 1971	**Atletico Madrid 1** (Adelardo) **Legia Warsaw 0**
24 March 1971	**Legia Warsaw 2** (Pieszko, Stachirski) **Atletico Madrid 1** (Salcedo)
	Atletico Madrid won on away goals.

SEMI-FINALS

14 April 1971	**Red Star Belgrade 4** (Jankovic, Ostojic 3) **Panathinaikos 1** (Kamaras)
28 April 1971	**Panathinaikos 3** (Antoniadis 2, Kamaras) **Red Star Belgrade 0**
	Panathinaikos won on away goals.
14 April 1971	**Atletico Madrid 1** (Irureta) **Ajax 0**
28 April 1971	**Ajax 3** (Keizer, Suurbier, Neeskens) **Atletico Madrid 0**

FINAL

2 June 1971 Wembley	**Ajax 2** (Van Dijk, Haan) **Panathinaikos 0**
	Ajax: Stuy, Suurbier, Neeskens, Vasovic, Rijnders (Blankenburg), Hulshoff, Swart (Haan), Van Dijk, Cruyff, Muhren, Keizer.
	Panathinaikos: Oeconomopoulos, Tomaras, Vlahos, Elefterakis, Kamaras, Sourpis, Grammos, Filakouris, Antoniadis, Domazos, Kapsis.
	Referee: Taylor (Eng)
	Attendance: 90,000.

Seventeenth season – 1971–72

PRELIMINARY ROUND

19 August 1971	**Valencia 3** (Claramunt, Quino 2) **US Luxembourg 1** (Braun)
26 August 1971	**US Luxembourg 0** **Valencia 1** (Lico)

FIRST ROUND

15 September 1971	**Stromgodset Drammen 1** (S. Pettersen) **Arsenal 3** (Simpson, Kelly, Marinello)
	Stromgodset: Thun, Wolner, Mathison, Alsaker-Noestdahl, Eriksen, Amundsen, Olsen, Andersen, S. Pettersen, Rorvik, Presberg (I. Pettersen).

Arsenal: Wilson, Rice, McNab, Roberts, McLintock, Simpson, Marinello (Davies), Kelly, Radford, Kennedy, Graham.

29 September 1971

Arsenal 4 (Kennedy, Radford 2, Armstrong)
Stromgodset Drammen 0

Arsenal: Wilson, Rice, Nelson, Kelly, Simpson, Roberts, Armstrong, George, Radford, Kennedy, Graham.

Stromgodset: Thun, Wolner, Mathison (Backstrom), Alsaker-Noestdahl, Eriksen, Amundsen, Rorvik (Henriksen), Olsen, Andersen, S. Pettersen, I. Pettersen.

15 September 1971

BK 1903 Copenhagen 2 (Johansen 2)
Celtic 1 (Macari)

BK 1903: Jensen, Nielsen I, Petersen, Westergaard, Andersen, Sjolberg, Thygesen, Mathiesen (Kristensen), Forsing, Aabling, Johansen.

Celtic: Marshall, Craig, Gemmell, Murdoch, McNeill, Connelly, Johnstone (Wallace), Dalglish, Macari, Callaghan, Lennox.

29 September 1971

Celtic 3 (Wallace 2, Callaghan)
BK 1903 Copenhagen 0

Celtic: Williams, Craig, Brogan, Hay, McNeill, Connelly, Johnstone, Wallace, Macari, Callaghan, Lennox (Hughes).

BK 1903: Jensen, Nielsen I, Petersen (Christiansen), Westergaard, Andersen, Sjolberg, Nielsen II, Mathiesen, Forsing, Aabling, Johansen.

15 September 1971

Standard Liège 2 (Semmeling, Takac)
Linfield 0

Standard Liège: Piot, Beurlet, Dewalque, Jeck, Dolmans, Van Moer, Svensson, Pilot, Semmeling, Henrotay, Takac.

Linfield: McGonigal, Fraser, Patterson, Larmour, McAllister, Bowyer, McAteer, Peacock, Magee, Andrews, Cathcart.

29 September 1971

Linfield 2 (Magee, Larmour)
Standard Liège 3 (Van Moer, Takac, Pilot pen)

Linfield: McGonigal, Fraser, Patterson, Larmour, McAllister, Bowyer, McAteer, Peacock (Andrews), Magee, Scott, Cathcart.

Standard Liège: Piot, Beurlet, Dolmans, Labarbe, Dewalque, Pilot, Semmeling, Van Moer, Henrotay, Svensson, Takac (Cvetler).

15 September 1971

Valencia 0
Hajduk Split 0

29 September 1971

Hajduk Split 1 (Anibal og)
Valencia 1 (Claramunt)

Valencia won on away goals.

15 September 1971

Cork Hibernians 0
Borussia Moenchengladbach 5 (Wloka 2, Heynckes, Lefevre 2)

29 September 1971

Borussia Moenchengladbach 2 (Sieloff, Wimmer)
Cork Hibernians 1 (Dennehy)

15 September 1971

Ujpest Dozsa 4 (A. Dunai, Bene 3)
Malmo FF 0

29 September 1971

Malmo FF 1 (Tapper pen)
Ujpest Dozsa 0

15 September 1971

Olympique Marseille 2 (Wrazy og, Skoblar)
Gornik Zabrze 1 (Lubanski)

29 September 1971

Gornick Zabrze 1 (Anczok)
Olympique Marseille 1 (Skoblar)

15 September 1971

Innsbruck 0
Benfica 4 (Graca, Jorge 2, Eusebio)

29 September 1971

Benfica 3 (Adolfo, Jorge, Simoes)
Innsbruck 1 (Jara)

15 September 1971

Lahden Reipas 1 (Lindholm)
Grasshoppers 1 (Ohlhauser)

29 September 1971

Grasshoppers 8 (Muller 4, Groebli, P. Meyer, A. Meyer, Schneeberger)
Lahden Reipas 0

15 September 1971

Galatasaray 1 (Aydin)
CSKA Moscow 1 (Kopeikin)

29 September 1971

CSKA Moscow 3 (Dorofeyev 2, Oglobin)
Galatasaray 0

15 September 1971

CSKA Sofia 3 (Atanassov, Nikodimov pen, Marashliev)
Partizan Tirana 0

29 September 1971	**Partizan Tirana 0** **CSKA Sofia 1** (Atanassov)
15 September 1971	**Ajax 2** (Swart, Keizer) **Dynamo Dresden 0**
29 September 1971	**Dynamo Dresden 0** **Ajax 0**
15 September 1971	**Dinamo Bucharest 0** **Spartak Trnava 0**
29 September 1971	**Spartak Trnava 2** (Dobias, Adamec) **Dinamo Bucharest 2** (Popescu 2) *Dinamo Bucharest won on away goals.*
15 September 1971	**Internazionale 4** (Mazzola, Facchetti, Jair, Boninsegna pen) **AEK Athens 1** (Pamonis)
29 September 1971	**AEK Athens 3** (Venturis, Papoiannu, Nikolaidis) **Internazionale 2** (Karafeskos og, Boninsegna)
15 September 1971	**Feyenoord 8** (Maiwald 2, Van Hanegem, Schoenmaker 3, Israel, Schneider) **Olympiakos Nicosia 0**
22 September 1971 Rotterdam	**Olympiakos Nicosia 0** **Feyenoord 9** (Israel 3, Van Hanegem 2, Posthumus 2, Hasil, Wery)
26 September 1971 Malta	**Akranes 0** **Sliema Wanderers 4** (Loporto 2, Vincent 2)
29 September 1971	**Sliema Wanderers 0** **Akranes 0**

SECOND ROUND

20 October 1971	**Grasshoppers 0** **Arsenal 2** (Kennedy, Graham) *Grasshoppers:* Deck, Staudenmann, Ruegg, Citherlet, Groebli, P. Meyer, Winiger, Ohlauser, A. Meyer, Muller, Schneeberger. *Arsenal:* Wilson, Rice, Nelson, Kelly, McLintock, Roberts, Armstrong, George, Radford, Kennedy, Graham.
3 November 1971	**Arsenal 3** (Kennedy, George, Radford) **Grasshoppers 0** *Arsenal:* Wilson, Rice, Nelson, Storey, Roberts (Simpson), McLintock (McNab), Armstrong, George, Radford, Kennedy, Graham. *Grasshoppers:* Deck, Winiger, Staudenmann, Citherlet, Ruegg, Groebli (Niggl), P. Meyer, A. Meyer, Ohlhauser, Muller, Schneeberger.
20 October 1971	**Celtic 5** (Gemmell, Macari 2, Hood, Brogan) **Sliema Wanderers 0** *Celtic:* Williams, Hay, Gemmell, Murdoch (Davidson), Connelly, Brogan, Johnstone, Dalglish, Hood (Lennox), Callaghan, Macari. *Sliema:* Pearson, Spiteri, J. Aquilina, Serge, Micallef, Briffa, Vella (Caruana), Darmanin, Cocks, E. Aquilina, Falzon.
3 November 1971	**Sliema Wanderers 1** (Cocks) **Celtic 2** (Hood, Lennox) *Sliema:* Pearson, Borg, J. Aquilina, Serge, Micallef, Darmanin, Vassallo, Briffa, Cocks, Falzon, E. Aquilina. *Celtic:* Williams, Craig, Gemmell, Callaghan, McNeill, Connelly, Dalglish, Hood, Macari, Davidson (Hancock), Lennox.
20 October 1971	**Olympique Marseille 1** (Gress) **Ajax 2** (Keizer, Cruyff)
3 November 1971	**Ajax 4** (Couécou og, Swart, Haan, Cruyff) **Olympique Marseille 1** (Couécou)
20 October 1971	**Valencia 0** **Ujpest Dozsa 1** (Zambo)
3 November 1971	**Ujpest Dozsa 2** (A. Dunai 2) **Valencia 1** (Valdez)
20 October 1971	**CSKA Moscow 1** (Kopeikin) **Standard Liège 0**
3 November 1971	**Standard Liège 2** (Takac 2) **CSKA Moscow 0**
20 October 1971	**Benfica 2** (Rodriguez, Jorge) **CSKA Sofia 1** (Jekov)

3 November 1971	**CSKA Sofia 0** **Benfica 0**
20 October 1971	**Dinamo Bucharest 0** **Feyenoord 3** (Wery, Maiwald, Schneider)
3 November 1971	**Feyenoord 2** (Nunweiler og, Schoenmaker) **Dinamo Bucharest 0**
20 October 1971	**Borussia Moenchengladbach 7** (Heynckes 2, Lefevre 2, Netzer 2, Sieloff pen) **Internazionale 1** (Boninsegna) *This match was declared void due to an incident in the 29th minute when Boninsegna was struck by a soft-drink can thrown from the crowd. A replay was ordered on a neutral ground. The score at the time was 2–1 to Borussia.*
3 November 1971	**Internazionale 4** (Bellugi, Boninsegna, Jair, Ghio) **Borussia Moenchengladbach 2** (Lefevre, Wittkamp)
1 December 1971 Berlin	**Borussia Moenchengladbach 0** **Internazionale 0**

QUARTER FINALS

8 March 1972	**Ajax 2** (Muhren 2 – 1 pen) **Arsenal 1** (Kennedy) *Ajax:* Stuy, Suurbier, Krol, Blankenburg, Hulshoff, Haan, Swart, Muhren, Cruyff, Van Dijk (Rep), Keizer. *Arsenal:* Wilson, Rice, Nelson, Storey, McLintock, Simpson, Armstrong, George, Radford, Kennedy, Graham.
22 March 1972	**Arsenal 0** **Ajax 1** (Graham og) *Arsenal:* Wilson, Rice, Nelson (Roberts), Storey, McLintock, Simpson, Marinello, George, Kennedy, Graham, Armstrong. *Ajax:* Stuy, Suurbier, Krol, Blankenburg, Hulshoff, Neeskens, Swart, Muhren, Cruyff, Haan, Keizer.
8 March 1972	**Ujpest Dozsa 1** (Horvath) **Celtic 2** (Horvath og, Macari) *Ujpest:* Szentmihalyi, Nosko, Maurer, Juhasz, E. Dunai, Horvath, Fazekas, Zambo, Bene, A. Dunai (Nagy), Toth. *Celtic:* Williams, McGrain, Brogan, Murdoch, McNeill, Connelly, Dalglish, Hay, Hood, Macari, Lennox.
22 March 1972	**Celtic 1** (Macari) **Ujpest Dozsa 1** (A. Dunai) *Celtic:* Williams, McGrain, Brogan (Johnstone), Murdoch, McNeill, Connelly, Dalglish, Hay, Hood, Macari, Lennox. *Ujpest:* Szentmihalyi, Kapostza, Maurer, Juhasz, E. Dunai, Horvath, Fazekas, Zambo, Bene, A. Dunai, Toth (Gorocs).
8 March 1972	**Feyenoord 1** (Laseroms) **Benfica 0**
22 March 1972	**Benfica 5** (Nene 3, Eusebio, Jordao) **Feyenoord 1** (Posthumus)
8 March 1972	**Internazionale 1** (Jair) **Standard Liège 0**
22 March 1972	**Standard Liège 2** (Cvetler, Takac pen) **Internazionale 1** (Mazzola) *Internazionale won on away goals.*

SEMI-FINALS

5 April 1972	**Internazionale 0** **Celtic 0** *Internazionale:* Vieri, Bellugi, Facchetti, Bertini, Oriali, Burgnich, Jair, Pellizzaro (Ghio), Boninsegna, Mazzola, Frustalupi. *Celtic:* Williams, Craig, Brogan (P. McCluskey), Murdoch, McNeill, Connelly, Johnstone, Dalglish, Macari, Callaghan, Lennox.
19 April 1972	**Celtic 0** **Internazionale 0** *After extra time Internazionale won on penalties.* *Celtic:* Williams, Craig, P. McCluskey, Murdoch, McNeill, Connelly, Johnstone, Daglish (Deans), Macari, Callaghan, Lennox. *Internazionale:* Vieri, Bellugi, Facchetti, Oriali, Giubertoni, Burgnich, Jair, Bedin, Bertini (Pellizzaro). Mazzola, Frustalupi.

5 April 1972	**Ajax 1** (Swart) **Benfica 0**
19 April 1972	**Benfica 0** **Ajax 0**

FINAL

31 May 1972 Rotterdam	**Ajax 2** (Cruyff 2) **Internazionale 0**

Ajax: Stuy, Suurbier, Krol, Blankenburg, Hulshoff, Neeskens, Swart. Muhren, Cruyff, Haan, Keizer.

Internazionale: Bordon, Burgnich, Facchetti, Bellugi, Giubertoni (Bertini), Oriali, Jair (Pellizzaro), Bedin, Boninsegna, Mazzola, Frustalupi.

Referee: Héliès (Fra)

Attendance: 61,000.

Eighteenth season – 1972–73

FIRST ROUND

Byes: Ajax, Spartak Trnava.

13 September 1972	**Derby County 2** (McFarland, Gemmill) **Zeljeznicar Sarajevo 0**

Derby County: Boulton, Powell, Daniel, Hennessy, McFarland, Todd, McGovern, Gemmill, O'Hare, Hector, Hinton.

Zeljeznicar: Janjus, D. Kojovic, Becirspahic, Derakovic, Katalinski, Jelusic, Bratic, Jankovic (S. Kojovic), Bukal, Spreco, Radovic (Saracevic).

27 September 1972	**Zeljeznicar Sarajevo 1** (Spreco) **Derby County 2** (Hinton, O'Hare)

Zeljeznicar: Janjus, D. Kojovic, Becirspahic, Bratic, Saracevic, Karalinski, Jelusic, Jankovic, Bukal (Radovic), Spreco. Derakovic (S. Kojovic).

Derby County: Boulton, Daniel, Robson, Hennessy, McFarland, Todd, McGovern, Gemmill, O'Hare, Hector, Hinton.

13 September 1972	**Celtic 2** (Macari, Deans) **Rosenborg 1** (Wirkola)

Celtic: Williams, McGrain, Callaghan, Murdoch, McNeill, Connelly, Hood, Dalglish, Deans, Macari, Wilson (Lennox).

Rosenborg: Karlsen (Torp), Meirik, Ronnes, Rime, Warmdahl, Christiansen, Ness, Lindseth, Sunde, Wirkola, Odegaard (Hansen).

27 September 1972	**Rosenborg 1** (Christiansen) **Celtic 3** (Macari, Hood, Dalglish)

Rosenborg: Torp, Meirik, Ronnes, Rime, Warmdahl, Christiansen, Ness, Lindseth, Sunde, Wirkola, Odegaard.

Celtic: Williams, McGrain, P. McCluskey, Murdoch, McNeill, Connelly, Johnstone, Dalglish, Macari, Hood, Callaghan.

13 September 1972	**Real Madrid 3** (Santillana 2, Grande) **IBK Keflavik 0**
27 September 1972	**IBK Keflavik 0** **Real Madrid 1** (Verdugo)
13 September 1972	**Anderlecht 4** (Ejderstedt, Rensenbrink 2, Van Himst) **Vejle BK 2** (Johanssen 2)
27 September 1972	**Vejle BK 0** **Anderlecht 3** (Wolters, Rensenbrink 2)
13 September 1972	**Ujpest Dozsa 2** (Horvath, Zambo) **Basle 0**
27 September 1972	**Basle 3** (Hasler, Balmer 2) **Ujpest Dozsa 2** (Bene 2)
13 September 1972	**Galatasaray 1** (Bulent) **Bayern Munich 1** (Müller)
27 September 1972	**Bayern Munich 6** (Müller 2, Hoeness, Schneider, Roth, Beckenbauer pen) **Galatasaray 0**
13 September 1972 Lyons	**Olympique Marseille 1** (Bonnel) **Juventus 0**
27 September 1972	**Juventus 3** (Bettega 2, Haller) **Olympique Marseille 0**

13 September 1972	**Malmo FF 1** (Bo Larsson) **Benfica 0**
27 September 1972	**Benfica 4** (Eusebio 2 – 1 pen, Jordao, Simoes) **Malmo FF 1** (Tapper pen)
13 September 1972	**Innsbruck 0** **Dynamo Kiev 1** (Kolotov)
27 September 1972	**Dynamo Kiev 2** (Puzasch, Damin) **Innsbruck 0**
13 September 1972	**CSKA Sofia 2** (Kolev pen, Yankov) **Panathinaikos 1** (Veron)
27 September 1972	**Panathinaikos 2** (Veron, Domelo) **CSKA Sofia 1** (Trankov) *This match was declared void because of an infringement of the provisions governing the penalty competition.*
26 October 1972	**Panathinaikos 0** **CSKA Sofia 2** (Jekov, Stankov)
13 September 1972	**Sliema Wanderers 0** **Gornik Zabrze 5** (Lubanski 3, Banas, Wilczek)
27 September 1972	**Gornik Zabrze 5** (Szoltysik, Lubanski, Oslizlo, Szarmach 2) **Sliema Wanderers 0**
13 September 1972	**FC Magdeburg 6** (Mewes, Pommerenke, Seguin, Sparwasser 2, Jalonen og) **Turun Palloseura 0**
27 September 1972	**Turun Palloseura 1** (Toivola) **FC Magdeburg 3** (Sparwasser 2, Pommerenke)
13 September 1972	**Aris Bonnevoie 0** **Arges Pitesti 2** (Rosu, Jercan)
27 September 1972	**Arges Pitesti 4** (Dobrin 2, Radu 2) **Aris Bonnevoie 0**
13 September 1972	**Waterford 2** (Hale 2) **Omonia Nicosia 1** (Rotides)
27 September 1972	**Omonia Nicosia 2** (Chelebis 2) **Waterford 0**

SECOND ROUND

25 October 1972	**Derby County 3** (McFarland, Hector, McGovern) **Benfica 0** *Derby County:* Boulton, Daniel, Robson, Hennessy, McFarland, Todd, McGovern, Gemmill, O'Hare, Hector, Hinton. *Benfica:* Henrique, Da Silva, Humberto, Messias, Adolfo, Graca, Nene, Toni, Batista (Jordao). Eusebio, Simoes.
8 November 1972	**Benfica 0** **Derby County 0** *Benfica:* Henrique, Da Silva, Humberto, Messias, Adolfo, Graca, Nene (Jorge), Toni, Batista (Rodriguez), Eusebio, Simoes. *Derby County:* Boulton, Webster, Robson, Hennessy, McFarland, Todd, McGovern, Gemmill, O'Hare, Hector, Hinton.
25 October 1972	**Celtic 2** (Dalglish 2) **Ujpest Dozsa 1** (Bene) *Celtic:* Williams, Hay, McGrain, Connelly, McNeill, Callaghan, Johnstone (Lennox), Dalglish, Deans, Macari, Hood (P. McCluskey). *Ujpest:* Szentmihalyi, Kolar, Harsanyi, Toth, E. Dunai, Horvath, Fazekas, Juhasz (Nagy), Bene, A. Dunai, Zambo (Kellner).
8 November 1972	**Ujpest Dozsa 3** (Bene 2, Fazekas pen) **Celtic 0** *Ujpest:* Borbely, Nosko (Kolar), Harsanyi, Juhasz (Nagy), E. Dunai, Horvath, Fazekas, Toth, Bene, A. Dunai, Zambo. *Celtic:* Williams, McGrain (Deans), Brogan, Hay, McNeill, P. McCluskey, Johnstone, Callaghan, Dalglish, Connelly, Lennox (Hood).
24 October 1972	**Bayern Munich 9** (Müller 5, Schneider 2, Hoeness, Roth) **Omonia Nicosia 0**
26 October 1972 Augsburg	**Omonia Nicosia 0** **Bayern Munich 4** (Roth, Müller 2, Hoffmann)

25 October 1972	**Arges Pitesti 2** (Dobrin, Prepurgel) **Real Madrid 1** (Anzarda)
9 November 1972	**Real Madrid 3** (Santillana 2, Grande) **Arges Pitesti 1** (Radu)
25 October 1972	**Spartak Trnava 1** (Kabat) **Anderlecht 0**
8 November 1972	**Anderlecht 0** **Spartak Trnava 1** (Masrna)
25 October 1972	**Dynamo Kiev 2** (Muntijan pen, Puzasch) **Gornik Zabrze 0**
8 November 1972	**Gornik Zabrze 2** (Szoltysik, Gorgon) **Dynamo Kiev 1** (Blokhin)
25 October 1972	**Juventus 1** (Anastasi) **FC Magdeburg 0**
8 November 1972	**FC Magdeburg 0** **Juventus 1** (Cuccureddu)
8 November 1972	**CSKA Sofia 1** (Jekov) **Ajax 3** (Swart, Keizer, Haan)
29 November 1972	**Ajax 3** (Cruyff 2, Blankenburg) **CSKA Sofia 0**

QUARTER-FINALS

7 March 1973	**Spartak Trnava 1** (Horvath) **Derby County 0** *Spartak Trnava:* Keketi, Dobias, Majernik, Varadin, Hrusecky, Fandel, Masrna, Horvath, Hagara, Adamec, Kabat. *Derby County:* Boulton, Powell, Nish, O'Hare, McFarland, Todd, McGovern, Gemmill, Davies, Hector, Durban.
21 March 1973	**Derby County 2** (Hector 2) **Spartak Trnava 0** *Derby County:* Boulton, Webster, Nish, O'Hare, McFarland, Todd, McGovern, Gemmill, Davies, Hector, Hinton. *Spartak Trnava:* Keketi, Dobias, Majernik, Kuna, Hagara, Hrusecky, Horvath (Varadin), Masrna (Martinkovic), Fandel, Adamec, Kabat.
7 March 1973	**Juventus 0** **Ujpest Dozsa 0**
21 March 1973	**Ujpest Dozsa 2** (Bene, Toth) **Juventus 2** (Altafini, Anastasi) *Juventus won on away goals.*
7 March 1973	**Dynamo Kiev 0** **Real Madrid 0**
21 March 1973	**Real Madrid 3** (Santillana, Aguilar, Amancio) **Dynamo Kiev 0**
7 March 1973	**Ajax 4** (Haan 2, Muhren, Cruyff) **Bayern Munich 0**
21 March 1973	**Bayern Munich 2** (Müller 2) **Ajax 1** (Keizer)

SEMI-FINALS

11 April 1973	**Juventus 3** (Altafini 2, Causio) **Derby County 1** (Hector) *Juventus:* Zoff, Spinosi, Marchetti, Furino, Morini, Salvadore, Causio, Cuccureddu (Haller), Anastasi, Capello, Altafini. *Derby County:* Boulton, Webster, Nish, Durban, McFarland, Todd, McGovern, Gemmill, O'Hare, Hector, Powell.
25 April 1973	**Derby County 0** **Juventus 0** *Derby County:* Boulton, Webster, Nish, Powell (Durban), Daniel (Sims), Todd, McGovern, O'Hare, Davies, Hector, Hinton. *Juventus:* Zoff, Spinosi, Marchetti, Furino, Morini, Salvadore, Causio, Cuccureddu (Longobucco), Anastasi, Capello, Altafini.
11 April 1973	**Ajax 2** (Hulshoff, Krol) **Real Madrid 1** (Pirri)

25 April 1973	**Real Madrid 0** **Ajax 1** (Muhren)
FINAL	
30 May 1973 Belgrade	**Ajax 1** (Rep) **Juventus 0**

Ajax: Stuy, Suurbier, Krol, Blankenburg, Hulshoff, Neeskens, Haan, Muhren, Cruyff, Rep, Keizer.

Juventus: Zoff, Longobucco, Marchetti, Furino, Morini, Salvadore, Causio (Cuccureddu), Altafini, Anastasi, Capello, Bettega (Haller).

Referee; Gugulovic (Yug)

Attendance: 93,000.

Nineteenth season – 1973–74

FIRST ROUND

Bye: Ajax.

19 September 1973	**Jeunesse Esch 1** (Dussier) **Liverpool 1** (Hall)

Jeunesse: R. Hoffman, Schaul, Schmit (Mond), Morocutti, Da Grava, Hnatow, Langer, Zwalli (Dussier), J. Hoffman, Reiland, Di Genova.

Liverpool: Clemence, Lawler, Smith, Thompson, Lloyd, Hughes, Keegan, Hall, Heighway, Boersma, Callaghan.

3 October 1973	**Liverpool 2** (Mond og, Toshack) **Jeunesse Esch 0**

Liverpool: Clemence, Lawler, Lindsay, Smith, Lloyd, Hughes, Keegan, Hall, Heighway, Toshack, Callaghan.

Jeunesse: R. Hoffman, Schaul, Schmit, Morocutti, Da Grava, Mond, Langer, Zwalli, J. Hoffman, Reiland, Di Genova.

19 September 1973	**Turun Palloseura 1** (Andelmin pen) **Celtic 6** (Callaghan 2, Hood, Johnstone, Connelly, Deans)

Turun: Enckelman (Kokkonen), Kymalainen, Saari, Nummi, Nummelin, Toivanen, Salama, Lindholm, Haittu, Andelmin, Suhonen.

Celtic: Hunter, McGrain, Brogan, Murray, McNeill, Connelly, Johnstone, Hay, Hood (Deans), Callaghan, Wilson (Davidson).

3 October 1973	**Celtic 3** (Deans, Johnstone 2) **Turun Palloseura 0**

Celtic: Hunter, P. McCluskey, Brogan, Murray, McNeill, Connelly, Johnstone, Davidson, Deans, Dalglish (McNamara), Wilson.

Turun: Enckelman, Kymalainen, Saari, Nummi, Salonen, Toivanen, Salama, Lindholm, Haittu, Andelmin, Saarinan.

19 September 1973	**Crusaders 0** **Dinamo Bucharest 1** (Cooke og)

Crusaders: Nicholson, Cooke, Beckett, McFarland, Flanagan, McPolin, Cullen, McFeeley, McQuillan, Todd, Lennox (subs used were Woods and Macklin).

Dinamo: Cava, Delenua, Satmareanu, Lucuta, Sandu, Radu, Moldovan, Salceanu, Dudu, Custov, Dumitrescu (subs used were Constantinescu and Dobrau).

3 October 1973	**Dinamo Bucharest 11** (Georgescu 4, Dumitrache, Dinu, Nunweiler 3, Beckett og, Todd og) **Crusaders 0**

Dinamo: Cava, Delenau, Gabriel, Lucuta, Dobrau, Dinu, Moldovan, Georgescu, Dumitrache, Satmareanu, Nunweiler (subs used were Duha and Custov).

Crusaders: Nicholson, Cooke, McFarland, Flanagan, Beckett, McPolin, Todd, Woods, Macklin, McQuillan, Lennox (subs used were Cullen and Hunter).

18 September 1973	**Basle 5** (Cubillas, Balmer 2, Hasler, Demarmels) **Fram Reykjavik 0**
20 September 1973 Olten, Switzerland	**Fram Reykjavik 2** (Leifson, Eliasson) **Basle 6** (Tanner 2, Cubillas, Wampfler, Stohler, Geirsson og)
19 September 1973	**Waterford 2** (Kirby, O'Neill) **Ujpest Dozsa 3** (Zambo, Fazekas, Nagy)
3 October 1973	**Ujpest Dozsa 3** (A. Dunai, Fazekas, Nagy) **Waterford 0**
19 September 1973	**Bayern Munich 3** (Müller 2, Olsson og) **Atvidaberg 1** (Dürnberger og)
3 October 1973	**Atvidaberg 3** (Torstensson 2, Wallinder) **Bayern Munich 1** ((Hoeness)

After extra time. Bayern won on penalties.

19 September 1973	**Benfica 1** (Messias) **Olympiakos Piraeus 0**
3 October 1973	**Olympiakos Piraeus 0** **Benfica 1** (Nene)
19 September 1973	**Dynamo Dresden 2** (Kreische, Schade) **Juventus 0**
3 October 1973	**Juventus 3** (Furino, Altafini, Cuccureddu) **Dynamo Dresden 2** (Capello og, Sachse)
19 September 1973	**Zaria Voroshilovgrad 2** (Kouznetsov 2) **Apoel Nicosia 0**
3 October 1973	**Apoel Nicosia 0** **Zaria Voroshilovgrad 1** (Kouznetsov)
19 September 1973	**Red Star Belgrade 2** (Petrovic, Karasi) **Stal Mielec 1** (Lato)
3 October 1973	**Stal Mielec 0** **Red Star Belgrade 1** (Lazarevic)
19 September 1973	**Bruges 8** (Lambert 3, Lefevre, Carteus 2, Russmann, Houwaert) **Floriana 0**
3 October 1973	**Floriana 0** **Bruges 2** (Thio, Houwaert)
19 September 1973	**Atletico Madrid 0** **Galatasaray 0**
3 October 1973	**Galatasaray 0** **Atletico Madrid 1** (Falceto) *After extra time.*
19 September 1973	**Viking Stavanger 1** (Kvia) **Spartak Trnava 2** (Adamec, Martinkovic)
3 October 1973	**Spartak Trnava 1** (Martinkovic) **Viking Stavanger 0**
19 September 1973	**Vejle 2** (Markussen, Lund) **Nantes 2** (Rampillon, Couécou)
3 October 1973	**Nantes 0** **Vejle 1** (Norregaard)
19 September 1973	**CSKA Sofia 3** (Maraschliev, Denev, Shekov) **Innsbruck 0**
3 October 1973	**Innsbruck 0** **CSKA Sofia 1** (Shekov)

SECOND ROUND

24 October 1973

Red Star Belgrade 2 (Jankovic, Bogicevic)
Liverpool 1 (Lawler)

Red Star: O. Petrovic, Krivokuca, Bogicevic, Pavlovic, Dojinovski, Baralic, Jankovic (Keri), Karasi, Lazarevic, Acimovic (Jovanovic), V. Petrovic.

Liverpool: Clemence, Lawler, Lindsay, Smith, Lloyd, Hughes, Keegan, Cormack, Heighway, Toshack, Callaghan.

6 November 1973

Liverpool 1 (Lawler)
Red Star Belgrade 2 (Lazarevic, Jankovic)

Liverpool: Clemence, Lawler, Lindsay, Thompson, Lloyd, Hughes, Keegan, McLaughlin (Hall), Heighway (Boersma), Toshack, Callaghan.

Red Star: O. Petrovic, Jovanovic, Bogicevic, Pavlovic, Dojinovski, Baralic, Jankovic, Karasi, Lazarevic, Acimovic, V. Petrovic.

24 October 1973

Celtic 0
Vejle 0

Celtic: Hunter, McGrain, Hay, Murray, Connelly, P. McCluskey, Johnstone, Hood (Wilson), Dalglish, Callaghan, Lennox.

Vejle: Wodsku, J. Jensen, F. Hansen, Serritslev, G. Jensen, Sorrensen, T. Hansen, Markusson, Huttel, Pedersen, Norregaard (Johansen).

6 November 1973

Vejle 0
Celtic 1 (Lennox)

Vejle: Wodsku, J. Jensen, F. Hansen, Serritslev, G. Jensen, Sorensen, Norregaard, T. Hansen, Markussen, Fritsen, Andersen.

Celtic: Hunter, McGrain, Brogan, P. McCluskey, McNeill, Connelly, Lennox, Murray, Deans, Hay, Dalglish.

24 October 1973	**Benfica 1** (Eusebio) **Ujpest Dozsa 1** (Toth)
7 November 1973	**Ujpest Dozsa 2** (Bene, Kolar) **Benfica 0**
24 October 1973	**Spartak Trnava 0** **Zaria Voroshilovgrad 0**
7 November 1973	**Zaria Voroshilovgrad 0** **Spartak Trnava 1** (Martinkovic)
24 October 1973	**Bruges 2** (Carteus, Thio) **Basle 1** (Odermatt)
7 November 1973	**Basle 6** (Hasler, Balmer, Wampfler 2, Hitzfeld 2) **Bruges 4** (Lambert 3 – 1 pen, Carteus)
24 October 1973	**Dinamo Bucharest 0** **Atletico Madrid 2** (Becerra, Eusebio)
7 November 1973	**Atletico Madrid 2** (Ayala, Capon) **Dinamo Bucharest 2** (Lucescu, Georgescu)
24 October 1973	**Ajax 1** (Mulder) **CSKA Sofia 0**
7 November 1973	**CSKA Sofia 2** (Maraschliev, Mikhailov) **Ajax 0** *After extra time.*
24 October 1973	**Bayern Munich 4** (Hoffman, Dürnberger, Roth, Müller) **Dynamo Dresden 3** (Sachse 2, Heidler)
7 November 1973	**Dynamo Dresden 3** (Waetzlich, Schade, Hafner) **Bayern Munich 3** (Hoeness 2, Müller)

QUARTER-FINALS

27 February 1974

Basle 3 (Hitzfeld 2 –1 pen, Odermatt)
Celtic 2 (Wilson, Dalglish)

Basle: Laufenburger, Munschin, Fischli, Rahmen, Demarmels, Odermatt (Wampfler), Hasler, Stohler, Balmer, Hitzfeld, Wenger (Tanner).
Celtic: Williams, McGrain, Brogan, Connelly, McNeill, Hay, Murray, Dalglish, Hood, Deans (Callaghan), Wilson.

20 March 1974

Celtic 4 (Dalglish, Deans, Callaghan, Murray)
Basle 2 (Munschin, Balmer)

After extra time.
Celtic: Connaghan, Hay, Brogan, Murray, McNeill, Connelly (P. McCluskey), Johnstone, Hood, Deans, Callaghan, Dalglish.
Basle: Laufenburger (Kunz), Rahmen, Stohler, Hasler, Fischli, Munschin, Balmer, Odermatt, Hitzfeld, Wampfler, Tanner.

5 March 1974

Bayern Munich 4 (Torstensson 2, Beckenbauer, Müller)
CSKA Sofia 1 (Maraschliev)

20 March 1974

CSKA Sofia 2 (Kolev pen, Denev)
Bayern Munich 1 (Breitner pen)

6 March 1974

Red Star Belgrade 0
Atletico Madrid 2 (Luis, Garate)

21 March 1974

Atletico Madrid 0
Red Star Belgrade 0

6 March 1974

Spartak Trnava 1 (Kabat)
Ujpest Dozsa 1 (Toth pen)

20 March 1974

Ujpest Dozsa 1 (Fekete)
Spartak Trnava 1 (Adamec)

After extra time. Ujpest won on penalties.

SEMI-FINALS

10 April 1974

Celtic 0
Atletico Madrid 0

Celtic: Connaghan, Hay, Brogan, Murray, McNeill, P. McCluskey, Johnstone, Dalglish, Hood, Deans (Wilson), Callaghan.
Atletico: Reina, Melo, Diaz, Benegas, Ovejero, Eusebio, Heredia, Adelardo, Garate (Quique), Irureta (Alberto), Ayala.

24 April 1974

Atletico Madrid 2 (Garate, Adelardo)
Celtic 0

Atletico: Reina, Benegas, Capon, Adelardo, Heredia (Bermejo), Eusebio, Ufarte, Luis (Cabrero), Garate, Irureta, Becerra.

Celtic: Connaghan, McGrain, Brogan, Hay, McNeill, P. McCluskey, Johnstone, Murray, Dalglish, Hood, Lennox.

10 April 1974

Ujpest Dozsa 1 (Fazekas)
Bayern Munich 1 (Torstensson)

24 April 1974
FINAL

Bayern Munich 3 (Torstensson, Müller 2)
Ujpest Dozsa 0

15 May 1974
Brussels

Bayern Munich 1 (Schwarzenbeck)
Atletico Madrid 1 (Luis)

After extra time. Score at 90 minutes, 0–0.

Bayern: Maier, Hansen, Breitner, Schwarzenbeck, Beckenbauer, Roth, Torstensson (Dürnberger), Zobel, Müller, Hoeness, Kapelmann.

Atletico: Reina, Melo, Capon, Adelardo, Heredia, Eusebio, Ufarte (Becerra), Luis, Garate, Irureta, Salcedo (Alberto).

Referee: Loraux (Bel)

Attendance 65,000.

Replay

17 May 1974
Brussels

Bayern Munich 4 (Hoeness 2, Müller 2)
Atletico Madrid 0

Bayern: Maier, Hansen, Breitner, Schwarzenbeck, Beckenbauer, Roth, Torstensson, Zobel, Müller, Hoeness, Kapelmann.

Atletico: Reina, Melo, Capon, Adelardo (Benegas), Heredia, Eusebio, Salcedo, Luis, Garate, Alberto (Ufarte), Becerra.

Referee: Delcourt (Bel)

Attendance: 23,000.

Note: This was the first time the European Cup final had ever gone to a replay.

Twentieth season – 1974–75

FIRST ROUND

Byes: Bayern Munich, FC Magdeburg.

18 September 1974

Leeds United 4 (Clarke 2, Lorimer pen, Jordan)
FC Zurich 1 (Katic)

Leeds United: Harvey, Reaney, Cooper, Yorath, McQueen, Hunter, Lorimer, Clarke, Jordan, Giles, Madeley.

Zurich: Grob, Heer, Rutschmann (Marti), Zigerlig, Bionda, Kuhn, Martinelli, Katic, Jeandupeux, Stierli, Botteron.

2 October 1974

FC Zurich 2 (Katic, Rutschmann pen)
Leeds United 1 (Clarke)

Zurich: Grob, Heer, Bionda, Zigerlig, Stierli, Martinelli, Rutschmann, Kuhn, Katic, Jeandupeux, Botteron.

Leeds United: Harvey, Reaney, Cherry, Yorath, Madeley, Hunter, Lorimer, Clarke, Jordan, Bates, F. Gray (Hampton).

18 September 1974

Celtic 1 (Wilson)
Olympiakos Piraeus 1 (Viera)

Celtic: Connaghan, McGrain, Brogan (Lennox), Murray, McNeill, P. McCluskey, Johnstone, Hood, Dalglish, Callaghan, Wilson.

Olympiakos: Kelessidis, Kyrastas, Angelis, Siokos, Glezos, Persidis, Losanda, Viera, Kritikopoulos, Delikaris, Stavropoulos.

2 October 1974

Olympiakos Piraeus 2 (Kritikopoulos, Stavropoulos)
Celtic 0

Olympiakos: Kelessidis, Liolios, Siokos, Glezos, Angelis, Persidis, Kyrastas, Delikaris, Losanda, Kritikopoulos, Savropoulos (Davroulis).

Celtic: Connaghan, McGrain, Brogan, Murray, McNeill, P. McCluskey, Dalglish (Lennox), Callaghan, Johnstone (Hood), Deans, Wilson.

18 September 1974

Feyenoord 7 (Schoenmaker, Kreuz 3, Van Hanegem 2, Ressel)
Coleraine 0

Feyenoord: Treytel, Schneider, Everse, De Jong, Vos, Olsen, Jansen, Ressel, Kreuz, Van Hanegem, Schoenmaker.

Coleraine: Crossan, McCurdy, McNutt, Campbell, Jackson, Murray, Cochrane, Jennings, Simpson, Dickson, Hutton (Guy)

2 October 1974

Coleraine 1 (Simpson)
Feyenoord 4 (Schoenmaker 3 – 1 pen, Kreuz)

Coleraine: Crossan, McCurdy, McNutt (Tweed), Campbell, Jackson, Murray, Cochrane, Jennings, Guy, Dickson, Simpson.

Feyenoord: Treytel, Schneider, De Jong, Everse, Vos, Van Daele, Jansen, Ressel, Kreuz, Schoenmaker, Van Til.

18 September 1974

Levski Spartak 0
Ujpest Dozsa 3 (Horvath, Bene, A. Dunai)

2 October 1974

Ujpest Dozsa 4 (Bene 2, A. Dunai 2)
Levski Spartak 1 (Voinov)

18 September 1974

Viking Stavanger 0
Ararat Erevan 2 (Makarov 2)

2 October 1974

Ararat Erevan 4 (Makarov 3. Bonderenko)
Viking Stavanger 2 (Knutsen, Berland)

18 September 1974

Hvidovre 0
Ruch Chorzow 0

2 October 1974

Ruch Chorzow 2 (Bula 2)
Hvidovre 1 (Pedersen)

18 September 1974

Saint Etienne 2 (H. Revelli, Bereta)
Sporting Lisbon 0

2 October 1974

Sporting Lisbon 1 (Yazalde)
Saint Etienne 1 (Synaeghel)

18 September 1974

Slovan Bratislava 4 (Novotny, Masny 2, Svehlik)
Anderlecht 2 (Coeck, Van Himst)

2 October 1974

Anderlecht 3 (Van Himst, Coeck, Thissen)
Slovan Bratislava 1 (Masny)

Anderlecht won on away goals.

18 September 1974

Valletta 1 (Magno)
HJK Helsinki 0

2 October 1974

HJK Helsinki 4 (Rahja, Pettoniemi, Hamalainen, Forsell)
Valletta 1 (Iglio)

18 September 1974

Universitatea Craiova 2 (Oblemenco 2)
Atvidaberg 1 (Augustsson)

3 October 1974

Atvidaberg 3 (Andersson, Ahlqvist 2 – 1 pen)
Universitatea Craiova 1 (Balin)

18 September 1974

Jeunesse Esch 2 (Mond, Melle)
Fenerbahce 3 (Osman 2, Cemil)

2 October 1974

Fenerbahce 2 (Cemil, Yilmaz)
Jeunesse Esch 0

18 September 1974

Voest Linz 0
Barcelona 0

2 October 1974

Barcelona 5 (Asensi, Clares 2, Juan Carlos, Rexach pen)
Voest Linz 0

19 September 1974
Split

IBK Keflavik 1 (Rozic og)
Hajduk Split 7 (Zungul 2, Surjak 2, Jerkovic, Buljan, Boljat)

24 September 1974

Hajduk Split 2 (Dzoni, Mijac)
IBK Keflavik 0

Cork Celtic Walkover
Omonia Nicosia Withdrew

SECOND ROUND

23 October 1974

Ujpest Dozsa 1 (Fazekas pen)
Leeds United 2 (Lorimer, McQueen)

Ujpest: Rothernel, Kellner, Harsanyi, Nagy, Horvath, E. Dunai, Fazekas, Toth, Zambo (A. Dunai), Fekete, Bene.

Leeds United: Harvey, Reaney, Cooper, Madeley, McQueen, Hunter, Lorimer, Yorath, Jordan, Giles, McKenzie.

6 November 1974

Leeds United 3 (McQueen, Bremner, Yorath)
Ujpest Dozsa 0

Leeds United: Harvey, Reaney, Cooper, Bremner, McQueen, Hunter (Cherry), Lorimer (Harris), Clarke, Madeley, Giles, Yorath.

Ujpest: Szigeti, Kolar, Kellner, E. Dunai, Sarlos, Toth, Fazekas, Zambo, Fekete (A. Dunai), Bene, Nagy (Torocsik).

22 October 1974	**Feyenoord 0** **Barcelona 0**
5 November 1974	**Barcelona 3** (Rexach 3) **Feyenoord 0**
23 October 1974	**Anderlecht 5** (Rensenbrink 3 – 2 pens, Ladinsky, Van der Elst) **Olympiakos Piraeus 1** (Persidis pen)
6 November 1974	**Olympiakos Piraeus 3** (Galakos 3) **Anderlecht 0**
23 October 1974	**Ruch Chorzow 2** (Kopicera, Beniger) **Fenerbahce 1** (Niazi)
6 November 1974	**Fenerbahce 0** **Ruch Chorzow 2** (Kopicera, Chojnacki)
23 October 1974	**Bayern Munich 3** (Müller 3 – 1 pen) **FC Magdeburg 2** (Hansen og, Sparwasser)
6 November 1974	**FC Magdeburg 1** (Sparwasser) **Bayern Munich 2** (Müller 2)
23 October 1974	**HJK Helsinki 0** **Atvidaberg 3** (Almqvist 2, Hasselberg)
6 November 1974	**Atvidaberg 1** (Almqvist) **HJK Helsinki 0**
23 October 1974	**Hajduk Split 4** (Jerkovic 2, Zungul, Mijac) **Saint Etienne 1** (H. Revelli)
6 November 1974	**Saint Etienne 5** (Triantafilos 2, Bathenay, Larqué, Bereta pen) **Hajduk Split 1** (Jovanic) *After extra time.*
23 October 1974	**Cork Celtic 1** (Tambling) **Ararat Erevan 2** (Zanazanyan, Kazaryan)
6 November 1974	**Ararat Erevan 5** (Pogosyan 2, Zanazanyan, Ishtoyan, Andriassian) **Cork Celtic 0**

QUARTER-FINALS

5 March 1975

Leeds United 3 (Jordan, McQueen, Lorimer)
Anderlecht 0

Leeds United: Stewart, Madeley, F. Gray, Bremner (Yorath), McQueen, Hunter, Lorimer, Clarke, Jordan, Giles, E. Gray.

Anderlecht: Ruiter, Van Binst, Broos, Van den Daele, Thissen, Dockx, Verheyen, Van der Elst, Coeck, Van Himst, Rensenbrink.

19 March 1975

Anderlecht 0
Leeds United 1 (Bremner)

Anderlecht: Barth, Dockx, Broos, Van den Daele, Thissen, Nicolaes (Denul), Van der Elst, Coeck, Ladinsky, Van Himst, Rensenbrink.

Leeds United: Stewart, Reaney, F. Gray, Bremner, McQueen, Hunter, Lorimer, Clarke, Jordan, Yorath, Madeley.

4 March 1975
Barcelona

Barcelona 2 (Marinho, Clares)
Atvidaberg 0

11 March 1975
Barcelona

Atvidaberg 0
Barcelona 3 (Gallego, Asensi, Neeskens)

5 March 1975

Ruch Chorzow 3 (Masczyk, Beniger, Bula pen)
Saint Etienne 2 (Larqué, Triantafilos)

19 March 1975

Saint Etienne 2 (Janvion, H. Revelli, pen)
Ruch Chorzow 0

5 March 1975

Bayern Munich 2 (Hoeness, Torstensson)
Ararat Erevan 0

19 March 1975

Ararat Erevan 1 (Andriassian)
Bayern Munich 0

SEMI-FINALS

9 April 1975

Leeds United 2 (Bremner, Clarke)
Barcelona 1 (Asensi)

Leeds United: Stewart, Reaney, F. Gray, Bremner, McQueen, Madeley, Yorath, Clarke, Jordan, Giles, E. Gray.

Barcelona: Sadurni, de la Cruz, Marinho, Migueli, Gallego, Costas (Rife), Neeskens (Juan Carlos), Heredia, Cruyff, Asensi, Rexach.

23 April 1975

Barcelona 1 (Clares)
Leeds United 1 (Lorimer)

Barcelona: Sadurni, de la Cruz, Marinho, Migueli, Gallego, Neeskens, Heredia, Clares, Cruyff, Asensi (Rife), Rexach.

Leeds United: Stewart, Cherry, F. Gray, Bremner, McQueen, Hunter, Lorimer, Clarke, Jordan, Yorath, Madeley.

9 April 1975

Saint Etienne 0
Bayern Munich 0

23 April 1975

Bayern Munich 2 (Beckenbauer, Dürnberger)
Saint Etienne 0

FINAL
28 May 1975
Paris

Bayern Munich 2 (Roth, Müller)
Leeds United 0

Bayern: Maier, Andersson (Weiss), Dürnberger, Schwarzenbeck, Beckenbauer, Zobel, Torstensson, Roth, Müller, Hoeness (Wunder), Kapellmann.

Leeds United: Stewart, Reaney, F. Gray, Bremner, Madeley, Hunter, Lorimer, Clarke, Jordan, Giles, Yorath (E. Gray).

Referee: Kitabdjian (Fra)

Attendance: 48,000.

Twenty-first season – 1975–76

FIRST ROUND

17 September 1975

Slovan Bratislava 1 (Masny)
Derby County 0

Slovan: Vencel, Pivarnik, Gogh, Ondrus, Josef Capkovic, Medvid, Pekarik (Haraslin), Masny, Svehlik, Novotny, Jan Capkovic.

Derby County: Boulton, Thomas, Nish, Powell, McFarland, Todd, H. Newton, Gemmill, Lee (Bourne), Rioch, George.

1 October 1975

Derby County 3 (Bourne, Lee 2)
Slovan Bratislava 0

Derby County: Boulton, Thomas, Nish, Rioch, McFarland, Todd, H. Newton (Bourne), Gemmill, Lee, Hector, George.

Slovan: Vencel, Elefant, Gogh, Ondrus, Josef Capkovic, Medvid (Haraslin), Masny, Svehlik, Pekarik, Novotny, Jan Capkovic.

17 September 1975

Glasgow Rangers 4 (Fyfe, Stein, O'Hara, Johnstone)
Bohemians 1 (Flanagan)

Rangers: McCloy, Denny, Miller, Greig, Jackson, Johnstone, Fyfe, O'Hara, Parlane, Stein, Young.

Bohemians: Smyth, Doran, O'Brien, Kelly, Burke, Fullam, Byrne, P. O'Connor, T. O'Connor, Flanagan, Mitten.

1 October 1975

Bohemians 1 (T. O'Connor)
Glasgow Rangers 1 (Johnstone)

Bohemians: Smyth, Gregg, O'Brien, Kelly, Burke, Fullam, Byrne, P. O'Connor, T. O'Connor, Martin, Mitten.

Rangers: McCloy, Miller, Dawson, Greig, Jackson, Young, McLean, MacDonald, Parlane, Johnstone, Fyfe.

17 September 1975

Linfield 1 (P. Malone)
PSV Eindhoven 2 (W. Van der Kerkhof, Edström)

Linfield: Barclay, McVeigh, Porter, Fraser, Bowyer, Bell (Patterson), M. Malone, Magee, Campbell, P. Malone, Rafferty.

PSV Eindhoven: Van Beveren, Deyckers, Poortvliet, Edström, Strik, Lubse, R. Van der Kerkhof (Francois). W. van der Kerfhof, Van Kray, Krijgh, Van der Kuylen (Quaars).

1 October 1975

PSV Eindhoven 8 (Edström, Deacy 2, Lubse 2, Dahlqvist, Van der Kuylen. W. Van der Kerkhof)
Linfield 0

PSV Eindhoven: Van Beveren, Krijgh, Poortvliet, Van Kraay, Deyckers, W. Van der Kerkhof, Van der Kuylen, Lubse, R. Van der Kerkhof, Edström, Dahlqvist (Deacy).

Linfield: Barclay, Fraser, McVeigh, Campbell, Crozier, Bowyer, Bell, Porter, M. Malone, Magee, McKee.

17 September 1975

Ujpest Dozsa 4 (Fazekas, A. Dunai, Toth pen, Keleman)
FC Zurich 0

1 October 1975

FC Zurich 5 (Katic, Risi 3, Kuhn)
Ujpest Dozsa 1 (Nagy)
Ujpest won on away goals.

17 September 1975

Real Madrid 4 (Santillana 2, Roberto Martinez, Netzer)
Dinamo Bucharest 1 (Lucescu)

1 October 1975

Dinamo Bucharest 1 (Satmareanu)
Real Madrid 0

17 September 1975

KB Copenhagen 0
Saint Etienne 2 (P. Revelli, Larqué)

1 October 1975

Saint Etienne 3 (Rocheteau, P. Revelli, Larqué)
KB Copenhagen 1 (Petersen)

17 September 1975

Olympiakos Piraeus 2 (Kritikopoulos, Aidiniou)
Dynamo Kiev 2 (Kolotov, Burjak)

1 October 1975

Dynamo Kiev 1 (Onishenko)
Olympiakos Piraeus 0

17 September 1975

Ruch Chorzow 5 (Marx 2, Bula, Beniger, Kopicera)
Kuopion Palloseura 0

1 October 1975

Kuopion Palloseura 2 (Toernroos, Heiskanen)
Ruch Chorzow 2 (Chojnacki, Faber)

17 September 1975

Benfica 7 (Sheu, Nene 3, Jordao 3)
Fenerbahce 0

1 October 1975

Fenerbahce 1 (Engin)
Benfica 0

17 September 1975

Jeunesse Esch 0
Bayern Munich 5 (Wunder, Schuster 2, Rummenigge 2)

1 October 1975

Bayern Munich 3 (Schuster 3)
Jeunesse Esch 1 (Zwally)

17 September 1975

RWD Molenbeek 3 (Boskamp, Teugals, Wellens)
Viking Stavanger 2 (Johansson, Kvia)

1 October 1975

Viking Stavanger 0
RWD Molenbeek 1 (Nielson)

17 September 1975

Borussia Moenchengladbach 1 (Simonsen pen)
Innsbruck 1 (Welzl)

1 October 1975

Innsbruck 1 (Flindt)
Borussia Moenchengladbach 6 (Stielike, Simonsen, Heynckes 4)

17 September 1975

CSKA Sofia 2 (Denev, Maraschliev)
Juventus 1 (Anastasi)

1 October 1975

Juventus 2 (Furino, Anastasi)
CSKA Sofia 0

17 September 1975

Floriana 0
Hajduk Split 5 (Zungul 3, Buljan, Surjak)

1 October 1975

Hajduk Split 3 (Buljan, Djordjevic, Savlov)
Floriana 0

17 September 1975

Malmo FF 2 (Cervin, Bo Larsson)
FC Magdeburg 1 (Hoffmann)

1 October 1975

FC Magdeburg 2 (Hoffmann, Streich)
Malmo FF 1 (Andersson)
After extra time. Malmo won on penalties.

21 September 1975

Omonia Nicosia 2 (Philippou 2)
Akranes 1 (Alfredsson)

28 September 1975

Akranes 4 (Hallgrimsson 2, T. Thordarson, K. Thordarson)
Omonia Nicosia 0

SECOND ROUND

22 October 1975

Derby County 4 (George 3 – 2 pens, Nish)
Real Madrid 1 (Pirri)

Derby County: Boulton, Thomas, Nish, Rioch, McFarland, Todd, H. Newton, Gemmill, Lee, Hector (Bourne), George (Davies).

Real Madrid: Miguel Angel, Sol, Rubinan, Pirri, Camacho, Velazquez, Amancio, Breitner, Del Bosque, Netzer, Roberto Martinez.

5 November 1975

Real Madrid 5 (Roberto Martinez 2, Santillana 2, Pirri pen)
Derby County 1 (George)
After extra time.

Real Madrid: Miguel Angel, Sol, Camacho, Pirri, Benito, Del Bosque, Amancio (Rubinan), Breitner, Santillana, Netzer, Roberto Martinez.

Derby County: Boulton, Thomas, Nish, Powell, McFarland, Todd, H. Newton, Gemmill, Davies, Hector (Bourne) (Hinton), George.

22 October 1975

Saint Etienne 2 (P. Revelli, Bathenay)
Glasgow Rangers 0

Saint Etienne: Curkovic, Janvion, Farison, Piazza, Lopez, Bathenay, Synaeghel, Larqué, H. Revelli, Rocheteau, P. Revelli.

Rangers: Kennedy, Jardine, Miller, Greig, Jackson, T. Forsyth, McLean, Stein, Parlane, MacDonald, Johnstone.

5 November 1975

Glasgow Rangers 1 (MacDonald)
Saint Etienne 2 (Rocheteau, H. Revelli)

Rangers: Kennedy, Jardine, Greig, T. Forsyth, Jackson, MacDonald, McLean, Stein, Parlane, Johnstone, Young.

Saint Etienne: Curkovic, Janvion, Farison (Repellini), Piazza, Lopez, Bathenay, Rocheteau, Larqué, H. Revelli, Synaeghel, Schaer (Santini).

22 October 1975

Borussia Moenchengladbach 2 (Heynckes, Simonsen)
Juventus 0

5 November 1975

Juventus 2 (Gori, Bettega)
Borussia Moenchengladbach 2 (Danner, Simonsen)

22 October 1975

Dynamo Kiev 3 (Burjak 2, Blokhin)
Akranes 0

5 November 1975

Akranes 0
Dynamo Kiev 2 (Onischenko, Gunnlaugsson og)

22 October 1975

Ruch Chorzow 1 (Bula)
PSV Eindhoven 3 (Lubse, Edström, R. van der Kerkhof)

5 November 1975

PSV Eindhoven 4 (R. van der Kerkhof, Lubse, Van der Kuylen2)
Ruch Chorzow 0

22 October 1975

Benfica 5 (Moinhos, Sheu, Batista 2, Toni)
Ujpest Dozsa 2 (A. Dunai, Fazekas)

5 November 1975

Ujpest Dozsa 3 (Bene 2, Nagy)
Benfica 1 (Nene)

22 October 1975

Hajduk Split 4 (Zungul, Rozic, Surjak, Mijak)
RWD Molenbeek 0

5 November 1975

RWD Molenbeek 2 (Teugels, Nielsen pen)
Hajduk Split 3 (Surjak, Zungul, Jovanic)

22 October 1975

Malmo FF 1 (T. Andersson)
Bayern Munich 0

5 November 1975

Bayern Munich 2 (Dürnberger pen, Torstensson)
Malmo FF 0

QUARTER-FINALS

3 March 1976

Benfica 0
Bayern Munich 0

17 March 1976

Bayern Munich 5 (Dürnberger 2, Rummenigge, Müller 2)
Benfica 1 (Barros)

3 March 1976

Dynamo Kiev 2 (Konkov, Blokhin)
Saint Etienne 0

17 March 1976

Saint Etienne 3 (H. Revelli, Larqué, Rocheteau)
Dynamo Kiev 0

After extra time.

3 March 1976

Hajduk Split 2 (Mijac, Surjak)
PSV Eindhoven 0

17 March 1976

PSV Eindhoven 3 (Dahlqvist, Lubse, Van der Kuylen)
Hajduk Split 0

After extra time.

3 March 1976

Borussia Moenchengladbach 2 (Jensen, Wittkamp)
Real Madrid 2 (Roberto Martinez, Pirri)

17 March 1976

Real Madrid 1 (Santillana)
Borussia Moenchengladbach 1 (Heynckes)

Real Madrid won on away goals.

SEMI-FINALS

31 March 1976	**Saint Etienne 1** (Larqué) **PSV Eindhoven 0**
14 April 1976	**PSV Eindhoven 0** **Saint Etienne 0**
31 March 1976	**Real Madrid 1** (Roberto Martinez) **Bayern Munich 1** (Müller)
14 April 1976	**Bayern Munich 2** (Müller 2) **Real Madrid 0**

FINAL

12 May 1976
Hampden Park, Glasgow

Bayern Munich 1 (Roth)
Saint Etienne 0

Bayern: Maier, Hansen, Horsmann, Schwarzenbeck, Beckenbauer, Roth, Kapellmann, Dürnberger. Müller, Hoeness, Rummenigge.

Saint Etienne: Curkovic, Janvion, Repellini, Piazza, Lopez, Bathenay, Santini, Larqué, P. Revelli, H. Revelli, Sarramagna (Rocheteau).

Referee: Palotai (Hun)

Attendance: 54,684.

Twenty-second season – 1976–77

FIRST ROUND

14 September 1976

Liverpool 2 (Neal pen, Toshack)
Crusaders 0

Liverpool: Clemence, Neal, Jones, Smith, R. Kennedy, Hughes, Keegan, Johnson, Heighway, Toshack, Callaghan.

Crusaders: McDonald, Strain, Gorman, McFarland, Gillespie, McPolin, Lennox, McAteer, Kirk, Cooke, McCann.

28 September 1976

Crusaders 0
Liverpool 5 (Johnson 2, Keegan, McDermott, Heighway)

Crusaders: McDonald, Strain, Gorman, McFarland, Gillespie, McPolin, Lennox (McQuillan), McAteer, Kirk, Cooke, McCann (Collins).

Liverpool: Clemence, Neal, Jones, Smith, R. Kennedy, Hughes, Keegan, Johnson, Heighway, Case (McDermott), Callaghan.

15 September 1976

Glasgow Rangers 1 (Parlane)
FC Zurich 1 (Cucinotta)

Rangers: McCloy, Miller, Denny, Greig, T. Forsyth, MacDonald, McLean, Jardine, Parlane, McKean, Johnstone.

Zurich: Grob, Heer, Fischbach, Zigerlig, Chapuisat, Kuhn, Martinelli (Stierli), Cucinotta (Aliesch), Risi, Weller, Botteron.

29 September 1976

FC Zurich 1 (Martinelli)
Glasgow Rangers 0

Zurich: Grob, Heer, Fischbach, Zigerlig, Chapuisat, Kuhn, Martinelli (Rutschmann), Weller, Cucinotta, Scheiwiler (Stierli), Botteron.

Rangers: McCloy, Miller, Jardine, Greig, T. Forsyth, Jackson (Denny), MacDonald, Hamilton (McKean), McLean, Parlane, Johnstone.

15 September 1976

Akranes 1 (Sveinsson)
Trabzonspor 3 (Perikli, Ali Kemal 2)

29 September 1976

Trabzonspor 3 (Huseyin 2, Engin)
Akranes 2 (Pogarson 2 – 1 pen)

15 September 1976

Austria WAC 1 (Daxbacher)
Borussia Moenchengladbach 0

29 September 1976

Borussia Moenchengladbach 3 (Stielike, Bonhof pen, Heynckes)
Austria WAC 0

(Austria WAC formerly appeared as FK Austria)

15 September 1976

Bruges 2 (Davies pen, Verbeeke)
Steaua Bucharest 1 (Troi)

29 September 1976

Steaua Bucharest 1 ((Vigu)
Bruges 1 (Lambert)

15 September 1976

CSKA Sofia 0
Saint Etienne 0

29 September 1976

Saint Etienne 1 (Piazza)
CSKA Sofia 0

15 September 1976	**Dynamo Dresden 2** (Kotte pen, Riedel) **Benfica 0**
29 September 1976	**Benfica 0** **Dynamo Dresden 0**
15 September 1976	**Dundalk 1** (McDowell) **PSV Eindhoven 1** (Van der Kuylen)
29 September 1976	**PSV Eindhoven 6** (Van der Kuylen, Postuma, R. Van der Kerkhof 4) **Dundalk 0**
15 September 1976	**Ferencvaros 5** (Nyilasi 2, Magyar, Onhaus, Ebedli) **Jeunesse Esch 1** (Giuliani)
29 September 1976	**Jeunesse Esch 2** (Zwally 2) **Ferencvaros 6** (Nyilasi 2 – 1 pen, Pusztai 2, Szabo 2 – 1 pen)
15 September 1976	**Dynamo Kiev 3** (Onishenko, Troshkin, Blokhin pen) **Partizan Belgrade 0**
29 September 1976	**Partizan Belgrade 0** **Dynamo Kiev 2** (Muntijan pen, Slobodan)
15 September 1976	**Omonia Nicosia 0** **PAOK Salonika 2** (Koudas, Sarafis)
29 September 1976	**PAOK Salonika 1** (Sarafis) **Omonia Nicosia 1** (Philippos pen)
15 September 1976	**Stal Mielec 1** (Sekulski) **Real Madrid 2** (Santillana, Del Bosque)
29 September 1976 Valencia	**Real Madrid 1** (Pirri) **Stal Mielec 0**
15 September 1976	**Viking Stavanger 2** (Valen, Johanssen) **Banik Ostrava 1** (Slany)
29 September 1976	**Banik Ostrava 2** (Vojacek 2) **Viking Stavanger 0**
15 September 1976	**Torino 2** (Mozzini, Graziani) **Malmo FF 1** (Jonsson)
29 September 1976	**Malmo FF 1** (Ljungberg pen) **Torino 1** (C. Sala)
15 September 1976	**Koge BK 0** **Bayern Munich 5** (Torstensson 2, Müller 2, Dürnberger)
29 September 1976	**Bayern Munich 2** (Beckenbauer, Torstensson) **Koge BK 1** (Poulsen)
15 September 1976	**Sliema Wanderers 2** (E. Aquilina 2) **Turun Palloseura 1** (Mannien)
29 September 1976	**Turun Palloseura 1** (Suhonen) **Sliema Wanderers 0**

Turun Palloseura won on away goals.

SECOND ROUND

20 October 1976	**Trabzonspor 1** (Cemil pen) **Liverpool 0**

Trabzonspor: Senol, Turgay, Necati, Kadir, Cemil, Ali Yavuz (Engin), Bekir, Huseyin, Ali Kemal Necmi, Ahmet.

Liverpool: Clemence, Smith, Jones, Thompson, R. Kennedy, Hughes, Keegan, McDermott, Heighway (Fairclough), Toshack (Johnson), Callaghan.

3 November 1976	**Liverpool 3** (Heighway, Johnson, Keegan) **Trabzonspor 0**

Liverpool: Clemence, Neal, Jones, Thompson, R. Kennedy, Hughes, Keegan, McDermott, Heighway, Johnson, Callaghan.

Trabzonspor: Senol, Turgay, Necati, Bekir, Cemil, Engin, Yavuz, Huseyin (M. Cemil), Ali Kemal, Necmi, Ahmet.

20 October 1976	**Dynamo Kiev 4** (Burjak 2, Kolotov, Slobodan) **PAOK Salonika 0**
3 November 1976	**PAOK Salonika 0** **Dynamo Kiev 2** (Kolotov, Blokhin)
20 October 1976	**Ferencvaros 1** (Onhaus) **Dynamo Dresden 0**

3 November 1976	**Dynamo Dresden 4** (Heidler, Schmuck, Riedel, Kotte) **Ferencvaros 0**
20 October 1976 Malaga	**Real Madrid 0** **Bruges 0**
3 November 1976	**Bruges 2** (Le Fevre, Camacho og) **Real Madrid 0**
20 October 1976	**Saint Etienne 1** (Piazza) **PSV Eindhoven 0**
3 November 1976	**PSV Eindhoven 0** **Saint Etienne 0**
20 October 1976	**Torino 1** (Wittkamp og) **Borussia Moenchengladbach 2** (Vogts, Klinkhammer)
3 November 1976	**Borussia Moenchengladbach 0** **Torino 0**
20 October 1976	**FC Zurich 2** (Cucinotta, Scheiwiler) **Turun Palloseura 0**
3 November 1976	**Turun Palloseura 0** **FC Zurich 1** (Cucinotta)
20 October 1976	**Banik Ostrava 2** (Lorenc, Licka) **Bayern Munich 1** (Müller)
3 November 1976	**Bayern Munich 5** (Müller 2, Rummenigge, Kapellmann, Torstensson) **Banik Ostrava 0**

QUARTER-FINALS

2 March 1977	**Saint Etienne 1** (Bathenay) **Liverpool 0** *Saint Etienne:* Curkovic, Janvion, Farison, Piazza, Lopez, Bathenay, Rocheteau, Larqué, Santini, Synaeghel, P. Revelli. *Liverpool:* Clemence, Neal, Jones, Thompson, R. Kennedy, Hughes, McDermott, Case, Heighway, Toshack (Smith), Callaghan.
16 March 1977	**Liverpool 3** (Keegan, Kennedy, Fairclough) **Saint Etienne 1** (Bathenay) *Liverpool:* Clemence, Neal, Jones, Smith, R. Kennedy, Hughes, Keegan, Case, Heighway, Toshack (Fairclough), Callaghan. *Saint Etienne:* Curkovic, Janvion, Farison, Merchadier (H. Revelli), Lopez, Bathenay, Rocheteau, Larqué, P. Revelli, Synaeghel, Santini.
2 March 1977	**Bayern Munich 1** (Kunkel) **Dynamo Kiev 0**
16 March 1977	**Dynamo Kiev 2** (Burjak pen, Slobodan) **Bayern Munich 0**
2 March 1977	**Borussia Moenchengladbach 2** (Kulik, Simonsen) **Bruges 2** (Cools, Courant)
16 March 1977	**Bruges 0** **Borussia Moenchengladbach 1** (Hannes)
2 March 1977	**FC Zurich 2** (Cucinotta, Risi) **Dynamo Dresden 1** (Kreische)
16 March 1977	**Dynamo Dresden 3** (Schade pen, Kreische 2) **FC Zurich 2** (Cucinotta, Risi) *FC Zurich won on away goals.*

SEMI-FINALS

6 April 1977	**FC Zurich 1** (Risi pen) **Liverpool 3** (Neal 2 – 1 pen, Heighway) *Zurich:* Grob, Heer, Fischbach, Zigerlig, Chapuisat, Kuhn, Rutschmann (Dickenmann), Scheiwiler, Risi, Weller (Aliesch), Botteron. *Liverpool:* Clemence, Neal, Jones, Smith, R. Kennedy, Hughes, Keegan, Case, Heighway, Fairclough, McDermott.
20 April 1977	**Liverpool 3** (Case 2, Keegan) **FC Zurich 0** *Liverpool:* Clemence, Neal, Jones, Smith, R. Kennedy, Hughes, Keegan, Case, Heighway (Waddle), McDermott, Johnson. *Zurich:* Grob, Heer, Fischbach, Zigerlig, Chapuisat, Kuhn, Weller, Botteron, Stierli, Cucinotta, Risi.
6 April 1977	**Dynamo Kiev 1** (Onishenko) **Borussia Moenchengladbach 0**

20 April 1977

FINAL

25 May 1977
Rome

Borussia Moenchengladbach 2 (Bonhof pen, Wittkamp)
Dynamo Kiev 0

Liverpool 3 (McDermott, Smith, Neal pen)
Borussia Moenchengladbach 1 (Simonsen)

Liverpool: Clemence, Neal, Jones, Smith, R. Kennedy, Hughes, Keegan, Case, Heighway, McDermott, Callaghan.

Moenchengladbach: Kneib, Vogts, Klinkhammer, Wittkamp, Bonhof, Wohlers (Hannes), Simonsen, Wimmer (Kulik), Stielike, Schafer, Heynckes.

Referee: Wurtz (Fra)

Attendance: 57,000.

Twenty-third season – 1977–78

FIRST ROUND

Bye: Liverpool.

14 September 1977

Celtic 5 (McDonald, Wilson, Craig 2, McLaughlin)
Jeunesse Esch 0

Celtic: Latchford, McGrain, Lynch, Edvaldsson, McDonald, McWilliams, Doyle (Lennox), Glavin (McLaughlin), Craig, Aitken, Wilson.

Jeunesse Esch: Rogues, Pigat, Rohmann, Mond, Redding, Di Pentima (Richelli), Meld, Koster, Zwally, Robert, Noel.

28 September 1977

Jeunesse Esch 1 (Giuliani)
Celtic 6 (Lennox, Edvaldsson 2, Glavin 2, Craig)

Jeunesse Esch: Rogues (Hoffman), Pigat, Rohmann, Mond, Cornaro, Di Pentima, Meld, Koster (Redding), Zwally, Giuliani, Noel.

Celtic: Latchford, McGrain, Kay, Casey (Edvaldsson), McDonald, Aitken, Glavin, Wilson (G. McCluskey), Craig, Burns, Lennox.

15 September 1977

Valur 1 (Bergs)
Glentoran 0

Valur: Dagsson, Kjartansson, Saemundsson, Hilmarsson, D. Gundmundsson, Bergs, Albertsson, Edvaldsson, A. Gundmundsson, Thorbjoernsson, Alfonsson.

Glentoran: Matthews, McCreery, R. McFall, Walsh, Robson, Stewart, Dickinson, Moreland, Caskey, Jamison, Feeney.

29 September 1977

Glentoran 2 (Robson, Jamison)
Valur 0

Glentoran: Matthews, McCreery, R. McFall, Walsh, Robson, Moreland, Dickinson, Jamison, Caskey, Q. McFall, Feeney.

Valur: Dagsson, Alfonsson, Saemundsson, Hilmarsson, D. Gundmundsson, Bergs, Albertsson, Edvaldsson, A. Gundmundsson, Thorbjoernsson, Petursson.

14 September 1977

Red Star Belgrade 3 (Dzajic 2, Filipovic)
Sligo Rovers 0

28 September 1977

Sligo Rovers 0
Red Star Belgrade 3 (Filipovic 2, Jovanovic)

14 September 1977

Lillestrom 2 (Lonsdal, Johansen)
Ajax 0

28 September 1977

Ajax 4 (Birkelund og, Geels, La Ling 2)
Lillestrom 0

14 September 1977

Basle 1 (Von Wartburg)
Innsbruck 3 (Welzl 2 – 1 pen, Constantini)

28 September 1977

Innsbruck 0
Basle 1 (Miessen)

14 September 1977

Vasas Budapest 0
Borussia Moenchengladbach 3 (Schafer, Simonsen, Wohlers)

28 September 1977

Borussia Moenchengladbach 1 (Simonsen)
Vasas Budapest 1 (Izso)

14 September 1977

Omonia Nicosia 0
Juventus 3 (Bettega, Fanna, Virdis)

28 September 1977

Juventus 2 (Boninsegna, Virdis)
Omonia Nicosia 0

14 September 1977

Trabzonspor 1 (Necdet)
BK 1903 Copenhagen 0

28 September 1977	**BK 1903 Copenhagen 2** (Francker 2) **Trabzonspor 0**
14 September 1977	**Kuopion Palloseura 0** **Bruges 4** (Vandereycken, Cools, Lambert, Davies)
28 September 1977	**Bruges 5** (Davies 2, Vandereycken, Simoen, Maes) **Kuopion Palloseura 2** (Rissanen, Laikonen)
14 September 1977	**Levski Spartak 3** (Panov, Milanov 2) **Slask Wroclaw 0**
28 September 1977	**Slask Wroclaw 2** (Pawlowsky, Kopycky) **Levski Spartak 2** (Panov 2)
14 September 1977	**Floriana 1** (G. Xuereb) **Panathinaikos 1** (Aslanidis)
28 September 1977	**Panathinaikos 4** (Alvarez, Antoniadis 2 – 1 pen, Gonios) **Floriana 0**
14 September 1977	**Dukla Prague 1** (Vizek) **Nantes 1** (Amisse)
28 September 1977	**Nantes 0** **Prague 0** *Nantes won on away goals.*
14 September 1977	**Dynamo Dresden 2** (Heidler, Schade) **Halmstad 0**
28 September 1977	**Halmstad 2** (Johansson, Larsson) **Dynamo Dresden 1** (Heidler)
14 September 1977	**Benfica 0** **Moscow Torpedo 0**
28 September 1977	**Moscow Torpedo 0** **Benfica 0** *After extra time. Benfica won on penalties.*
15 September 1977	**Dinamo Bucharest 2** (Vrinceanu, Georgescu) **Atletico Madrid 1** (Luis Pereira)
28 September 1977	**Atletico Madrid 2** (Benegas, Ruben Cano) **Dinamo Bucharest 0**

SECOND ROUND

19 October 1977	**Liverpool 5** (Hansen, Case 2, Neal pen, R. Kennedy) **Dynamo Dresden 1** (Hafner) *Liverpool:* Clemence, Neal, Jones, Hansen, R. Kennedy, Hughes, Dalglish, Case, Heighway, Toshack, Callaghan. *Dresden:* Boden, K. Muller (Helm), Dorner, Schmuck, Weber, Hafner, Schade, Kreische, M. Muller, Kotte (Riedel), Heidler.
2 November 1977	**Dynamo Dresden 2** (Kotte, Sachse) **Liverpool 1** (Heighway) *Dresden:* Boden (Jacubowski), Helm, Dorner, Schmuck, Weber, Hafner, Schade, Riedel, M. Muller, Kotte, Sachse (Richter). *Liverpool:* Clemence, Neal, Jones, Hansen, R. Kennedy, Hughes, Dalglish, Case, Heighway, McDermott (Fairclough), Callaghan.
19 October 1977	**Celtic 2** (Craig, Burns) **Innsbruck 1** (Kriess) *Celtic:* Latchford, Aitken, Lynch, Edvaldsson, McDonald, Casey, Doyle, Craig, Burns, Wilson, Conn (Lennox). *Innsbruck:* Koncilia, Kriess, Constantini, P. Schwarz, Pezzey, Stering, Zanon, Forstinger, Welzl, W. Schwarz, Oberacher.
2 November 1977	**Innsbruck 3** (Welzl, Stering, Oberacher) **Celtic 0** *Innsbruck:* Koncilia, Kriess, Constantini, P. Schwarz, Pezzey, Stering, Zanon, Forstinger, Welzl, W. Schwarz, Oberacher. *Celtic:* Latchford, Aitken, Lynch, Glavin, McDonald, Casey, Doyle, Edvaldsson, Craig, Burns, Wilson.
19 October 1977	**Glentoran 0** **Juventus 1** (Causio) *Glentoran:* Matthews, McCreery, R. McFall, Walsh, Robson, Moreland, Dougan (Stewart), Jamison, Caskey, Q. McFall, Feeney.

Juventus: Zoff, Cuccureddu, Gentile (Cabrini), Furino, Morini, Scirea, Causio, Tardelli, Boninsegna, Benetti, Bettega (Virdis).

2 November 1977

Juventus 5 (Virdis 2, Boninsegna, Fanna, Benetti)
Glentoran 0

Juventus: Zoff, Gentile, Cabrini, Furino, Spinosi, Scirea, Fanna, Causio (Cuccureddu), Virdis, Benetti (Boninsegna), Bettega.

Glentoran: Matthews, McCreery, R. McFall, Walsh, Robson, Moreland, Stewart (O'Neill), Jamison, Caskey, Q. McFall, Feeney.

19 October 1977

Levski Spartak 1 (Voinov pen)
Ajax 2 (Geels, Erkens)

2 November 1977

Ajax 2 (Lerby, Geels)
Levski Spartak 1 (Milanov)

19 October 1977

Red Star Belgrade 0
Borussia Moenchengladbach 3 (Schafer, Heynckes, Simonsen)

2 November 1977

Borussia Moenchengladbach 5 (Simonsen 2, Heynckes, Nikolic og, Wittkamp)
Red Star Belgrade 1 (Susic)

19 October 1977

Bruges 2 (Davies pen, Cools)
Panathinaikos 0

2 November 1977

Panathinaikos 1 (Gonios)
Bruges 0

19 October 1977

Benfica 1 (Pietra pen)
BK 1903 Copenhagen 0

2 November 1977

BK 1903 Copenhagen 0
Benfica 1 (Pietra)

19 October 1977

Nantes 1 (Lacombe)
Atletico Madrid 1 (Marcial)

2 November 1977

Atletico Madrid 2 (Ruben Cano, Luis Pereira)
Nantes 1 (Lacombe)

QUARTER-FINALS

1 March 1978

Benfica 1 (Nene)
Liverpool 2 (Case, Hughes)

Benfica: Bento, Bastos-Lopes, Humberto, Alberto, Eurico, Pietra, Toni, Celso, Nene, Sheu (Wilson), Cavungi.

Liverpool: Clemence, Neal, Smith, Thompson (Hansen), R. Kennedy, Hughes, Dalglish, Case, Heighway, McDermott, Callaghan.

15 March 1978

Liverpool 4 (Callaghan, Dalglish, McDermott, Neal)
Benfica 1 (Nene)

Liverpool: Clemence, Neal, Smith, Thompson, R. Kennedy, Hughes, Dalglish, Case, Heighway, McDermott, Callaghan.

Benfica: Bento, Bastos-Lopes, Humberto, Alberto (Wilson), Eurico, Pietra, Rui Lopes, Toni, Nene, Sheu, Jose Luis.

1 March 1978

Innsbruck 3 (P. Koncilia, Kriess, W. Schwarz)
Borussia Moenchengladbach 1 (Heynckes)

15 March 1978

Borussia Moenchengladbach 2 (Bonhof pen, Heynckes)
Innsbruck 0

Moenchengladbach won on away goals.

1 March 1978

Ajax 1 (Van Dord)
Juventus 1 (Causio)

15 March 1978

Juventus 1 (Tardelli)
Ajax 1 (La Ling)

After extra time. Juventus won on penalties.

1 March 1978

Bruges 2 (Courant, De Cubber)
Atletico Madrid 0

15 March 1978

Atletico Madrid 3 (Benegas, Marcial 2)
Bruges 2 (Cools, Lambert)

SEMI-FINALS

29 March 1978

Borussia Moenchengladbach 2 (Hannes, Bonhof)
Liverpool 1 (Johnson)

Moenchengladbach: Kleff, Vogts, Hannes, Wohlers, Bonhof, Nielsen, Del Haye, Wimmer, Lienen (Danner), Kulik, Heynckes.

Liverpool: Clemence, Neal, Smith, Thompson, R. Kennedy, Hughes, Dalglish, Case, Heighway (Souness), McDermott (Johnson), Callaghan.

12 April 1978

Liverpool 3 (R. Kennedy, Dalglish, Case)
Borussia Moenchengladbach 0

Liverpool: Clemence, Neal, Smith, Thompson, R. Kennedy, Hughes, Dalglish, Case, Heighway, McDermott, Souness.
Moenchengladbach: Kleff, Vogts, Hannes, Wittkamp, Bonhof, Wohlers (Schafer), Del Haye, Wimmer (Lienen), Nielsen, Kulik, Heynckes.

29 March 1978

Juventus 1 (Bettega)
Bruges 0

12 April 1978

Bruges 2 (Bastijns, Vandereycken)
Juventus 0
After extra time.

FINAL

10 May 1978
Wembley

Liverpool 1 (Dalglish)
Bruges 0

Liverpool: Clemence, Neal, Hughes, Thompson, R. Kennedy, Hansen, Dalglish, Case (Heighway), Fairclough, McDermott, Souness.
Bruges: Jensen, Bastijns, Maes (Volder), Krieger, Leekens, Cools, De Cubber, Vandereycken, Simoen, Ku (Sanders), Sorensen.
Referee: Corver (Nth)
Attendance: 92,000.

Twenty-fourth season – 1978–79

PRELIMINARY ROUND

15 August 1978

AS Monaco 3 (Onnis, Nogues, Zorzetto)
Steaua Bucharest 0

30 August 1978

Steaua Bucharest 2 (Troi 2)
AS Monaco 0

FIRST ROUND

13 September 1978

Nottingham Forest 2 (Birtles, Barrett)
Liverpool 0

Nottingham Forest: Shilton, Anderson, Barrett, McGovern, Lloyd, Burns, Gemmill, Bowyer, Birtles, Woodcock, Robertson.
Liverpool: Clemence, Neal, A. Kennedy, Thompson, R. Kennedy, Hughes, Dalglish, Case, Heighway, McDermott (Johnson), Souness.

27 September 1978

Liverpool 0
Nottingham Forest 0

Liverpool: Clemence, Neal, A. Kennedy, Thompson, R. Kennedy, Hughes, Dalglish, Case (Fairclough), Heighway, McDermott (Johnson), Souness.
Nottingham Forest: Shilton, Anderson, Clark, McGovern, Lloyd, Burns, Gemmill, Bowyer, Birtles, Woodcock, Robertson.

13 September 1978

Juventus 1 (Virdis)
Glasgow Rangers 0

Juventus: Zoff, Cuccureddu, Cabrini, Furino, Morini, Scirea, Causio, Tardelli, Virdis, Benetti (Fanna), Bettega.
Rangers: McCloy, Jardine, A. Forsyth, T. Forsyth, Jackson, MacDonald, Miller, Russell, Parlane, Smith, Watson.

27 September 1978

Glasgow Rangers 2 (MacDonald, Smith)
Juventus 0

Rangers: McCloy, Jardine, A. Forsyth, T. Forsyth, Jackson, MacDonald, McLean, Russell, Parlane, Johnstone, Smith.
Juventus: Zoff, Cuccureddu, Cabrini, Furino (Benetti), Morini, Scirea, Causio, Tardelli (Fanna), Virdis, Gentile, Bettega.

13 September 1978

Linfield 0
Lillestrom 0

Linfield: Barclay, Fraser, Garrett, Coyle, Rafferty, Dornan, Nixon, Jameson, Martin, Kirk, Murray.
Lillestrom: Amundsen, Hammer, Birkelund, Kordahl, Berg, Gronlund, L. Hansen, Lonstad, V. Hansen, Lund, Tomteberget.

27 September 1978

Lillestrom 1 (Lonstad)
Linfield 0

Lillestrom: Amundsen, Hammer, Birkelund, Kordahl, Berg, Gronlund, L. Hansen (Dokken), Lonstad, V. Hansen, Lund, Tomteberget.

Linfield: Barclay, Fraser, Garrett, Kirk, Rafferty, Dornan, Nixon, Jameson, Martin, Hewitt (Dunlop), Murray.

13 September 1978	**Real Madrid 5** (Jensen, Juanito 2, Wolff, Del Bosque) **Progres Niedercorn 0**
27 September 1978	**Progres Niedercorn 0** **Real Madrid 7** (Pirri, Jensen, Stielike, Santillana 2, Garcia Hernandez, Bossi og)
13 September 1978	**AEK Athens 6** (Bajevic 2, Ardizoglou, Tassos, Nikolau, Mavros) **FC Porto 1** (Oliveira)
27 September 1978	**FC Porto 4** (Vital 2, Teixeira, Gomes) **AEK Athens 1** (Bajevic)
13 September 1978	**Fenerbahce 2** (Rasit, Cemil) **PSV Eindhoven 1** (Brandts)
27 September 1978	**PSV Eindhoven 6** (Van der Kuylen 4, Deyckers 2) **Fenerbahce 1** (Rasit)
13 September 1978	**Vllaznia 2** (Zhega, Ballgijni) **Austria WAC 0**
27 September 1978	**Austria WAC 4** (Parits, Schachner 2, R. Sara) **Vllaznia 1** (Hafizi)
13 September 1978	**Malmo FF 0** **AS Monaco 0**
27 September 1978	**AS Monaco 0** **Malmo FF 1** (Kinnvall)
13 September 1978	**Cologne 4** (Littbarski, Neumann 2, Konopka) **Akranes 1** (Hallgrimsson)
27 September 1978	**Akranes 1** (Hein og) **Cologne 1** (Van Gool)
13 September 1978	**Zbrojovka Brno 2** (Kroupa, Janecka) **Ujpest Dozsa 2** (Fekete, Torocsik)
27 September 1978	**Ujpest Dozsa 0** **Zbrojovka Brno 2** (Dosek, Kroupa)
13 September 1978	**Partizan Belgrade 2** (Prekazi, Djurovic) **Dynamo Dresden 0**
27 September 1978	**Dynamo Dresden 2** (Dörner, Weber) **Partizan Belgrade 0** *After extra time. Dynamo Dresden won on penalties.*
13 September 1978	**Grasshoppers 8** (Sulser 5, Ponte 2, Wehrli) **Valletta 0**
27 September 1978	**Valletta 3** (Seychell, Agius, Farrugia) **Grasshoppers 5** (Sulser, Ponte, Heinz Hermann, Traber 2)
13 September 1978	**Bruges 2** (Ceulemans, Cools) **Wisla Krakow 1** (Kapka)
27 September 1978	**Wisla Krakow 3** (Kmiecik, Lipka, Krupinski) **Bruges 1** (Vandereycken)
13 September 1978	**Odense 2** (M. Jensen 2) **Lokomotiv Sofia 2** (Kolev, Veliotzkov)
27 September 1978	**Lokomotiv Sofia 2** (Mihailov, Kostov) **Odense 1** (Erikson)
13 September 1978	**Valkeakosken Haka 0** **Dynamo Kiev 1** (Boltatsha)
27 September 1978	**Dynamo Kiev 3** (Veremeev, Khapsalis, Burjak) **Valkeakosken Haka 1** (Ronkainen)
13 September 1978	**Omonia Nicosia 2** (Kanaris, Gootkrtou) **Bohemians 1** (O'Connor)
27 September 1978	**Bohemians 1** (Joyce) **Omonia Nicosia 0** *Bohemians won on away goals.*

SECOND ROUND

18 October 1978	**AEK Athens 1** (Tassos pen) **Nottingham Forest 2** (McGovern, Birtles)

AEK: Stergioudas, Moussouris, Intzoglou (Damianidis), Ravousis, Nikolaou, Viera, Tassos (Tsamis), Nikoloudis, Bajevic, Ardizoglou, Mavros.

Nottingham Forest: Shilton, Anderson, Clark, McGovern, Lloyd, Burns, Bowyer, Gemmill, Birtles, Woodcock, Robertson.

1 November 1978

Nottingham Forest 5 (Needham, Woodcock, Anderson, Birtles 2)
AEK Athens 1 (Bajevic)

Nottingham Forest: Shilton, Anderson, Clark (Mills), O'Hare, Lloyd, Needham, Gemmill, Bowyer, Birtles, Woodcock, Robertson.

AEK: Christidis, Moussouris, Intzoglou, Ravousis, Nikolaou, Domazos, Tassos, Nikoloudis, Bajevic, Ardizoglou, Mavros.

18 October 1978

Glasgow Rangers 0
PSV Eindhoven 0

Rangers: McCloy, Jardine, A. Forsyth, T. Forsyth, Jackson (Miller), MacDonald, McLean, Russell, Parlane (Cooper), Johnstone, Smith.

PSV: Van Engelen, Deyckers, Stevens, Brandts, Poortvliet, Lubse, Posthuma, W. Van der Kerkhof (Hooyer), Van Kraay, Krigh, Van der Kuylen (Jansen).

1 November 1978

PSV Eindhoven 2 (Lubse, Deyckers)
Glasgow Rangers 3 (MacDonald, Johnstone, Russell)

PSV: Van Engelen, Krigh (Smits), Stevens, Van Kraay, Brandts, W. Van der Kerkhof, Jansen, Poortvliet, R. Van der Kerkhof, Lubse, Deyckers.

Rangers: McCloy, Jardine, A. Forsyth, T. Forsyth, Johnstone, MacDonald, McLean, Russell, Parlane, Smith, Watson.

18 October 1978

Real Madrid 3 (Juanito, Garcia Hernandez, Santillana)
Grasshoppers 1 (Sulser)

1 November 1978

Grasshoppers 2 (Sulser 2)
Real Madrid 0

Grasshoppers won on away goals.

18 October 1978

Dynamo Kiev 0
Malmo FF 0

1 November 1978

Malmo FF 2 (Kinnvall, Cervin)
Dynamo Kiev 0

18 October 1978

Lokomotiv Sofia 0
Cologne 1 (Zimmerman)

1 November 1978

Cologne 4 (D. Muller 2, Van Gool, Glowacz)
Lokomotiv Sofia 0

18 October 1978

Bohemians 0
Dynamo Dresden 0

1 November 1978

Dynamo Dresden 6 (Trautmann 2, Dörner, Riedel, Schmuck, Kotte)
Bohemians 0

18 October 1978

Austria WAC 4 (Gasselich 2, R. Sara, Schachner)
Lillestrom 1 (Dokker)

1 November 1978

Lillestrom 0
Austria WAC 0

18 October 1978

Zbrojovka Brno 2 (Pesice, Kroupa)
Wisla Krakow 2 (Kmiecik, Maculewicz)

1 November 1978

Wisla Krakow 1 (Kapka)
Zbrojovka Brno 1 (Dosek)

Wisla Krakow won on away goals.

QUARTER-FINALS

7 March 1979

Nottingham Forest 4 (Birtles, Robertson pen, Gemmill, Lloyd)
Grasshoppers 1 (Sulser)

Nottingham Forest: Shilton, Anderson, Clark, McGovern, Lloyd, Needham, O'Neill, Gemmill, Birtles, Woodcock, Robertson.

Grasshoppers: Berbig, Wehrli, Heinz Hermann, Montandon, Hey, Bauer, Egli, Sulser, Ponte, Herbert Hermann.

21 March 1979

Grasshoppers 1 (Sulser pen)
Nottingham Forest 1 (O'Neill)

Grasshoppers: Berbig, Wehrli, Heinz Hermann, Montandon, Hey, Bauer, Meyer, Egli, Sulser, Ponte, Herbert Hermann.

Nottingham Forest: Shilton, Anderson, Barrett, McGovern, Lloyd, Needham, O'Neill, Gemmill, Birtles, Woodcock, Robertson.

6 March 1979

Cologne 1 (D. Muller)
Glasgow Rangers 0

Cologne: Schumacher, Konopka, Zimmerman, Schuster, Gerber, Cullmann, Glowacz (Prestin). Flohe, D. Muller, Neumann, Littbarski.

Rangers: McCloy, Jardine, Dawson, T. Forsyth, Jackson, MacDonald, McLean, Russell, Parlane (Urquhart), Smith, Denny (Miller).

22 March 1979

Glasgow Rangers 1 (McLean)
Cologne 1 (D. Muller)

Rangers: McCloy, Jardine, Dawson (Johnstone), T. Forsyth, Jackson, MacDonald, McLean, Russell, Urquhart (Parlane), Smith, Cooper.

Cologne: Schumacher, Konopka, Zimmerman, Strack (Prestin), Gerber, Cullmann, Schuster, Flohe, D. Muller, Neumann, Van Gool (Glowacz).

7 March 1979

Wisla Krakow 2 (Nawalka, Kmiecik)
Malmo FF 1 (Hansson)

21 March 1979

Malmo FF 4 (Ljungberg 3 –2 pens, Cervin)
Wisla Krakow 1 (Kmiecik)

7 March 1979

Austria WAC 3 (Schachner 2, Zach)
Dynamo Dresden 1 (Weber)

21 March 1979

Dynamo Dresden 1 (Riedel pen)
Austria WAC 0

SEMI-FINALS

11 April 1979

Nottingham Forest 3 (Birtles, Bowyer, Robertson)
Cologne 3 (Van Gool, D. Muller, Okudera)

Nottingham Forest: Shilton, Barrett, Bowyer, McGovern, Lloyd, Needham, O'Neill, Gemmill (Clark), Birtles, Woodcock, Robertson.

Cologne: Schumacher, Konopka, Zimmerman, Schuster, Gerber, Cullmann, Van Gool, Glowacz (Okudera), D. Muller, Neumann, Prestin.

25 April 1979

Cologne 0
Nottingham Forest 1 (Bowyer)

Cologne: Schumacher, Konopka, Zimmerman, Strack, Schuster, Cullmann, Van Gool, Glowacz (Okudera), D. Muller (Flohe), Neumann, Prestin.

Nottingham Forest: Shilton, Anderson, Clark, McGovern, Lloyd, Burns, O'Neill, Bowyer, Birtles, Woodcock, Robertson.

11 April 1979

Austria WAC 0
Malmo FF 0

25 April 1979

Malmo FF 1 (Hansson)
Austria WAC 0

FINAL

30 May 1979
Munich

Nottingham Forest 1 (Francis)
Malmo FF 0

Nottingham Forest: Shilton, Anderson, Clark, McGovern, Lloyd, Burns, Francis, Bowyer, Birtles, Woodcock, Robertson.

Malmo: Moller, R. Andersson, Jonsson, M. Andersson, Erlandsson, Tapper (Malmberg), Ljungberg, Prytz, Kinnvall, Hansson (T. Andersson), Cervin.

Referee: Linemayr (Aut)

Attendance: 57,500.

Twenty-fifth season – 1979–80

PRELIMINARY ROUND

29 August 1979

Dundalk 1 (Devine)
Linfield 1 (Feeney)

Dundalk: Blackmore, McConville, Dunning, Keely, Martin Lawlor, Flanagan, Mick Lawlor, Byrne, Daly, Muckian, Carlyle (Devine).

Linfield: Dunlop, Garrett, Rafferty, Dornan, Hayes, Jameson, McKeown, Nixon (Koch), McCurdy, McKee, Feeney.

5 September 1979
Haarlem

Linfield 0
Dundalk 2 (Muckian 2)

Linfield: Dunlop, Garrett, Hayes, Jameson, Rafferty, Dornan (Parks), Nixon, McKeown, McCurdy, McKee, Feeney.

Dundalk: Blackmore, McConville, Martin Lawlor, Keely, Dunning, Flanagan, Daly, Mick Lawlor, Carlyle, Byrne (Dainty), Muckian.

FIRST ROUND

19 September 1979

Liverpool 2 (Johnson, Case)
Dynamo Tblisi 1 (Chivadze)

Liverpool: Clemence, Neal, A. Kennedy, Thompson, Irwin, McDermott, Fairclough (Heighway), Case, Dalglish, Johnson, Souness.

Tblisi: Gabeliya, G. Machaidze, Chivadze, Khinchagashvili, Chilaia, Daraseliya, M. Machaidze, Sulakvelidze, Gutsaev, Kipiani, Shengeliya.

3 October 1979 **Dynamo Tblisi 3** (Gutsaev, Shengeliya, Chivadze pen)
Liverpool 0

Tblisi: Gabeliya, G. Machaidze, Chivadze, Khinchagashvili, Chilaia, Daraseliya, Koridze, M. Machaidze, Gutsaev, Kipiani, Shengeliya.

Liverpool: Clemence, Neal, Irwin, Thompson, R. Kennedy, Hansen, Dalglish, Case (Fairclough), Johnson, McDermott, Souness.

19 September 1979 **Nottingham Forest 2** (Bowyer 2)
Osters IF 0

Nottingham Forest: Shilton, Anderson, Gray, McGovern, Lloyd, Burns, O'Neill, Bowyer, Birtles, Woodcock, Robertson.

Osters: Hagberg, Gustavsson, Bild, Ravelli, Björklund, Hallen, Nilsson, Svensson, Thordarson, Nordgren, Ewesson.

3 October 1979 **Osters IF 1** (Nordgren)
Nottingham Forest 1 (Woodcock)

Osters: Hagberg, Gustavsson, Bild (Schroder), Bergqvist, Hallen, Nordgren (Johansson), Nilsson, Andersson, Björklund, Thordarson, Ewesson.

Nottingham Forest: Shilton, Anderson, Gray, McGovern, Lloyd, Burns, O'Neill (Bowyer), Mills, Birtles, Woodcock, Robertson.

19 September 1979 **Partizan Tirana 1** (Murati)
Celtic 0

Tirana: Musta, Milani, Hyfi, Spiro, Berisha, Ragani, Safedini, Lame, Breta, Murati, Shyqeriu.

Celtic: Latchford, Sneddon, McGrain, Aitken, McAdam, Conroy, Provan, Davidson, G. McCluskey (Doyle), MacLeod, Lennox.

3 October 1979 **Celtic 4** (McDonald, Aitken 2, Davidson)
Partizan Tirana 1 (Sneddon og)

Celtic: Latchford, Sneddon, McGrain, Aitken, McDonald, McAdam, Provan, Davidson, G. McCluskey (Lennox), MacLeod, Doyle.

Tirana: Musta, Bachi, Cocoli, Starova, Berisha, Ahmeti, Braho, Lame, Breta, Murati, Ballgjini (Hado).

19 September 1979 **Dundalk 2** (Carlyle, Devine)
Hibernians (Malta) 0

26 September 1979 **Hibernians 1** (C. Vella)
Dundalk 0

19 September 1979 **Levski Spartak 0**
Real Madrid 1 (Roberto Martinez)

3 October 1979 **Real Madrid 2** (Del Bosque, Cunningham pen)
Levski Spartak 0

19 September 1979 **Arges Pitesti 3** (Nicolae 2, Radu)
AEK Athens 0

3 October 1979 **AEK Athens 2** (Ivan og, Vladic)
Arges Pitesti 0

19 September 1979 **Start Kristiansand 1** (Ervik)
Racing Strasbourg 2 (Piasecki 2)

3 October 1979 **Racing Strasbourg 4** (Bianchi 3, Decastel)
Start Kristiansand 0

19 September 1979 **Dynamo Berlin 4** (Netz, Pelka 2, Riediger)
Ruch Chorzow 1 (Wycislik)

3 October 1979 **Ruch Chorzow 0**
Dynamo Berlin 0

19 September 1979 **Upjest Dozsa 3** (Sarlos, Nagy, Fazekas pen)
Dukla Prague 2 (Gajdusek, Nehoda)

3 October 1979 **Dukla Prague 2** (Vizek, Nehoda)
Ujpest Dozsa 0

19 September 1979 **Red Boys Differdange 2** (Di Domenico pen, Wagner)
Omonia Nicosia 1 (Patikis)

3 October 1979 **Omonia Nicosia 6** (Kaiafas 4 – 2 pen, Philippos. Canaris)
Red Boys Differdange 1 (Schmit)

19 September 1979 **HJK Helsinki 1** (Ismail Atik)
Ajax 8 (Lerby 2, Tahamata 2, Arnesen 2, Krol pen, La Ling)

3 October 1979	**Ajax 8** (Krol 2 – 1 pen, Blanker 4, Everse, Lerby) **HJK Helsinki 1** (Toivola)
19 September 1979	**Valur 0** **Hamburg 3** (Hrubesch 2, Buljan)
3 October 1979	**Hamburg 2** (Hrubesch, Wehmeyer) **Valur 1** (Edvaldsson)
19 September 1979	**Hajduk Split 1** (Primorac pen) **Trabzonspor 0**
3 October 1979	**Trabzonspor 0** **Hajduk Split 1** (Djordjevic)
19 September 1979	**Vejle 3** (Andersen, Rasmussen, Sorensen pen) **Austria WAC 2** (Baumeister, Schachner)
3 October 1979	**Austria WAC 1** (Gasselich) **Vejle 1** (Brylle)
19 September 1979	**FC Porto 0** **AC Milan 0**
3 October 1979	**AC Milan 0** **FC Porto 1** (Duda)
19 September 1979	**Servette 3** (Van Genechten og, Coutaz, Hamberg) **Beveren 1** (Janssens)
3 October 1979	**Beveren 1** (Albert pen) **Servette 1** (Barberis)

SECOND ROUND

24 October 1979	**Nottingham Forest 2** (Woodcock, Birtles) **Arges Pitesti 0** *Nottingham Forest:* Shilton, Anderson, Gray, McGovern, Lloyd, Burns, Mills, Bowyer, Birtles, Woodcock, Robertson. *Arges:* Cristian, Zamfir, Moisescu, Ivan, Stancu, Cirstea, Chivescu, Iovanescu, Toma, Dobrin, Nicolae.
7 November 1979	**Arges Pitesti 1** (Barbulescu pen) **Nottingham Forest 2** (Bowyer, Birtles) *Arges:* Cristian, Barbulescu, Toma, Ivan, Stancu, Cirstea, Chivescu, Iovanescu (Ralai), Radu, Dobrin (Turcu), Nicolae. *Nottingham Forest:* Shilton, Anderson, Gray, McGovern, Lloyd, Burns, O'Hare (Mills), Bowyer, Birtles, Woodcock, Robertson.
24 October 1979	**Celtic 3** (McDonald, G. McCluskey, Burns) **Dundalk 2** (Muckian, Mick Lawlor) *Celtic:* Latchford, McGrain, McAdam, McDonald, Lynch, Aitken, MacLeod, Davidson (Lennox), Provan, G. McCluskey, Burns. *Dundalk:* Blackmore, McConville, Keely, Dunning, Martin Lawlor, Dainty, Byrne, Devine, Flanagan, Muckian, Daly (Mick Lawlor).
7 November 1979	**Dundalk 0** **Celtic 0** *Dundalk:* Blackmore, McConville, Martin Lawlor (McKenna), Keely, Dunning, Flanagan, Mick Lawlor (Daly), Devine, Muckian, Byrne, Dainty. *Celtic:* Latchford, McGrain, Aitken, McAdam, McDonald, MacLeod, Provan, Conroy, Edvaldsson, Lennox, Burns (Davidson).
24 October 1979	**Dynamo Berlin 2** (Pelka, Netz) **Servette 1** (Cucinotta)
7 November 1979	**Servette 2** (Hamberg, Barberis) **Dynamo Berlin 2** (Brillat, Terletzki)
24 October 1979	**Dukla Prague 1** (Vizek pen) **Racing Strasbourg 0**
7 November 1979	**Racing Strasbourg 2** (Piasecki, Decastel) **Dukla Prague 0** *After extra time.*
24 October 1979	**Hamburg 3** (Mudschiri og, Keegan, Hartwig) **Dynamo Tblisi 1** (Kipiani)
7 November 1979	**Dynamo Tblisi 2** (Gutsaev, Kipiani) **Hamburg 3** (Keegan, Hrubesch, Buljan)
24 October 1979	**Hajduk Split 3** (Surjak, Cevi, Salov) **Vejle 0**

7 November 1979	**Vejle 2** (Brylle, Ostersen) **Hajduk Split 1** (Zlatko Vujovic)
24 October 1979	**Ajax 10** (Lerby 5, Blanker 3, Krol pen, Arnesen) **Omonia Nicosia 0**
7 November 1979	**Omonia Nicosia 4** (Tsikkos, Demetriou, Kaiafas 2) **Ajax 0**
24 October 1979	**FC Porto 2** (Gomes 2 – 1 pen) **Real Madrid 1** (Cunningham)
7 November 1979	**Real Madrid 1** (Benito) **FC Porto 0**

Real Madrid won on away goals.

QUARTER-FINALS

5 March 1980

Nottingham Forest 0
Dynamo Berlin 1 (Riediger)

Nottingham Forest: Shilton, Gunn, Gray, McGovern, Lloyd, Burns, O'Neill, Bowles, Birtles, Francis, Robertson.

Dynamo: Rudwaleit, Noack, Ullrich, Trieloff, Troppa, Strasser, Terletzki, Lauck, Riediger, Pelka (Schulz), Netz (Brillat).

19 March 1980

Dynamo Berlin 1 (Terletzki pen)
Nottingham Forest 3 (Francis 2, Robertson pen)

Dynamo: Rudwaleit, Noack, Ullrich, Trieloff, Troppa, Strasser, Terletzki, Brillat, Riediger, Pelka, Netz.

Nottingham Forest: Shilton, Anderson, Gray, McGovern, Lloyd, Needham, O'Neill, Bowyer, Birtles, Francis, Robertson.

5 March 1980

Celtic 2 (G. McCluskey, Doyle)
Real Madrid 0

Celtic: Latchford, Sneddon, McGrain, Aitken, McDonald, McAdam, Provan, G. McCluskey, Lennox, MacLeod, Doyle.

Real Madrid: Garcia Remon; Sabido, Camacho, Stielike, Benito, Del Bosque, Juanito, Angel, Santillana, Garcia Hernandez, Cunningham.

19 March 1980

Real Madrid 3 (Santillana, Stielike, Juanito)
Celtic 0

Real Madrid: Garcia Remon; Sabido, Camacho, Pirri, Benito, Del Bosque, Juanito, Angel, Santillana, Stielike, Cunningham.

Celtic: Latchford, Sneddon, McGrain, Aitken, McDonald, McAdam, Provan, G. McCluskey, Lennox, MacLeod, Doyle.

5 March 1980

Hamburg 1 (Reimann)
Hajduk Split 0

19 March 1980

Hajduk Split 3 ((Zlatko Vujovic, Djordjevic, Primorac)
Hamburg 2 (Hrubesch, Hieronymus)

5 March 1980

Strasbourg 0
Ajax 0

19 March 1980

Ajax 4 (Schoenaker, Arnesen, Lerby, La Ling)
Strasbourg 0

SEMI-FINALS

9 April 1980

Nottingham Forest 2 (Francis, Robertson pen)
Ajax 0

Nottingham Forest: Shilton, Anderson, Gray, McGovern, Lloyd, Burns, O'Neill, Bowles, Birtles, Francis, Robertson.

Ajax: Schrijvers, Wijnberg, Zwamborn, Krol, Boeve, Schoenaker, Arnesen, Lerby, La Ling (Bonsink), Jensen, Tahamata.

23 April 1980

Ajax 1 (Lerby)
Nottingham Forest 0

Ajax: Schrijvers, Meutstege (Zwamborn), Krol, Wijnberg, Boeve, Schoenaker, Lerby, Arnesen, La Ling, Bonsink, Jensen.

Nottingham Forest; Shilton, Anderson, Gray, McGovern, Lloyd, Burns, Francis, O'Neill, Birtles, Bowyer, Robertson.

9 April 1980

Real Madrid 2 (Santillana 2)
Hamburg 0

23 April 1980

Hamburg 5 (Kaltz 2 – 1 pen, Hrubesch 2, Memering)
Real Madrid 1 (Cunningham)

FINAL

28 May 1980
Madrid

Nottingham Forest 1 (Robertson)
Hamburg 0

Nottingham Forest: Shilton, Anderson, Gray (Gunn), McGovern, Lloyd, Burns, O'Neill, Bowyer, Birtles, Mills (O'Hare), Robertson.

Hamburg: Kargus, Kaltz, Nogly, Jakobs, Buljan, Hieronymus (Hrubesch), Keegan, Memering, Milewski, Magath, Reimann.

Referee: Garrido (Por)

Attendance: 51,000.

APPENDIX TWO

25 EUROPEAN CUP FINALS AT A GLANCE

1955–56

13 June 1956
Paris

Real Madrid 4 (Di Stefano, Rial 2, Marquitos)
Stade De Reims 3 (Leblond, Hidalgo, Templin)

Real Madrid: Alonso, Atienza, Lesmes, Muñoz, Marquitos, Zarraga, Joseito, Marsal, Di Stefano, Rial, Gento.

Stade De Reims: Jacquet, Zimny. Giraudo, Leblond, Jonquet, Siatka, Hidalgo, Glovacki, Kopa, Bliard, Templin.

Referee: Ellis (Eng)

Attendance: 38,000.

1956–57

30 May 1957
Madrid

Real Madrid 2 (Di Stefano – pen, Gento)
Fiorentina 0

Real Madrid: Alonso, Torres, Lesmes, Muñoz, Marquitos, Zarraga, Kopa, Mateos, Di Stefano, Rial, Gento.

Fiorentina: Sarti, Magnini, Cervato, Scaramucci, Orzan, Segato, Julinho, Gratton, Virgili, Montuori, Bizzarri.

Referee: Horn (Nth)

Attendance: 124,000.

1957–58

28 May 1958
Brussels

Real Madrid 3 (Di Stefano, Rial, Gento)
AC Milan 2 (Schiaffino, Grillo)

After extra time.

Real Madrid: Alonso, Atienza, Lesmes, Santisteban, Santamaria, Zarraga, Kopa, Joseito, Di Stefano, Rial, Gento.

AC Milan: Soldan, Fontana, Beraldo, Bergamaschi, Maldini, Radice, Danova, Liedholm, Schiaffino, Grillo, Cuccharoni.

Referee: Alsteen (Bel)

Attendance: 67,000.

1958–59

3 June 1959
Stuttgart

Real Madrid 2 (Mateos, Di Stefano)
Stade De Reims 0

Real Madrid: Dominguez, Marquitos, Zarraga, Santisteban, Santamaria, Ruiz, Kopa, Mateos, Di Stefano, Rial, Gento.

Stade De Reims: Colonna, Rodzik, Giraudo, Penverne, Jonquet, Leblond, Lamartine, Bliard, Fontaine, Piantoni, Vincent.

Referee: Dusch (GFR)

Attendance: 80,000.

1959–60

18 May 1960
Glasgow

Real Madrid 7 (Di Stefano 3, Puskas 4 – 1 pen)
Eintracht Frankfurt 3 (Kress, Stein 2)

Real Madrid: Dominguez, Marquitos, Pachin, Vidal, Santamaria, Zarraga, Canario, Del Sol, Di Stefano, Puskas, Gento.

Eintracht Frankfurt: Loy, Lutz, Hofer, Weilbacher, Eigenbrodt, Stinka, Kress, Lindner, Stein, Pfaff, Meier.

Referee: Mowat (Sco)

Attendance: 127,621.

1960–61

31 May 1961
Berne

Benfica 3 (Aguas, Gensana og, Coluna)
Barcelona 2 (Kocsis, Czibor)

Benfica: Costa Pereira, Joao, Angelo, Neto, Germano, Cruz, Augusto, Santana, Aguas, Coluna, Cavem.

Barcelona: Ramallets, Foncho, Gracia, Verges, Garay, Gensana, Kubala, Kocsis, Evaristo, Suarez, Czibor.

Referee: Dienst (Swi)

Attendance: 33,000.

1961–62

2 May 1962
Amsterdam

Benfica 5 (Eusebio 2 – 1 pen, Aguas, Cavem, Coluna)
Real Madrid 3 (Puskas 3)

Benfica: Costa Pereira, Joao, Angelo, Cavem, Germano, Cruz, Augusto, Eusebio, Aguas, Coluna, Simoes.

Real Madrid: Araquistain, Casado, Miera, Felo, Santamaria, Pachin, Tejada, Del Sol, Di Stefano, Puskas, Gento.

Referee: Horn (Nth)

Attendance: 68,000.

1962–63

22 May 1963
Wembley

AC Milan 2 (Altafini 2)
Benfica 1 (Eusebio)

AC Milan: Ghezzi, David, Trebbi, Benitez, Maldini, Trapattoni, Pivatelli, Dino Sani, Altafini, Rivera, Mora.

Benfica: Costa Pereira, Cavem, Cruz, Humberto, Raul, Coluna, Augusto, Santana, Torres, Eusebio, Simoes.

Referee: Holland (Eng)

Attendance: 45,000.

1963–64

27 May 1964
Vienna

Internazionale 3 (Mazzola 2, Milani)
Real Madrid 1 (Felo)

Internazionale: Sarti, Burgnich, Facchetti, Tagnin, Guarneri, Picchi, Jair, Mazzola, Milani, Suarez, Corso.

Real Madrid: Vicente, Isidro, Pachin, Muller, Santamaria, Zoco, Amancio, Felo, Di Stefano, Puskas, Gento.

Referee: Stoll (Aut)

Attendance: 72,000.

1964–65

27 May 1965
Milan

Internazionale 1 (Jair)
Benfica 0

Internazionale: Sarti, Burgnich, Facchetti, Bedin, Guarneri, Picchi, Jair, Mazzola, Peiro, Suarez, Corso.

Benfica: Costa Pereira, Cavem, Cruz, Neto, Germano, Raul, Augusto, Eusebio, Torres, Coluna, Simoes.

Referee: Dienst (Swi)

Attendance: 80,000.

1965–66

11 May 1966
Brussels

Real Madrid 2 (Amancio, Serena)
Partizan Belgrade 1 (Vasovic)

Real Madrid: Araquistain, Pachin, Sanchos, Pirri, De Felipe, Zoco, Serena, Amancio, Grosso, Valazquez, Gento.

Partizan: Soskic, Jusufi, Mihailovic, Becejac, Rasovic, Vasovic, Bajic, Kovacevic, Hasanagic, Galic, Pirmajer.

Referee: Kreitlein (GFR)

Attendance: 55,000.

1966–67

25 May 1967
Lisbon

Celtic 2 (Gemmell, Chalmers)
Internazionale 1 (Mazzola – pen)

Celtic: Simpson, Craig, Gemmell, Murdoch, McNeill, Clark, Johnstone, Wallace, Chalmers, Auld, Lennox.

Internazionale: Sarti, Burgnich, Facchetti, Bedin, Guarneri, Picchi, Domenghini, Bicicli, Mazzola, Cappellini, Corso.

Referee: Tschenscher (GFR)

Attendance: 55,000.

1967–68

29 May 1968
Wembley

Manchester United 4 (Charlton 2, Best, Kidd)
Benfica 1 (Graca)

After extra time.

Manchester United: Stepney, Brennan, Dunne, Crerand, Foulkes, Stiles, Best, Kidd, Charlton, Sadler, Aston.

Benfica: Henrique, Adolfo, Humberto, Jacinto, Cruz, Graca, Coluna, Augusto, Eusebio, Torres, Simoes.

Referee: Lo Bello (Ita)

Attendance: 100,000.

1968–69

28 May 1969
Madrid

AC Milan 4 (Prati 3, Sormani)
Ajax 1 (Vasovic – pen)

AC Milan: Cudicini, Anquilletti, Schnellinger, Maldera, Rosata, Trapattoni, Hamrin, Lodetti, Sormani, Rivera, Prati.

Ajax: Bals, Suurbier (Nuninga), Vasovic, Van Duivenbode, Hulshoff, Pronk, Groot, Swart, Cruyff, Danielsson, Keizer.

Referee: de Mendibil (Spn)

Attendance: 50,000.

1969–70

6 May 1970
Milan

Feyenoord 2 (Israel, Kindvall)
Celtic 1 (Gemmell)

After extra time.

Feyenoord: Pieters-Graafland, Romeyn (Haak), Israel, Laseroms, Jansen, Van Duivenbode, Hasil, Van Hanegem, Wery, Kindvall, Moulijn.

Celtic: Williams, Hay, Gemmell, Murdoch, McNeill, Brogan, Johnstone, Wallace, Hughes, Auld (Connelly), Lennox.

Referee: Lo Bello (Ita)

Attendance: 53,187.

1970–71

2 June 1971
Wembley

Ajax 2 (Van Dijk, Haan)
Panathinaikos 0

Ajax: Stuy, Neeskens, Vasovic, Hulshoff, Suurbier, Rijnders (Blankenburg), G. Muhren, Swart (Haan), Cruyff, Van Dijk, Keizer.

Panathinaikos: Oeconomopoulos, Tomaras, Vlahos, Elefterakis, Kamaras, Sourpis, Grammos, Filakouris, Antoniadis, Domazos, Kapsis.

Referee: Taylor (Eng)

Attendance: 90,000.

1971–72

31 May 1972
Rotterdam

Ajax 2 (Cruyff 2)
Internazionale 0

Ajax: Stuy, Suurbier, Hulshoff, Blankenburg, Krol, Neeskens, G. Muhren, Swart, Haan, Cruyff, Keizer.

Internazionale: Bordon, Bellugi, Burgnich, Giubertoni (Bertini), Facchetti, Oriali, Mazzola, Bedin, Jair (Pellizzaro), Boninsegna, Frustalupi.

Referee: Helies (Fra)

Attendance: 61,000.

1972–73

30 May 1973
Belgrade

Ajax 1 (Rep)
Juventus 0

Ajax: Stuy, Suurbier, Hulshoff, Blankenburg, Krol, Neeskens, Haan, G. Muhren, Rep, Cruyff, Keizer.

Juventus: Zoff, Longobucco, Marchetti, Furino, Morini, Salvadore, Causio (Cuccureddu), Altafini, Anastasi, Capello, Bettega (Haller).

Referee: Gugulovic (Yug)

Attendance: 93,000.

1973–74

15 May 1974
Brussels

Bayern Munich 1 (Schwarzenbeck)
Atletico Madrid 1 (Luis)

After extra time.

Bayern Munich: Maier, Hansen, Breitner, Schwarzenbeck, Beckenbauer, Roth, Torstensson (Dürnberger), Zobel, Müller, Hoeness, Kapelmann.

Atletico Madrid: Reina, Melo, Capon, Adelardo, Heredia, Eusebio, Ufarte (Becerra), Luis, Garate, Irureta, Salcedo (Alberto).

Referee: Loraux (Bel)

Attendance: 65,000.

Replay
17 May 1974
Brussels

Bayern Munich 4 (Hoeness 2, Müller 2)
Atletico Madrid 0

Bayern Munich: Maier, Hansen, Breitner, Schwarzenbeck, Beckenbauer, Roth, Torstensson, Zobel, Müller, Hoeness, Kapelmann.

Atletico Madrid: Reina, Melo, Capon, Adelardo (Benegas), Heredia, Eusebio, Becerra, Luis, Garate, Alberto (Ufarte), Becerra.

Referee: Delcourt (Bel)

Attendance: 23,000.

1974–75

28 May 1975
Paris

Bayern Munich 2 (Roth, Müller)
Leeds United 0

Bayern Munich: Maier, Beckenbauer, Dürnberger, Schwarzenbeck, Andersson (Weiss), Zobel, Roth, Kapelmann, Torstensson, Müller, Hoeness (Wunder).

Leeds United: Stewart, Reaney, Madeley, Hunter, F. Gray, Bremner, Giles, Yorath (E. Gray), Lorimer, Clarke, Jordan.

Referee: Kitabdjian (Fra)

Attendance: 48,000.

1975–76

12 May 1976
Glasgow

Bayern Munich 1 (Roth)
St Etienne 0

Bayern Munich: Maier, Hansen, Schwarzenbeck, Beckenbauer, Horsmann, Roth, Durnberger, Kapelmann, Rummenigge, Müller, Hoeness.

St Etienne: Curkovic, Repellini, Piazza, Lopez, Janvion, Bathenay, Santini, Larqué , P. Revelli, H. Revelli, Sarramagna (Rocheteau).

Referee: Palotai (Hun)

Attendance: 54,684.

1976–77

25 May 1977
Rome

Liverpool 3 (McDermott, Smith, Neal – pen)
Borussia Moenchengladbach 1 (Simonsen)

Liverpool: Clemence, Neal, Jones, Smith, R. Kennedy, Hughes, Keegan, Case, Heighway, McDermott, Callaghan.

Borussia: Kneib, Vogts, Klinkhammer, Wittkamp, Bonhof, Wohlers (Hannes), Simonsen, Wimmer (Kulik), Stielike, Schaffer, Heynckes.

Referee: Wurtz (Fra)

Attendance: 57,000.

1977–78

10 May 1978
Wembley

Liverpool 1 (Dalglish)
Bruges 0

Liverpool: Clemence, Neal, Thompson, Hansen, Hughes, McDermott, R. Kennedy, Souness, Case (Heighway), Fairclough, Dalglish.

Bruges: Jensen, Bastijns, Krieger, Leekens, Maes (Volder), Cools, De Cubber, Vandereycken, Ku (Sanders), Simoen, Sorensen.

Referee: Corver (Nth)

Attendance: 92,000.

1978–79

30 May 1979
Munich

Nottingham Forest 1 (Francis)
Malmo 0

Nottingham Forest: Shilton, Anderson, Lloyd, Burns, Clark, McGovern, Bowyer, Francis, Birtles, Woodcock, Robertson.

Malmo: Möller, Roland Andersson, Jonsson, M. Andersson, Erlandsson, Tapper (Malmberg), Ljungberg, Prytz, Kinnvall, Hansson (T. Andersson), Cervin.

Referee: Linemayr (Aut)

Attendance: 57,500.

1979–80

28 May 1980
Madrid

Nottingham Forest 1 (Robertson)
Hamburg 0

Nottingham Forest: Shilton, Anderson, Gray (Gunn), McGovern, Lloyd, Burns, O'Neill, Bowyer, Birtles, Mills (O'Hare), Robertson.

Hamburg: Kargus, Kaltz, Nogly, Jakobs, Buljan, Hieronymus (Hrubesch), Keegan, Memering, Milewski, Magath, Reimann.

Referee: Garrido (Por)

Attendance: 51,000.

APPENDIX THREE

TOP 30 GOALSCORERS IN THE EUROPEAN CUP 1955–1980

1	Di Stefano (Real Madrid)	49
2	Eusebio (Benfica)	46
3	G. Müller (Bayern Munich)	37
4	Puskas (Honved, Real Madrid)	36
5	Gento (Real Madrid)	31
6	J. Augusto (Benfica)	25
7	Altafini (AC Milan, Juventus)	24
8	Van Himst (Anderlecht)	20
9	Amancio (Real Madrid)	19
	Torres (Benfica)	19
11	Aguas (Benfica)	18
	Cruyff (Ajax)	18
	Kostic (Red Star Belgrade)	18
14	Pirri (Real Madrid)	17
	Santillana (Real Madrid)	17
16	Adamec (Dukla Prague, Spartak Trnava)	16
	Mazzola (Internazionale)	16
18	Bene (Ujpest Dozsa)	15
	Lubanski (Gornik)	15
20	Heynckes (Borussia Moenchengladbach)	14
	Law (Manchester United)	14
	Rial (Real Madrid)	14
23	Antoniadis (Panathinaikos)	13
	Viollet (Manchester United)	13
25	Coluna (Benfica)	12
	Jair (Internazionale)	12
	Keizer (Ajax)	12
	Luis (Atletico Madrid)	12
	Mraz (Sparta Prague, Dukla Prague)	12
	Torstensson (Atvidaberg, Bayern Munich)	12

APPENDIX FOUR

CLUB RANKING LIST 1955–80

The following merit table has been calculated on the imaginary number of points won by each club in the competition. For this purpose the score at the end of normal or extra time is considered the 'final' result of each match, irrespective of the toss of a coin, penalty kicks etc. Where points and goal difference are equal, priority has been given to the club scoring more goals, then by the club playing fewer matches, and finally by alphabetical order.

		P	W	D	L	F	A	Pt
1	Real Madrid (Spn)	127	76	17	34	319	146	169
2	Benfica (Por)	92	46	20	26	197	110	112
3	Ajax (Nth)	65	39	12	14	135	60	90
4	Glasgow Celtic (Sco)	64	36	12	16	127	59	84
5	Manchester United (Eng)	41	26	7	8	100	45	59
6	AC Milan (Ita)	46	26	6	14	116	60	58
7	Bayern Munich (GFR)	40	25	7	8	93	37	57
8	Internazionale (Ita)	41	23	10	8	93	37	57
9	Juventus (Ita)	45	22	9	14	58	46	53
10	CSKA Sofia (Bul)	52	22	9	21	83	80	53
11	Dukla Prague (Cze)	43	21	10	12	73	55	52
12	Feyenoord (Nth)	37	20	9	8	89	39	49
13	Atletico Madrid (Spn)	39	21	7	11	65	39	49
14	Liverpool (Eng)	38	21	6	11	74	40	48
15	Red Star Belgrade (Yug)	43	21	6	16	92	68	48
16	Glasgow Rangers (Sco)	43	20	5	18	72	77	45

		P	W	D	L	F	A	Pt
17	Saint Etienne (Fra)	39	19	6	14	49	41	44
18	Ujpest Dozsa (Hun)	38	17	8	13	65	38	42
19	Dynamo Kiev (USSR)	32	18	6	8	45	25	42
20	Standard Liège (Bel)	32	20	1	11	55	33	41
21	Borussia Moenchengladbach (GFR)	31	15	10	6	69	31	40
22	Anderlecht (Bel)	44	16	6	22	84	89	38
23	Gornik Zabrze (Pol)	31	17	3	11	52	45	37
24	Barcelona (Spn)	26	15	6	5	60	25	36
25	Rapid Vienna (Aut)	33	15	4	14	53	49	34
26	Spartak Trnava (Cze)	24	13	7	4	44	20	33
27	Stade de Reims (Fra)	24	14	3	7	63	30	31
28	Vasas Budapest (Hun)	27	12	6	9	62	34	30
29	Dinamo Bucharest (Rom)	30	13	4	13	52	55	30
30	PSV Eindhoven (Nth)	24	12	5	7	51	25	29
31	Nottingham Forest (Eng)	18	12	4	2	32	12	28
32	Hajduk Split (Yug)	18	12	2	4	41	18	26
33	Leeds United (Eng)	17	12	1	4	42	11	25
34	FC Bruges (Bel)	21	11	3	7	43	24	25
35	Partizan Belgrade (Yug)	29	11	3	15	49	49	25
36	Panathinaikos (Gre)	31	8	9	14	40	42	25
37	Austria/WAC (Aut)	29	10	5	14	38	45	25
38	Legia Warsaw (Pol)	18	11	2	5	29	16	24
39	Dynamo Dresden (GDR)	22	10	4	8	38	30	24
40	Malmö FF (Swe)	25	10	4	11	27	38	24
41	IFC Cologne (GFR)	17	7	8	2	27	19	22
42	Galasataray (Tur)	25	8	6	11	29	39	22
43	FC Zurich (Swi)	25	10	2	13	33	46	22
44	Borussia Dortmund (GFR)	18	8	3	7	44	31	19
45	SV Hamburg (GFR)	16	9	1	6	34	21	19
46	Vorwaerts (GDR)	22	9	1	12	35	33	19
47	Ferencvaros (Hun)	16	8	2	6	36	28	18
48	Fiorentina (Ita)	13	7	4	2	14	11	18
49	Sparta Prague (Cze)	12	7	3	2	23	17	17
50	Young Boys (Swi)	15	6	5	4	27	26	17
51	Sporting Lisbon (Por)	20	7	3	10	35	40	17
52	Fenerbahce (Tur)	25	7	3	15	23	53	17
53	OGC Nice (Fra)	14	7	2	5	29	25	16
54	Basle (Swi)	18	7	2	9	37	37	16
55	Wismut Aue (GDR)	16	5	4	7	26	23	14
56	Derby County (Eng)	12	6	2	4	18	22	14
57	Grasshoppers (Swi)	14	5	3	6	34	23	13
58	Ruch Chorzow (Pol)	12	5	3	4	18	19	13
59	Slovan Bratislava (Cze)	12	6	1	5	17	19	13
60	Aarhus (Den)	14	5	3	6	18	22	13
61	AEK Athens (Gre)	16	5	3	8	27	35	13
62	Jeunesse Esch (Lux)	29	5	3	21	37	97	13
63	Wiener Sportklub (Aut)	12	4	4	4	21	18	12
64	Servette (Swi)	13	5	2	6	23	26	12
65	Linfield (NI)	21	3	6	12	26	52	12
66	IFC Nuremburg (GFR)	8	5	1	2	16	14	11
67	Omonia Nicosia (Cyp)	18	5	1	12	20	53	11
68	Ararat Erevan (USSR)	6	5	0	1	14	5	10
69	Eintracht Frankfurt (GFR)	7	4	2	1	23	15	10
70	Dundee (Sco)	8	5	0	3	20	14	10
71	Carl Zeiss Jena (GDR)	8	5	0	3	12	11	10
72	Olympiakos Piraeus (Gre)	14	3	4	7	14	21	10
73	DWS Amsterdam (Nth)	6	4	1	1	13	4	9
74	Tottenham Hotspur (Eng)	8	4	1	3	21	13	9
75	MTK Budapest (Hun)	8	4	1	3	24	18	9
76	Everton (Eng)	8	2	5	1	12	6	9
77	Atletico Bilbao (Spn)	6	4	1	1	16	14	9
78	Vasas Gyor (Hun)	8	4	1	3	16	15	9
79	Vojvodina (Yug)	7	4	1	2	8	7	9
80	Nantes (Fra)	12	2	5	5	17	21	9
81	IFK Norköpping (Swe)	12	2	5	5	14	20	9
82	Vejle (Den)	10	3	3	4	11	17	9
83	Gothenburg (Swe)	14	4	1	9	24	36	9
84	Dundalk (Ire)	12	3	3	6	11	25	9
85	Arsenal (Eng)	6	4	0	2	13	4	8
86	Arges Pitesti (Rom)	8	4	0	4	13	10	8
87	Dynamo Berlin (GDR)	6	3	2	1	10	7	8
88	Schalke 04 (GFR)	7	3	2	2	13	13	8
89	Atvidaberg (Swe)	8	4	0	4	12	12	8
90	Trabzonspor (Tur)	8	4	0	4	8	10	8
91	Levski Spartak (Bul)	14	3	2	9	22	30	8

		P	W	D	L	F	A	Pt
92	Steaua Bucharest (Rom)	12	3	2	7	13	24	8
93	Hibernians (Sco)	6	3	1	2	9	5	7
94	RC Strasbourg (Fra)	6	3	1	2	8	6	7
95	IFK Malmö (Swe)	6	3	1	2	7	7	7
96	Lokomotiv Sofia (Bul)	8	3	1	4	19	21	7
97	FC Porto (Por)	10	3	1	6	12	18	7
98	SW Innsbruck (Aut)	14	3	1	10	13	28	7
99	Sliema Wanderers (Mal)	14	3	1	10	10	36	7
100	Ipswich Town (Eng)	4	3	0	1	16	5	6
101	TSV 1860 Munich (GFR)	4	3	0	1	12	4	6
102	Werder Bremen (GFR)	4	3	0	1	11	3	6
103	Magdeburg (GDR)	8	3	0	5	15	11	6
104	Sparta Rotterdam (Nth)	6	3	0	3	12	11	6
105	Valencia (Spn)	6	2	2	2	6	5	6
106	Monaco (Fra)	10	2	2	6	16	16	6
107	Spartak Kralove (Cze)	5	2	2	1	5	5	6
108	Wisla Krakow (Pol)	6	2	2	2	10	11	6
109	KB Copenhagen (Den)	9	3	0	6	14	18	6
110	Wolverhampton Wanderers (Eng)	8	2	2	4	12	16	6
111	Seville (Spn)	6	2	2	2	9	13	6
112	Polonia Bytom (Pol)	6	3	0	3	8	12	6
113	Lilleström (Nor)	6	2	2	2	4	8	6
114	Partizan Tirana (Alb)	10	2	2	6	5	16	6
115	Glentoran (NI)	12	1	4	7	10	22	6
116	Lahden Reipas (Fin)	8	2	2	4	8	30	6
117	Waterford (Ire)	14	3	0	11	15	47	6
118	Red Star Bratislava (Cze)	4	2	1	1	8	6	5
119	Zbrojorka Brno (Cze)	4	1	3	0	7	5	5
120	CSKA Moscow (USSR)	4	2	1	1	5	3	5
121	Sarja Voroshilovgrad (USSR)	4	2	1	1	3	1	5
122	Hvidovre (Den)	6	1	3	2	9	12	5
123	BK 1903 Copenhagen (Den)	8	2	1	5	7	11	5
124	Olympique Marseille (Fra)	6	2	1	3	6	11	5
125	Petrolul Ploesti (Rom)	8	2	1	5	8	15	5
126	Djurgarden (Swe)	8	2	1	5	7	16	5
127	Valur (Ice)	10	1	3	6	8	30	5
128	Sarajevo (Yug)	4	1	2	1	6	5	4
129	BK 1913 Odense (Den)	4	2	0	2	14	14	4
130	Burnley (Eng)	4	2	0	2	8	8	4
131	Cagliari (Ita)	4	2	0	2	5	5	4
132	Eintracht Brunswick (GFR)	5	2	0	3	5	5	4
133	Torino (Ita)	4	1	2	1	4	4	4
134	RWD Molenbeek (Bel)	4	2	0	2	6	9	4
135	Gwardia Warsaw (Pol)	5	1	2	2	6	9	4
136	Banik Ostrava (Cze)	4	2	0	2	5	8	4
137	Kilmarnock (Sco)	4	1	2	1	4	7	4
138	La Chaux-de-Fonds (Swi)	4	1	2	1	5	9	4
139	Akranes (Ice)	10	1	2	7	10	22	4
140	Bohemians (Ire)	6	1	2	3	4	13	4
141	Hibernians (Mal)	8	1	2	5	4	19	4
142	Esbjerg (Den)	8	1	2	5	6	23	4
143	Lyn Oslo (Nor)	10	2	0	8	14	41	4
144	Rapid Bucharest (Rom)	4	1	1	2	3	3	3
145	Spartak Plovdiv (Bul)	4	1	1	2	3	3	3
146	Bologna (Ita)	3	1	1	1	2	2	3
147	Akademisk (Den)	4	1	1	2	4	5	3
148	PAOK Salonika (Gre)	4	1	1	2	3	7	3
149	Nendori Tirana (Alb)	6	0	3	3	3	9	3
150	Besiktas (Tur)	8	1	1	6	3	15	3
151	Frederikstad (Nor)	8	1	1	6	6	22	3
152	Spartak Moscow (USSR)	2	1	0	1	4	4	2
153	Dynamo Tbilisi (USSR)	4	1	0	3	7	8	2
154	Universitatea Craiova (Rom)	2	1	0	1	3	4	2
155	Vllaznia (Alb)	2	1	0	1	3	4	2
156	Trakia Plovdiv (Bul)	2	1	0	1	2	3	2
157	Saarbrucken (Saar)	2	1	0	1	5	7	2
158	Red Boys Differdange (Lux)	2	1	0	1	3	7	2
159	LKS Lodz (Pol)	2	1	0	1	2	6	2
160	Torpedo Moscow (USSR)	4	0	2	2	1	5	2
161	Derry City (NI)	3	1	0	2	8	15	2
162	Hearts (Sco)	4	1	0	3	4	11	2
163	Viking Stavanger (Nor)	8	1	0	7	7	16	2
164	VT Arad (Rom)	6	0	2	4	3	17	2
165	Spora Luxembourg (Lux)	5	1	0	4	7	27	2

		P	W	D	L	F	A	Pt
166	Valetta (Mal)	6	1	0	5	5	25	2
167	Valkeakosken (Fin)	8	1	0	7	7	28	2
168	Drumcondra (Ire)	6	1	0	5	3	25	2
169	HJK Helsinki (Fin)	8	1	0	7	8	31	2
170	Turun Palloseura (Fin)	10	1	0	9	4	28	2
171	Floriana (Mal)	12	0	2	10	3	49	2
172	Honved (Hun)	2	0	1	1	5	6	1
173	Csepel (Hun)	2	0	1	1	3	4	1
174	Dynamo Zagreb (Yug)	2	0	1	1	3	4	1
175	Odense BK (Den)	2	0	1	1	3	4	1
176	Manchester City (Eng)	2	0	1	1	1	2	1
177	Skeid (Nor)	2	0	1	1	1	2	1
178	Admira (Aut)	2	0	1	1	0	1	1
179	Beveren (Bel)	2	0	1	1	2	4	1
180	Slask Wroclaw (Pol)	2	0	1	1	2	5	1
181	Valerengen (Nor)	2	0	1	1	2	5	1
182	Glenavon (NI)	2	0	1	1	0	3	1
183	Oesters Vaxjo (Swe)	4	0	1	3	2	6	1
184	Rot-Weiss Essen (GFR)	2	0	1	1	1	5	1
185	Lausanne (Swi)	2	0	1	1	0	4	1
186	Distillery (NI)	2	0	1	1	3	8	1
187	Voest Linz (Aut)	2	0	1	1	0	5	1
188	Rosenborg (NI)	6	0	1	5	6	18	1
189	Shamrock Rovers (Ire)	6	0	1	5	5	18	1
190	BK 1909 Odense (Den)	6	0	1	5	6	21	1
191	Kuopion Palloseura (Fin)	6	0	1	5	4	21	1
192	Aris Bonnevoie (Lux)	6	0	1	5	6	25	1
193	Olympiakos Nicosia (Cyp)	6	0	1	5	4	36	1
194	DOS Utrecht (Nth)	2	0	0	2	4	6	0
195	Rapid Heerlen (Nth)	2	0	0	2	3	6	0
196	ASK Linz (Aut)	2	0	0	2	2	5	0
197	Karl-Marx-Stadt (GDR)	2	0	0	2	2	5	0
198	Halmstadt (Swe)	2	0	0	2	2	5	0
199	Zeljeznicar Sarajevo (Yug)	2	0	0	2	1	4	0
200	Chemie Leipzig (GDR)	2	0	0	2	2	6	0
201	Stal Mielec (Pol)	4	0	0	4	2	6	0
202	Anorthosis (Cyp)	2	0	0	2	1	6	0
203	Start Kristiansand (Nor)	2	0	0	2	1	6	0
204	Lierse (Bel)	2	0	0	2	0	5	0
205	Cork Celtic (Ire)	2	0	0	2	1	7	0
206	Cork Hibs (Ire)	2	0	0	2	1	7	0
207	Koge BK (Den)	2	0	0	2	1	7	0
208	Shelbourne (Ire)	2	0	0	2	1	7	0
209	Stromsgodset (Nor)	2	0	0	2	1	7	0
210	Sligo Rovers (Ire)	2	0	0	2	0	6	0
211	HIFK Helsinki (Fin)	4	0	0	4	5	12	0
212	Ards (NI)	2	0	0	2	3	10	0
213	Limerick (Ire)	2	0	0	2	2	9	0
214	Antwerp (Bel)	2	0	0	2	1	8	0
215	Helsinki Palloseura (Fin)	2	0	0	2	0	7	0
216	Avenir Beggen (Lux)	2	0	0	2	0	8	0
217	Fram (Ice)	2	0	0	2	2	11	0
218	Coleraine (NI)	2	0	0	2	1	11	0
219	AEL (Cyp)	2	0	0	2	0	12	0
220	Progres Niedercorn (Lux)	2	0	0	2	0	12	0
221	Apoel (Cyp)	4	0	0	4	0	13	0
222	Kokkolan (Fin)	2	0	0	2	0	14	0
223	EPA (Cyp)	2	0	0	2	0	16	0
224	Union Luxembourg (Lux)	4	0	0	4	1	18	0
225	Crusaders (NI)	2	0	0	2	0	19	0
226	KR Reykjavik (Ice)	6	0	0	6	7	35	0
227	IBK Keflavik (Ice)	8	0	0	8	5	35	0
228	Stade Dudelange (Lux)	4	0	0	4	1	32	0

APPENDIX FIVE

EUROPEAN FOOTBALLER OF THE YEAR

The European Footballer of the Year award is based on an annual poll conducted among leading football journalists on the continent by the French magazine, *France Football*. Their votes are gathered to determine who, at the end of each calendar year, has proved himself the outstanding player in Europe. It is no co-incidence that many of the winners, and those finishing in second and third place, have staked a major part of their claim by stirring performances in the European Cup – quite often in the final itself.

The award was introduced in 1956, fittingly the first year that the European Cup final took place. However the first winner, England's legendary Stanley Matthews, never kicked a ball in the competition. He is unique, because all those who have succeeded him in winning what the French call *Le Ballon d'Or* have taken part in the European Cup.

The table includes the winner, the runner-up and the player finishing in third place, with their respective clubs at the time of their award noted in brackets.

1956	Stanley Matthews (Blackpool)	Alfredo Di Stefano (Real Madrid)	Raymond Kopa (Reims)
1957	Alfredo Di Stefano (Real Madrid)	Billy Wright (Wolverhampton Wanderers)	Raymond Kopa (Real Madrid)
1958	Raymond Kopa (Real Madrid)	Helmut Rahn (Rot-Weiss Essen)	Juste Fontaine (Reims)
1959	Alfredo Di Stefano (Real Madrid)	Raymond Kopa (Reims)	John Charles (Juventus)
1960	Luis Suarez (Barcelona)	Ferenc Puskas (Real Madrid)	Uwe Seeler (SV Hamburg)
1961	Omar Sivori (Juventus)	Luis Suarez (Internazionale)	Johnny Haynes (Fulham)
1962	Josef Masopust (Dukla Prague)	Eusebio (Benfica)	Karl-Heinz Schnellinger (Cologne)
1963	Lev Yashin (Moscow Dynamo)	Gianni Rivera (AC Milan)	Jimmy Greaves (Tottenham Hotspur)
1964	Denis Law (Manchester United)	Luis Suarez (Internazionale)	Amancio (Real Madrid)
1965	Eusebio (Benfica)	Giacinto Facchetti (Internazionale)	Luis Suarez (Internazionale)
1966	Bobby Charlton (Manchester United)	Eusebio (Benfica)	Franz Beckenbauer (Bayern Munich)
1967	Florian Albert (Ferencvaros)	Bobby Charlton (Manchester United)	Jimmy Johnstone (Celtic)
1968	George Best (Manchester United)	Bobby Charlton (Manchester United)	Dragan Dzajic (Red Star Belgrade)
1969	Gianni Rivera (AC Milan)	Luigi Riva (Cagliari)	Gerd Muller (Bayern Munich)
1970	Gerd Muller (Bayern Munich)	Bobby Moore (West Ham United)	Luigi Riva (Cagliari)
1971	Johan Cruyff (Ajax)	Sandro Mazzola (Internazionale)	George Best (Manchester United)
1972	Franz Beckenbauer (Bayern Munich)	Gerd Muller (Bayern Munich)	Günter Netzer (Borussia Moenchengladbach)
1973	Johan Cruyff (Barcelona)	Dino Zoff (Juventus)	Gerd Müller (Bayern Munich)
1974	Johan Cruyff (Barcelona)	Franz Beckenbauer (Bayern Munich)	Kazimierz Deyna (Legia Warsaw)
1975	Oleg Blokhin (Dynamo Kiev)	Franz Beckenbauer (Bayern Munich)	Johan Cruyff (Barcelona)
1976	Franz Beckenbauer (Bayern Munich)	Robbie Rensenbrink (Anderlecht)	Ivo Viktor (Dukla Prague)
1977	Allan Simonsen (Borussia Moenchengladbach)	Kevin Keegan (SV Hamburg)	Michel Platini (Nancy-Lorraine)
1978	Kevin Keegan (SV Hamburg)	Hans Krankl (Barcelona)	Robbie Rensenbrink (Anderlecht)
1979	Kevin Keegan (SV Hamburg)	Karl-Heinz Rummenigge (Bayern Munich)	Ruud Krol (Ajax)

BIBLIOGRAPHY

The first 12 seasons of the competition are comprehensively covered by Roger MacDonald in *Britain versus Europe* (Pelham, 1968) which includes a section on the other two club tournaments and a useful appendix. Also of interest to students of the early years of the European Cup are Willy Meisl's chapter in volume four of *Association Football* (Caxton, 1960) and Jacques Ferran's own account of the role of *L'Equipe* in *Les Coupes D'Europe* (Editions Famot, Genève, 1978).

The list of club histories continues to grow season by season, Manchester United being particularly well documented. Their early excursions into Europe, together with the effects of the Munich air disaster, are dealt with in Frank Taylor's *The Day A Team Died* (Stanley Paul, 1960), and more recently by John Roberts in *The Team That Wouldn't Die* (Arthur Barker, 1975).

Liverpool's various campaigns are described by John Keith in *Liverpool, Champions of Europe* (Duckworth Elmswood, 1977), while John Lawson chronicles Nottingham Forest's first victory in *Forest – The 1979 Season* (Wensum, 1979). Perhaps the best short account of the influence of Real Madrid on the tournament is in Brian Glanville's *Soccer: A Panorama* (Eyre and Spottiswoode, 1969).

The *Rothman's Football Year Book* (Queen Anne Press) has proved a valuable source of statistics since it was first published in 1970, and the early editions are already becoming collector's items. The now defunct *World Football Handbook* (first edition: Hodder and Stoughton, 1964) contained useful summaries of the European Cup, while in recent seasons, the monthly magazine *World Soccer* has featured round-by-round details of the competition. In addition *World Soccer from A to Z* edited by Norman Barrett (Book Club Associates, 1973) includes useful portraits of the major clubs and their players.

There have been many accounts published of the more dramatic European Cup games, but perhaps the most illuminating versions are the television match recordings, of which by far the best collection is held by the BBC.

INDEX